EXPLORING AMERICA

PERSPECTIVES ON CRITICAL ISSUES

HARVEY MINKOFF
Hunter College

EVELYN MELAMED
Hunter College

HARCOURT BRACE COLLEGE PUBLISHERS

Fort Worth   Philadelphia   San Diego   New York   Orlando   Austin   San Antonio
Toronto   Montreal   London   Sydney   Tokyo

PUBLISHER	Ted Buchholz
SENIOR ACQUISITIONS EDITOR	Michael Rosenberg
DEVELOPMENTAL EDITOR	Tia Black
PROJECT EDITOR	Deanna M. Johnson
PRODUCTION MANAGER	Thomas Urquhart IV
ART DIRECTOR	Peggy Young

COVER IMAGE: Dick Patrick, represented by Celeste Cuomo. Dallas, Texas.

For Jackie and Dinah and Irene

ISBN: 0-15-500981-8

Library of Congress Catalog Card Number: 93-80867

ADDRESS FOR EDITORIAL CORRESPONDENCE
Harcourt Brace College Publishers
301 Commerce Street, Suite 3700
Fort Worth, TX 76102.

ADDRESS FOR ORDERS:
Harcourt Brace & Company
6277 Sea Harbor Drive
Orlando, FL 32887-6777
1-800-782-4479, or
1-800-433-0001 (in Florida).

PREFACE

"What is an American?" asked Michel-Guillaume Jean de Crèvecoeur two centuries ago. The history of the United States since then has been, in effect, an attempt to answer that question. Politics, economics and morality, debates over religion, slavery, women's rights, and immigration—all confronted what it means to be an American. Today, Americans argue over abortion, sexuality, welfare, civil rights, and multiculturalism. And these disagreements too arise form the same core question.

Goals

This book, *Exploring America,* invites students to become informed participants in these public debates and to clarify their opinions by examining five critical issues underlying the current controversies: the question of whether America has a mission, the problem of identity, the promise of equality, the relationship of the individual to the state, and the place of religion in a secular state.

By introducing students to aspects of America's social and cultural history, the book allows them to formulate and argue their point of view with breadth, depth, and perspective.

Philosophy

Students are understandably most concerned with issues that affect them personally. They must face a complicated world, and they want to deal with it in their own way. A major premise of this book, however, is that making informed decisions requires knowing how things came to be the way they are. We can question the notion that there is nothing new under the sun, but it is wrong to believe that everything under the sun is new. Seemingly new ideas come from somewhere. The first women's rights convention was not in the 1970s, but in 1848.

Problems and solutions do not exist in a vacuum. Problems have causes, and solutions have consequences. Feminists argue, for example, that electing more women to public office will bring greater morality to politics. The reading selections raise some pertinent questions: What is the basis for believing that women are more virtuous than men? Where did this idea come from? What has been its effect? Who has benefited from it? Is it to women's advantage to embrace a stereotype that justifies the sexual double standard? An intelligent response to a current issue therefore requires understanding historical antecedents.

A second premise is that people, texts, and ideas cross paths. Consciously or subconsciously, most thinkers are attuned to the spirit of the times, whether they embrace or reject it. Something affecting women may influence African-Americans, who may in turn make demands that cause society to redefine national identity. Moreover, the intersection of people and ideas is often surprising. The women activists at the Seneca Falls Convention of 1848 built on the Declaration of Independence of 1776; on the dais at that convention was Frederick Douglass, an escaped slave and abolitionist leader. To allow students to experience the historical context of ideas, reading selections are arranged chronologically. For those who would rather trace the evolution of a single idea, an alternative table of contents groups the readings thematically.

Reading Selections

This book aims to create fluent, thoughtful readers by introducing students to important texts from a number of disciplines and in various styles. Selections come from history, autobiography, and belles lettres. Authors represent various perspectives, from the mainstream to famous dissents to lesser-known opposing views. Occasional boxes offer "Another Voice" as a complement or counterpoint to the readings. In many cases, selections explicitly address each other; in all cases, students are led to see the implicit connections.

Apparatus

Students learn the elements of critical thinking and reading through example and practice. In *Exploring America,* annotated passages illustrate how a reader engages a text, moving from mere comprehension to a fuller appreciation. In particular, students see how good readers return to a text and annotate again on the basis of later reading. Introductions to each chapter set the historical stage; headnotes to each selection place it in context. Study questions help students explore the text—including the main idea, supporting evidence, and the author's purpose, assumptions, and relationship to the audience. Suggestions for written responses and essays encourage students to make connections among readings, and to investigate the relevance of selections to a larger context and contemporary issues. Such research is aided by bibliographies and keywords for data searches.

Acknowledgments

We wish to thank publicly the many people who helped us in writing this book. Special gratitude goes to our students in "The Literature of American Values and Ideals" and to colleagues in the City University of New York Faculty Seminar on Incorporating Women of Color into the Curriculum.

Invaluable, and always gracious, assistance came from the librarians at Hunter College and the Mahopac Library: Suzanne Siegel, Pat Chase Kaufman, Maria Brech, Marsha DeBlasi, and Ping Fu.

Our editors were especially helpful. With a firm and sure hand, Michael Rosenberg maintained the integrity of our vision and enhanced it through his suggestions. Tia Black's insightful criticism at every stage of a long project accounts for much of the book's final shape. Her gentle wit and charming diplomacy smoothed many rough moments. Peggy Young contributed the book's artistic form, and Deanna Johnson guided it through production. Important comments came also from Judith Lee, Rutgers University; Alfred Zucker, Los Angeles Valley College; Todd Gernes, Michigan State University; Anna Joy, Sacramento City College; Anne C. Myers, State University of New York at Cobleskill; Michael Kuelker, St. Charles County Community College; Gayle Davis-Culp, Santa Monica College.

Finally, thanks to our children, Dinah and Jackie, who bravely bore the disruption in their lives and provided encouragement when it was most needed.

$\mathscr{C}$ONTENTS

OTHER VOICES:

$\mathcal{T}$HEMATIC CONTENTS

THE QUESTION OF MISSION

THE PROBLEM OF IDENTITY

THE PLACE OF RELIGION IN A SECULAR SOCIETY

1

$\mathcal{I}$NTRODUCING CRITICAL ISSUES

"**W**e hold these truths to be self evident: that all men are created equal."

DECLARATION OF INDEPENDENCE, 1776

"**W**e hold these truths to be self-evident: that all men and women are created equal."

SENECA FALLS DECLARATION, 1848

"**W**hat to the American slave is your Fourth of July?"

FREDERICK DOUGLASS, 1852

Critical Issues in the American Experience

The United States is rare, perhaps unique, in its status as a nation created by signatures on a document explaining philosophical principles. Rather than being a defined territory, a spoil of war, or a homeland for an already existing tribe, religion, ethnic group, or language community, the United States was formed when representatives, most of them elected, of thirteen British colonies agreed—after much debate and compromise—to unite. The inhabitants of these colonies practiced different religions and political traditions, and, in joining together, they separated themselves from people sharing similar backgrounds and languages—not only the distant English, but even the neighboring colonists in Canada. From its very start, this new nation housed communities in which other languages, including German and Dutch, were more common than English. Its rapid expansion, by treaty and purchase, encompassed huge areas settled by the French and Spanish. In addition, this sea of European settlement contained islands of Native American cultures and societies. The United States, then, was an experiment in Enlightenment theory—an attempt to prove that diverse people can unite for the peace, profit, and greater good of all.

When we investigate the characteristic ideas of this nation and their implementation over the centuries, we discover issues that have been addressed repeatedly in the past, and which are still relevant today. At the very core is the question asked two hundred years ago by the French immigrant Michel-Guillaume Jean de Crèvecoeur: What is an American? Is there a shared heritage, a common bond, uniting hundreds of millions of individuals into a national community, or are we just diverse men and women, Europeans, Africans, Asians, laborers, merchants, professionals, living in isolated proximity?

Such all-encompassing questions are best investigated by isolating a few contributing issues.

CRITICAL ISSUES IN THE AMERICAN EXPERIENCE

The question of mission

The problem of identity

The promise of equality

The relationship between the individual and the state

The place of religion in a secular society

These issues, in turn, may be approached by considering several questions:

The Question of Mission:
Is the United States special in some way?

How does this country differ from colonial powers?

What, if anything, is its mission?

Does foreign policy always mean "Us versus Them"?

What are "American" values?

The Problem of Identity:
How is identity determined or defined?

Are we one people or many?

When do "They" became part of "Us"?

What are the roles of gender, race, and ethnicity?

The Promise of Equality:
Does America offer equality to all?

In what sense are people equal?

Is the goal to provide equality of opportunity or equality of result?

What roles do social class and wealth play?

How is a balance achieved between majority rule and minority rights?

The Relationship between the Individual and the State:
Where do individual rights originate?

What does an individual owe to the community?

What does the government owe to its citizens?

When is civil disobedience justified?

When is armed revolution justified?

What parts should the individual and the government play in assigning social class and wealth?

The Place of Religion in a Secular Society:
What is America's religious heritage?

Is the objective to provide freedom *of* religion or freedom *from* religion?

Can values be separated from religion?

How is the balance maintained between private religion and public policy?

Critical Issues in Context

How one explores these issues or attempts to answer these questions depends, of course, upon individual perspective. Until about thirty years ago, history was the study of leaders, great ideas, and wars: According to this view, leaders conceived ideas or were moved by them, and ideas clashed quite literally as civilizations invaded, conquered, and overwhelmed one another. The American experience, in this context, included competition among European maritime powers during the age of discovery, a search for religious freedom during an era of religious wars, the French and Indian War during a struggle for colonial empire, the Revolutionary War, War of 1812, Mexican-American War, Civil War, Spanish-American War, World Wars I and II, the Korean War, the Vietnam War. Perhaps connected to the counterculture of the 1960s, however, an interest developed in social history, the story of ordinary people leading ordinary lives. Now scholars search archives for tax rolls, real estate transactions, police blotters, and records of marriages, births, adoptions, and deaths to learn and interpret the history of work, social class, family, childhood, aging, prejudice, and crime. This new information obviously affects our understanding of America and the important issues of our day.

The United States, like other nations, has evolved its own mythology—a system of stories and images that embody cultural ideals. The Founding Fathers, in fact, believed that public education should inculcate these ideals and thereby create a citizenry appropriate for and worthy of the republic they envisioned. Generations of schoolchildren learned about the honesty of George Washington, the inventions of Benjamin Franklin, and the persistence of Abraham Lincoln, because honesty, creativity and hard work were judged to be valuable characteristics—distinctively American—along with respect, justice, fairness, individualism, open-mindedness, and the beliefs in progress, compromise, and human perfectibility.

But has America lived up to its promise?

> *While the Declaration of Independence said, "We hold these truths to be self evident: that all men are created equal," the Seneca Falls Declaration said, "We hold these truths to be self-evident: that all men and women are created equal."*

While some critics point to the persistence of poverty or racism as reasons to dismiss America's ideals as the fantasy of white males from Western Europe, others argue that not achieving ideals is distinct from not *having* ideals. The values we respect and hold up as models inevitably influence our behavior. A nation that idealizes personal rights, unlike one that subordinates the individual to the state, will eventually be called to account for violating its duties to its citizens. A government that bases its authority upon a compact among free men and women has obligations that are simply denied by governments that claim individual rights exist only if they grant them. So too, unlike countries that blatantly remove certain groups from the protection of the law, a nation that preaches equality for all will one day confront the injustice of racism or religious tests for public office. Thus, it was entirely proper, and ultimately successful, when the Woman's Rights Movement brought the implied promise of the Declaration of Independence to its logical conclusion.

Defining the American Experience

Individual scholars and other investigators can examine the same material and yet reach contrasting conclusions because personal experience shapes our perspective. What we believe about America, what we understand when we read its formative documents, is influenced by our feelings about how America has treated us or those important to us.

Of course, who is included in the category of "us" is one of the critical issues we want to explore. Assimilation into the American majority or mainstream culture has long been a goal of immigrants. Crèvecoeur did not invent the melting pot he spoke of with such approval: Americans of English, Irish, German, Scandinavian, and French extraction do, in fact, mix freely; what he called intermarriage among them is now so much the norm it is not even conceptualized as intermarriage anymore; fourth- or fifth-generation descendants of non–English-speaking immigrants from these groups would be hard-pressed to construct a sentence in their ancestral language. Their values, beliefs, occupations, and life-styles are today characterized as typically "American." They do not check a separate ethnic box on governmental forms.

This is not the case with other groups. Catholics, Jews, Italians, and Poles, although white Europeans, have been, and often still are, distinguished from other Americans. Hispanics, the earliest colonists of Florida, Louisiana, and the Southwest, are still treated like outsiders by many. And, whether because of distinctive racial features or linguistic and cultural attachments, or both, Americans of aboriginal, African, and Asian extraction are generally recognized—either by choice or by outside imposition—as separate or "other." Their experience of America is therefore very different from that of whites, because the possibility of assimilation is either not available when desired, or offered at too great a price.

Though the French immigrant Crèvecoeur wrote, "Here individuals of all nations are melted into a new race of men," the Seneca chief Red Jacket protested, "You have got our country, but are not satisfied; you want to force your religion upon us."

Within these groups, women form a special subset. Frequently they share the economic, social, and political liabilities of their racial or ethnic community; but often they experience distinct privileges and pay a distinct price for them. When black men are unemployed or kept in the field, black women might be employed as housekeepers, babysitters, and nurses, living—often at great personal sacrifice—almost as part of the employer's family. While Chinese men were symbolically emasculated by working as cooks and laundrymen, Chinese women were mythologized as the hypersexual "erotic Oriental." The experience of these women therefore differs significantly from that of the men in their community.

> *Many groups would empathize with Frederick Douglass, an escaped slave, who asked, "What to the American slave is your Fourth of July?"*

Exploring the Critical Issues

In addition to the experience of the author, each reader brings his or her own experiences, knowledge, and opinions to the act of reading. What one reader considers commonplace, another may find insightful. What one praises as patriotism another may condemn as chauvinism. What one accepts as straightforward another may interpret as ironic. Where one focuses on the romance of the rich heroine another may be more interested in the poor servants in the background. To take one recent example, the image of Columbus in the 1990s is very different from the perception of fifty or a hundred years ago: During the celebration of the four hundredth anniversary of his discovery of America, there was no public opposition to the terms "celebration" and "discovery," no concern with whether he was Italian or Spanish, and no accusations that he destroyed the environment. In 1895, Henry Stanley characterized criticism of American expansion as absurd. "We shall presently find ourselves blaming Columbus for discovering America," he warned. In 1992, many Americans were doing just that.

Obviously, the meaning or impact of a piece of writing reflects the interplay of an author, a topic, an audience, and a context. It is almost impossible to imagine what *Uncle Tom's Cabin,* for example, would have been like if it had been written by a pro-slavery Southerner; it might have been a story about slaves, or even a noble slave, but it could not have been anything remotely similar to Stowe's tragic novel, an anti-slavery polemic of such emotional and religious power that President Lincoln said it caused the Civil War. Going a step further, an American in 1900 would simply not have written the novel, for there would have been no reason. To approach the novel, therefore, a reader must know at least about the existence of slavery. But to appreciate it fully, the reader would also have to know about issues that are presupposed, but not explained, in the novel: the divisions in and among Christian churches over the Biblical justification for slavery, the role of women in abolitionism, and the debate among abolitionists over how to treat millions of freed slaves. Numerous asides in the novel directly address the reader—and most of them assume the reader to be a woman. The attempt to understand the reason for this assumption might lead the reader to research contemporary literacy among men and women, the availability of time for reading, theories about the moral natures of women and men, women's self-improvement societies, or a number of other background issues.

Moreover, as illustrated by the boxed quotations in the previous sections, important documents must often be understood in terms of other important documents. That is, earlier historical or literary works provide background or context for later works. The Seneca Falls Declaration consciously quotes the Declaration of Independence; in fact, it virtually throws the ringing words back in the face of the men who cherished them. A reader who does not know both the line "All men are created equal" and its source cannot possibly grasp the power of the Seneca Falls emendation: "We hold these truths to be self-evident: that all men *and women* are created equal."

In other words, what you need to know in order to read and understand important works is not limited to what is contained in the texts themselves. Authors make assumptions about what their audience knows and believes. Consequently, you, as a reader, must be able to place what you read within a cultural and historical context.

Finally, major works seldom address only one carefully selected issue. The relationship between the individual and the state will often be formulated in terms of America's mission or religious heritage, or couched in arguments about race and identity. Part of understanding what you read lies in noticing how the interplay and relative importance of these critical issues changes over time and from author to author.

Features of This Book

One student recently asked a professor, "How do you know all this and how are we supposed to know it?" The answer, of course, is that we learn from experience, practice, and repeated exposure. Students are not expected to "know all this" coming into a course, or even upon college graduation. What you should know, however, is that critical reading should be your goal. Good readers are not content merely to understand the text they are currently reading. An essay, story, or legal document resonates with a host of associations, encouraging a good reader to seek the answers to a multitude of new questions.

Perhaps the most important characteristic of good readers is that they expect—in fact, demand—that the text they are reading make sense. In so doing, they make demands upon themselves. Good readers do not accept failure or mystification. They look up the definitions of unfamiliar words, cross-reference allusions, and research any remaining questions. This book directs you in this kind of reading process and provides you with the opportunity to practice all of the important elements of critical reading.

In order to help you build a context for each selection, the text is organized chronologically so that you can see what currents were swirling about each of the authors. Each chapter offers a historical setting; each selection has its own introduction. In addition, short passages labeled *Another Voice* offer complements and counterpoints to the readings, enriching the context and providing leads for essay topics and further research.

Accompanying each selection are three types of questions. *Exploring Issues in the Text* precedes each reading and helps you focus on its thesis, details, evidence, and technique. After the selection, *Building Context* points out connections to other selections in this book, and *Further Study* suggests topics for outside investigation. To assist your research, there are brief bibliographies and a list of keywords for computer searches.

Because the questions refer you to related selections, the book can be read thematically as well as chronologically. It is possible to start with any selection and trace the treatment of significant ideas through other readings.

Each chapter ends with suggested topics to explore through writing. These broad and open-ended topics cannot be "done" in a short essay. Rather, they are meant to offer directions worth exploring. Once on your way, you can then focus on a manageable point that interests you. You might even return to an idea later, after reading something that provides it with another perspective. In addition, preparing short answers to the questions that follow the reading selections will provide notes and ideas from which additional essay topics may emerge.

Finally, the text illustrates the creative aspect of writing. Whether writing fiction, autobiography, history, or science, an author does not simply record or transmit facts. Instead, from the myriad events occurring daily to individuals and nations, the author chooses certain ones as significant within a particular framework. Moreover, he or she will almost certainly try to distinguish cause and effect from mere sequence—that is, A *caused* B, not simply, A *preceded* B. Needless to say, no two authors will write identical accounts of a given event because each has differing interests and points of view.

For example, the explorer John Smith and a minister's wife, Mary Rowlandson, have both written what have come to be called "captivity narratives," describing life among their Indian captors. Yet their stories are very different. Smith's story stresses his courage, resourcefulness, and ultimate friendship with Pocahontas, the Indian princess who saved his life. Rowlandson's narrative emphasizes the cruelty of the Indians, the suffering of the victims, and the saving power of God. Recent scholarship has also found in these accounts the influence of gender on perception and the political power of survivors.

The reading selections in this book explore critical issues in America—mission, identity, equality, religion, the individual and the state—in a variety of ways, from vastly different perspectives. Some of the selections contain voices from the mainstream: white men, upperclass women, and black men who have won general acceptance. In others, the frequently ignored women, minorities, and less privileged speak for and about themselves. We have tried to introduce you to a few important issues while providing you with additional written sources so you can develop your own informed opinion. We have not attempted to write "Everything You Need to Know to Be Culturally Literate." Rather, we hope that by exploring these important issues through critical thinking and reading, you will continue to investigate them and thus realize their relevance to all aspects of American life.

Critical Thinking

Even if you have not heard the term, you are familiar with critical thinking. Perhaps an advertisement offered an expensive VCR at an unbelievable price and you said sarcastically, "Oh, sure." Or a mere acquaintance told you a personal story and you thought, "Why are you telling me this?" These are instances in which you did not simply accept what you were told—you were critical about what you heard and decided that the facts did not add up.

Though you may not have analyzed your behavior in these types of situations, critical thinking includes several steps:

Analysis:
1. identifying a main point or purpose
2. distinguishing fact from opinion
3. discerning assumption from proof

Evaluation:
1. considering the credibility of the source
2. weighing the facts
3. considering the logic of the conclusion

Making Connections:
1. associating this situation with your own experiences
2. relating this situation to what you have heard

Forming a Judgment or an Opinion:
1. choosing the best explanation of the facts
2. creating an informed opinion

Critical Reading

Critical reading applies these same skills to written text. Good readers make sense of what they are reading by focusing on several components:

Content:
1. identifying the main idea
2. distinguishing the main idea from supporting details
3. summarizing the text concisely

Author:
1. recognizing the author's purpose
2. perceiving the author's assumptions
3. determining the author's credibility

Audience:
1. identifying the author's readers
2. clarifying their relationship to the author
3. determining what knowledge is assumed
4. recognizing what beliefs are assumed
5. comparing this audience to oneself

Technique:
1. understanding the organization of the text
2. recognizing the author's point of view

PREVIEWING

Before they even start reading, readers can get a sense of a selection by finding out more about its author, the author's purpose, and the time period in which it was written. Such information, provided by headnotes in this book, can alert you to many of the variables we have been discussing. Some readers also skim sections of the text, looking especially for topic sentences and transitional words, in order to determine the thesis and the author's method of developing it.

UNDERLINING

Unless a book is expensive or does not belong to you, you should underline small passages that capture the point of a selection concisely. Good readers underline sparingly—only those phrases or words that are truly vital. Underlining whole sentences or paragraphs obscures the useful information you want to highlight and therefore defeats the purpose.

ANNOTATING

You should write notes to yourself in the margins or in a notebook. These notes should explain why you underlined passages, show how ideas are developed, and make connections to other books and articles.

Exploring Critical Issues through Writing

As you will see again and again in the reading selections, writing involves more than just the recording of facts. In a good essay, a writer addresses an audience about a certain topic. The writer's reasons for discussing this particular topic with this particular audience will affect the content and shape of the essay. Details that the writer considers relevant are included, while others, however interesting they may seem in the abstract, are omitted. You should clarify, therefore, why a topic matters to you, why it should matter to your audience, and why you believe a particular detail is worth including.

This book asks you to engage five critical issues. As valuable as your opinion is, developing it into an essay requires evidence, the sort of information that is found within the reading selections and elsewhere. You can mine an article for statistics or arguments to strengthen a position you already hold. You can compare and contrast several sources in order to clarify an issue or appreciate its complexity.

Your purpose, not the purpose of the source, must determine how you use information in your essay. When the Seneca Falls Convention declared, "We hold these truths to be self-evident: that all men *and women* are created equal," there was a direct reference to the Declaration of Independence. But Jefferson's purpose in the Declaration was not to defend women's rights in 1848. The women at Seneca Falls adapted his work for their own purpose. Similarly, the boxed quotations in this chapter were chosen to highlight our point about the need to read each selection in relation to other writings. Thus, the quotations from the Declaration of Independence and the Seneca Falls Convention focus on the issue of equality, while those from Michel-Guillaume Jean de Crèvecoeur and Red Jacket offer different perspectives regarding the desirability of assimilation. If your purpose is to compare the importance of religion in two works, or to explain another issue you found particularly meaningful, other quotations will be required to support your argument. When drawing from a source you must consider the needs of your essay and include only those elements that serve your purpose. As you read, therefore, you should mark the passages that catch your eye or promise to be useful.

PREWRITING

You should view class discussions and writing assignments as opportunities to engage what you have read. After each selection, this text asks you to react, evaluate, and form connections by writing summaries, short answers, or notes for class discussion. These questions help you see what others have found significant and suggest ways to develop your own response. But you should not limit your expression to these questions—your goal is to find points and quotations that are meaningful to you.

BRAINSTORMING

Deciding what to write about is often the most discomfiting aspect of the writing process. Very few people can sit down and write an essay from beginning to end on the first try. Some writers find it helpful simply to play with ideas for awhile, either in their heads or by jotting them down on paper. Students often find it productive to work with their friends, so that each one can offer ideas that jog the imaginations of the others. Class discussions in which students respond to each other freely instead of addressing only their instructor also help. The goal of brainstorming is to generate promising leads and examples.

RESEARCH

Sometimes the impetus that you need is in the library. If a subject piques your interest and you want ideas for an essay topic, libraries and computer services are invaluable resources. Because you may not yet know a topic well enough to go directly to important sources, we recommend looking at the tracings at the end of library card-catalog entries, and following the links offered by a computer search.

For example, if you want to write about civil rights, you might start by looking for books under the subject heading "King, Martin Luther, Jr." There, you are likely to find *Parting the Waters: America in the King Years, 1954–63,* by Taylor Branch. But this book is only a beginning. The tracings tell you that more information can be found by looking under the Library of Congress subject headings at the end of the listing:

"Afro-Americans—Civil rights."

"Civil rights movements—United States—History—20th century."

"United States—History—1953–1961."

Branch, Taylor.
Parting the waters: America in the King years, 1954–63/Taylor Branch.
p. cm.
Bibliography: p.
Includes index.
ISBN 0-671-46097-8 (v. 1)
1. Afro-Americans—Civil rights. 2. Civil rights
movements—United States—History—20th century.
3. King, Martin Luther, Jr., 1929-1968.
4. United States—History—1953-1961. I. Title.

Tracings

E185.61.B7914 1988
973'0496073—dc19

88-24033
CIP

Similarly, the tracings in the listing for *Coming to America: A History of Immigration and Ethnicity in American Life,* by Roger Daniels, direct you to these subject headings:

"Ethnology—United States—History."

"United States—Emigration and immigration."

"Immigrants—United States—History."

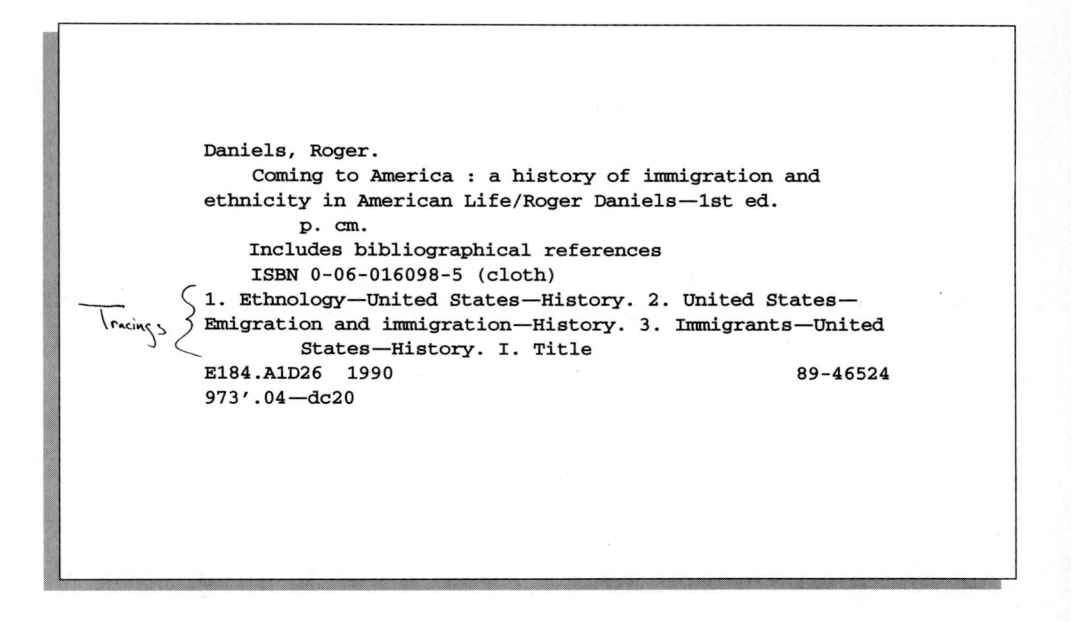

And by following the links offered in a computer search of the name "Red Jacket" you would discover:

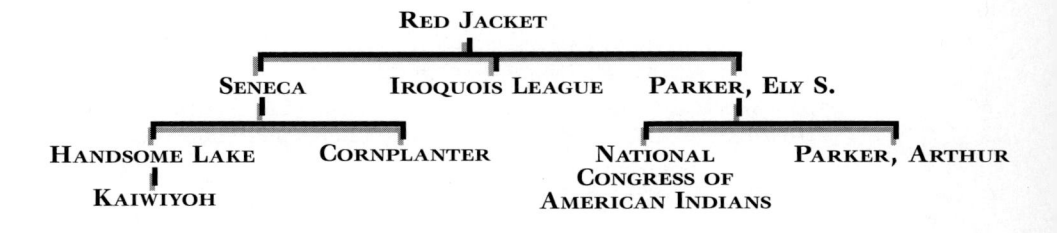

Any one of these headings will lead you to fascinating material that you might not have originally known about and which may now suggest a new essay topic.

PEER CRITIQUING

To discover if your essay topic will interest a reader, you can ask a friend to look at it. The peer who is doing this critiquing should focus on your ideas, insights, and examples, and offer an opinion about whether this is a topic worth developing into a paper that someone else would want to read. After you have drafted an essay, you can ask a friend to critique this as well.

THESIS AND EVIDENCE

Whether you are writing an expository essay or autobiographical sketch, you must have a clear main point, or thesis, to help you determine what to include or omit. Conversely, the information available to you will limit the breadth of your thesis. At this stage, it is probably best for you to state your thesis explicitly, usually in the first or second paragraph, to offer direction to both yourself and your readers. Later, you might experiment with more subtle or inferential techniques. In all cases, however, you will need evidence to support your position, just as a lawyer needs Exhibits A, B, and so on to persuade a jury. Your evidence is contained in the reading selections and in the additional notes and summaries you write. You should feel free to draw upon these valuable resources.

Understanding how all of these concepts and techniques function in practice is the topic of the next chapter.

2

EXPLORING ISSUES IN CONTEXT

"Pocahontas, the King's dearest daughter . . . got his head in her arms and laid her own upon his to save him from death."

JOHN SMITH

"I don't like being put under a magnifying glass and having cute liberal terms describe who I am."

BARBARA CAMERON

"Indian captivity narratives have mirrored the aspirations and anxieties of successive generations."

ANNETTE KOLODNY

We saw in the previous chapter that a piece of writing shows the interaction of an author, a topic, and an audience; and that not everything a thoughtful reader needs is contained in the text itself. In this chapter we will read a few selections about the early European settlement of the Atlantic coast of North America. By analyzing the writings as a group, we will see how the techniques of critical thinking and critical reading help us to make additional discoveries, gleaning significance from the methods authors use to present their specific topic to their intended audience.

The selections in this chapter include the narratives of John Smith and Mary Rowlandson; essays by Dale Van Every, a white male historian, and Barbara Cameron, a Native-American woman radical, that provide two modern perspectives on European-Indian relations; and, finally, a study by Annette Kolodny explaining how authors and their audience create diverse interpretations of the same material.

We have already mentioned that the works of John Smith and Mary Rowlandson are similar in that each describes the author's capture by Indians, but are different in what they tell us about the influence of gender on perception, the importance of religion to the individual and community, the political power of the victims and survivors. We will examine how the contexts of these and other works reflect the dynamic interplay of ideas about America's mission, personal identity, equality, religion, and the individual and the state. In doing this, we will apply the techniques of critical thinking and reading that we outlined in the previous chapter.

JOHN SMITH
The General History of Virginia (1624)

"Pocahontas, the King's dearest daughter . . . got his head in her arms and laid her own upon his to save him from death."

John Smith's swashbuckling adventures are the stuff of legend—and the models for scores of movies. According to his own accounts, by the age of twenty-six he had joined the English army, fought in the Netherlands and Hungary, been captured and sold into slavery by the Turks, escaped with the aid of a beautiful lady, and made his way back to England. As a soldier and survivor, he was a natural choice to be one of the leaders of the settlement that the English wanted to establish in North America to compete with the Spanish.

Virginia in 1607 was a wilderness, filled with known and unknown dangers. Within a year, only 38 of the original 105 settlers were still alive. Smith led hunting and foraging parties into the wilderness to find food. On one of these expeditions, he was captured by the natives. His story, told in the following selection, has become a mainstay of American mythology.

Some modern scholars view this part of Smith's *History* with skepticism for a number of reasons: his is the only version of the event; it bears striking resemblances to his accounts of his earlier adventures; Pocahontas is not mentioned in his first book about Virginia; Smith emerges as the most intelligent and hardworking council member; and at the time of publication he was negotiating (unsuccessfully as it turned out) to lead other colonists to America. Other scholars, however, find no basis in fact for these suspicions.

The following questions will help focus your reading:

Text: *The General History of Virginia, New England, and the Summer Isles;* from *Heritage of American Literature,* vol. 1; ed. by James E. Miller, Jr., Harcourt Brace Jovanovich, 1991.

EXPLORING ISSUES IN THE TEXT

1. What is Smith's purpose in telling this story? How does his intent relate to his use of the terms Indian "nations" and "king," and his referring to Powhatan as an Emperor and Pocahontas as a princess?

2. What does Smith see as his purpose in Jamestown? How does he view himself? How does this view help shape the content and organization of his narrative?

3. How does Smith view the Indians? Are they his equals? Are they fully human? Mark passages in which he describes them or comments on their behavior.

4. What part does religion play in Smith's narrative?

THE GENERAL HISTORY
OF VIRGINIA

1   The President and Captain Archer not long after intended also to have abandoned the country, which project also was curbed and suppressed by Smith.

2   The Spaniard never more greedily desired gold than he victual, nor his soldiers more to abandon the country than he to keep it. But [he found] plenty of corn in the river of Chickahominy, where hundreds of savages in divers places stood with baskets expecting his coming.

3   And now the winter approaching, the rivers became so covered with swans, geese, ducks, and cranes that we daily feasted with good bread, Virginia peas, pumpkins, and putchamins, fish, fowl, and divers sort of wild beasts as fast as we could eat them, so that none of our tuftaffety humorists desired to go for England.

4   But our comedies never endured long without a tragedy, some idle exceptions being muttered against Captain Smith for not discovering the head of Chickahominy river and [being] taxed by the Council to be too slow in so worthy an attempt. The next voyage he proceeded so far that with much labor by cutting of trees asunder he made his passage, but when his barge could pass no farther, he left her in a broad bay out of danger of shot, commanding none should go ashore till his return; himself with two English and two savages went up higher in a canoe, but he was not long absent but his men went ashore, whose want of government gave both occasion and opportunity to the savages to surprise one George Cassen whom they slew and much failed not to have cut off the boat and all the rest.

5   Smith little dreaming of that accident, being got to the marshes at the river's head twenty miles in the desert, had his two men slain (as is supposed) sleeping by the canoe, while himself by fowling sought them victual, who finding he was beset with 200 savages, two of them he slew, still defending himself with the aid of a savage his guide, whom he bound to his arm with his garters and used him as a buckler, yet he was shot in his thigh a little, and had many arrows that stuck in his clothes but no great hurt, till at last they took him prisoner.

6   When this news came to Jamestown, much was their sorrow for his loss, few expecting what ensued.

7   Six or seven weeks those barbarians kept him prisoner, many strange triumphs and conjurations they made of him, yet he so demeaned himself amongst them, as he not only diverted them from surprising the fort, but procured his own liberty, and got himself and his company such estimation amongst them, that those savages admired him more than their own Quiyouckosucks.

8   The manner how they used and delivered him is as followeth:

The savages having drawn from George Cassen whither Captain Smith was gone, prosecuting that opportunity they followed him with 300 bowmen, conducted by the King of Pamunkey, who in divisions searching the turnings of the river found Robinson and Emry by the fireside; those they shot full of arrows and slew. Then finding the Captain, as is said, that used the savage that was his guide as his shield (three of them being slain and divers others so galled), all the rest would not come near him. Thinking thus to have returned to his boat, regarding them, as he marched, more than his way, [he] slipped up to the middle in an oozy creek and his savage with him, yet dared they not come to him till being near dead with cold he threw away his arms. Then according to their composition they drew him forth and led him to the fire where his men were slain. Diligently they chafed his benumbed limbs.

9   He demanding for their captain, they showed him Opechancanough, King of Pamunkey, to whom he gave a round ivory double compass dial. Much they marveled at the playing of the fly and needle, which they could see so plainly and yet not touch it because of the glass that covered them. But when he demonstrated by that globe-like jewel the roundness of the earth and skies, the sphere of the sun, moon, and stars, and how the sun did chase the night round about the world continually, the greatness of the land and sea, the diversity of nations, variety of complexions, and how we were to them antipodes and many other such like matters, they all stood as amazed with admiration.

10   Notwithstanding, within an hour after, they tied him to a tree, and as many as could stand about him prepared to shoot him, but the King holding up the compass in his hand, they all laid down their bows and arrows and in a triumphant manner led him to Orapaks where he was after their manner kindly feasted and well used.

11   Their order in conducting him was thus: Drawing themselves all in file, the King in the midst had all their pieces and swords borne before him. Captain Smith was led after him by three great savages holding him fast by each arm, and on each side six went in file with their arrows nocked. But arriving at the town (which was but only thirty or forty hunting houses made of mats, which they remove as they please, as we our tents), all the women and children staring to behold him, the soldiers first all in file performed the form of a bissom so well as could be, and on each flank, officers as sergeants to see them keep their orders. A good time they continued this

exercise and then cast themselves in a ring, dancing in such several postures and singing and yelling out such hellish notes and screeches; being strangely painted, every one [had] his quiver of arrows and at his back a club, on his arm a fox or an otter's skin or some such matter for his vambrace, their heads and shoulders painted red with oil and pocones mingled together, which scarlet-like color made an exceeding handsome show, his bow in his hand and the skin of a bird with her wings abroad, dried, tied on his head, a piece of copper, a white shell, a long feather with a small rattle growing at the tails of their snakes tied to it, or some such like toy. All this while, Smith and the King stood in the midst, guarded as before is said, and after three dances they all departed. Smith they conducted to a long house where thirty or forty tall fellows did guard him, and ere long more bread and venison was brought him than would have served twenty men. I think his stomach at that time was not very good; what he left they put in baskets and tied over his head. About midnight they set the meat again before him; all this time not one of them would eat a bit with him, till the next morning they brought him as much more, and then did they eat all the old and reserved the new as they had done the other, which made him think they would fat him to eat him. Yet in this desperate estate, to defend him from the cold, one Maocassater brought him his gown in requital of some beads and toys Smith had given him at his first arrival in Virginia.

12   Two days after, a man would have slain him (but that the guard prevented it) for the death of his son, to whom they conducted him to recover the poor man then breathing his last. Smith told them that at Jamestown he had a water would do it, if they would let him fetch it, but they would not permit that, but made all the preparations they could to assault Jamestown, craving his advice, and for recompence he should have life, liberty, land, and women. In part a table book he wrote his mind to them at the fort, what was intended, how they should follow that direction to affright the messengers, and without fail send him such things as he wrote for. And an inventory with them. The difficulty and danger, he told the savages, of the mines, great guns, and other engines exceedingly affrighted them, yet according to his request they went to Jamestown in as bitter weather as

could be of frost and snow, and within three days returned with an answer.

13   But when they came to Jamestown, seeing men sally
out as he had told them they would, they fled, yet in the
night they came again to the same place where he had
told them they should receive an answer and such
things as he had promised them, which they found accordingly, and with which they returned with no small
expedition to the wonder of them all that heard it, that
he could either divine, or the paper could speak. . . .

14   At last they brought him to Werowocomoco, where was
Powhatan, their Emperor. Here more than two hundred of
those grim courtiers stood wondering at him, as [if] he had
been a monster, till Powhatan and his train had put themselves in their greatest braveries. Before a fire upon a seat
like a bedstead, he sat covered with a great robe made of
raccoon skins and all the tails hanging by. On either hand
did sit a young wench of sixteen or eighteen years and
along on each side [of] the house, two rows of men and behind them as many women, with all their heads and
shoulders painted red, many of their heads bedecked with
the white down of birds, but every one with something,
and a great chain of white beads about their necks.

15   At his entrance before the King, all the people gave a
great shout. The Queen of Appomattoc was appointed to
bring him water to wash his hands, and another brought
him a bunch of feathers, instead of a towel, to dry them;
having feasted him after their best barbarous manner
they could, a long consultation was held, but the conclusion was, two great stones were brought before Powhatan;
then as many as could, laid hands on him, dragged him to
them, and thereon laid his head and being ready with
their clubs to beat out his brains, Pocahontas, the King's
dearest daughter, when no entreaty could prevail, got his
head in her arms and laid her own upon his to save him
from death, whereat the Emperor was contented he
should live to make him hatchets, and her bells, beads,
and copper, for they thought him as well of all occupations as themselves. For the King himself will make his
own robes, shoes, bows, arrows, pots; plant, hunt, or do
anything so well as the rest.

> They say he bore a pleasant show,
> But sure his heart was sad.
> For who can pleasant be, and rest,

> That lives in fear and dread:
> And having life suspected, doth
> It still suspected lead.

16 Two days after, Powhatan, having disguised himself in the most fearfulest manner he could, caused Captain Smith to be brought forth to a great house in the woods and there upon a mat by the fire to be left alone. Not long after, from behind a mat that divided the house, was made the most dolefulest noise he ever heard; then Powhatan more like a devil than a man, with some two hundred more as black as himself, came unto him and told him now they were friends, and presently he should go to Jamestown to send him two great guns and a grindstone for which he would give him the country of Capahowasic and forever esteem him as his son Nantaquond.

17 So to Jamestown with twelve guides Powhatan sent him. That night they quartered in the woods, he still expecting (as he had done all this long time of his imprisonment) every hour to be put to one death or other, for all their feasting. But almighty God (by His divine providence) had mollified the hearts of those stern barbarians with compassion. The next morning betimes they came to the fort, where Smith having used the savages with what kindness he could, he showed Rawhunt, Powhatan's trusty servant, two demi-culverins and a millstone to carry [to] Powhatan; they found them somewhat too heavy, but when they did see him discharge them, being loaded with stones, among the boughs of a great tree loaded with icicles, the ice and branches came so tumbling down that the poor savages ran away half dead with fear. But at last we regained some conference with them and gave them such toys and sent to Powhatan, his women, and children such presents as gave them in general full content.

18 Now in Jamestown they were all in combustion, the strongest preparing once more to run away with the pinnace; which, with the hazard of his life, with saker falcon and musket shot, Smith forced now the third time to stay or sink.

19 Some, no better than they should be, had plotted with the President the next day to have him put to death by the Levitical law, for the lives of Robinson and Emry; pretending the fault was his that had led them to their ends; but he quickly took such order with such lawyers that he laid them by their heels till he sent some of them prisoners for England.

20   Now every once in four of five days, Pocahontas with her attendants brought him so much provision that saved many of their lives, that else for all this had starved with hunger.

> Thus from numb death our good God
>   sent relief,
> The sweet assuager of all other grief.

21   His relation of the plenty he had seen, especially at Werowocomoco, and of the state and bounty of Powhatan (which till that time was unknown), so revived their dead spirits (especially the love of Pocahontas) as all men's fear was abandoned.

22   Thus you may see what difficulties still crossed any good endeavour; and the good success of the business being thus oft brought to the very period of destruction; yet you see by what strange means God hath still delivered it.

BUILDING CONTEXT

After you read a selection, you should try to place it within a larger context that includes the works of other authors. Thus, for example, you might want to keep these questions in mind when you read Rowlandson's narrative:

1. How does Rowlandson's self-image compare to Smith's? How do their differing feelings about themselves connect to the central purposes of the two accounts?

2. How do Smith and Rowlandson use references to God and religion?

In addition, you should note ideas or leads that may warrant further study—for example, references that you did not recognize or statements that interested, intrigued, or angered you. While individual tastes vary, these points merit consideration.

FURTHER STUDY

1. What accounts for the popularity of the story of Pocahontas? Why is John Smith a central image in American mythology?

2. Columbus arrived in America in 1492. Jamestown, the first successful English colony in Virginia, was established in 1607. What happened during the intervening 115 years? How did this history affect Smith's purpose in writing his *History of Virginia* and his presentation of the material? Could his purpose suggest why he calls Powhatan an emperor and Pocahontas a princess?

3. In a later chapter Smith writes that Pocahontas converted to Christianity, married an Englishman, bore a child by him, and traveled to England. Why does he include this information? What purpose does it serve in his narrative, and how does it influence later attitudes toward his story?

4. Some people claim that Smith was a self-promoter, selling himself as much as Virginia. What evidence in the text supports or refutes this contention? How does his account compare with current "insider" books and political memoirs?

An Annotated Reading of Smith's History

The questions we have asked acted as part of the previewing for a first reading of this selection. However, you should always read a selection more than once, because the importance of an early passage may not become clear until a later passage clarifies its purpose; for example, the fact that paragraph 4 is a legal defense of Smith's behavior on the ill-fated mission does not become clear until we learn in paragraph 19 that his opponents had hoped to court-martial him for the deaths of his men. Now, read the selection again, underlining and annotating those passages that address the questions or that pique your interest. Then compare your results to the following sample.

THE GENERAL HISTORY
OF VIRGINIA

1 The President and Captain Archer not long after intended also to have abandoned the country, which project also was curbed and suppressed by Smith.

Other leaders are cowards; Smith is hero.

2 The Spaniard never more greedily desired gold than he victual, nor his soldiers more to abandon the country than he to keep it. But [he found] plenty of corn in the river of Chickahominy, where hundreds of savages in divers places stood with baskets expecting his coming.

Negative view of Spain— England's longtime enemy

3 And now the winter approaching, the rivers became so covered with swans, geese, ducks, and cranes that we daily feasted with good bread, Virginia peas, pumpkins, and putchamins, fish, fowl, and divers sort of wild beasts as fast as we could eat them, so that none of our tuftaffety humorists desired to go for England.

Contempt for other leaders

4 But our comedies never endured long without a tragedy, some idle exceptions being muttered against Captain Smith for not discovering the head of Chickahominy river and [being] taxed by the Council to be too slow in so

Cause of later deaths is false accusations

worthy an attempt. The next voyage he proceeded so far that with much labor by cutting of trees asunder he made his passage, but when his barge could pass no farther, he left her in a broad bay out of danger of shot, commanding none should go ashore till his return; himself with two English and two savages went up higher in a canoe, but he was not long absent but his men went ashore, whose want of government gave both occasion and opportunity to the savages to surprise one George Cassen whom they slew and much failed not to have cut off the boat and all the rest.

5 Smith little dreaming of that accident, being got to the marshes at the river's head twenty miles in the desert, had his two men slain (as is supposed) sleeping by the canoe, while himself by fowling sought them victual, who finding he was beset with 200 savages, two of them he slew, still defending himself with the aid of a savage his guide, whom he bound to his arm with his garters and used him as a buckler, yet he was shot in his thigh a little, and had many arrows that stuck in his clothes but no great hurt, till at last they took him prisoner.

6 When this news came to Jamestown, much was their sorrow for his loss, few expecting what ensued.

7 Six or seven weeks those barbarians kept him prisoner, many strange triumphs and conjurations they made of him, yet he so demeaned himself amongst them, as he not only diverted them from surprising the fort, but procured his own liberty, and got himself and his company such estimation amongst them, that those savages admired him more than their own Quiyouckosucks.

8 The manner how they used and delivered him is as followeth:

The savages having drawn from George Cassen whither Captain Smith was gone, prosecuting that opportunity they followed him with 300 bowmen, conducted by the King of Pamunkey, who in divisions searching the turnings of the river found Robinson and Emry by the fireside; those they shot full of arrows and slew. Then finding the Captain, as is said, that used the savage that was his guide as his shield (three of them being slain and divers others so galled), all the rest would not come near him. Thinking thus to have returned to his boat, regarding them, as he marched, more than his way, [he] slipped up to the middle in an oozy creek and his savage with him, yet dared they

---

Handwritten marginal notes:

Like a true leader, Smith leaves his men in safety and pushes on, even hunting for their food.

Uses "savage" as human shield. His guide is not his equal — or even "human."

Modern demeanor Not demeaning

Smith is hero. Saves fort, and establishes good relations. This is the purpose of the whole story.

200 in par. 5

2 savage guides in par. 4 2 in par. 15

what happened to him? Is he dead? Allowed to drown?

not come to him till being near dead with cold he threw away his arms. Then according to their composition they drew him forth and led him to the fire where his men were slain. Diligently they chafed his benumbed limbs.

9   He <u>demanding for their captain,</u> they showed him Opechancanough, <u>King of Pamunkey,</u> to whom he gave a round ivory double compass dial. Much they marveled at the playing of the fly and needle, which they could see so plainly and yet not touch it because of the glass that covered them. But when he <u>demonstrated by that</u> <u>globe-like jewel</u> the <u>roundness of the earth</u> and skies, the sphere of the sun, moon, and stars, and <u>how the sun did</u> <u>chase</u> the night round about the world continually, the <u>greatness of the land and sea,</u> the <u>diversity of nations,</u> variety of complexions, and how we were to them antipodes and many other such like matters, <u>they all stood</u> <u>as amazed with admiration.</u>

Sees Indians in European terms

How did he explain these things to them? In what language? How did they know what the compass pictures meant?

10   Notwithstanding, within an hour after, they tied him to a tree, and as many as could stand about him prepared to shoot him, but the King holding up the compass in his hand, they all laid down their bows and arrows and in a triumphant manner led him to Orapaks where he was after their manner kindly feasted and well used.

11   Their order in conducting him was thus: Drawing themselves all in file, the King in the midst had all their pieces and swords borne before him. Captain Smith was led after him by three great savages holding him fast by each arm, and on each side six went in file with their arrows nocked. But arriving at the town (which was but only thirty or forty hunting houses made of mats, which they remove as they please, as we our tents), all the women and children staring to behold him, the <u>soldiers</u> first all in file performed the form of a bissom so well as could be, and on each flank, <u>officers as sergeants</u> to see them keep their orders. A good time they continued this exercise and then cast themselves in a ring, dancing in such several postures and singing and yelling out such <u>hellish notes and screeches;</u> being <u>strangely painted,</u> every one [had] his quiver of arrows and at his back a club, on his arm a fox or an otter's skin or some such matter for his vambrace, their <u>heads and shoulders</u> <u>painted red</u> with oil and pocones mingled together, which scarlet-like color made an <u>exceeding handsome</u> <u>show,</u> his bow in his hand and the skin of a bird with her wings abroad, dried, tied on his head, a piece of copper,

European perspective

Hellish savages, but nonetheless, attractive in their way

a white shell, a long feather with a small rattle growing at the tails of their snakes tied to it, or some such like toy. All this while, Smith and the King stood in the midst, guarded as before is said, and after three dances they all departed. Smith they conducted to a long house where thirty or forty tall fellows did guard him, and ere long more bread and venison was brought him than would have served twenty men. I think his stomach at that time was not very good; what he left they put in baskets and tied over his head. About midnight they set the meat again before him; all this time not one of them would eat a bit with him, till the next morning they brought him as much more, and then did they eat all the old and reserved the new as they had done the other, which made him think they would fat him to eat him. Yet in this desperate estate, to defend him from the cold, one Maocassater brought him his gown in requital of some beads and toys Smith had given him at his first arrival in Virginia.

12 Two days after, a man would have slain him (but that the guard prevented it) for the death of his son, to whom they conducted him to recover the poor man then breathing his last. Smith told them that at Jamestown he had a water would do it, if they would let him fetch it, but they would not permit that, but made all the preparations they could to assault Jamestown, craving his advice, and for recompence he should have life, liberty, land, and women. In part a table book he wrote his mind to them at the fort, what was intended, how they should follow that direction to affright the messengers, and without fail send him such things as he wrote for. And an inventory with them. The difficulty and danger, he told the savages, of the mines, great guns, and other engines exceedingly affrighted them, yet according to his request they went to Jamestown in as bitter weather as could be of frost and snow, and within three days returned with an answer.

13 But when they came to Jamestown, seeing men sally out as he had told them they would, they fled, yet in the night they came again to the same place where he had told them they should receive an answer and such things as he had promised them, which they found accordingly, and with which they returned with no small expedition to the wonder of them all that heard it, that he could either divine, or the paper could speak. . . .

14   At last they brought him to Werowocomoco, where was
Powhatan, their Emperor. Here more than two hundred of
those grim courtiers stood wondering at him, as [if] he had
been a monster, till Powhatan and his train had put themselves in their greatest braveries. Before a fire upon a seat
like a bedstead, he sat covered with a great robe made of
raccoon skins and all the tails hanging by. On either hand
did sit a young wench of sixteen or eighteen years and
along on each side [of] the house, two rows of men and behind them as many women, with all their heads and
shoulders painted red, many of their heads bedecked with
the white down of birds, but every one with something,
and a great chain of white beads about their necks.

15   At his entrance before the King, all the people gave a
great shout. The Queen of Appomattoc was appointed to
bring him water to wash his hands, and another brought
him a bunch of feathers, instead of a towel, to dry them;
having feasted him after their best barbarous manner
they could, a long consultation was held, but the conclusion was, two great stones were brought before Powhatan;
then as many as could, laid hands on him, dragged him to
them, and thereon laid his head and being ready with
their clubs to beat out his brains, Pocahontas, the King's
dearest daughter, when no entreaty could prevail, got his
head in her arms and laid her own upon his to save him
from death, whereat the Emperor was contented he
should live to make him hatchets, and her bells, beads,
and copper, for they thought him as well of all occupations as themselves. For the King himself will make his
own robes, shoes, bows, arrows, pots; plant, hunt, or do
anything so well as the rest.

> They say he bore a pleasant show,
> But sure his heart was sad.
> For who can pleasant be, and rest,
> That lives in fear and dread:
> And having life suspected, doth
> It still suspected lead.

16   Two days after, Powhatan, having disguised himself in
the most fearfulest manner he could, caused Captain
Smith to be brought forth to a great house in the woods
and there upon a mat by the fire to be left alone. Not long
after, from behind a mat that divided the house, was made
the most dolefulest noise he ever heard; then Powhatan
more like a devil than a man, with some two hundred

[Margin annotations: "European perspective"; "Crisis!"; "Saved by the native princess."]

more as black as himself, came unto him and told him now they were friends, and presently he should go to Jamestown to send him two great guns and a grindstone for which he would give him the country of Capahowasic and forever esteem him as his son Nantaquond.

17   So to Jamestown with twelve guides Powhatan sent him. That night they quartered in the woods, he still expecting (as he had done all this long time of his imprisonment) every hour to be put to one death or other, for all their feasting. But almighty God (by His divine providence) had mollified the hearts of those stern barbarians with compassion. The next morning betimes they came to the fort, where Smith having used the savages with what kindness he could, he showed Rawhunt, Powhatan's trusty servant, two demi-culverins and a millstone to carry [to] Powhatan; they found them somewhat too heavy, but when they did see him discharge them, being loaded with stones, among the boughs of a great tree loaded with icicles, the ice and branches came so tumbling down that the poor savages ran away half dead with fear. But at last we regained some conference with them and gave them such toys and sent to Powhatan, his women, and children such presents as gave them in general full content.

18   Now in Jamestown they were all in combustion, the strongest preparing once more to run away with the pinnace; which, with the hazard of his life, with saker falcon and musket shot, Smith forced now the third time to stay or sink.

19   Some, no better than they should be, had plotted with the President the next day to have him put to death by the Levitical law for the lives of Robinson and Emry; pretending the fault was his that had led them to their ends; but he quickly took such order with such lawyers that he laid them by their heels till he sent some of them prisoners for England.

20   Now every once in four of five days, Pocahontas with her attendants brought him so much provision that saved many of their lives, that else for all this had starved with hunger.

> Thus from numb death our good God
>   sent relief,
> The sweet assuager of all other grief.

21   His relation of the plenty he had seen, especially at Werowocomoco, and of the state and bounty of Powhatan

(which till that time was unknown), <u>so revived their dead</u> <u>spirits</u> (especially the love of Pocahontas) as all men's fear was abandoned.

22   Thus you may see what difficulties still crossed any good endeavour; and the good success of the business being thus oft brought to the very period of destruc- tion; yet <u>you see by what strange means God hath still</u> <u>delivered it.</u>

Ends on pious note

∽

Discussion of Smith Annotations

The questions we asked were meant as a guide, not a quiz in which they should be answered one by one. In the following discussion we will address the points we raised in order to illustrate the process of critical thinking and reading. There is much more to the selection, however, some of which can be found in other writings, and some that is still waiting to be discov- ered by readers with new perspectives—including you.

As we understand the narrative, Smith's purpose in telling this story is to prove that he saved the colony in the face of incompetent leaders, hostile enemies, and natural disasters. Smith hoped to lead other expeditions to the New World, but the deaths of his men while he was elsewhere had to be explained. His opponents accused him of dereliction of duty and hoped to court-martial him (par. 19). He, in turn, argued (par. 4) that pressure to dis- cover the source of the Chickahominy River forced him to proceed farther than was prudent, but nonetheless he left his men in a protected area and undertook the arduous mission himself, with only two guides and two oth- ers. Then, while he was hunting for food for his sleeping men, they were killed and he was captured. For six or seven weeks he not only resisted of- fers to spare his life if he betrayed the colony, he also carried himself with such dignity (par. 7) that he won over his captors (par. 15), who now came regularly to supply the English with food (par. 20). The fact that the story is told in the third person—seemingly *about* him rather than *by* him—gives the account an air of objectivity, like a legal defense.

Smith's mission was to make the colony succeed, thereby giving England a foothold in America, where the Spanish enemy was already firmly estab- lished. The other leaders (par. 1) and the soldiers (par. 2) wanted to abandon the colony, but because of his efforts—and some good luck—even the "tuf- taffety humorists" were staying on. As much as the Spanish (and perhaps also some English colonists) were motivated by the hope of easy wealth, he was driven by the desire to feed his charges (par. 2). Like a good leader, or parent, he undertook dangerous missions (pars. 4, 5, and 8) to provide for them.

The details and structure of the narrative combine to make Smith stand out as the only competent, honest, and devoted leader of the colony—eventually its savior. Like a funnel, the opening paragraphs narrow the focus from all the colonists, to the exploring party on the barge, to the five men in the canoe, and finally to Smith alone. In captivity, he impresses the Indians with his demeanor, dazzles them with his tools, and wins them over to his side. By the end of the story he has been adopted by the Emperor and has arranged for the colony to be regularly fed by an Indian princess.

Smith is ambivalent towards the Indians: They are savages (par. 4 and elsewhere), hellish (par. 11), cannibals (par. 11), and cowards (pars. 12, 13); but they are also noble (par. 14), compassionate (par. 15), and generous (par. 20). This ambivalence reflects the function of the Indians in the story: They are the problem that must be overcome through a proper leader like Smith, but, once allied with Smith, they are the guarantee that his leadership will make the colony succeed. Seldom, however, is an Indian the equal of a European. At times they are not even human, serving, for example, as a shield (par. 5) and disappearing without a word of explanation or regret (par. 8).

Bringing a European perspective to his view of the Indians, Smith speaks of "nations" and "kings," ironically conferring equal status on the people that he considers to be inferior in other ways. However, calling Powhatan an emperor and Pocahontas a princess enhances the position of Smith, who is their friend, and promises safety to any colony he leads.

The occasional, brief references to God seem to be mere formalities, perhaps because the audience expects such nods to religion. While they may be sincere, there is no indication that Smith is crediting anything but his own skill for his success.

The previous questions for further study represent possible topics for research and essays and have proved valuable avenues of investigation for other readers. Of course, you may decide to explore a path that has gone unnoticed by other scholars.

Scholars and previous students have suggested several reasons for the appeal of Smith's narrative to Americans. It has a happy ending, thus proving once again that things work out in the end and that America always comes out on top. It reinforces the belief that America is the product of brave individuals who faced challenges and overcame them. It is a well-written adventure story, with dangers, crises, close calls with death and a beautiful native princess. There is even the hint of romance in that many people mistakenly believe that Smith married Pocahontas.

Jamestown was an experiment in colonization. While the Spanish had successfully colonized Mexico, Central America and several Caribbean islands, previous English attempts to plant settlements in America had failed. Smith, a young adventurer who had already experienced war, capture, enslavement and escape in the Mediterranean, was one of the leaders of the English at Jamestown. If the settlement succeeded, his career would prosper. But prospective colonists knew the realities of America: a wild land filled with hostile savages, separated by a trackless ocean from the comforts of civilization. Smith acknowledges these drawbacks, but emphasizes his ability to overcome them and survive. He portrays himself as the perfect leader for such an undertaking. By the end of the story, after all the close calls with death, he is friends with the Indian emperor and his small town is regularly visited and looked after by an Indian princess. Moreover, the princess shows her love for his people by converting to Christianity and marrying an Englishman.

Smith's "History of Virginia" is thus an advertisement for the colony and its savior, what we might now label a self-promotional "infomercial." Smith contrasts his own competence and faithfulness to the leaders and soldiers who were ready to abandon the colony (pars. 1, 2, 18). He also defends himself against charges (pars. 4, 5, 19) that may have reached England and threatened his career. Smith makes it clear that without him the colony would have failed (pars. 2, 20, 21) or been attacked (pars. 7, 12).

MARY ROWLANDSON
A Narrative of the Captivity and Restoration of Mrs. Mary Rowlandson (1682)

"Little do many think what is the savageness and brutishness of this barbarous enemy, Ay, even . . . the Praying Indians."

Mary Rowlandson was both the daughter of one of the founders of Lancaster, Massachusetts, and the wife of its first minister. Frontier settlements like Lancaster, thirty miles west of Boston, brought the Puritans into conflict with the Wampanoags and their allies. In 1675, colonial authorities at Plymouth executed three Wampanoags for the murder of a Christian Indian who was spying for the English. To Metacomet, called King Philip by the English, this was one more affront to his people and a threat to their survival as a sovereign nation. King Philip's War, which followed, was a series of surprise attacks, hit-and-run ambushes, and massacres, resulting in the killing of 600 colonists and 3,000 Indians—a frightening proportion of both populations. The war ended with the death of Metacomet and the sale of his surviving people into slavery in the West Indies.

Rowlandson was captured in an attack on Lancaster during King Philip's War. After her release, she moved with her family to Connecticut, where she is believed to have lived until her death in 1711. Her *Narrative* was published in 1682 to great acclaim, and became the model for other "captivity narratives," including James Fenimore Cooper's *The Last of the Mohicans.* Her own purpose in writing it, however, is given in the title: "The Sovereignty and Goodness of God, Together with the Faithfulness of His Promises Displayed; Being a Narrative of the Captivity and Restoration of Mrs. Mary Rowlandson, Commended by Her, to All That Desire to Know the Lord's Doings to, and Dealings with Her . . . Now Made Public at the Earnest Desire of Some Friends, and for the Benefit of the Afflicted."

A Narrative of the Captivity and Restoration of Mrs. Mary Rowlandson; from *Heritage of American Literature,* vol. 1; edited by James E. Miller, Jr.; Harcourt Brace Jovanovich, 1991.

EXPLORING ISSUES IN THE TEXT

1. What was Rowlandson's probable purpose in writing this account? What effect do you think it had on its readers? As you understand her narrative, is it about Indians, religion, personal feelings, or something else?

2. How does Rowlandson see herself? How does this view help shape the content and organization of the narrative?

3. How does Rowlandson view the Indians? What words does she use to describe them? What were the "praying Indians"? What is Rowlandson's attitude toward them?

4. How do Rowlandson's religious beliefs influence her reaction to and interpretation of her ordeal?

A NARRATIVE OF THE CAPTIVITY AND RESTORATION OF MRS. MARY ROWLANDSON

1 On the tenth of February 1675, came the Indians with great numbers upon Lancaster: their first coming was about sunrising; hearing the noise of some guns, we looked out; several houses were burning, and the smoke ascending to heaven. There were five persons taken in one house; the father, and the mother and a sucking child, they knocked on the head; the other two they took and carried away alive. There were two others, who being out of their garrison upon some occasion were set upon; one was knocked on the head, the other escaped. Another there was who running along was shot and wounded, and fell down; he begged of them his life, promising them money (as they told me) but they would not hearken to him but knocked him in head, and stripped him naked, and split open his bowels. Another, seeing many of the Indians about his barn, ventured and went out, but was

quickly shot down. There were three others belonging to the same garrison who were killed; the Indians' getting up upon the roof of the barn, had advantage to shoot down upon them over their fortification. Thus these murderous wretches went on, burning, and destroying before them.

2 At length they came and beset our own house, and quickly it was the dolefulest day that ever mine eyes saw. The house stood upon the edge of a hill; some of the Indians got behind the hill, others into the barn, and others behind anything that could shelter them; from all which places they shot against the house, so that the bullets seemed to fly like hail; and quickly they wounded one man among us, then another, and then a third. About two hours (according to my observation, in that amazing time) they had been about the house before they prevailed to fire it (which they did with flax and hemp, which they brought out of the barn, and there being no defense about the house, only two flankers at two opposite corners and one of them not finished); they fired it once and one ventured out and quenched it, but they quickly fired it again, and that took. Now is the dreadful hour come, that I have often heard of (in time of war, as it was the case of others), but now mine eyes see it. Some in our house were fighting for their lives, others wallowing in their blood, the house on fire over our heads, and the bloody heathen ready to knock us on the head, if we stirred out. Now might we hear mothers and children crying out for themselves, and one another, "Lord, what shall we do?" Then I took my children (and one of my sisters', hers) to go forth and leave the house: but as soon as we came to the door and appeared, the Indians shot so thick that the bullets rattled against the house, as if one had taken an handful of stones and threw them, so that we were fain to give back. We had six stout dogs belonging to our garrison, but none of them would stir, though another time, if any Indian had come to the door, they were ready to fly upon him and tear him down. The Lord hereby would make us the more to acknowledge His hand, and to see that our help is always in Him. But out we must go, the fire increasing, and coming along behind us, roaring, and the Indians gaping before us with their guns, spears, and hatchets to devour us. No sooner were we out of the house, but my brother-in-law (being before wounded, in defending the house, in or near the throat) fell down dead, whereat the Indians scornfully shouted, and hal-

lowed, and were presently upon him, stripping off his clothes, the bullets flying thick, one went through my side, and the same (as would seem) through the bowels and hand of my dear child in my arms. One of my elder sister's children, named William, had then his leg broken, which the Indians perceiving, they knocked him on [the] head. Thus were we butchered by those merciless heathen, standing amazed, with the blood running down to our heels. My eldest sister being yet in the house, and seeing those woeful sights, the infidels haling mothers one way, and children another, and some wallowing in their blood; and her elder son telling her that her son William was dead, and myself was wounded, she said, "And Lord, let me die with them," which was no sooner said, but she was struck with a bullet, and fell down dead over the threshold. I hope she is reaping the fruit of her good labors, being faithful to the service of God in her place. In her younger years she lay under much trouble upon spiritual accounts, till it pleased God to make the precious scripture take hold of her heart, 2 Cor. 12:9, "And he said unto me, my Grace is sufficient for thee." More than twenty years after, I have heard her tell how sweet and comfortable that place was to her. But to return: the Indians laid hold of us, pulling me one way, and the children another, and said, "Come go along with us"; I told them they would kill me; they answered, if I were willing to go along with them, they would not hurt me.

3   Oh the doleful sight that now was to behold at this house! "Come, behold the works of the Lord, what desolations he has made in the Earth." Of thirty-seven persons who were in this one house, none escaped either present death, or a bitter captivity, save only one, who might say as he, Job 1:15. "And I only am escaped alone to tell the News." There were twelve killed, some shot, some stabbed with their spears, some knocked down with their hatchets. When we are in prosperity, Oh the little that we think of such dreadful sights, and to see our dear friends and relations lie bleeding out their heart-blood upon the ground. There was one who was chopped into the head with a hatchet, and stripped naked, and yet was crawling up and down. It is a solemn sight to see so many Christians lying in their blood, some here, and some there, like a company of sheep torn by wolves, all of them stripped naked by a company of hell-hounds, roaring, singing, ranting, and insulting, as if they would have torn our very

hearts out; yet the Lord by His almighty power preserved a number of us from death, for there were twenty-four of us taken alive and carried captive.

4   I had often before this said that if the Indians should come, I should choose rather to be killed by them than taken alive, but when it came to the trial my mind changed; their glittering weapons so daunted my spirit, that I chose rather to go along with those (as I may say) ravenous beasts, than that moment to end my days; and that I may the better declare what happened to me during that grievous captivity, I shall particularly speak of the several removes we had up and down the wilderness.

The First Remove

5   Now away we must go with those barbarous creatures, with our bodies wounded and bleeding, and our hearts no less than our bodies. About a mile we went that night, up upon a hill within sight of the town, where they intended to lodge. There was hard by a vacant house (deserted by the English before, for fear of the Indians). I asked them whether I might not lodge in the house that night, to which they answered, "What, will you love English men still?" This was the dolefulest night that ever my eyes saw. Oh the roaring, and singing and dancing, and yelling of those black creatures in the night, which made the place a lively resemblance of hell. And as miserable was the waste that was there made of horses, cattle, sheep, swine, calves, lambs, roasting pigs, and fowl (which they had plundered in town), some roasting, some lying and burning, and some boiling to feed our merciless enemies; who were joyful enough, though we were disconsolate. To add to the dolefulness of the former day, and the dismalness of the present night, my thoughts ran upon my losses and sad bereaved condition. All was gone, my husband gone (at least separate from me, he being in the bay; and to add to my grief, the Indians told me they would kill him as he came homeward), my children gone, my relations and friends gone, our house and home and all our comforts, within door and without—all was gone (except my life), and I knew not but the next moment that might go too. There remained nothing to me but one poor wounded babe, and it seemed at present worse than death that it was in such a pitiful condition, bespeaking compassion, and I had no refreshing for it, nor suitable things to revive

it. Little do many think what is the savageness and brutishness of this barbarous enemy. Ay, even those that seem to profess more than others among them, when the English have fallen into their hands.

6   Those seven that were killed at Lancaster the summer before upon a Sabbath day, and the one that was afterward killed upon a week day, were slain and mangled in a barbarous manner, by one-eyed John, and Marlborough's Praying Indians, which Capt. Mosely brought to Boston, as the Indians told me. . . .

The Third Remove

7   The morning being come, they prepared to go on their way. One of the Indians got up upon a horse, and they set me up behind him, with my poor sick babe in my lap. A very wearisome and tedious day I had of it; what with my own wound, and my child's being so exceeding sick, and in a lamentable condition with her wound. It may be easily judged what a poor feeble condition we were in, there being not the least crumb of refreshing that came within either of our mouths from Wednesday night to Saturday night, except only a little cold water. This day in the afternoon, about an hour by sun, we came to the place where they intended, *viz.* an Indian town, called Wenimesset, northward of Quabaug. When we were come, Oh the number of pagans (now merciless enemies) that there came about me, that I may say as David, Psalm 27:13, "I had fainted, unless I had believed, etc." The next day was the sabbath. I then remembered how careless I had been of God's holy time, how many sabbaths I had lost and misspent, and how evilly I had walked in God's sight; which lay so close unto my spirit, that it was easy for me to see how righteous it was with God to cut off the thread of my life and cast me out of His presence for ever. Yet the Lord still showed mercy to me, and upheld me; and as He wounded me with one hand, so he healed me with the other. This day there came to me one Robert Pepper (a man belonging to Roxbury) who was taken in Captain Beers his fight, and had been now a considerable time with the Indians; and up with them almost as far as Albany, to see king Philip, as he told me, and was now very lately come into these parts. Hearing, I say, that I was in this Indian town, he obtained leave to come and see me. He told me he himself was wounded in the leg at

Captain Beers his fight; and was not able some time to go, but as they carried him, and as he took oaken leaves and laid to his wound, and through the blessing of God he was able to travel again. Then I took oaken leaves and laid to my side, and with the blessing of God it cured me also; yet before the cure was wrought, I may say, as it is in Psalm 38:5–6 "My wounds stink and are corrupt, I am troubled, I am bowed down greatly, I go mourning all the day long." I sat much alone with a poor wounded child in my lap, which moaned night and day, having nothing to revive the body, or cheer the spirits of her, but instead of that, sometimes one Indian would come and tell me one hour that "your master will knock your child in the head," and then a second, and then a third, "your master will quickly knock your child in the head."

8   This was the comfort I had from them, miserable comforters are ye all, as he said. Thus nine days I sat upon my knees, with my babe in my lap, till my flesh was raw again; my child being even ready to depart this sorrowful world, they bade me carry it out to another wigwam (I suppose because they would not be troubled with such spectacles) whither I went with a very heavy heart, and down I sat with the picture of death in my lap. About two hours in the night, my sweet babe like a lamb departed this life on Feb. 18, 1675. It being about six years, and five months old. It was nine days from the first wounding, in this miserable condition, without any refreshing of one nature or other, except a little cold water. I cannot but take notice how, at another time, I could not bear to be in the room where any dead person was, but now the case is changed; I must and could lie down by my dead babe, side by side all the night after. I have thought since of the wonderful goodness of God to me in preserving me in the use of my reason and senses in that distressed time, that I did not use wicked and violent means to end my own miserable life. In the morning, when they understood that my child was dead, they sent for me home to my master's wigwam (by my master in this writing, must be understood Quanopin, who was a Sagamore, and married King Philip's wife's sister; not that he first took me, but I was sold to him by another Narraganset Indian, who took me when first I came out of the garrison). I went to take up my dead child in my arms to carry it with me, but they bid me let it alone; there was no resisting, but go I must and leave

it. When I had been at my master's wigwam, I took the first opportunity I could get to go look after my dead child. When I came I asked them what they had done with it; then they told me it was upon the hill. Then they went and showed me where it was, where I saw the ground was newly digged, and there they told me they had buried it. There I left that child in the wilderness, and must commit it, and myself also in this wilderness-condition, to Him who is above all. . . .

9   God having taken away this dear child, I went to see my daughter Mary, who was at this same Indian town, at a wigwam not very far off, though we had little liberty or opportunity to see one another. She was about ten years old, and taken from the door at first by a Praying Ind. and afterward sold for a gun. When I came in sight, she would fall aweeping; at which they were provoked, and would not let me come near her, but bade me be gone; which was a heart-cutting word to me. I had one child dead, another in the wilderness, I knew not where, the third they would not let me come near to: "Me (as he said) have ye bereaved of my Children, Joseph is not, and Simeon is not, and ye will take Benjamin also, all these things are against me." I could not sit still in this condition, but kept walking from one place to another. And as I was going along, my heart was even overwhelmed with the thoughts of my condition, and that I should have children, and a nation which I knew not, ruled over them. Whereupon I earnestly entreated the Lord, that He would consider my low estate, and show me a token for good, and if it were His blessed will, some sign and hope of some relief.

10   And indeed quickly the Lord answered, in some measure, my poor prayers; for as I was going up and down mourning and lamenting my condition, my son came to me, and asked me how I did. I had not seen him before, since the destruction of the town, and I knew not where he was, till I was informed by himself, that he was amongst a smaller parcel of Indians, whose place was about six miles off. With tears in his eyes, he asked me whether his sister Sarah was dead; and told me he had seen his sister Mary; and prayed me, that I would not be troubled in reference to himself. The occasion of his coming to see me at this time, was this: there was, as I said, about six miles from us, a small plantation of Indians, where it seems he had been during his captivity; and at this time, there were some forces of the Ind. gathered

out of our company, and some also from them (among whom was my son's master) to go to assault and burn Medfield. In this time of the absence of his master, his dame brought him to see me. I took this to be some gracious answer to my earnest and unfeigned desire.

11 The next day, *viz.* to this, the Indians returned from Medfield, all the company, for those that belonged to the other small company, came through the town that now we were at. But before they came to us, Oh! the outrageous roaring and whooping that there was. They began their din about a mile before they came to us. By their noise and whooping they signified how many they had destroyed (which was at that time twenty-three). Those that were with us at home were gathered together as soon as they heard the whooping, and every time that the other went over their number, these at home gave a shout, that the very earth rung again. And thus they continued till those that had been upon the expedition were come up to the Sagamore's wigwam; and then, Oh, the hideous insulting and triumphing that there was over some Englishmen's scalps that they had taken (as their manner is) and brought with them.

12 I cannot but take notice of the wonderful mercy of God to me in those afflictions, in sending me a Bible. One of the Indians that came from Medfield fight, had brought some plunder, came to me, and asked me, if I would have a Bible; he had got one in his basket. I was glad of it, and asked him, whether he thought the Indians would let me read? He answered, yes. So I took the Bible, and in that melancholy time, it came into my mind to read first the 28th Chap. of Deuteronomy, which I did, and when I had read it, my dark heart wrought on this manner: that there was no mercy for me, that the blessings were gone, and the curses come in their room, and that I had lost my opportunity. But the Lord helped me still to go on reading till I came to Chap. 30, the seven first verses, where I found, there was mercy promised again, if we would return to Him by repentance; and though we were scattered from one end of the earth to the other, yet the Lord would gather us together, and turn all those curses upon our enemies. I do not desire to live to forget this Scripture, and what comfort it was to me.

13 Now the Ind. began to talk of removing from this place, some one way, and some another. There were now besides myself nine English captives in this place

(all of them children, except one woman). I got an opportunity to go and take my leave of them. They being to go one way, and I another, I asked them whether they were earnest with God for deliverance. They told me they did as they were able, and it was some comfort to me, that the Lord stirred up children to look to Him. The woman, *viz.* goodwife Joslin, told me she should never see me again, and that she could find in her heart to run away. I wished her not to run away by any means, for we were near thirty miles from any English town, and she very big with child, and had but one week to reckon, and another child in her arms, two years old, and bad rivers there were to go over, and we were feeble, with our poor and coarse entertainment. I had my Bible with me; I pulled it out, and asked her whether she would read. We opened the Bible and lighted on Psalm 27, in which Psalm we especially took notice of that, *ver. ult.,* "Wait on the Lord, Be of good courage, and he shall strengthen thine Heart, wait I say on the Lord."

[Return Home]

14 So I took my leave of them, and in coming along my heart melted into tears, more than all the while I was with them, and I was almost swallowed up with the thoughts that ever I should go home again. About the sun going down, Mr. Hoar, and myself, and the two Indians came to Lancaster, and a solemn sight it was to me. There had I lived many comfortable years amongst my relations and neighbors, and now not one Christian to be seen, or one house left standing. We went on to a farmhouse that was yet standing, where we lay all night, and a comfortable lodging we had, though nothing but straw to lie on. The Lord preserved us in safety that night, and raised us up again in the morning, and carried us along, that before noon, we came to Concord. Now was I full of joy, and yet not without sorrow: joy to see such a lovely sight, so many Christians together, and some of them my neighbors. There I met with my brother, and my brother-in-law, who asked me, if I knew where his wife was? Poor heart! he had helped to bury her, and knew it not. She being shot down by the house was partly burnt, so that those who were at Boston at the desolation of the town, and came back afterward, and buried the dead, did not know her. Yet I was not without sorrow, to think how

many were looking and longing, and my own children amongst the rest, to enjoy that deliverance that I had now received, and I did not know whether ever I should see them again. Being recruited with food and raiment we went to Boston that day, where I met with my dear husband, but the thoughts of our dear children, one being dead, and the other we could not tell where, abated our comfort each to other. I was not before so much hemmed in with the merciless and cruel heathen, but now as much with pitiful, tender-hearted and compassionate Christians. In that poor, and distressed, and beggarly condition I was received in, I was kindly entertained in several houses. So much love I received from several (some of whom I knew, and others I knew not) that I am not capable to declare it. . . .

15 I can remember the time when I used to sleep quietly without workings in my thoughts, whole nights together, but now it is other ways with me. When all are fast about me, and no eye open, but His who ever waketh, my thoughts are upon things past, upon the awful dispensation of the Lord towards us, upon His wonderful power and might, in carrying of us through so many difficulties, in returning us in safety, and suffering none to hurt us. I remember, in the night season, how the other day I was in the midst of thousands of enemies, and nothing but death before me. It is then hard work to persuade myself, that ever I should be satisfied with bread again. But now we are fed with the finest of wheat, and as I may say, with honey out of the rock. Instead of the husk, we have the fatted calf. The thoughts of these things in the particulars of them, and of the love and goodness of God towards us, make it true of me, what David said of himself, Psalm 6:6, "I watered my Couch with my tears." Oh! the wonderful power of God that mine eyes have seen, affording matter enough for my thoughts to run in, that when others are sleeping mine eyes are weeping.

16   I have seen the extreme vanity of this world: One hour I have been in health, and wealth, wanting nothing. But the next hour in sickness and wounds, and death, having nothing but sorrow and affliction.

17   Before I knew what affliction meant, I was ready sometimes to wish for it. When I lived in prosperity, having the comforts of the world about me, my relations by

me, my heart cheerful, and taking little care for anything, and yet seeing many, whom I preferred before myself, under many trials and afflictions, in sickness, weakness, poverty, losses, crosses, and cares of the world. I should be sometimes jealous lest I should have my portion in this life, and that scripture would come to my mind, Hebrews 12:6, "For whom the Lord loveth he chasteneth, and scourgeth every Son whom he receiveth." But now I see the Lord had His time to scourge and chasten me. The portion of some is to have their afflictions by drops, now one drop and then another; but the dregs of the cup, the wine of astonishment, like a sweeping rain that leaveth no food, did the Lord prepare to be my portion. Affliction I wanted, and affliction I had, full measure (I thought), pressed down and running over. Yet I see, when God calls a person to anything, and through never so many difficulties, yet He is fully able to carry them through and make them see, and say they have been gainers thereby. And I hope I can say in some measure, as David did, "It is good for me that I have been afflicted." The Lord hath showed me the vanity of these outward things. That they are the vanity of vanities, and vexation of spirit, that they are but a shadow, a blast, a bubble, and things of no continuance. That we must rely on God Himself, and our whole dependence must be upon Him. If trouble from smaller matters begin to arise in me, I have something at hand to check myself with, and say, why am I troubled? It was but the other day that if I had had the world, I would have given it for my freedom, or to have been a servant to a Christian. I have learned to look beyond present and smaller troubles, and to be quieted under them. As Moses said, Exodus 14:13, "Stand still and see the salvation of the Lord."

BUILDING CONTEXT

1. Compare Rowlandson's narrative stance—that is, tone and perspective—to Smith's. How do the contrasts contribute to the distinct meaning and impact of their works?

2. Compare Rowlandson's self-image to Smith's. Show the connection between self-image and the purpose of the two narratives.

3. Compare the role of religion in Rowlandson's and Smith's narratives.

FURTHER STUDY

1. Try to explain Smith's and Rowlandson's accounts in the context of their time and place—Virginia in 1607 and Massachusetts in the 1670s.

2. Why do you think the story of John Smith and Pocahontas has found a place in American mythology while the ordeal of Mary Rowlandson is now largely forgotten? Is Smith's story better written? More realistic? More exciting? More useful?

3 Point out the typical (or stereotypical) feminine aspects of Rowlandson's story. What effect did these elements probably have on the readers of her day?

4. In his *Sketchbook,* Washington Irving included several studies of American Indians, including one of King Philip. You might want to read "Philip of Pokanoket" and "Traits of Indian Character" to see Irving's analysis of accounts like Rowlandson's.

Annotating Rowlandson; Re-annotating Smith

The study questions preceding the Rowlandson selection should have guided you in making annotations as you read the text. Now compare your notes to those in the following excerpt.

A NARRATIVE OF
THE CAPTIVITY AND
RESTORATION OF
MRS. MARY ROWLANDSON

2   . . . Now is the dreadful hour come, that I have often heard of (in time of war, as it was the case of others), but now mine eyes see it. Some in our house were fighting for their lives, others wallowing in their blood, the house on fire over our heads, and the bloody heathen ready to knock us on the head, if we stirred out. Now might we hear mothers and children crying out for themselves, and one another, "Lord, what shall we do?" Then I took my children (and one of my sisters', hers) to go forth and leave the house: but as soon as we came to the door and appeared, the Indians shot so thick that the bullets rattled against the house, as if one had taken an handful of stones and threw them, so that we were fain to give back. We had six stout dogs belonging to

Heathen vs. Christian

our garrison, but none of them would stir, though another time, if any Indian had come to the door, they were ready to fly upon him and tear him down. The Lord hereby would make us the more to acknowledge His hand, and to see that our help is always in Him. But out we must go, the fire increasing, and coming along behind us, roaring, and the Indians gaping before us with their guns spears and hatchets to devour us. No sooner were we out of the house, but my brother-in-law (being before wounded, in defending the house, in or near the throat) fell down dead whereat the Indians scornfully shouted, and hallowed, and were presently upon him, stripping off his clothes, the bullets flying thick, one went through my side, and the same (as would seem) through the bowels and hand of my dear child in my arms. One of my elder sister's children, named William, had then his leg broken; which the Indians perceiving, they knocked him on [the] head. Thus were we butchered by those merciless heathen, standing amazed, with the blood running down to our heels. My eldest sister being yet in the house, and seeing those woeful sights, the infidels haling mothers one way, and children another, and some wallowing in their blood; and her elder son telling her that her son William was dead, and myself was wounded, she said, "And Lord, let me die with them," which was no sooner said, but she was struck with a bullet, and fell down dead over the threshold. I hope she is reaping the fruit of her good labors, being faithful to the service of God in her place. In her younger years she lay under much trouble upon spiritual accounts, till it pleased God to make that precious scripture take hold of her heart, 2 Cor. 12:9, "And he said unto me, my Grace is sufficient for thee." More than twenty years after, I have heard her tell how sweet and comfortable that place was to her. But to return: the Indians laid hold of us, pulling me one way, and the children another, and said, "Come go along with us"; I told them they would kill me; they answered, if I were willing to go along with them, they would not hurt me.

3   Oh the doleful sight that now was to behold at this house! "Come, behold the works of the Lord, what desolations he has made in the Earth." Of thirty-seven persons who were in this one house, none escaped either present death, or a bitter captivity, save only one, who might say as he, Job 1:15, "And I only am escaped alone to tell the News." There were twelve killed, some shot, some

stabbed with their spears, some knocked down with their hatchets. When we are in prosperity, Oh the little that we think of such dreadful sights, and to see our dear friends and relations lie bleeding out their heart-blood upon the ground. There was one who was chopped into the head with a hatchet, and stripped naked, and yet was crawling up and down. It is a solemn sight to see so many Christians lying in their blood, some here, and some there, like a company of sheep torn by wolves, all of them stripped naked by a company of hell-hounds, roaring, singing, ranting, and insulting, as if they would have torn our very hearts out; yet the Lord by His almighty power preserved a number of us from death, for there were twenty-four of us taken alive and carried captive. . . .

[margin note: Images of martyrdom]

[margin note: Captivity (rather than death) is God's grace]

15 I can remember the time when I used to sleep quietly without workings in my thoughts, whole nights together, but now it is other ways with me. When all are fast about me, and no eye open, but His who ever waketh, my thoughts are upon things past, upon the awful dispensation of the Lord towards us, upon His wonderful power and might, in carrying of us through so many difficulties, in returning us in safety, and suffering none to hurt us. I remember, in the night season, how the other day I was in the midst of thousands of enemies, and nothing but death before me. It is then hard work to persuade myself, that ever I should be satisfied with bread again. But now we are fed with the finest of the wheat, and, as I may say, with honey out of the rock. Instead of the husk, we have the fatted calf. The thoughts of these things in the particulars of them, and of the love and goodness of God towards us, make it true of me, what David said of himself, Psalm 6:6, "I watered my Couch with my tears." Oh! the wonderful power of God that mine eyes have seen, affording matter enough for my thoughts to run in, that when others are sleeping mine eyes are weeping.

[margin note: Religious view. Though God controls all things, she thanks him for the good; even the bad is good because of the lesson she learns.]

16 I have seen the extreme vanity of this world: One hour I have been in health, and wealth, wanting nothing. But the next hour in sickness and wounds, and death, having nothing but sorrow and affliction.

17 Before I knew what affliction meant, I was ready sometimes to wish for it. When I lived in prosperity, having the comforts of the world about me, my relations by me, my heart cheerful, and taking little care for any-

thing, and yet seeing many, whom I preferred before myself, under many trials and afflictions, in sickness, weakness, poverty, losses, crosses, and cares of the world. I should be sometimes jealous lest I should have my portion in this life, and that scripture would come to my mind, Hebrews 12:6, "For whom the Lord loveth he chasteneth, and scourgeth every Son whom he receiveth." But now I see the Lord had His time to scourge and chasten me. The Portion of some is to have their afflictions by drops, now one drop and then another; but the dregs of the cup, the wine of astonishment, like a sweeping rain that leaveth no food, did the Lord prepare to be my portion. Affliction I wanted, and affliction I had, full measure (I thought), pressed down and running over. Yet I see, when God calls a person to anything, and through never so many difficulties, yet He is fully able to carry them through and make them see, and say they have been gainers thereby. And I hope I can say in some measure, as David did, "It is good for me that I have been afflicted." The Lord hath showed me the vanity of these outward things. That they are the vanity of vanities, and vexation of spirit, that they are but a shadow, a blast, a bubble, and things of no continuance. That we must rely on God Himself, and our whole dependence must be upon Him. If trouble from smaller matters begin to arise in me, I have something at hand to check myself with, and say, why am I troubled? It was but the other day that if I had had the world, I would have given it for my freedom, or to have been a servant to a Christian. I have learned to look beyond present and smaller troubles, and to be quieted under them. As Moses said, Exodus 14:13, "Stand still and see the salvation of the Lord."

[handwritten marginal note: Compare to Smith par. 7]

Because you read Smith's narrative first, you almost inevitably read and annotated Rowlandson in light of your knowledge of Smith. Now, you should re-read Smith and see if any passages take on new meaning in relation to Rowlandson's work. You will want to add annotations such as the following that cross-reference Smith's work to Rowlandson's.

4   But our comedies never endured long without a tragedy, some idle exceptions being muttered against Captain Smith for not discovering the head of Chickahominy river and [being] taxed by the Council to be too slow in so worthy an attempt. The next voyage he proceeded so far

[handwritten marginal note: Compare to Rowlandson par. 2]

that with much labor by cutting of trees asunder he made his passage, but when his barge could pass no farther, he left her in a broad bay out of danger of shot, commanding none should go ashore till his return; himself with two English and two savages went up higher in a canoe, but he was not long absent but his men went ashore, whose want of government gave both occasion and opportunity to the savages to surprise one George Cassen whom they slew and much failed not to have cut off the boat and all the rest.

5 Smith little dreaming of that accident, being got to the marshes at the river's head twenty miles in the desert, had his two men slain (as is supposed) sleeping by the canoe, while himself by fowling sought them victual, who finding he was beset with 200 savages, two of them he slew, still defending himself with the aid of a savage his guide, whom he bound to his arm with his garters and used him as a buckler, yet he was shot in his thigh a little, and had many arrows that stuck in his clothes but no great hurt, till at last they took him prisoner.

6 When this news came to Jamestown, much was their sorrow for his loss, few expecting what ensued.

7 Six or seven weeks those barbarians kept him prisoner, many strange triumphs and conjurations they made of him, yet he so demeaned himself amongst them, as he not only diverted them from surprising the fort, but procured his own liberty, and got himself and his company such estimation amongst them, that those savages admired him more than their own Quiyouckosucks.

Compare to Rowlandson par. 10 + 17

∽

17 So to Jamestown with twelve guides Powhatan sent him. That night they quartered in the woods, he still expecting (as he had done all this long time of his imprisonment) every hour to be put to one death or other, for all their feasting. But almighty God (by His divine providence) had mollified the hearts of those stern barbarians with compassion. The next morning betimes they came to the fort, where Smith having used the savages with what kindness he could, he showed Rawhunt, Powhatan's trusty servant, two demi-culverins and a millstone to carry [to] Powhatan; they found them somewhat too heavy, but when they did see him discharge them, being loaded with stones, among the boughs of a great tree loaded with icicles, the ice and branches came so tumbling down that the

Compare to Rowlandson par. 2 + 3

poor savages ran away half dead with fear. But at last we regained some conference with them and gave them such toys and sent to Powhatan, his women, and children such presents as gave them in general full content.

Smith and Rowlandson in Context

While we will not answer the study questions about Rowlandson individually, we should note that critics have made the following observations in discussing her work and Smith's. Smith is a man; Rowlandson is a woman. Smith ends on an upbeat note; Rowlandson concludes in a sad tone. Smith ultimately befriends his Indian enemies; Rowlandson nurses her enmity toward them. Smith stresses adventure and survival; Rowlandson emphasizes God's intervention in human affairs. These contrasts provide insights into Smith's and Rowlandson's purposes in writing and the reception that their books received.

As we have already mentioned, Virginia in 1607 was an early experiment in colonization. If, despite the many dangers, the settlement succeeded, Smith's career would prosper. He therefore emphasizes his devotion to his mission and his ability to overcome obstacles. Moreover, having been adopted by the Indian emperor and befriended by an Indian princess, he can assure the safety of those who follow him to America.

The situation was very different seventy years later. As settlers pushed inland from the coast, they drove the Indians before them. In Massachusetts, where Puritans sought a Promised Land in which to establish God's kingdom on earth, Indians led by King Philip rose up against them. To Rowlandson, such an attempt to interfere with God's plan meant that the Indians were agents of the devil, or, from a different theological perspective, the vehicle of God's anger against his saints, who were at the center of human history. The Indians, in this view, were not equals, or even real people; their motivation or concerns were given no thought. Like the Biblical Canaanites, they had to be uprooted and destroyed because they stood between God's chosen and the Promised Land. Thus, while Smith refers to God's guidance in pious passing, Rowlandson is consumed with searching the Scriptures for clues to God's hand in the events of her own life and the life of the community of saints.

The two stories, therefore, had—and continue to have—different effects on their readers. The enduring scene from Smith's *History* is that of Pocahontas saving him from death—the white hunter rescued by the beautiful Indian princess.

> "*Pocahontas . . . laid her own [head] upon his to save him from death.*"

Another Voice

"PHILIP OF POKANOKET"
WASHINGTON IRVING

The nature of the contest that ensued was such as too often distinguishes the warfare between civilized men and savages. On the part of the whites it was conducted with superior skill and success; but with a wastefulness of the blood, and disregard of the natural rights of their antagonists: on the part of the Indians it was waged with the desperation of men fearless of death, and who had nothing to expect from peace, but humiliation, dependence, and decay.

The events of the war are transmitted to us by a worthy clergyman of the time; who dwells with horror and indignation on every hostile act of the Indians, however justifiable, whilst he mentions with applause the most sanguinary atrocities of the whites. Philip is reviled as a murderer and a traitor; without considering that he was a true born prince, gallantly fighting at the head of his subjects to avenge the wrongs of his family; to retrieve the tottering power of his line; and to deliver his native land from the oppression of usurping strangers. . . .

. . . The Indians were driven from one post to another. They disputed their ground inch by inch, fighting with the fury of despair. Most of their veterans were cut to pieces; and after a long and bloody battle, Philip and Canonchet, with a handful of surviving warriors, retreated from the fort, and took refuge in the thickets of the surrounding forest.

The victors set fire to the wigwams and the fort; the whole was soon in a blaze; many of the old men, the women and the children perished in the flames. This last outrage overcame even the stoicism of the savage. The neighboring woods resounded with the yells of rage and despair uttered by the fugitive warriors, as they beheld the destruction of their dwellings, and heard the agonizing cries of their wives and offspring. "The burning of the wigwams," says a contemporary writer, "the shrieks and cries of the women and children, and the yelling of the warriors, exhibited a most horrible and affecting scene, so that it greatly moved some of the soldiers." The same writer cautiously adds, "they were in *much doubt* then, and afterwards seriously inquired, whether

continued

continued from previous page

burning their enemies alive could be consistent with humanity, and the benevolent principles of the Gospel."

. . . If, however, we consider even the prejudiced anecdotes furnished us by his enemies, we may perceive in them traces of amiable and lofty character sufficient to awaken sympathy for his fate, and respect for his memory. We find that, amidst all the harassing cares and ferocious passions of constant warfare, he was alive to the softer feelings of connubial love and paternal tenderness, and to the generous sentiment of friendship. The captivity of his "beloved wife and only son" are mentioned with exultation as causing him poignant misery: the death of any near friend is triumphantly recorded as a new blow on his sensibilities; but the treachery and desertion of many of his followers, in whose affections he had confided, is said to have desolated his heart, and to have bereaved him of all further comfort. He was a patriot attached to his native soil—a prince true to his subjects, and indignant of their wrongs—a soldier, daring in battle, firm in adversity, patient of fatigue, of hunger, of every variety of bodily suffering, and ready to perish in the cause he had espoused. Proud of heart, and with an untamable love of natural liberty, he preferred to enjoy it among the beasts of the forests or in the dismal and famished recesses of swamps and morasses, rather than bow his haughty spirit to submission, and live dependent and despised in the ease and luxury of the settlements. With heroic qualities and bold achievements that would have graced a civilized warrior, and have rendered him the theme of the poet and the historian; he lived a wanderer and a fugitive in his native land, and went down, like a lonely bark foundering amid darkness and tempest—without a pitying eye to weep his fall, or a friendly hand to record his struggle.

The Sketch Book, 1819

Rowlandson, in contrast, harbored undying hatred toward the Indians.

"What is the savageness and brutishness of this barbarous enemy."

Smith's tale of survival and success reinforces a popular image of Americans as winners, unafraid of challenge, brave in the face of death, and saved in the end by cunning, luck, or providence. Some critics even say that Smith's story fulfills a primal male fantasy. Rowlandson's story is very different. Throughout, she is a victim of external forces—never in control of events and always awaiting salvation. By stressing divine providence, she minimizes people's contributions to their own destiny. This message may have justified the destruction of the Native American "Canaanites" and comforted those who considered themselves saints, but it did not serve the purposes of later generations. Even those who were convinced that Americans were the chosen people in a country destined for greatness envisioned a more secular providence. Daring, ruggedness, skill, a pioneering spirit, and hard work replaced the hand of God in guaranteeing success. Despite its importance in American life, religion for later generations of Americans was supposed to be less heavy-handed.

Expanding the Context

We have already said that the context of a text is not limited to its original time and place. Almost 200 years ago, the American writer Washington Irving showed his awareness of how the work of Rowlandson and others was being manipulated. As you can see in the excerpts on pages 50–51 and 52–53, he portrays Philip not as a demonic savage, but as a prince defending his doomed nation. In contrast to stories of Indian atrocities, he describes the English burning Indian women and children in their wigwams. And, most significantly, he indicts writers who contributed to the destruction of the Native Americans through biased and inflammatory reporting.

Irving's reminder that history contains a point of view, not merely a list of events, introduces the following two selections by Dale Van Every and Barbara Cameron.

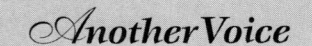

"TRAITS OF INDIAN CHARACTER"
WASHINGTON IRVING

It has been the lot of the unfortunate aborigines of America, in the early periods of colonization, to be doubly wronged by the white men. They have been dispossessed of their hereditary pos-

continued

continued from previous page

sessions by mercenary and frequently wanton warfare; and their characters have been traduced by bigoted and interested writers. The colonist often treated them like beasts of the forest; and the author has endeavored to justify him in his outrages. The former found it easier to exterminate than to civilize; the latter, to vilify than to discriminate. The appellations of savage and pagan were deemed sufficient to sanction the hostilities of both; and thus the poor wanderers of the forest were persecuted and defamed, not because they were guilty, but because they were ignorant.

The rights of the savage have seldom been properly appreciated or respected by the white man. In peace he has too often been the dupe of artful traffic; in war he has been regarded as a ferocious animal, whose life or death was a question of mere precaution and convenience. Man is cruelly wasteful of life when his own safety is endangered, and he is sheltered by impunity; and little mercy is to be expected from him when he feels the sting of the reptile and is conscious of the power to destroy.

The Sketch Book, 1819

DALE VAN EVERY
Disinherited: The Lost Birthright of the American Indian (1966)

"The basic Indian weakness . . . was . . . failure to recognize the community of their interests."

Born in Michigan, Van Every served as an ambulance driver during World War I and then studied history at Stanford. He worked as a reporter and editor for United Press and as a writer and producer in Hollywood before devoting himself to full-time writing. Van Every published almost a score of fiction and nonfiction books, among them *A Company of Heroes, Forth to the Wilderness,* and *The Frontier People of America,* a four-volume chronicle of the settlement of the West.

In Chapter 2 of his book *Disinherited,* most of which is reprinted here, Van Every examines the reasons that the Indians did not unite during the seventeenth and eighteenth centuries against their enemies, the white colonists.

Text: Dale Van Every; *Disinherited: The Lost Birthright of the American Indian;* New York: William Morrow, 1966.

EXPLORING ISSUES IN THE TEXT

1. What is Van Every's explanation for the plight of the Indians? To what extent is it accurate to say that he is blaming the victims?

2. According to Van Every, what role did war play in Indian culture (pars. 2–4)? How did the Indian concept of war differ from that of the Europeans? How did the arrival of Europeans change the Indian approach to war (pars. 5–7)?

3. What contrast does Van Every make between the intentions—or missions—of the French and English in North America (pars. 8–9)? How is this difference significant?

DISINHERITED: THE LOST BIRTHRIGHT OF THE AMERICAN INDIAN

1   So complete a disaster as befell the Indian occupants of what had become the eastern half of the United States leads to speculation upon the degree of their responsibility for their own misfortunes. There can be but one answer. Guiltless as they may have been when overwhelmed by the culminating disaster of the 1830's, they had during the preceding two centuries, while there was still scope for Indian action which might at least have postponed their decline, taken every action calculated to accelerate their downfall. They had made every mistake that an endangered people can make. Judged by the harsh law governing survival of any species, their total failure to adapt to new circumstances had amounted to an embrace of extinction. They had persisted in this suicidal course until in 1830 their sole remaining hope was reliance on the magnanimity of their white conquerors. This proved a hope as vain as had been their former illusions.

2   The basic Indian weakness in coping with the ever-growing threat to their existence as a people was from the outset their failure to recognize the community of their interests as a people. They were confronted by an

appalling and unmistakable clear and present danger. Their homeland was being overrun by alien invaders bent upon their extermination. Yet, from the days of the first white appearance on the continent to the days when the last flickers of Indian resistance were being extinguished, Indians exhibited no urgent impulse to combine in their common defense. Occasional inspired leaders of the stature of Pontiac, Brant and Tecumseh, preaching the doctrine of Indian union with compelling eloquence, succeeded only in contriving temporary, regional confederations which dissolved at the first strain. No Indian nation was too insignificant in numbers or power to consider its interests as distinct from those of its Indian neighbors. Throughout the period of progressively accelerating white conquest Indians continued to devote much more energy to their wars upon each other than to efforts to resist the invaders. In the last frontier wars fought east of the Mississippi Indians were still fighting Indians.

3   The preoccupation of Indians with making war on each other was among the first and strongest impressions of the new world gained by the first white men to set foot on its shores. Everywhere, from the St. Lawrence to the Gulf of Mexico, the natives were discovered to be engaged in obscure but persistent wars with their neighbors. No sooner did nearer Indians begin to appreciate the superiority of white weapons than they sought the assistance of the newly arrived aliens in attacks on their more distant rivals. No sooner did proximity permit them to be first to trade for possession of those weapons than invariably and relentlessly they employed their new arms against other Indians who had not yet gained that advantage. This eccentricity in Indian diplomatic and military policy immensely gratified the early colonists. Had tidewater Indians instead combined to set up a united resistance most colonies must have been short-lived. The economic returns from newly founded colonies were at first so scant that their parent governments must soon have tired of their support and the colonization of the eastern seaboard been indefinitely delayed, perhaps until the Indians through commercial contacts had developed defense capabilities enabling them to negotiate as equals.

4   Intertribal Indian hostility had not been a consequence of the white man's approach. Since long before the white era war-making had been as inherent a feature of the Indian way of life as hunting. The young Indian male was expected to demonstrate his skill as hunter by taking game. Community opinion committed him as completely to the demonstration of his courage as a man by the taking of scalps or captives. Wars were fought not for territory or trade advantage but to prove the private valor of the participants. They tended to be desultory and intermittent and to consist largely of raids, surprises and feats of individual daring, as each new generation of young warriors strove to attain personal status.

5   The advent of white men did, however, introduce a new element into Indian warfare almost as destructive to the prospects of Indian survival as was the devastating exposure to new diseases. The moment that Indians

became aware of the superiority of white tools, utensils and weapons they were consumed by a desire to possess them. This compulsion was accompanied by a collateral compulsion to deny trade goods to their Indian neighbors in order to augment their own relative power or to gain for themselves the profits of middlemen. Intertribal war had ceased to be a hazardous sport dedicated to the education of young men to become instead a struggle for material advantage, for trade monopoly, for control of trade routes or for the exaction of tribute. With these more sophisticated incentives, it was waged with a formerly unknown ardor and persistence.

6 These Indian trade wars produced a portentous train of consequences with a decisive influence not only upon Indian survival but upon the rate of white expansion into the center of the continent. They became so merciless that whole nations which otherwise might have assisted Indian resistance to the spread of white settlement were obliterated or their remnants driven into helpless wanderings among distant refuges. In the north the Iroquois by their remarkable 17th century conquests sought to establish a trade empire covering the entire region of the Hudson, the St. Lawrence, the Susquehanna and the Great Lakes and in the course of their tireless aggressions all but exterminated their nearer rivals, the Huron, the Erie, the Mohican and the Susquehannock. In the warmer south where furs had less value in payment for the coveted white man's goods the Indian nations of the region fell upon one another to gain war captives who might be sold as slaves to white buyers on the seacoast for shipment to the West Indies or New England. In the process the powerful Yamassee nation was destroyed, the Catawba reduced to insignificance, the Shawnee and Tuscarora driven into northern exile, and the energies of the Cherokee, Creek, Choctaw and Chickasaw dissipated.

7 The Indian trade wars had been an unalloyed blessing to early colonists struggling to develop their scattered beachheads along the Atlantic coast. From Maine to Georgia they had denied the Indian occupants of the coastal lowlands every opportunity to repel the intrusion while the intruders were still weak. Their aftermath was so destructive to any later Indian hope that a line of resistance might somewhere be found that it became a controlling factor in the continuing westward thrust of white settlement.

8 In the north the Iroquois grasp at trade empire had succeeded in barring French advance into the upper Ohio Valley for more than a century. No development could have had a more serious long term effect on the Indian cause. The French penetration of the interior was a type of exploitation which permitted the maintenance of Indian culture and Indian independence. The penetration of France's English rival, on the other hand, was one committed to the seizure of land and total Indian dispossession. As a result of the Iroquois attempt at trade monopoly the French had not reached the headwaters of the Ohio until the English colonies had gained an importance that prompted England to make the successful effort to drive France altogether from the North American

mainland. The Indians were left to cope with the victors without the support of their former patrons.

9   In the south the aftermath of persistent Indian trade wars had been as fatal. The flight of Shawnee and Tuscarora to northern sanctuaries had precipitated a half century of conflict between northern and southern Indians. During the critical period of the white frontier's approach to the mountain barrier the two most militarily potent Indian nations, the Iroquois in the north and the Cherokee in the south, absorbed in this endless, long range war with each other, ignored the white threat. Under the stresses of this war the entire area between the Ohio and the Tennessee became an unpopulated no-man's land inviting eventual white occupation. In the ensuing French and Indian war both Iroquois and Cherokee took the English side in opposition to their fellow Indians of the interior who were allied with the French, thus helping to insure that what remained of the Indian world would thereafter be dominated not by indulgent French missionaries and traders but by land-seeking English settlers.

10   Even greater policy mistakes were to follow. A cluster of Indian opportunities to stem white expansion at the Appalachian mountain barrier was squandered in rapid succession. Pontiac's rebellion against English rule ravaged the frontier, captured every English position in the west except Pittsburgh and Detroit and cost 3,000 English lives. Yet these dramatic victories roused no general Indian response. Instead, his striking effort to promote Indian union was throttled by a general Indian demand for a resumption of normal trade relations. Meanwhile a frantic British cabinet had by imperial dictate established the Proclamation Line along the crest of the mountains, prohibiting the extension of settlement west of it and reserving the interior to undisturbed Indian occupancy. The Line was designed not so much to protect Indians as to render the increasingly restive colonies more manageable but in any event the Indians themselves struck aside the proffered advantage. The Iroquois and Cherokee, each with some dim idea that all that they were sacrificing was the other's interests, by formal treaties promoted the isolation of the Shawnee and breached the mountain barrier by opening Kentucky and Tennessee to white settlement.

11   This monumental fallacy in Indian calculations marked the supreme crisis in Indian affairs. Their last opportunity was fading. In the immediately ensuing Revolution Indians for the first time mustered at least the semblance of united action. In sporadic concert both northern and southern Indians threw themselves upon the white frontier. For the next 20 years they were able to hold the line of the Tennessee and the Ohio and to inflict untold miseries on the intruding settlers. But Indian awakening had come too late. Through the gap in the mountain barrier that they themselves had breached poured more settlers by the thousands, and then by the hundreds of thousands. The Battle of Fallen Timbers in 1794 crushed the last significant hope that the tide of white settlement might ever be stemmed.

12   The Indians who in 1830 were appalled by the dread specter of removal were guided by few memories and less comprehension of these mistakes of their ancestors. They could not evade, however, the sharpest recollection and the most remorseful understanding of their own generation's mistakes which had been as grievous. They were falling into a pit which they themselves had dug.

13   The southern Indians were being afforded one last opportunity to realize that their interests were inseparable and that those interests might only be protected were this realized. The great Shawnee, Tecumseh, had been striving for years to reactivate the confederation of northern Indians that Brant had briefly assembled in the years of Indian militancy after the Revolution. In August of 1811, foreseeing the imminent outbreak of war between the United States and Great Britain, he embarked upon a tour of the southern nations to preach the absolute necessity of Indian union in the approaching crisis. With the prospective support of British military power, he maintained, there had appeared a last chance to require the Americans to recognize Indian right to what remained of their homeland.

14   Tecumseh was a legitimate spokesman for any all-Indian policy. He was neither a northern nor a southern Indian. His mother was a Cherokee living with the Creek, he had been born in the south and in his youth he had fought as often on the southern frontier as the northern. He represented in experience, viewpoint and heritage as near an approach to a universal Indian leader as the race was ever to produce.

15   He was accompanied on his embassy by an entourage of northern Indians as devoted as he to the extension of Indian confederation to all Indians exposed to American aggressiveness. Every care was taken to impress the multitudes who gathered to hear him with the dramatic immediacy of his doctrine. His every entrance and exit was theatrically contrived to satisfy Indian appreciation of ceremony and pageantry. His disciples performed nightlong rituals and dances. The beating of drums and the chanting of ancient songs never ceased. To drive home his major premise, he himself always wore as his sole regalia of leadership two crane feathers, one white and one red. The white symbolized the imperative need that all Indians keep the peace with one another, the red that they must remember that the white man was their only enemy. In his progress across Mississippi, Alabama, Florida and Georgia he preached his crusade to rapt assemblages of many thousands. But nowhere could he linger to press his point or deal with doubt. He had no time. The imminence of the British-American war compelled him continually to hasten on, for he had still to deliver his message to the Indians west of the Mississippi.

16   In his wake the southern Indians grappled with their problem. It was a moment for the most excruciating soul-searching. If any failed to realize the gravity of the hour they were reminded by terrifying natural portents. Unprecedented storms swept the region. A comet blazed in the sky. The Great Earthquake shook the very hills. In countless and endless council meetings every town and every nation debated the issue. Witch doctors,

conjurors and prophets vied with chiefs, elders and warriors in beseeching a frantic public's attention. Then, July 18, 1812, the United States declared war on Great Britain and there was no more time for debate.

17   The months spent in discussion without decision had sealed the failure of Tecumseh's crusade. Everywhere his appearance and his message had stirred the enthusiasm of the multitude but everywhere also the more prominent and influential figures in the community had held aloof, each still as reluctant as in the past to risk the interests of his town or nation for the sake of the general Indian cause. The great debate generated by Tecumseh's plea for unity had degenerated into an aggravation of disunity, particularly among the Creek, the most populous of Indian nations. They were torn by a long-standing and increasingly embittered cleavage between a progressive faction which believed the Creek future could only be assured by an accelerated adoption of the white man's ways and a conservative faction which believed that only by clinging to primitive customs and traditions could the integrity of the Creek people be preserved. With the outbreak of the British-American war, the conservatives, better known as Red Sticks, could no longer contain their impatience. Accepting British arms, they attempted to force their still pacific progressive neighbors to share their belligerence. The dissension erupted into a Creek civil war. In the course of a hot pursuit of a party of their rivals, Red Sticks overwhelmed a white stockade, Fort Mims, in which the fugitives had sought sanctuary along with some hundreds of white settlers. In the ensuing massacre more than 400 died. Revolted by the outrage, the United States and adjacent states launched three invading armies into the Creek country, from Mississippi, from Georgia and from Tennessee.

18   The other southern nations, subjected to the combined pressures of the British-American and Creek-American wars, were compelled to take positions with reference to both. To their agitated councils two supportable courses were open. They could move to defend the Creek, by this defiance of the United States accepting an alliance with Great Britain, as had Tecumseh's northern Indians, a course which could prove of incalculable value were Great Britain to win the war. Or they could maintain a stubborn neutrality, clinging to an attitude permitting later negotiation with whoever proved the victor. They adopted neither of these courses but instead elected a third. They joined the American invaders and vigorously assisted in the destruction of their Creek neighbor.

19   The Cherokee debate had been the most protracted and their decision of by far the most consequence. They possessed a significant residue of their traditional military power. Their determination was precipitated by the persistent arguments of Ridge, one of their more influential chiefs. Unlike many Cherokee leaders, who were the part white descendants of early intermarriages between Cherokee women and colonial officers or traders, he was a full blood. His record of patriotic devotion to Cherokee territorial integrity was unassailable. Five years before he had assisted in the execution of a fellow chief, Doublehead, who had been accused of a land sale

unauthorized by the Cherokee National Council. In this greater crisis the burden of Ridge's argument was that every future Cherokee hope of maintaining possession of their homeland depended upon American favor and that the Creek War offered an extraordinary opportunity to cultivate it. He advocated, therefore, a full scale Cherokee association with the American attack on the Creek. The distracted Cherokee Council hesitated but, with the assistance of a coincidental Creek murder of a Cherokee woman, his earnest plea finally carried the day.

20   Of the three American armies striking at the heart of the Creek country in central Alabama, the most important was the column of regulars and militia from Tennessee commanded by Andrew Jackson. Nearly a thousand Cherokee warriors flocked to his standard. The Creek, forced into unity by the extremity of this external danger, defended themselves with despairing valor. Frustrated by the unreliability and misbehavior of his military, Jackson was twice compelled to retreat to his base while the weight of his campaign was carried by his Cherokee allies. His eventual victory at Horseshoe Bend, where more than a thousand Creek died in the flames of their central stronghold, was won, after his frontal assault by white troops had been repulsed, by the impetuosity of his Cherokee battalions who swam the river to take the defenders in the rear.

21   Jackson's Indian allies had won for him those first victories which had in turn opened to him his sensational opportunity at the ensuing Battle of New Orleans where in one fearful half hour he gained the military reputation which made him the west's great hero. These services the Indians began immediately and bitterly to regret. As in every former instance of white victories gained with Indian assistance the fruits of victory were reserved entirely for whites. Jackson's response to the allegiance of his Indian allies was to appoint himself their chief adversary. At the peace conference ending the Creek War he dictated a cession opening a wide corridor to white settlement leading through the center of the Indian country from the Tennessee to the Gulf. Thereafter he began at once to insist that not only the Creek but all southern Indians take themselves off forthwith to the far west. He pressed this insistence with a relentless vigor that was made irresistible by the executive power he wielded during the eight years he occupied the White House.

22   The pit the southern Indians had dug for one another had become a chasm engulfing them all.

BUILDING CONTEXT

1. Compare Van Every's discussion of Indians to the selections by Smith and Rowlandson. Which of the many possible aspects of the Indian story

does each choose to discuss? How do these choices reflect each writer's time, place, and concerns?

2. Compare the criteria used by Van Every and Rowlandson to define group identity. What importance does each author place on race and religion? Pay particular attention to Van Every's portraits of Tecumseh and Ridge, and Rowlandson's attitude toward "praying Indians."

FURTHER STUDY

1. What was happening in the 1960s that might have motivated Van Every to write about the Indian's "lost birthright" and to treat it in the manner he did? Which popular views of that period is he rejecting or dismissing?

2. What assumption does Van Every make about group identity? Why does he think that it would have been "natural" for Indians to oppose whites but not other Indians? Why are wars among Indian nations less understandable than wars between England and France, Catholics and Protestants, or Christians and Muslims?

3. Is group identity or membership in a community defined from the inside or the outside? To which group, for example, would, or should, a female African-American teacher feel most affinity? Explore current ideas about group identity among women, African Americans, Hispanics, workers, gays, or other groups.

> **BARBARA CAMERON**
> *"Gee, You Don't Seem Like an Indian from the Reservation"* (1988)

"I don't like being put under a magnifying glass and having cute liberal terms describe who I am."

The quest for community and personal identity is at the heart of this essay by a lesbian Indian activist from South Dakota. Cameron recalls her childhood exposure to racism, her early hatred of whites, and her odyssey in search of understanding, acceptance, or inner peace. The essay originally appeared in *This Bridge Called My Back: Writings by Radical Women of Color*, a title that reflects the complexity of defining community.

Text: Cherrie Morraga and Ana Castillo, eds.; *This Bridge Called My Back: Writings by Radical Women of Color*; San Francisco: ISM Press, 1988.

EXPLORING ISSUES IN THE TEXT

1. Why, at her first pow-wow (par. 4), did Cameron keep asking, "Where are the Indians?" What is the significance of this question? What stereotypes about Indians does Cameron confront in her experience? What stereotypes about whites does she seem to accept (pars. 2–3)?

2. Why does Cameron say (par. 9) that she has difficulty with the words "alienation" and "assimilation"? Why does she have trouble writing about racism (par. 13)?

3. Trace how Cameron moves from discussing white racism to Third World racism to antigay attitudes. What is happening to the concept of group identity during this evolution?

"GEE, YOU DON'T SEEM LIKE AN INDIAN FROM THE RESERVATION"

1   One of the very first words I learned in my Lakota language was *wasicu* which designates white people. At that early age, my comprehension of *wasicu* was gained from observing and listening to my family discussing the wasicu. My grandmother always referred to white people as the "wasicu sica" with emphasis on *sica,* our word for terrible or bad. By the age of five I had seen one Indian man gunned down in the back by the police and was a silent witness to a gang of white teenage boys beating up an elderly Indian man. I'd hear stories of Indian ranch hands being "accidentally" shot by white ranchers. I quickly began to understand the wasicu menace my family spoke of.

2   My hatred for wasicu was solidly implanted by the time I entered first grade. Unfortunately in first grade I became teacher's pet so my teacher had a fondness for hugging me which always repulsed me. I couldn't stand the idea of a white person touching me. Eventually I realized that it wasn't the white skin that I hated, but it was their culture of deceit, greed, racism, and violence.

3   During my first memorable visit to a white town, I was appalled that they thought of themselves as superior to my people. Their manner of living appeared devoid of life and bordered on hostility even for one another. They were separated from each other by their perfectly, politely fenced square plots of green lawn. The only lawns on my reservation were the

lawns of the BIA [Bureau of Indian Affairs] officials or white christians. The white people always seemed so loud, obnoxious, and vulgar. And the white parents were either screaming at their kids, threatening them with some form of punishment or hitting them. After spending a day around white people, I was always happy to go back to the reservation where people followed a relaxed yet respectful code of relating with each other. The easy teasing and joking that were inherent with the Lakota were a welcome relief after a day with the plastic faces.

4   I vividly remember two occasions during my childhood in which I was cognizant of being an Indian. The first time was at about three years of age when my family took me to my first pow-wow. I kept asking my grandmother, "Where are the Indians? Where are the Indians? Are they going to have bows and arrows?" I was very curious and strangely excited about the prospect of seeing real live Indians even though I myself was one. It's a memory that has remained with me through all these years because it's so full of the subtleties of my culture. There was a sweet wonderful aroma in the air from the dancers and from the traditional food booths. There were lots of grandmothers and grandfathers with young children running about. Pow-wows in the Plains usually last for three days, sometimes longer, with Indian people traveling from all parts of our country to dance, to share food and laughter, and to be with each other. I could sense the importance of our gathering times and it was the beginning of my awareness that my people are a great and different nation.

5   The second time in my childhood when I knew very clearly that I am Indian occurred when I was attending an all white (except for me) elementary school. During Halloween my friends and I went trick or treating. At one of the last stops, the mother knew all of the children except for me. She asked me to remove my mask so she could see who I was. After I removed my mask, she realized I was an Indian and quite cruelly told me so, refusing to give me the treats my friends had received. It was a stingingly painful experience.

6   I told my mother about it the next evening after I tried to understand it. My mother was outraged and explained the realities of being an Indian in South Dakota. My mother paid a visit to the woman which resulted in their expressing a barrage of equal hatred for one another. I remember sitting in our pick-up hearing the intensity of the anger and feeling very sad that my mother had to defend her child to someone who wasn't worthy of her presence.

7   I spent a part of my childhood feeling great sadness and helplessness about how it seemed that Indians were open game for the white people, to kill, maim, beat up, insult, rape, cheat, or whatever atrocity the white people wanted to play with. There was also a rage and frustration that has not died. When I look back on reservation life it seems that I spent a great deal of time attending the funerals of my relatives or friends of my family. During one year I went to funerals of four murder victims. Most of

my non-Indian friends have not seen a dead body or have not been to a funeral. Death was so common on the reservation that I did not understand the implications of the high death rate until after I moved away and was surprised to learn that I've seen more dead bodies than my friends will probably ever see in their lifetime.

8   Because of experiencing racial violence, I sometimes panic when I'm the only non-white in a roomful of whites, even if they are my closest friends; I wonder if I'll leave the room alive. The seemingly copacetic gay world of San Francisco becomes a mere dream after the panic leaves. I think to myself that it's truly insane for me to feel the panic. I want to scream out my anger and disgust with myself for feeling distrustful of my white friends and I want to banish the society that has fostered those feelings of alienation. I wonder at the amount of assimilation which has affected me and how long my "Indianness" will allow me to remain in a city that is far removed from the lives of many Native Americans.

9   "Alienation" and "assimilation" are two common words used to describe contemporary Indian people. I've come to despise those two words because what leads to "alienation" and "assimilation" should not be so concisely defined. And I generally mistrust words that are used to define Native Americans and Brown People. I don't like being put under a magnifying glass and having cute liberal terms describe who I am. The "alienation" or "assimilation" that I manifest is often in how I speak. There isn't necessarily a third world language but there is an Indian way of talking that is an essential part of me. I like it, I love it, yet I deny it. I "save" it for when I'm around other Indians. It is a way of talking that involves "Indian humor" which I know for sure non-Indian people would not necessarily understand.

10   *Articulate. Articulate.* I've heard that word used many times to describe third world people. White people seem so surprised to find brown people who can speak fluent english and are even perhaps educated. We then become "articulate." I think I spend a lot of time being articulate with white people. Or as one person said to me a few years ago, "Gee, you don't seem like an Indian from the reservation."

11   I often read about the dilemmas of contemporary Indians caught between the white and Indian worlds. For most of us, it is an uneasy balance to maintain. Sometimes some of us are not so successful with it. Native Americans have a very high suicide rate.

> When I was about 20, I dreamt of myself at the age of 25–26, standing at a place on my reservation, looking to the North, watching a glorious, many-colored horse galloping toward me from the sky. My eyes were riveted and attracted to the beauty and overwhelming strength of the horse. The horse's eyes were staring directly into mine, hypnotizing me and holding my attention. Slowly from the East, an eagle was gliding toward the horse. My attention began to be drawn toward the calm of the eagle but I still did not want to lose sight of the horse. Finally the two met with the eagle sailing into the horse causing it to disintegrate. The eagle flew gently on.

12   I take this prophetic dream as an analogy of my balance between the white (horse) and Indian (eagle) world. Now that I am 26, I find that I've gone as far into my exploration of the white world as I want. It doesn't mean that I'm going to run off to live in a tipi. It simply means that I'm not interested in pursuing a society that uses analysis, research, and experimentation to concretize their vision of cruel destinies for those who are not bastards of the Pilgrims; a society with arrogance rising, moon in oppression, and sun in destruction.

13   Racism is not easy for me to write about because of my own racism toward other people of color, and because of a complex set of "racisms" within the Indian community. At times animosity exists between half-breed, full-blood, light-skinned Indians, dark-skinned Indians, and non-Indians who attempt to pass as Indians. The U.S. government has practiced for many years its divisiveness in the Indian community by instilling and perpetuating these Indian vs. Indian tactics. Native Americans are the foremost group of people who continuously fight against pre-meditated cultural genocide.

14   I've grown up with misconceptions about Blacks, Chicanos, and Asians. I'm still in the process of trying to eliminate my racist pictures of other people of color. I know most of *my* images of other races come from television, books, movies, newspapers, and magazines. Who can pinpoint exactly where racism comes from? There are certain political dogmas that are excellent in their "analysis" of racism and how it feeds the capitalist system. To intellectually understand that it is wrong or politically incorrect to be racist leaves me cold. A lot of poor or working class white and brown people are just as racist as the "capitalist pig." We are *all* continually pumped with gross and inaccurate images of everyone else and we *all* pump it out. I don't think there are easy answers or formulas. My personal attempts at eliminating my racism have to start at the base level of those mind-sets that inhibit my relationships with people.

15   Racism among third world people is an area that needs to be discussed and dealt with honestly. We form alliances loosely based on the fact that we have a common oppressor, yet we do not have a commitment to talk about our own fears and misconceptions about each other. I've noticed that liberal, consciousness-raised white people tend to be incredibly polite to third world people at parties or other social situations. It's almost as if they make a point to SHAKE YOUR HAND or to introduce themselves and then run down all the latest right-on third world or Native American books they've just read. On the other hand it's been my experience that if there are several third world gay people at a party, we make a point of avoiding each other, and spend our time talking to the whites to show how sophisticated and intelligent were are. I've always wanted to introduce myself to other third world people but wondered how I would introduce myself or what would I say. There are so many things I would want to say, except sometimes I don't want to remember I'm Third World or Native American. I don't want to remember sometimes because it means recognizing that we're outlaws.

16   At the Third World Gay Conference in October 1979, the Asian and Native American people in attendance felt the issues affecting us were not adequately included in the workshops. Our representation and leadership had minimal input which resulted in a skimpy educational process about our struggles. The conference glaringly pointed out to us the narrow definition held by some people that third world means black people only. It was a depressing experience to sit in the lobby of Harambee House with other Native Americans and Asians, feeling removed from other third world groups with whom there is supposed to be this automatic solidarity and empathy. The Indian group sat in my motel room discussing and exchanging our experiences within the third world context. We didn't spend much time in workshops conducted by other third world people because of feeling unwelcomed at the conference and demoralized by having an invisible presence. What's worse than being invisible among your own kind?

17   It is of particular importance to us as third world gay people to begin a serious interchange of sharing and educating ourselves about each other. We not only must struggle with the racism and homophobia of straight white america, but must often struggle with the homophobia that exists within our third world communities. Being third world doesn't always connote a political awareness of activism. I've met a number of third world and Native American lesbians who've said they're just into "being themselves" and that politics has no meaning in their lives. I agree that everyone is entitled to "be themselves" but in a society that denies respect and basic rights to people because of their ethnic background, I feel that individuals cannot idly sit by and allow themselves to be co-opted by the dominant society. I don't know what moves a person to be politically active or to attempt to raise the quality of life in our world. I only know what motivates my political responsibility . . . the death of Anna Mae Aquash—Native American freedom fighter—"mysteriously" murdered by a bullet in the head; Raymond Yellow Thunder—forced to dance naked in front of a white VFW club in Nebraska—murdered; Rita Silk-Nauni—imprisoned for life for defending her child; my dear friend Mani Lucas-Papago—shot in the back of the head outside of a gay bar in Phoenix. The list could go on and on. My Native American History, recent and past, moves me to continue as a political activist.

18   And in the white gay community there is rampant racism which is never adequately addressed or acknowledged. My friend Chrystos from the Menominee Nation gave a poetry reading in May 1980, at a Bay Area feminist bookstore. Her reading consisted of poems and journal entries in which she wrote honestly from her heart about the many "isms" and contradictions in most of our lives. Chrystos' bluntly revealing observations on her experiences with the white-lesbian-feminist-community are similar to mine and are probably echoed by other lesbians of color.

19   Her honesty was courageous and should be representative of the kind of forum our community needs to openly discuss mutual racism. A few days

following Chrystos' reading, a friend who was in the same bookstore overhead a white lesbian denounce Chrystos' reading as anti-lesbian and racist.

20 A few years ago, a white lesbian telephoned me requesting an interview, explaining that she was taking Native American courses at a local university, and that she needed data for her paper on gay Native Americans. I agreed to the interview with the idea that I would be helping a "sister" and would also be able to educate her about Native American struggles. After we completed the interview, she began a diatribe on how sexist Native Americans are, followed by a questioning session in which I was to enlighten her mind about why Native Americans are so sexist. I attempted to rationally answer her inanely racist and insulting questions, although my inner response was to tell her to remove herself from my house. Later it became very clear how I had been manipulated as a sounding board for her ugly and distorted views about Native Americans. Here arrogance and disrespect were characteristic of the racist white people in South Dakota. If I tried to point it out, I'm sure she would have vehemently denied her racism.

21 During the Brigg's Initiative scare, I was invited to speak at a rally to represent Native American solidarity against the initiative. The person who spoke prior to me expressed a pro-Bakke sentiment which the audience booed and hissed. His comments left the predominantly white audience angry and in disruption. A white lesbian stood up demanding that a third world person address the racist comments he had made. The MC, rather than taking responsibility for restoring order at the rally, realized that I was the next speaker and I was also T-H-I-R-D-W-O-R-L-D!! I refused to address the remarks of the previous speaker because of the attitudes of the MC and the white lesbian that only third world people are responsible for speaking out against racism. *It is inappropriate for progressive or liberal white people to expect warriors in brown armor to eradicate racism.* There must be co-responsibility from people of color and white people to equally work on this issue. It is not just MY responsibility to point out and educate about racist activities and beliefs.

22 Redman, redskin, savage, heathen, injun, american indian, first americans, indigenous peoples, natives, amerindian, native american, nigger, negro, black, wet back, greaser, mexican, spanish, latin, hispanic, chicano, chink, oriental, asian, disadvantaged, special interest group, minority, third world, fourth world, people of color, illegal aliens—oh yes about them, will the U.S. government recognize that the Founding Fathers (you know George Washington and all those guys) are this country's first illegal aliens.

23 *We are named by others and we are named by ourselves.*

Epilogue . . .

24 Following writing most of this, I went to visit my home in South Dakota. It was my first visit in eight years. I kept putting off my visit year after year because I could not tolerate the white people there and the ruralness

and poverty of the reservation. And because in the eight years since I left home, I came out as a lesbian. My visit home was overwhelming. Floods and floods of locked memories broke. I rediscovered myself there in the hills, on the prairies, in the sky, on the road, in the quiet nights, among the stars, listening to the distant yelps of coyotes, walking on Lakota earth, seeing Bear Butte, looking at my grandparents' cragged faces, standing under wakiyan, smelling the Paha Sapa (Black Hills), and being with my previous circle of relatives.

25   My sense of time changed, my manner of speaking changed, and a certain freedom with myself returned.

26   I was sad to leave but recognized that a significant part of myself has never left and never will. And that part is what gives me strength—the strength of my people's enduring history and continuing belief in the sovereignty of our lives.

BUILDING CONTEXT

1. Compare Cameron's discussion of Indians to those of Van Every, Smith, or Rowlandson. What issues does she choose to focus on in her writing? How do these different choices made by the writers reflect their purposes and concerns?

2. Compare how one of the issues we are exploring—mission, identity, equality, religion, or the individual and the state—is treated by two or three of the writers in the selections we have read.

3. Cameron's essay does not follow the rigid structure of thesis–development–conclusion that is usually taught in composition classes. What is the organizing principle? How does it reinforce her purpose or message? Analyze the possibility that she is rejecting a "white male" style of writing.

FURTHER STUDY

1. What was going on in the 1980s that might have motivated Cameron to write about this topic? Which aspects of her essay would she probably have omitted twenty years earlier? Why did she, or why could she, include them?

2. Discuss Cameron's views about the label "Third World." What is her attitude toward the belief that "people of color" constitute a natural community? What do you believe about the "natural" affinity of blacks, Hispanics, and Asians?

3. In the best-seller *You Just Don't Understand: Women and Men in Conversation,* Deborah Tannen analyzes the possibility that women and men speak (and write) differently. Using the works of Smith, Van Every, Rowlandson,

and Cameron, try to find evidence that supports or disproves the existence of sex-based writing styles.

Van Every and Cameron in Context

As we have pointed out, there are no definitive answers to the study questions. Instead, we offer some thoughts that may help you form your own appreciation of each of the selections.

The Civil Rights movement of the 1960s and the Gay Rights campaign of the 1980s clearly influenced Van Every and Cameron. The rights of minorities became a visible issue when African Americans refused to remain second-class citizens. As the white majority slowly accepted the justice of black claims, other groups found their own voices—at first in solidarity with blacks, but then as their antagonists. What many had envisioned as a "Rainbow Coalition"—a massive group with broad membership—broke into many competing factions, each narrowly defined: Cubans and blacks fought for power in Miami, blacks turned against Koreans in Los Angeles, and women began to question whether they owed their allegiance to their color, their gender or their sexual orientation. In addition, demands for toleration of differences eventually became an aggressive celebration of diversity, often accompanied by a mythology that romanticized ethnic perfection and demonized white male Europeans. Many people no longer sought a common denominator to offer them membership in ever-larger groups; instead, they defined their identity in ever-narrower terms.

Thus, it is not surprising that in the 1960s, at the beginning of this period, Van Every could assume that Indians should "naturally" have perceived themselves as a single group in conflict with a monolithic white enemy. Though he rejects the romantic view of noble savages living in harmony, he nevertheless minimizes the differences among the numerous Native Americans that caused wars and decimation long before the arrival of the Europeans—as well as the differences among the warring whites themselves. Since the colonists perceived the Indians as a group, he seems to say, the Indians ought to have done so too. That they did not led to their destruction.

On the other hand, Cameron writes during a period celebrating diversity. She traces her own pilgrimage from the reservation to San Francisco back to the reservation, that is, from wanting to be accepted in the mainstream, through recognizing the racism of white lesbians and the homophobia of straight ethnics, to finding comfort in her Indian heritage. While Van Every takes group identity for granted, Cameron's essay illustrates her search for a group, or community, that will nourish her personal identity.

Writing about Critical Issues in Context

As our discussion has shown, ideas occur in the context of the writer, and they continue to exist—usually after some transformation—in the context of the reader. Essays and books speak to each other because later writers inherit the world shaped by their predecessors. When you read and write, you join this world and share in this tradition. Almost any of the questions following the reading selections could become the topic of an essay; many could lead to exciting research papers. Only you know what a selection will mean to you, in light of your personality, background, and training. Other readers are eager to learn about how your experiences and perceptions differ from their own.

We are all affected differently by events because of who we are. As you have seen, John Smith and Mary Rowlandson reacted to their captivity in ways that reflected their personalities, beliefs, and needs. Smith wrote a story about a brave soldier who survived adversity to civilize the wilderness. Rowlandson portrayed a mother's grief at the loss of her children and her reconciliation to God's will. Smith hoped his story of survival and friendship with an Indian emperor would help solidify his career as a guide to the New World. Rowlandson offered consolation to Christians by relating God's hand in human experience, even the deaths of helpless women and children. How readers—such as yourself—of varying backgrounds, at different times respond to these narratives is a topic for a provocative essay, as you can see in the following selection.

ANNETTE KOLODNY
*"A*mong the Indians: The Uses of Captivity" **(1993)**

---

*"I*ndian captivity narratives have mirrored the aspirations and anxieties of successive generations."

After summarizing Rowlandson's *Narrative,* Annette Kolodny, a professor at the University of Arizona, surveys how captivity narratives have been crafted, received, and used over the years. She then describes how her students—whites, African Americans, Native Americans, men, women, '60s flower children, Vietnam veterans—have experienced these narratives in very personal ways.

Text: Annette Kolodny; "Among the Indians: The Uses of Captivity"; *The New York Times;* January 31, 1993; *Book Review,* 1, 26–29.

EXPLORING ISSUES IN THE TEXT

1. Why, according to Kolodny, did captivity narratives become so popular? How were they enlisted for service in America's various missions?

2. Describe how Indians became both a model and a metaphor in the Revolutionary War era. Explain how this development shows an idea being transformed by a new context.

3. Analyze how the reactions of Kolodny's students illustrate the ways in which readers bring their own context to what they are reading.

AMONG THE INDIANS: THE USES OF CAPTIVITY

1 . . . Never mentioned in Rowlandson's account of her captivity is the fact that the raid on Lancaster had been part of a continuing offensive to inflict retribution on the British for the massacre of more than 600 Narragansett men, women and children in their winter home in the swamps of central Rhode Island the previous November. "There were hundreds of *wigwams* . . . which our Souldiers set on fire, in the which men, women and Children (no man knoweth how many hundreds of them) were burnt to death," reported the most influential Puritan minister in Boston, Increase Mather, in "A Brief History of the War With the Indians in New-England" (1676). In a later history of that same encounter, Mather's son Cotton noted gleefully that the Narragansetts had been "Berbikew'd."

2 For Rowlandson, the meaning of her ordeal lay in its spiritual context. She was, after all, the wife of Lancaster's minister (who, ironically, had been in Boston at the time of the raid to plead for greater protection against the Indian threat). She shared the Puritans' view of themselves as a chosen people divinely ordained to subdue and possess "the howling wilderness" of the New World. As such, "the many trials and afflictions" she endured amid her "satanic" captors represented a chastening of her vanity and a testing of her faith. Her narrative strives to reveal "the wonderful power of God" in sustaining and finally redeeming her, and it unquestioningly affirms Increase Mather's declaration in "A Brief History" (published the very year of her captivity) that this was the "land the Lord God of our Fathers hath given to us for a rightfull Possession."

3 "A True History of the Captivity and Restoration of Mrs. Mary Rowlandson," the first printed account of a New Englander captured by Indians (though Rowlandson was not the first from the Massachusetts Bay Colony to be captured), sold out four editions when it appeared in Boston in 1682 and initiated the colonial reading public into a voracious taste for vivid reports of the experiences of settlers who were captured by American Indians.

4   Stories of captivity did not begin with the British, of course. When Cortés landed in Yucatan in 1519, one of his exploratory parties encountered two Spaniards who had been living with a coastal tribe since a shipwreck eight years before. One greeted the Spaniards as rescuers, because he had been enslaved by the Indians, but the other resolutely refused to rejoin his countrymen because he had married, fathered three children and adopted the local customs. According to contemporaneous Spanish accounts, what most provoked Cortés was that the man was now serving as a warrior and military tactician for his adoptive tribe.

5   Such incidents in New Spain did not result in extended written narratives, however. That fell to the British, beginning with the explorer John Smith's eagerness to enhance his reputation for heroism by exploiting his claim that he had been captured outside the Jamestown settlement in 1607 and condemned to death by the chief of the Pamunkey tribe. But while Smith's dramatic rescue by Powhatan's daughter, Pocahontas, later figured prominently in his "Generall Historie of Virginia" (1624), it was not until Mary White Rowlandson defied Puritan sanctions against a woman making public statements that an account of captivity was published as a single book.

6   Generally regarded by scholars as one of the few distinctively American literary genres, the Indian captivity narrative continued to show the influence of Rowlandson's original shaping imagination. Subsequent captivity narratives, framed by the drama of the capture at the outset and the release of the captive through escape, rescue or ransom at the end, followed Rowlandson in detailing the rituals, social organization and daily life of an unknown culture to which the captive had temporarily gained access. Whether as a fearful prisoner anticipating death or as a cherished member adopted into full kinship, most captives—male and female, adults and children alike—provided their readers with intimate glimpses into the workings of an alien society, all the while struggling to make sense of their special experience.

7   In later decades, authentic narratives competed for popularity with wholly fictional works, sometimes serving up images of happy adaptations to an almost idyllic Indian existence, while at other times detailing hideous tortures of male captives, sexual violation of females and the murderous scalping of pioneers on the Overland Trail. In most narratives, the Indian represented a threat to the ideals of "civilization," but in other narratives the Indian stood as an embattled, and sometimes noble, emblem of a vanishing wilderness. With the closing of the frontier in 1890, the numbers of new captivity accounts decreased markedly, even as older ones continued to be reprinted; relatively few new titles appeared in the 20th century.

8   When modern readers first encounter these narratives, there is often an immediate shock of recognition. The imprint of these narratives seems to be everywhere: obvious in popular movies like John Ford's classic "The

Searchers" (1956) or Kevin Costner's "Dances With Wolves" (1990) and more subtly etched in the media treatment of the Patricia Hearst kidnapping, the portrayal of American hostages released from the Middle East and accounts of what is now called the Stockholm syndrome, the psychiatric label for the experience of prisoners who come to identify with their captors.

9   From the first, for both their authors and their readers, Indian captivity narratives have mirrored the aspirations and anxieties of successive generations, revealing new meanings and lending themselves to startling new interpretations over time.

10   For the Puritans, captivity narratives served as vehicles for moral instruction. In sermons and published tracts, ministers like the Mathers represented individual captives as metaphors for the entire community, deserving of "scourging" for momentary backsliding but eventually destined for rescue and divine redemption. The Puritan emphasis on the "satanic" brutality of the Indians toward their pious Christian captives was used to justify not only the conversion of the "savages" but their removal as well.

11   Toward the middle of the 18th century, the religious tenor of the narratives was replaced by politics. The recurring military engagements that marked territorial disputes between the British and French in North America, dating roughly from 1689 through 1763 and known by the British as the French and Indian Wars, resulted in large numbers of captives on both sides. In the English colonies, highly sensationalized captivity narratives stirred war fever by inciting hatred of both the Catholic French and their Indian allies.

12   By the Revolutionary era, these patterns were so much a staple of the colonial imagination that they provided ready images for those who began to see themselves as captives of a tyrant no less arbitrary in his exercise of power than the exaggerated sachems (tribal leaders) of the Indian captivity narratives. Once the fighting began, British occupation took on the features of captivity in the popular press, and the rhetoric of revolution repeatedly compared the British troops to "savage" Indians even as the rebellious partisans donned Indian dress for the Boston Tea Party in 1773 and employed native allies and native fighting strategies to defeat the redcoats.

13   When "The Narrative of Colonel Ethan Allen's Captivity" appeared in 1779, it borrowed heavily from the Indian captivity tradition in offering the first account by an American of a prisoner-of-war experience. Detailing his capture by the British and by Indians in Montreal in 1775 and the ensuing starvation and humiliation in Canadian stockades and in British prison ships anchored off New York Harbor, Allen's book about his three-year imprisonment opened with his capture by a "savage" with shaven head and a "hellish visage." What distinguished Allen's account from its forebears was his portrayal of his captivity as a test of patriotic loyalty rather than a trial

of religious faith. Like its models, Allen's narrative was also immediately successful, going through an estimated 20 editions within two years.

14 Along with the reprintings and revisions of the older captivity narratives, the tastes of the late 18th century gave rise to captivity works that were often wholly fictional and generally so melodramatic as to resemble the popular sentimental novels of the day. By the close of the century, Charles Brockden Brown, the new nation's first professional author, was incorporating captivity episodes into his novels. In the 19th century, James Fenimore Cooper invented captivity incidents for his Leatherstocking series. Lurid illustrations of young white women about to be scalped or captured accompanied a number of 19th-century narratives, increasing their sales and reinforcing the Government's avowedly expansionist intentions.

15 Despite its opening encomium to the "intrepid and brave General Jackson," whose troops rescued the narrative's heroine, "An Affecting Narrative of the Captivity and Sufferings of Mrs. Mary Smith" (1815) otherwise followed patterns that were now familiar and, in addition, incorporated all the elements that came to characterize the most sensationalized captivity stories of the 19th century. According to an anonymous "gentleman in the Western Country" who recorded her 60-day ordeal, in 1814 Mary Smith, her husband and their daughters were taken captive on the west bank of the Mississippi, in the vicinity of New Orleans, by a roving band of Kickapoo Indians. Soon after their capture, Mrs. Smith and her daughters were compelled to witness the "horrid spectacle" of the torture of her husband and his death. Days later, "the Savages . . . dragged" Smith's two daughters, "the oldest in her 19th and the youngest in the 11th year of their age, shrieking from the embraces of their helpless mother." Stripped, tortured and "set on fire," these "helpless virgins" endured a three-hour agony in full view of their mother, who afterward "remained in a state of delirium for two or three days."

16 Finally, an elderly chief offered Smith the choice between a similar death or taking "the place of his squaw, who with his two children had been killed by the whites." "To gratify the wishes of one of these vile monsters, was as I conceived, although shocking in the extreme, not quite so bad as to endure their savage torture," Smith wrote, surrendering to what she viewed as "the necessity of becoming a prostitute in order to prevent the most cruel death."

17 For most contemporary readers, the torture and death of Mary Smith's husband and daughters, as well as her coerced marriage, not only justified Smith's eventual fatal knifing of "the old Indian" sleeping beside her, but, more important, reinforced the narrative's praise of Andrew Jackson for "exterminating the Indians of the Creek Nations." If the native inhabitants were no more than "ferocious cannibals," capable of the atrocities so graphically depicted by Smith's "gentleman" reporter, then readers need not ponder the morality of genocidal campaigns like Jackson's or, even less, question the policy of removing tribes from their traditional lands.

18   Sympathy for the Indian—or even squeamishness at the disease and starvation that accompanied the Indians' confinement within stockades or on reservations with poor soil and limited water—was constrained by the captivity narrative's appeal in behalf of "the poor distressed mother . . . witnessing the horrid sacrifice of her tender offspring." There can be no doubt that the Smith narrative also helped bolster popular support for Jackson's campaign against the Seminoles of Florida three years later.

19   But even as official Government policy echoed John Quincy Adams's observation in 1814 that it was unthinkable "to condemn vast regions of territory to perpetual barrenness that a few hundred savages might find wild beasts to hunt upon it," one nagging fact of Euro-American and native relations became increasingly and embarrassingly evident. As J. Hector St. John Crèvecoeur summed it up in 1782 in his "Letters From an American Farmer," "There must be in their social bond something singularly captivating, and far superior to anything to be boasted of among us; for thousands of Europeans are Indians, and we have no examples of even one of those Aborigines having from choice become Europeans."

20   Benjamin Franklin made a similar observation in a 1753 letter to a friend in England: "When white persons of either sex have been taken prisoners young by the Indians, and have lived a while among them, tho' ransomed by their Friends, and treated with all imaginable tenderness to prevail with them to stay . . . yet in a Short time they become disgusted with our manner of life, and the care and pains that are necessary to support it, and take the first good Opportunity of escaping again into the Woods, from whence there is no reclaiming them."

21   The reverse, however, was never true. "When an Indian Child has been brought up among us, taught our language and habituated to our Customs, yet if he goes to see his relations and make one Indian Ramble with them, there is no perswading him ever to return," Franklin added.

22   Moreover, it was not only those taken young who refused repatriation. A British colonel overseeing an exchange of captives in 1764 reported to his superiors that "it must not be denied that there were even some grown persons who shewed an unwillingness to return."

23   The tantalizing possibility that life among the Indians might offer an attractive alternative to what Franklin had called "the care and pains . . . necessary to support" European civilization had been suggested by a number of narratives, although never as powerfully as in those attributed to Daniel Boone and Mary Jemison. In 1784, John Filson appended to a promotional tract for Kentucky a first-person narrative entitled "The Adventures of Col. Daniel Boone, one of the first Settlers." Supposedly taken down by Filson from Boone's dictation (though probably largely invented by Filson himself), the book included two captivity episodes.

24   It was well known, of course, that Boone had been captured during the early days of Kentucky's settlement and then again during the Revolutionary War, when a Shawnee chief rejected a generous ransom offer from the British lieutenant governor of Detroit and decided, instead, to

adopt Boone as his son. Although Boone was hardly the first white man to reveal that he had been adopted, he was the first *famous* figure openly to take pleasure from that fact. The Indians' "affection for me was . . . great," Boone boasted. He "was adopted, according to their custom, into a family where I became a son, and had a great share in the affection of my new parents, brother, sisters, and friends."

25 While Boone's narrative, in various edited versions, sold steadily from the late 18th century into our own, the unrivaled publishing success of 1824 was "A Narrative of the Life of Mrs. Mary Jemison Who Was Taken by the Indians in the Year 1755 When Only About Twelve Years of Age and Has Continued to Reside Amongst Them to the Present," which outsold the works of Sir Walter Scott and James Fenimore Cooper for the rest of the decade.

26 At the time her narrative appeared, Jemison was already in her 80's, living with her children in upstate New York on land that had been deeded to her just after the Revolution by her former Seneca captors. Although she was no longer with the tribe (many of the Seneca having sided with the British during the Revolution, the survivors were removed to reservations by the victorious Americans), her long life among them was recalled with definite nostalgia. "No people can live more happy than the Indians did in times of peace," she insisted.

27 Like Boone, Mary Jemison dictated her story to a local schoolteacher named James Everett Seaver. Like Boone, she emphasized the close affectional ties between her and her adoptive family, carefully detailing for Seaver the steps by which she was given new clothes, a new name, patiently taught the Seneca language and instructed in the skills required of a Seneca woman, all under the tutelage of two sisters by whom "I was ever considered and treated . . . as a real sister, the same as though I had been born of their mother."

28 Jemison, like Boone, also portrayed a world of seasonal repetitions in which her assigned tasks were "not severe." Where Boone took pleasure in competing with his adoptive male relatives in hunting and contests of marksmanship, Jemison fondly remembered how "in the summer season, we planted, tended and harvested our corn, and generally had all our children with us; but had no master to oversee or drive us, so that we could work as leisurely as we pleased."

29 Together, the Boone and Jemison narratives confirmed a suspicion that dated back to the Puritans. As John Eliot, the first English missionary to preach to the native people in a native tongue, put it in a letter to a fellow minister, Thomas Shepard of Boston, in 1647, "We labour and work in building, planting, clothing our selves, &c. and they doe not." In the paradisal garden of the New World, it appeared, some human beings had been spared the curse of Adam, living exempt from the necessity to toil by the sweat of one's brow. But European colonists clung to the virtue of labor, equating toil with civilization, and scorned the Indians as uncivi-

lized for what the whites interpreted as their willful "idleness." "In this they are sufficiently revenged on us," William Penn explained to his English partners. "We sweat and toil to live; their pleasure feeds them, I mean, their Hunting, Fishing, and Fowling."

30   The portrait of a harmonious society governed by seasonal change and unburdened by either toil or material wealth did not, by itself, account for the popularity of the many different editions of the Boone narrative or the phenomenal sales of the Jemison account. Boone was already a figure of legend, and what arrested attention in the Jemison story—and distinguished it from any previous narrative—was Jemison's insistence that she *loved* an Indian husband.

31   Only Lydia Maria Child's fictional historical romance, "Hobomok: A Tale of Early Times," published in 1824 (the same year as Jemison's narrative), had dared to depict consensual marriage between a white woman and an Indian. And even Child shied away from suggesting that her heroine actually loved her "unlettered" mate. Not so with Jemison. Although she admits that she first felt uneasy at the prospect of such a union, nonetheless she finds herself won over by "his good nature, generosity, tenderness, and friendship towards me." Her husband, a member of the Delaware tribe, "soon gained my affection," she declares, and "Strange as it may seem, I loved him!"

32   Ever since the first reported abductions, there had been avid speculation about the sexual fate of female captives. One anonymous male historian of the Indian wars pronounced, unequivocally, in 1675, "Any Women they take alive, they Defile." Jemison's account, however, accorded with the testimony of every female captive before her, substantiating the view of Elizabeth Hanson, who had been briefly captured and then ransomed in 1724, that "the Indians are seldom guilty of any indecent carriage toward their captive women."

33   Even Mary Rowlandson, ill disposed as she was toward her captors— "those roaring Lions and Savage Bears, that feared neither God nor Man, nor the Devil"—had acknowledged that "by night and day, alone and in company, sleeping all sorts together . . . not one of them ever offered the least abuse or unchastity to me in word or action." Among the tribes east of the Mississippi, societal injunctions against coercive sex were so powerful that female captives might choose to marry—as did Jemison and, less willingly, Mary Smith—but they otherwise remained untouched. After participating in American punitive expeditions against the Iroquois in New York in 1779, Gen. James Clinton concluded, "Bad as the savages are, they never violate the chastity of any women their prisoners."

34   But in the second half of the 19th century, several instances of white women raped by their Indian captors were reported, especially among the Plains tribes west of the Mississippi. Dime novels exploited such incidents, as did a number of fictitious captivity narratives, circulating a renewed image of the Indian as inherently bestial and depraved. Army

wives posted to the frontier after the Civil War confided to their diaries a dread of being taken by "devilish" Indians. When Camp Cooke in the Montana Territory was under attack, one officer's wife recorded in her diary that the women "held a 'council of war'" and determined that if the fort was overrun, "we preferred to be shot by our own officers rather than to be taken captive."

35   While the image of the predatory savage deserving of extinction clearly served the purposes of territorial expansion, benign portrayals continued to appear in at least some of the authentic captivity narratives of the period. Recounting her "six weeks in Sioux tepees," following the Sioux uprising of 1863, Sarah Wakefield asserted in "A Narrative of Indian Captivity" that "the Indians were as respectful towards me as any white man would be towards a lady: and now, when I hear all the Indians abused, it aggravates me, for I know some are as manly, honest, and noble, as our own race."

36   From the 18th century onward, captivity narratives offered conflicting and contradictory images of the Indian. In some instances, those contradictions stood side by side within a single text. J. D. Bemis, who printed the first edition of Mary Jemison's narrative, for example, obviously thought he had contracted for a fairly conventional account and so promised on the title page that it would contain the "barbarities of the Indians in the French and Revolutionary Wars." The schoolteacher to whom Jemison told her story was similarly unprepared. "The vices of the Indians, she appeared disposed not to aggravate," Seaver noted with surprise in his introduction, while she "seemed to take pride in extoling their virtues."

37   All its internal contradictions notwithstanding, in dozens of reprintings throughout the 19th century, Jemison's narrative offered thousands of readers a more complicated view of captivity than was elsewhere available. For what Jemison made clear was the precariousness of Indian survival under the dual pressures of European diseases and invasion.

38   To be sure, raiding for captives predated the arrival of the Europeans. There was a long tradition of adopting individuals from another tribe in order to compensate a family for a member lost during hostilities. But when imported diseases decimated populations and European military practices destroyed entire villages, including crops, stores and livestock, the survival of the remaining band was in jeopardy.

39   During the Continental Army's campaign against the tribes of western New York in 1779, Jemison recalled that the Americans' destruction of one Seneca camp had been so complete that there remained "not a mouthful of any kind of sustenance, not even enough to keep a child one day from perishing from hunger." Under exigencies like this, taking captives for ransom provided the means with which to buy or trade for food, and adopted captives allowed a group threatened with extinction to replenish its numbers.

⌒

40 Because of their singular popularity and unique longevity in American letters, and because of their influence on major canonical authors—from James Fenimore Cooper in "The Last of the Mohicans" to William Faulkner in "Red Leaves"—I introduced Indian captivity narratives into my American literature courses when I first began teaching in the late 1960's. In those heady political times, many college students were attracted to overarching cultural critiques. As a result, my classes found in these narratives rationalizations for the European invasion of the New World, symbolic expressions of the Puritan obsession with the testing of the chosen and racist justifications for Manifest Destiny.

41   Some students who went beyond the two or three narratives assigned as required reading asserted that they understood why, despite the tortures to which some captives were subjected, many chose to remain with the Indians. For these flower children, tribal life seemed to offer adventure and freedom, a strong sense of community, genuine affectional ties and an unfailing integrity in personal relations. Many of my Native American students flinched at such explanations, hearing in them the latest romanticized version of the noble savage. In response they would try to impress on their non-Indian classmates that there are, even today, 500 different native cultures in the United States and that tribal life differed markedly in the forests, on the Great Plains and in the pueblos.

42   With the introduction of women's studies courses in the 1970's, women students, especially, began to bristle at the habit of Puritan ministers' equating communal spiritual vulnerability with the graphic image of a helpless captive white woman languishing in the wilderness. As more men became attuned to feminist analysis, they joined the women in examining the different treatment accorded by white society to those who had had intimate relations with Indians.

43   Traders, trappers and mountain men who abandoned their "squaw" wives could easily reenter the white world and even marry a respectable woman of their own kind and raise another family. But white women who had married Indian men were regarded as tainted and "unchaste," their mixed-blood children unwelcome by white relations. For some students, the concept of a double standard had never been more stark. But the most interesting outcome of these discussions was the discovery that, for native peoples, acceptance into the group was determined solely by acculturation, while for Euro-Americans there was always a racial requirement.

44   In the 1980's, responses to the narratives were often more personal. One student who had returned to school years after serving in the Vietnam War astonished a class by reading aloud from Mary Rowlandson's closing confession that "when others are sleeping mine eyes are weeping." This student identified with Rowlandson, ransomed and safely returned to Boston, who years later was still recalling "in the night season,

how the other day I was in the midst of thousands of enemies, and nothing but death before me."

45   The 14-page "Narrative of the Uncommon Sufferings, and Surprizing Deliverance of Briton Hammon, a Negro Man,—Servant to General Winslow, of Marshfield, in New England," originally printed in Boston in 1760, always elicited an equally powerful response from African-American students. As these readers were quick to point out, the first autobiographical work by an African-American in the colonies dared not protest that most pernicious of captivities, chattel slavery. Yet the text cries out against "horrid cruelty and inhuman Barbarity," even if its apparent target is a native tribe from southern Florida who carried off Hammon after a shipwreck. After five weeks with the Indians, "during which Time they us'd me pretty well," Hammon admits, he made his escape with the aid of the master of a Spanish schooner.

46   Nowadays, in increasingly racially mixed and ethnically diverse classrooms, my students empathize with both captor and captive, recognizing in each the trauma of losing a secure cultural identity. Nobody's world was left unaltered by such contacts and intimacies, they contend. For these students, captivity narratives reflect what they experience daily. The confusion and fear of the captives and the sometimes obvious gestures of frustration, anger and impatience on the part of the captors feel very familiar to those who are themselves trying to communicate across the barriers of custom, tradition, religion and language.

47   Captivity narratives offer no illusion that such contacts will ever be easy, my students say, but at least they don't deny the possibility of respect and affection even where mutual understanding is imperfect. As the nation seeks to digest the passionate debates that accompanied last year's Columbian quincentenary, this strikes me as an important insight.

BUILDING CONTEXT

1. Kolodny asserts that Rowlandson's narrative is sufficiently different from Smith's in form and content to be considered the first true "captivity narrative." What are the features of this genre? How does Rowlandson's work differ from Smith's in these features? Explain why you agree or disagree with Kolodny's assertion.

2. Who were (or are) the "flower children" (par. 41)? Why do you think they idealized tribal life? Why do you think many Native American students were offended, rather than flattered, by this reaction to their culture? Compare their feelings to Cameron's anger with "liberals."

3. How does the fact that 500 Native American cultures exist today help us to evaluate Van Every's argument that the Indians shared a community of interest?

FURTHER STUDY

1. Kolodny assumes (par. 8) that her readers are familiar with the movies *The Searchers* and *Dances with Wolves*. What does this assumption say about how a writer imagines an audience? Summarize the main topics of these movies and show their relevance to her discussion. Compare how the two movies depict whites, Indians, the treatment of captives, and race relations. Why do they present the heroes and villains so differently?

2. Kolodny refers to a "romanticized version of the noble savage" (par. 41). Describe this idea and explain its history. What is its attraction? What does "romanticized" mean in this context? How is it related to the philosophy of romanticism? How do these concepts illuminate Washington Irving's portrait of King Philip and the popular movie *Dances with Wolves?*

3. Why do you think that Kolodny's Native American students flinched during discussions of the noble savage? Why would they be unhappy about positive images of their culture? Consider the popularity and impact of all stereotypes. What other groups might now flinch at positive portraits of themselves? Why?

4. Kolodny speaks of the "Puritan sanctions against a woman making public statements" (par. 5). Explore the reasons for and practical consequences of this stricture. How did it affect other women of that time, such as the preacher Anne Hutchinson (1591–1643) or the poet Anne Bradstreet (1612?–1672). Explore how these or other women in America "found their voices."

EXPLORING CRITICAL ISSUES THROUGH WRITING

It is now time for you to mold your own essay from all of the summaries, notes, and answers that you have been writing. The following thoughts can help you create essay topics that draw on the five selections in this chapter. The questions are meant to aid or direct your thinking; do not feel compelled to answer each one of them, or their parts, in your essay.

You should also be able to come up with other topics that interest you. Your essay should emerge from what you have been reading and present your own understanding of a single aspect of the five critical issues that have been our focus: mission, identity, equality, religion, and the individual and the state.

1. Compare and contrast how two, three, or all of the reading selections treat one of the following issues: America's mission, the formation of

identity, equality in America, the role of religion in America, and the relationship between the individual and the state.

2. Trace the evolution of the American attitude(s) toward one of the critical issues we have been discussing.

3. How is the canon—the "great books"—of a society determined? Why do you think the story of John Smith and Pocahontas has found a place in American mythology while Rowlandson's narrative has not? How do these two works and their reception shed light on ideas about America's mission and self-image, or the role of gender in our society?

4. How has religion figured in the history of the United States? How has it helped to define America's mission and self-image, and the treatment of various groups? How have the concepts of religion and Christianity, and their roles, changed in the course of our history? How is religious imagery used in defining or portraying particular groups? What current public issues are discussed in religious terms?

5. What is the significance of the terms *nation, clan,* and *tribe?* What do these terms tell us about cultural assumptions and the attitudes of the people who use them toward certain groups? What is the difference between a tribe and a clan? Examine how newspapers and broadcast news programs use these words. As an alternative, you might consider pairs such as *farmer* and *peasant* or *commando* and *terrorist.*

6. Compare and contrast ideas about group identity among women, African Americans, Hispanics, workers, gays, or another group. Is group identity or membership in a community defined from the inside or the outside?

7. Discuss the label "Third World." How is it defined? Who applies it to whom? Do "people of color" constitute a natural community? Is there a "natural" affinity among blacks, Hispanics, and Asians? Why are Hispanics—a language community with many whites—often classified as people of color?

8. Trace how women or various minority groups "found their voice" in America. To what extent has free speech been guaranteed to unpopular or non-mainstream voices?

9. What do scholars say are the characteristics of a typically male or female writing style? Why are some books popular among men and others among women? Explore the same kinds of questions about African-American, Jewish, Southern, Western, gay or other writers.

3

COLONIAL FOUNDATIONS: 1492–1800

"Having undertaken for the Glory of God and advancement of the Christian Faith . . . a Voyage to plant the First Colony . . ."

MAYFLOWER COMPACT

"Christopher Columbus, representing the Spanish Crown, arrived in 1492 . . ."

EDNA ACOSTA-BELÉN

"He has waged cruel war against human nature itself, violating its sacred rights of life and liberty . . ."

THOMAS JEFFERSON

Who settled in America, and why? In the popular imagination, the history of America begins with the Pilgrims. Their voyage to the New World in search of religious freedom is commemorated on Thanksgiving and invoked by politicians of all parties. In fact, however, this image ignores not only the older English settlement of Virginia but also the contributions of the Spanish, French, Dutch, Portuguese, and, of course, Native Americans and Africans.

The voyage of Columbus in 1492 opened a new chapter in the histories of Europe and America. In the following century soldiers and adventurers, traders and missionaries encountered the people Columbus mistakenly called Indians. Whether motivated by greed or the best of intentions, these Europeans replaced the native cultures with their own or with new, mixed cultures, as in the process of *mestizaje* described by Edna Acosta-Belén.

Europe in the sixteenth century was fragmented along religious fissures. Even as Columbus sailed for America, his Spanish patrons, the "Catholic Monarchs" Ferdinand and Isabella, were unifying their domain by expelling Muslims and Jews. But within a generation, the teachings of Martin Luther created a religious Reformation that shattered the solidarity of the Catholic world. Among the new Protestant denominations, Henry VIII established the Church of England. Some of the English, dissatisfied with this Anglican Church, hoped to purify it; hence the name Puritans. Others left the Church entirely, becoming Dissenters or Separatists. Religious wars and persecution wracked Europe, with Spain and France emerging as defenders of the Papacy and bitter enemies of England.

The Europeans who left for America were a varied people, with varied motives. But for all, the New World was a place of special promise, perhaps even the Promised Land. Some came to expand the empire of their earthly sovereign, others to build God's kingdom on earth, still others to find their fortune or because they had nothing to keep them in Europe. The Spanish Conquistadors, in particular, inflamed the popular imagination with shiploads of gold and slaves and stories of fabulous cities filled with booty.

Early English attempts to match the rival Spaniards ended in failure, or disaster, as at the lost colony of Roanoke Island in 1587. The only riches the English found came from raids along the Spanish Main by pirates and privateers. Virginia, the first successful English colony, was a joint stock company, a venture of private investors hoping to profit from the natural resources of America. Encouraged by this success, the Pilgrims sought religious freedom in the vastness of America, as their leader William Bradford explains. After them came the Puritans, whose identification of themselves with the Biblical Chosen People and Promised Land, notes Conor Cruise O'Brien, still resonates in America's sense of having a divine mission.

From the very beginning English colonists were predominantly merchants, artisans, and dissidents, with only a small representation from the nobility. The commercial arrangement between Virginia and its English stockholders provided a market for agricultural products. With endless land waiting to be cultivated, increased production required only additional laborers. When the Indians refused to work, and transported convicts proved insufficient, large numbers of African slaves were imported, a solution which changed the nature of the colony and created a small group of wealthy aristocrats. Though slavery had opponents almost from its inception, it flourished, and later proved an obstacle to adoption of the Declaration of Independence, as Thomas Jefferson, a member of the Virginia aristocracy, reports in his autobiography.

Another Voice

RELIGIOUS PERSECUTION RUINS NEW FRANCE
FRANCIS PARKMAN

Sometimes considered America's best historian, Francis Parkman was certainly the master of the narrative tradition. His training in literature, history and law are evident in the sweep of his narratives and the detailed weighing of evidence. France and England in North America, *a massive multivolume history published between 1865 and 1892, illustrates both the strengths and biases of his Puritan New England heritage. His glorification of things English and disdain for Latin culture is evident in the following excerpts, which capture the context which Bradford lived in and which Acosta-Belen decries.*

. . . . it has been argued that the success of the English colonies and the failure of the French was not due to difference of religious and political systems, but simply to numerical preponderance. But this preponderance itself grew out of a difference of systems. We have said before, and it cannot be said too often, that in making Canada a citadel of the state religion,—a holy of holies of exclusive Roman Catholic orthodoxy,—the clerical monitors of the Crown robbed their country of a trans-Atlantic empire. New France could not grow with a priest on guard at the gate to let in none but such as pleased him. One of the ablest of Canadian governors, La Galissonière, seeing the feebleness of the colony compared with the vastness of its claims, advised the King to send ten thousand peasants to occupy the valley of the Ohio, and hold back the British swarm that was just then pushing its advance-guard

continued

continued from previous page

over the Alleghanies. It needed no effort of the King to people his waste domain, not with ten thousand peasants, but with twenty times ten thousand Frenchmen of every station,—the most industrious, most instructed, most disciplined by adversity and capable of self-rule, that the country could boast. While La Galissonière was asking for colonists, the agents of the Crown, set on by priestly fanaticism, or designing selfishness masked with fanaticism, were pouring volleys of musketry into Huguenot congregations, imprisoning for life those innocent of all but their faith. . . .

France and England in North America, 1884

WILLIAM BRADFORD
Of Plymouth Plantation
(1630)

"Having undertaken for the Glory of God and advancement of the Christian Faith . . . a Voyage to plant the First Colony . . ."

Although they were not the first Europeans in what was to become the United States, nor even the first English settlers, the Pilgrims who landed at Plymouth in 1620 occupy a special place in the mythology of America. Unlike the Puritans who hoped to purify the Church of England (hence their name), the Separatists considered the Church beyond repair, rejecting it, and, by implication, the king who reigned over it. Driven by conscience to wander from England to Holland to the New World, they became Pilgrims: quintessential seekers of religious freedom and models for all later immigrants to the Promised Land.

Thirty-year-old William Bradford, one of the leaders who had arranged the passage from Leyden to America, was elected governor of Plymouth when the first governor died soon after their arrival, along with Bradford's wife and almost half the group. He remained leader of the colony for thirty-three of the next thirty-seven years, guiding its economic policies and extending equal rights to all settlers.

In the following excerpt, Bradford explains the decision to leave Holland for Virginia. Landing by accident in Massachusetts, the Pilgrims were beyond the authority of the Virginia Company. They therefore drew up an agreement with each other to establish and be bound by laws of their own devising. Essentially a response to a crisis, the Mayflower Compact adapted the familiar church covenant to civil law, and represents a model of government based on consent of the governed—at a time when most of Europe still lived under the feudal system.

Text: William Bradford; *Of Plymouth Plantation;* ed. Samuel E. Morison; NY: Knopf, 1952.

EXPLORING ISSUES IN THE TEXT

1. What were the arguments against going to America (pars. 7–8)? In the face of such adversity, why did the Pilgrims choose to come to America (par. 9)?

2. What were the Pilgrims' religious considerations for leaving Holland? For going to America? How do these ideas connect to a sense of mission?

3. What image of the Indian does Bradford present in this passage (par. 7)? Of the Spanish (par. 9)?

4. Summarize the reasons for the Mayflower Compact and its provisions (pars. 11–12). In what way was the Compact "more sure" than the original patent? Explain the significance of this belief and of the Compact itself.

OF PLYMOUTH PLANTATION

Chapter IV

1 After they had lived in this city about some eleven or twelve years (which is the more observable being the whole time of that famous truce between that state and the Spaniards) and sundry of them were taken away by death and many others began to be well stricken in years (the grave mistress of Experience having taught them many things), those prudent governors with sundry of the sagest members began both deeply to apprehend their present dangers and wisely to foresee the future and think of timely remedy. In the agitation of their thoughts, and much discourse of things hereabout, at length they began to incline to this conclusion: of removal to some other place. Not out of any newfangledness or other such like giddy humor by which men are oftentimes transported to their great hurt and danger, but for sundry weighty and solid reasons, some of the chief of which I will here briefly touch.

2   And first, they saw and found by experience the hardness of the place and country to be such as few in comparison would come to them, and fewer that would bide it out and continue with them. For many that came to them, and many more that desired to be with them, could not endure

that great labour and hard fare, with other inconveniences which they underwent and were contented with. But though they loved their persons, approved their cause and honored their sufferings, yet they left them as it were weeping, as Orpah did her mother-in-law Naomi, or as the Romans did Cato in Utica who desired to be excused and borne with, though they could not all be Catos. For many, though they desired to enjoy the ordinances of God in their purity and the liberty of the gospel with them, yet (alas) they admitted of bondage with danger of conscience, rather than to endure these hardships. Yea, some preferred and chose the prisons in England rather than this liberty in Holland with these afflictions. But it was thought that if a better and easier place of living could be had, it would draw many and take away these discouragements. Yea, their pastor would often say that many of those who both wrote and preached now against them, if they were in a place where they might have liberty and live comfortably, they would often practice as they did.

3   Secondly. They saw that though the people generally bore all these difficulties very cheerfully and with a resolute courage, being in the best and strength of their years; yet old age began to steal on many of them; and their great and continual labours, with other crosses and sorrows, hastened it before the time. So as it was not only probably thought, but apparently seen, that within a few years more they would be in danger to scatter, by necessities pressing them, or sink under their burdens, or both. And therefore according to the divine proverb, that a wise man seeth the plague when it cometh, and hideth himself, Proverbs xxii.3, so they like skillful and beaten soldiers were fearful either to be entrapped or surrounded by their enemies so as they should neither be able to fight nor fly. And therefore thought it better to dislodge betimes to some place of better advantage and less danger, if any such could be found.

4   Thirdly. As necessity was a taskmaster over them so they were forced to be such, not only to their servants but in a sort to their dearest children, the which as it did not a little wound the tender hearts of many a loving father and mother, so it produced likewise sundry sad and sorrowful effects. For many of their children that were of best dispositions and gracious inclinations, having learned to bear the yolk in their youth and willing to bear part of their parents' burden, were oftentimes so oppressed with their heavy labors that though their minds were free and willing, yet their bodies bowed under the weight of the same, and became decrepit in their early youth, the vigour of nature being consumed in the very bud as it were. But that which was more lamentable, and of all sorrows most heavy to be borne, was that many of their children, by these occasions and the great licentiousness of youth in that country, and the manifold temptations of the place, were drawn away by evil examples into extravagant and dangerous courses, getting the reins off their necks and departing from their parents. Some became soldiers, others took upon them far voyages by sea, and others some worse courses tending to dissoluteness and the danger of their

souls, to the great grief of their parents and dishonor of God. So that they saw their posterity would be in danger to degenerate and be corrupted.

5   Lastly (and which was not least), a great hope and inward zeal they had of laying some good foundation, or at least to make some way thereunto, for the propagating and advancing the gospel of the kingdom of Christ in those remote parts of the world; yea, though they should be but even as stepping-stones unto others for the performing of so great a work.

6   These and some other like reasons moved them to undertake this resolution of their removal; the which they afterward prosecuted with so great difficulties, as by the sequel will appear.

7   The place they had thoughts on was some of those vast and unpeopled countries of America, which are fruitful and fit for habitation, being devoid of all civil inhabitants, where there are only savage and brutish men which range up and down, little otherwise than the wild beasts of the same. This proposition being made public and coming to the scanning of all, it raised many variable opinions amongst men and caused many fears and doubts amongst themselves. Some, from their reasons and hopes conceived, laboured to stir up and encourage the rest to undertake and prosecute the same; others again, out of their fears, objected against it and sought to divert from it; alleging many things, and those neither unreasonable nor unprobable; as that it was a great design and subject to many unconceivable perils and dangers; as, besides the casualties of the sea (which none can be freed from), the length of the voyage was such as the weak bodies of women and other persons worn out with age and travail (as many of them were) could never be able to endure. And yet if they should, the miseries of the land which they should be exposed unto, would be too hard to be borne and likely, some or all of them together, to consume and utterly ruinate them. For there they should be liable to famine and nakedness and the want, in a manner, of all things. The change of air, diet and drinking of water would infect their bodies with sore sicknesses and grievous diseases. And also those which should escape or overcome these difficulties should yet be in continual danger of the savage people, who are cruel, barbarous and most treacherous, being most furious in their rage and merciless where they overcome; not being content only to kill and take away life, but delight to torment men in the most bloody manner that may be; flaying some alive with the shells of fishes, cutting off the members and joints of others by piecemeal and broiling on the coals, eat the collops of their flesh in their sight whilst they live, with other cruelties horrible to be related.

8   And surely it could not be thought but the very hearing of these things could not but move the very bowels of men to grate within them and make the weak to quake and tremble. It was further objected that it would require greater sums of money to furnish such a voyage and to fit them with necessaries, than their consumed estates would amount to; and yet they must as well look to be seconded with supplies as presently to be transported. Also many precedents of ill success and lamentable

miseries befallen others in the like designs were easy to be found, and not forgotten to be alleged; besides their own experience, in their former troubles and hardships in their removal into Holland, and how hard a thing it was for them to live in that strange place, though it was a neighbour country and a civil and rich commonwealth.

9   It was answered, that all great and honourable actions are accompanied with great difficulties and must be both enterprised and overcome with answerable courages. It was granted the dangers were great, but not desperate. The difficulties were many, but not invincible. For though there were many of them likely, yet they were not certain. It might be sundry of the things feared might never befall; others by provident care and the use of good means might in a great measure be prevented; and all of them, through the help of God, by fortitude and patience, might either be borne or overcome. True it was that such attempts were not to be made and undertaken without good ground and reason, not rashly or lightly as many have done for curiosity or hope of gain, etc. But their condition was not ordinary, their ends were good and honourable, their calling lawful and urgent; and therefore they might expect the blessing of God in their proceeding. Yea, though they should lose their lives in this action, yet might they have comfort in the same and their endeavours would be honourable. They lived here but as men in exile and in a poor condition, and as great miseries might possibly befall them in this place; for the twelve years of truce were now out and there was nothing but beating of drums and preparing for war, the events whereof are always uncertain. The Spaniard might prove as cruel as the savages of America, and the famine and pestilence as sore here as there, and their liberty less to look out for remedy.

10   After many other particular things answered and alleged on both sides, it was fully concluded by the major part to put this design in execution and to prosecute it by the best means they could.

Chapter XI

11   I shall a little return back, and begin with a combination made by them before they came ashore; being the first foundation of their government in this place. Occasioned partly by the discontented and mutinous speeches that some of the strangers amongst them had let fall from them in the ship: That when they came ashore they would use their own liberty, for none had power to command them, the patent they had being for Virginia and not for New England, which belonged to another government, with which the Virginia Company had nothing to do. And partly that such an act by them done, this their condition considered, might be as firm as any patent, and in some respects more sure.

The form was as followeth:

IN THE NAME OF GOD, AMEN.

12 We whose names are underwritten, the loyal subjects of our dread Sovereign Lord King James, by the Grace of God of Great Britain, France, and Ireland King, Defender of the Faith, etc.

Having undertaken, for the Glory of God and advancement of the Christian Faith and Honour of our King and Country, a Voyage to plant the First Colony in the Northern Parts of Virginia, do by these presents solemnly and mutually in the presence of God and one of another, Covenant and Combine ourselves together into a Civil Body Politic, for our better ordering and preservation and furtherance of the ends aforesaid; and by virtue hereof to enact, constitute and frame such just and equal Laws, Ordinances, Acts, Constitutions and Offices, from time to time, as shall be thought most meet and convenient for the general good of the Colony, unto which we promise all due submission and obedience. In witness whereof we have hereunder subscribed our names at Cape Cod, the 11th of November, in the year of the reign of our Sovereign Lord King James, of England, France, and Ireland the eighteenth, and of Scotland the fifty-fourth. Anno Domini 1620.

13   After this they chose, or rather confirmed, Mr. John Carver (a man godly and well approved amongst them) their Governor for that year. And after they had provided a place for their goods, or common store (which were long in unlading for want of boats, foulness of the winter weather and sickness of divers) and begun some small cottages for their habitation; as time would admit, they met and consulted laws and orders, both for their civil and military government as the necessity of their condition did require, still adding thereunto as urgent occasion in several times, and as cases did require.

14   In those hard and difficult beginnings they found some discontents and murmurings arise amongst some, and mutinous speeches and carriages in other; but they were soon quelled and overcome by the wisdom, patience, and just and equal carriage of things, by the Governor and better part, which clave faithfully together in the main.

BUILDING CONTEXT

1. Why, despite all they had suffered in England, did the Pilgrims seek permission to settle on English territory in America? Explain what this says about their sense of identity.

2. Why didn't the Pilgrims simply assume that they were English citizens bound by English law? What is the significance of the Mayflower Compact to America's image of itself?

3. Discuss how Bradford adapts Biblical language and imagery to the Pilgrims. Compare this to how Smith and Rowlandson use the Bible in their

writings. Explore the significance of such Biblical identification to America's self-image.

FURTHER STUDY

1. Explore the significance of the Mayflower Compact as a theory of government.
2. At the time of Bradford's account, what was the status of Spain in America? In Europe? How does the seventeenth-century relationship between Spain and England color later American attitudes? What light does Acosta-Belén shed on these questions?

ADDITIONAL RESOURCES

Daniels, Roger. *Coming to America: A History of Immigration and Ethnicity in American Life.* New York: HarperCollins, 1990

Dinnerstein, Leonard, Roger L. Nichols, David M. Reimers. *Natives and Strangers: Ethnic Groups and the Building of America.* New York: Oxford University Press, 1979.

O'Brien, Conor Cruise. *Godland: Reflections on Religion and Nationalism.* Cambridge: Harvard University Press, 1988.

RESEARCH KEYWORDS

Pilgrims
Mayflower Compact

EDNA ACOSTA-BELÉN
"From Settlers to Newcomers: The Hispanic Legacy in the United States" (1988)

"Christopher Columbus, representing the Spanish Crown, arrived in 1492. . . ."

The history of the United States has been traditionally interpreted as starting from the English settlements on the East Coast and spreading to the west and south, absorbing French Louisiana and the Spanish West Coast. Acosta-

Belén offers an alternative perspective: Her account originates in the Spanish island of Puerto Rico, from which—almost 100 years before the English settled Jamestown—Juan Ponce de León launched an expedition to Florida, founding St. Augustine, the first European city in North America, in 1565.

Acosta-Belén also surveys the Spanish exploration of what is now the American Southwest. She argues that Spanish missions like San Francisco and Santa Fe—established to bring the true Catholic faith to the natives—became centers of trade and enabled later colonists to develop the territories by introducing cattle, sheep, and horses. She is especially angered that the Spanish contribution to the cause of the American Revolution is ignored and that, having lost their land to their one-time ally, Hispanics are now made to feel like foreigners in their own homes.

Text: Edna Acosta-Belén; *The Hispanic Experience in the United States;* New York: Praeger, 1988.

EXPLORING ISSUES IN THE TEXT

1. Discuss the significance of the title "From Settlers to Newcomers." How does this capture Acosta-Belén's thesis?

2. Summarize the religious aspect of Spanish colonization (pars. 2, 9–10). What effect did this have on the native populations and the later development of the United States?

3. Explain the *mestizaje* process as described by Acosta-Belén (par. 4). What is its significance to the history of the American Southwest and to the United States as a whole?

FROM SETTLERS TO NEWCOMERS: THE HISPANIC LEGACY IN THE UNITED STATES

The Settlers

1 Hispanics are not newcomers to the United States. Their history in this land began long before the arrival of the Pilgrims at Plymouth Rock and the founding of the 13 British colonies. Hence, it is fitting to say that the first wheels that turned on American soil were Spanish in origin.

2 Almost 500 years ago Christopher Columbus, representing the Spanish Crown, arrived in 1492 in what later became the New World, or America. He claimed the "discovered" lands for Spain, which at the time was consolidating its political, economic, and religious hegemony within its own territory. This effort culminated in 1492 under the monarchy of the Catholic rulers Ferdinand and Isabella, with the expulsion of the Jews and the defeat of the Moors in Granada. Inspired by Marco Polo's adventures in the lands of the Great Khan two centuries before, and by a crusader's sense of mission to spread the Catholic faith, find new wealth

and commercial routs to the Orient, and prove his own navigational theories, Columbus believed that he had arrived in the exotic islands of the Far East known as the Indies. Instead, he had opened up a new continent to European explorers, adventurers, merchants, and immigrants in search of wealth and prosperity.

3   When the Spanish explored the new lands, they found a wide variety of aboriginal groups exhibiting varying degrees of cultural and socioeconomic development. From the magnificence of the Maya, Aztec, and Inca civilizations—civilizations much older than those of Europe—to the more rudimentary lives of the Tainos or the Caribs, Indian groups experienced the conquest as one of the largest immolations to be recorded in human history. War, forced labor, mistreatment, illness, and suicide all played a substantial role in the decimation of the native populations of the New World.

4   In areas where the indigenous populations had been larger, their descendants survived and amalgamated to a large extent with the Spanish conquerors; in other areas, such as the Caribbean islands, the Indian populations were almost totally extinct by the end of the first century of colonization. Slaves from Africa were introduced early in the sixteenth century to replace or supplement the decreasing Indian labor force in agriculture, mining, and domestic service. Black slaves also intermingled with the Spanish and Indian groups, creating through the centuries new cultures and a mixed population in the Americas that integrated the three races to varying degrees. The *mestizaje* (race mixture) produced by the fusion of the white, Indian, and black races and cultures is one of the most distinctive features of the Spanish conquest and colonization of the Americas, and hence of Latin American and U.S. Hispanic cultures.

5   The mentality of the Spanish conquistador was one permeated with myths, legends, and preconceptions from a variety of sources, among which were chivalry novels, medieval legends, classical myths, and biblical tales. The mythological world of the indigenous populations also fed into those preconceptions, and propelled many explorers into a chivalric view of the conquest—a world of adventure, danger, and heroism where monsters were often seen, where there were windmills blurring the lines between fantasy and reality. Others were motivated primarily by greed, and the gold and wealth they found in some of the first explored territories only increased their thirst for more.

6   Spanish exploration and colonization of the North and South American continents extended across a large portion of the territory that constitutes the United States as we know it today. In 1513, Juan Ponce de León, then governor of the island of San Juan Bautista (later known as Puerto Rico), brought an expedition to a land he called "la Pascua florida" (Spanish for Easter, the day of his arrival), in search of the legendary fountain of youth. In the area explored by Ponce de León, the Spanish founded St. Augustine in 1565, the first city of North America which later became one of the most important Spanish military garrisons on that

part of the continent. (The San Marcos Castle, built between 1672 and 1756, stands today as a monument to the Spanish colonization and settlement of this region.)

7   In 1527–28 Pánfilo de Narváez led an ill-fated expedition to the lands of the north and reached the Gulf Coast. Caught by a storm, his ships were destroyed and most of his men perished. One of the few men who survived the shipwreck, Álvar Núñez Cabeza de Vaca, faced all kinds of calamities (among them being captured by the Indians) before he made his 3000-mile journey by foot, which lasted almost nine years, through territories on both sides of the Mississippi River and a good part of what is known today as the U.S. Southwest. He wrote about his odyssey in his *Naufragios,* first published in 1542, a work that has become one of the most important and interesting narratives in the body of literature known as the Chronicles of the Indies. His adventures in the vast wilderness inspired other explorers to follow his footsteps. One of them, Francisco Vásquez de Coronado, searched for the Seven Cities of Cíbola, the seven cities of great splendor where, according to the tales of the time, gold was abundant. In 1540, he reached the territories that later became New Mexico and Colorado. Instead of seven cities of gold, however, he found the villages of the Pueblo Indians. The year before, Hernando de Soto headed an expedition through the territories along the Mississippi River, where he met his death. During the same period, Hernando de Alarcón arrived in a land that was named California because it reminded its explorers of the marvelous imaginary island of the same name inhabited by Amazons, which they had read about in a popular chivalry novel.

8   These pioneer explorations opened the door to Spanish civilization on the North American continent and to what would become, more than two centuries later, the United States of America.

9   Settlement of some of the explored territories to the north was largely due to the efforts of Spanish missionary friars. The scattered missions they established in California, Arizona, and New Mexico during the seventeenth and eighteenth centuries began to open up the territories to the west for more settlement. One of the most remembered missionaries is Fray Junipero Serra, who established a mission in 1776 where the majestic city of San Francisco stands today. The missions were crucial to the settlement process, since most major cities were built around them. They contributed to the pacification, Christianization, and education of the Indians, and the development and spread of methods for the cultivation and irrigation of the lands.

10   Spanish policies of subjugation of native populations and religious conversion aroused hostilities among many of the North American Indian groups who resisted the conquistadors. Among those groups that were subdued, a process of *mestizaje* took place; and in New Mexico, for instance, the Spanish built their settlements on Indian foundations, causing a degree of Hispanization among the Pueblo Indians. . . .

11   Spain maintained control of its North American territories until the first half of the eighteenth century. By then, the 13 British colonies had shared the North American continent with the Spanish, the Dutch, and the French for more than a century. The relationship between the Spanish and the English colonists had been strained at times because of their economic rivalry, their concern with territorial encroachment, and their religious differences. In 1776, the colonies declared their independence from England, and after the Revolutionary War, in which England was defeated, they constituted themselves in 1787 into the federation of the United States of America.

12   One of the most downplayed facts in U.S. history is the large degree of Spanish participation in the Revolutionary War. When the colonists declared their desire to be free of British colonial rule in 1776, both Spain and France became major supporters of the revolutionaries, anticipating mutual economic benefits from trade with the new nation. During the first two years of the war, Spain's support of the colonists was tacit and most aid was covert, in order to avoid its own war with the English.

13   A great deal of recognition has been given to the role of the Marquis de Lafayette in the success of the Revolutionary War. In contrast, the figure of Bernardo de Gálvez, Spanish governor of Louisiana, has not received the same prominence. Between 1779 and 1781, he commanded an army that defeated the English in Louisiana, Alabama, and Florida. His mestizo army included not only Spanish but also Indian and black soldiers, and its military actions kept major Gulf ports open for communications and the flow of weapons and other supplies to the colonists. The Spanish also gained command of Mississippi, frustrating British attempts to encircle and isolate the southern front of the 13 colonies. From the early stages of the American Revolution, money and supplies from Spain and its colonies contributed to turning the tide in favor of the revolutionary forces. The Spanish colonies of Cuba and Puerto Rico were granted permission by Spain to trade with the American colonists, particularly in products such as sugar, which had been available to them before the war from the British-controlled West Indies. Toward the end of the war, Cuban citizens supplied funds that helped Washington's troops in the decisive Battle of Yorktown.

14   A few decades after the American Revolution, Spain faced wars of independence waged by its New World colonies. Liberalism and its democratic ideals of equality and the sovereignty of the people, embodied in the republican form of government, had been espoused by European intellectuals of the Enlightenment and provided the ideological foundations of the American and French Revolutions of 1776 and 1789, respectively. The Enlightenment's ideology of liberal democracy and representative government inspired the emerging creole bourgeoisies in the North and South American colonies in their efforts to topple the colonial empires of the European monarchies. Independence was also the assertion that the

socioeconomic interests of the mother countries no longer represented, and in fact were antagonistic to, the expanding socioeconomic interests of the Creoles. For the people of Latin America the successful American Revolution became a source of inspiration in their own struggle for independence, and the U.S. Constitution served as a model of political and moral virtues, and democratic rule.

15   Spain's position as an important European power suffered a major setback with Napoleon's invasion of 1808. A few years earlier, in 1803, Spain had sold Louisiana to the French, who in turn sold it to the United States. Then came the purchase and annexation of Florida by the United States in 1819. These two incidents served as the first indicators of U.S. intentions and future policies for territorial expansion to the west and south. Manifest Destiny was unmistakably emerging as a doctrine that guided the young U.S. nation in its conviction that it was destined to rule the entire North American continent to its natural borders.

16   In the Monroe Doctrine of 1823, the United States warned the imperialist-minded European nations to stay out of the Western Hemisphere. But the credo "America for the Americans" did not turn into a mere condemnation of imperialism; it became an instrument of U.S. national policy and an assertion that a new power was set to dominate the Americas. The doctrine would not prevent the United States from infringing on the sovereign rights of the new Latin American nations during the decades that followed. In the final analysis, it became a natural complement to Manifest Destiny.

17   By the 1830s all of the Spanish colonies in Central and South America, with the exception of the Hispanic Caribbean islands, had become independent nations. The Spanish territories to the southwest of the United States, which had constituted a part of the viceroyalty of New Spain during Spanish colonial rule, had become part of the nation of Mexico when its independence was granted by Spain in 1821. Relations between the United States and the new nation of Mexico were initially amicable, but began to deteriorate when U.S. expansionist policies continued throughout the continent, encroaching upon Mexican territory. . . .

18   War between Mexico and the United States broke out in 1846, and in 1847, U.S. troops invaded and captured Mexico City. As part of the 1848 Treaty of Guadalupe Hidalgo, Mexico was forced to yield almost half of its land; all the territory north of the Rio Grande was then transferred to the United States. Mexico lost what is now California, Arizona, New Mexico, and the territory from which the states of Colorado, Kansas, Nevada, Oklahoma, Utah, and Wyoming were formed.

19   The hispanos, people of Hispanic descent who remained in the new U.S. Southwest, became through the years a segregated minority with the increasing flux of Anglo citizens. Although the peace treaty between Mexico and the United States stipulated that the Hispanic population of the Southwest would have the right to continue its cultural traditions and use

of Spanish, the second-class treatment of this population became commonplace. Laws were often passed to drive the Hispanic population out
of these territories, and legal disputes over property ownership usually
found Hispanics on the losing end. Mexicans gradually became outsiders
in what had been their own land.

BUILDING CONTEXT

1. Describe the Indians encountered by the first Spanish explorers (par. 3).
   How does this information help you to evaluate Van Every's argument
   about Indians having a community of interest?

2. Compare the Spanish treatment of the Indians to that of the English, as
   described by Smith or Rowlandson. Explore the historical significance
   of this contrast—for example, the absence of an English counterpart to
   mestizaje.

3. Why was the Spanish involvement in the Revolutionary War, in Acosta-
   Belén's words, "one of the most downplayed facts in U.S. history"? Try to
   think of other minimized or ignored contributors to American history.
   What accounts for their lack of historical attention?

4. Read Thoreau's reaction to the war with Mexico. What significance should
   you place on the fact that Thoreau is of Anglo, not Hispanic, heritage?

FURTHER STUDY

1. Define "Manifest Destiny" (par. 15). Discuss how such a belief could have
   evolved from religious views like those of Rowlandson and Bradford.

2. What is the Monroe Doctrine (par. 16)? Contrast how it is viewed by
   Acosta-Belén to its portrayal in a number of high-school or college textbooks.

ADDITIONAL RESOURCES

Borjas, George J. and Marta Tienda, eds. *Hispanics in the U.S. Economy.*
   New York: Academic Press, 1985.
Nabakov, Peter, ed. *Native American Testimony.* New York: Viking, 1991.
Moquin, Wayne, and Charles Van Doren, eds. *Great Documents in American
   Indian History.* New York: Praeger, 1973.

RESEARCH KEYWORDS

Jesuits	Missions
North America—Exploration	Indians—North America

CONOR CRUISE
O'BRIEN
Godland (1988)

"...as the influence of religion in general weakened in the second half of the eighteenth century, confidence in the proposition of America as the Promised Land appears stronger . . ."

An Irish legislator and diplomat, Conor Cruise O'Brien was for many years an internationally respected troubleshooter for the Untied Nations. He is particularly knowledgeable about the role of religion and mythology in conflicts among nations.

In the following selection, O'Brien discusses how America has defined its mission in religious terms. He observes that early writers, recognizing the hardships to be faced, considered America anything but a Promised Land; later writers, however, identified themselves with the Biblical Israelites and transformed America from a howling wilderness into the Promised Land. He further notes that once this identification was solidified, it survived even the loss of religious commitment that marks the history of Christianity in America.

Text: Conor Cruise O'Brien; *Godland: Reflections on Religion and Nationalism;* Cambridge: Harvard University Press, 1988.

EXPLORING ISSUES IN THE TEXT

1. Trace the evolution of the belief in America as the Promised Land. What was the earlier view (par. 1)? Why did this change (pars. 2–4)? What connection does this evolution have to the concept of America's mission?

2. Explain the evolution of the idea that Americans are a Chosen People (par. 8). How has this idea affected the treatment of immigrants (pars. 17–18)? Explain the effect on American identity, especially the definition of "us" and "them."

3. Explain the connection between Protestant theology and political dissent (pars. 13–14). What does this theory imply about dissent in Catholic or Muslim countries?

GODLAND

1   In Governor Bradford's account of the landing of the Pilgrim Fathers, the notion of Plymouth as a Promised Land is explicitly rejected: "Besides what could they see but a hideous and desolate wilderness, full of wild beasts and wild men? . . . Neither could they, as it were, go up to the top of Pisgah to view from the wilderness a more Godly country to feed their hopes (Deut. 3:27), for which way soever they turned their eyes (save upward to the heavens) they could have little solace or content in respect of any outward objects." And Governor Winthrop, in *A Model of Christian Charity,* written aboard the *Arbella* bound for Massachusetts Bay, stresses the need for "strict performance" by the settlers of their side of the covenant with God, if they are to expect the grace, rather than the wrath of God. "We shall find that the God of Israel is on our side when ten of us shall be able to resist a thousand of our enemies." In its context, that sounds much more like a warning than a promise.

2   It was only as the wilderness began to be subdued that people began to become confident about identifying New England with the Promised Land. Richard Mather, a spiritual leader of the original settlers, lived long enough to sense the new mood and to be troubled by it. In a sermon of 1650, Richard Mather, as Robert Middlekauff, biographer of the Mathers, puts it, "reminded his church that men must not confuse holiness with geography." Holiness did not reside in the landscape, "neither Jerusalem nor any other place" was holy.

3   But the thing was too strong. Richard Mather was not even able to save his own son, Increase, from confusing holiness with geography. In a 1677 sermon Increase Mather asked: "Where was there ever a place so like unto new Jerusalem as New England hath been?" Twenty years later, dismayed—as his father had been long before—by evidence of increasing worldliness, Increase Mather suggested that New England "served the Lord as a type of Hell, an emblem for the edification of other nations still capable of profiting by its dismal example."

4   The "dismal example" theory did not catch on; the Promised Land theory did. It is remarkable that, as the influence of religion in general weakened in the second half of the eighteenth century, confidence in the proposition of America as the Promised Land appears stronger than it was among the Puritan Fathers. It is almost as if the object of faith is shifting from Heaven to earth, in an emerging cult of America itself, with the notion of the Promised Land there as a bridge, joining the memories of the old religion to the reality of the new, and also as a veil, obscuring the transformation of the object of worship.

5   Faith in America the chosen was manifest on the eve of the Revolution, and during its course. In November 1775 Ebenezer Baldwin prophesied: "I would suppose these colonies to be the foundation of a great and mighty empire; the largest the world ever saw, to be founded on such principles of liberty and freedom, both civil and religious, as never before

took place in the world; which shall be the principal seat of that glorious kingdom which Christ shall erect upon earth in the latter days." On 16 March 1776 the Continental Congress resolved "that it may please the Lord of Hosts, the God of America, to animate our officers and soldiers with invincible fortitude, earnestly beseeching him to . . . grant that a spirit of incorruptible patriotism and undefiled religion may universally prevail."

6   Patriotism and religion are fused in that momentous hour in the service of the Lord of Hosts, the God of America.

7   After the Revolution, Timothy Dwight, later President of Yale, and an indefatigable versifier of verse, celebrated George Washington in the role of Joshua, conqueror of the new Canaan.

> The chief whose arm to Israel's chosen Band
> Gave the fair empire of the Promised Land
> Ordain'd by Heaven to hold the sacred sway
> Demands my voice and animates my lay.

"Animates" may be pitching it a bit high, but you get the idea.

8   While the Promised Land identification was taking hold, the concept of the Chosen People had shifted. In the beginning, both in England and in New England, the Chosen were a spiritual elite, "visible saints," those who had undergone, or were believed to have undergone, conversion to a living faith in Christ. But the acceptance of infant baptism by the second half of the seventeenth century made the "visible saints" concept impossible to sustain in practice, though it was defended in theory long after it had in fact broken down. In the late seventeenth century, Solomon Stoddard of Northampton was teaching that "the entire nation comprised the Church, because the entire nation, saints and sinners alike, enjoyed a special covenant with God." This was revolutionary doctrine in terms of earlier Puritan teaching, though some English Puritans, under Oliver Cromwell, seemed to have been moving in the same general direction. In New England, Increase Mather resisted the Stoddard doctrinal innovations. But Stoddard's doctrine of "saints and sinners alike" fell in with the logic of infant baptism, and the demands of parents to have their children baptized were so strong as to prevail over the misgivings of the clergy.

9   Babies were now members of the Chosen People. And babies are *not* saints, visibly or audibly.

10 We have already contemplated the phenomenon of the perceived genetic transmission of *un*holiness in the cases of Jews and blacks. In seventeenth-century New England we can contemplate the phenomenon of the perceived genetic transmission of *holiness*. (Not in strict theory of course, since baptism, not birth, brought the child within the covenant,

but since baptism followed automatically on birth, the theoretical distinction lacked practical significance.)

11   "Christenings make not Christians." Roger Williams, the most determined American opponent of the tendency toward sanctified nationalism, said that. Williams is, I think, the most determined, eloquent, and consistent antinationalist to appear anywhere.

12   In our own time Simone Weil went to greater lengths in the sheer fervor of her antinationalism. But hers was a self-destructive fervor, a disgust for all forms of human bonding, which culminated in fasting to death. The antinationalism of Roger Williams, on the other hand, was compatible with life, and even with some very shrewd politicking and diplomacy.

13   Williams, being among those who like to read the Bible and make up their own minds, disregarded the deallegorizing of Luther and Calvin; wholeheartedly interpreted the Old Testament in the old typological way, as predictive of the New; and at the same time adamantly opposed the new nationalistic typology of contemporary Puritans like John Cotton. His strict typological approach, like that of some of the early Fathers, filtered nationalism out of the Old Testament. But even filtered, the Old Testament, according to Williams was not really necessary: "Christ Jesus and his Testament are enough for Christians, although we had never heard of Moses" or "the whole Old Testament." Basing himself on the New Testament alone, Williams resisted the nationalizing tendencies in Britain and America. In 1644, in a letter to "the Commissioners of the General Assembly (so-called) of the Church of Scotland," he posed this question: "Where find you evidence of a whole nation converted to the Faith . . . ?" He wrote of "the great Mysterie of the Church's sleepe," when, after Constantine, "the Leaders of Christ's Churches turned into the Wildernesse of National Religion." "The *bodies* of all nations," said Williams, "are a part of the *world,* and although the Holy Spirit of God in every nation where the Word comes washeth white some Blackamores and changeth some Leopard spots, yet the bodies and bulks of nations cannot by all the Acts and Statutes under Heaven put off the Blackamore skin and the Leopard spots." Specifically addressing himself to New England, he wrote that Canaan ought not to be taken as "a Pattern for all Lands; it was a non-such," and when the Bay Colony used the pattern of Israel, "here they lost the path and themselves!" Nationalism appeared to Williams as one among a number of symptoms of a general idolatry, which a later age would call materialism. "The truth is," he wrote, "the great Gods of this world are God-belly, God-peace, God-wealth, God-honor, God-pleasure, etc." And, for New England, he added to the list: "God Land." I take him to have had in mind both idolatry of land in general and also that idea of a divine promise of land, the idea for which the Bay Colony had "lost the path and themselves."

14   Roger Williams' teachings on the separation of church and state are a familiar and respected landmark in the approved American cultural

retrospect. His vigorous assaults on divinely sanctioned nationlism have left much less of a mark, though they formed the basis of his teachings on church and states. Apparently his utterances on "the Wildernesse of National Religion" remained inaudible, even to editors of his collected work. The seven-volume edition published in the 1960s and currently in use incorporates in facsimile the text of the six-volume nineteenth-century Narragansett edition.

15   The introduction to that collection quotes, without any qualifying note by either nineteenth-century or twentieth-century editor, a poem by John Durfee, which depicts the great seventeenth-century dissident as a stock Puritan out of Central Casting, a typological nationalist cherishing the conventional Israelite analogy.

> Beside the good man lay his Bible's fair
> Broad open page upon the accustom'd stand
> And many a message had he noted there
> Of Israel wandering the wild wastes of sand
> And each assurance had he marked with care
> Made by Jehovah of the promised land.

16   In the context it is made clear that the promised land is now New England. The conversion of Roger Williams into a Chosen-People—Promised-Land buff is a conspicuous miracle of holy nationalism. Williams' teaching on these matters had been neither accepted nor rebutted, but his person had been iconographically incorporated into the tradition which he abhorred, and which had prevailed.

17 The specific linkage with ancient Israel long endured, though it became less conspicuous outside New England, and in a developing and partially more secular America, containing a high proportion of non-Protestants. But the basic notion of the United States as a nation peculiarly blessed by God not only survived but flourished exceedingly. The new immigrants took to the notion of the holy nation like ducks to water. Or rather, in many cases new immigrants, like the Puritan settlers themselves, brought faith in a holy nation—Ireland or Poland, say—along with them, and simply transferred its location, along with their persons, without necessarily being aware that they were doing so.

18   Basically the immigrants made only one stipulation concerning the holy nation: that the holy nation had henceforward to be understood as including *them.* This stipulation was not always easily made good; and before it was, the immigrants had to make concessions, adapting themselves to an American ethos of Protestant formation. In the late nineteenth century John Ireland, Catholic Archbishop of St. Paul, Minnesota, liked to stress that America had been shaped by the Puritans. He was telling his flock something about what they had to adapt themselves to.

And they did. Of the more successful cases of adaptation, one might almost say that an American Catholic is a Protestant who goes to Mass. The name of John F. Kennedy comes to mind.

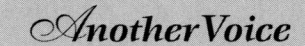

LIBERTY OF CONSCIENCE
ROGER WILLIAMS

Roger Williams opposed the common practice of fining, imprisoning or even executing people for their religious beliefs. Banished from Massachusetts Bay in 1636, he founded the colony of Rhode Island. Williams was accused of fostering anarchy by undermining the power of the state to define crime and punish criminals. He responded:

That ever I should speak or write a tittle, that tends to such an infinite liberty of conscience, is a mistake, and which I have ever disclaimed and abhorred. To prevent such mistakes, I shall at present only propose this case: there goes many a ship to sea, with many hundred souls in one ship, whose weal and woe is common, and is a true picture of a commonwealth, or a human combination or society. It hath fallen out sometimes, that both Papists and Protestants, Jews and Turks, may be embarked in one ship; upon which supposal I affirm, that all the liberty of conscience, that ever I pleaded for, turns upon these two hinges—that none of the Papists, Protestants, Jews, or Turks be forced to come to the ship's prayers or worship, nor compelled from their own particular prayers or worship, if they practice any. I further add, that I never denied, that notwithstanding this liberty, the commander of this ship ought to command the ship's course, yea, and also command that justice, peace and sobriety be kept and practiced, both among the seamen and all the passengers. If any of the seamen refuse to perform their services, or passengers to pay their freight; if any refuse to help, in person or purse, towards the common charges or defense; if any refuse to obey the common laws and orders of the ship, concerning their common peace or preservation; if any shall mutiny and rise up against their commanders and officers; if any should preach or

continued

continued from previous page

write that there ought to be no commanders or officers, because all are equal in Christ, therefore no masters nor officers, no laws nor orders, nor corrections nor punishments; I say, I never denied, but in such cases, whatever is pretended, the commander or commanders may judge, resist, compel and punish such transgressors, according to their deserts and merits.

"Letter to the Town of Providence," 1655

BUILDING CONTEXT

1. In light of the debate that Bradford records concerning emigration to America, show how his selection supports or contradicts O'Brien's theory about the Promised Land.

2. Compare the Chosen People motifs in the works of Rowlandson and Bradford. Show how these selections either support or contradict O'Brien's theory.

FURTHER STUDY

1. Discuss current manifestations of the United States as the Promised Land. Explain whether they are mostly religious or secular.

2. Explain the significance of the reference to John F. Kennedy in the discussion of adaptation to American myths (par. 18).

3. Explore the writings and work of Roger Williams. What was his relationship with the Puritan leaders in Massachusetts? With the Indians? What is his significance in American history?

ADDITIONAL RESOURCES

Anderson, Lydia. *Immigration.* New York: Franklin Watts Inc., 1981.
Eliade, Mircea, ed. *The Encyclopedia of Religion.* New York: Macmillan, 1987.
Marty, Martin E. *Religion and Republic: The American Circumstance.* Boston: Beacon Press, 1987.

RESEARCH KEYWORDS

United States—Religion
Immigration
Ethnic Relations

> *"He has waged cruel war against human nature itself, violating its most sacred rights of life and liberty in the persons of a distant people . . . carrying them into slavery in another hemisphere. . . ."*

The Declaration of Independence is, of course, one of the most important documents in American history. In listing the rights and privileges violated by King George, it implicitly presents a theory of government: The monarch is constrained by the rule of law, and citizens may expect just treatment from the state. The significance of the Declaration to the course of modern history is also great; by articulating principles of liberty and equality it kindled a desire for freedom throughout the world and created the legal framework for other colonies to break from their mother countries.

After complaining for years about taxes and other matters, in 1774 some of the English colonies in America agreed to boycott British goods and unite for mutual defense. King George, declaring the colonies in rebellion, ordered his troops to confiscate the arms stored by the colonial militia in Concord, Massachusetts. Fighting broke out in 1775. By 1776 many colonials believed that a complete break from Britain was necessary and inevitable; Virginia instructed its delegates to present a declaration of independence to the Continental Congress. Adoption of the Declaration, however, was not certain, with the condemnation of slavery proving the most controversial passage. Many delegates opposed Jefferson's first draft; some even objected to the final version. In this excerpt from his *Autobiography,* Jefferson describes the debate and revisions.

Text: Adrienne Koch and William Peden, eds.; *The Life and Selected Writings of Thomas Jefferson;* New York: Modern Library, 1944.

EXPLORING ISSUES IN THE TEXT

1. Summarize the reasons given for opposing the Declaration of Independence (pars. 5–23). Try to group them by topic and rate them according to their importance.

2. List the arguments in support of the Declaration of Independence (pars. 24–50). As in question 1, group them by topic and rate them according to their importance.

3. Evaluate the assertion about slavery in paragraph 74 in light of paragraph 52.

4. Analyze the changes made to the draft of the Declaration in order to gain wider support. What insights can be gained from these changes?

THE DECLARATION OF INDEPENDENCE

In Congress, Friday, June 7, 1776

1 The delegates from Virginia moved, in obedience to instructions from their constituents, that the Congress should declare that these United colonies are, and of right ought to be, free and independent states, that they are absolved from all allegiance to the British crown, and that all political connection between them and the state of Great Britain is, and ought to be, totally dissolved; that measures should be immediately taken for procuring the assistance of foreign powers, and a Confederation be formed to bind the colonies more closely together.

2 The House being obliged to attend at that time to some other business, the proposition was referred to the next day, when the members were ordered to attend punctually at ten o'clock.

3 *Saturday, June 8.* They proceeded to take it into consideration, and referred it to a committee of the whole, into which they immediately resolved themselves, and passed that day and Monday, the 10th, in debating on the subject.

4 It was argued by Wilson, Robert R. Livingston, E. Rutledge, Dickinson, and others—

5 That, though they were friends to the measures themselves, and saw the impossibility that we should ever again be united with Great Britain, yet they were against adopting them at this time:

6 That the conduct we had formerly observed was wise and proper now, of deferring to take any capital step till the voice of the people drove us into it:

7 That they were our power, and without them our declarations could not be carried into effect:

8 That the people of the middle colonies (Maryland, Delaware, Pennsylvania, the Jerseys and New York) were not yet ripe for bidding adieu to British connection, but that they were fast ripening, and, in a short time, would join in the general voice of America:

9 That the resolution, entered into by this House on the 15th of May, for suppressing the exercise of all powers derived from the crown, had shown, by the ferment into which it had thrown these middle colonies, that they had not yet accommodated their minds to a separation from the mother country:

10 That some of them had expressly forbidden their delegates to consent to such a declaration, and others had given no instructions, and consequently no powers to give such consent:

11 That if the delegates of any particular colony had no power to declare such colony independent, certain they were, the others could not declare it for them; the colonies being as yet perfectly independent of each other:

12 That the assembly of Pennsylvania was now sitting above stairs, their convention would sit within a few days, the convention of New York was now sitting, and those of the Jerseys and Delaware counties would meet on the Monday following, and it was probable these bodies would take up the question of Independence, and would declare to their delegates the voice of their state:

13 That if such a declaration should now be agreed to, these delegates must retire, and possibly their colonies might secede from the Union:

14 That such a secession would weaken us more than could be compensated by any foreign alliance:

15 That in the event of such a division, foreign powers would either refuse to join themselves to our fortunes, or, having us so much in their power as that desperate declaration would place us, they would insist on terms proportionably more hard and prejudicial:

16 That we had little reason to expect an alliance with those to whom alone, as yet, we had cast our eyes:

17 That France and Spain had reason to be jealous of that rising power, which would one day certainly strip them of all their American possessions:

18 That it was more likely they should form a connection with the British court, who, if they should find themselves unable otherwise to extricate themselves from their difficulties, would agree to a partition of our territories, restoring Canada to France, and the Floridas to Spain, to accomplish for themselves the recovery of these colonies:

19 That it would not be long before we should receive certain information of the disposition of the French court, from the agent whom we had sent to Paris for that purpose:

20 That if this disposition should be favorable, by waiting the event of the present campaign, which we all hoped would be successful, we should have reason to expect an alliance on better terms:

21 That this would in fact work no delay of any effectual aid from such ally, as, from the advance of the season and distance of our situation, it was impossible we could receive any assistance during this campaign:

22 That it was prudent to fix among ourselves the terms on which we should form alliance, before we declared we would form one at all events:

23 And that if these were agreed on, and our Declaration of Independence ready by the time our Ambassador should be prepared to sail, it would be as well as to go into that Declaration at this day.

24 On the other side, it was urged by J. Adams, Lee, Wythe, and others, that no gentleman had argued against the policy or the right of sepa-

ration from Great Britain, nor had supposed it possible we should ever renew our connection; that they had only opposed its being now declared:

25 That the question was not whether, by a Declaration of Independence, we should make ourselves what we are not; but whether we should declare a fact which already exists:

26 That, as to the people or parliament of England, we had always been independent of them, their restraints on our trade deriving efficacy from our acquiescence only, and not from any rights they possessed of imposing them, and that so far, our connection had been federal only, and was now dissolved by the commencement of hostilities:

27 That, as to the King, we had been bound to him by allegiance, but that this bond was now dissolved by his assent to the last act of Parliament, by which he declares us out of his protection, and by his levying war on us, a fact which had long ago proved us out of his protection; it being a certain position in law, that allegiance and protection are reciprocal, the one ceasing when the other is withdrawn:

28 That James the Second never declared the people of England out of his protection, yet his actions proved it, and the Parliament declared it:

29 No delegates then can be denied, or ever want, a power of declaring an existing truth:

30 That the delegates from the Delaware counties having declared their constituents ready to join, there are only two colonies, Pennsylvania and Maryland, whose delegates are absolutely tied up, and that these had, by their instructions, only reserved a right of confirming or rejecting the measure:

31 That the instructions from Pennsylvania might be accounted for from the times in which they were drawn, near a twelve-month ago, since which the face of affairs has totally changed:

32 That within that time, it had become apparent that Britain was determined to accept nothing less than a *carte-blanche,* and that the King's answer to the Lord Mayor, Aldermen and Common Council of London, which had come to hand four days ago, must have satisfied every one of this point:

33 That the people wait for us to lead the way:

34 That *they* are in favor of the measure, though the instructions given by some of their *representatives* are not:

35 That the voice of the representatives is not always consonant with the voice of the people, and that this is remarkably the case in these middle colonies:

36 That the effect of the resolution of the 15th of May has proved this, which, raising the murmurs of some in the colonies of Pennsylvania and Maryland, called forth the opposing voice of the freer part of the people, and proved them to be the majority even in these colonies:

37 That the backwardness of these two colonies might be ascribed, partly to the influence of proprietary power and connections, and partly, to their having not yet been attacked by the enemy:

38   That these causes were not likely to be soon removed, as there seemed no probability that the enemy would make either of these the seat of this summer's war:

39   That it would be vain to wait either weeks or months for perfect unanimity, since, it was impossible that all men should ever become of one sentiment on any question:

40   That the conduct of some colonies, from the beginning of this contest, had given reason to suspect it was their settled policy to keep in the rear of the confederacy, that their particular prospect might be better, even in the worst event:

41   That, therefore, it was necessary for those colonies who had thrown themselves forward and hazarded all from the beginning, to come forward now also, and put all again to their own hazard:

42   That the history of the Dutch Revolution, of whom three states only confederated at first, proved that a secession of some colonies would not be so dangerous as some apprehended:

43   That a Declaration of Independence alone could render it consistent with European delicacy, for European powers to treat with us, or even to receive an Ambassador from us:

44   That till this, they would not receive our vessels into their ports, nor acknowledge the adjudications of our courts of admiralty to be legitimate, in cases of capture of British vessels:

45   That though France and Spain may be jealous of our rising power, they must think it will be much more formidable with the addition of Great Britain; and will therefore see it their interest to prevent a coalition; but should they refuse, we shall be but where we are; whereas without trying, we shall never know whether they will aid us or not:

46   That the present campaign may be unsuccessful, and therefore we had better propose an alliance while our affairs wear a hopeful aspect:

47   That to wait the event of this campaign will certainly work delay, because, during the summer, France may assist us effectually, by cutting off those supplies of provisions from England and Ireland, on which the enemy's armies here are to depend; or by setting in motion the great power they have collected in the West Indies, and calling our enemy to the defence of the possessions they have there:

48   That it would be idle to lose time in settling the terms of alliance, till we had first determined we would enter into alliance:

49   That it is necessary to lose no time in opening a trade for our people, who will want clothes, and will want money too, for the payment of taxes:

50   And that the only misfortune is, that we did not enter into alliance with France six months sooner, as, besides opening her ports for the vent of our last year's produce, she might have marched an army into Germany, and prevented the petty princes there, from selling their unhappy subjects to subdue us.

51   It appearing in the course of these debates, that the colonies of New York, New Jersey, Pennsylvania, Delaware, Maryland, and South Carolina

were not yet matured from falling from the parent stem, but that they were fast advancing to that state, it was thought most prudent to wait a while for them, and to postpone the final decision to July 1st; but, that this might occasion as little delay as possible, a committee was appointed to prepare a Declaration of Independence. The committee were John Adams, Dr. Franklin, Roger Sherman, Robert R. Livingston, and myself. Committees were also appointed, at the same time, to prepare a plan of confederation for the colonies, and to state the terms proper to be proposed for foreign alliance. The committee for drawing the Declaration of Independence, desired me to do it. It was accordingly done, and being approved by them, I reported it to the House on Friday, the 28th of June, when it was read, and ordered to lie on the table. On Monday, the 1st of July, the House resolved itself into a committee of the whole, and resumed the consideration of the original motion made by the delegates of Virginia, which, being again debated through the day, was carried in the affirmative by the votes of New Hampshire, Connecticut, Massachusetts, Rhode Island, New Jersey, Maryland, Virginia, North Carolina and Georgia. South Carolina and Pennsylvania voted against it. Delaware had but two members present, and they were divided. The delegates from New York declared they were for it themselves, and were assured their constituents were for it; but that their instructions having been drawn near a twelve-month before, when reconciliation was still the general object, they were enjoined by them to do nothing which should impede that object. They, therefore, thought themselves not justifiable in voting on either side, and asked leave to withdraw from the question; which was given them. The committee rose and reported their resolution to the House. Mr. Edward Rutledge, of South Carolina, then requested the determination might be put off to the next day, as he believed his colleagues, though they disapproved of the resolution, would then join in it for the sake of unanimity. The ultimate question, whether the House would agree to the resolution of the committee, was accordingly postponed to the next day, when it was again moved, and South Carolina concurred in voting for it. In the meantime, a third member had come post from the Delaware counties and turned the vote of that colony in favor of the resolution. Members of a different sentiment attending that morning from Pennsylvania also, her vote was changed, so that the whole twelve colonies who were authorized to vote at all, gave their voices for it; and within a few days, the convention of New York approved of it, and thus supplied the void occasioned by the withdrawing of the delegates from the vote.

52   Congress proceeded the same day to consider the Declaration of Independence, which had been reported and lain on the table the Friday preceding, and on Monday referred to a committee of the whole. The pusillanimous idea that we had friends in England worth keeping terms with, still haunted the minds of many. For this reason, those passages which conveyed censures on the people in England were struck out, lest they should give them offence. The clause too, reprobating the enslaving

of the inhabitants of Africa, was struck out in complaisance to South Carolina and Georgia, who had never attempted to restrain the importation of slaves, and who, on the contrary, still wished to continue it. Our northern brethren also, I believe, felt a little tender under those censures; for though their people had very few slaves themselves, yet they had been pretty considerable carriers of them to others. The debates, having taken up the greater parts of the 2d, 3d, and 4th days of July, were, on the evening of the last, closed; the Declaration was reported by the committee, agreed to by the House, and signed by every member present, except Mr. Dickinson. As the sentiments of men are known not only by what they receive, but what they reject also, I will state the form of the Declaration as originally reported. The parts struck out by Congress shall be distinguished by a black line drawn under them; and those inserted by them shall be placed in the margin, or in a concurrent column.

A Declaration by the Representatives of the United States of America, in General Congress Assembled

53   When in the course of human events it becomes necessary for one people to dissolve the political bands which have connected them with another, and to assume among the powers of the earth the separate and equal station to which the laws of nature and of nature's God entitle them, a decent respect to the opinions of mankind requires that they should declare the causes which impel them to the separation.

54   We hold these truths to be self-evident: that all men are created equal; that they are endowed by their Creator with <u>inherent and</u> inalienable rights; that among   **certain** these are life, liberty, and the pursuit of happiness; that to secure these rights, governments are instituted among men, deriving their just powers from the consent of the governed; that whenever any form of government becomes destructive of these ends, it is the right of the people to alter or abolish it, and to institute new government, laying its foundation on such principles, and organizing its powers in such form, as to them shall seem most likely to effect their safety and happiness. Prudence indeed will dictate that governments long established should not be changed for light and transient causes; and accordingly all experience hath shown that mankind are more disposed to suffer while evils are sufferable, then to right themselves by abolishing the forms to which they are accustomed. But when a long train of

abuses and usurpations begun at a distinguished period and pursuing invariably the same object, evinces a design to reduce them under absolute despotism, it is their right, it is their duty to throw off such government, and to provide new guards for their future security. Such has been the patient sufferance of these colonies; and such is now the necessity which constrains them to expunge **alter** their former systems of government. The history of the present king of Great Britain is a history of unremitting **repeated** injuries and usurpations, among which appears no soli- **all having** tary fact to contradict the uniform tenor of the rest but all have in direct object the establishment of an absolute tyranny over these states. To prove this let facts be submitted to a candid world for the truth of which we pledge a faith yet unsullied by falsehood.

55   He has refused his assent to laws the most wholesome and necessary for the public good.

56   He has forbidden his governors to pass laws of immediate and pressing importance, unless suspended in their operation till his assent should be obtained; and when so suspended, he has utterly neglected to attend to them.

57   He has refused to pass other laws for the accommodation of large districts of people, unless those people would relinquish the right of representation in the legislature, a right inestimable to them, and formidable to tyrants only.

58   He has called together legislative bodies at places unusual, uncomfortable, and distant from the depository of their public records, for the sole purpose of fatiguing them into compliance with his measures.

59   He has dissolved representative houses repeatedly and continually for opposing with manly firmness his invasions on the rights of the people.

60   He has refused for a long time after such dissolutions to cause others to be elected, whereby the legislative powers, incapable of annihilation, have returned to the people at large for their exercise, the state remaining in the meantime exposed to all the dangers of invasion from without and convulsions within.

61   He has endeavored to prevent the population of these states; for that purpose obstructing the laws for naturalization of foreigners, refusing to pass others to encourage their migrations hither, and raising the conditions of new appropriations of lands.

62   He has <u>suffered</u> the administration of justice <u>totally to</u>   **obstructed/by**
<u>cease in some of these states</u> refusing his assent to laws
for establishing judiciary powers.

63   He has made our judges dependent on his will alone,
for the tenure of their offices, and the amount and payment of their salaries.

64   He has erected a multitude of new offices <u>by a self-as-</u>
<u>sumed power</u> and sent hither swarms of new officers to
harass our people and eat out their substance.

65   He has kept among us in times of peace standing armies
<u>and ships of war</u> without the consent of our legislatures.

66   He has affected to render the military independent
of, and superior to, the civil power.

67   He has combined with others to subject us to a jurisdiction foreign to our constitutions and unacknowledged
by our laws, giving his assent to their acts of pretended
legislation for quartering large bodies of armed troops
among us; for protecting them by a mock-trial from punishment for any murders which they should commit on
the inhabitants of these states; for cutting off our trade
with all parts of the world; for imposing taxes on us with-
out our consent; for depriving us [ ] of the benefits of trial   **in many cases**
by jury; for transporting us beyond seas to be tried for
pretended offences; for abolishing the free system of English laws in a neighboring province, establishing therein
an arbitrary government, and enlarging its boundaries, so
as to render it at once an example and fit instrument for
introducing the same absolute rule into these <u>states</u>; for   **colonies**
taking away our charters, abolishing our most valuable
laws, and altering fundamentally the forms of our governments; for suspending our own legislatures, and declaring
themselves invested with power to legislate for us in all
cases whatsoever.

68   He has abdicated government here <u>withdrawing his</u>   **by declaring**
<u>governors, and declaring us out of his allegiance and</u>   **us out of his**
<u>protection</u>.   **protection,
and waging
war against us.**

69   He has plundered our seas, ravaged our coasts, burnt
our towns, and destroyed the lives of our people.

70   He is at this time transporting large armies of foreign
mercenaries to complete the works of death, desolation
and tyranny already begun with circumstances of cruelty
and perfidy [ ] unworthy the head of a civilized nation.   **scarcely
paralleled
in the most
barbarous**

71   He has constrained our fellow citizens taken captive   **paralleled**
on the high seas to bear arms against their country, to   **in the most**
become the executioners of their friends and brethren,   **barbarous**
or to fall themselves by their hands.   **ages, and
totally**

72   He has [ ] endeavored to bring on the inhabitants of our frontiers the merciless Indian savages, whose known rule of warfare is an undistinguished destruction of all ages, sexes, and conditions of existence.

excited domestic insurrection among us, and has

73   He has incited treasonable insurrections of our fellow-citizens, with the allurements of forfeiture and confiscation of our property.

74   He has waged cruel war against human nature itself, violating its most sacred rights of life and liberty in the persons of a distant people who never offended him, captivating and carrying them into slavery in another hemisphere, or to incur miserable death in their transportation thither. This piratical warfare, the opprobrium of INFIDEL powers, is the warfare of the CHRISTIAN king of Great Britain. Determined to keep open a market where MEN should be bought and sold, he has prostituted his negative for suppressing every legislative attempt to prohibit or to restrain this execrable commerce. And that this assemblage of horrors might want no fact of distinguished die, he is now exciting those very people to rise in arms among us, and to purchase that liberty of which he has deprived them, by murdering the people on whom he also obtruded them: thus paying off former crimes committed against the LIBERTIES of one people, with crimes which he urges them to commit against the LIVES of another.

75   In every stage of these oppressions we have petitioned for redress in the most humble terms: our repeated petitions have been answered only by repeated injuries.

76   A prince whose character is thus marked by every act which may define a tyrant is unfit to be the ruler of a [ ] people who mean to be free. Future ages will scarcely believe that the hardiness of one man adventured, within the short compass of twelve years only, to lay a foundation so broad and so undisguised for tyranny over a people fostered and fixed in principles of freedom.

free

77   Nor have we been wanting in attention to our British brethren. We have warned them from time to time of attempts by their legislature to extend a jurisdiction over these our states. We have reminded them of the circumstances of our emigration and settlement here, no one of which could warrant so strange a pretension: that these were effected at the expense of our own blood and treasure, unassisted by the wealth or the strength of Great Britain: that in constituting indeed our several forms of government, we had adopted one common king, thereby

an unwarrantable

us

laying a foundation for perpetual league and amity with them: but that submission to their parliament was no part of our constitution, nor ever in idea, if history may be credited: and, we [ ] appealed to their native justice and magnanimity as well as to the ties of our common kindred to disavow these usurpations which were likely to interrupt our connection and correspondence. They too have been deaf to the voice of justice and of consanguinity, and when occasions have been given them, by the regular course of their laws, of removing from their councils the disturbers of our harmony, they have, by their free election, re-established them in power. At this very time too they are permitting their chief magistrate to send over not only soldiers of our common blood, but Scotch and foreign mercenaries to invade and destroy us. These facts have given the last stab to agonizing affection, and manly spirit bids us to renounce forever these unfeeling brethren. We must endeavor to forget our former love for them, and hold them as we hold the rest of mankind, enemies in war, in peace friends. We might have been a free and a great people together; but a communication of grandeur and of freedom it seems is below their dignity. Be it so, since they will have it. The road to happiness and to glory is open to us too. We will tread it apart from them, and acquiesce in the necessity which denounces our eternal separation [ ]!

have
and we have
conjured them
by
would
inevitably

We must
therefore
and hold them
as we hold the
rest of man-
kind, enemies
in war, in
peace friends.

78   We therefore the representatives of the United States of America in General Congress assembled do in the name and by authority of the good people of these states reject and renounce all allegiance and subjection to the kings of Great Britain and all others who may hereafter claim by, through or under them: we utterly dissolve all political connection which may heretofore have subsisted between us and the people or parliament of Great Britain: and finally we do assert and declare these colonies to be free and independent states, and that as free and independent states, they have full power to levy war, conclude peace, contract alliances, establish commerce, and to do all other acts and things which independent states may of right do.

We therefore the representatives of the United States of America in General Congress assembled, appealing to the supreme judge of the world for the rectitude of our intentions, do in the name, and by the authority of the good people of these colonies, solemnly publish and declare that these united colonies are and of right ought to be free and independent states; that they are absolved from all allegiance to the British crown, and that all political connection between them and the state of Great Britain is, and ought to be, totally dissolved; and that as free and independent states they have full power to levy war, conclude peace, contract alliances, establish commerce and to do all other acts and things which independent states may of right do.

79 And for the support of this declaration we mutually pledge to each other our lives, our fortunes, and our sacred honor.

And for the support of this declaration, with a firm reliance on the protection of divine providence we mutually pledge to each other our lives, our fortunes, and our sacred honor.

80 The Declaration thus signed on the 4th, on paper was engrossed on parchment, and signed again on the 2d. of August.

BUILDING CONTEXT

1. How did the Mayflower Compact influence the Declaration of Independence (pars. 54, 78)?
2. Compare the roles that divinity plays in both the Mayflower Compact and the Declaration.
3. Analyze the image of the Indians presented in the Declaration. Compare this image to the portrayals of Indians by Smith and Rowlandson.

FURTHER STUDY

1. What are natural rights? Where did Jefferson get the idea that people have inalienable rights that even a government cannot take away? What is the status of this idea in America today? How does it relate to the concepts of outlaw states or war crimes?
2. Why was it possible that France and Spain might have supported either the Americans or the British in the issue of independence? As it turned out, what effect did the American Revolution have on France and Spain? You might want to consider Acosta-Belén's essay in your answer.
3. Discuss the place of slavery in the deliberations over the adoption of the Declaration. How did the debate and resolution of the slavery question foreshadow the Civil War?

ADDITIONAL RESOURCES

Bernstein, Richard B. *Are We to Be a Nation?* Cambridge: Harvard University Press, 1987.

De Ruggiero, Guido. *The History of European Liberalism.* Boston: Beacon Press, 1959 (orig. 1927).

Jordan, Winthrop D. *White over Black: American Attitudes toward the Negro, 1550–1812.* Chapel Hill, N.C.: University of North Carolina Press, 1968.

RESEARCH KEYWORDS

Natural Law
Natural Rights
Liberalism

WRITING ABOUT THE CRITICAL ISSUES

1. Compare and contrast how two or three of the reading selections treat one of the following issues: America's mission, the formation of identity, equality in America, the role of religion in America, the relation of the individual and the state.

2. Trace the evolution of the American attitude(s) toward one of the critical issues we have been discussing.

3. Discuss the significance of the Mayflower Compact as a theory of government. Explain why the settlers didn't simply assume that they were English citizens bound by English law. Explore the significance of the Compact to America's image of itself.

4. Analyze the influence of the Mayflower Compact on the Declaration of Independence. Trace the origin and history of such ideas as compact and consent of the governed.

5. Discuss how Biblical language and imagery have been adapted to the history of the United States. Examine the significance of such Biblical identification to America's self-image.

6. Compare the Spanish treatment of the Indians to that of the English, as described for example by Smith and Rowlandson. Explore the historical significance of this contrast.

7. Examine whether the contribution of certain groups is downplayed. Try to account for any example you find.

8. Explore the Promised Land and Chosen People motifs in American history. Discuss whether current manifestations of the United States as the Promised Land are mostly religious or secular.

9. Explore an idea that caught your interest, or that charmed or provoked you, or that supported or challenged your own beliefs. Try to place the issue in a larger context and explain its significance.

4

EIGHTEENTH CENTURY LIVES: 1700–1800

"... I conceiv'd the bold and arduous Project of arriving at moral Perfection."

BENJAMIN FRANKLIN

"Here individuals of all nations are melted into a new race of men."

MICHEL-GUILLAUME JEAN DE CRÈVECOEUR

The earliest period of English colonization in America coincided with momentous events in England and Europe. John Smith was in Virginia at the same time Shakespeare was staging his great plays in England and during the period when the King James Version of the Bible was being published. The planting of Massachusetts Bay Colony, the founding of Harvard College, and the publication of the Bay Psalms Book marked the expansion to the New World of the Puritan revolution that swept out the English monarchy and established the Commonwealth. Meanwhile, the Dutch were using Manhattan island as a trading post, were sending settlers to the West Indies, and, being newly independent from Spain, were trying to wrest control of Brazil from Spain's ally Portugal.

All this converged—some might say as part of a divine plan—to lay the basis for democracy and religious tolerance in the English colonies. The Pilgrims, who had found refuge in Holland during a truce with Spain, feared the resumption of the war and chose to seek religious freedom in the New World. The Puritans, in contrast, hoped to build God's kingdom for His chosen, keeping out the undesirables who threatened their purity in England. As it happened, however, the Pilgrims comprised only a third of the passengers on the Mayflower, the rest being soldiers, traders, adventurers, and assorted misfits and outcasts; and the Puritans had a constant struggle to rid themselves of the unorthodox thinkers that their own Protestant theology virtually guaranteed. Moreover, when the Mayflower landed in the wrong place, the Pilgrims felt compelled to put their signatures to an agreement that bound each individual to the decisions of the group. For their part, the Puritans in Massachusetts used the upheaval of the English Civil War to assume in practice, if not in law, that they were independent of the government that had granted them their land and the commercial company that had sent them.

In addition, Church of England loyalists settled in Virginia, Catholics in Maryland, and Jews—many from families that had been expelled from Spain and Portugal—in the Dutch colonies. When the last Dutch stronghold in Brazil fell to the Portuguese, Jews found haven in the Dutch West Indies and New Amsterdam. When the English conquered New Amsterdam in 1664 and renamed it New York, all Dutch citizens were guaranteed their rights. Thus, while Jews were officially barred from living in England, they were able to live freely in the English colony of New York.

There was certainly the possibility that the religious wars of Europe would be replayed in America. And to an extent that almost occurred. An Inquisition was established in Spain's colonies to root out heretics. The Puritans burned witches and expelled the likes of Anne Hutchinson and Roger Williams. But in America there was room to move. Nothing compelled a freethinker to stay in Boston, or anywhere else. The endless frontier acted as a safety valve for malcontents. And, of course, most of the settlers had been drawn by the promise of wealth—gold, furs, land. To them, live and let live made the most sense.

Ingrained ideas did not die; they were transformed. As the Puritans rose to leadership in New England, absorbing the Pilgrims and others before losing power, their religious outlook influenced even those who opposed them. At the heart of their theology was the principle of interpreting the Holy Scripture for oneself. Each individual had the same authority as a priest or church hierarchy because God could touch anyone. The implications of this position were inescapable: Even as the Puritan leaders tried to enforce their own view, their central dogma contained the rationale for dissent, or democracy. Protestant theology fed and was fed by Enlightenment humanism, leading to the secular, yet Puritan, morality of Benjamin Franklin and, according to Max Weber, the origins of capitalism and the work ethic. Significantly, this secularized religion, bordering on indifference, struck the French immigrant Michel-Guillaume Jean de Crèvecoeur as one of the great strengths of the English colonies.

As Crèvecoeur notes, the absence of religious division allowed a broadening of group identity. People were able to see their commonality because they were not distracted by irrelevant differences. This inclusiveness, unfortunately, did not usually extend to African slaves. We have already seen that condemnation of slavery proved an obstacle to adoption of the Declaration of Independence. How slavery and its white practitioners looked to slaves themselves is the subject of Olaudah Equiano's autobiography.

Another Voice

THE PROMISE OF AMERICA
HENRY ADAMS

In his *History of the United States,* written at the end of the nineteenth century, Henry Adams, of the family that produced two presidents, captured the promise of America in its youth:

"In the early days of colonization, every new settlement represented an idea and proclaimed a mission. Virginia was founded by a great, liberal movement aiming at the spread of English liberty and empire. The Pilgrims of Plymouth, the Puritans of Boston, the Quakers of Pennsylvania, all avowed a moral purpose, and began making institutions that consciously reflected a moral ideal."

BENJAMIN FRANKLIN
Autobiography (1771)

" . . . *I conceiv'd the bold and arduous Project of arriving at moral Perfection."*

Author, printer, inventor, and politician, Benjamin Franklin (1706–1790) was one of the first Americans with an international reputation. His career began while he was still a teenager in Boston, with the clever Dogood essays that he submitted anonymously to his brother's newspaper. After moving to Philadelphia, he started his own printing business. His *Poor Richard's Almanack* popularized such proverbs as "God helps them that help themselves" and "Early to bed and early to rise makes a man healthy, wealthy, and wise." Indicative of Franklin's sense of humor, he parodied his famous work in "The Way to Wealth," an essay in which "a plain clean old man with white locks" named Father Abraham explains the economic virtues by stringing together Poor Richard's maxims. By the time Franklin went to France to represent the interests of the emerging United States, he had already been corresponding for many years with some of the greatest minds in Europe.

Franklin states in the introduction to his *Autobiography* that friends suggested he write about his life so that following generations of Americans would learn from his rags-to-riches experience. In the excerpt reprinted here, he describes the plan he devised for personal improvement. That the book is written at least partially tongue in cheek is evident from his observation that he worked for years to overcome his excessive pride—and is now proud of his humility.

Like many of the Founding Fathers, Franklin rejected his early religious training and tended toward Deism, a belief in an Almighty that excludes ritual and dogma. His *Autobiography* follows the format of Puritan introspection, acknowledging his own faults and seeking divine guidance in overcoming them. Franklin, however, replaces the Divinity with literary sources and equates religious virtues with good citizenship.

Text: Benjamin Franklin; *The Autobiography of Benjamin Franklin;* ed. R. Jackson Wilson; New York: Modern Library, 1981.

Another Voice

STRIVING FOR PERFECTION
JONATHAN EDWARDS

The most stirring accounts for Puritan audiences were of a sinner being granted Grace—often through illness or suffering—to recognize previous errors and thenceforth live the life of a visible saint. A famous example comes from Jonathan Edwards, a minister and president of The College of New Jersey (now Princeton):

. . . it pleased God, in my last year at college, at a time when I was in the midst of many uneasy thoughts about the state of my soul, to seize me with a pleurisy; in which he brought me nigh to the grave, and shook me over the pit of hell. . . .

My longings after God and holiness, were much increased. Pure and humble, holy and heavenly Christianity appeared exceeding amiable to me. I felt in me a burning desire to be in everything a complete Christian, and conformed to the blessed image of Christ, and that I might live in all things, according to the pure, sweet and blessed rules of the gospel. I had an eager thirsting after progress in these things. My longings after it put me upon pursuing and pressing after them. It was my continual strife day and night, and constant inquiry, how I should be more holy, and live more holily, and more becoming a child of God, and disciple of Christ. I sought an increase of grace and holiness, and that I might live an holy life with vastly more earnestness than ever I sought grace, before I had it. I used to be continually examining myself, and studying and contriving for likely ways and means how I should live holily with far greater diligence and earnestness than ever I pursued anything in my life.

Personal Narrative, 1740

EXPLORING ISSUES IN THE TEXT

1. What were Franklin's religious principles (pars. 1–2, 15)? Why did he hold these after rejecting the dogmas of his early training? What flaw did he find in the sermons of his friend, the Presbyterian minister? How did he relate religion to good citizenship?

2. What were the virtues Franklin sought in his project for arriving at moral perfection (pars. 4–5)? How did he arrive at them? How do these virtues and the discovery process illuminate his concept of morality?

3. Why did Franklin add a thirteenth virtue to his original list of twelve (par. 16)? Explain the humor or irony in his discussion of this last virtue. What insight (or warning) should this give you about reading Franklin's autobiography (or anything else)?

AUTOBIOGRAPHY

1 I had been religiously educated as a Presbyterian, and tho' some of the Dogmas of the Persuasion, such as the Eternal Decrees of God, Election, Reprobation, etc., appear'd to me unintelligible, others doubtful, and I early absented myself from the Public Assemblies of the Sect, Sunday being my Studying-Day, I never was without some religious Principles; I never doubted, for instance, the Existance of the Deity, that he made the World, and govern'd it by his Providence; that the most acceptable Service of God was the doing Good to Man; that our Souls are immortal; and that all Crime will be punished and Virtue rewarded either here or hereafter; these I esteem'd the Essentials of every Religion, and being to be found in all the Religions we had in our Country I respected them all, tho' with different degrees of Respect as I found them more or less mix'd with other Articles which without any Tendency to inspire, promote or confirm Morality, serv'd principally to divide us and make us unfriendly to one another. This Respect to all, with an Opinion that the worst had some good Effects, induc'd me to avoid all Discourse that might tend to lessen the good Opinion another might have of his own Religion; and as our Province increas'd in People and new Places of worship were continually wanted, and generally erected by voluntary Contribution, my Mite for such purpose, whatever might be the Sect, was never refused.

2   Tho' I seldom attended any Public Worship, I had still an Opinion of its Propriety, and of its Utility when rightly conducted, and I regularly paid my annual Subscription for the Support of the only Presbyterian Minister or Meeting we had in Philadelphia. He us'd to visit me sometimes as a Friend, and admonish me to attend his Administrations, and I was now and then prevail'd on to do so, once for five Sundays successively. Had he been, *in my Opinion,* a good Preacher perhaps I might have continued, notwithstanding the occasion I had for the Sunday's Leisure in my Course of Study: But his Discourses were chiefly either polemic Arguments, or Explications of the peculiar Doctrines of our Sect, and were all to me very dry, uninteresting and unedifying, since not a single moral Principle was inculcated or enforc'd, their Aim seeming to be rather to make us Presbyterians than good Citizens. At length he took for his Text that Verse of the 4th Chapter of Philippians, *Finally, Brethren, Whatsoever Things are true,*

honest, just, pure, lovely, or of good report, if there be any virtue, or any praise, think on these Things; and I imagin'd in a Sermon on such a Text, we could not miss of having some Morality: But he confin'd himself to five Points only as meant by the Apostle, viz. 1. Keeping holy the Sabbath Day. 2. Being diligent in Reading the Holy Scriptures. 3. Attending duly the Publick Worship. 4. Partaking of the Sacrament. 5. Paying a due Respect to God's Ministers. These might be all good Things, but as they were not the kind of good Things that I expected from that Text, I despaired of ever meeting with them from any other, was disgusted, and attended his Preaching no more. I had some Years before compos'd a little Liturgy or Form of Prayer for my own private Use, viz, in 1728, entitled, *Articles of Belief and Acts of Religion.* I return'd to the Use of this, and went no more to the public Assemblies. My Conduct might be blameable, but I leave it without attempting farther to excuse it, my present purpose being to relate Facts, and not to make Apologies for them.

3   It was about this time that I conceiv'd the bold and arduous Project of arriving at moral Perfection. I wish'd to live without committing any Fault at any time; I would conquer all that either Natural Inclination, Custom, or Company might lead me into. As I knew, or thought I knew, what was right and wrong, I did not see why I might not *always* do the one and avoid the other. But I soon found I had undertaken a Task of more Difficulty than I had imagined. While my *Attention was taken up* in guarding against one Fault, I was often surpriz'd by another. Habit took the Advantage of Inattention. Inclination was sometimes too strong for Reason. I concluded at length, that the mere speculative Conviction that it was our Interest to be compleatly virtuous, was not sufficient to prevent our Slipping, and that the contrary Habits must be broken and good ones acquired and established, before we can have any Dependance on a steady uniform Rectitude of Conduct. For this purpose I therefore contriv'd the following Method.

4   In the various Enumerations of the moral Virtues I had met with in my Reading, I found the Catalogue more or less numerous, as different Writers included more or fewer Ideas under the same Name. Temperance, for Example, was by some confin'd to Eating and Drinking, while by others it was extended to mean the moderating every other Pleasure, Appetite, Inclination or Passion, bodily or mental, even to our Avarice and Ambition. I propos'd to myself, for the sake of Clearness, to use rather more Names with fewer Ideas annex'd to each, than a few Names with more Ideas; and I included under Thirteen Names of Virtues all that at that time occurr'd to me as necessary or desirable, and annex'd to each a short Precept, which fully express'd the Extent I gave to its Meaning.

5   These Names of Virtues with their Precepts were

1. TEMPERANCE.

Eat not to Dulness.
Drink not to Elevation.

2. SILENCE.

Speak not but what may benefit others or yourself. Avoid trifling Conversation.

3. ORDER.

Let all your Things have their Places. Let each Part of your Business have its Time.

4. RESOLUTION.

Resolve to perform what you ought. Perform without fail what you resolve.

5. FRUGALITY.

Make no Expence but to do good to others or yourself: i.e. Waste nothing.

6. INDUSTRY.

Lose no Time. Be always employ'd in something useful. Cut off all unnecessary Actions.

7. SINCERITY.

Use no hurtful Deceit.
Think innocently and justly; and, if you speak, speak accordingly.

8. JUSTICE.

Wrong none, by doing Injuries or omitting the Benefits that are your Duty.

9. MODERATION.

Avoid Extreams. Forbear resenting Injuries so much as you think they deserve.

10. CLEANLINESS.

Tolerate no Uncleanness in Body, Cloaths or Habitation.

11. TRANQUILITY.

Be not disturbed at Trifles, or at Accidents common or unavoidable.

12. CHASTITY.

Rarely use Venery but for Health or Offspring; Never to Dulness, Weakness, or the Injury of your own or another's Peace or Reputation.

13. HUMILITY.

Imitate Jesus and Socrates.

6   My Intention being to acquire the *Habitude* of all these Virtues, I judg'd it would be well not to distract my Attention by attempting the whole at once, but to fix it on one of them at a time, and when I should be Master of that, then to proceed to another, and so on till I should have gone thro' the thirteen. And as the previous Acquisition of some might facilitate the Acquisition of certain others, I arrang'd them with that View as they stand above. *Temperance* first, as it tends to procure that Coolness and Clearness of Head, which is so necessary where constant Vigilance was to be kept up, and Guard maintained, against the unremitting Attraction of ancient Habits, and the Force of perpetual Temptations. This being acquir'd and establish'd, *Silence* would be more easy, and my Desire being to gain Knowledge at the same time that I improv'd in Virtue, and considering that in Conversation it was obtain'd rather by the use of the Ears than of the Tongue, and therefore wishing to break a Habit I was getting into of Prattling, Punning and Joking, which only made me acceptable to trifling Company, I gave *Silence* the second Place. This, and the next, *Order,* I expected would allow me more Time for attending to my Project and my Studies; RESOLUTION, once become habitual, would keep me firm in my Endeavours to obtain all the subsequent Virtues; *Frugality* and *Industry,* by freeing me from my remaining Debt, and producing Affluence and Independance, would make more easy the Practice of *Sincerity* and *Justice,* etc. Conceiving then that agreable to the Advice of Pythagoras in his Golden Verses daily Examination would be necessary, I contriv'd the following Method for conducting that Examination.

7   I made a little Book in which I allotted a Page for each of the Virtues. I rul'd each Page with red Ink, so as to have seven Columns, one for each Day of the Week, marking each Column with a Letter for the Day. I cross'd these Columns with thirteen red Lines, marking the Beginning of each Line with the first Letter of one of the Virtues, on which Line and in its proper Column I might mark by a little black Spot every Fault I found upon Examination to have been committed respecting that Virtue upon that Day.

8   I determined to give a Week's strict Attention to each of the Virtues successively. Thus in the first Week my great Guard was to avoid every the least Offence against Temperance, leaving the other Virtues to their ordinary Chance, only marking every Evening the Faults of the Day. Thus if in the first Week I could keep my first Line marked T clear of

Spots, I suppos'd the Habit of that Virtue so much strengthen'd and its opposite weaken'd, that I might venture extending my Attention to include the next, and for the following Week keep both Lines clear of Spots. Proceeding thus to the last, I could go thro' a Course compleat in Thirteen Weeks, and four Courses a Year. And like him who having a Garden to weed, does not attempt to eradicate all the bad Herbs at once, which would exceed his Reach and his Strength, but works on one of the Beds at a time, and having accomplish'd the first proceeds to a Second; so I should have, (I hoped) the encouraging Pleasure of seeing on my Pages the Progress I made in Virtue, by clearing successively my Lines of their Spots, till in the End by a Number of Courses, I should be happy in viewing a clean Book after thirteen Weeks daily Examination. . . .

9   I entered upon the execution of this plan for self-examination, and continued it with occasional intermissions for some time. I was surprised to find myself so much fuller of faults than I had imagined, but I had the satisfaction of seeing them diminish. To avoid the trouble of renewing now and then my little book, which, by scraping out the marks on the paper of old faults to make room for new ones in a new course, became full of holes, I transferred my tables and precepts to the ivory leaves of a memorandum book, on which the lines were drawn with red ink that made a durable stain, and on those lines I marked my faults with a black lead pencil, which marks I could easily wipe out with a wet sponge. After a while I went through one course only in a year, and afterward only one in several years, till at length I omitted them entirely, being employed in voyages and business abroad, with a multiplicity of affairs that interfered; but I always carried my little book with me.

10   My scheme of ORDER gave me the most trouble; and I found that, though it might be practicable where a man's business was such as to leave him the disposition of his time, that of a journeyman printer, for instance, it was not possible to be exactly observed by a master who must mix with the world and often receive people of business at their own hours. *Order,* too, with regard to places for things, papers, etc., I found extremely difficult to acquire. I had not been early accustomed to it, and, having an exceeding good memory, I was not so sensible of the inconvenience attending want of method. This article, therefore, cost me so much painful attention, and my faults in it vexed me so much, and I made so little progress in amendment, and had such frequent relapses, that I was almost ready to give up the attempt, and content myself with a faulty character in that respect, like the man who, in buying an ax of a smith, my neighbor, desired to have the whole of its surface as bright as the edge. The smith consented to grind it bright for him if he would turn the wheel; he turned while the smith pressed the broad face of the ax hard and heavily on the stone which made the turning of it very fatiguing. The man came every now and then from the wheel to see how the work went on and at length would take his ax as it was, without farther

grinding. "No," said the smith, "turn on, turn on; we shall have it bright by and by; as yet, it is only speckled." "Yes," says the man, *"but I think I like a speckled ax best."* And I believe this may have been the case with many who, having, for want of some such means as I employed, found the difficulty of obtaining good and breaking bad habits in other points of vice and virtue, have given up the struggle, and concluded that *a speckled ax was best;* for something, that pretended to be reason, was every now and then suggesting to me that such extreme nicety as I exacted of myself might be a kind of foppery in morals, which, if it were known, would make me ridiculous; that a perfect character might be attended with the inconvenience of being envied and hated; and that a benevolent man should allow a few faults in himself, to keep his friends in countenance.

11   In truth, I found myself incorrigible with respect to *Order;* and now I am grown old, and my memory bad, I feel very sensibly the want of it. But, on the whole, though I never arrived at the perfection I had been so ambitious of obtaining, but fell far short of it, yet I was, by the endeavor, a better and a happier man than I otherwise should have been if I had not attempted it; as those who aim at perfect writing by imitating the engraved copies, though they never reach the wished-for excellence of those copies, their hand is mended by the endeavor, and is tolerable while it continues fair and legible.

12   It may be well my posterity should be informed that to this little artifice, with the blessing of God, their ancestor owed the constant felicity of his life, down to his 79th year in which this is written. What reverses may attend the remainder is in the hand of Providence; but, if they arrive, the reflection on past happiness enjoyed ought to help his bearing them with more resignation. To *Temperance* he ascribes his long-continued health, and what is still left to him of a good constitution. To *Industry* and *Frugality,* the early easiness of his circumstances and acquisition of his fortune, with all that knowledge that enabled him to be a useful citizen, and obtained for him some degree of reputation among the learned. To *Sincerity* and *Justice,* the confidence of his country, and the honorable employs it conferred upon him. And to the joint influence of the whole mass of the virtues, even in the imperfect state he was able to acquire them, all that evenness of temper, and that cheerfulness in conversation, which makes his company still sought for and agreeable even to his younger acquaintance. I hope, therefore, that some of my descendants may follow the example and reap the benefit.

13   It will be remark'd that, tho' my Scheme was not wholly without Religion there was in it no Mark of any of the distinguishing Tenets of any particular Sect. I had purposely avoided them; for being fully persuaded of the Utility and Excellency of my Method, and that it might be serviceable to People in all Religions, and intending some time or other to publish it, I would not have any thing in it that should prejudice any one of any Sect against it. I purposed writing a little Comment on each Virtue,

in which I would have shown the Advantages of possessing it, and the Mischiefs attending its opposite Vice; and I should have called my Book the ART *of Virtue,* because it would have shown the *Means* and *Manner* of obtaining Virtue, which would have distinguish'd it from the mere Exhortation to be good, that does not instruct and indicate the Means; but is like the Apostle's Man of verbal Charity, who only, without showing to the Naked and the Hungry *how* or where they might get Cloaths or Victuals, exhorted them to be fed and clothed. *James* II, 15, 16.

14   But it so happened that my Intention of writing and publishing this Comment was never fulfilled. I did indeed, from time to time put down short Hints of the Sentiments, Reasonings, etc., to be made use of in it; some of which I have still by me: But the necessary close Attention to private Business in the earlier part of Life, and public Business since, have occasioned my postponing it. For it being connected in my Mind with a *great and extensive Project* that required the whole Man to execute, and which an unforeseen Succession of Employs prevented my attending to, it has hitherto remain'd unfinish'd.

15   In this Piece it was my Design to explain and enforce this Doctrine, that vicious Actions are not hurtful because they are forbidden, but forbidden because they are hurtful, the Nature of Man alone consider'd: That it was therefore every one's Interest to be virtuous, who wish'd to be happy even in this World. And I should from this Circumstance, there being always in the World a Number of rich Merchants, Nobility, States and Princes, who have need of honest Instruments for the Management of their Affairs, and such being so rare have endeavoured to convince young Persons, that no Qualities were so likely to make a poor Man's Fortune as those of Probity and Integrity.

16   My List of Virtues contain'd at first but twelve: But a Quaker Friend having kindly inform'd me that I was generally thought proud; that my Pride show'd itself frequently in Conversation; that I was not content with being in the right when discussing any Point, but was overbearing and rather insolent; of which he convinc'd me by mentioning several Instances; I determined endeavouring to cure myself if I could of this Vice or Folly among the rest, and I add *Humility* to my List, giving an extensive Meaning to the Word. I cannot boast of much Success in acquiring the *Reality* of this Virtue; but I had a good deal with regard to the *Appearance* of it. I made it a Rule to forbear all direct Contradiction to the Sentiments of others, and all positive Assertion of my own. I even forbid myself agreable to the old Laws of our Junto, the Use of every Word or Expression in the Language that imported a fix'd Opinion; such as *certainly, undoubtedly,* etc., and I adopted instead of them, *I conceive, I apprehend,* or *I imagine* a thing to be so or so, or it so appears to me at present. When another asserted something, that I thought an Error, I deny'd my self the Pleasure of contradicting him abruptly, and of showing immediately some Absurdity in his Proposition; and in answering I began by observing that in certain Cases or Circumstances his Opinion

would be right, but that in the present case there *appear'd* or *seem'd* to me some Difference, etc. I soon found the Advantage of this Change in my Manners. The Conversations I engag'd in went on more pleasantly. The modest way in which I propos'd my Opinions, procur'd them a readier Reception and less Contradiction; I had less Mortification when I was found to be in the wrong, and I more easily prevail'd with others to give up their Mistakes and join with me when I happen'd to be in the right. And this Mode, which I at first put on, with some violence to natural Inclination, became at length so easy and so habitual to me, that perhaps for these Fifty Years past no one has ever heard a dogmatical Expression escape me. And to this Habit (after my Character of Integrity) I think it principally owing, that I had early so much Weight with my Fellow Citizens, when I proposed new Institutions, or Alterations in the old; and so much Influence in public Councils when I became a Member. For I was but a bad Speaker, never eloquent, subject to much Hesitation in my choice of Words, hardly correct in Language, and yet I generally carried my Points.

17   In reality there is perhaps no one of our natural Passions so hard to subdue as *Pride*. Disguise it, struggle with it, beat it down, stifle it, mortify it as much as one pleases, it is still alive, and will every now and then peep out and show itself. You will see it perhaps often in this History. For even if I could conceive that I had compleatly overcome it, I should probably [be] proud of my Humility.

BUILDING CONTEXT

1. Compare Franklin's and Rowlandson's attitudes toward religion as a personal matter. Compare Franklin's beliefs about religious mission to those of the Pilgrims.

2. Analyze the different details that two or three writers include in their autobiographies—for example, Franklin, Eaton, Equiano, and Cahan. What can you infer about each writer's purpose?

FURTHER STUDY

1. Although the United States is a secular republic, religion has played an important role as both an overt force and a source of basic assumptions in this country. Examine how religion shaped Franklin's secular morality. Consider how it influenced the abolitionists and the Civil Rights movement of the 1960s.

2. Consider how the relationship between religious virtue and civic values or communal friction is described in other colonial religious autobiographies—for example, the *Personal Narrative* of Jonathan Edwards or *Some Account of the Fore-Part of the Life of Elizabeth Ashbridge*. Trace how these

virtues became secularized by Franklin and later generations of Americans. Examine their current manifestations.

ADDITIONAL RESOURCES

Brooks, Van Wyck. *The Flowering of New England.* New York: E. P. Dutton, 1952.
Davidson, Edward H. *Jonathan Edwards: The Narrative of a Puritan Mind.* Boston: Houghton Mifflin, 1966.
Miller, Perry, ed. *The American Puritans: Their Prose and Poetry.* Garden City, N.Y.: Doubleday, 1956.

RESEARCH KEYWORDS

Statesmen—U.S.   Periodicals—U.S.
Freemasonry   Deism

MAX WEBER
The Protestant Ethic and the Spirit of Capitalism
(1904)

" . . . the earning of more and more money, combined with the strict avoidance of all spontaneous enjoyment of life . . . is thought of so purely as an end in itself . . . it appears entirely transcendental."

Max Weber was an early pioneer of sociology and political economics. Impressed by the industrial strength of Germany, Great Britain, and the United States at the end of the nineteenth century, he tried to explain what these countries had in common that distinguished them from so many others. His answer was capitalism, and he theorized that it developed in the West because of the Protestant religious tradition. Weber reasoned as follows: Puritans believed that worldly success was a sign of being chosen as one of God's elect; however, wealth is a temptation to sinful pleasures; therefore, the best way to use wealth is for the creation of more wealth, which increases the proof of being one of the elect. "To wish to be poor," he explained, "was the same as wishing to be unhealthy; it is objectionable as a glorification of works and derogatory to the glory of God." Moreover, constant self-examination and introspection led Puritans to look for God's signs in all things at all times. Thus, "if that God, whose hand the Puritan sees in all occurrences of life, shows one of His elect a chance of profit, he must do it with a purpose."

Weber's concept of the "Protestant work ethic" is now applied to Americans in general, without regard to their religion. Of particular interest is that he used Benjamin Franklin as his model of secularized religion.

Text: *The Protestant Ethic and the Spirit of Capitalism.* 1930.

EXPLORING ISSUES IN THE TEXT

1. What aspects of Franklin's philosophy form the focus of par. 2–10? How are these maxims related to capitalism?

2. Why was Franklin so easy to satirize as the model Yankee (par. 11). Which aspects of his creed did critics find offensive? How does your understanding of Franklin compare to this negative view?

3. Explain what Weber means by the statement that Franklin's morality is "coloured with utilitarianism" (par. 13). To what extent is this an American trait? What danger does Weber see in it?

4. Examine how Weber traces the line of descent from Puritanism to Franklin. How is this indicative of the secularization of religion in America?

THE PROTESTANT ETHIC AND THE SPIRIT OF CAPITALISM

1   . . . if we try to determine the object, the analysis and historical explanation of which we are attempting, it cannot be in the form of a conceptual definition, but at least in the beginning only a provisional description of what is here meant by the spirit of capitalism. Such a description is, however, indispensable in order clearly to understand the object of the investigation. For this purpose we turn to a document of that spirit which contains what we are looking for in almost classical purity, and at the same time has the advantage of being free from all direct relationship to religion, being thus for our purposes, free of preconceptions.

2   "Remember, that *time* is money. He that can earn ten shillings a day by his labour, and goes abroad, or sits idle, one half of that day, though he spends but sixpence during his diversion or idleness, ought not to reckon *that* the only expense; he has really spent, or rather thrown away, five shillings besides.

3   "Remember, that *credit* is money. If a man lets his money lie in my hands after it is due, he gives me the interest, or so much as I can make

of it during that time. This amounts to a considerable sum where a man has good and large credit, and makes good use of it. . . .

4   "The most trifling actions that affect a man's credit are to be regarded. The sound of your hammer at five in the morning, or eight at night, heard by a creditor, makes him easy six months longer; but if he sees you at a billiard-table, or hears your voice at a tavern, when you should be at work, he sends for his money the next day; demands it, before he can receive it, in a lump.

5   "It shows, besides, that you are mindful of what you owe; it makes you appear a careful as well as an honest man, and that still increases your credit.

6   "For six pounds a year you may have the use of one hundred pounds, provided you are a man of known prudence and honesty.

7   "He that spends a groat a day idly, spends idly above six pounds a year, which is the price for the use of one hundred pounds.

8   "He that wastes idly a groat's worth of his time per day, one day with another, wastes the privilege of using one hundred pounds each day.

9   "He that idly loses five shillings' worth of time, loses five shillings, and might as prudently throw five shillings into the sea.

10   "He that loses five shillings, not only loses that sum, but all the advantage that might be made by turning it in dealing, which by the time that a young man become old, will amount to a considerable sum of money."

11   It is Benjamin Franklin who preaches to us in these sentences, the same which Ferdinand Kürnberger satirizes in his clever and malicious *Picture of American Culture* as the supposed confession of faith of the Yankee. That it is the spirit of capitalism which here speaks in characteristic fashion, no one will doubt, however little we may wish to claim that everything which could be understood as pertaining to that spirit is contained in it. Let us pause a moment to consider this passage, the philosophy of which Kürnberger sums up in the words, "They make tallow out of cattle and money out of men." The peculiarity of this philosophy of avarice appears to be the ideal of the honest man of recognized credit, and above all the idea of a duty of the individual toward the increase of his capital, which is assumed as an end in itself. Truly what is here preached is not simply a means of making one's way in the world, but a peculiar ethic. The infraction of its rules is treated not as foolishness but as forgetfulness of duty. This is the essence of the matter. It is not mere business astuteness, that sort of thing is common enough, it is an ethos. *This* is the quality which interests us.

12   When Jacob Fugger, in speaking to a business associate who had retired and who wanted to persuade him to do the same, since he had made enough money and should let others have a chance, rejected that as pusillanimity and answered that "he (Fugger) thought otherwise, he wanted to make money as long as he could", the spirit of this statement is evidently quite different from that of Franklin. What in the former case was an expression of commercial daring and a personal inclination morally neutral,

in the latter takes on the character of an ethically coloured maxim for the conduct of life. The concept spirit of capitalism is here used in this specific sense, it is the spirit of modern capitalism. For that we are here dealing only with Western European and American capitalism is obvious from the way in which the problem was stated. Capitalism existed in China, India, Babylon, in the classic world, and in the Middle Ages. But in all these cases, as we shall see, this particular ethos was lacking.

13   Now, all Franklin's moral attitudes are coloured with utilitarianism. Honesty is useful, because it assures credit; so are punctuality, industry, frugality, and that is the reason they are virtues. A logical deduction from this would be that where, for instance, the appearance of honesty serves the same purpose, that would suffice, and an unnecessary surplus of this virtue would evidently appear to Franklin's eyes as unproductive waste. And as a matter of fact, the story in his autobiography of his conversion to those virtues, or the discussion of the value of a strict maintenance of the appearance of modesty, the assiduous belittlement of one's own deserts in order to gain general recognition later, confirms this impression. According to Franklin, those virtues, like all others, are only in so far virtues as they are actually useful to the individual, and the surrogate of mere appearance is always sufficient when it accomplished the end in view. It is a conclusion which is inevitable for strict utilitarianism. The impression of many Germans that the virtues professed by Americanism are pure hypocrisy seems to have been confirmed by this striking case. But in fact the matter is not by any means so simple. Benjamin Franklin's own character, as it appears in the really unusual candidness of his autobiography, belies that suspicion. The circumstance that he ascribes his recognition of the utility of virtue to a divine revelation which was intended to lead him in the path of righteousness, shows that something more than mere garnishing for purely egocentric motives is involved.

14   In fact, the *summum bonum* of this ethic, the earning of more and more money, combined with the strict avoidance of all spontaneous enjoyment of life, is above all completely devoid of any eudaemonistic, not to say hedonistic, admixture. It is thought of so purely as an end in itself, that from the point of view of the happiness of, or utility to the single individual, it appears entirely transcendental and absolutely irrational. Man is dominated by the making of money, by acquisition as the ultimate purpose of his life. Economic acquisition is no longer subordinated to man as the means for the satisfaction of his material needs. This reversal of what we should call the natural relationship, so irrational from a naïve point of view, is evidently as definitely a leading principle of capitalism as it is foreign to all peoples not under capitalistic influence. At the same time it expresses a type of feeling which is closely connected with certain religious ideas. If we thus ask, *why* should "money be made out of men", Benjamin Franklin himself, although he was a colourless deist, answers in his autobiography with a quotation from the Bible, which his strict Calvinistic

father drummed into him again and again in his youth: "Seest thou a man diligent in his business? He shall stand before kings" (Prov. xxii. 29). The earning of money within the modern economic order is, so long as it is done legally, the result and the expression of virtue and proficiency in a calling; and this virtue and proficiency are, as it is now not difficult to see, the real Alpha and Omega of Franklin's ethic, as expressed in the passages we have quoted, as well as in all his works without exception.

15   And in truth this peculiar idea, so familiar to us to-day, but in reality so little a matter of course, of one's duty in a calling, is what is most characteristic of the social ethic of capitalistic culture, and is in a sense the fundamental basis of it. It is an obligation which the individual is supposed to feel and does feel towards the content of his professional activity, no matter in what it consists, in particular no matter whether it appears on the surface as a utilization of his personal powers, or only of his material possessions (as capital).

BUILDING CONTEXT

1. Compare the quotations from Franklin in this selection to the project Franklin describes in his *Autobiography*. What can you infer about Franklin's character and Weber's analysis of Franklin?

2. Compare Weber's statement that Franklin's morality is "utilitarian" to Franklin's statement about the "utility" of religion. To what extent is Weber accurate in his understanding of Franklin and to what extent is he being unfair? Try to supply other examples, historical or current, of American religion being utilitarian.

3. Compare Weber's argument that Puritan ethics became secularized into a work ethic to O'Brien's theory about religious ideas that have become secularized. Try to add other religious behaviors to their lists.

FURTHER STUDY

1. Read the "Parable of the Talents" in The Gospel of Matthew, chapter 25. Explain the relevance of this passage to Weber's theory about the Puritan approach to money. Compare it also to the theory of work in John Milton's poem "On His Blindness."

2. To what extent is the work ethic Protestant? What accounts for the economic success of Japan, Korea, and people from other cultures?

ADDITIONAL RESOURCES

Robertson, H. M. *Aspects of the Rise of Economic Individualism,* 1933
Eliade, Mircea, ed. *The Encyclopedia of Religion.* New York: Macmillan, 1987.

RESEARCH KEYWORDS

Capitalism   Puritanism
Calvinism   Utilitarianism

MICHEL-GUILLAUME
JEAN DE CRÈVECOEUR
"What Is an American?"
(1782)

"Here individuals of all nations are melted into a new race of men."

The well-educated child of a distinguished aristocratic family, Michel-Guillaume Jean de Crèvecoeur (1734–1813) served as a cartographer with the French army in Canada, near the Great Lakes and Ohio. After some traveling, he became a citizen of New York in 1765, living sixty miles north of New York City, as a gentleman farmer under the name Hector St. John. Though he was sympathetic to the ideals of the American Revolution, he was nonetheless an aristocrat whose oath of citizenship had been sworn to Britain. Morally unable to choose sides, he was suspected by both, and returned to France in 1780. With the help of Benjamin Franklin and others, he was appointed French consul after the war and served in the United States from 1783 to 1790, before retiring to Normandy.

In 1782, he published *Letters from an American Farmer.* In it he portrayed an idyllic life of equality and tolerance, a reflection of his living close to the land and far from the evils of an entrenched ruling class. He was particularly hopeful that America would not repeat the errors that had led to centuries of religious and factional wars in Europe, believing instead that in America, people of differing origins "melted" into a new race. While his picture of American life—classless, enlightened, and progressive—is dismissed by some critics as too idealized, it is a classic statement that has helped shape a self-image that many Americans continue to cherish.

Text: Michel-Guillaume Jean de Crèvecoeur; *Letters from an American Farmer;* ed. A. E. Stone; NY: Penguin Books, 1981.

EXPLORING ISSUES IN THE TEXT

1. Summarize the advantages Crèvecoeur ascribes to America and American society (par. 1). Explain the contrasts between America and Europe, especially concerning personal freedom and governmental control.

2. According to Crèvecoeur, what is the process by which the outcasts of Europe became the promise of the future in America (par. 3)? Explain the significance of *Ubi panis ibi patria* (par. 4).

3. What does Crèvecoeur mean by "Here individuals of all nations are melted into a new race of men" (par. 4)? What does he see as the significance of this melting?

4. Examine Crèvecoeur's use of inclusive and exclusive references—for example, "we" versus "they." Show how this rhetorical usage supports or undermines his thesis.

WHAT IS AN AMERICAN?

1 I wish I could be acquainted with the feelings and thoughts which must agitate the heart and present themselves to the mind of an enlightened Englishman when he first lands on this continent. He must greatly rejoice that he lived at a time to see this fair country discovered and settled; he must necessarily feel a share of national pride when he views the chain of settlements which embellish these extended shores. When he says to himself, "This is the work of my countrymen, who, when convulsed by factions, afflicted by a variety of miseries and wants, restless and impatient, took refuge here. They brought along with them their national genius, to which they principally owe that liberty they enjoy and what substance they possess." Here he sees the industry of his native country displayed in a new manner and traces in their works the embryos of all the arts, sciences, and ingenuity which flourish in Europe. Here he beholds fair cities, substantial villages, extensive fields, an immense country filled with decent houses, good roads, orchards, meadows, and bridges where an hundred years ago all was wild, woody, and uncultivated! What a train of pleasing ideas this fair spectacle must suggest; it is a prospect which must inspire a good citizen with the most heart-felt pleasure. The difficulty consists in the manner of viewing so extensive a scene. He is arrived on a new continent; a modern society offers itself to his contemplation, different from what he had hitherto seen. It is not composed, as in Europe, of great lords who possess everything and of a herd of people who have nothing. Here are no aristocratical families, no courts, no kings, no bishops, no ecclesiastical dominion, no invisible power giving to a few a very visible one, no great manufactures employing thousands, no great refinements of luxury. The rich and the poor are not so far removed from each other as they are in Eu-

rope. Some few towns excepted, we are all tillers of the earth, from Nova Scotia to West Florida. We are a people of cultivators scattered over an immense territory, communicating with each other by means of good roads and navigable rivers, united by the silken bands of mild government, all respecting the laws without dreading their power, because they are equitable. We are all animated with the spirit of an industry which is unfettered and unrestrained, because each person works for himself. If he travels through our rural districts, he views not the hostile castle and the haughty mansion, contrasted with the clay-built hut and miserable cabin, where cattle and men help to keep each other warm and dwell in meanness, smoke, and indigence. A pleasing uniformity of decent competence appears throughout our habitations. The meanest of our log-houses is a dry and comfortable habitation. Lawyer or merchant are the fairest titles our towns afford; that of a farmer is the only appellation of the rural inhabitants of our country. It must take some time ere he can reconcile himself to our dictionary, which is but short in words of dignity and names of honour. There, on a Sunday, he sees a congregation of respectable farmers and their wives, all clad in neat homespun, well mounted, or riding in their own humble waggons. There is not among them an esquire, saving the unlettered magistrate. There he sees a parson as simple as his flock, a farmer who does not riot on the labour of others. We have no princes for whom we toil, starve, and bleed; we are the most perfect society now existing in the world. Here man is free as he ought to be, nor is this pleasing equality so transitory as many others are. Many ages will not see the shores of our great lakes replenished with inland nations, nor the unknown bounds of North America entirely peopled. Who can tell how far it extends? Who can tell the millions of men whom it will feed and contain? For no European foot has as yet travelled half the extent of this mighty continent!

2   The next wish of this traveller will be to know whence came all these people. They are a mixture of English, Scotch, Irish, French, Dutch, Germans, and Swedes. From this promiscuous breed, that race now called American have arisen. . . .

3   In this great American asylum, the poor of Europe have by some means met together, and in consequence of various causes; to what purpose should they ask one another what countrymen they are? Alas, two thirds of them had no country. Can a wretch who wanders about, who works and starves, whose life is a continual scene of sore affliction or pinching penury—can that man call England or any other kingdom his country? A country that had no bread for him, whose fields procured him no harvest, who met with nothing but the frowns of the rich, the severity of the laws, with jails and punishments, who owned not a single foot of the extensive surface of this planet? No! Urged by a variety of motives, here they came. Everything has tended to regenerate them: new laws, a new mode of living, a new social system; here they are become men: in Europe they were as so many useless plants, wanting vegetative

mould and refreshing showers; they withered, and were mowed down by want, hunger, and war; but now, by the power of transplantation, like all other plants they have taken root and flourished! Formerly they were not numbered in any civil lists of their country, except in those of the poor; here they rank as citizens. By what invisible power hath this surprising metamorphosis been performed? By that of the laws and that of their industry. The laws, the indulgent laws, protect them as they arrive, stamping on them the symbol of adoption; they receive ample rewards for their labours; these accumulated rewards procure them lands; those lands confer on them the title of freemen, and to that title every benefit is affixed which men can possibly require. This is the great operation daily performed by our laws. Whence proceed these laws? From our government. Whence that government? It is derived from the original genius and strong desire of the people ratified and confirmed by the crown. This is the great chain which links us all, this is the picture which every province exhibits. Nova Scotia excepted. There the crown has done all; either there were no people who had genius or it was not much attended to; the consequence is that the province is very thinly inhabited indeed; the power of the crown in conjunction with the musketos has prevented men from settling there. Yet some parts of it flourished once, and it contained a mild, harmless set of people. But for the fault of a few leaders, the whole was banished. The greatest political error the crown ever committed in America was to cut off men from a country which wanted nothing but men!

4   What attachment can a poor European emigrant have for a country where he had nothing? The knowledge of the language, the love of a few kindred as poor as himself, were the only cords that tied him; his country is now that which gives him his land, bread, protection, and consequence; *Ubi panis ibi patria* [Where bread is, there one's country is] is the motto of all emigrants. What, then, is the American, this new man? He is neither an European nor the descendant of an European; hence that strange mixture of blood, which you will find in no other country. I could point out to you a family whose grandfather was an Englishman, whose wife was Dutch, whose son married a French woman, and whose present four sons have now four wives of different nations. *He* is an American, who, leaving behind him all his ancient prejudices and manners, receives new ones from the new mode of life he has embraced, the new government he obeys, and the new rank he holds. He becomes an American by being received in the broad lap of our great Alma Mater. Here individuals of all nations are melted into a new race of men, whose labours and posterity will one day cause great changes in the world. Americans are the western pilgrims who are carrying along with them that great mass of arts, sciences, vigour, and industry which began long since in the East; they will finish the great circle. The Americans were once scattered all over Europe; here they are incorporated into one of the finest systems of population which

has ever appeared, and which will hereafter become distinct by the power of the different climates they inhabit. The American ought therefore to love this country much better than that wherein either he or his forefathers were born. Here the rewards of his industry follow with equal steps the progress of his labour; his labour is founded on the basis of nature, self-interest; can it want a stronger allurement? Wives and children, who before in vain demanded of him a morsel of bread, now, fat and frolicsome, gladly help their father to clear those fields whence exuberant crops are to arise to feed and to clothe them all, without any part being claimed, either by a despotic prince, a rich abbot, or a mighty lord. Here religion demands but little of him: a small voluntary salary to the minister and gratitude to God; can he refuse these? The American is a new man, who acts upon new principles; he must therefore entertain new ideas and form new opinions. From involuntary idleness, servile dependence, penury, and useless labour, he has passed to toils of a very different nature, rewarded by ample subsistence. This is an American. . . .

5   As I have endeavoured to show you how Europeans become Americans, it may not be disagreeable to show you likewise how the various Christian sects introduced wear out and how religious indifference becomes prevalent. When any considerable number of a particular sect happen to dwell contiguous to each other, they immediately erect a temple and there worship the Divinity agreeably to their own peculiar ideas. Nobody disturbs them. If any new sect springs up in Europe, it may happen that many of its professors will come and settle in America. As they bring their zeal with them, they are at liberty to make proselytes if they can and to build a meeting and to follow the dictates of their consciences; for neither the government nor any other power interferes. If they are peaceable subjects and are industrious, what is it to their neighbours how and in what manner they think fit to address their prayers to the Supreme Being? But if the sectaries are not settled close together, if they are mixed with other denominations, their zeal will cool for want of fuel, and will be extinguished in a little time. Then, the Americans become as to religion what they are as to country, allied to all. In them the name of Englishman, Frenchman, and European is lost, and in like manner, the strict modes of Christianity as practised in Europe are lost also. This effect will extend itself still farther hereafter, and though this may appear to you as a strange idea, yet it is a very true one. I shall be able, perhaps, hereafter to explain myself better; in the meanwhile, let the following example serve as my first justification.

6   Let us suppose you and I to be travelling; we observe that in this house, to the right, lives a Catholic, who prays to God as he has been taught and believes in transubstantiation; he works and raises wheat, he has a large family of children, all hale and robust; his belief, his prayers, offend nobody. About one mile farther on the same road, his next neighbour may be a good, honest, plodding German Lutheran, who addresses himself to the

same God, the God of all, agreeable to the modes had has been educated in, and believes in consubstantiation; by so doing, he scandalizes nobody; he also works in his field, embellishes the earth, clears swamps, etc. What has the world to do with his Lutheran principles? He persecutes nobody, and nobody persecutes him; he visits his neighbours, and his neighbours visit him. Next to him lives a seceder, the most enthusiastic of all sectaries; his zeal is hot and fiery, but separated as he is from others of the same complexion, he has no congregation of his own to resort to where he might cabal and mingle religious pride with worldly obstinacy. He likewise raises good crops, his house is handsomely painted, his orchard is one of the fairest in the neighbourhood. How does it concern the welfare of the country, or of the province at large, what this man's religious sentiments are, or really whether he has any at all? He is a good farmer, he is a sober, peaceable, good citizen; William Penn himself would not wish for more. This is the visible character; the invisible one is only guessed at, and is nobody's business. Next, again, lives a Low Dutchman, who implicitly believes the rules laid down by the synod of Dort. He conceives no other idea of a clergyman than that of an hired man; if he does his work well, he will pay him the stipulated sum; if not, he will dismiss him, and do without his sermons, and let his church be shut up for years. But notwithstanding this coarse idea, you will find his house and farm to be the neatest in all the country; and you will judge by his waggon and fat horses that he thinks more of the affairs of this world than of those of the next. He is sober and laborious; therefore, he is all he ought to be as to the affairs of this life. As for those of the next, he must trust to the great Creator. Each of these people instruct their children as well as they can, but these instructions are feeble compared to those which are given to the youth of the poorest class in Europe. Their children will therefore grow up less zealous and more indifferent in matters of religion than their parents. The foolish vanity or, rather, the fury of making proselytes is unknown here; they have no time, the seasons call for all their attention, and thus in a few years this mixed neighborhood will exhibit a strange religious medley that will be neither pure Catholicism nor pure Calvinism. A very perceptible indifference, even in the first generation, will become apparent; and it may happen that the daughter of the Catholic will marry the son of the seceder and settle by themselves at a distance from their parents. What religious education will they give their children? A very imperfect one. If there happens to be in the neighbourhood any place of worship, we will suppose a Quaker's meeting; rather than not show their fine clothes, they will go to it, and some of them may perhaps attach themselves to that society. Others will remain in a perfect state of indifference; the children of these zealous parents will not be able to tell what their religious principles are, and their grandchildren still less. The neighbourhood of a place of worship generally leads them to it, and the action of going thither is the strongest evidence they can give of their attachment to any sect. The Quakers are the only people who retain a fondness for their own mode of worship; for be they ever so far separated from each other, they hold a sort of communion with the society and seldom depart from its rules, at least in this country. Thus all sects are mixed, as well as all nations; thus religious indifference is imperceptibly disseminated from one end of the continent to the other, which is at present one of the strongest characteristics of the Americans. Where this will reach no one can tell; perhaps it may leave a vacuum fit to receive other systems. Persecution, religious pride, the love of contradiction, are the food of what the world commonly calls religion. These motives have ceased here; zeal in Europe is confined; here it evaporates in the great distance it has to travel; there it is a grain of powder inclosed; here it burns away in the open air and consumes without effect.

BUILDING CONTEXT

1. Compare Crèvecoeur's attitude toward citizenship to that of Bradford or Franklin.

2. What does Crèvecoeur see as the best aspect of religion in America? Given the history of religious wars in Europe, explain why he feels this way. Compare Crèvecoeur's attitude toward group identity to that of Rowlandson or Cameron.

FURTHER STUDY

1. While Crèvecoeur described the melting together of many nations into a new race, *The Melting Pot* is actually the title of a 1909 play by Israel Zangwill about Jewish immigration: "America is God's crucible, the great melting-pot where all the races of Europe are melting and reforming." Explore the history of this belief. Which groups came to America to protect their special identities, and which sought to conform to others? What is the current feeling about the reality and desirability of the melting pot?

2. In paragraph 3, Nova Scotia is singled out as different from the other English colonies—the site of the "greatest political error the crown ever committed in America." What happened in Nova Scotia? (You may want to read Henry Wadsworth Longfellow's *Evangeline.*)

ADDITIONAL RESOURCES

Anderson, Lydia. *Immigration.* New York: Franklin Watts Inc., 1981.

Daniels, Roger. *Coming to America: A History of Immigration and Ethnicity in American Life.* New York: HarperCollins, 1990.

Dinnerstein, Leonard, and David M. Reimers. *Ethnic Americans: A History of Immigration and Assimilation.* New York: Dodd, Mead, 1975.

RESEARCH KEYWORDS

Melting Pot   Assimilation
Immigration   Multiculturalism

> **OLAUDAH EQUIANO**
> *The Interesting Narrative of Olaudah Equiano, the African, Written by Himself* (1789)

"I asked them if we were not to be eaten by those white men with horrible looks, red faces, and long hair."

When he was about eleven years old, Olaudah Equiano (1745?–1801?), whose own family owned slaves, was kidnapped by black slave traders from his village in Nigeria. Sold from master to master, he moved steadily toward the Atlantic coast; there he was sold to traders, the first white men he had ever seen, and taken to America. Under a series of owners, he experienced chattel slavery: whether treated ill or well he was someone's property, subject to another's whim. He was freed in 1766 and began a life of travel and adventure. In 1774 he joined the Methodist Church and went to Central America as a missionary for three years. Though he was often befriended by white sailors and colleagues, he also experienced prejudice and the risk of renewed enslavement.

Equiano's account shares many features with captivity narratives, such as those of Smith and Rowlandson: astonishment at the strangeness of "others," the assumption that "they" are capable of the worst behavior, interest in documenting outlandish behavior. An additional element, however, is significant: at a time when slavery was defended on the grounds that blacks were not capable of intelligent thought, Equiano published his story, "written by himself." He therefore became a popular lecturer among abolitionists. This and later slave narratives influenced such writers as Harriet Beecher Stowe, author of *Uncle Tom's Cabin,* and twentieth-century black authors like Ralph Ellison and Toni Morrison.

Text: *The Classic Slave Narratives;* ed. Henry L. Gates; New York: New American Library, 1987.

EXPLORING ISSUES IN THE TEXT

1. According to Equiano, what was the difference between being owned by blacks and whites? Compare, for example, the punishments for not eating (pars. 3, 10).

2. What does Equiano mean by "the languages of different nations" were not "so copious as those of the Europeans" (par. 6)? Analyze the belief that certain languages are primitive or childish. What does it say about Equiano's perception of his own people that he accepts this view?

THE INTERESTING NARRATIVE OF THE LIFE OF OLAUDAH EQUIANO

Chapter II

1 I have already acquainted the reader with the time and place of my birth. My father, besides many slaves, had a numerous family, of which seven lived to grow up, including myself and a sister, who was the only daughter. As I was the youngest of the sons, I became, of course, the greatest favourite with my mother, and was always with her, and she used to take particular pains to form my mind. I was trained up from my earliest years in the art of war: my daily exercise was shooting and throwing javelins; and my mother adorned me with emblems, after the manner of our greatest warriors. In this way I grew up till I was turned the age of eleven, when an end was put to my happiness in the following manner:—When the grown people in the neighbourhood were gone far in the fields to labour, the children generally assembled together in some of the neighbours' premises to play; and some of us often used to get up into a tree to look out for any assailant, or kidnapper, that might come upon us. For they sometimes took those opportunities of our parents' absence, to attack and carry off as many as they could seize. One day, as I was watching at the top of a tree in our yard, I saw one of those people come into the yard of our next neighbour but one, to kidnap, there being many stout young people in it. Immediately on this I gave the alarm of the rogue, and he was surrounded by the stoutest of them, who entangled him with cords, so that he could not escape till some of the grown people came and secured him.

2 But alas! ere long it was my fate to be thus attacked, and to be carried off, when none of the grown people were nigh. One day, when all our people were gone out to their work as usual, and only I and my sister were left to mind the house, two men and a woman got over our walls, and in a moment seized us both; and without giving us time to cry out, or to make any resistance, they stopped our mouths and ran off with us

into the nearest wood. Here they tied our hands, and continued to carry us as far as they could, till night came on, when we reached a small house, where the robbers halted for refreshment and spent the night. We were then unbound, but were unable to take any food; and being quite overpowered by fatigue and grief, our only relief was some sleep, which allayed our misfortune for a short time. The next morning we left the house, and continued travelling all the day. For a long time we had kept the woods, but at last we came into a road which I believed I knew. I had now some hopes of being delivered; for we had advanced but a little way before I discovered some people at a distance, on which I began to cry out for their assistance; but my cries had no other effect than to make them tie me faster and stop my mouth; they then put me into a large sack. They also stopped my sister's mouth, and tied her hands; and in this manner we proceeded till we were out of sight of these people.

3   When we went to rest the following night, they offered us some victuals; but we refused it; and the only comfort we had was in being in one another's arms all that night, and bathing each other with tears. But alas! we were soon deprived of even the small comfort of weeping together. The next day proved one of greater sorrow than I had yet experienced; for my sister and I were then separated, while we lay clasped in each other's arms. It was in vain that we besought them not to part us; she was torn from me, and immediately carried away, while I was left in a state of distraction not to be described. I cried and grieved continually; and for several days did not eat any thing but what they forced into my mouth. At length, after many days' travelling, during which I had often changed masters, I got into the hands of a chieftain, in a pleasant country. This man had two wives and some children; and they all used me extremely well, and did all they could to comfort me; particularly the first wife, who was something like my mother. Although I was a great many days' journey from my father's house, yet these people spoke exactly the same language with us. This first master of mine, as I may call him, was a smith, and my principal employment was working his bellows, which were the same kind as I had seen in my vicinity. They were in some respects not unlike the stoves here in gentlemen's kitchens; and were covered over with leather, and in the middle of that leather a stick was fixed, and a person stood up and worked it, in the same manner as is done to pump water out of a cask with a hand pump. I believe it was gold he worked, for it was of a lovely bright yellow colour, and was worn by the women on their wrists and ankles.

4   I was there, I suppose, about a month, and they at length used to trust me some little distance from the house. I employed this liberty in embracing every opportunity to inquire the way to my own home: and I also sometimes, for the same purpose, went with the maidens, in the cool of the evenings, to bring pitchers of water from the springs for the use of the house. I had also remarked where the sun rose in the morning, and set in the evening, as I had travelled along: and had observed that my father's house was towards the rising of the sun. I therefore determined to seize

the first opportunity of making my escape, and to shape my course for that quarter; for I was quite oppressed and weighed down by grief after my mother and friends; and my love of liberty, ever great, was strengthened by the mortifying circumstance of not daring to eat with the free-born children, although I was mostly their companion. . . .

5   Soon after this my master's only daughter and child by his first wife, sickened and died, which affected him so much that for some time he was almost frantic, and really would have killed himself, had he not been watched and prevented. However, in a small time afterwards he recovered, and I was again sold. I was now carried to the left of the sun's rising, through many dreary wastes and dismal woods, amidst the hideous roaring of wild beasts. The people I was sold to used to carry me very often, when I was tired, either on their shoulders or on their backs. I saw many convenient well-built sheds along the road, at proper distances, to accommodate the merchants and travellers. They lie in those buildings along with their wives, who often accompany them: and they always go well armed.

6   From the time I left my own nation I always found somebody that understood me till I came to the sea coast. The languages of different nations did not totally differ, nor were they so copious as those of the Europeans, particularly the English. They were therefore easily learned; and, while I was journeying thus through Africa, I acquired two or three different tongues. In this manner I had been travelling for a considerable time, when one evening, to my great surprise, whom should I see brought to the house where I was, but my dear sister? As soon as she saw me she gave a loud shriek, and ran into my arms. I was quite overpowered: neither of us could speak; but for a considerable time, clung to each other in mutual embraces, unable to do any thing but weep. Our meeting affected all who saw us; and indeed I must acknowledge, in honour of those sable destroyers of human rights, that I never met with any ill treatment, or saw any offered to their slaves, except tying them, when necessary, to keep them running away. . . .

7   All the nations and people I had hitherto passed through resembled our own in their manners, customs, and language: but I came at length to a country, the inhabitants of which differed from us in all these particulars. I was very much struck with this difference, especially when I came among a people who did not circumcise, and who ate without washing their hands. They cooked their provisions also in iron pots, and had European cutlasses and cross bows, which were unknown to us; and fought with their fists among themselves. Their women were not so modest as ours, for they ate, drank, and slept with their men. But, above all, I was amazed to see no sacrifices or offerings among them. In some of those places the people ornamented themselves with scars, and likewise filed their teeth very sharp. They sometimes wanted to ornament me in the same manner, but I would not suffer them; hoping that I might sometime be among a people who did not thus disfigure themselves, as I thought

they did. At last I came to the banks of a large river, covered with canoes, in which the people appeared to live, with their household utensils, and provisions of all kinds. I was beyond measure astonished at this, as I had never before seen any water larger than a pond or a rivulet: and my surprise was mingled with no small fear when I was put into one of these canoes, and we began to paddle and move along the river. We continued going on thus till night; and when we came to land, and made fires on the banks, each family by themselves, some dragged their canoes on shore, other cooked in theirs, and laid in them all night. Those on the land had mats, of which they made tents, some in the shape of little houses: in these we slept: and after the morning meal, we embarked again, and proceeded as before. I was often very much astonished to see some of the women as well as the men, jump into the water, dive to the bottom, come up again, and swim about. Thus I continued to travel, both by land and by water, through different countries and various nations, till at the end of six or seven months after I had been kidnapped, I arrived at the sea coast.

8   It would be tedious and uninteresting to relate all the incidents which befell me during this journey, and which I have not yet forgotten, or to mention the various lands I passed through, and the manners and customs of the different people among whom I lived: I shall therefore only observe, that in all the places where I was, the soil was exceedingly rich; the pomkins, aedas, plantains, yams, &c. &c. were in great abundance, and of incredible size. There were also large quantities of different gums, though not used for any purpose; and every where a great deal of tobacco. The cotton even grew quite wild; and there was plenty of red wood. I saw no mechanics whatever in all the way, except such as I have mentioned. The chief employment in all these countries was agriculture, and both the males and females, as with us, were brought up to it, and trained in the arts of war.

9   The first object that saluted my eyes when I arrived on the coast was the sea, and a slave ship, which was then riding at anchor, and waiting for its cargo. These filled me with astonishment, that was soon converted into terror, which I am yet at a loss to describe, and much more the then feelings of my mind when I was carried on board. I was immediately handled and tossed up to see if I was sound, by some of the crew; and I was now persuaded that I had got into a world of bad spirits, and that they were going to kill me. Their complexions too, differing so much from ours, their long hair, and the language they spoke, which was very different from any I had ever heard, united to confirm me in this belief. Indeed such were the horrors of my views and fears at the moment, that if ten thousand worlds had been my own, I would have freely parted with them all to have exchanged my condition with the meanest slave in my own country. When I looked round the ship too, and saw a large furnace or copper boiling and a multitude of black people, of every description, chained together, every one of their countenances expressing dejection

and sorrow, I no longer doubted of my fate; and, quite overpowered with horror and anguish, I fell motionless on the deck, and fainted. When I recovered a little, I found some black people about me, who I believed were some of those who brought me on board, and had been receiving their pay: they talked to me in order to cheer me, but all in vain. I asked them if we were not to be eaten by those white men with horrible looks, red faces, and long hair. They told me I was not: and one of the crew brought me a small portion of spirituous liquor in a wine glass; but, being afraid of him, I would not take it out of his hand. One of the blacks therefore took it from him and gave it to me, and I took a little down my palate, which, instead of reviving me, as they thought it would, threw me into the greatest consternation at the strange feeling it produced, having never tasted any such liquor before.

10   Soon after this the blacks who brought me on board went off, and left me abandoned to despair. I now saw myself deprived of all chance of returning to my native country, or even the least glimpse of gaining the shore, which I now considered as friendly; and I even wished for my former slavery, in preference to my present situation, which was filled with horrors of every kind, still heightened by my ignorance of what I was to undergo. I was not long suffered to indulge my grief. I was soon put down under the decks, and there I received such a salutation in my nostrils as I had never experienced in my life: so that, with the loathsomeness of the stench, and with my crying together, I became so sick and low that I was not able to eat, nor had I the least desire to taste any thing. I now wished for the last friend, death, to relieve me; but soon, to my grief, two of the white men offered me eatables; and, on my refusing to eat, one of them held me fast by the hands, and laid me across, I think, the windlass, and tied my feet, while the other flogged me severely. I had never experienced any thing of this kind before, and although, not being used to the water, I naturally feared that element the first time I saw it, yet nevertheless, could I have got over the nettings, I would have jumped over the side, but I could not; and besides the crew used to watch us very closely, who were not chained down to the decks, lest we should leap into the water. I have seen some of those poor African prisoners most severely cut for attempting to do so, and hourly whipped for not eating. This indeed was often the case with myself. In a little time after, amongst the poor chained men, I found some of my own nation, which in a small degree gave ease to my mind. I inquired of these what was to be done with us. They gave me to understand we were to be carried to these white people's country to work for them. I was then a little revived, and thought if it were no worse than working, my situation was not so desperate. But still I feared I should be put to death, the white people looked and acted, as I thought, in so savage a manner; for I had never seen among any people such instances of brutal cruelty: and this is not only shewn towards us blacks, but also to some of the whites themselves.

One white man in particular I saw, when we were permitted to be on deck, flogged so unmercifully with a large rope near the foremast, that he died in consequence of it; and they tossed him over the side as they would have done a brute. This made me fear these people the more; and I expected nothing less than to be treated in the same manner. . . .

BUILDING CONTEXT

1. Discuss Equiano's first impression of whites (pars. 9–10). In what ways does this epitomize universal reactions to the unknown? Compare Smith's reaction to Indians, Cameron's reaction to whites.
2. Equiano's journey of discovery and growth has been compared to Franklin's. Compare and contrast the two autobiographies.

FURTHER STUDY

1. What kind of person does Equiano seem to be? Why do you think he was so successful as an abolitionist lecturer? Compare his career to that of other black Abolitionists, for example Frederick Douglass.
2. Investigate the influence of slave narratives on later African American writers. Trace the significance of "finding your voice" and "naming yourself."

ADDITIONAL RESOURCES

Genovese, Eugene. *Black History and the History of Slavery.* Berkeley: University of California Press, 1970.

Jordan, Winthrop D. *White Over Black: American Attitudes toward the Negro, 1550–1812.* Chapel Hill, NC: University of North Carolina Press, 1968.

Katz, William L., ed. *Five Slave Narratives.* New York: Arno Press, 1969.

RESEARCH KEYWORDS

Slavery

Racism

African-Americans in literature

WRITING ABOUT THE CRITICAL ISSUES

1. Compare and contrast how two or three of the reading selections treat one of the following issues: America's mission, the formation of identity, equality in America, the role of religion in America, the relation of the individual and the state.

2. Trace the evolution of the American attitude(s) toward one of the critical issues we have been discussing.

3. Though the United States is a secular republic, religion has played an important role as both an overt force and a source of basic assumptions. Examine how religion shapes secular morality.

4. Discuss the "utilitarian" thread in American character. Supply examples, historical or current, of this characteristic in American religion, politics or foreign relations.

5. Discuss the secularization of American religion. Show how de-ritualized religion has been applied to public issues. Explore whether this trend is still active.

6. Discuss the history of the "melting pot" ideal. What is the current feeling about its reality and desirability?

7. Explore the process of discovery and growth in various autobiographical works. What makes a successful autobiography?

8. Discuss first impressions. Are there universal reactions to the unknown? Compare how we see ourselves and our groups to how others see us.

9. Explore an idea that caught your interest, or that charmed or provoked you, or that supported or challenged your own beliefs. Try to place the issue in a larger context and explain its significance.

5

DEFINING THE NEW REPUBLIC: 1800–1850

"You have got our country, but are not satisfied; you want to force your religion upon us."

RED JACKET

"What do you expect from society and its government? We must be clear about that."

ALEXIS DE TOCQUEVILLE

"The only obligation which I have a right to assume is to do at any time what I think right."

HENRY DAVID THOREAU

It would be difficult to overstate the significance of the American Revolution. It was not simply a revolution on the battlefield. It was a revolution in colonial policy, government, and society.

From the earliest European colonies in the New World, purpose and hierarchy were implicit. Colonies existed to serve the mother country. They fulfilled economic and military requirements of the empire and received protection and support in return. The possibility that colonists might consider themselves citizens of the colony rather than the empire, that colonies had the right to engage in trade for their own benefit, that there should be a mechanism for turning colonies into independent nations—all this was unthinkable. Within a generation of the American Revolution, however, wars of independence shattered the colonial empires of Spain and Portugal, as Venezuela, Mexico, and Brazil followed the lead of the United States.

After independence comes governing, and here too the United States was revolutionary. Everywhere, the existing model was monarchy; many Americans therefore felt that they should choose their own king and be a nation like other nations. In contrast, Republicans and Democrats—that is, supporters of representative and egalitarian government (and not to be confused with the modern political parties with these names)—struggled to put Rationalist and Enlightenment theories into practice. They believed that by applying scientific methods they could create a government that would embody the bold principles of freedom and equality, of progress and human perfectability. The result was the Constitution, with its logical structure and balance of powers.

And, finally, American society was revolutionary. Alexis de Tocqueville, a visiting French statesman, was among many who recognized the central question: "What do you expect from society and its government?" Americans were convinced that they had defeated not only England, but an outdated world view. Europe, they said, was archaic, decrepit, the past. America was young, strong, and held the promise of the future. A people that would be a light unto the nations had to strive for perfection; self-improvement societies flourished, along with temperance leagues. Many ordinary citizens believed, as one told a French diplomat, "that nothing good is done, and that no one has any brains, except in America." In 1796 the House of Representatives debated whether to proclaim the American nation "the freest and most enlightened in the world." The educator and lexicographer Noah Webster wrote an *American* dictionary of the English language; his *Reader,* which contained speeches by America's war heroes, dominated schools for decades. And in an 1837 speech with the provocative title "The American Scholar," Ralph Waldo Emerson, one of the most influential Americans of the nineteenth century, told the students of Harvard: "We have listened too long to the courtly muses of Europe."

Emerson and his colleagues developed an American philosophy, Transcendentalism, a mystical belief in the power of the individual to rise above—to transcend—reality. They taught that feelings, rather than logic, should guide behavior. And because each individual, as a part of Nature, is directly connected to the Divine, they saw little need for organized religion or government, and no justification for following laws that violate the individual's conscience. It is in this context that Emerson's friend, Henry David Thoreau, could say, "The only obligation which I have a right to assume is to do at any time what I think right." And this same faith in the individual informed advocates of woman's rights to declare, in a deliberate echo of the Declaration of Independence, "We hold these truths to be self-evident: that all men and women are created equal."

Other forces were also at work shaping the new nation. In the spirit of egalitarianism, many Americans wanted just treatment of the Indian "nations" in their midst. Missionaries sought to bring salvation to the Native Americans, not noticing, as Red Jacket tried to explain on more than one occasion, that adopting another religion destroyed the Indians' way of life. By rejecting assimilation, however, the Native Americans simply provided additional proof to their white enemies that it was pointless to deal nicely with savages.

The Industrial Revolution also changed society. New machines and steam-driven transportation promised to free workers from the drudgery of labor and to improve the standard of living by bringing decent food and clothing to even the most rural settlers. Many young women, in particular, saw freedom in employment at the new textile mills. They could earn their own money and spend it as they pleased; they could also improve themselves through education and social clubs. But they were eventually opposed by male workers who feared they would take away jobs from heads of households. Ironically, these working women had little contact with the woman's rights reformers at Seneca Falls, who gave only passing consideration to worries about earning a living.

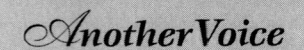

AMERICAN SOCIETY
HENRY ADAMS

American society might be both sober and sad, but except for negro slavery it was sound and healthy in every part. Stripped for the hardest work, every muscle firm and elastic, every ounce of brain ready for use, and not a trace of superfluous flesh on his nervous and supple body, the American stood in the world a new order of man. . . . Not only were artificial barriers carefully removed, but every influence that could appeal to ordinary ambition was applied. . . . Few human beings, however sluggish,

continued

continued from previous page

could long resist the temptation to acquire power; and the elements of power were to be had in America for the asking. Reversing the old-world system, the American stimulant increased in energy as it reached the lowest and most ignorant class, dragging and whirling them upward as in a blast furnace. The penniless and homeless Scotch or Irish immigrant was caught and consumed by it; for every stroke of the axe and the hoe made him a capitalist, and made gentlemen of his children.

History of the United States, 1889–1891

Another Voice

THE AMERICAN SCHOLAR
RALPH WALDO EMERSON

The scholar is that man who must take up into himself all the ability of the time, all the contributions of the past, all the hopes of the future. He must be an university of knowledges. If there be one lesson more than another which should pierce his ear, it is, The world is nothing, the man is all; in yourself is the law of all nature, and you know not yet how a globule of sap ascends; in yourself lumbers the whole of Reason; it is for you to know all, it is for you to dare all. Mr. President and Gentlemen, this confidence in the unsearched might of man, belongs by all motives, by all prophecy, by all preparation, to the American Scholar. We have listened too long to the courtly muses of Europe. The spirit of the American freeman is already suspected to be timid, imitative, tame. . . . Not so, brothers and friends,— please God, ours shall not be so. We will walk on our own feet; we will work with our own hands; we will speak our own minds. The study of letters shall be no longer a name for pity, for doubt, and for sensual indulgence. The dread of man and the love of man shall be a wall of defence and a wreath of joy around all. A nation of men will for the first time exist, because each believes himself inspired by the Divine Soul which also inspires all men.

1837

RED JACKET
Speech to the Missionaries (1805)

"You have got our country, but are not satisfied; you want to force your religion upon us."

Sa-Go-Ye-Wat-Ha (1758–1830), a chief of the Senecas, was a flamboyant and shrewd political leader who devoted his energies to maintaining tribal customs and protecting the legal autonomy of his people. In accordance with the decision of the Iroquois League, he fought on the side of the British during the Revolutionary War. Though he received the name Red Jacket because of the uniform that he continued to wear, after the war he made peace with the United States and supported the Americans in the War of 1812.

In 1799, a time of cultural crisis for the Iroquois, Handsome Lake, a Senecan visionary, expounded a combination of Christian and Native American religious and moral teachings. Many Iroquois embraced his Kaiwiyoh, or "Good Message," but Christian missionaries opposed it and sought permission in 1805 to preach among the six nations of the League. Recognized as a defender of tribal traditions and highly regarded as an orator, Red Jacket was chosen to deliver the Indian response. His speech contains a Native American view of early colonization, religious philosophy, and cultural assimilation, as well as biting observations concerning the behavior of Christians.

All interpretations of the multifaceted contact between Native Americans and Christianity are controversial. On the one hand, most missionaries who braved the dangers of the wilderness sincerely wished to bring what they considered the gift of salvation to the Indians. On the other, there is no doubt that Christianity served as one more tool to pacify the Indians and destroy their indigenous cultures.

Bear in mind when reading the following selection that Red Jacket was not speaking from a written English text; a transcript of his speech was edited by a printer.

Text: William L. Stone; *Life and Times of Sa-Go-Ye-Wat-Ha;* NY: Wiley and Putnam; 1866.

EXPLORING ISSUES IN THE TEXT

1. What is Red Jacket's view of Indian-European history (pars. 4–5)?

2. How does Red Jacket answer the missionaries? What are his objections to accepting Christianity (pars. 7–12)?

3. Summarize Red Jacket's attitude toward assimilation (pars. 9–11).

4. What is Red Jacket's view about the purpose of religion? What is your reaction to the way he presents his case?

SPEECH TO THE MISSIONARIES

1 FRIEND AND BROTHER: It was the will of the Great Spirit that we should meet together this day. He orders all things, and has given us a fine day for our Council. He has taken his garment from before the sun, and caused it to shine with brightness upon us. Our eyes are opened, that we see clearly; our ears are unstopped, that we have been able to hear distinctly the words you have spoken. For all these favors we thank the Great Spirit, and HIM *only.*

2 BROTHER: This council fire was kindled by you. It was at your request that we came together at this time. We have listened with attention to what you have said. You requested us to speak our minds freely. This gives us great joy; for we now consider that we stand upright before you, and can speak what we think. All have heard your voice, and all speak to you now as one man. Our minds are agreed.

3 BROTHER: You say you want an answer to your talk before you leave this place. It is right you should have one, as you are a great distance from home, and we do not wish to detain you. But we will first look back a little, and tell you what our fathers have told us, and what we have heard from the white people.

4 BROTHER: Listen to what we say. There was a time when our forefathers owned this great island. Their seats extended from the rising to the setting sun. The Great Spirit had made it for the use of Indians. He had created the buffalo, the deer, and other animals for food. He had made the bear and the beaver. Their skins served us for clothing. He had scattered them over the country, and taught us how to take them. He had caused the earth to produce corn for bread. All this HE had done for his red children, because HE loved them. If we had some disputes about our hunting ground, they were generally settled without the shedding of much blood. But an evil day came upon us. Your forefathers crossed the great water and landed on this island. Their numbers were small. They found friends and not enemies. They told us they had fled from their own country for fear of wicked men, and had come here to enjoy their religion. They asked for a small seat. We took pity on them, granted their request; and they sat down amongst us. We gave them corn and meat; they gave us poison in return.

5 The white people, BROTHER, had now found our country. Tidings were carried back, and more came amongst us. Yet we did not fear them. We

took them to be friends. They called us brothers. We believed them and gave them a larger seat. At length their numbers had greatly increased. They wanted more land; they wanted our country. Our eyes were opened, and our minds became uneasy. Wars took place. Indians were hired to fight against Indians, and many of our people were destroyed. They also brought strong liquor amongst us. It was strong and powerful, and has slain thousands.

6   BROTHER: Our seats were once large and yours were small. You have now become a great people, and we have scarcely a place left to spread our blankets. You have got our country, but are not satisfied; you want to force your religion upon us.

7   BROTHER: Continue to listen. You say that you are sent to instruct us how to worship the Great Spirit agreeably to his mind, and, if we do not take hold of the religion which you white people teach, we shall be unhappy hereafter. You say that you are right and we are lost. How do we know this to be true? We understand that your religion is written in a book. If it was intended for us as well as you, why has not the Great Spirit given to us, and not only to us, but why did he not give to our forefathers, the knowledge of that book, with the means of understanding it rightly? We only know what you tell us about it. How shall we know when to believe, being so often deceived by the white people?

8   BROTHER: You say there is but one way to worship and serve the Great Spirit. If there is but one religion, why do you white people differ so much about it? Why not all agreed, as you can all read the book?

9   BROTHER: We do not understand these things. We are told that your religion was given to your forefathers, and has been handed down from father to son. We also have a religion, which was given to our forefathers, and has been handed down to us their children. We worship in that way. It teaches us to be thankful for all the favors we receive; to love each other, and to be united. We never quarrel about religion.

10   BROTHER: The Great Spirit has made us all, but HE has made a great difference between his white and red children. HE has given us different complexions and different customs. To you HE has given the arts. To these HE has not opened our eyes. We know these things to be true. Since HE has made so great a difference between us in other things, why may we not conclude that he has given us a different religion according to our understanding? The Great Spirit does right. HE knows what is best for his children; we are satisfied.

11   BROTHER: We do not wish to destroy your religion, or take it from you. We only want to enjoy our own.

12   BROTHER: You say you have not come to get our land or our money, but to enlighten our minds. I will now tell you that I have been at your meetings, and saw you collect money from the meeting. I cannot tell what this money was intended for, but suppose that it was for your minister, and if we should conform to your way of thinking, perhaps you may want some from us.

13　BROTHER: We are told that you have been preaching to the white people in this place. These people are our neighbors. We are acquainted with them. We will wait a little while, and see what effect your preaching has upon them. If we find it does them good, makes them honest and less disposed to cheat Indians, we will then consider again of what you have said.

14　BROTHER: You have now heard our answer to your talk, and this is all we have to say at present. As we are going to part, we will come and take you by the hand, and hope the Great Spirit will protect you on your journey, and return you safe to your friends.

BUILDING CONTEXT

1. Compare Red Jacket's outline of Indian-European contact to those by Smith and Van Every. What does each writer say about the initial reception of the whites? About relations among the Native Americans before the arrival of Europeans?

2. Compare Red Jacket's attitude toward cultural assimilation to the writings of Cameron, Booker T. Washington, or Du Bois.

3. Compare Red Jacket's observations about religious differences to Crèvecoeur's or Tocqueville's.

FURTHER STUDY

1. Why are the words "Him" (par. 1) and "He" (par. 4) capitalized? Since Red Jacket did not write his speech in English, why do you think the printer did this? What is the effect of this spelling? Research instances in which newspapers or magazines use spelling in quotations to shape the reader's opinion; for example, writing "gonna" or "wuz" instead of "going to" and "was" in quoted *speech* (not quoted written text). What is the effect of this practice? Why do you think it is done?

2. Investigate the careers of Ely S. Parker, Red Jacket's "clan grandson," and Arthur C. Parker, grandnephew of Ely. How did they advance Red Jacket's beliefs? How did their lives contradict or validate Red Jacket's views? You might want to pay special attention to Ely's work in the Bureau of Indian Affairs and Arthur's as founder of the National Congress of American Indians.

3. Investigate the work of the Bureau of Indian Affairs or the Bureau of American Ethnology. Why were they established, what was their mandate, how did (or do) they operate, and how were (or are) they perceived by Native Americans?

ADDITIONAL RESOURCES

Annual Report[s] of the Bureau of American Ethnology.

Brotherston, Gordon. *Image of the New World: The American Continent Portrayed in Native Texts.* London: Thames and Hudson, 1979.

Bureau of American Ethnology Bulletin.

Nabokov, Peter, ed. *Native American Testimony.* New York: Viking, 1991.

Parker, Arthur C. *Red Jacket: Last of the Senecas.* New York: McGraw-Hill, 1952.

Wallace, Anthony F. C. *The Death and Rebirth of the Seneca.* New York: Knopf, 1970.

RESEARCH KEYWORDS

Red Jacket

Iroquois League

National Congress of American Indians

Parker (Arthur C.)

Indians—History—Sources

Seneca

Handsome Lake

Parker (Ely S.)

Bureau of Indian Affairs

Indians—Literature

ALEXIS DE TOCQUEVILLE
Democracy in America
(1835)

"What do you expect from society and its government? We must be clear about that."

Alexis de Tocqueville (1805–1859), was a French politician and writer. In 1831, while a lawyer for the government, he was sent to the United States to study the penal system. His travels, however, were not limited to his official mission, and in 1835 he published *Democracy in America,* a wide-ranging study of political philosophy and social conditions.

Tocqueville embraced the liberalism of his day (not to be equated with late–twentieth-century liberalism), which placed humanity, not God, at the center of the universe. Though he was an aristocrat, he accepted the belief that human freedoms are a product of natural law—and that the privileges of the nobility and church are a perversion of it. In contrast to France, which he believed was stifled by class divisions, he portrayed America as the inevitable model for the future, a land of equality and opportunity where the reign of reason would lead to personal and societal improvement. Nonetheless, Tocqueville feared what he called the "tyranny of the majority"; he felt it threatened creativity and culture, and that unbridled individualism undermined patriotism and public order. Most troubling to him was the inherent danger that democracy raised hopes that could not be satisfied.

Text: Alexis de Tocqueville; *Democracy in America;* ed. J. P. Mayer; trans. George Lawrence; New York: Harper & Row, 1966.

EXPLORING ISSUES IN THE TEXT

1. What advantage does Tocqueville find in granting rights to as many citizens as possible (pars. 4–7)? What connection does he draw between rights and religion (pars. 10–12)?

2. Summarize the possible goals of society and government (pars. 16–22). Which does Tocqueville support? Why?

3. What surprised Tocqueville about religion in the United States (pars. 23–27)? What explanation does he give for this situation (pars. 28–38)? Does Tocqueville seem more concerned with protecting religion from governmental interference or protecting government from religious interference?

DEMOCRACY IN AMERICA

The Advantages of Democratic Government

1 The idea of rights is nothing but the conception of virtue applied to the world of politics.

2 By means of the idea of rights men have defined the nature of license and of tyranny. Guided by its light, we can each of us be independent without arrogance and obedient without servility. When a man submits to force, that surrender debases him; but when he accepts the recognized right of a fellow mortal to give him orders, there is a sense in which he rises above the giver of the commands. No man can be great without virtue, nor any nation great without respect for rights; one might almost say that without it there can be no society, for what is a combination of rational and intelligent beings held together by force alone?

3 I keep asking myself how, in our day, this conception may be taught to mankind and made, so to say, palpable to their senses; and I find one only, namely, to give them all the peaceful use of certain rights. One can see how this works among children, who are men except in strength and in experience; when a baby first begins to move among things outside

himself, instinct leads him to make use of anything his hands can grasp; he has no idea of other people's property, not even that it exists; but as he is instructed in the value of things and discovers that he too may be despoiled, he becomes more circumspect, and in the end is led to respect for others that which he wishes to be respected for himself.

4   As for a child with his toys, so it is later for a man with all his belongings. Why is it that in America, the land par excellence of democracy, no one makes that outcry against property in general that often echoes through Europe? Is there any need to explain? It is because there are no proletarians in America. Everyone, having some possession to defend, recognizes the right to property in principle.

5   It is the same in the world of politics. The American man of the people has conceived a high idea of political rights because he has some; he does not attack those of others, in order that his own may not be violated. Whereas the corresponding man in Europe would be prejudiced against all authority, even the highest, the American uncomplainingly obeys the lowest of his officials.

6   This truth is illustrated even in the smallest details of a nation's life. In France there are few pleasures exclusively reserved for the higher classes of society; the poor man is admitted almost everywhere where the rich can go, so one finds him behaving decently and with proper consideration for pleasures in which he shares. In England, where enjoyment is the privilege of the rich, who also monopolize power, people complain that when a poor man does furtively steal into the exclusive haunts of the rich he has a taste for causing pointless damage there. Why be surprised at that? Trouble has been taken to see that he has nothing to lose.

7   Democratic government makes the idea of political rights penetrate right down to the least of citizens, just as the division of property puts the general idea of property rights within reach of all. That, in my view, is one of its greatest merits.

8   I am not asserting it to be an easy matter to teach all men to make use of political rights; I only say that when that can happen, the results are important.

9   And I would add that if ever there was a century in which such an attempt should be made, that century is ours.

10   Do you not see that religions are growing weak and that the conception of the sanctity of rights is vanishing? Do you not see that mores are changing and that the moral conception of rights is being obliterated with them?

11   Do you not notice how on all sides beliefs are giving way to arguments, and feelings to calculations? If amid this universal collapse you do not succeed in linking the idea of rights to personal interest, which provides the only stable point in the human heart, what other means will be left to you to govern the world, if not fear?

12   So, then, when I am told that laws are feeble and the governed turbulent, that passions are lively and virtue powerless, and that in this situation one must not dream of increasing the rights of democracy, I answer

that it is for these very reasons that one must consider doing so, and in truth, I think the governments have an even greater interest in doing this than has society, for governments perish but society cannot die. . . .

13   It is incontestible that the people often manage public affairs very badly, but their concern therewith is bound to extend their mental horizon and shake them out of the rut of ordinary routine. A man of the people, when asked to share the task of governing society, acquires a certain self-esteem. Since he then has power, the brains of very enlightened people are put at his disposal. Constant efforts are made to enlist his support, and he learns from a thousand different efforts to deceive him. In politics he takes a part in undertakings he has not thought of, and they give him a general taste for enterprise. Daily new improvements to communal property are suggested to him, and that starts him wishing to improve his own. He may not be more virtuous or happier than his forebears, but he is more enlightened and active. I have no doubt that democratic institutions, combined with the physical nature of the land, are the indirect reason, and not, as is often claimed, the direct one, for the prodigious industrial expansion seen in the United States. It is not the laws' creation, but the people have learned to achieve it by making the laws.

14   When the enemies of democracy claim that a single man does his appointed task better than the government of all, I think they are right. There is more consistency in one man's rule than in that of a multitude, assuming equal enlightenment on either side; one man is more persevering, has more idea of the whole problem, attends more closely to details, and is a better judge of men. Anyone who denies that either has never seen a democratic republic or bases his view on too few examples. Democracy, even when local circumstances and the character of the people allow it to maintain itself, does not display a regular or methodical form of government. That is true. Democratic freedom does not carry its undertakings through as perfectly as an intelligent despotism would; it often abandons them before it has reaped the profit, or embarks on perilous ones; but in the long run it produces more; each thing is less well done, but more things are done. Under its sway it is not especially the things accomplished by the public administration that are great, but rather those things done without its help and beyond its sphere. Democracy does not provide a people with the most skillful of governments, but it does that which the most skillful government often cannot do: it spreads throughout the body social a restless activity, superabundant force, and energy never found elsewhere, which, however little favored by circumstance, can do wonders. Those are its true advantages.

15   In this century, when the destinies of the Christian world seem in suspense, some hasten to assail democracy as a hostile power while it is still growing; others already worship this new deity emerging from chaos. But both parties have an imperfect knowledge of the object of their hate or their desire; they fight in the dark and strike at random.

16   What do you expect from society and its government? We must be clear about that.

17   Do you wish to raise mankind to an elevated and generous view of the things of this world? Do you want to inspire men with a certain scorn of material goods? Do you hope to engender deep convictions and prepare the way for acts of profound devotion?

18   Are you concerned with refining mores, elevating manners, and causing the arts to blossom? Do you desire poetry, renown, and glory?

19   Do you set out to organize a nation so that it will have a powerful influence over all others? Do you expect it to attempt great enterprises and, whatever be the result of its efforts, to leave a great mark on history?

20   If in your view that should be the main object of men in society, do not support democratic government; it surely will not lead you to that goal.

21   But if you think it profitable to turn man's intellectual and moral activity toward the necessities of physical life and use them to produce well-being, if you think that reason is more use to men than genius, if your object is not to create heroic virtues but rather tranquil habits, if you would rather contemplate vices than crimes and prefer fewer transgressions at the cost of fewer splendid deeds, if in place of a brilliant society you are content to live in one that is prosperous, and finally, if in your view the main object of government is not to achieve the greatest strength or glory for the nation as a whole but to provide for every individual therein the utmost well-being, protecting him as far as possible from all afflictions, then it is good to make conditions equal and to establish a democratic government.

22   But if there is no time left to make a choice, and if a force beyond human control is already carrying you along regardless of your desires toward one of these types of government, then at least seek to derive from it all the good that it can do; understanding its good instincts as well as its evil inclinations, try to restrain the latter and promote the former.

Causes Tending to Maintain a Democratic Republic

23   Eighteenth-century philosophers had a very simple explanation for the gradual weakening of beliefs. Religious zeal, they said, was bound to die down as enlightenment and freedom spread. It is tiresome that the facts do not fit this theory at all.

24   There are sections of the population in Europe where unbelief goes hand in hand with brutishness and ignorance, whereas in America the most free and enlightened people in the world zealously perform all the external duties of religion.

25   The religious atmosphere of the country was the first thing that struck me on arrival in the United States. The longer I stayed in the country, the more conscious I became of the important political consequences resulting from this novel situation.

26   In France I had seen the spirits of religion and of freedom almost always marching in opposite directions. In America I found them intimately linked together in joint reign over the same land.

27   My longing to understand the reason for this phenomenon increased daily.

28   So long as a religion derives its strength from sentiments, instincts, and passions, which are reborn in like fashion in all periods of history, it can brave the assaults of time, or at least it can only be destroyed by another religion. But when a religion chooses to rely on the interests of this world, it becomes almost as fragile as all earthly powers. Alone, it may hope for immortality; linked to ephemeral powers, it follows their fortunes and often falls together with the passions of a day sustaining them.

29   Hence any alliance with any political power whatsoever is bound to be burdensome for religion. It does not need their support in order to live, and in serving them it may die.

30   The danger I have just pointed out exists at all times but is not always equally obvious.

31   There are centuries when governments appear immortal and others when society's existence seems frailer than that of a man.

32   Some constitutions keep the citizens in a sort of lethargic slumber, while others force them into feverish agitation.

33   When governments seem so strong and laws so stable, men do not see the danger that religion may run by allying itself with power.

34   When governments are clearly feeble and laws changeable, the danger is obvious to all, but often then there is no longer time to avoid it. One must therefore learn to perceive it from afar.

35   When a nation adopts a democratic social state and communities show republican inclinations, it becomes increasingly dangerous for religion to ally itself with authority. For the time is coming when power will pass from hand to hand, political theories follow one another, and men, laws, and even constitutions vanish or alter daily, and that not for a limited time but continually. Agitation and instability are natural elements in democratic republics, just as immobility and somnolence are the rule in absolute monarchies.

36   If the Americans, who change the head of state every four years, elect new legislators every two years and replace provincial administrators every year, and if the Americans, who have handed over the world of politics to the experiments of innovators, had not placed religion beyond their reach, what could it hold on to in the ebb and flow of human opinions? Amid the struggle of parties, where would the respect due to it be? What would become of its immortality when everything around it was perishing?

37   The American clergy were the first to perceive this truth and to act in conformity with it. They saw that they would have to give up religious influence if they wanted to acquire political power, and they preferred to lose the support of authority rather than to share its vicissitudes.

38   In America religion is perhaps less powerful than it has been at certain times and among certain peoples, but its influence is more lasting. It restricts itself to its own resources, of which no one can deprive it; it functions in one sphere only, but it pervades it and dominates there without effort.

BUILDING CONTEXT

1. Compare Tocqueville's observations about the American attitude to property with those of Franklin or Sinclair.

2. How does Tocqueville's analysis of religion in America compare to Crèvecoeur's? What significance can you find in the fact that both of these writers come from France?

3. Try to reconcile Tocqueville's observation about the lack of religious involvement in American politics with the views of Douglass, Stowe, or another writer.

Another Voice

THE UNITED STATES: THE GREATEST POEM
WALT WHITMAN

The Americans of all nations at any time upon the earth have probably the fullest poetical nature. The United States themselves are essentially the greatest poem. In the history of the earth hitherto the largest and most stirring appear tame and orderly to their ampler largeness and stir. Here at last is something in the doings of man that corresponds with the broadcast doings of the day and night. Here is not merely a nation but a teeming nation of nations. Here is action untied from strings necessarily blind to particulars and details magnificently moving in vast masses. Here is the hospitality which forever indicates heroes. . . . Here are the roughs and beards and space and ruggedness and nonchalance that the soul loves. Here the performance disdaining the trivial unapproached in the tremendous audacity of its crowds and groupings and the push of its perspective spreads with crampless and flowing breadth and showers its prolific and splendid extravagance. One sees it must indeed own the riches of the summer and winter, and need never be bankrupt while corn grows from the ground or the orchards drop apples or the bays contain fish or men beget children upon women.

Leaves of Grass, 1855

FURTHER STUDY

1. Place Tocqueville's views within the context of the Enlightenment or nineteenth-century liberalism.

2. Explore differing theories of the state—for example, those implied by isolationism, imperialism, or the belief "My country, right or wrong." List examples of countries that embody contrasting theories.

ADDITIONAL RESOURCES

Commager, Henry Steele. *Commager on Tocqueville.* Columbia: University of Missouri Press, 1993.

Eisenstadt, Abraham S., ed. *Reconsidering Tocqueville's Democracy in America.* New Brunswick: Rutgers University Press, 1988.

Masugi, Ken, ed. *Interpreting Tocqueville's Democracy in America.* Savage, Md.: Rowman & Littlefield Publishers, 1991.

Probst, George E., ed. *The Happy Republic: A Reader in Tocqueville's America.* New York: Harper, 1962.

RESEARCH KEYWORDS

Tocqueville	Democracy in America	Liberalism
State (Political Philosophy)	Social Democracy	Sociology
Natural Law	Locke (John)	Mill (John Stuart)

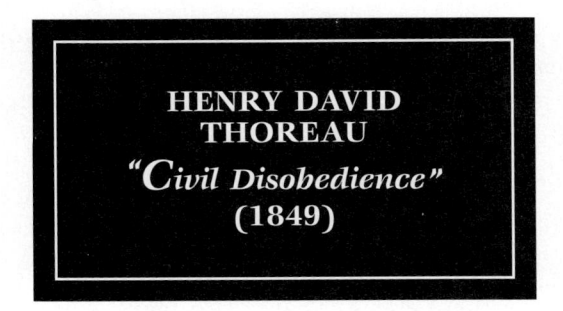

HENRY DAVID
THOREAU
"Civil Disobedience"
(1849)

"The only obligation which I have a right to assume is to do at any time what I think right."

Abolitionist, environmentalist, and quintessential individualist, Henry David Thoreau (1817–1862) championed personal ethics over conformity. *Walden* describes his two years of solitary life in a cabin in the woods—an experiment to prove that he could separate himself from society if necessary.

"Civil Disobedience," his protest against the Mexican War of 1846–48, became a basic text of the nonviolent protests of Martin Luther King, Jr., during the 1960s.

After graduating from Harvard College in 1837, Thoreau worked unsuccessfully at teaching, tutoring, and several menial jobs, all the while keeping a journal. His friend Ralph Waldo Emerson urged him to concentrate on his writing, and published many of his poems and essays in *The Dial*. The journals containing Thoreau's observations on nature grew to over two million words, and when published in 1906 filled fourteen volumes; the sections on the flora and fauna of Concord, Massachusetts, are still among the most complete natural history of any area in America.

An ardent abolitionist, Thoreau opposed the war with Mexico because it would have enlarged the slave territory. In protest, in 1846, while living at Walden, he refused to pay the poll tax and was imprisoned until his aunt paid it for him the next day. This experience led to a pamphlet entitled "Resistance to Civil Government," later reprinted as "Civil Disobedience." Thoreau continued his antislavery activities throughout his life; in violation of the Fugitive Slave Act he aided escaped slaves in reaching safety in Canada, and he supported John Brown's 1859 raid on Harpers Ferry.

Text: Henry David Thoreau; *Walden and Other Writings;* William Howarth, ed.; New York: Modern Library, 1981.

EXPLORING ISSUES IN THE TEXT

1. What are Thoreau's views of government (pars. 1–2) and majority rule (par. 4)? What practical implications do you find in these theories?

2. Explain why resistance to the government is the only proper course for an abolitionist (pars. 16–17).

3. Summarize Thoreau's understanding of the relationship between the individual and the state.

CIVIL DISOBEDIENCE

1 I heartily accept the motto,—"That government is best which governs least;" and I should like to see it acted up to more rapidly and systematically. Carried out, it finally amounts to this, which also I believe,—"That government is best which governs not at all;" and when men are prepared for it, that will be the kind of government which they will have. Government is at best but an expedient; but most governments are usually, and all governments are sometimes, inexpedient. The objections which have been brought against a standing army, and they are many and weighty, and deserve to prevail, may also at last be brought against a

standing government. The standing army is only an arm of the standing government. The government itself, which is only the mode which the people have chosen to execute their will, is equally liable to be abused and perverted before the people can act through it. Witness the present Mexican war, the work of comparatively a few individuals using the standing government as their tool; for, in the outset, the people would not have consented to this measure.

2   This American government,—what is it but a tradition, though a recent one, endeavoring to transmit itself unimpaired to posterity, but each instant losing some of its integrity? It has not the vitality and force of a single living man; for a single man can bend it to his will. It is a sort of wooden gun to the people themselves. But it is not the less necessary for this; for the people must have some complicated machinery or other, and hear its din, to satisfy that idea of government which they have. Governments show thus how successfully men can be imposed on, even impose on themselves, for their own advantage. It is excellent, we must all allow. Yet this government never of itself furthered any enterprise, but by the alacrity with which it got out of its way. *It* does not keep the country free. *It* does not settle the West. *It* does not educate. The character inherent in the American people has done all that has been accomplished; and it would have done somewhat more, if the government had not sometimes got in its way. For government is an expedient by which men would fain succeed in letting one another alone; and, as has been said, when it is most expedient, the governed are most let alone by it. Trade and commerce, if they were not made of India-rubber, would never manage to bounce over the obstacles which legislators are continually putting in their way; and, if one were to judge these men wholly by the effects of their actions and not partly by their intentions, they would deserve to be classed and punished with those mischievous persons who put obstructions on the railroads.

3   But, to speak practically and as a citizen, unlike those who call themselves no-government men, I ask for, not at once no government, but *at once* a better government. Let every man make known what kind of government would command his respect, and that will be one step toward obtaining it.

4   After all, the practical reason why, when the power is once in the hands of the people, a majority are permitted, and for a long period continue, to rule is not because they are most likely to be in the right, nor because this seems fairest to the minority, but because they are physically the strongest. But a government in which the majority rule in all cases cannot be based on justice, even as far as men understand it. Can there not be a government in which majorities do not virtually decide right and wrong, but conscience?—in which majorities decide only those questions to which the rule of expediency is applicable? Must the citizen ever for a moment, or in the least degree, resign his conscience to the legislator? Why has every man a conscience, then? I think that we should be men

first, and subjects afterward. It is not desirable to cultivate a respect for the law, so much as for the right. The only obligation which I have a right to assume is to do at any time what I think right. It is truly enough said, that a corporation has no conscience; but a corporation of conscientious men is a corporation *with* a conscience. Law never made men a whit more just; and, by means of their respect for it, even the well-disposed are daily made the agents of injustice. A common and natural result of an undue respect for law is, that you may see a file of soldiers, colonel, captain, corporal, privates, powdermonkeys, and all, marching in admirable order over hill and dale to the wars, against their wills, ay, against their common sense and consciences, which makes it very steep marching indeed, and produces a palpitation of the heart. They have no doubt that it is a damnable business in which they are concerned; they are all peaceably inclined. Now, what are they? Men at all? or small movable forts and magazines, at the service of some unscrupulous man in power? Visit the Navy-Yard, and behold a marine, such a man as an American government can make, or such as it can make a man with its black arts,—a mere shadow and reminiscence of humanity, a man laid out alive and standing, and already, as one may say, buried under arms with funeral accompaniments, though it may be,—

> "Not a drum was heard, not a funeral note,
> As his corse to the rampart we hurried;
> Not a soldier discharged his farewell shot
> O'er the grave where our hero we buried."

5   The mass of men serve the state thus, not as men mainly, but as machines, with their bodies. They are the standing army, and the militia, jailors, constables, posse comitatus, etc. In most cases there is no free exercise whatever of the judgment or of the moral sense; but they put themselves on a level with wood and earth and stones; and wooden men can perhaps be manufactured that will serve the purpose as well. Such command no more respect than men of straw or a lump of dirt. They have the same sort of worth only as horses and dogs. Yet such as these even are commonly esteemed good citizens. Others—as most legislators, politicians, lawyers, ministers, and office-holders—serve the state chiefly with their heads; and, as they rarely make any moral distinctions, they are as likely to serve the Devil, without *intending* it, as God. A very few, as heroes, patriots, martyrs, reformers in the great sense, and *men,* serve the state with their consciences also, and so necessarily resist it for the most part; and they are commonly treated as enemies by it. A wise man will only be useful as a man, and will not submit to be "clay," and "stop a hole to keep the wind away," but leave that office to his dust at least:—

> "I am too high-born to be propertied,
> To be a secondary at control,

> Or useful serving-man and instrument
> To any sovereign state throughout the world."

6   He who gives himself entirely to his fellow-men appears to them useless and selfish; but he who gives himself partially to them is pronounced a benefactor and philanthropist.

7   How does it become a man to behave toward this American government to-day? I answer, that he cannot without disgrace be associated with it. I cannot for an instant recognize that political organization as *my* government which is the *slave's* government also.

8   All men recognize the right of revolution; that is, the right to refuse allegiance to, and to resist, the government, when its tyranny or its inefficiency are great and unendurable. But almost all say that such is not the case now. But such was the case, they think, in the Revolution of '75. If one were to tell me that this was a bad government because it taxed certain foreign commodities brought to its ports, it is most probable that I should not make an ado about it, for I can do without them. All machines have their friction; and possibly this does enough good to counterbalance the evil. At any rate, it is a great evil to make a stir about it. But when the friction comes to have its machine, and oppression and robbery are organized, I say, let us not have such a machine any longer. In other words, when a sixth of the population of a nation which has undertaken to be the refuge of liberty are slaves, and a whole country is unjustly overrun and conquered by a foreign army, and subjected to military law, I think that it is not too soon for honest men to rebel and revolutionize. What makes this duty the more urgent is the fact that the country so overrun is not our own, but ours is the invading army. . . .

9   It is not a man's duty, as a matter of course, to devote himself to the eradication of any, even the most enormous wrong; he may still properly have other concerns to engage him; but it is his duty, at least, to wash his hands of it, and, if he gives it no thought longer, not to give it practically his support. If I devote myself to other pursuits and contemplations, I must first see, at least, that I do not pursue them sitting upon another man's shoulders. I must get off him first, that he may pursue his contemplations too. See what gross inconsistency is tolerated. I have heard some of my townsmen say, "I should like to have them order me out to help put down an insurrection of the slaves, or to march to Mexico;—see if I would go;" and yet these very men have each, directly by their allegiance, and so indirectly, at least, by their money, furnished a substitute. The soldier is applauded who refuses to serve in an unjust war by those who do not refuse to sustain the unjust government which makes the war; is applauded by those whose own act and authority he disregards and sets at naught; as if the state were penitent to that degree that it

hired one to scourge it while it sinned, but not to that degree that it left off sinning for a moment. Thus, under the name of Order and Civil Government, we are all made at last to pay homage to and support our own meanness. After the first blush of sin comes its indifference; and from immoral it becomes, as it were, *unmoral*, and not quite unnecessary to that life which we have made.

10   The broadest and most prevalent error requires the most disinterested virtue to sustain it. The slight reproach to which the virtue of patriotism is commonly liable, the noble are most likely to incur. Those who, while they disapprove of the character and measures of a government, yield to it their allegiance and support are undoubtedly its most conscientious supporters, and so frequently the most serious obstacles to reform. Some are petitioning the state to dissolve the Union, to disregard the requisitions of the President. Why do they not dissolve it themselves,—the union between themselves and the state,—and refuse to pay their quota into its treasury? Do not they stand in the same relation to the state that the state does to the Union? And have not the same reasons prevented the state from resisting the Union which have prevented them from resisting the state?

11   How can a man be satisfied to entertain an opinion merely, and enjoy *it?* Is there any enjoyment in it, if his opinion is that he is aggrieved? If you are cheated out of a single dollar by your neighbor, you do not rest satisfied with knowing that you are cheated, or with saying that you are cheated, or even with petitioning him to pay you your due; but you take effectual steps at once to obtain the full amount, and see that you are never cheated again. Action from principle, the perception and the performance of right, changes things and relations; it is essentially revolutionary, and does not consist wholly with anything which was. It not only divides states and churches, it divides families; ay, it divides the *individual,* separating the diabolical in him from the divine.

12   Unjust laws exist: shall we be content to obey them, or shall we endeavor to amend them, and obey them until we have succeeded, or shall we transgress them at once? Men generally, under such a government as this, think that they ought to wait until they have persuaded the majority to alter them. They think that, if they should resist, the remedy would be worse than the evil. But it is the fault of the government itself that the remedy *is* worse than the evil. *It* makes it worse. Why is it not more apt to anticipate and provide for reform? Why does it not cherish its wise minority? Why does it cry and resist before it is hurt? Why does it not encourage its citizens to be on the alert to point out its faults, and *do* better than it would have them? Why does it always crucify Christ, and excommunicate Copernicus and Luther, and pronounce Washington and Franklin rebels?

13   One would think, that a deliberate and practical denial of its authority was the only offense never contemplated by government; else, why has

it not assigned its definite, its suitable and proportionate penalty? If a man who has no property refuses but once to earn nine shillings for the state, he is put in prison for a period unlimited by any law that I know, and determined only by the discretion of those who placed him there; but if he should steal ninety times nine shillings from the state, he is soon permitted to go at large again.

14   If the injustice is part of the necessary friction of the machine of government, let it go, let it go: perchance it will wear smooth,—certainly the machine will wear out. If the injustice has a spring, or a pulley, or a rope, or a crank, exclusively for itself, then perhaps you may consider whether the remedy will not be worse than the evil; but if it is of such a nature that it requires you to be the agent of injustice to another, then, I say, break the law. Let your life be a counter friction to stop the machine. What I have to do is to see, at any rate, that I do not lend myself to the wrong which I condemn.

15   As for adopting the ways which the state has provided for remedying the evil, I know not of such ways. They take too much time, and a man's life will be gone. I have other affairs to attend to. I came into this world, not chiefly to make this a good place to live in, but to live in it, be it good or bad. A man has not everything to do, but something; and because he cannot do *everything,* it is not necessary that he should do *something* wrong. It is not my business to be petitioning the Governor or the Legislature any more than it is theirs to petition me; and if they should not hear my petition, what should I do then? But in this case the state has provided no way: its very Constitution is the evil. This may seem to be harsh and stubborn and unconciliatory; but it is to treat with the utmost kindness and consideration the only spirit that can appreciate or deserves it. So is all change for the better, like birth and death, which convulse the body.

16   I do not hesitate to say, that those who call themselves Abolitionists should at once effectually withdraw their support, both in person and property, from the government of Massachusetts and not wait till they constitute a majority of one, before they suffer the right to prevail through them. I think that it is enough if they have God on their side, without waiting for that other one. Moreover, any man more right than his neighbors constitutes a majority of one already.

17   I meet this American government, or its representative, the state government, directly, and face to face, once a year—no more—in the person of its tax-gatherer; this is the only mode in which a man situated as I am necessarily meets it; and it then says distinctly, Recognize me; and the simplest, most effectual, and, in the present posture of affairs, the indispensablest mode of treating with it on this head, of expressing your little satisfaction with and love for it, is to deny it then. My civil neighbor, the tax-gatherer, is the very man I have to deal with,—for it is, after all, with

men and not with parchment that I quarrel,—and he has voluntarily chosen to be an agent of the government. How shall he ever know well what he is and does as an officer of the government, or as a man, until he is obliged to consider whether he shall treat me, his neighbor, for whom he has respect, as a neighbor and well-disposed man, or as a maniac and disturber of the peace, and see if he can get over this obstruction to his neighborliness without a ruder and more impetuous thought or speech corresponding with his action. I know this well, that if one thousand, if one hundred, if ten men whom I could name,—if ten *honest* men only,— ay, if *one* HONEST man, in this State of Massachusetts, *ceasing to hold slaves,* were actually to withdraw from this copartnership, and be locked up in the county jail therefor, it would be the abolition of slavery in America. For it matters not how small the beginning may seem to be: what is once well done is done forever. But we love better to talk about it: that we say is our mission. Reform keeps many scores of newspapers in its service, but not one man. If my esteemed neighbor, the State's ambassador, who will devote his days to the settlement of the question of human rights in the Council Chamber, instead of being threatened with the prisons of Carolina, were to sit down the prisoner of Massachusetts, that State which is so anxious to foist the sin of slavery upon her sister,— though at present she can discover only an act of inhospitality to be the ground of a quarrel with her,—the Legislature would not wholly waive the subject the following winter.

18   Under a government which imprisons any unjustly, the true place for a just man is also a prison. The proper place to-day, the only place which Massachusetts has provided for her freer and less desponding spirits, is in her prisons, to be put out and locked out of the State by her own act, as they have already put themselves out by their principles. It is there that the fugitive slave, and the Mexican prisoner on parole, and the Indian come to plead the wrongs of his race should find them; on that separate, but more free and honorable ground, where the State places those who are not *with* her, but *against* her,—the only house in a slave State in which a free man can abide with honor. If any think that their influence would be lost there, and their voices no longer afflict the ear of the State, that they would not be as an enemy within its walls, they do not know by how much truth is stronger than error, nor how much more eloquently and effectively he can combat injustice who has experienced a little in his own person. Cast your whole vote, not a strip of paper merely, but your whole influence. A minority is powerless while it conforms to the majority; it is not even a minority then; but it is irresistible when it clogs by its whole weight. If the alternative is to keep all just men in prison, or give up war and slavery, the State will not hesitate which to choose. If a thousand men were not to pay their tax-bills this year, that would not be a violent and bloody measure, as it would be to pay them, and enable the State to com-

mit violence and shed innocent blood. This is, in fact, the definition of a peaceable revolution, if any such is possible. If the tax-gatherer, or any other public officer, asks me, as one has done, "But what shall I do?" my answer is, "If you really wish to do anything, resign your office." When the subject has refused allegiance, and the officer has resigned his office, then the revolution is accomplished. But even suppose blood should flow. Is there not a sort of blood shed when the conscience is wounded? Through this wound a man's real manhood and immortality flow out, and he bleeds to an everlasting death. I see this blood flowing now.

19   I have contemplated the imprisonment of the offender, rather than the seizure of his goods,—though both will serve the same purpose,—because they who assert the purest right, and consequently are most dangerous to a corrupt State, commonly have not spent much time in accumulating property. To such the State renders comparatively small service, and a slight tax is wont to appear exorbitant, particularly if they are obliged to earn it by special labor with their hands. If there were one who lived wholly without the use of money, the State itself would hesitate to demand it of him. But the rich man—not to make any invidious comparison—is always sold to the institution which makes him rich. Absolutely speaking, the more money, the less virtue; for money comes between a man and his objects, and obtains them for him; and it was certainly no great virtue to obtain it. It puts to rest many questions which he would otherwise be taxed to answer; while the only new question which it puts is the hard but superfluous one, how to spend it. Thus his moral ground is taken from under his feet. The opportunities of living are diminished in proportion as what are called the "means" are increased. The best thing a man can do for his culture when he is rich is to endeavor to carry out those schemes which he entertained when he was poor. Christ answered the Herodians according to their condition. "Show me the tribute-money," said he;—and one took a penny out of his pocket;—if you use money which has the image of Cæsar on it and which he has made current and valuable, that is, *if you are men of the State,* and gladly enjoy the advantages of Cæsar's government, then pay him back some of his own when he demands it. "Render therefore to Cæsar that which is Cæsar's, and to God those things which are God's,"— leaving them no wiser than before as to which was which; for they did not wish to know.

20   When I converse with the freest of my neighbors, I perceive that, whatever they may say about the magnitude and seriousness of the question, and their regard for the public tranquillity, the long and the short of the matter is, that they cannot spare the protection of the existing government, and they dread the consequences to their property and families of disobedience to it. For my own part, I should not like to think that I ever rely on the protection of the State. But, if I deny the authority of the State

when it presents its tax-bill, it will soon take and waste all my property, and so harass me and my children without end. This is hard. This makes it impossible for a man to live honestly, and at the same time comfortably, in outward respects. It will not be worth the while to accumulate property; that would be sure to go again. You must hire or squat somewhere, and raise but a small crop, and eat that soon. You must live within yourself, and depend upon yourself always tucked up and ready for a start, and not have many affairs. A man may grow rich in Turkey even, if he will be in all respects a good subject of the Turkish government. Confucius said: "If a state is governed by the principles of reason, poverty and misery are subjects of shame; if a state is not governed by the principles of reason, riches and honors are the subjects of shame." No: until I want the protection of Massachusetts to be extended to me in some distant Southern port, where my liberty is endangered, or until I am bent solely on building up an estate at home by peaceful enterprise, I can afford to refuse allegiance to Massachusetts, and her right to my property and life. It costs me less in every sense to incur the penalty of disobedience to the State than it would to obey. I should feel as if I were worth less in that case.

21   Some years ago, the State met me in behalf of the Church, and commanded me to pay a certain sum toward the support of a clergyman whose preaching my father attended, but never I myself. "Pay," it said, "or be locked up in the jail." I declined to pay, But, unfortunately, another man saw fit to pay it. I did not see why the schoolmaster should be taxed to support the priest, and not the priest the schoolmaster; for I was not the State's schoolmaster, but I supported myself by voluntary subscription. I did not see why the lyceum should not present its tax-bill, and have the State to back its demand, as well as the Church. However, at the request of the selectmen, I condescended to make some such statement as this in writing:—"Know all men by these presents, that I, Henry Thoreau, do not wish to be regarded as a member of any incorporated society which I have not joined." This I gave to the town clerk; and he has it. The State, having thus learned that I did not wish to be regarded as a member of that church, has never made a like demand on me since; though it said that it must adhere to its original presumption that time. If I had known how to name them, I should then have signed off in detail from all the societies which I never signed on to; but I did not know where to find a complete list.

22   I have paid no poll-tax for six years. I was put into a jail once on this account, for one night; and, as I stood considering the walls of solid stone, two or three feet thick, the door of wood and iron, a foot thick, and the iron grating which strained the light, I could not help being struck with the foolishness of that institution which treated me as if I were mere flesh and blood and bones, to be locked up. I wondered that it should have concluded at length that this was the best use it could put me to, and had never thought to avail itself of my services in some way.

I saw that, if there was a wall of stone between me and my townsmen, there was a still more difficult one to climb or break through before they could get to be as free as I was. I did not for a moment feel confined, and the walls seemed a great waste of stone and mortar. I felt as if I alone of all my townsmen had paid my tax. They plainly did not know how to treat me, but behaved like persons who are underbred. In every threat and in every compliment there was a blunder; for they thought that my chief desire was to stand the other side of that stone wall. I could not but smile to see how industriously they locked the door on my meditations, which followed them out again without let or hindrance, and *they* were really all that was dangerous. As they could not reach me, they had resolved to punish my body; just as boys, if they cannot come at some person against whom they have a spite, will abuse his dog. I saw that the State was half-witted, that it was timid as a lone woman with her silver spoons, and that it did not know its friends from its foes, and I lost all my remaining respect for it, and pitied it. . . .

23 When I came out of prison,—for some one interfered, and paid that tax,— I did not perceive that great changes had taken place on the common, such as he observed who went in a youth and emerged a tottering and gray-headed man; and yet a change had to my eyes come over the scene,—the town, and State, and country,—greater than any that mere time could effect. I saw yet more distinctly the State in which I lived. I saw to what extent the people among whom I lived could be trusted as good neighbors and friends; that their friendship was for summer weather only; that they did not greatly propose to do right; that they were a distinct race from me by their prejudices and superstitions, as the Chinamen and Malays are; that in their sacrifices to humanity they ran no risks, not even to their property; that after all they were not so noble but they treated the thief as he had treated them, and hoped, by a certain outward observance and a few prayers, and by walking in a particular straight though useless path from time to time, to save their souls. This may be to judge my neighbors harshly; for I believe that many of them are not aware that they have such an institution as the jail in their village.

24   It was formerly the custom in our village, when a poor debtor came out of jail, for his acquaintances to salute him, looking through their fingers, which were crossed to represent the grating of a jail window, "How do ye do?" My neighbors did not thus salute me, but first looked at me, and then at one another, as if I had returned from a long journey. I was put into jail as I was going to the shoemaker's to get a shoe which was mended. When I was let out the next morning, I proceeded to finish my errand, and, having put on my mended shoe, joined a huckleberry party, who were impatient to put themselves under my conduct; and in half an hour,—for the horse was soon tackled,—was in the midst of a huckleberry

field, on one of our highest hills, two miles off, and then the State was
nowhere to be seen.

25   This is the whole history of "My Prisons."

BUILDING CONTEXT

1. Try to explain the connection between Thoreau's experiment at Walden
   and his theory of civil disobedience.
2. Discuss how the function of government in the United States has changed
   since the time of Thoreau. Consider, for example, modern education and
   other tax-supported services.
3. Try to place Thoreau's idea of moral resistance within American values.

FURTHER STUDY

1. Investigate transcendentalism. Why did this philosophy appeal to many
   American intellectuals? How did it influence American values? What
   has become of it?
2. Explore Thoreau's influence on Dr. Martin Luther King, Jr., and the Civil
   Rights and Anti-War Movements of the 1960s.
3. Explore the history of environmentalism in America. How does it fit in
   with other American values? What have been the contributions of both
   Thoreau and Theodore Roosevelt?

ADDITIONAL RESOURCES

Madden, Edward H. *Civil Disobedience and Moral Law in Nineteenth-Century
American Philosophy.* Seattle: University of Washington Press, 1968.
Porte, Joel. *Transcendentalists in Conflict.* Middletown, Conn.: Wesleyan
University Press, 1966.
Richardson, Robert D. *Henry Thoreau: A Life of the Mind.* Berkeley: Univer-
sity of California Press, 1986.
Weber, David R., ed. *Civil Disobedience in America: A Documentary History.*
Ithaca, N.Y.: Cornell University Press, 1978.

RESEARCH KEYWORDS

Civil Disobedience
Government—Resistance to
King (Martin Luther, Jr.)
Transcendentalism
Walden
Environmentalism

Pacifism and Nonviolent Movements
Gandhi
Individualism
Emerson (Ralph Waldo)
Natural History

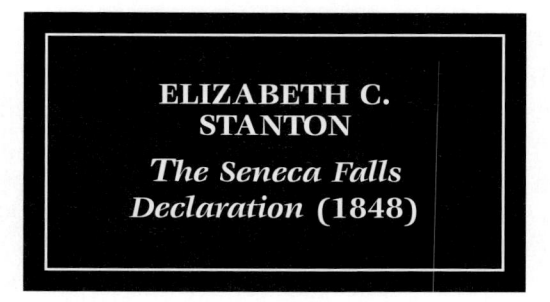

ELIZABETH C. STANTON

The Seneca Falls Declaration (1848)

"*We* hold these truths to be self-evident: that all men and women are created equal."

It might be said that Elizabeth Cady Stanton (1815–1902) had all the advantages of birth—except being male. Her maternal grandfather was a Revolutionary War hero. Her father was a member of the New York State legislature. She studied Greek, enjoyed outdoor sports, and was a skilled equestrian. Yet, when her only brother died when she was eleven, her father went into perpetual mourning. None of her accomplishments, or those of her four sisters, mattered to him. "I never felt more keenly the degradation of my sex," she wrote. "To think that all in me of which my father would have felt proper pride had I been a man is deeply mortifying because I am a woman."

Other degradations abounded. Though she excelled in mathematics and classics, no college accepted women. Though she observed close at hand her sister's unhappy marriage, New York allowed divorce only in cases of adultery, and then awarded the children to the husband. Though she married Henry Stanton, an abolitionist lecturer, and spent her honeymoon at the World Anti-Slavery Convention in London, she and other women delegates were excluded. She realized then that her life's work would focus on the "emancipation of women from the dogmas of the past, political, religious, and social."

In Boston, while insisting on being called Elizabeth Cady Stanton, rather than Mrs. Henry Stanton, she nonetheless settled into keeping house and raising her seven children. However, the presence of domestic help allowed her to attend concerts, theaters, and lectures in a city alive with the ideas of Ralph Waldo Emerson, William Lloyd Garrison, and other transcendentalists and abolitionists. But this ended when her husband moved the family to the small town of Seneca Falls in western New York. Here she experienced the lot of most women: "I now fully understood the practical difficulties women had to contend with in the isolated household and the impossibility of woman's best development if in contact the chief part of her life with servants and children."

A visit from Lucretia Mott burst the dam of frustration and revived the idea of emancipating women. The first Woman's Rights Convention was held five days later.

Text: Elizabeth C. Stanton, et al.; *History of Woman Suffrage;* Rochester, N.Y.: Charles Mann, 1881.

EXPLORING ISSUES IN THE TEXT

1. Consider the significance of the fact that the women who called the meeting considered themselves "fortunately organized and conditioned" (par. 2). How did this affect their priorities?

2. How serious do you find the charge that "Your grievances must be grievous indeed, when you are obliged to go to books in order to find them out" (par. 3)?

3. Explain the significance of using the Declaration of Independence as the model for the Declaration of Sentiments.

4. What do you make of the fact that men were asked to "take the laboring oar" (par. 4)?

THE SENECA FALLS DECLARATION

1   WOMAN'S RIGHTS CONVENTION.—A Convention to discuss the social, civil, and religious condition and rights of woman, will be held in the Wesleyan Chapel, at Seneca Falls, N.Y., on Wednesday and Thursday, the 19th and 20th of July, current; commencing at 10 o'clock A.M. During the first day the meeting will be exclusively for women, who are earnestly invited to attend. The public generally are invited to be present on the second day, when Lucretia Mott, of Philadelphia, and other ladies and gentlemen, will address the convention.

2   This call, without signature, was issued by Lucretia Mott, Martha C. Wright, Elizabeth Cady Stanton, and Mary Ann McClintock. At this time Mrs. Mott was visiting her sister Mrs. Wright, at Auburn, and attending the Yearly Meeting of Friends in Western New York. Mrs. Stanton, having recently removed from Boston to Seneca Falls, finding the most congenial associations in Quaker families, met Mrs. Mott incidentally for the first time since her residence there. They at once returned to the topic they had so often discussed, walking arm in arm in the streets of London, and Boston, "the propriety of holding a woman's convention." These four ladies, sitting round the tea-table of Richard Hunt, a prominent Friend near Waterloo, decided to put their long-talked-of resolution into action, and before the twilight deepened into night, the call was written, and sent to the *Seneca County Courier.* On Sunday morning they met in Mrs. McClintock's parlor to write their declaration, resolutions, and to consider subjects for speeches. As the convention was to assemble in three days, the time was short for such productions; but having no experience in the *modus operandi* of getting up conventions, nor in that kind of literature, they were quite innocent of the herculean labors they proposed. On the first attempt to frame a resolution; to crowd a complete thought, clearly and concisely, into three lines; they felt as helpless and hopeless as if they had been suddenly asked to construct a steam engine. And the

humiliating fact may as well now be recorded that before taking the initiative step, those ladies resigned themselves to a faithful perusal of various masculine productions. The reports of Peace, Temperance, and Anti-Slavery conventions were examined, but all alike seemed too tame and pacific for the inauguration of a rebellion such as the world had never before seen. They knew women had wrongs, but how to state them was the difficulty, and this was increased from the fact that they themselves were fortunately organized and conditioned; they were neither "sour old maids," "childless women," nor "divorced wives," as the newspapers declared them to be. While they had felt the insults incident to sex, in many ways, as every proud, thinking woman must, in the laws, religion, and literature of the world, and in the invidious and degrading sentiments and customs of all nations, yet they had not in their own experience endured the coarser forms of tyranny resulting from unjust laws, or association with immoral and unscrupulous men, but they had souls large enough to feel the wrongs of others, without being scarified in their own flesh.

3   After much delay, one of the circle took up the Declaration of 1776, and read it aloud with much spirit and emphasis, and it was at once decided to adopt the historic document, with some slight changes such as substituting "all men" for "King George." Knowing that women must have more to complain of than men under any circumstances possibly could, and seeing the Fathers had eighteen grievances, a protracted search was made through statute books, church usages, and the customs of society to find that exact number. Several well-disposed men assisted in collecting the grievances, until, with the announcement of the eighteenth, the women felt they had enough to go before the world with a good case. One youthful lord remarked, "Your grievances must be grievous indeed, when you are obliged to go to books in order to find them out."

4   The eventful day dawned at last, and crowds in carriages and on foot, wended their way to the Wesleyan church. When those having charge of the Declaration, the resolutions, and several volumes of the Statutes of New York arrived on the scene, lo! the door was locked. However, an embryo Professor of Yale College was lifted through an open window to unbar the door; that done, the church was quickly filled. It had been decided to have no men present, but as they were already on the spot, and as the women who must take the responsibility of organizing the meeting, and leading the discussions, shrank from doing either, it was decided, in a hasty council around the altar, that this was an occasion when men might make themselves pre-eminently useful. It was agreed they should remain, and take the laboring oar through the Convention.

5   James Mott, tall and dignified, in Quaker costume, was called to the chair; Mary McClintock appointed Secretary, Frederick Douglass, Samuel Tillman, Ansel Bascom, E. W. Capron, and Thomas McClintock took part throughout in the discussions. Lucretia Mott, accustomed to public speaking in the Society of Friends, stated the objects of the Convention, and in taking a survey of the degraded condition of woman the world over,

showed the importance of inaugurating some movement for her education and elevation. Elizabeth and Mary McClintock, and Mrs. Stanton, each read a well-written speech; Martha Wright read some satirical articles she had published in the daily papers answering the diatribes on woman's sphere. Ansel Bascom, who had been a member of the Constitutional Convention recently held in Albany, spoke at length on the property bill for married women, just passed the Legislature, and the discussion on woman's rights in that Convention. Samuel Tillman, a young student of law, read a series of the most exasperating statutes for women, from English and American jurists, all reflecting the *tender mercies* of men toward their wives, in taking care of their property and protecting them in their civil rights.

6   The Declaration having been freely discussed by many present, was re-read by Mrs. Stanton, and with some slight amendments adopted.

7   *Declaration of Sentiments.* When, in the course of human events, it becomes necessary for one portion of the family of man to assume among the people of the earth a position different from that which they have hitherto occupied, but one to which the laws of nature and of nature's God entitle them, a decent respect to the opinions of mankind requires that they should declare the causes that impel them to such a course.

8   We hold these truths to be self-evident: that all men and women are created equal; that they are endowed by their Creator with certain inalienable rights; that among these are life, liberty, and the pursuit of happiness; that to secure these rights governments are instituted, deriving their just powers from the consent of the governed. Whenever any form of government becomes destructive of these ends, it is the right of those who suffer from it to refuse allegiance to it, and to insist upon the institution of a new government, laying its foundation on such principles, and organizing its powers in such form, as to them shall seem most likely to effect their safety and happiness. Prudence, indeed, will dictate that governments long established should not be changed for light and transient causes; and accordingly all experience hath shown that mankind are more disposed to suffer, while evils are sufferable, than to right themselves by abolishing the forms to which they were accustomed. But when a long train of abuses and usurpations, pursuing invariably the same object evinces a design to reduce them under absolute despotism, it is their duty to throw off such government, and to provide new guards for their future security. Such has been the patient sufferance of the women under this government, and such is now the necessity which constrains them to demand the equal station to which they are entitled.

9   The history of mankind is a history of repeated injuries and usurpations on the part of man toward woman, having in direct object the establishment of an absolute tyranny over her. To prove this, let facts be submitted to a candid world.

10   He has never permitted her to exercise her inalienable right to the elective franchise.

11   He has compelled her to submit to laws, in the formation of which she had no voice.

12   He has withheld from her rights which are given to the most ignorant and degraded men—both natives and foreigners.

13   Having deprived her of this first right of a citizen, the elective franchise, thereby leaving her without representation in the halls of legislation, he has oppressed her on all sides.

14   He has made her, if married, in the eye of the law, civilly dead.

15   He has taken from her all right in property, even to the wages she earns.

16   He has made her, morally, an irresponsible being, as she can commit many crimes with impunity, provided they be done in the presence of her husband. In the covenant of marriage, she is compelled to promise obedience to her husband, he becoming, to all intents and purposes, her master—the law giving him power to deprive her of her liberty, and to administer chastisement.

17   He has so framed the laws of divorce, as to what shall be the proper causes, and in case of separation, to whom the guardianship of the children shall be given, as to be wholly regardless of the happiness of women—the law, in all cases, going upon a false supposition of the supremacy of man, and giving all power into his hands.

18   After depriving her of all rights as a married woman, if single, and the owner of property, he has taxed her to support a government which recognizes her only when her property can be made profitable to it.

19   He has monopolized nearly all the profitable employments, and from those she is permitted to follow, she receives but a scanty remuneration. He closes against her all the avenues to wealth and distinction which he considers most honorable to himself. As a teacher of theology, medicine, or law, she is not known.

20   He has denied her the facilities for obtaining a thorough education, all colleges being closed against her.

21   He allows her in Church, as well as State, but a subordinate position, claiming Apostolic authority for her exclusion from the ministry, and, with some exceptions, from any public participation in the affairs of the Church.

22   He has created a false public sentiment by giving to the world a different code of morals for men and women, by which moral delinquencies which exclude women from society, are not only tolerated, but deemed of little account in man.

23   He has usurped the prerogative of Jehovah himself, claiming it as his right to assign for her a sphere of action, when that belongs to her conscience and to her God.

24   He has endeavored, in every way that he could, to destroy her confidence in her own powers, to lessen her self-respect, and to make her willing to lead a dependent and abject life.

25 Now, in view of this entire disfranchisement of one-half the people of this country, their social and religious degradation—in view of the unjust laws above mentioned, and because women do feel themselves aggrieved, oppressed, and fraudulently deprived of their most sacred rights, we insist that they have immediate admission to all the rights and privileges which belong to them as citizens of the United States.

26 In entering upon the great work before us, we anticipate no small amount of misconception, misrepresentation, and ridicule; but we shall use every instrumentality within our power to effect our object. We shall employ agents, circulate tracts, petition the State and National legislatures, and endeavor to enlist the pulpit and the press in our behalf. We hope this Convention will be followed by a series of Conventions embracing every part of the country.

27 The following resolutions were discussed by Lucretia Mott, Thomas and Mary Ann McClintock, Amy Post, Catharine A. F. Stebbins, and others, and were adopted:

28 WHEREAS, The great precept of nature is conceded to be, that "man shall pursue his own true and substantial happiness." Blackstone in his Commentaries remarks, that this law of Nature being coeval with mankind, and dictated by God himself, is of course superior in obligation to any other. It is binding over all the globe, in all countries and at all times; no human laws are of any validity if contrary to this, and such of them as are valid, derive all their force, and all their validity, and all their authority, mediately and immediately, from this original; therefore,

29 *Resolved,* That such laws as conflict, in any way, with the true and substantial happiness of woman, are contrary to the great precept of nature and of no validity, for this is "superior in obligation to any other."

30 *Resolved,* That all laws which prevent woman from occupying such a station in society as her conscience shall dictate, or which place her in a position inferior to that of man, are contrary to the great precept of nature, and therefore of no force or authority.

31 *Resolved,* That woman is man's equal—was intended to be so by the Creator, and the highest good of the race demands that she should be recognized as such.

32 *Resolved,* That the women of this country ought to be enlightened in regard to the laws under which they live, that they may no longer publish their degradation by declaring themselves satisfied with their present position, nor their ignorance, by asserting that they have all the rights they want.

33 *Resolved,* That inasmuch as man, while claiming for himself intellectual superiority, does accord to woman moral superiority, it is pre-eminently his duty to encourage her to speak and teach, as she has an opportunity, in all religious assemblies.

34   *Resolved,* That the same amount of virtue, delicacy, and refinement of behavior that is required of woman in the social state, should also be required of man, and the same transgressions should be visited with equal severity on both man and woman.

35   *Resolved,* That the objection of indelicacy and impropriety, which is so often brought against woman when she addresses a public audience, comes with a very ill-grace from those who encourage, by their attendance, her appearance on the stage, in the concert, or in feats of the circus.

36   *Resolved,* That woman has too long rested satisfied in the circumscribed limits which corrupt customs and a perverted application of the Scriptures have marked out for her, and that it is time she should move in the enlarged sphere which her great Creator has assigned her.

37   *Resolved,* That it is the duty of the women of this country to secure to themselves their sacred right to the elective franchise.

38   *Resolved,* That the equality of human rights results necessarily from the fact of the identity of the race in capabilities and responsibilities.

39   *Resolved, therefore,* That, being invested by the Creator with the same capabilities, and the same consciousness of responsibility for their exercise, it is demonstrably the right and duty of woman, equally with man, to promote every righteous cause by every righteous means; and especially in regard to the great subjects of morals and religion, it is self-evidently her right to participate with her brother in teaching them, both in private and in public, by writing and by speaking, by any instrumentalities proper to be used, and in any assemblies proper to be held; and this being a self-evident truth growing out of the divinely implanted principles of human nature, any custom or authority adverse to it, whether modern or wearing the hoary sanction of antiquity, is to be regarded as a self-evident falsehood, and at war with mankind.

40 At the last session Lucretia Mott offered and spoke to the following resolution:

41   *Resolved,* That the speedy success of our cause depends upon the zealous and untiring efforts of both men and women, for the overthrow of the monopoly of the pulpit, and for the securing to woman an equal participation with men in the various trades, professions, and commerce.

42   The only resolution that was not unanimously adopted was the ninth, urging the women of the country to secure to themselves the elective franchise. Those who took part in the debate feared a demand for the right to vote would defeat others they deemed more rational, and make the whole movement ridiculous.

43   But Mrs. Stanton and Frederick Douglass seeing that the power to choose rulers and make laws, was the right by which all others could be

secured, persistently advocated the resolution, and at last carried it by a small majority.

44   Thus it will be seen that the Declaration and resolutions in the very first Convention, demanded all the most radical friends of the movement have since claimed—such as equal rights in the universities, in the trades, and professions; the right to vote; to share in all political offices, honors, and emoluments; to complete equality in marriage, to personal freedom, property, wages, children; to make contracts; to sue, and be sued; and to testify in courts of justice. At this time the condition of married women under the Common Law, was nearly as degraded as that of the slave on the Southern plantation. The Convention continued through two entire days, and late in the evenings. The deepest interest was manifested to its close.

45   The proceedings were extensively published, unsparingly ridiculed by the press, and denounced by the pulpit, much to the surprise and chagrin of the leaders. Being deeply in earnest, and believing their demands pre-eminently wise and just, they were wholly unprepared to find themselves the target for the jibes and jeers of the nation. The Declaration was signed by one hundred men, and women, many of whom withdrew their names as soon as the storm of ridicule began to break. The comments of the press were carefully preserved, and it is curious to see that the same old arguments, and objections rife at the start, are reproduced by the press of to-day. But the brave protests sent out from this Convention touched a responsive chord in the hearts of women all over the country.

BUILDING CONTEXT

1. Which charges in paragraphs 9–24 could Elizabeth Cady Stanton formulate without having to search through law books?

2. Describe your reaction to the charges referred to in question 1. Which of them do you find to be true today?

3. Explain the assertion that "man, while claiming for himself intellectual superiority, does accord to woman moral superiority" (par. 33). What is the practical effect of this belief? Who benefits from it? Consider the attitudes of Stowe and Millett.

FURTHER STUDY

1. Analyze the contribution of the Quakers or abolitionists to the Woman's Movement. Research the contributions of African Americans, such as Frederick Douglass.

2. Investigate the impact of the Woman's Rights Movement on the Women's Labor Movement, and the role of working-class women in feminism.

What are the goals of the two movements? How do these goals determine allies and antagonists?

ADDITIONAL RESOURCES

Foner, Philip S., ed. *Frederick Douglass on Women's Rights.* Westport, Conn.: Greenwood Press, 1976.

Hersh, Blanche Glassman. *The Slavery of Sex: Feminist-Abolitionists in America.* Urbana: University of Illinois Press, 1978.

Rossi, Alice, ed. *The Feminist Papers: From Adams to Beauvoir.* Boston: Northeastern University Press, 1973.

Ruether, Rosemary Radford, and Rosemary Skinner Keller, ed. *Women and Religion in America.* San Francisco: Harper & Row, 1981.

RESEARCH KEYWORDS

Feminism   Woman's Rights
Abolitionism   Friends (Society of)

CAROL HYMOWITZ AND MICHAELE WEISSMAN
"On the Loom: The First Factory Women" (1978)

"When the mills were new, many of the women who worked in them felt a pioneering spirit—a sense . . . that they were contributing to the widening of woman's sphere."

Classification means grouping items according to similar traits. But which traits? How do we decide whether a trait is significant or merely coincidental? Is it more important to an Irish woman factory worker that she is a woman, a factory worker, Irish, or white? The following excerpt illustrates some of the problems of personal identification and group formation. The first women who worked in the textile mills saw themselves as pioneers creating a new world for women—that of financial and social independence. Yet they did not immediately collaborate with black and immigrant Irish women. The mill workers believed that marriage would free them from the labor force; black and immigrant women expected to work throughout their lives. On the other hand, working-class men did not sympathize with working women, whom they saw primarily as women, not fellow workers. And finally, the Woman's Rights Movement gave little thought to working women because, as a class, their concerns differed from those of the early feminists.

Text: Carol Hymowitz and Michaele Weissman; *A History of Women in America;* New York: Bantam Books, 1978.

EXPLORING ISSUES IN THE TEXT

1. Examine the relationship between work and values (pars. 6–8). Why were some factory jobs immediately defined as being for women only?

2. What is the implication of the effort to protect the morals of the workers (pars. 11–13)? Why did the workers need protecting?

3. Analyze the movement for self-improvement among factory workers (pars. 19–22). What were its goals? What form did it take?

4. Review the factors that led to disillusionment and the rise of labor unrest (pars. 23–27). What light does the early labor movement shed on the formation of group identity (pars. 28–32)?

ON THE LOOM: THE FIRST FACTORY WOMEN

1   The development of an industrial economy in the 1800s changed the definition of women's work. All women continued to work in their homes, but only those who earned money for their labor were called working women.

2   Working women in the 1800s were usually schoolteachers, seamstresses, domestics, and factory operatives. None of these jobs provided women with status or a decent wage. Teaching was the most respectable job available to an unmarried woman who needed to earn a living. Most female schoolteachers began working while still in their teens. Those who did not marry and remained schoolteachers were doomed to a life of genteel poverty because of extremely low wages.

3   Throughout the 1800s household service provided employment for more women than any other occupation. Because few native-born white women were willing to do domestic work outside their own homes, it was generally new arrivals and free black women who worked as household servants. Domestics worked long hours, their pay was meager, and privacy and leisure time were practically nonexistent.

4   The emergence of an industrial economy created new conditions for working women. From the start of the Industrial Revolution women were needed to mass-produce the goods they had once produced for

their families. Manufacturing was done both in the home and in factories. In general, married women who needed to earn wages worked at home while single women were hired to work in factories.

5 The most common home-manufacturing trade for women was sewing for the emerging ready-made clothing industry. In Troy, New York, the "collar and cuff capital" of the nation, hundreds of women worked at home making these items. Troy manufacturers delivered the raw materials to women at home and later picked up the finished products.

6 In the early 1800s home sewing for the ready-made clothing industry was considered "respectable" work for native-born white women. The work was considered an extension of women's traditional roles, since they had always sewn for their families. Now, doing the same kind of work on a larger scale, they could earn wages.

7 By the mid-1800s the nature of the home sewing industry had changed drastically; the work was done only by the poorest of native-born and immigrant women. In large cities such as New York and Chicago clothing manufacturers bought whole blocks of tenements and leased them to workers. Within these tenement sweatshops women and children labored for starvation wages.

8 This same pattern can be seen in the employment of single women in the textile mills of New England. In the 1820s and 1830s, after the invention of the spinning jenny and the power loom, textile mills sprang up in towns throughout New England, wherever there was a river to supply water power. Work in the mills was considered an excellent opportunity for unmarried women. There seemed to be little difference between a woman working a spinning wheel at home and a woman working a loom in a mill. The added attraction was that now women could earn money for their work. It was said that the mills would save young women from "idleness and its inseparable attendants, vice and guilt." The "golden opportunity" that the mills seemed to promise, however, proved to be illusory.

9 Francis Cabot Lowell, scion of an illustrious American family and a pioneer in the American textile industry, promoted the idea of female factory workers when he founded what was to become the most famous mill town in the nation. Young single women were in many ways the most likely candidates for employment by Lowell. Most of the New England men were needed on farms, and married women had families to care for. Single women who had finished school but were not yet absorbed in households of their own were available and already skilled in the work of making cloth. They could be recruited at one-third to one-half the wages demanded by men.

10 During the 1820s and 1830s single women from Massachusetts, New Hampshire, Vermont, and Maine traveled to the mill towns to sign up for work. The mill owners demanded twelve to thirteen hours of labor a day, six days a week, and each worker had to agree to work for at least one year. There was no shortage of workers. Most of the women were between

the ages of sixteen and twenty-five, the daughters of poor farmers, fiancees of seamen, and young widows. These women, with such "old fashioned country names" as Samantha, Leafy, and Almaretta, girls with yearnings for town culture and independence from their families, were easily convinced that both could be found in the mills. . . .

11   During these early years women workers were treated to a heavy dose of paternalism. Mill owners were eager to show the public that factory labor and life in the mill towns would not damage the morals of young women. To "protect" the women, they watched over them at all times, outside the mills as well as within them. All mill girls were required to live in company-built boarding houses, each housing twelve to thirteen workers. The atmosphere within the boarding house was like that in a strict girls' seminary. Widows who leased and managed the houses were instructed to report the names of any girls who stayed out late (after 10 o'clock at night) or complained in any way about their work or life in the mill towns. Anyone who was reported was promptly fired.

12   Women workers were lectured on the importance of honesty, cleanliness, frugality, and punctuality. Workers in Lowell, the show place of the textile industry, were expected to uphold the company's reputation. They were required to sign contracts promising to demonstrate "on all occasions, both in their work and by their actions . . . that they are penetrated by a laudable love of temperance and virtue and animated by their moral and social obligations." They were also required to attend church regularly. Those who did not purchase pews had their pay docked and were refused mail service at the company post office.

13   For the most part the first generation of mill girls complied with the rules and regulations. They came from Yankee, Puritan families and had been reared on hard work, duty, and usefulness. Before they could enter the mills, they had to convince their parents that they would not succumb to the temptations of town life such as fine clothes, dancing, or gossiping.

14   When the mills were new, many of the women who worked in them felt a pioneering spirit—a sense, as Harriet Robinson noted, that they were contributing to the widening of woman's sphere. They were opening the way for unmarried women to live on their own, independent of parents or husbands. Most important, these first factory women thought of their work as temporary. They hoped to stay in the mills for a few years, save money, and move on. Some wanted to continue their educations, some to find better work, others to marry.

15   This feeling of impermanence among mill workers was extremely beneficial to mill owners. As long as women did not think of themselves as permanently bound to the mills, they did not spend much time questioning the inequities of the factory system. As long as they had families to return to, they could leave the mills when they were worn out or ill. "Upon any embarrassment," wrote one Lowell company backer, "they return to

their country homes and do not sink down here a helpless caste clamoring for work, starving unless employed, and hence ready for a riot."

16   So long as mill girls could leave the factory, they did not think of themselves as being very different from the majority of American women, who lived on farms. But factory women were aware that they were not members of the new class of town ladies; very often they wrote about being "mistaken for ladies" when they went to church or walked about the town. Concerning this awareness, Lucy Larcom remarked, "We did not forget that we were working girls, wearing coarse aprons, and that there was some danger of our becoming drudges."

17   In whatever ways they could, the early mill girls sought to guard themselves against that danger. Women who worked in the mills for four, five, or even eight years insisted that "at longest our employment was only to be temporary." They clung to the belief that they as much as any American women had the right to be ladies. And they nurtured the hope of finding prosperous middle-class husbands who would support them in ladylike style.

18   Many of the early mill girls spent their hard-earned wages on fashionable clothing, so that in church no one could tell the difference between them and "the daughters of the first families of the town." They read *Godey's Lady's Book* and spouted all the pious, romantic and domestic sentiments espoused by Sarah Hale. Their advice to men, wrote Harriet Robinson, was, "Treat every maiden with respect, for you do not know whose *wife* she shall be."

19   Becoming a lady through marriage was one way of guarding against the "danger of becoming drudges." The other way was through self-improvement. In the early days mill girls believed fervently in the power of religion, culture, and learning. Eager for education and determined to benefit from life in the towns, they devoted themselves to numerous self-improvement activities. They read avidly, even in the mills where books were forbidden. Lucy Larcom tore pages from her Bible, sneaked them into the mills, and read them at her loom whenever the overseer was not watching.

20   In the evenings, after twelve to thirteen hours of work, mill girls somehow found the energy to meet in groups where they studied literature and foreign languages. They flocked to lectures, making up two-thirds of the Lyceum audiences in Lowell throughout the 1830s and 1840s. On Sundays, their one free day, the girls went both to church and to church school. In 1843 Lowell had fourteen religious societies. Ten of these were Sabbath Schools, containing over five thousand teachers and students. Three-quarters of these were mill girls.

21   Nowhere was the theme of self-improvement more touted than in the pages of the Lowell *Offering,* a monthly magazine edited by two former mill operatives, which began publication in 1841. Editor Harriet Farley believed that as long as workers achieved learning and culture, they did

not need to worry about conditions in the factory. The purpose of the *Offering* was "to provide mill girls with sweetness and light" and to prove to the world that there was "Mind Among the Spindles."

22   The *Offering* claimed to be the voice of the mill girls, but as a rule it spoke for factory owners. Some operatives did submit stories and poetry; only those that stressed virtue and gentility were printed. By the 1840s mill girls had a message to communicate which the *Offering* would never publish. . . .

23   By the 1840s some mill girls were beginning to realize that they might be stuck in the mills for much longer than they had imagined. Many girls no longer had families to return to, as their fathers had lost their farms during the depression of 1837. At the same time, the deteriorating conditions in the factories did away with the dream of self-improvement as an escape. By the 1840s few mill girls had the money to buy church pews, let alone the energy to attend study groups in the evenings.

24   Harriet Farley, editor of the *Offering,* insisted that if mill girls would arm themselves with learning and culture, they could protect themselves from the "power of the machine." Most of the women saw this argument as a whitewash of factory conditions. But Farley refused to print the many articles stressing the need for factory improvements. Wages and hours, Farley insisted, were matters over which "workers have no control." Improvements would come in time as a result of the kindheartedness of the owners.

25   At this juncture several mill girls denounced the *Offering* as a company mouthpiece and began publishing their own "Factory Tracts" in which they could write freely. Such papers as the *Factory Girl,* the *Factory Girls' Album,* and most especially the *Voice of Industry,* begun in 1845 and for a time edited and managed by Lowell workers, marked the beginning of the American labor press. These journals encouraged mill girls to think about the inequities of the factory system. "What glorious privilege we enjoy in this boasted republican land," wrote one girl. "Here I am a healthy New England girl, quite well behaved, bestowing just half of all my hours, including Sundays, upon a company for less than two cents an hour." This and similar articles helped to promote a new organization among mill workers—the Female Labor Reform Association. Twelve workers in Lowell started the first association in 1845. Within six months it had five hundred members, all rallying to their motto, "Try Again."

26   Sarah Bagley, a weaver who had worked in the mills for eight years, was elected president. She was a highly effective leader, who played a major role in organizing women in Lowell and many other New England mill towns. When owners tried to blacklist Association members, Bagley used the *Voice of Industry* to trumpet her outrage. . . .

27   Though working women sought alliances with working men in such groups as the New England Workingman's Association, and though they

supported the struggles of men to win economic rights, men did not consider women equals in this struggle. There were a number of reasons why working men failed to support their female counterparts. Many men believed that economic justice would be achieved when they could afford to keep their daughters and wives out of the factories. The object was to rid factories of women rather than improve conditions for them. Other trade unionists were convinced that because working women were paid one-third to one-half of men's wages, they were underbidding male salaries and threatening jobs for men. The easiest solution to this imagined threat was to drive women from the trades and bar them from unions. That is exactly what happened when national unions began emerging at the time of the Civil War. Of the thirty such labor groups that existed in 1873, only two admitted women.

28   In reality few women posed a threat to men's jobs. Women did not work in such heavy "central" industries as railroads, steel, or mining, and jobs in factories and the manufacturing industries were sex-segregated. When employers hired women, they hired them for the least skilled jobs, which were marked "Female Only." Some working men understood the situation, but they failed to recognize the importance of organizing the lowest level of workers. Only a few far-sighted working men realized that their own success depended on "strengthening the weakest part of the labor forces, for the main strength of the capitalist class consisted in the divisions existing in labor's ranks."

29   Unfortunately the women's rights movement was equally blind to the predicament of working women. In 1848, while the Female Labor Reform Association was dying, the women's rights movement was being born. In her Declaration of Rights and Sentiments, Elizabeth Cady Stanton spoke out for the rights of working women. Several female factory workers and women in the home manufacturing trades, such as Charlotte Woodward, attended the Seneca Falls convention. However, none of the founding feminists made contact with women workers in the mills and other industries, nor did Bagley and her followers get in touch with feminists. The interests of feminists and working women were different. Feminists wanted rights their men already had, while the central issue for working women—economic inequity—was one they shared with their men.

30   The myth of the comfortable and healthy life led by women who worked in the mills survived for twenty years. By the late 1840s no one believed any longer that factory work was a blessing. The population of factory workers was changing; and with that change, conditions deteriorated further.

31   Millions of new immigrants were beginning to arrive in America. Among them were Irish men and women driven out of their country by the catastrophic famine of 1846. The availability of poor Irish women enabled mill owners to get rid of native-born operatives, who had begun to

assert themselves. Between 1845 and 1850 the population in the mills changed dramatically. In 1845, 90 percent of the mill girls were native-born, and only 7 percent were Irish. Five years later, 50 percent were Irish.

32   In time Irish mill workers fought for improved conditions just as the Yankee operatives had, facing many of the same difficulties. Irish-American working women in other industries—such women as Augusta Lewis of the typesetters and Kate Mullaney of the Troy collar and cuff workers—followed in the tradition of Sarah Bagley, becoming leaders of the women's labor movement in the decades following the Civil War.

BUILDING CONTEXT

1. Contrast the concerns of women factory workers and the women at the Seneca Falls convention. What accounts for their differences?

2. Compare the concerns of women and men workers, as explained, for example, by Hymowitz and Weissman on the one hand, and Dawley and Faler on the other. How does Millett's theory of sexual politics shed light on the differences?

3. What do you think accounts for the popularity of self-improvement societies among women? Consider, for example, the reading clubs mentioned by Hymowitz and Weissman, the temperance movement, or the interest in literature discussed by Howells.

FURTHER STUDY

1. Investigate attitudes toward women in the nineteenth century. What did contemporary writers—both men and women—consider to be a woman's nature and role in society? What was expected of them? What part did class play in defining the place of women? You might want to explore "the cult of true womanhood."

2. Examine the contribution of women to the labor movement or the contribution of working women to the Woman's Rights Movement. Consider especially whether the situation has changed between the early and current stages of these movements.

ADDITIONAL RESOURCES

Cott, Nancy F., ed. *Root of Bitterness.* New York: Dutton, 1972.

Welter, Barbara. "The Cult of True Womanhood, 1820–1860." *American Quarterly,* XVIII (Summer 1966), 151–174.

Yellowitz, Irwin. *Industrialization and the American Labor Movement.* Port Washington, N.Y.: Kennikat, 1977.

RESEARCH KEYWORDS

Labor and Laboring Classes   Working Class   Women in America
Woman's Rights   Immigration

EXPLORING CRITICAL ISSUES THROUGH WRITING

1. Try to find instances in which newspapers or magazines place misspelled words in quoted *speech* (not quoted written text)—for example, "gonna" or "wuz" instead of "going to" and "was." What is the effect of this practice? Why do you think print media do it? What does it say about the relationship between the writer and the audience and the person being quoted?

2. Examine the problem of translating from one language to another. To what extent does a writer in any language presuppose shared knowledge and experience with the audience? To what extent does the very act of translating distort such cultural sharing?

3. Investigate the work of the Bureau of Indian Affairs or the Bureau of American Ethnology. Why were they established, what was their mandate, how did (or do) they operate in practice, and how were (or are) they perceived by Native Americans?

4. Explore differing theories of the state—for example, those implied by isolationism, imperialism, or the belief "My country, right or wrong." Try to find examples of countries that embody contrasting theories.

5. Study transcendentalism. Why did this philosophy appeal to many American intellectuals? How did it influence American values? What has become of it?

6. Consider the roles that self-improvement societies have played in America.

7. Explore Thoreau's influence on Dr. Martin Luther King, Jr., and the Civil Rights and Anti-War Movements of the 1960s.

8. Explore the history of environmentalism in America. How does it conform to other American values? What have been the contributions of both Thoreau and Theodore Roosevelt?

9. Investigate the contribution of the Quakers or abolitionists to the Woman's Rights Movement. Research the contributions of African Americans, such as Frederick Douglass.

10. Research attitudes toward women in the nineteenth century. What was thought of women—by both men and women? What was expected of them? What part did class play in defining the place of women? You might want to explore "the cult of true womanhood."

11. Evaluate the contribution of women to the labor movement or the contribution of working women to the Woman's Rights Movement. Consider especially how the situation has changed over the years.

12. Explore an idea from the reading selections that caught your interest, charmed or provoked you, or supported or challenged your own beliefs. Try to place this issue within a larger context, and explain its significance.

6

SLAVERY: 1800–1860

"If God has bestowed beauty upon her, it will prove her greatest curse. That which commands admiration in the white woman only hastens the degradation of the female slave."

HARRIET JACOBS

"Does not every American Christian owe to the African race some effort at reparation for the wrongs that the American nation has brought upon them?"

HARRIET BEECHER STOWE

"Lincoln's history-making modification of Jefferson was to apply this Jeffersonian idea to the issue of slavery. . . ."

CUSHING STROUT

In 1619 a group of Africans was sold at Jamestown, although whether they were sold as slaves or as indentured servants is not clear. By 1660 however, black slavery was entrenched in Virginia and other English colonies in America.

At first, European servants were preferred because they shared the language and culture of their masters. Toward the end of the seventeenth century, however, a healthy English economy reduced the number of laborers interested in relocating to the New World. At the same time, landowners realized that in order to buy manufactured goods, they would need a cash crop. In Virginia, tobacco—which Spanish explorers had introduced to Europe—promised to be the needed export. Growing tobacco, however, is labor intensive. Thus, the use of slaves seemed the best way to guarantee a profit. In the Carolinas, rice served as a cash crop. Since free workers refused to stand all day bent over in knee-deep water, slaves provided the solution here as well. By 1730, 30 percent of the population in the southern colonies consisted of African slaves; in many counties and even a few colonies, slaves soon outnumbered the whites.

To maintain their psychological equanimity, slaveowners had to dehumanize, and even demonize, the Africans. How else could they believe themselves to be Christians and moral gentlemen? Many churches offered Biblical support: blackness was equated with sin and evil. Africans were accused of being naturally violent and of lusting after white women. It was even argued that they were incapable of thought or learning. Ironically, as we see in the narrative of Harriet Jacobs, it was the white masters who forced themselves on their female slaves. And as Frederick Douglass notes, numerous laws intended to restrict them proved that—if given a chance—the blacks would indeed elevate themselves.

Opposition to slavery existed almost from the beginning. In 1688, Mennonites in Germantown, Pennsylvania, released a resolution against the kidnapping and selling of Africans, invoking the Biblical commandment to do unto others as you would have them do unto you. And a century later, Thomas Jefferson's draft of the Declaration of Independence objected to allowing slavery in the American colonies.

Slavery remained a sore point after independence as well. To create the Union and to keep it from tearing apart, one compromise after another had to be negotiated. The importation of slaves was banned in 1808. Settlement of the West was divided into free and slave territories. But as each side pushed for another concession, new problems arose. Because the law allowed slavery, slaves were legal property; therefore, anyone who helped them escape was an accessory to theft. This logic resulted in the Fugitive Slave Act, which required all citizens to respond to a lawful request for assistance in returning property—that is, escaped slaves. This Southern victory radicalized many people, such as Harriet Beecher Stowe, who until then were content to passively dislike slavery.

The conflict over slavery led to the Civil War. Opposing the image of Abraham Lincoln as the "Great Emancipator," some claim that the Civil War was fought to save the Union, not just free the slaves. This argument overlooks the fact that without the fight over slavery, there would have been no threat to the Union. Nevertheless, it should be noted that Lincoln, like most whites of his time—including abolitionists—held views that would be considered racist by modern standards.

Africans were not considered equal to Europeans in accomplishment, civilization, or, perhaps, intelligence. Therefore, what to do with the freed slaves was itself a problem. One solution was to return them to Africa, where they would be in their natural element. Another, espoused by Frederick Douglass, an American slave with a white father, was to grant them full equality immediately. This debate raged on long after the Civil War ended.

Another Voice

GERMANTOWN MENNONITE RESOLUTION AGAINST SLAVERY, 1688

. . . Now, though they are black, we cannot conceive there is more liberty to have them slaves, as it is to have other white ones. There is a saying, that we should do to all men like as we will be done ourselves; making no difference of what generation, descent, or colour they are. And those who steal or rob men, and those who buy or purchase them, are they not all alike? Here is liberty of conscience, which is right and reasonable; here ought to be likewise liberty of the body, except of evildoers, which is another case. But to bring men hither, or to rob and sell them against their will, we stand against. In Europe there are many oppressed for conscience-sake; and here there are those oppressed which are of a black colour. And we who know that men must not commit adultery—some do commit adultery *in* others, separating wives from their husbands, and giving them to others: and some sell the children of these poor creatures to other men. Ah! do consider well this thing, you who do it, if you would be done at this manner—and if it is done according to Christianity! . . .

continued

continued from previous page

You surpass Holland and Germany in this thing. This makes an ill report in all those countries of Europe, where they hear of (it), that the Quakers do here handel men as they handel there the cattle. And for that reason some have no mind or inclination to come hither. And who shall maintain this your cause, or plead for it? Truly, we cannot do so, except you shall inform us better hereof, viz.: that Christians have liberty to practice these things. Pray, what thing in the world can be done worse towards us, than if men should rob or steal us away, and sell us for slaves to strange countries; separating husbands from their wives and children. Being now this is not done in the manner we would be done at; therefore, we contradict, and are against this traffic of men-body. And we who profess that it is not lawful to steal, must, likewise, avoid to purchase such things as are stolen, but rather help to stop this robbing and stealing, if possible. And such men ought to be delivered out of the hands of the robbers, and set free as in Europe. Then is Pennsylvania to have a good report, instead, it hath now a bad one, for this sake, in other countries; especially whereas the Europeans are desirous to know in what manner *the Quakers* do rule in *their* province; and most of them do look upon us with an envious eye. But if this is done well, what shall we say is done evil?

If once these slaves (which they say are so wicked and stubborn men) should join themselves—fight for their freedom, and handel their masters and mistresses, as they did handel them before; will these masters and mistresses take the sword at hand and war against these poor slaves, like, as we are able to believe, some will not refuse to do? Or, have these poor negers not as much right to fight for their freedom, as you have to keep them slaves?

Now consider well this thing, if it is good or bad. And in case you find it to be good to handel these blacks in that manner, we desire and require you hereby lovingly, that you may inform us herein, which at this time never was done, viz., that Christians have such a liberty to do so. To the end we shall be satisfied on this point, and satisfy likewise our good friends and acquaintances in our native country, to whom it is a terror, or fearful thing, that men should be handelled so in Pennsylvania.

This is from our meeting at Germantown, held ye 18th of the 2d month, 1688, to be delivered to the monthly meeting at Richard Worrell's.

Garret Henderich,
Derick op de Graeff,
Francis Daniel Pastorius,
Abram op de Graeff.

ALICE DANA ADAMS
The Neglected Period of Anti-Slavery in America, 1808–1831 (1908)

"Notwithstanding . . . a true anti-slavery sentiment among churches in this period, it is not to be contested that the great religious bodies did little, as such, to aid in the abolition of slavery."

Nineteenth-century histories of Abolitionism commonly labeled the years 1808–1831 as "the Period of Stagnation." They believed that the passage in 1807 of the African Slave Trade Act, which outlawed the importation of slaves, led to the mistaken belief that slavery would soon disappear by itself; only when this failed to occur did the anti-slavery movement come to life again, with the trumpet call of William Lloyd Garrison. As a student at Radcliffe College learning research methods under the guidance of Harvard Professor Albert Bushnell Hart, Alice Dana Adams pored over the primary sources from this era and discovered that this popular view was wrong. Society rolls, newspaper editorials and church conferences supplied evidence of anti-slavery sentiment where none appeared in history books, even of violent agitation where none had been reported. This led Adams to publish her findings under the label "the neglected period"—meaning neglected by historians.

The fact that Adams was working with a Harvard professor is itself noteworthy. With only limited opportunities for women to pursue higher education, Harvard faculty began lecturing to women in 1879; this led to the formation of the Society for the Collegiate Instruction of Women in 1882, and two years later to official connection with Harvard and to the name Radcliffe College, in honor of Ann Radcliffe, patron of the first scholarship at Harvard, in 1643. Adam's work was published as Radcliffe College Monograph No. 14.

The selection that follows is Chapter 9, "The Attitude of the Churches."

Text: Alice Dana Adams, *The Neglected Period of Anti-Slavery in America, 1808–1831.* Radcliffe College Monographs, 1908.

EXPLORING ISSUES IN THE TEXT

1. What is the moral contradiction that Adams establishes in par. 1? How does this lead to the main idea of the selection in par. 2?

2. Summarize the position of the Methodists toward slavery (par. 5). How did the Methodists and Friends differ from other denominations in this respect? What accounted for this difference?

3. Summarize the response of the Society of Friends to slavery (pars. 11–12). Account for the irony that the Society itself owned slaves.

THE NEGLECTED PERIOD OF ANTI-SLAVERY IN AMERICA, 1808–1831

The Attitude of the Churches

1   On a question involving so many moral issues, appealing so directly to the fundamental principles of Christianity, it seems natural to expect from the churches and their spiritual guides an interest and an influence in anti-slavery measures. As a whole, however, they showed great indifference towards the matter. Indeed, in many cases it was worse than indifference; clergymen presented reasoned apologies for the system, they carefully prepared arguments in its behalf, they even actively participated in its horrors. Because of these undeniable facts, the entire clergy and all the religious societies are often accused of, at best, a weak yielding to the greater power of the slaveholder, and an upholding or a sharing of his deeds for the sake of self-protection.

2   Whatever the ground for blame against the clergymen of the United States during this period, it is not true that decided efforts to check the evils of slavery or to prohibit it utterly were entirely wanting either among them or among the churches to whom they ministered. The action of a good number of Southern ministers in leaving their homes for new ones in the free state of Ohio, and their labors in behalf of abolition, have already been spoken of. Some of these so influenced their Southern churches that they emigrated to free states either as individuals or as a body.

3   The attitude of a comparatively small number of clergymen and of a few local churches cannot be taken as proofs of the attitude of the religious bodies to which they belong. It is therefore important to seek clear proof both of anti-slavery sentiment among larger religious bodies, and of their distinct expression of this sentiment. David Thomas, a resident of New York, stated, in a book published in 1819, that whole religious societies had relinquished the practice of slavery. "The Genius of Universal Emancipation," in an editorial written in 1827, said that though the Methodists and Friends were the most active in this direction, there were many Presbyterians, Baptists, and other denominations interested. Evan Lewis, in a paper printed in 1831 but written earlier, spoke of the Society of Friends in Pennsylvania, and of the Baptists in the West, as taking up the question of slavery as a religious duty, and said of the Presbyterians in the West: "Their resolution appears to be formed never to cease their efforts until their society is purged from the sin of slavery."

4   The Methodists had a well equipped system of state conferences which had power to lay down rules of discipline for the churches, and many of their leaders were anti-slavery men. Bishop Asbury stated in his Journal that in North Carolina the masters were afraid of the influence of the Methodists over the blacks. Candler recalled a casual conversation in Virginia, about 1824, with a farmer who was sure that the traveler was a "Methodist parson" because he professed to think labor not degrading to the whites.

5   More definite and convincing are the votes of the organized bodies. In 1812 the General Conference of the Methodist Church, meeting in New York, adopted a resolution providing that no slaveholder should be eligible to the office of local elder in any state or territory in which he could legally manumit his slaves. In 1824 a clause was added stating that if a traveling preacher should in any way become the owner of slaves, he must "forfeit his ministerial character . . . unless he execute if it be practicable, a legal emancipation of such slaves, conformably to the laws of the state in which he lives." The Quarterly Conference of the Cambridge Circuit, Maryland, adopted in 1826 unanimous resolutions which denounced slavery and pointed out the inconsistency of allowing the lay-members of the churches to hold slaves while the officials were forbidden to do so. They also declared their intention to use all possible efforts to obtain from the General Conference a rule forbidding the admission to church membership of a slaveholder who would not manumit his slaves, where the law allowed. Even in the cotton states the Methodists had something of this feeling, for in 1825 the Bishop of Georgia told a traveler that the Methodists in the state were considering the advisability of making a rule requiring all of their members to free their slaves. Unfortunately the Methodist Church of the South eventually felt itself bound to protect and defend slavery, even to the point of complete separation from its denominational brethren in the North.

6   The Presbyterian Church was well qualified to influence public opinion through its annual General Assembly, the most powerful ecclesiastical body in America; and among its leading men were some prominent opponents of slavery. Comparatively few of the churches were in the slave states; hence, perhaps, the somewhat more decided though spasmodic action. In answer to a petition in 1815 the General Assembly reported that they were not strong enough as a body for decided action on the subject of slavery, but a resolution was passed regretting the continuance of the institution and recommending the education of slaves as a preparation for future emancipation. In 1816 they went backward, by erasing some strong words against manstealing adopted in 1795. In 1818 the anti-slavery element obtained a larger influence. By a unanimous vote they declared slavery "a gross violation of the most precious and sacred rights of human nature; as utterly inconsistent with the law of God . . . and as totally irreconcileable with the spirit and principles of the gospel of Christ," the Golden Rule. They

expressed their sympathy with those in the slave states who were doing all they legally could for their slaves, recommended patronage of the Colonization Society, education of slaves, the discountenancing of all cruelty, and the suspension of any church member who should sell a Christian slave. They still admitted slaveholders to church office, however. In 1823 or 1824 unsuccessful resolutions were introduced to exclude slaveholders from the ministry, and to deny the communion to slave traders. "The very making of them was a good symptom," although they were both negatived.

7   The action of the individual synods and presbyteries was much more distinctly anti-slavery than that of the General Assembly. The Synod of Kentucky recommended the American Colonization Society in 1823, and in 1830 enjoined the churches to raise money for Liberia. In 1825 it directed the ministers to pay more attention to the religious education of the slaves, and in 1826 there were fifteen schools for colored children reported within its limits. In 1828 the Synod of Indiana sent a memorial to the General Assembly, emphasizing the immorality of slaveholding. They quoted the language of the General Assembly in 1815 and 1818, and concluded that the toleration of slavery there found was only intended to make more sure the preparation of the slave for freedom. They entreat that measures be now taken for speedy (though gradual) emancipation.

8   The Associate Synod adopted in 1811 at Cannonsburg, Pennsylvania, these resolutions: 1. To hold negroes is a moral evil. 2. All slaveholding members must emancipate their slaves unless prohibited by civil law; in which case they should treat them well and pay them wages. 3. Those refusing to follow the preceding rule cannot be admitted or retained in fellowship. 4. Members may buy negroes for the purpose of emancipation, and hold them as slaves until they have paid for themselves, provided the negroes consent. In 1821 it was noticed by the Synod that the resolutions of 1811 had been neglected, and new resolutions were passed. 1. All members of the Synod holding slaves on April 1, 1822, shall be considered as suspended from office. 2. All Elders holding slaves on April 1, 1823, shall be considered unworthy of membership. 3. If any one sells a slave in the meantime he shall not be readmitted to membership without special treatment of his case. This action in Pennsylvania is more radical than in any other state except among the Presbyterians of southern Ohio, whose attitude against slavery has already been treated in an earlier chapter.

9   In 1826 the Synod of Ohio, in a session at Columbus, held a discussion on the question "Is the holding of slaves manstealing?" and a large majority decided in the affirmative. In 1827 the same Synod considered whether slaveholding was a sufficiently great sin to exclude a man from the communion. No advocate or justifier of slavery appeared in the meeting, and a resolution was passed declaring that slavery could "no longer be tolerated within the jurisdiction of this Synod." The only reason given against such action was the fear of offending some slaveholder,—a reason deemed utterly insufficient. . . .

10   There is less testimony as to the work of other sects in the United States, with the exception of the Friends. The Episcopalians and Catholics were apparently neutral. The German, or High Dutch, Church at Pleasant Run, Ohio, was one of the few anti-slavery churches of which we have mention, and carried their opposition to the institution "so far that they would hold no slaves themselves, nor have any communion or fellowship with those who did." Nearly all the members were from Virginia, whence the church had as a body emigrated to Ohio in 1801. A congregation of Lutherans, probably in Tennessee, passed in 1822 or 1823 a resolution declaring their abhorrence of slavery.

11   The Friends were by far the most active opponents of slavery during this period. They furnished the leaders in the "American Convention" and in the greater number of the Abolition Societies in the country, while many individual members were renowned as friends of the slave. The traveler Blane thought the Quakers the only people in the United States who were seriously striving to abolish slavery, or who were exerting "themselves to the utmost to alleviate its horrors." Knight is less positive, yet says: "The Quakers, emphatically, and to their unfading honor, have ever been the foremost against slavery." [Wm. N. Blane: "An Excursion through the United States and Canada," p. 26; Henry C. Knight (Arthur Singleton, Esq.): "Letters from the South and West," p. 17.] Among the few memorials to Congress during this period are two from a Quaker Yearly Meeting; one in 1819 expressed their disapprobation of slavery extension, and a second, in December, 1823, prayed for the amelioration of the condition of the slaves, especially in regard to the marriage relation. Candler said in 1824 that slaveholding was not tolerated among the Friends of Long Island. [Isaac Candler: "A Summary View of the United States," p. 322.] A remonstrance in 1826 from the Monthly Meeting of Friends to the Legislature of Delaware solicits attention to the subject of slavery, denounces the system, and blames Delaware for her participation in the crime. It demands an immediate action of the powers of the Legislature for abolition in the state.

12   The relation of the Friends of North Carolina and Virginia to slavery has been fully treated in a recent monograph, and a few facts may be briefly quoted. Quakers in the former state were not all anti-slavery men; some who married outside the Society, and took slaves as their wives' dower, became the hardest class to deal with. As a denomination, however, they freed their slaves, and since the laws in that state against unconditional emancipation were so rigid, the Society itself became a slaveholder in 1808, receiving slaves from masters who wished to be rid of them, and giving them virtual freedom, sometimes sending them to the free states. In 1809 the Yearly Meeting decided to give up this custom, but it was soon recommenced, and continued till the Civil War. In 1814 they had 350 negroes whom they held in trust in this way. It was not deemed advisable to purchase these slaves at their full value, or to receive them from persons outside of the Society. A report in 1830 gave

the number sent to free governments since the beginning of the custom as 652, at an expense of $12,769.81, and the number still under their care as 402. Other than this there was little work done even by the Quakers in North Carolina. Petitions to Congress in 1816 and 1823, which had but little success, and some effort to educate the negroes are about all that is noted. Between 1825 and 1831 they were especially interested in the work of the American Colonization Society, although some members looked upon it as an aid to the slave power. In 1826 nearly $5000 was given to the North Carolina Yearly Meeting to send negroes from the states, and several vessels were fitted out and sent with emigrants.

13   In Virginia slavery attracted little attention from the Quakers after the beginning of the nineteenth century. The Society in that state never became a slaveholder, and it did no aggressive work.

14   Notwithstanding these and other facts showing a true anti-slavery sentiment among the churches in this period, it is not to be contested that the great religious bodies did little, as such, to aid in the abolition of slavery. The real work of the Quakers was in the Abolition Societies, which will be considered later, and in individual work, some of which has already been described.

BUILDING CONTEXT

1. Compare the data in this selection to what Frederick Douglass says about the church and slavery.

2. Explore how the information in this selection sets the scene for Stowe's appeal to Christian conscience in *Uncle Tom's Cabin*.

FURTHER STUDY

1. Investigate the response of the large religious denominations to slavery. Explore the religious arguments in favor of slavery.

2. Investigate the place of religion in the lives of the slaves themselves. How many slaves were Christians? How did they become Christian? What part did Christianity play in their lives? Did it contribute to their hopes for freedom or help resign them to their plight?

3. Explore the place of Christianity in the modern Civil Rights Movement and in black liberation and nationalism movements.

ADDITIONAL RESOURCES

Fogel, Robert W., and Stanley L. Engerman. *Time on the Cross: The Economics of American Negro Slavery*. Boston: Little, Brown, 1974.

Gutman, Herbert G. *Slavery and the Numbers Game: A Critique of Time on the Cross.* Urbana, IL: University of Illinois Press, 1976.

Reist, Benjamin. *Theology in Red, White, and Black.* Philadelphia: Westminster Press, 1975.

Stampp, Kenneth. *The Peculiar Institution: Slavery in the Ante-Bellum South.* New York: Knopf, 1956.

RESEARCH KEYWORDS

Methodism	Friends (Society of)
Evangelicalism	Pietism
African Methodist Episcopal Church	Abolitionism
Race—Religious Aspects	Civil Rights
Black Nationalism	

FREDERICK DOUGLASS
Fourth of July Oration
(1852)

"What, to the American slave, is your 4th of July? I answer; a day that reveals to him, more than all other days in the year, the gross injustice and cruelty to which he is the constant victim."

Frederick Douglass (1818?–1895)—born Frederick Bailey on a plantation in Tuckahoe, Maryland—was the most prominent African-American abolitionist. His mother, Harriet Bailey, was a slave; his father was a white man. Douglass comments in his autobiography that rumor said his master was his father, but as he was separated from his mother as an infant, he had no certain knowledge of this. At the age of eight he was sent to work for a family in Baltimore, where he secretly learned to read. After returning to the plantation in 1833, Douglass tried unsuccessfully to escape. He was then apprenticed as a ship caulker and in 1838, carrying papers identifying him as a free Negro sailor, escaped to New York City. There he took the name Douglass and married Anna Murray, the free black woman who had aided his escape.

After moving to New Bedford, Massachusetts, where he hoped to find work in the shipyards, Douglass became active in church life and abolitionism. In 1839 he presided at a meeting of African-American abolitionists opposing the colonization of freedmen in Africa, an opposition espoused also by William Lloyd Garrison. Two years later Douglass became part of Garrison's circle and a lecturer for the Massachusetts Anti-Slavery Society. Because his eloquence led to charges that he was not really a slave, in 1845 he published *Narrative of the Life of Frederick Douglass, an American Slave.* Having revealed details of his early life, however, he was in danger of being returned to slavery; he fled to England, where he stayed until sympathizers bought his freedom.

Back in America he attended the Woman's Rights Convention at Seneca Falls and began publishing a series of abolitionist weeklies that continued until the Civil War. His support for woman's suffrage meshed naturally with his growing belief that slavery could be fought through the ballot; this position destroyed his friendship with Garrison, who felt that voting acknowledged the legitimacy of an immoral government. When the war broke out, Douglass urged that blacks be allowed to enlist in the Union army; his sons Lewis and Charles served in the renowned Fifty-fourth Massachusetts Volunteers. After the war, he served in a number of government posts while continuing the struggle for equal rights for both African Americans and women. In 1884, two years after Anna's death, Douglass married Helen Pitts, a white woman—an act that Douglass defended as proof of racial equality, but which many of his followers condemned as betrayal.

In 1852, the Rochester, New York, Ladies' Anti-Slavery Society invited Douglass to deliver a Fourth of July Oration. He agreed to speak, but for reasons explained in the speech, insisted on delaying it one day. The speech that follows is therefore sometimes called the Fifth of July Oration.

Text: Frederick Douglass; *Oration, Delivered in Corinthian Hall, Rochester, July 5, 1852;* Rochester: Lee, Mann & Co., 1852.

Another Voice

SLAVES OF THEIR OWN FATHERS
FREDERICK DOUGLASS

The whisper that my master was my father, may or may not be true; and, true or false, it is of but little consequence to my purpose whilst the fact remains, in all its glaring odiousness, that

continued

continued from previous page

slaveholders have ordained, and by law established, that the children of slave women shall in all cases follow the condition of their mothers; and this is done too obviously to administer to their own lusts, and make a gratification of their wicked desires profitable as well as pleasurable; for by this cunning arrangement, the slaveholder, in cases not a few, sustains to his slaves the double relation of master and father.

I know of such cases; and it is worthy of remark that such slaves invariably suffer greater hardships, and have more to contend with, than others. They are, in the first place, a constant offence to their mistress. She is ever disposed to find fault with them; they can seldom do any thing to please her; she is never better pleased than when she sees them under the lash, especially when she suspects her husband of showing to his mulatto children favors which he withholds from his black slaves. The master is frequently compelled to sell this class of his slaves, out of deference to the feelings of his white wife; and, cruel as the deed may strike any one to be, for a man to sell his own children to human fleshmongers, it is often the dictate of humanity for him to do so; for, unless he does this, he must not only whip them himself, but must stand by and see one white son tie up his brother, of but few shades darker complexion than himself, and ply the gory lash to his naked back; and if he lisp one word of disapproval, it is set down to his paternal partiality, and only makes a bad matter worse, both for himself and the slave whom he would protect and defend.

Every year brings with it multitudes of this class of slaves. It was doubtless in consequence of a knowledge of this fact, that one great statesman of the south predicted the downfall of slavery by the inevitable laws of population. Whether this prophecy is ever fulfilled or not, it is nevertheless plain that a very different-looking class of people are springing up at the south, and are now held in slavery, from those originally brought to this country from Africa.

Narrative of the Life of Frederick Douglass, 1845

EXPLORING ISSUES IN THE TEXT

1. How does Douglass use the concept of group identity (pars. 1–3) to make his point? How does he employ the idea of America's mission (pars. 5–8)?

2. Explain Douglass's religious allusions and references to Psalm 137 (pars. 3–4). Douglass quotes only the first verses of the psalm. Look up the

verses that follow. What was Douglass implying? What is his attitude toward Christianity (par. 16ff.)?

3. Analyze the rhetorical questions asked by Douglass in paragraphs 8–10. Why is this more effective than actually answering the charges of his critics?

FOURTH OF JULY ORATION

1   Fellow-citizens, pardon me, allow me to ask, why am I called upon to speak here to-day? What have I, or those I represent, to do with your national independence? Are the great principles of political freedom and of natural justice, embodied in that Declaration of Independence, extended to us? and am I, therefore, called upon to bring our humble offering to the national altar, and to confess the benefits and express devout gratitude for the blessings resulting from your independence to us?

2   Would to God, both for your sakes and ours, that an affirmative answer could be truthfully returned to these questions! Then would my task be light, and my burden easy and delightful. For *who* is there so cold, that a nation's sympathy could not warm him? Who so obdurate and dead to the claims of gratitude, that would not thankfully acknowledge such priceless benefits? Who so stolid and selfish, that would not give his voice to swell the hallelujahs of a nation's jubilee, when the chains of servitude had been torn from his limbs? I am not that man. In a case like that, the dumb might eloquently speak, and the "lame man leap as an hart."

3   But, such is not the state of the case. I say it with a sad sense of the disparity between us. I am not included within the pale of this glorious anniversary! Your high independence only reveals the immeasurable distance between us. The blessings in which you, this day, rejoice, are not enjoyed in common.—The rich inheritance of justice, liberty, prosperity and independence, bequeathed by your fathers, is shared by you, not by me. The sunlight that brought life and healing to you, has brought stripes and death to me. This Fourth of July, is *yours,* not *mine. You* may rejoice, *I* must mourn. To drag a man in fetters into the grand illuminated temple of liberty, and call upon him to join you in joyous anthems, were inhuman mockery and sacrilegious irony. Do you mean, citizens, to mock me, by asking me to speak to-day? If so, there is a parallel to your conduct. And let me warn you that it is dangerous to copy the example of a nation whose crimes, towering up to heaven, were thrown down by the breath of the Almighty, burying that nation in irrecoverable ruin! I can to-day take up the plaintive lament of a peeled and woe-smitten people!

4   "By the rivers of Babylon, there we sat down. Yea! we wept when we remembered Zion. We hanged our harps upon the willows in the midst

thereof. For there, they that carried us away captive, required of us a song; and they who wasted us required of us mirth, saying, Sing us one of the songs of Zion. How can we sing the Lord's song in a strange land? If I forget thee, O Jerusalem, let my right hand forget her cunning. If I do not remember thee, let my tongue cleave to the roof of my mouth."

5   Fellow-citizens; above your national, tumultuous joy, I hear the mournful wail of millions! whose chains, heavy and grievous yesterday, are, today, rendered more intolerable by the jubilee shouts that reach them. If I do forget, if I do not faithfully remember those bleeding children of sorrow this day, "may my right hand forget her cunning, and may my tongue cleave to the roof of my mouth!" To forget them, to pass lightly over their wrongs, and to chime in with the popular theme, would be treason most scandalous and shocking, and would make me a reproach before God and the world. My subject, then, fellow-citizens, is AMERICAN SLAVERY. I shall see, this day, and its popular characteristics, from the slave's point of view. Standing, there, identified with the American bondman, making his wrongs mine, I do not hesitate to declare, with all my soul, that the character and conduct of this nation never looked blacker to me than on this 4th of July! Whether we turn to the declarations of the past, or to the professions of the present, the conduct of the nation seems equally hideous and revolting. America is false to the past, false to the present, and solemnly binds herself to be false to the future. Standing with God and the crushed and bleeding slave on this occasion, I will, in the name of humanity which is outraged, in the name of liberty which is fettered, in the name of the constitution and the Bible, which are disregarded and trampled upon, dare to call in question and to denounce, with all the emphasis I can command, everything that serves to perpetuate slavery—the great sin and shame of America! "I will not equivocate; I will not excuse;" I will use the severest language I can command; and yet not one word shall escape me that any man, whose judgment is not blinded by prejudice, or who is not at heart a slaveholder, shall not confess to be right and just.

6   But I fancy I hear some one of my audience say, it is just in this circumstance that you and your brother abolitionists fail to make a favorable impression on the public mind. Would you argue more, and denounce less, would you persuade more, and rebuke less, your cause would be much more likely to succeed. But, I submit, where all is plain there is nothing to be argued. What point in the anti-slavery creed would you have me argue? On what branch of the subject do the people of this country need light? Must I undertake to prove that the slave is a man? That point is conceded already. Nobody doubts it. The slaveholders themselves acknowledge it in the enactment of laws for their government. They acknowledge it when they punish disobedience on the part of the slave. There are seventy-two crimes in the State of Virginia, which, if committed by a black man, (no matter how ignorant he be,) subject him

to the punishment of death; while only two of the same crimes will subject a white man to the like punishment.—What is this but the acknowledgement that the slave is a moral, intellectual and responsible being? The manhood of the slave is conceded. It is admitted in the fact that Southern statute books are covered with enactments forbidding, under severe fines and penalties, the teaching of the slave to read or to write.— When you can point to any such laws, in reference to the beasts of the field, then I may consent to argue the manhood of the slave. When the dogs in your streets, when the fowls of the air, when the cattle on your hills, when the fish of the sea, and the reptiles that crawl, shall be unable to distinguish the slave from a brute, *then* will I argue with you that the slave is a man!

7   For the present, it is enough to affirm the equal manhood of the negro race. Is it not astonishing that, while we are ploughing, planting and reaping, using all kinds of mechanical tools, erecting houses, constructing bridges, building ships, working in metals of brass, iron, copper, silver and gold; that, while we are reading, writing and cyphering, acting as clerks, merchants and secretaries, having among us lawyers, doctors, ministers, poets, authors, editors, orators and teachers; that, while we are engaged in all manner of enterprises common to other men, digging gold in California, capturing the whale in the Pacific, feeding sheep and cattle on the hill-side, living, moving, acting, thinking, planning, living in families as husbands, wives and children, and, above all, confessing and worshipping the Christian's God, and looking hopefully for life and immortality beyond the grave, we are called upon to prove that we are men!

8   Would you have me argue that man is entitled to liberty? that he is the rightful owner of his own body? You have already declared it. Must I argue the wrongfulness of slavery? Is that a question for Republicans? Is it to be settled by the rules of logic and argumentation, as a matter beset with great difficulty, involving a doubtful application of the principle of justice, hard to be understood? How should I look to-day, in the presence of Americans, dividing, and subdividing a discourse, to show that men have a natural right to freedom? speaking of it relatively, and positively, negatively, and affirmatively. To do so, would be to make myself ridiculous, and to offer an insult to your understanding.—There is not a man beneath the canopy of heaven, that does not know that slavery is wrong *for him.*

9   What, am I to argue that it is wrong to make men brutes, to rob them of their liberty, to work them without wages, to keep them ignorant of their relations to their fellow men, to beat them with sticks, to flay their flesh with the lash, to load their limbs with irons, to hunt them with dogs, to sell them at auction, to sunder their families, to knock out their teeth, to burn their flesh, to starve them into obedience and submission to their masters? Must I argue that a system thus marked with blood, and stained with pollution, *is wrong?* No! I will not. I have better employment for my time and strength, than such arguments would imply.

10   What, then, remains to be argued? Is it that slavery is not divine; that God did not establish it; that our doctors of divinity are mistaken? There is blasphemy in the thought. That which is inhuman, cannot be divine! *Who* can reason on such a proposition? They that can, may; I cannot. The time for such argument is past.

11   At a time like this, scorching irony, not convincing argument, is needed. O! had I the ability, and could I reach the nation's ear, I would, to-day, pour out a fiery stream of biting ridicule, blasting reproach, withering sarcasm, and stern rebuke. For it is not light that is needed, but fire; it is not the gentle shower, but thunder. We need the storm, the whirlwind, and the earthquake. The feeling of the nation must be quickened; the conscience of the nation must be roused; the propriety of the nation must be startled; the hypocrisy of the nation must be exposed; and its crimes against God and man must be proclaimed and denounced.

12   What, to the American slave, is your 4th of July? I answer; a day that reveals to him, more than all other days in the year, the gross injustice and cruelty to which he is the constant victim. To him, your celebration is a sham; your boasted liberty, an unholy license; your national greatness, swelling vanity; your sounds of rejoicing are empty and heartless; your denunciations of tyrants, brass fronted impudence; your shouts of liberty and equality, hollow mockery; your prayers and hymns, your sermons and thanksgivings, with all your religious parade, and solemnity, are, to him, mere bombast, fraud, deception, impiety, and hypocrisy—a thin veil to cover up crimes which would disgrace a nation of savages. There is not a nation on the earth guilty of practices, more shocking and bloody, than are the people of these United States, at this very hour.

13   Go where you may, search where you will, roam through all the monarchies and despotisms of the old world, travel through South America, search out every abuse, and when you have found the last, lay your facts by the side of the every day practices of this nation, and you will say with me, that, for revolting barbarity and shameless hypocrisy, America reigns without a rival. . . .

14   By an act of American Congress, not yet two years old, slavery has been nationalized in its most horrible and revolting form. By that act, Mason & Dixon's line has been obliterated; New York has become as Virginia: and the power to hold, hunt, and sell men, women and children, as slaves, remains no longer a mere state institution, but is now an institution of the whole United States. The power is co-extensive with the star-spangled banner, and American Christianity. Where these go, may also go the merciless slave-hunter. Where these are, man is not sacred. He is a bird for the sportsman's gun. By that most foul and fiendish of all human decrees, the liberty and person of every man are put in peril. Your broad republican domain is hunting ground for *men. Not* for thieves and robbers, enemies of society, merely, but for men guilty of no crime. Your law-makers have commanded all good citizens to engage in this

hellish sport. Your President, your Secretary of State, your *lords, nobles,* and ecclesiastics, enforce, as a duty you owe to your free and glorious country, and to your God, that you do this accursed thing. Not fewer than forty Americans, have, within the past two years, been hunted down, and, without a moment's warning, hurried away in chains, and consigned to slavery, and excruciating torture. Some of these have had wives and children, dependent on them for bread: but of this no account was made. The right of the hunter to his prey, stands superior to the right of marriage, and to *all* rights in this republic, the rights of God included! For black men there are neither law, justice, humanity, nor religion. The Fugitive Slave *Law* makes MERCY TO THEM, A CRIME: and bribes the judge who tries them. An American JUDGE GETS TEN DOLLARS FOR EVERY VICTIM HE CONSIGNS to slavery, and five, when he fails to do so. The oath of any two villains is sufficient, under this hell-black enactment, to send the most pious and exemplary black man into the remorseless jaws of slavery! His own testimony is nothing. He can bring no witnesses for himself. The minister of American justice is bound, by the law to hear but *one* side; and *that* side, is the side of the oppressor. Let this damning fact be perpetually told. Let it be thundered around the world, that, in tyrant-killing, king-hating, people-loving, democratic, Christian America, the seats of justice are filled with judges, who hold their offices under an open and palpable *bribe,* and are bound, in deciding in the case of a man's liberty, *to hear only his accusers!*

15　In glaring violation of justice, in shameless disregard of the forms of administering law, in cunning arrangement to entrap the defenceless, and in diabolical intent, this Fugitive Slave Law stands alone in the annals of tyrannical legislation. I doubt if there be another nation on the globe, having the brass and the baseness to put such a law on the statute-book. If any man in this assembly thinks differently from me in this matter, and feels able to disprove my statements, I will gladly confront him at any suitable time and place he may select.

16　I take this law to be one of the grossest infringements of Christian Liberty, and, if the churches and ministers of our country were not stupidly blind, or most wickedly indifferent, they, too, would so regard it.

17　At the very moment that they are thanking God for the enjoyment of civil and religious liberty, and for the right to worship God according to the dictates of their own consciences, they are utterly silent in respect to a law which robs religion of its chief significance, and makes it utterly worthless to a world lying in wickedness. Did this law concern the *"mint, anise* and *cummin"*—abridge the right to sing psalms, to partake of the sacrament, or to engage in any of the ceremonies of religion, it would be smitten by the thunder of a thousand pulpits. A general shout would go up from the church, demanding *repeal, repeal, instant repeal!*—And it would go hard with that politician who presumed to solicit the votes of the people without inscribing this motto on his banner. Further, if this demand were not complied with, another Scotland would be added to the history of religious liberty, and the stern old covenanters would be thrown into the shade. A John Knox would be seen at every church door, and heard from every pulpit, and Fillmore would have no more quarter than was shown by Knox, to the beautiful, but treacherous Queen Mary of Scotland.—The fact that the church of our country, (with fractional exceptions,) does not esteem "the Fugitive Slave Law" as a declaration of war against religious liberty, implies that that church regards religion simply as a form of worship, an empty ceremony, and *not* a vital principle, requiring active benevolence, justice, love and good will towards man. It esteems sacrifice above mercy; psalm-singing above right doing; solemn meetings above practical righteousness. A worship that can be conducted by persons who refuse to give shelter to the houseless, to give bread to the hungry, clothing to the naked, and who enjoin obedience to a law forbidding these acts of mercy, is a curse, not a blessing to mankind. The Bible addresses all such persons as "scribes, pharisees, hypocrites, who pay tithe of *mint, anise,* and *cummin,* and have omitted the weightier matters of the law, judgment, mercy and faith."

18   But the church of this country is not only indifferent to the wrongs of the slave, it actually takes sides with the oppressors. It has made itself the bulwark of American slavery, and the shield of American slave-hunters. Many of its most eloquent Divines, who stand as the very lights of the church, have shamelessly given the sanction of religion, and the bible, to the whole slave system.—They have taught that man may, properly, be a slave; that the relation of master and slave is ordained of God; that to send back an escaped bondman to his master is clearly the duty of all the followers of the Lord Jesus Christ; and this horrible blasphemy is palmed off upon the world for christianity.

19   For my part, I would say, welcome infidelity! welcome atheism! welcome anything! in preference to the gospel, *as preached by those Divines!* They convert the very name of religion into an engine of tyranny, and barbarous cruelty, and serve to confirm more infidels, in this age, than all the infidel writings of Thomas Paine, Voltaire, and Bolingbroke, put together, have done. These ministers make religion a cold and flinty-hearted thing, having neither principles of right action, nor bowels of compassion. They strip the love of God of its beauty, and leave the throne of religion a huge, horrible, repulsive form. It is a religion for oppressors, tyrants, man-stealers, and *thugs.* It is not that *"pure and undefiled religion"* which is from above, and which is *"first pure, then peaceable, easy to be entreated,* full of mercy and good fruits, *without partiality, and without hypocrisy.* But a religion which favors the rich against the poor;

which exalts the proud above the humble; which divides mankind into two classes, tyrants and slaves; which says to the man in chains, *stay there;* and to the oppressor, *oppress on;* it is a religion which may be professed and enjoyed by all the robbers and enslavers of mankind; it makes God a respecter of persons, denies his fatherhood of the race, and tramples in the dust the great truth of the brotherhood of man. All this we affirm to be true of the popular church, and the popular worship of our land and nation—a religion, a church and a worship which, on the authority of inspired wisdom, we pronounce to be an abomination in the sight of God. In the language of Isaiah, the American church might be well addressed, "Bring no more vain oblations; incense is an abomination unto me: the new moons and Sabbaths, the calling of assemblies, I cannot away with; it is iniquity, even the solemn meeting. Your new moons, and your appointed feasts my soul hateth. They are a trouble to me; I am weary to bear them; and when ye spread forth your hands I will hide mine eyes from you. Yea! when ye make many prayers, I will not hear. YOUR HANDS ARE FULL OF BLOOD; cease to do evil, learn to do well, seek judgment; relieve the oppressed; judge for the fatherless; plead for the widow."

20   The American church is guilty, when viewed in connection with what it is doing to uphold slavery; but it is superlatively guilty when viewed in connection with its ability to abolish slavery.

21   The sin of which it is guilty is one of omission as well as of commission. Albert Barnes but uttered what the common sense of every man at all observant of the actual state of the case will receive as truth, when he declared that "There is no power out of the church that could sustain slavery an hour, if it were not sustained in it."

22   Let the religious press, the pulpit, the sunday school, the conference meeting, the great ecclesiastical, missionary, bible and tract associations of the land array their immense powers against slavery, and slave-holding; and the whole system of crime and blood would be scattered to the winds, and that they do not do this involves them in the most awful responsibility of which the mind can conceive.

23   In prosecuting the anti-slavery enterprise, we have been asked to spare the church, to spare the ministry; but *how,* we ask, could such a thing be done? We are met on the threshold of our efforts for the redemption of the slave, by the church and ministry of the country, in battle arrayed against us; and we are compelled to fight or flee. From *what* quarter, I beg to know, has proceeded a fire so deadly upon our ranks, during the last two years, as from the Northern pulpit? As the champions of oppressors, the chosen men of American theology have appeared—men, honored for their so called piety, and their real learning. The LORDS of Buffalo, the SPRINGS of New York, the LATHROPS of Auburn, the COXES and SPENCERS of Brooklyn, the GANNETS and SHARPS of Boston, the DEWEYS of Washington,

and other great religious lights of the land, have, in utter denial of the authority of *Him,* by whom they professed to be called to the ministry, deliberately taught us, against the example of the Hebrews, and against the remonstrance of the Apostles, they teach *that we ought to obey man's law before the law of God.*

24   My spirit wearies of such blasphemy; and how such men can be supported, as the "standing types and representative of Jesus Christ," is a mystery which I leave others to penetrate. In speaking of the American church, however, let it be distinctly understood that I mean the *great mass* of the religious organizations of our land. There are exceptions, and I thank God that there are. Noble men may be found, scattered all over these Northern States, of whom Henry Ward Beecher, of Brooklyn, Samuel J. May, of Syracuse, and my esteemed friend [Rev. R. R. Raymond.], on the platform, are shining examples; and let me say further, that, upon these men lies the duty to inspire our ranks with high religious faith and zeal, and to cheer us on in the great mission of the slave's redemption from his chains.

25   One is struck with the difference between the attitude of the American church towards the anti-slavery movement, and that occupied by the churches in England towards a similar movement in that country. There, the church, true to its mission of ameliorating, elevating, and improving the condition of mankind, came forward promptly, bound up the wounds of the West Indian slave, and restored him to his liberty. There, the question of emancipation was a high religious question. It was demanded, in the name of humanity, and according to the law of the living God. The Sharps, the Clarksons, the Wilberforces, the Buxtons, the Burchells, and the Knibbs, were alike famous for their piety, and for their philanthropy. The anti-slavery movement *there,* was not an anti-church movement, for the reason that the church took its full share in prosecuting that movement: and the anti-slavery movement in this country will cease to be an anti-church movement, when the church of this country shall assume a favorable, instead of a hostile position towards that movement.

26   Americans! your republican politics, not less than your republican religion, are flagrantly inconsistent. You boast of your love of liberty, your superior civilization, and your pure christianity, while the whole political power of the nation, (as embodied in the two great political parties,) is solemnly pledged to support and perpetuate the enslavement of three millions of your countrymen. You hurl your anathemas at the crowned headed tyrants of Russia and Austria, and pride yourselves on your Democratic institutions, while you yourselves consent to be the mere *tools* and *body-guards* of the tyrants of Virginia and Carolina. You invite to your shores fugitives of oppression from abroad, honor them with banquets, greet them with ovations, cheer them, toast them, salute them,

protect them, and pour out your money to them like water; but the fugitives from your own land, you advertise, hunt, arrest, shoot and kill. You glory in your refinement, and your universal education; yet you maintain a system as barbarous and dreadful, as ever stained the character of a nation—a system begun in avarice, supported in pride, and perpetuated in cruelty. You shed tears over fallen Hungary, and make the sad story of her wrongs the theme of your poets, statesmen and orators, till your gallant sons are ready to fly to arms to vindicate her cause against her oppressors; but, in regard to the ten thousand wrongs of the American slave, you would enforce the strictest silence, and would hail him as an enemy of the nation who dares to make those wrongs the subject of public discourse! You are all on fire at the mention of liberty for France or for Ireland; but are as cold as an iceberg at the thought of liberty for the enslaved of America.—You discourse eloquently on the dignity of labor; yet, you sustain a system which, in its very essence, casts a stigma upon labor. You can bare your bosom to the storm of British artillery, to throw off a threepenny tax on tea; and yet wring the last hard earned farthing from the grasp of the black laborers of your country. You profess to believe, "that, of one blood, God made all nations of men to dwell on the face of all the earth," and hath commanded all men, everywhere to love one another; yet you notoriously hate, (and glory in your hatred,) all men whose skins are not colored like your own. You declare, before the world, and are understood by the world to declare, that you *"hold these truths to be self evident, that all men are created equal; and are endowed by their Creator with certain inalienable rights; and that, among these are, life, liberty, and the pursuit of happiness;"* and yet, you hold securely, in a bondage, which according to your own Thomas Jefferson, *"is worse than ages of that which your fathers rose in rebellion to oppose, a seventh part* of the inhabitants of your country.

27   Fellow-citizens! I will not enlarge further on your national inconsistencies. The existence of slavery in this country brands your republicanism as a sham, your humanity as a base pretence, and your christianity as a lie. It destroys your moral power abroad; it corrupts your politicians at home. It saps the foundation of religion; it makes your name a hissing, and a bye-word to a mocking earth. It is the antagonistic force in your government, the only thing that seriously disturbs and endangers your *Union.* It fetters your progress; it is the enemy of improvement, the deadly foe of education; it fosters pride; it breeds insolence; it promotes vice; it shelters crime; it is a curse to the earth that supports it; and yet, you cling to it, as if it were the sheet anchor of all your hopes. Oh! be warned! be warned! a horrible reptile is coiled up in your nation's bosom; the venomous creature is nursing at the tender breast of your youthful republic; *for the love of God, tear away,* and fling from you the hideous monster, and *let the weight of twenty millions, crush and destroy it forever!*

Another Voice

WILLIAM LLOYD GARRISON
ATTACKS FREDERICK DOUGLASS

Jaundiced in vision, and inflamed with passion, he affects to regard us as the "disparager"(!) of the colored race, and artfully endeavors to excite their jealousy and opposition by utterly perverting the meaning of our language. We said, that "the Anti-Slavery cause, both religiously and politically, has transcended the ability of the sufferers from American slavery and prejudice, *as a class,* to keep pace with it, or to perceive what are its demands, or to understand the philosophy of its operations"—meaning by this, that the cause requires religious and political sacrifices, which, "as a class," they do not yet see, or, seeing, are not yet prepared to make, even though they are the victims to be delivered—and also meaning that what was at first supposed to be local, is now seen to have a worldwide bearing, and must be advocated upon world-wide principles, irrespective of complexional differences. There is nothing really or intentionally invidious in a statement like this: and yet, how does Mr. Douglass treat it? "The colored man," he says, "ought to feel profoundly grateful for this magnificent compliment to their high moral worth and breadth of comprehension, so generously bestowed by William Lloyd Garrison! Who will doubt, hereafter, the *natural* inferiority of the Negro, when the great champion of the Negroes' rights *thus broadly concedes all that is claimed respecting the Negro's inferiority by the bitterest despisers of the Negro race"* !!! Now, if this were blundering stupidity, it might readily be pardoned; but it is unmitigated baseness, and therefore inexcusable.

Again we said—"It does not follow, that, because a man is or has been a slave, or because he is identified with a class meted out and trodden under foot, therefore he will be the truest to the cause of human freedom"—a truism which nothing can make plainer. Yet Mr. Douglass presumes upon the color of his skin to vindicate his superior fidelity to that cause, and to screen himself from criticism and rebuke! This trick cannot succeed. Of the colored people he says—"What is theory to others, is practice to them. Every day and hour is crowded with lessons to them on the subject, to which the whites, as a class, are strangers." Very true—but what then? Does it

continued

continued from previous page

indicate the same regard for universal justice, for those who are oppressed to desire to gain their freedom, as it does for others, not of
their complexion, and not involved in their suffering, to encounter
deadly perils and make liberal sacrifices in seeking their liberation? The former may be animated by motives limited to a narrow
selfishness; the latter must be actuated by feelings of disinterested
benevolence and world-wide philanthropy.

BUILDING CONTEXT

1. Compare what the audience expects to hear about America's mission on
   the Fourth of July to what Douglass tells them. Compare his opinion
   about America's mission to that of such writers as Crèvecoeur, Tocqueville, or Thoreau.

2. Relate what Douglass says about the attitude of the churches to slavery
   to Stowe's writing. What evidence is there for Douglass's charge that the
   church "takes sides with the oppressors" (par. 18)?

3. Examine how both Douglass and Thoreau treat the issue of placing conscience over law. According to Douglass, why is there a conflict between
   morality and law?

FURTHER STUDY

1. Read the autobiography of Frederick Douglass. Why is it significant that he
   calls himself "an American slave"? Compare his saga as a self-named, self-
   made man to the stories of such American icons as Benjamin Franklin.

2. Investigate Douglass's contribution to African-American literature and
   thought—for example, the significance of choosing one's own name, or
   of gaining self-respect by fighting for freedom.

3. Douglass's marriage to a white woman in 1884 has been both attacked as
   a betrayal of black women, and defended as the ultimate success of his
   campaign for a color-blind society. Investigate the debate over Douglass
   as a role model.

4. Investigate the work of the American Colonization Society. Compare
   Douglass's plans for the freed slaves to those of Stowe or Lincoln.

ADDITIONAL RESOURCES

Douglass, Frederick. *Narrative of the Life of Frederick Douglass, an American
Slave, Written by Himself.* 1845.
———. *Life and Times of Frederick Douglass, Written by Himself.* 1881.

Foner, Philip S., ed. *Frederick Douglass on Women's Rights.* Westport, Conn.: Greenwood Press, 1976.

Quarles, Benjamin. *Black Abolitionists.* New York: Oxford University Press, 1969.

Sundquist, Eric J., ed. *Frederick Douglass: New Literary and Historical Essays.* New York: Cambridge University Press, 1990.

RESEARCH KEYWORDS

Abolitionism	Garrison (William Lloyd)
Friends (Society of)	Slavery—U.S.
Freedmen—American	Slave Act
American Colonization Society	Feminism

HARRIET JACOBS
Incidents in the Life of a Slave Girl (1861)

"If God has bestowed beauty upon her, it will prove her greatest curse. That which commands admiration in the white woman only hastens the degradation of the female slave."

Harriet Jacobs (1813–1897) was born into slavery in North Carolina—her grandmother, a freed slave, having been falsely re-enslaved. Under her first mistress, she wrote, "I was so fondly shielded that I never dreamed I was a piece of merchandise." She was even taught to read and write. Her situation changed, however, when this mistress died and Jacobs was inherited by a three-year-old whose father had sexual designs on the young slave. To gain protection from this enemy, she became the mistress of a white lawyer and bore him two children. Still, her master pursued her, and she finally ran away, hiding in the tiny attic of her grandmother's house for seven years. In 1842 she escaped to the North, eventually gaining her freedom and reuniting with her children.

Abolitionist friends urged her to publish her story. While men had told of their slavery, the unique victimization of women in slavery had been hidden.

As Jacobs wrote in the preface to *Incidents,* "it would have been more pleasant to me to have been silent about my own history. . . . But I do earnestly desire to rouse the women of the North to a realizing sense of the condition of two millions of women at the South, still in bondage, suffering what I suffered, and most of them far worse." This sentiment was echoed by the popular writer and abolitionist Lydia Maria Child: "This peculiar phase of Slavery has generally been kept veiled; but the public ought to be made acquainted with its monstrous features." She helped Jacobs publish the book, Child said, "for the sake of my sisters in bondage, who are suffering wrongs so foul . . . [and] with the hope of arousing conscientious and reflecting women at the North to a sense of their duty in the exertion of moral influence on the question of slavery."

Jacobs's book had long been labeled fiction, but research by Jean F. Yellin in the 1980s proved that, while names had been changed, the events were real. *Incidents* thus documents the sexual abuse of women slaves and the consequent degradation of Southern white women and domestic life.

Text: Harriet Jacobs; *Incidents in the Life of a Slave Girl;* V. Smith, ed.; N.Y.: Oxford University Press, 1988.

EXPLORING ISSUES IN THE TEXT

1. Why does Jacobs believe that the mistress "ought to protect the helpless victim" (par. 1)? What point does she make in the chapter entitled "The Jealous Mistress"?

2. Why was Dr. Flint, a white man, afraid of the girl's grandmother, a former slave (par. 3)? What does Jacobs imply by describing his fear?

3. What does Jacobs accomplish by stepping outside of the story and directly addressing the audience (pars. 4–7, 20–23)? How does this technique serve her purpose?

INCIDENTS IN THE LIFE OF A SLAVE GIRL

Chapter V: The Trials of Girlhood

1 During the first years of my service in Dr. Flint's family, I was accustomed to share some indulgences with the children of my mistress. Though this seemed to me no more than right, I was grateful for it, and tried to merit the kindness by the faithful discharge of my duties. But I now entered on my fifteenth year—a sad epoch in the life of a slave girl. My master began to whisper foul words in my ear. Young as I was, I could not remain ignorant of their import. I tried to treat them with indifference or contempt. The master's age, my extreme youth, and the fear that his conduct would be reported to my grandmother, made him bear this treatment for many

months. He was a crafty man, and resorted to many means to accomplish his purposes. Sometimes he had stormy, terrific ways, that made his victims tremble; sometimes he assumed a gentleness that he thought must surely subdue. Of the two, I preferred his stormy moods, although they left me trembling. He tried his utmost to corrupt the pure principles my grandmother had instilled. He peopled my young mind with unclean images, such as only a vile monster could think of. I turned from him with disgust and hatred. But he was my master. I was compelled to live under the same roof with him—where I saw a man forty years my senior daily violating the most sacred commandments of nature. He told me I was his property; that I must be subject to his will in all things. My soul revolted against the mean tyranny. But where could I turn for protection? No matter whether the slave girl be as black as ebony or as fair as her mistress. In either case, there is no shadow of law to protect her from insult, from violence, or even from death; all these are inflicted by fiends who bear the shape of men. The mistress, who ought to protect the helpless victim, has no other feelings towards her but those of jealousy and rage. The degradation, the wrongs, the vices, that grow out of slavery, are more than I can describe. They are greater than you would willingly believe. Surely, if you credited one half the truths that are told you concerning the helpless millions suffering in this cruel bondage, you at the north would not help to tighten the yoke. You surely would refuse to do for the master, on your own soil, the mean and cruel work which trained bloodhounds and the lowest class of whites do for him at the south.

2   Every where the years bring to all enough of sin and sorrow; but in slavery the very dawn of life is darkened by these shadows. Even the little child, who is accustomed to wait on her mistress and her children, will learn, before she is twelve years old, why it is that her mistress hates such and such a one among the slaves. Perhaps the child's own mother is among those hated ones. She listens to violent outbreaks of jealous passion, and cannot help understanding what is the cause. She will become prematurely knowing in evil things. Soon she will learn to tremble when she hears her master's footfall. She will be compelled to realize that she is no longer a child. If God has bestowed beauty upon her, it will prove her greatest curse. That which commands admiration in the white woman only hastens the degradation of the female slave. I know that some are too much brutalized by slavery to feel the humiliation of their position; but many slaves feel it most acutely, and shrink from the memory of it. I cannot tell how much I suffered in the presence of these wrongs, nor how I am still pained by the retrospect. My master met me at every turn, reminding me that I belonged to him, and swearing by heaven and earth that he would compel me to submit to him. If I went out for a breath of fresh air, after a day of unwearied toil, his footsteps dogged me. If I knelt by my mother's grave, his dark shadow fell on me even there. The light heart which nature had given me became heavy with sad forebodings. The

other slaves in my master's house noticed the change. Many of them pitied me; but none dared to ask the cause. They had no need to inquire. They knew too well the guilty practices under that roof; and they were aware that to speak of them was an offence that never went unpunished.

3   I longed for some one to confide in. I would have given the world to have laid my head on my grandmother's faithful bosom, and told her all my troubles. But Dr. Flint swore he would kill me, if I was not as silent as the grave. Then, although my grandmother was all in all to me, I feared her as well as loved her. I had been accustomed to look up to her with a respect bordering upon awe. I was very young, and felt shamefaced about telling her such impure things, especially as I knew her to be very strict on such subjects. Moreover, she was a woman of high spirit. She was usually very quiet in her demeanor; but if her indignation was once roused, it was not very easily quelled. I had been told that she once chased a white gentleman with a loaded pistol, because he insulted one of her daughters. I dreaded the consequences of a violent outbreak; and both pride and fear kept me silent. But though I did not confide in my grandmother, and even evaded her vigilant watchfulness and inquiry, her presence in the neighborhood was some protection to me. Though she had been a slave, Dr. Flint was afraid of her. He dreaded her scorching rebukes. Moreover, she was known and patronized by many people; and he did not wish to have his villainy made public. It was lucky for me that I did not live on a distant plantation, but in a town not so large that the inhabitants were ignorant of each other's affairs. Bad as are the laws and customs in a slaveholding community, the doctor, as a professional man, deemed it prudent to keep up some outward show of decency.

4   O, what days and nights of fear and sorrow that man caused me! Reader, it is not to awaken sympathy for myself that I am telling you truthfully what I suffered in slavery. I do it to kindle a flame of compassion in your hearts for my sisters who are still in bondage, suffering as I once suffered.

5   I once saw two beautiful children playing together. One was a fair white child; the other was her slave, and also her sister. When I saw them embracing each other, and heard their joyous laughter, I turned sadly away from the lovely sight. I foresaw the inevitable blight that would fall on the little slave's heart. I knew how soon her laughter would be changed to sighs. The fair child grew up to be a still fairer woman. From childhood to womanhood her pathway was blooming with flowers, and overarched by a sunny sky. Scarcely one day of her life had been clouded when the sun rose on her happy bridal morning.

6   How had those years dealt with her slave sister, the little playmate of her childhood? She, also, was very beautiful; but the flowers and sunshine of love were not for her. She drank the cup of sin, and shame, and misery, whereof her persecuted race are compelled to drink.

7   In view of these things, why are ye silent, ye free men and women of the north? Why do your tongues falter in maintenance of the right? Would that I had more ability! But my heart is so full, and my pen is so weak! There are noble men and women who plead for us, striving to help those who cannot help themselves. God bless them! God give them strength and courage to go on! God bless those, every where, who are laboring to advance the cause of humanity!

VI: *The Jealous Mistress*

8 I would ten thousand times rather that my children should be the half-starved paupers of Ireland than to be the most pampered among the slaves of America. I would rather drudge out my life on a cotton plantation, till the grave opened to give me rest, than to live with an unprincipled master and a jealous mistress. The felon's home in a penitentiary is preferable. He may repent, and turn from the error of his ways, and so find peace; but it is not so with a favorite slave. She is not allowed to have any pride of character. It is deemed a crime in her to wish to be virtuous.

9   Mrs. Flint possessed the key to her husband's character before I was born. She might have used this knowledge to counsel and to screen the young and the innocent among her slaves; but for them she had no sympathy. They were the objects of her constant suspicion and malevolence. She watched her husband with unceasing vigilance; but he was well practised in means to evade it. What he could not find opportunity to say in words he manifested in signs. He invented more than were ever thought of in a deaf and dumb asylum. I let them pass, as if I did not understand what he meant; and many were the curses and threats bestowed on me for my stupidity. One day he caught me teaching myself to write. He frowned, as if he was not well pleased; but I suppose he came to the conclusion that such an accomplishment might help to advance his favorite scheme. Before long, notes were often slipped into my hand. I would return them, say, "I can't read them, sir." "Can't you?" he replied; "then I must read them to you." He always finished the reading by asking, "Do you understand?" Sometimes he would complain of the heat of the tea room, and order his supper to be placed on a small table in the piazza. He would seat himself there with a well-satisfied smile, and tell me to stand by and brush away the flies. He would eat very slowly, pausing between the mouthfuls. These intervals were employed in describing the happiness I was so foolishly throwing away, and in threatening me with the penalty that finally awaited my stubborn disobedience. He boasted much of the forbearance he had exercised towards me, and reminded me that there was a limit to his patience. When I succeeded in avoiding opportunities for him to talk to me at home, I was ordered to come to his office, to do some errand. When there, I was obliged to stand and listen to such language as he saw fit to address to me. Sometimes I so openly expressed my contempt for him that he would

become violently enraged, and I wondered why he did not strike me. Circumstanced as he was, he probably thought it was better policy to be forbearing. But the state of things grew worse and worse daily. In desperation I told him that I must and would apply to my grandmother for protection. He threatened me with death, and worse than death, if I made any complaint to her. Strange to say, I did not despair. I was naturally of a buoyant disposition, and always I had a hope of somehow getting out of his clutches. Like many a poor, simple slave before me, I trusted that some threads of joy would yet be woven into my dark destiny.

10   I had entered my sixteenth year, and every day it became more apparent that my presence was intolerable to Mrs. Flint. Angry words frequently passed between her and her husband. He had never punished me himself, and he would not allow any body else to punish me. In that respect, she was never satisfied; but, in her angry moods, no terms were too vile for her to bestow upon me. Yet I, whom she detested so bitterly, had far more pity for her than he had, whose duty it was to make her life happy. I never wronged her, or wished to wrong her; and one word of kindness from her would have brought me to her feet.

11   After repeated quarrels between the doctor and his wife, he announced his intention to take his youngest daughter, then four years old, to sleep in his apartment. It was necessary that a servant should sleep in the same room, to be on hand if the child stirred. I was selected for that office, and informed for what purpose that arrangement had been made. By managing to keep within sight of people, as much as possible, during the day time, I had hitherto succeeded in eluding my master, though a razor was often held to my throat to force me to change this line of policy. At night I slept by the side of my great aunt, where I felt safe. He was too prudent to come into her room. She was an old woman and had been in the family many years. Moreover, as a married man, and a professional man, he deemed it necessary to save appearances in some degree. But he resolved to remove the obstacle in the way of his scheme; and he thought he had planned it so that he should evade suspicion. He was well aware how much I prized my refuge by the side of my old aunt, and he determined to dispossess me of it. The first night the doctor had the little child in his room alone. The next morning, I was ordered to take my station as nurse the following night. A kind Providence interposed in my favor. During the day Mrs. Flint heard of this new arrangement, and a storm followed. I rejoiced to hear it rage.

12   After a while my mistress sent for me to come to her room. Her first question was, "Did you know you were to sleep in the doctor's room?"

"Yes, ma'am."

"Who told you?"

"My master."

"Will you answer truly all the questions I ask?"

"Yes, ma'am."

"Tell me, then, as you hope to be forgiven, are you innocent of what I have accused you?"

"I am."

She handed me a Bible, and said, "Lay your hand on your heart, kiss this holy book, and swear before God that you tell me the truth."

I took the oath she required, and I did it with a clear conscience.

"You have taken God's holy word to testify your innocence," said she. "If you have deceived me, beware! Now take this stool, sit down, look me directly in the face, and tell me all that has passed between your master and you."

13   I did as she ordered. As I went on with my account her color changed frequently, she wept, and sometimes groaned. She spoke in tones so sad, that I was touched by her grief. The tears came to my eyes; but I was soon convinced that her emotions arose from anger and wounded pride. She felt that her marriage vows were desecrated, her dignity insulted; but she had no compassion for the poor victim of her husband's perfidy. She pitied herself as a martyr; but she was incapable of feeling for the condition of shame and misery in which her unfortunate, helpless slave was placed.

14   Yet perhaps she had some touch of feeling for me; for when the conference was ended, she spoke kindly, and promised to protect me. I should have been much comforted by this assurance if I could have confidence in it; but my experiences in slavery had filled me with distrust. She was not a very refined woman, and had not much control over her passions. I was an object of her jealousy, and, consequently, of her hatred; and I knew I could not expect kindness or confidence from her under the circumstances in which I was placed. I could not blame her. Slave-holders' wives feel as other women would under similar circumstances. The fire of her temper kindled from small sparks, and now the flame became so intense that the doctor was obliged to give up his intended arrangement.

15   I knew I had ignited the torch, and I expected to suffer for it afterwards; but I felt too thankful to my mistress for the timely aid she rendered me to care much about that. She now took me to sleep in a room adjoining her own. There I was an object of her especial care, though not of her especial comfort, for she spent many a sleepless night to watch over me. Sometimes I woke up, and found her bending over me. At other times she whispered in my ear, as though it was her husband who was speaking to me, and listened to hear what I would answer. If she startled me, on such occasions, she would glide stealthily away; and the next morning she would tell me I had been talking in my sleep, and ask who I was talking to. At last, I began to be fearful for my life. It had been often threatened; and you can imagine, better than I can describe, what an unpleasant sensation it must produce to wake up in the dead of night and find a jealous woman bending over you. Terrible as this experience was, I had fears that it would give place to one more terrible.

16   My mistress grew weary of her vigils; they did not prove satisfactory. She changed her tactics. She now tried the trick of accusing my master of crime, in my presence, and gave my name as the author of the accusation. To my utter astonishment, he replied, "I don't believe it; but if she did acknowledge it, you tortured her into exposing me." Tortured into exposing him! Truly, Satan had no difficulty in distinguishing the color of his soul! I understood his object in making this false representation. It was to show me that I gained nothing by seeking the protection of my mistress; that the power was still all in his own hands. I pitied Mrs. Flint. She was a second wife, many years the junior of her husband; and the hoary-headed miscreant was enough to try the patience of a wiser and better woman. She was completely foiled, and knew not how to proceed. She would gladly have had me flogged for my supposed false oath; but, as I have already stated, the doctor never allowed any one to whip me. The old sinner was politic. The application of a lash might have led to remarks that would have exposed him in the eyes of his children and grandchildren. How often did I rejoice that I lived in a town where all the inhabitants knew each other! If I had been on a remote plantation, or lost among the multitude of a crowded city, I should not be a living woman at this day.

17   The secrets of slavery are concealed like those of the Inquisition. My master was, to my knowledge, the father of eleven slaves. But did the mothers dare to tell who was the father of their children? Did the other slaves dare to allude to it, except in whispers among themselves? No, indeed! They knew too well the terrible consequences.

18   My grandmother could not avoid seeing things which excited her suspicions. She was uneasy about me, and tried various ways to buy me; but the never-changing answer was always repeated: "Linda does not belong to *me*. She is my daughter's property, and I have no legal right to sell her." The conscientious man! He was too scrupulous to *sell* me; but he had no scruples whatever about committing a much greater wrong against the helpless young girl placed under his guardianship, as his daughter's property. Sometimes my persecutor would ask me whether I would like to be sold. I told him I would rather be sold to any body than to lead such a life as I did. On such occasions he would assume the air of a very injured individual, and reproach me for my ingratitude. "Did I not take you into the house, and make you the companion of my children?" he would say. "Have I ever treated you like a negro? I have never allowed you to be punished, not even to please your mistress. And this is the recompense I get, you ungrateful girl!" I answered that he had reasons of his own for screening me from punishment, and that the course he pursued made my mistress hate me and persecute me. If I wept, he would say, "Poor child! Don't cry! don't cry! I will make peace for you with your mistress. Only let me arrange matters in my own way. Poor, foolish girl! you don't know what is for your own good. I would cherish you. I would make a lady of you. Now go, and think of all I have promised you."

19 I did think of it.

20 Reader, I draw no imaginary pictures of southern homes. I am telling you the plain truth. Yet when victims make their escape from this wild beast of Slavery, northerners consent to act the part of blood-hounds, and hunt the poor fugitive back into his dean, "full of dead men's bones, and all uncleanness." Nay, more, they are not only willing, but proud, to give their daughters in marriage to slaveholders. The poor girls have romantic notions of a sunny clime, and of the flowering vines that all the year round shade a happy home. To what disappointments are they destined! The young wife soon learns that the husband in whose hands she has placed her happiness pays no regard to his marriage vows. Children of every shade of complexion play with her own fair babies, and too well she knows that they are born unto him of his own household. Jealousy and hatred enter the flowery home, and it is ravaged of its loveliness.

21 Southern women often marry a man knowing that he is the father of many little slaves. They do not trouble themselves about it. They regard such children as property, as marketable as the pigs on the plantation; and it is seldom that they do not make them aware of this by passing them into the slave-trader's hands as soon as possible, and thus getting them out of their slight. I am glad to say there are some honorable exceptions.

22 I have myself known two southern wives who exhorted their husbands to free those slaves towards whom they stood in a "parental relation;" and their request was granted. These husbands blushed before the superior nobleness of their wives' natures. Though they had only counselled them to do that which it was their duty to do, it commanded their respect, and rendered their conduct more exemplary. Concealment was at an end, and confidence took the place of distrust.

23 Though this bad institution deadens the moral sense, even in white women, to a fearful extent, it is not altogether extinct. I have heard southern ladies say of Mr. Such a one, "He not only thinks it no disgrace to be the father of those little niggers, but he is not ashamed to call himself their master. I declare, such things ought not to be tolerated in any decent society!"

VII: *The Lover*

24 Why does the slave ever love? Why allow the tendrils of the heart to twine around objects which may at any moment be wrenched away by the hand of violence? When separations come by the hand of death, the pious soul can bow in resignation, and say, "Not my will, but thine be done, O Lord!" But when the ruthless hand of man strikes the blow, regardless of the misery he causes, it is hard to be submissive. I did not reason thus when I was a young girl. Youth will be youth. I loved, and I indulged the hope that the dark clouds around me would turn out a bright lining. I forgot that in the land of my birth the shadows are too dense for light to penetrate. A land

"Where laughter is not mirth; nor thought the mind;
Nor words a language; nor e'en men mankind.
Where cries reply to curses, shrieks to blows,
And each is tortured in his separate hell."

25   There was in the neighborhood a young colored carpenter; a free born man. We had been well acquainted in childhood, and frequently met together afterwards. We became mutually attached, and he proposed to marry me. I loved him with all the ardor of a young girl's first love. But when I reflected that I was a slave, and that the laws gave no sanction to the marriage of such, my heart sank within me. My lover wanted to buy me; but I knew that Dr. Flint was too willful and arbitrary a man to consent to that arrangement. From him, I was sure of experiencing all sorts of opposition, and I had nothing to hope from my mistress. She would have been delighted to have got rid of me, but not in that way. It would have relieved her mind of a burden if she could have seen me sold to some distant state, but if I was married near home I should be just as much in her husband's power as I had previously been,—for the husband of a slave has no power to protect her. Moreover, my mistress, like many others, seemed to think that slaves had no right to any family ties of their own; that they were created merely to wait upon the family of the mistress. I once heard her abuse a young slave girl, who told her that a colored man wanted to make her his wife. "I will have you peeled and pickled, my lady," she said, "if I ever hear you mention that subject again. Do you suppose that I will have you tending *my* children with the children of that nigger?" The girl to whom she said this had a mulatto child, of course not acknowledged by its father. The poor black man who loved her would have been proud to acknowledge his helpless offspring.

26   Many and anxious were the thoughts I revolved in my mind. I was at a loss what to do. Above all things, I was desirous to spare my lover the insults that had cut so deeply into my own soul. I talked with my grandmother about it, and partly told her my fears. I did not dare to tell her the worst. She had long suspected all was not right, and if I confirmed her suspicions I knew a storm would rise that would prove the overthrow of all my hopes.

27   This love-dream had been my support through many trials; and I could not bear to run the risk of having it suddenly dissipated. There was a lady in the neighborhood, a particular friend of Dr. Flint's who often visited the house. I had a great respect for her, and she had always manifested a friendly interest in me. Grandmother thought she would have great influence with the doctor. I went to this lady, and told her my story. I told her I was aware that my lover's being a freeborn man would prove a great objection; but he wanted to buy me; and if Dr. Flint would consent to that arrangement, I felt sure he would be willing to pay any reasonable price. She knew that Mrs. Flint disliked me; therefore, I ventured to suggest that

perhaps my mistress would approve of my being sold, as that would rid her of me. The lady listened with kindly sympathy, and promised to do her utmost to promote my wishes. She had an interview with the doctor, and I believe she pleaded my cause earnestly; but it was all to no purpose.

28 How I dreaded my master now! Every minute I expected to be summoned to his presence; but the day passed, and I heard nothing from him. The next morning, a message was brought to me: "Master wants you in his study." I found the door ajar, and I stood a moment gazing at the hateful man who claimed a right to rule me, body and soul. I entered, and tried to appear calm. I did not want him to know how my heart was bleeding. He looked fixedly at me, with an expression which seemed to say, "I have half a mind to kill you on the spot." At last he broke the silence, and that was a relief to both of us.

29 "So you want to be married, do you?" said he, "and to a free nigger."

"Yes, sir."

"Well, I'll soon convince you whether I am your master, or the nigger fellow you honor so highly. If you *must* have a husband, you may take up with one of my slaves."

What a situation I should be in, as the wife of one of *his* slaves, even if my heart had been interested!

I replied, "Don't you suppose, sir, that a slave can have some preference about marrying? Do you suppose that all men are alike to her?"

"Do you love this nigger?" said he, abruptly.

"Yes, sir."

"How dare you tell me so!" he exclaimed, in great wrath. After a slight pause, he added, "I supposed you thought more of yourself; that you felt above the insults of such puppies."

I replied, "If he is a puppy I am a puppy, for we are both of the negro race. It is right and honorable for us to love each other. The man you call a puppy never insulted me, sir; and he would not love me if he did not believe me to be a virtuous woman."

30 He sprang upon me like a tiger, and gave me a stunning blow. It was the first time he had ever struck me; and fear did not enable me to control my anger. When I had recovered a little from the effects, I exclaimed, "You have struck me for answering you honestly. How I despise you!"

31 There was silence for some minutes. Perhaps he was deciding what should be my punishment; or, perhaps, he wanted to give me time to reflect on what I had said, and to whom I had said it. Finally, he asked, "Do you know what you have said?"

"Yes, sir; but your treatment drove me to it."

"Do you know that I have a right to do as I like with you,—that I can kill you, if I please?'

"You have tried to kill me, and I wish you had; but you have no right to do as you like with me."

32   "Silence!" he exclaimed, in a thundering voice. "By heavens, girl, you forget yourself too far! Are you mad? If you are, I will soon bring you to your senses. Do you think any other master would bear what I have borne from you this morning? Many masters would have killed you on the spot. How would you like to be sent to jail for your insolence?"

33   "I know I have been disrespectful, sir," I replied; "but you drove me to it; I couldn't help it. As for the jail, there would be more peace for me there than there is here."

34   "You deserve to go there," said he, "and to be under such treatment, that you would forget the meaning of the word *peace.* It would do you good. It would take some of your high notions out of you. But I am not ready to send you there yet, notwithstanding your ingratitude for all my kindness and forbearance. You have been the plague of my life. I have wanted to make you happy, and I have been repaid with the basest ingratitude; but though you have proved yourself incapable of appreciating my kindness, I will be lenient towards you, Linda. I will give you one more chance to redeem your character. If you behave yourself and do as I require, I will forgive you and treat you as I always have done; but if you disobey me, I will punish you as I would the meanest slave on my plantation. Never let me hear that fellow's name mentioned again. If I ever know of your speaking to him, I will cowhide you both; and if I catch him lurking about my premises, I will shoot him as soon as I would a dog. Do you hear what I say? I'll teach you a lesson about marriage and free niggers! Now go, and let this be the last time I have occasion to speak to you on this subject."

35   Reader, did you ever hate? I hope not. I never did but once; and I trust I never shall again. Somebody has called it "the atmosphere of hell;" and I believe it is so.

36   For a fortnight the doctor did not speak to me. He thought to mortify me; to make me feel that I had disgraced myself by receiving the honorable addresses of a respectable colored man, in preference to the base proposals of a white man. But though his lips disdained to address me, his eyes were very loquacious. No animal ever watched its prey more narrowly than he watched me. He knew that I could write, though he had failed to make me read his letters; and he was now troubled lest I should exchange letters with another man. After a while he became weary of silence; and I was sorry for it. One morning, as he passed through the hall, to leave the house, he contrived to thrust a note into my hand. I thought I had better read it, and spare myself the vexation of having him read it to me. It expressed regret for the blow he had given me, and reminded me that I myself was wholly to blame for it. He hoped I had become convinced of the injury I was doing myself by incurring his displeasure. He wrote that he had made up his mind to go to Louisiana; that he should take several slaves with him, and intended I should be one of the number. My mistress would remain where she was; therefore I should have noth-

ing to fear from that quarter. If I merited kindness from him, he assured me that it would be lavishly bestowed. He begged me to think over the matter, and answer the following day.

37   The next morning I was called to carry a pair of scissors to his room. I laid them on the table, with the letter beside them. He thought it was my answer, and did not call me back. I went as usual to attend my young mistress to and from school. He met me in the street, and ordered me to stop at his office on my way back. When I entered, he showed me his letter, and asked me why I had not answered it. I replied, "I am your daughter's property, and it is in your power to send me, or take me, wherever you please." He said he was very glad to find me so willing to go, and that we should start early in the autumn. He had a large practice in the town, and I rather thought he had made up the story merely to frighten me. However that might be, I was determined that I would never go to Louisiana with him.

38   Summer passed away, and early in the autumn Dr. Flint's eldest son was sent to Louisiana to examine the country, with a view to emigrating. That news did not disturb me. I knew very well that I should not be sent with *him*. That I had not been taken to the plantation before this time, was owing to the fact that his son was there. He was jealous of his son; and jealousy of the overseer had kept him from punishing me by sending me into the fields to work. Is it strange that I was not proud of these protectors? As for the overseer, he was a man for whom I had less respect than I had for a bloodhound.

39   Young Mr. Flint did not bring back a favorable report of Louisiana, and I heard no more of that scheme. Soon after this, my lover met me at the corner of the street, and I stopped to speak to him. Looking up, I saw my master watching us from his window. I hurried home, trembling with fear. I was sent for, immediately, to go to his room. He met me with a blow. "When is mistress to be married?" said he, in a sneering tone. A shower of oaths and imprecations followed. How thankful I was that my lover was a free man! that my tyrant had no power to flog him for speaking to me in the street!

40   Again and again I revolved in my mind how all this would end. There was no hope that the doctor would consent to sell me on any terms. He had an iron will, and was determined to keep me, and to conquer me. My lover was an intelligent and religious man. Even if he could have obtained permission to marry me while I was a slave, the marriage would give him no power to protect me from my master. It would have made him miserable to witness the insults I should have been subjected to. And then, if we had children, I knew they must "follow the condition of the mother." What a terrible blight that would be on the heart of a free, intelligent father! For *his* sake, I felt that I ought not to link his fate with my own unhappy destiny. He was going to Savannah to see about a little property left him by an uncle; and hard as it was to bring my feelings to

it, I earnestly entreated him not to come back. I advised him to go to the Free States, where his tongue would not be tied, and where his intelligence would be of more avail to him. He left me, still hoping the day would come when I could be bought. With me the lamp of hope had gone out. The dream of my girlhood was over. I felt lonely and desolate.

BUILDING CONTEXT

1. Compare the purposes of Jacobs and Douglass in implying that certain people are, or are not, identified with a group.

2. How do both Jacobs and Douglass use religion in their writing? What assumptions do they share about their audience? What accusations do they make?

3. Compare several depictions of slave families, such as those in the works of Jacobs, Douglass, or Stowe.

FURTHER STUDY

1. Investigate the place in society of free blacks in the North and South before the Civil War. What rights did freedmen have? What was their attitude toward slaves?

2. Research nineteenth-century attitudes toward women and morality. Why, for example, would Lydia Maria Child refer to the obligation of women to exert moral influence?

3. Explore the relationship between abolitionism and feminism. To what extent, for example, is *Incidents* abolitionist? To what extent is it feminist?

ADDITIONAL RESOURCES

Cohen, David W., and Jack P. Green, eds. *Neither Slave nor Free: The Freedman of African Descent in the Slave Societies of the New World.* Baltimore: Johns Hopkins Press, 1972.

Genovese, Eugene. *Roll, Jordan, Roll: The World the Slaves Made.* New York: Pantheon Books, 1974.

Gutman, Herbert G. *The Black Family in Slavery and Freedom, 1750–1925.* New York: Pantheon, 1976.

Niemoeller, Adolph. *Sexual Slavery in America.* New York: Panurge Press, 1935.

RESEARCH KEYWORDS

Abolitionism	Feminism
Methodism	Child (Lydia Maria)
African Americans in Literature	Race Relations in Literature

HARRIET BEECHER STOWE
Uncle Tom's Cabin
(1851–52)

"What do you owe to these poor unfortunates, O Christians? Does not every American Christian owe to the African race some effort at reparation for the wrongs that the American nation has brought upon them?"

Uncle Tom's Cabin is one of those rare works of fiction that make history. Published serially in 1851–52, it achieved immediate success and was adapted into a popular play that traveled the country. The depiction of the horrors of slavery, the destruction of families, the degradation of women, the nobility of the saintly Uncle Tom, and the depravity of the satanic Simon Legree aided the abolitionist cause. When President Lincoln met the author during the Civil War he is supposed to have said, "So this is the little lady who made this big war."

Harriet Beecher Stowe (1811–1896) was the daughter of the prominent minister Lyman Beecher, and the sister of Henry Ward Beecher, a famous preacher, and Catherine Beecher, a champion of education for women. Her husband, the Reverend Calvin Ellis Stowe, taught at Lane Theological Seminary in Cincinnati. From here she observed the slavery across the river in Kentucky, though she was not at first an active abolitionist. According to her own account, the Fugitive Slave Act of 1850 radicalized her by requiring her—and all other Americans—to assist in the capture and return of escaped slaves. Anger at this imposition motivated her to write a novel exposing the evils of slavery and expounding the obligation of Christians to oppose it. In researching slave life, she sought information from Frederick Douglass, and this led to the belief—no longer held by most current scholars—that he was the model for Uncle Tom.

It is worth noting that despite the twentieth-century use of "Uncle Tom" as an epithet for a groveling black with no self-respect, the character in the book is clearly and frequently identified with Christ. In Stowe's eyes, at least, Uncle Tom was perfection personified, and slavery was the work of the devil.

The excerpt reprinted here is the Epilogue, in which Stowe addresses the reader directly, without the screen of fiction.

Text: Harriet Beecher Stowe; *Uncle Tom's Cabin;* New York: Signet, 1981.

EXPLORING ISSUES IN THE TEXT

1. Illustrate the connection between the Fugitive Slave Act and the writing of *Uncle Tom's Cabin* (par. 2). Analyze the religious foundations for Stowe's arguments (pars. 2–5). Explain the significance of the religious imagery in the conclusion (pars. 19–24).

2. Explain Stowe's basis for shifting her condemnation from Southerners to Northerners (pars. 6–7). Why does she make a special appeal to Northern women (pars. 6, 8)?

3. Explain the criteria Stowe uses for defining group membership. To what extent do whites and blacks belong in the same group?

UNCLE TOM'S CABIN

1 The author hopes she has done justice to that nobility, generosity, and humanity, which in many cases characterize individuals at the south. Such instances save us from utter despair of our kind. But, she asks any person who knows the world, are such characters *common,* anywhere?

2   For many years of her life, the author avoided all reading upon or allusion to the subject of slavery, considering it as too painful to be inquired into, and one which advancing light and civilization would certainly live down. But, since the legislative act of 1850, when she heard, with perfect surprise and consternation, Christian and humane people actually recommending the remanding escaped fugitives into slavery, as a duty binding on good citizens,—when she heard, on all hands, from kind, compassionate, and estimable people, in the free states of the north, deliberations and discussions as to what Christian duty could be on this head,—she could only think, These men and Christians cannot know what slavery is; if they did, such a question could never be open for discussion. And from this arose a desire to exhibit it in a *living dramatic reality.* She has endeavored to show it fairly, in its best and its worst phases. In its *best* aspect, she has, perhaps, been successful; but, oh! who shall say what yet remains untold in that valley and shadow of death that lies the other side?

3   To you, generous, noble-minded men and women, of the south,—you, whose virtue, and magnanimity, and purity of character, are the greater for the severer trial it has encountered,—to you is her appeal. Have you not, in your own secret souls, in your own private conversings, felt that there are woes and evils, in this accursed system, far beyond what are here shadowed, or can be shadowed? Can it be otherwise? Is *man* ever a creature to be trusted with wholly irresponsible power? And does not the slave system, by denying the slave all legal right of testimony, make every individual owner an irresponsible despot? Can anybody fail to

make the inference what the practical result will be? If there is, as we admit, a public sentiment among you, men of honor, justice, and humanity, is there not also another kind of public sentiment among the ruffian, the brutal, and debased? And cannot the ruffian, the brutal, the debased, by slave law, own just as many slaves as the best and purest? Are the honorable, the just, the high-minded and compassionate, the majority anywhere in this world?

4   The slave-trade is now, by American law, considered as piracy. But a slavetrade, as systematic as ever was carried on on the coast of Africa, is an inevitable attendant and result of American slavery. And its heart-break and its horrors, *can* they be told?

5   The writer has given only a faint shadow, a dim picture, of the anguish and despair that are, at this very moment, riving thousands of hearts, shattering thousands of families, and driving a helpless and sensitive race to frenzy and despair. There are those living who know the mothers whom this accursed traffic has driven to the murder of their children; and themselves seeking in death a shelter from woes more dreaded than death. Nothing of tragedy can be written, can be spoken, can be conceived, that equals the frightful reality of scenes daily and hourly on our shores, beneath the shadow of American law, and the shadow of the cross of Christ.

6   And now, men and women of America, is this a thing to be trifled with, apologized for, and passed over in silence? Farmers of Massachusetts, of New Hampshire, of Vermont, of Connecticut, who read this book by the blaze of your winter-evening fire,—strong-hearted, generous sailors and ship-owners of Maine,—is this a thing for you to countenance and encourage? Brave and generous men of New York, farmers of rich and joyous Ohio, and ye of the wide prairie states,—answer, is this a thing for you to protect and countenance? And you, mothers of America,—you, who have learned, by the cradles of your own children, to love and feel for all mankind,—by the sacred love you bear your child; by your joy in his beautiful, spotless infancy; by the motherly pity and tenderness with which you guide his growing years; by the anxieties of his education; by the prayers you breathe for his soul's eternal good;—I beseech you, pity the mother who has all your affections, and not one legal right to protect, guide, or educate the child of her bosom! By the sick hour of your child; by those dying eyes, which you can never forget; by those last cries, that wrung your heart when you could neither help nor save; by the desolation of that empty cradle, that silent nursery,—I beseech you, pity those mothers that are constantly made childless by the American slave-trade! And say, mothers of America, is this a thing to be defended, sympathized with, passed over in silence?

7   Do you say that the people of the free states have nothing to do with it, and can do nothing? Would to God this were true! But it is not true. The people of the free states have defended, encouraged, and participated;

and are more guilty for it, before God, than the south, in that they have *not* the apology or education of custom.

8   If the mothers of the free states had all felt as they should, in times past, the sons of the free states would not have been the holders, and, proverbially, the hardest masters of slaves; the sons of the free states would not have connived at the extension of slavery, in our national body; the sons of the free states would not, as they do, trade the souls and bodies of men as an equivalent to money, in their mercantile dealings. There are multitudes of slaves temporarily owned, and sold again, by merchants in northern cities; and shall the whole guilt or obloquy of slavery fall only on the south?

9   Northern men, northern mothers, northern Christians, have something more to do than denounce their brethren at the south; they have to look to the evil among themselves.

10   But, what can any individual do? Of that, every individual can judge. There is one thing that every individual can do,—they can see to it that *they feel right.* An atmosphere of sympathetic influence encircles every human being; and the man or woman who *feels* strongly, healthily, and justly on the great interests of humanity, is a constant benefactor to the human race. See, then, to your sympathies in this matter! Are they in harmony with the sympathies of Christ? or are they swayed and perverted by the sophistries of worldly policy?

11   Christian men and women of the north! still further,—you have another power; you can *pray!* Do you believe in prayer? or has it become an indistinct apostolic tradition? You pray for the heathen abroad; pray also for the heathen at home. And pray for those distressed Christians whose whole chance of religious improvement is an accident of trade and sale; from whom any adherence to the morals of Christianity is, in many cases, an impossibility, unless they have given them, from above, the courage and grace of martyrdom.

12   But, still more. On the shores of our free states are emerging the poor, shattered, broken remnants of families,—men and women, escaped, by miraculous providences, from the surges of slavery,—feeble in knowledge, and, in many cases, infirm in moral constitution, from a system which confounds and confuses every principle of Christianity and morality. They come to seek a refuge among you; they come to seek education, knowledge, Christianity.

13   What do you owe to these poor unfortunates, O Christians? Does not every American Christian owe to the African race some effort at reparation for the wrongs that the American nation has brought upon them? Shall the doors of churches and school-houses be shut upon them? Shall states arise and shake them out? Shall the Church of Christ hear in silence the taunt that is thrown at them, and shrink away from the helpless hand that they stretch out; and, by her silence, encourage the cruelty that would chase them from our borders? If it must be so, it will

be a mournful spectacle. If it must be so, the country will have reason to tremble, when it remembers that the fate of nations is in the hands of One who is very pitiful, and of tender compassion.

14 Do you say, "We don't want them here; let them go to Africa?"

15 That the providence of God has provided a refuge in Africa, is, indeed, a great and noticeable fact; but that is no reason why the Church of Christ should throw off that responsibility to this outcast race which her profession demands of her.

16 To fill up Liberia with an ignorant, inexperienced, half-barbarized race, just escaped from the chains of slavery, would be only to prolong, for ages, the period of struggle and conflict which attends the inception of new enterprises. Let the Church of the north receive these poor sufferers in the spirit of Christ; receive them to the educating advantages of Christian republican society and schools, until they have attained to somewhat of a moral and intellectual maturity, and then assist them in their passage to those shores, where they may put in practice the lessons they have learned in America.

17 There is a body of men at the north, comparatively small, who have been doing this; and, as the result, this country has already seen examples of men, formerly slaves, who have rapidly acquired property, reputation, and education. Talent has been developed, which, considering the circumstances, is certainly remarkable; and, for moral traits of honesty, kindness, tenderness of feeling,—for heroic efforts and self-denials, endured for the ransom of brethren and friends yet in slavery,—they have been remarkable to a degree that, considering the influence under which they were born, is surprising.

18 The writer has lived, for many years, on the frontier-line of slave states, and has had great opportunities of observation among those who formerly were slaves. They have been in her family as servants; and, in default of any other school to receive them, she has, in many cases, had them instructed in a family school, with her own children. She has also the testimony of missionaries, among the fugitives in Canada, in coincidence with her own experience; and her deductions, with regard to the capabilities of the race, are encouraging in the highest degree. . . .

19 This is an age of the world when nations are trembling and convulsed. A mighty influence is abroad, surging and heaving the world, as with an earthquake. And is America safe? Every nation that carries in its bosom great and unredressed injustice has in it the elements of this last convulsion.

20 For what is this mighty influence thus rousing in all nations and languages those groanings that cannot be uttered, for man's freedom and equality?

21 O Church of Christ, read the signs of the times! Is not this power the spirit of Him whose kingdom is yet to come, and whose will be done on earth as it is in heaven?

22   But who may abide the day of his appearing? "For that day shall burn as an oven: and he shall appear as a swift witness against those that oppress the hireling in his wages, the widow and the fatherless, and that *turn aside the stranger in his right:* and he shall break in pieces the oppressor."

23   Are not these dread words for a nation bearing in her bosom so mighty an injustice? Christians! every time that you pray that the kingdom of Christ may come, can you forget that prophecy associates in dread fellowship, the *day of vengeance* with the year of his redeemed?

24   A day of grace is yet held out to us. Both North and South have been guilty before God; and the *Christian Church* has a heavy account to answer. Not by combining together, to protect injustice and cruelty, and making a common capital of sin, is this Union to be saved,—but by repentance, justice and mercy; for, not surer is the eternal law by which the millstone sinks in the ocean, than that stronger law by which injustice and cruelty shall bring on nations the wrath of Almighty God!

BUILDING CONTEXT

1. Place Stowe's arguments within the religious context described by Alice Dana Adams.

2. Why does Stowe claim that women have a special moral responsibility to end slavery? How does her belief reflect nineteenth-century attitudes about women? Compare her views of women to those of Stanton and Millett.

3. Compare Stowe's plans for the freed slaves to those of Douglass or another writer.

FURTHER STUDY

1. Investigate the work of the American Colonization Society. Try to understand the motives of its supporters in the context of the nineteenth century. Compare the Society to modern black nationalist movements.

2. Analyze the concept that women are more moral than men. When and why did this view arise? How prevalent is it today? Who gains from this belief?

3. Research the role and position of women abolitionists. Explore the part they played in the Woman's Rights Movement.

ADDITIONAL RESOURCES

Caskey, Marie. *Chariot of Fire: Religion and the Beecher Family.* New Haven: Yale University Press, 1978.

Gosset, Thomas. *Uncle Tom's Cabin and American Culture.* Dallas: Southern Methodist University Press, 1985.

Hersch, Blanche Glassman. *The Slavery of Sex: Feminist-Abolitionists in America.* Urbana: University of Illinois Press, 1978.

Lerner, Gerda. *The Grimke Sisters from South Carolina.* New York: Schocken, 1971.

Sundquist, Eric J., ed. *New Essays on Uncle Tom's Cabin.* New York: Cambridge University Press, 1986.

RESEARCH KEYWORDS

Slavery and Slaves in Literature   African Americans in Literature
Women in Christianity—U.S.   Women—U.S.

CUSHING STROUT
*"American Dilemma:
Lincoln's Jefferson and
the Irony of History"*
(1990)

"*Lincoln's history-making modification of Jefferson was to apply this Jeffersonian idea to the issue of slavery. . . . Lincoln pointed out that the two parties had changed places with respect to Jefferson.*"

During the decades of debate over slavery preceding the Civil War, both sides claimed that they were protecting traditional values and sought support from the Founding Fathers. The early nineteenth-century ban on importing slaves was help up as proof both that the Founding Fathers wished slavery to end, and that they wanted to let it run its course. The Declaration of Independence was read as both a model for freedom for all people at all times, and a limited defense of the rights of white, male British subjects in America. Clearly, what the earlier leaders "really" believed—even if it could be discovered—was less important than their usefulness in the current confrontation.

As Cushing Strout, a professor of American Studies at Cornell University, argues, American writers and politicians had been creating revisions of American history from the very start, and continue the process today. Among the many examples he analyzes is Lincoln's use of Thomas Jefferson's writings. In particular, he shows how Lincoln focused on Jefferson's words in the Declaration of Independence while ignoring his career as a slave owner, and how Lincoln rejected Jefferson's defense of state's rights in defending the sanctity of the Union.

Text: Cushing Strout; *Making American Tradition: Visions and Revisions from Ben Franklin to Alice Walker;* New Brunswick: Rutgers University Press, 1990.

EXPLORING ISSUES IN THE TEXT

1. Summarize Lincoln's early position on slavery and racial equality (pars. 6–8), and trace its evolution (pars. 13–14).

2. Describe Lincoln's use of religious themes in his description of the Civil War (pars. 16–17). Show how he revised Jefferson's prediction about the consequence of slavery (par. 19).

3. Explain Strout's belief that "Lincoln's Jefferson was edited for Lincoln's political purposes" (par. 20). How is this similar to or different from the way all of us use literature and precedent?

AMERICAN DILEMMA: LINCOLN'S JEFFERSON AND THE IRONY OF HISTORY

1   It was the early Jefferson that Lincoln invoked, the Jefferson of the Declaration of Independence, the *Notes on the State of Virginia,* and the proposed Ordinance of 1784 for the settlement of future states. Lincoln's first great speech, in 1854 at Peoria, Illinois, laid out all the elements of his Republican position in a reply to Senator Stephen A. Douglas. In it Lincoln saluted Jefferson, "who was, is, and perhaps will continue to be, the most distinguished politician of our history." Lincoln noted that Jefferson conceived the germ of the Ordinance of 1787 that kept slavery out of the Northwestern Territory, thus establishing congressional responsibility for regulating the question of slavery in the territories. It was an important part of Lincoln's historical argument that Chief Justice Roger Taney and his supporters were quite wrong in their assumption that the founding fathers had no qualms whatever in making slaves property and never intended the Declaration of Independence to include black men. The Constitution had recognized slavery from necessity, but it had not sanctioned it by using the word "slavery" anywhere in the document; where it alluded to slavery, the term "person," not "property," was used instead.

2   Lincoln was passionately devoted to being worthy of his exalted vision of the Revolutionary generation. For him nothing was more truly Jeffer-

sonian than his hero's remark in the last year of his life that the Declaration of Independence would be "grounds of hope for others." It was meant to be, Lincoln argued, "a standard maxim for free society" to be "constantly approximated" in the future. Against Douglas, Lincoln ridiculed the absurdity that it could be reduced to meaning only that "all British subjects who were on this continent eighty-one years ago, were created equal to all British subjects born and then residing in Great Britain." Lincoln knew how to make political capital out of this reductionism when he spoke in Chicago about the German, Irish, French, and Scandinavian immigrants who cannot by ancestry "carry themselves back into that glorious epoch" of 1776 and "make themselves feel that they are part of us," but can discover their moral relation to those men through the moral sentiment of the Declaration's self-evident truths, "as though they were blood of the blood, and flesh of the flesh, of the men who wrote that Declaration, and so they are." Jefferson's ideas linked them like "an electric cord."

3   Lincoln went further in his application of the Declaration by arguing that "no man is good enough to govern another man without that other's consent," and this "sheet-anchor of American republicanism" he found expressed in the Declaration's assertion that governments derive "their just powers from the consent of the governed." Slavery was "a total violation of this principle." This move was audacious because his opponent Douglas would use the consent principle to justify his position that the territorial question of slavery should be left up to each territory's inhabitants by popular vote. Douglas might have appealed to the Declaration too, though he did not; it became Lincoln's standard by posing the "truth" of equality as a limit on popular sovereignty. Jefferson in his first inaugural address had endorsed "absolute acquiescence in the decisions of the majority" as "the vital principle of republics," but this characteristically sweeping phrase was balanced earlier in the same address by a characteristic qualification that while it is a "sacred principle, that though the will of the majority is in all cases to prevail, that will to be rightful must be reasonable; that the minority possess their equal rights, which equal law must protect, and to violate would be oppression." Lincoln's history-making modification of Jefferson was to apply this Jeffersonian idea to the issue of slavery in a political context and contest. Lincoln did not deny that the concern of the nation's fathers for the right of states to regulate their own domestic concerns had some reference to the existence of slavery among them. He did deny that their concern had reference to the carrying of slavery into new territories.

4   Writing to a group of Boston Republicans who had organized a meeting to honor Jefferson, Lincoln pointed out that the two parties had changed places with respect to Jefferson, who, like the Republicans, stressed "*personal* rights" rather than property rights, which were favored by the Douglas Democrats. The parties were like two drunken men who had each "fought himself *out* of his own coat and *into* that of the other."

For Lincoln "the principles of Jefferson are the definitions and axioms of free society." . . .

5   Jefferson also came to his aid in his dispute with Douglas about Chief Justice Taney's Dred Scott decision, defining slaves as the inalienable property of their owners. Lincoln saw in it not only the practical denial of the right of a territory to prohibit slavery, supposedly guaranteed by Douglas's Kansas-Nebraska principle of popular sovereignty, but also a hypothetical danger, pointing towards a future decision that might make it impossible even for a state to prohibit slavery. Douglas reasonably considered this possibility spurious as a practical matter, but he demagogically went further by trying to make Lincoln appear to be a lawless man who refused to respect the high court's judgment. Lincoln was able to cite Jefferson's refusal to let the United States Supreme Court be the last word on constitutionality, and he asserted the right of Republicans to regard Taney's argument as lacking legitimacy and therefore entitling voters and officials to support political measures that were not congruent with it, though they did not constitute civil disobedience.

6   Lincoln's opposition to slavery was not radical, as Abolitionist criticism and action often were. He accepted the legality of slavery where it existed in the states, agreed to the Fugitive Slave Law (though he found it distasteful to do so), accepted the provision that Utah and New Mexico could choose whether they would come into the union as slave or free states, because it had been so agreed in Henry Clay's Compromise of 1850, and attacked the Kansas-Nebraska Act mainly because it had reversed the Missouri Compromise of 1820, which he wanted to have restored as a basis for future settlement of the territories. His whole aim, he said, was to put slavery back to where it had been in the minds of the most liberal founders: not a permanent institution, but one slated for "ultimate extinction," even though "ultimate" might mean for Lincoln a hundred years in the future.

7   While his position was certainly a moderate one, Lord Charnwood has perceptively remarked that it was "a deadly moderation," knowing exactly and in detail where and why it stood where it did, and it would not compromise one iota on essential principles. Moreover, as J. R. Pole has pointed out, Lincoln's moderation arose from his observing not only "the moral scandal of slavery, but also the historical depth of the institution and the appalling complexity of the problem it presented." What is remarkable about his role in the debates with Douglas is not so much his eloquence, which is occasional, but rather his close historical reasoning and his persistent appeal to sober judgment and humane feeling. Lord Charnwood has also put his finger on what is distinguished and rare in Lincoln as a speaker, a respect for argument that must strike us as a lost art among politicians: "He put himself in a position in which if his argument were not sound nothing could save his speech from failure as a speech." (Radio and television would make that standard increasingly rare.)

8   True, from a modern point of view about racial equality, Lincoln shares much of Jefferson's prejudice about race. Like most of their contemporaries, they accepted the idea of white superiority and opposed amalgamation. Pressed by Douglas, who racially taunted Lincoln and his supporters by calling them "Black Republicans," Lincoln conceded that no more than Jefferson did he advocate political or social equality between blacks and whites; and he was equally devoted to a separation of the races. In a polemical reply to Douglas's alarms about racial mixture, Lincoln wryly said: "Why, Judge, if we do not let them get together in the Territories, they won't mix there. I should say at least that that is a self-evident truth." He wanted the new territories to be open to settlement by poor white people, including those from slave states.

9   No more than Jefferson, whom he quoted on "emancipation and deportation," did he (until 1863) have any policy except colonization for free blacks. Even so, though he did not make an issue out of racial discrimination against them, he did not follow Jefferson in meditating on their supposed natural inferiority. Lincoln's concessions to Douglas's racist tauntings were at the level of political and social institutions (the state and the family).

10   What then gives meaning to Lincoln's use of the theme of equality in the Declaration of Independence? Free blacks exist, he strongly insisted in his first major speech on slavery, because their owners have realized that "the poor Negro has some natural right to himself—that those who deny it and make mere merchandise of him deserve kickings, contempt, and death." Hence, the prejudice even among Southerners against the slave dealer. Ending the debates with Douglas, Lincoln put his case for Negro equality by defining slavery as the spirit that says, "You toil and work and earn bread, and I'll eat it." Just as the Declaration had identified the king as the political evil to be resisted, so did Lincoln make the spirit of slavery an analogue of a king's claim "to bestride the people of his own nation and live by the fruit of their labor." Refuting the demagogic charge that if he did not want a black woman for a slave, he must necessarily believe in racial mixture and therefore want her for a wife, Lincoln used a Lockean standard: "In some respects she certainly is not my equal; but in her natural right to eat the bread she earns with her own hands without asking leave of any one else, she is my equal, and the equal of all others." . . .

11   In practice, however, until 1863, Lincoln's condemnation of slavery issued in a containment policy that worked within constitutional limits by focusing on prohibiting the expansion of slavery into any new territory. That, he believed, would put slavery on the road to ultimate extinction by reinstating the principle of the Missouri Compromise that had previously kept it south of the 36–30 line. Like so many of the leaders of the American Revolution, he created a radically new historical situation by advocating a policy that was based on a conservative feeling for satisfactions

already enjoyed—in his case a respect for Henry Clay's Compromise of 1820 and a reverence for the principles of Jefferson's Declaration of Independence. In time, his policy seemed radical enough from the South's point of view to warrant secession.

12   He was firm in maintaining a refusal to compromise his containment principle, even after seven states had seceded and made actual Jefferson's darkest fear of what the future might bring. The Virginian had seen in the line marking off slave from free territory in 1820 a source of perpetual antagonism; by 1854, however, it seemed to Lincoln that its restoration was the only way to restore sectional peace. By 1860, it was clear that no widely accepted solution could be found for solving the problem of slavery in the territories or in the Union.

13   After his election, by a plurality of the popular vote in a four-way contest that gave him not a single Southern electoral vote, but a decisive electoral majority, Lincoln journeyed to Washington, giving speeches along the way. Nothing could be more appropriate than his speaking at Philadelphia in Independence Hall. He was much moved and extravagantly proclaimed that he had never had any political feeling that did not "spring from the sentiments embodied in the Declaration of Independence." The statement ignored his earlier career as a follower of Henry Clay, but it pointed to what had become the major issue between Douglas and himself about the interpretation of the Declaration in relation to slavery. He said he hoped the country could be saved by his democratic reading of what Jefferson had meant—a principle "which gave promise that in due time the weights should be lifted from the shoulders of all men, and that *all* should have an equal choice." He had already been informed of a plot against his life, and he ominously remarked that if the country could not be saved on that basis, he would "rather be assassinated on the spot than to surrender it."

14   Lincoln was moved by events to a more radical position. Already in his annual message to Congress in December 1862, he had eloquently defined the need for Americans to "think anew and act anew" in order to "rise with the occasion" in bearing an historic responsibility, in "the fiery trial through which we pass," either to "nobly save or meanly lose the last, best hope of earth." (Jefferson's phrase, "best hope," was less desperate.) The specific context of his rhetoric was a plan, addressed largely to the border states, for federally compensated emancipation to be voluntarily carried out at the state level sometime before the end of the century. The plan had no takers, but Lincoln stated then a rationale that the Emancipation Proclamation would make explicit and official a month later: "In giving freedom to the slave, we assure freedom to the free—honorable alike in what we give and what we preserve." After the Proclamation, "an act of justice" executed by executive authority as a military measure, Lincoln immediately encouraged the use of blacks in the Northern armies.

He wrote Andrew Johnson, the military governor of Tennessee, that the "colored population is the great available and yet unavailable force for restoring the Union." No longer did he propose plans for colonizing free Negroes.

15   His memorable eloquence at Gettysburg asserted that the dead would not have died in vain if the living were "dedicated" to "a new birth of freedom." Lincoln's use of "proposition" and "dedication" for Jefferson's "We hold these truths to be self-evident," points to the dynamic element in Lincoln's revision of the traditional theme. Equality is a task, not just an axiom or premise. To see it that way is to see how the Declaration of Independence can be regenerated.

16   Lincoln, in his debates with Douglas, had cited Jefferson's confession (in *Notes on the State of Virginia*) that "he trembled for his country when he remembered that God was just." Increasingly, in his reflections on the meaning of the Civil War, Lincoln resorted to similar biblical idiom. It seemed to him that God must have willed the contest and willed it to continue for his own reasons. Perhaps this idea helped diminish his sense of his own responsibility for consolidating sectional division over the territorial question of slavery. At any rate, the idea did not diminish the vigor of Lincoln's practical, political, and successful efforts to use his canniness to lobby for the Thirteenth Amendment, making the end of slavery a constitutional matter. He took pride in the fact that some one hundred and thirty thousand black soldiers fought for the Union cause, as the eventual result of the Emancipation Proclamation, but he also knew that he did not control events as much as they controlled him. Responding in a letter to a Kentuckian, who was indignant that slaves should serve in the armed forces, Lincoln pointed to the irony of history. No party or person had anticipated the nation's new condition: "God alone can claim it." If God willed that both sides should pay "for our complicity" in the wrong of slavery, then it was new evidence for "the justice and goodness of God."

17   Lincoln struck this religious note more poetically, more elaborately, and more solemnly almost a year later in his second inaugural address, the best expression of his political religion. In it Lincoln finds it strange that any Confederates should have prayed to God for help in "wringing their bread from the sweat of other men's faces," but the prayers of neither side have been fully answered, for "the Almighty has His own purposes." Yet, if we supposed that slavery was an offense, paid for by the application of "this terrible war," the accounting would still be the righteous judgment of a just God. That would be true, Lincoln asserted, indicating the enormity that faith would require us to believe, even if He willed the war to continue until the wealth lost would be equal to the bondsman's two hundred and fifty years of "unrequited toil," or until every drop of blood drawn by whipping slaves would be paid for by another "drawn with the sword." With this utterly chilling possibility dealt

with, Lincoln turned to encourage his listeners to finish the work, with charity and firmness, and "to bind up the nation's wounds." . . .

18 "Lacking Jefferson's education," Robert N. Bellah has written about Lincoln, "he was more deeply educated. His three greatest teachers were the two texts that shaped the consciousness of Americans in those days, the Bible and Shakespeare, and Jefferson himself." The rhetoric of the great Bach-like coda to Lincoln's second inaugural address is in some respects reminiscent of Jefferson's rhetoric in his letter to a French correspondent, advising him how to write about the failure of Virginia to include provision for gradual emancipation, at a time when Jefferson was absent on the legation to France. His advice used the religious language of a patient awaiting of an "overruling providence" to deliver "our suffering brethren" when "the measure of their tears shall be full, when their groans shall have involved heaven itself in darkness." Then "a god of justice will awaken to their distress" either by "diffusing light & liberality among their oppressors, or at length by his exterminating thunder" show his attention to "things of this world."

19 Jefferson, with his sanguine temperament, was more inclined to imagine the former alternative, but Lincoln, with his melancholic temperament, was less inclined to think that slaveholders would respond to light and liberality. He did overestimate their Union sentiment and also their willingness in the border states to emancipate during the war. But events taught him more harshly than they did Jefferson, who died shortly before the hardening of the sectional antagonism. Jefferson could not know that the "exterminating thunder" would be the Civil War, which Lincoln finally came to diagnose, as in a glass darkly, through the idiom of the Presbyterian church where he often attended. It was a divine affliction for the offense of slavery. Jefferson had been inclined to fear that the convulsion would be a race war between slaves and masters.

20 Lincoln's Jefferson was edited for Lincoln's political purposes. It was the exact opposite of the scurrilous forgery (which he exposed) of his supposed speech ridiculing Jefferson as a statesman who "dreampt of freedom in a slave's embrace." Lincoln's version of Jefferson left out the Virginian who in his draft of the Kentucky Resolutions in 1798 wrote that "every State has a natural right" to be the judge "in the last resort" of the powers exercised under the "compact" among the "co-States" and in the case where "powers are assumed which have not been delegated, a nullification of the act is the rightful remedy." Jefferson's nullifying ordinance, later to be tempered by Madison's Virginia Resolutions, was developed as a protest against the repressive legislation of the Alien and Sedition Laws, Federalist measures violating freedom of speech and immigration. When South Carolina led the movement for secession, based on the theory of state sovereignty, however, it did so because of the election of a President whose opinions and purposes, it protested, were hostile to slavery. Jefferson's tactics and con-

stitutional theory were thus deployed against a President for whom Jefferson's idealism had always been a source of inspiration in the campaign to contain slavery and set it on the long road to extinction.

21   As a result of South Carolina's expansion of the nullifying principle into secession, Lincoln became the major opponent of Jefferson's constitutional theory. Lincoln would insist as President that the Union is "perpetual" and is "much older than the Constitution," being formed in 1774 when the Continental Congress pledged to cease all importations from and exportations to Britain, to institute nonconsumption of British products, and to discontinue the slave trade. It followed from his nationalist's view that "no State upon its own mere motion can lawfully get out of the Union."

22   Jefferson might well have been astonished to discover his greatest legatee in this wartime role. Jefferson did not rule out a state deciding *"to stand to our arms"* against the federal government if it should act without any limitation on its powers, but would he have seen what South Carolina saw in the election of the man who venerated Jefferson's name? Jefferson in 1825, at least, was willing to use the amending process so that Congress could have the right "to make roads and canals of intercommunication between the States," precisely the program that Lincoln's Whig mentor Henry Clay called "the American system." How far Jefferson's practical acquiescence in the Southern slave system would have taken him thirty years later, when Lincoln became his champion as an antislavery Republican, is impossible to know.

23   What Lincoln made of Jefferson, however, is surely one of the most remarkable relationships in American culture between one man and his hero. Ironically, it was the man who revered Jefferson as the source of his own political idealism who would preside over the sectional war that his hero feared, the liberation of the slaves, and the end of the policy of deportation (which he, like Jefferson, had formerly endorsed). No wonder that Lincoln, looking the irony of history full in the face, could say of the War's outcome: "Only God can claim it."

BUILDING CONTEXT

1. Compare Lincoln's ideas about slavery to those that were omitted from Jefferson's draft of the Declaration of Independence. What can you infer about Jefferson's beliefs from the original draft?

2. Compare Lincoln's plans for the freed slaves to those of Douglass and Stowe.

3. Compare Lincoln's "revision" of Jefferson with another writer's use of tradition—for example, Stanton's use of the Declaration of Independence.

4. Lincoln noted that "the two parties had changed places." Trace the history of the names "Democratic" and "Republican" or the labels "liberal" and "conservative."

FURTHER STUDY

1. Evaluate the place of religion in political discourse in America. Has religion traditionally been used to support "liberal" or "conservative" positions? Consider its use in debates over slavery, civil rights, abortion, or other issues.

2. Explore the validity or fairness of judging past actions by modern standards. If, for example, Lincoln's views on racial equality are racist by modern standards, does that make him a racist in his own time? Consider, also, whether modern standards should be the criteria for judgment. Explore whether you would consider modern standards concerning pornography, sexuality, or school prayer superior or inferior to previous standards.

ADDITIONAL RESOURCES

Gerlach, Larry R., ed. *Legacies of the American Revolution.* Logan and Cedar City: Utah State University, 1978.

Horwitz, Robert H., ed. *The Moral Foundations of the American Republic.* Charlottesville: University Press of Virginia, 1986.

Jefferson, Thomas. *Notes on the State of Virginia.*

Oates, Stephen B. *Abraham Lincoln: The Man behind the Myths.* New York: New American Library, 1985.

RESEARCH KEYWORDS

Lincoln (Abraham)	Jefferson (Thomas)
Slavery	American Colonization Society
Race—U.S.	

Exploring critical issues through writing

1. Investigate the place of religion in the lives of the slaves themselves. How many slaves were Christians? How did they become Christian? What part did Christianity play in their lives? Did it contribute to their hopes for freedom or help resign them to their plight?

2. Discuss the place of Christianity in the modern Civil Rights Movement, as well as in black liberation and nationalist movements.

3. Examine the commitment of oppressed groups to the land of their oppression. Is it, for example, significant that Douglass calls himself "an American slave"?

4. Review the conflict between assimilation and separatism. Consider, for example, the debate over Frederick Douglass as a role model.

5. Research the work of the American Colonization Society. Place the motives of its supporters within the context of the nineteenth century. Compare it to modern black nationalist movements.

6. Elaborate upon the American myth of the self-made man. Look, for example, at the writings of Douglass, Franklin, and others.

7. Evaluate Douglass's contribution to African-American literature and thought—for example, the significance of choosing one's own name, or encouraging self-respect by fighting for freedom.

8. Investigate the place of free blacks in the North and South before the Civil War. What rights did freedmen have? What was their attitude toward slaves? You may want to pay special attention to the unique history of Louisiana.

9. Investigate the nineteenth-century attitudes toward women and morality. Why, for example, would Lydia Maria Child refer to the obligation of women to exert moral influence, or Harriet Beecher Stowe address her abolitionist plea to women?

10. Investigate the relationship between abolitionism and feminism. Explore, for example, the role and position of women abolitionists and what part they played in the Woman's Rights Movement.

11. Analyze the view that women are more moral than men. When and why did this view arise? How prevalent is it today? Who gains from this belief?

12. Trace the place of religion in political discourse in America. Has religion traditionally been used to support "liberal" or "conservative" positions? Comment upon its use in debates over slavery, civil rights, abortion, or other issues.

13. Assess the validity or fairness of judging past actions by modern standards. Consider, also, whether modern standards supply the appropriate criteria for these judgments.

14. Pursue an idea from the reading selections that caught your interest, charmed or provoked you, or supported or challenged your own beliefs. Try to place this issue within a larger context, and explain its significance.

7

REDEFINING AMERICA: 1860–1900

"It is useless to blame the white race for moving across the continent. . . . If we proceed in that manner, we shall presently find ourselves blaming Columbus for discovering America. . . ."

HENRY STANLEY

"The wisest of my race understand that the agitation of questions of social equality is the extremest folly."

BOOKER T. WASHINGTON

"If one race be inferior to the other socially, the Constitution . . . cannot put them upon the same plane. . . ."

PLESSY V. FERGUSON

The Civil War ended slavery, but it did not solve the problems wrought by the "peculiar institution." Freed slaves had no homes or jobs, and their former masters did not eagerly accept them as equals. Many whites preferred to import workers from Europe, where famine and war created thousands of potential immigrants.

The Constitution was amended to protect African-American citizens: The Thirteenth Amendment (1865) abolished slavery. The Fourteenth Amendment (1868) barred states from passing "any law which shall abridge the privileges or immunities of citizens" or deny "equal protection of the laws." The Fifteenth Amendment (1870) guaranteed the right to vote regardless of "race, color, or previous condition of servitude." The Military Reconstruction Act of 1867 stationed federal troops throughout the South to enforce the new civil rights laws. The eager participation of black voters, coupled with the disfranchisement of many former Confederates, resulted in African Americans winning election to southern legislatures for the first time.

The removal of the troops and a series of regressive Supreme Court decisions brought an end to black civil rights in the South. In the *Slaughter-house* cases of 1873, for example, the Court ruled that the Bill of Rights bound only the national government, not the states. In *United States* v. *Reese* it held that the Fifteenth Amendment did not ban limits on voting for such reasons as insufficient education or descent from a grandfather not qualified to vote. In the Civil Rights cases of 1883 the Court overturned federal laws against segregation. And in *Plessy* v. *Ferguson* (1896) the doctrine of "separate but equal" received judicial approval. In the face of these setbacks, Booker T. Washington, president of Tuskegee Institute, argued that vocational training was more important to African Americans than social integration. For this, he was condemned by many blacks.

In the West, the frontier continued to disappear under the plow. And when, by the end of the century, Native American tribes had been subdued in the last of the Indian wars, the explorer and reporter Henry Stanley lauded this as a sign of inevitable progress. But not everyone saw all progress as positive. William Dean Howells and Mark Twain opposed what they considered a drift toward imperialism, with Howells arguing that literature should inculcate proper moral values.

WILLIAM DEAN
HOWELLS
Criticism and Fiction
(1890)

*" . . . the question of how much or how little the American
novel ought to deal with certain facts of life which are not usually
talked of before young people, and especially young ladies."*

Prolific writer, discerning editor, and political functionary, William Dean
Howells (1837–1920) was a literary giant in his day. Born in Ohio, Howells
moved frequently as his father sought work as a printer and journalist; he
acquired his impressive education by reading voraciously. At the age of
twenty-three, after writing for newspapers for a number of years, he wrote
a biography of Abraham Lincoln for the 1860 campaign and was rewarded
with an appointment as an American consul in Venice. There he studied
Italian and developed a love for Italian literature, which he describes in *My
Literary Passions.* After the Civil War, he settled in Boston and assumed a series of editorships—at *The Atlantic Monthly, Harper's Monthly,* and *Harper's
Weekly*—in which he championed socially conscious realism and innovative
writers like Mark Twain and Henry James, who became his lifelong friends.
In the editor's columns he attempted to shape the nation's literary taste,
and these formed the basis for *Criticism and Fiction.*

Howells was particularly concerned with social and ethical problems.
For example, he was one of the few prominent writers to denounce the
death sentences against seven anarchists accused in the Haymarket Square
bombing of 1886, and along with Twain he was active in anti-imperialist cir-
cles. He believed that through didacticism, literature should contribute to
improving society. In his novel *The Rise of Silas Lapham* (1885), the protag-
onist gains wealth, but rises spiritually only when he loses it. And, like
James, he portrayed the often tragic consequences that ensue when the
modern, independent but innocent "American girl" flouts European mores,
and is misunderstood by conservative Europeans. Ironically, by the time of
his death in 1920, he was being dismissed as a relic of the genteel tradition.

Text: William Dean Howells; *Criticism and Fiction;* New York: Harper & Brother, 1910.

EXPLORING ISSUES IN THE TEXT

1. Evaluate Howells' belief that popular fiction is subject to the law of supply and demand (pars. 3, 16–17).

2. Comment on Howells' defense of prudishness (par. 6ff.). Do you think this position is motivated by ethics or by economics?

3. Analyze Howell's remark that one "sex . . . is supposed somehow to have purity in its keeping" (par. 6).

CRITICISM AND FICTION

XXI

1   IT used to be one of the disadvantages of the practice of romance in America, which Hawthorne more or less whimsically lamented, that there were so few shadows and inequalities in our broad level of prosperity; and it is one of the reflections suggested by Dostoïevsky's novel, *The Crime and the Punishment,* that whoever struck a note so profoundly tragic in American fiction would do a false and mistaken thing—as false and as mistaken in its way as dealing in American fiction with certain nudities which the Latin peoples seem to find edifying. Whatever their deserts, very few American novelists have been led out to be shot, or finally exiled to the rigors of a winter at Duluth; and in a land where journeymen carpenters and plumbers strike for four dollars a day the sum of hunger and cold is comparatively small, and the wrong from class to class has been almost inappreciable, though all this is changing for the worse. Our novelists, therefore, concern themselves with the more smiling aspects of life, which are the more American, and seek the universal in the individual rather than the social interests. It is worth while, even at the risk of being called commonplace, to be true to our well-to-do actualities; the very passions themselves seem to be softened and modified by conditions which formerly at least could not be said to wrong any one, to cramp endeavor, or to cross lawful desire. Sin and suffering and shame there must always be in the world, I suppose, but I believe that in this new world of ours it is still mainly from one to another one, and oftener still from one to one's self. We have death, too, in America, and a great deal of disagreeable and painful disease, which the multiplicity of our patent medicines does not seem to cure; but this is tragedy that comes in the very nature of things, and is not peculiarly American, as the large, cheerful average of health and success and happy life is. It will not do to boast, but it is well to be true to the facts, and to see that, apart from these purely mortal troubles, the race here has enjoyed conditions in which most of the ills that have darkened its annals might be averted by honest work and unselfish behavior.

2   Fine artists we have among us, and right-minded as far as they go; and we must not forget this at evil moments when it seems as if all the women had taken to writing hysterical improprieties, and some of the men were trying to be at least as hysterical in despair of being as improper. Other

traits are much more characteristic of our life and our fiction. In most American novels, vivid and graphic as the best of them are, the people are segregated if not sequestered, and the scene is sparsely populated. The effect may be in instinctive response to the vacancy of our social life, and I shall not make haste to blame it. There are few places, few occasions among us, in which a novelist can get a large number of polite people together, or at least keep them together. Unless he carries a snap-camera his picture of them has no probability; they affect one like the figures perfunctorily associated in such deadly old engravings as that of "Washington Irving and his Friends." Perhaps it is for this reason that we excel in small pieces with three or four figures, or in studies of rustic communities, where there is propinquity if not society. Our grasp of more urbane life is feeble; most attempts to assemble it in our pictures are failures, possibly because it is too transitory, too intangible in its nature with us, to be truthfully represented as really existent.

3   I am not sure that the Americans have not brought the short story nearer perfection in the all-round sense than almost any other people, and for reasons very simple and near at hand. It might be argued from the national hurry and impatience that it was a literary form peculiarly adapted to the American temperament, but I suspect that its extraordinary development among us is owing much more to more tangible facts. The success of American magazines, which is nothing less than prodigious, is only commensurate with their excellence. Their sort of success is not only from the courage to decide which ought to please, but from the knowledge of what does please; and it is probable that, aside from the pictures, it is the short stories which please the readers of our best magazines. The serial novels they must have, or course; but rather more of course they must have short stories, and by operation of the law of supply and demand, the short stories, abundant in quantity and excellent in quality, are forthcoming because they are wanted. By another operation of the same law, which political economists have more recently taken account of, the demand follows the supply, and short stories are sought for because there is a proven ability to furnish them, and people read them willingly because they are usually very good. The art of writing them is now so disciplined and diffused with us that there is no lack either for the magazines or for the newspaper "syndicates" which deal in them almost to the exclusion of the serials.

4   An interesting fact in regard to the different varieties of the short story among us is that the sketches and studies by the women seem faithfuller and more realistic than those of the men, in proportion to their number. Their tendency is more distinctly in that direction, and there is a solidity, an honest observation, in the work of such women, which often leaves little to be desired. I should, upon the whole, be disposed to rank American short stories only below those of such Russian writers as I have read, and I should praise rather than blame their free use of our different local par-

lances, or "dialects," as people call them. I like this because I hope that our inherited English may be constantly freshened and revived from the native sources which our literary decentralization will help to keep open, and I will own that as I turn over novels coming from Philadelphia, from New Mexico, from Boston, from Tennessee, from rural New England, from New York, every local flavor of diction gives me courage and pleasure. . . .

5   In fine, I would have our American novelists be as American as they unconsciously can. Matthew Arnold complained that he found no "distinction" in our life, and I would gladly persuade all artists intending greatness in any kind among us that the recognition of the fact pointed out by Mr. Arnold ought to be a source of inspiration to them, and not discouragement. We have been now some hundred years building up a state on the affirmation of the essential equality of men in their rights and duties, and whether we have been right or been wrong the gods have taken us at our word, and have responded to us with a civilization in which there is no "distinction" perceptible to the eye that loves and values it. Such beauty and such grandeur as we have is common beauty, common grandeur, or the beauty and grandeur in which the quality of solidarity so prevails that neither distinguishes itself to the disadvantage of anything else. It seems to me that these conditions invite the artist to the study and the appreciation of the common, and to the portrayal in every art of those finer and higher aspects which unite rather than sever humanity, if he would thrive in our new order of things. The talent that is robust enough to front the every-day world and catch the charm of its work-worn, care-worn, brave, kindly face, need not fear the encounter, though it seems terrible to the sort nurtured in the superstition of the romantic, the bizarre, the heroic, the distinguished, as the things alone worthy of painting or carving or writing. The arts must become democratic, and then we shall have the expression of America in art; and the reproach which Arnold was half right in making us shall have no justice in it any longer; we shall be "distinguished."

XXIII

6   One of the great newspapers the other day invited the prominent American authors to speak their minds upon a point in the theory and practice of fiction which had already vexed some of them. It was the question of how much or how little the American novel ought to deal with certain facts of life which are not usually talked of before young people, and especially young ladies. Of course the question was not decided, and I forget just how far the balance inclined in favor of a larger freedom in the matter. But it certainly inclined that way; one or two writers of the sex which is somehow supposed to have purity in its keeping (as if purity were a thing that did not practically concern the other sex, preoccupied with serious affairs) gave it a rather vigorous tilt to that side. In view of this fact it would not be the part of prudence to make an effort to dress the balance; and indeed I do not

know that I was going to make any such effort. But there are some things to say, around and about the subject, which I should like to have some one else say, and which I may myself possibly be safe in suggesting.

7   One of the first of these is the fact, generally lost sight of by those who censure the Anglo-Saxon novel for its prudishness, that it is really not such a prude after all; and that if it is sometimes apparently anxious to avoid those experiences of life not spoken of before young people, this may be an appearance only. Sometimes a novel which has this shuffling air, this effect of truckling to propriety, might defend itself, if it could speak for itself, by saying that such experiences happened not to come within its scheme, and that, so far from maiming or mutilating itself in ignoring them, it was all the more faithfully representative of the tone of modern life in dealing with love that was chaste, and with passion so honest that it could be openly spoken of before the tenderest society bud at dinner. It might say that the guilty intrigue, the betrayal, the extreme flirtation even, was the exceptional thing in life, and unless the scheme of the story necessarily involved it, that it would be bad art to lug it in, and as bad taste as to introduce such topics in a mixed company. It could say very justly that the novel in our civilization now always addresses a mixed company, and that the vast majority of the company are ladies, and that very many, if not most, of these ladies are young girls. If the novel were written for men and for married women alone, as in continental Europe, it might be altogether different. But the simple fact is that it is not written for them alone among us, and it is a question of writing, under cover of our universal acceptance, things for young girls to read which you would be put out-of-doors for saying to them, or of frankly giving notice of your intention, and so cutting yourself off from the pleasure—and it is a very high and sweet one—of appealing to these vivid, responsive intelligences, which are none the less brilliant and admirable because they are innocent.

8   One day a novelist who liked, after the manner of other men, to repine at his hard fate, complained to his friend, a critic, that he was tired of the restriction he had put upon himself in this regard; for it is a mistake, as can be readily shown, to suppose that others impose it. "See how free those French fellows are!" he rebelled. "Shall we always be shut up to our tradition of decency?"

9   "Do you think it's much worse than being shut up to their tradition of indecency?" said his friend.

10   Then that novelist began to reflect, and he remembered how sick the invariable motive of the French novel made him. He perceived finally that, convention for convention, ours was not only more tolerable, but on the whole was truer to life, not only to its complexion, but also to its texture. No one will pretend that there is not vicious love beneath the surface of our society; if he did, the fetid explosions of the divorce trials would refute him; but if he pretended that it was in any just sense characteristic of our society, he could be still more easily refuted. Yet it exists, and it is unquestion-

ably the material of tragedy, the stuff from which intense effects are wrought. The question, after owning this fact, is whether these intense effects are not rather cheap effects. I incline to think they are, and I will try to say why I think so, if I may do so without offence. The material itself, the mere mention of it, has an instant fascination; it arrests, it detains, till the last word is said, and while there is anything to be hinted. This is what makes a love intrigue of some sort all but essential to the popularity of any fiction. Without such an intrigue the intellectual equipment of the author must be of the highest, and then he will succeed only with the highest class of readers. But any author who will deal with a guilty love intrigue holds all readers in his hand, the highest with the lowest, as long as he hints the slightest hope of the smallest potential naughtiness. He need not at all be a great author; he may be a very shabby wretch, if he has but the courage or the trick of that sort of thing. The critics will call him "virile" and "passionate"; decent people will be ashamed to have been limed by him; but the low average will only ask another chance of flocking into his net. If he happens to be an able writer, his really fine and costly work will be unheeded, and the lure to the appetite will be chiefly remembered. There may be other qualities which make reputations for other men, but in his case they will count for nothing. He pays this penalty for his success in that kind; and every one pays some such penalty who deals with some such material.

11   But I do not mean to imply that his case covers the whole ground. So far as it goes, though, it ought to stop the mouths of those who complain that fiction is enslaved to propriety among us. It appears that of a certain kind of impropriety it is free to give us all it will, and more. But this is not what serious men and women writing fiction mean when they rebel against the limitations of their art in our civilization. They have no desire to deal with nakedness, as painters and sculptors freely do in the worship of beauty; or with certain facts of life, as the stage does, in the service of sensation. But they ask why, when the conventions of the plastic and histrionic arts liberate their followers to the portrayal of almost any phase of the physical or of the emotional nature, an American novelist may not write a story on the lines of *Anna Karénina* or *Madame Bovary.* They wish to touch one of the most serious and sorrowful problems of life in the spirit of Tolstoy and Flaubert, and they ask why they may not. At one time, they remind us, the Anglo-Saxon novelist did deal with such problems—De Foe in his spirit, Richardson in his, Goldsmith in his. At what moment did our fiction lose this privilege? In what fatal hour did the Young Girl arise and seal the lips of Fiction, with a touch of her finger, to some of the most vital interests of life?

12   Whether I wished to oppose them in their aspiration for greater freedom, or whether I wished to encourage them, I should begin to answer them by saying that the Young Girl has never done anything of the kind. The manners of the novel have been improving with those of its readers; that is all. Gentlemen no longer swear or fall drunk under the table, or abduct young ladies and shut them up in lonely country-houses, or so

habitually set about the ruin of their neighbors' wives, as they once did. Generally, people now call a spade an agricultural implement; they have not grown decent without having also grown a little squeamish, but they have grown comparatively decent; there is no doubt about that. They require of a novelist whom they respect unquestionable proof of his seriousness, if he proposes to deal with certain phases of life; they require a sort of scientific decorum. He can no longer expect to be received on the ground of entertainment only; he assumes a higher function, something like that of a physician or a priest, and they expect him to be bound by laws as sacred as those of such professions; they hold him solemnly pledged not to betray them or abuse their confidence. If he will accept the conditions, they give him their confidence, and he may then treat to his greater honor, and not at all to his disadvantage, of such experiences, such relations of men and women as George Eliot treats in *Adam Bede,* in *Daniel Deronda,* in *Romola,* in almost all her books; such as Hawthorne treats in *The Scarlet Letter;* such as Dickens treats in *David Copperfield;* such as Thackeray treats in *Pendennis,* and glances at in every one of his fictions; such as most of the masters of English fiction have at some time treated more or less openly. It is quite false or quite mistaken to suppose that our novels have left untouched these most important realities of life. They have only not made them their stock in trade; they have kept a true perspective in regard to them; they have relegated them in their pictures of life to the space and place they occupy in life itself, as we know it in England and America. They have kept a correct proportion, knowing perfectly well that unless the novel is to be a map, with everything scrupulously laid down in it, a faithful record of life in far the greater extent could be made to the exclusion of guilty love and all its circumstances and consequences.

13   I justify them in this view not only because I hate what is cheap and meretricious, and hold in peculiar loathing the cant of the critics who require "passion" as something in itself admirable and desirable in a novel, but because I prize fidelity in the historian of feeling and character. Most of these critics who demand "passion" would seem to have no conception of any passion but one. Yet there are several other passions: the passion of grief, the passion of avarice, the passion of pity, the passion of ambition, the passion of hate, the passion of envy, the passion of devotion, the passion of friendship; and all these have a greater part in the drama of life than the passion of love, and infinitely greater than the passion of guilty love. Wittingly or unwittingly, English fiction and American fiction have recognized this truth, not fully, not in the measure it merits, but in greater degree than most other fiction.

XXIV

14 Who can deny that fiction would be incomparably stronger, incomparably truer, if once it could tear off the habit which enslaves it to the

celebration chiefly of a single passion, in one phase or another, and could frankly dedicate itself to the service of all the passions, all the interests, all the facts? Every novelist who has thought about his art knows that it would, and I think that upon reflection he must doubt whether his sphere would be greatly enlarged if he were allowed to treat freely the darker aspects of the favorite passion. But, as I have shown, the privilege, the right to do this, is already perfectly recognized. This is proved again by the fact that serious criticism recognizes as masterworks (I will not push the question of supremacy) the two great novels which above all others have moved the world by their study of guilty love. If by any chance, if by some prodigious miracle, any American should now arise to treat it on the level of *Anna Karénina* and *Madame Bovary,* he would be absolutely sure of success, and of fame and gratitude as great as those books have won for their authors.

15   But what editor of what American magazine would print such a story?

16   Certainly I do not think any one would; and here our novelist must again submit to conditions. If he wishes to publish such a story (supposing him to have once written it), he must publish it as a book. A book is something by itself, responsible for its character, which becomes quickly known, and it does not necessarily penetrate to every member of the household. The father or the mother may say to the child, "I would rather you wouldn't read that book"; if the child cannot be trusted, the book may be locked up. But with the magazine and its serial the affair is different. Between the editor of a reputable English or American magazine and the families which receive it there is a tacit agreement that he will print nothing which a father may not read to his daughter, or safely leave her to read herself.

17   After all, it is a matter of business; and the insurgent novelist should consider the situation with coolness and common-sense. The editor did not create the situation; but it exists, and he could not even attempt to change it without many sorts of disaster. He respects it, therefore, with the good faith of an honest man. Even when he is himself a novelist, with ardor for his art and impatience of the limitations put upon it, he interposes his veto, as Thackeray did in the case of Trollope when a contributor approaches forbidden ground.

18   It does not avail to say that the daily papers teem with facts far fouler and deadlier than any which fiction could imagine. That is true, but it is true also that the sex which reads the most novels reads the fewest newspapers; and, besides, the reporter does not command the novelist's skill to fix impressions in a young girl's mind or to suggest conjecture. The magazine is a little despotic, a little arbitrary; but unquestionably its favor is essential to success, and its conditions are not such narrow ones. You cannot deal with Tolstoy's and Flaubert's subjects in the absolute artistic freedom of Tolstoy and Flaubert; since De Foe, that is unknown among us; but if you deal with them in the manner of George Eliot, of Thackeray, of Dickens, of society, you may deal with them even in the

magazines. There is no other restriction upon you. All the horrors and miseries and tortures are open to you; your pages may drop blood; sometimes it may happen that the editor will even exact such strong material from you. But probably he will require nothing but the observance of the convention in question; and if you do not yourself prefer bloodshed he will leave you free to use all sweet and peaceable means of interesting his readers.

19   It is no narrow field he throws open to you, with that little sign to keep off the grass up at one point only. Its vastness is still almost unexplored, and whole regions in it are unknown to the fictionist. Dig anywhere, and do but dig deep enough, and you strike riches; or, if you are of the mind to range, the gentler climes, the softer temperatures, the serener skies, are all free to you, and are so little visited that the chance of novelty is greater among them.

Another Voice

IMPERIALISM IS HOSTILE TO LIBERTY

We hold that the policy known as imperialism is hostile to liberty and tends toward militarism, an evil from which it has been our glory to be free. We regret that it has become necessary in the land of Washington and Lincoln to reaffirm that all men, of whatever race or color, are entitled to life, liberty, and the pursuit of happiness. We maintain that governments derive their just powers from the consent of the governed. We insist that the subjugation of any people is "criminal aggression" and open disloyalty to the distinctive principles of our government.

We earnestly condemn the policy of the present national administration in the Philippines. It seeks to extinguish the spirit of 1776 in those islands. We deplore the sacrifice of our soldiers and sailors, whose bravery deserves admiration even in an unjust war. We denounce the slaughter of the Filipinos as a needless horror. We protest against the extension of American sovereignty by Spanish methods.

We demand the immediate cessation of the war against liberty, begun by Spain and continued by us. We urge that Congress

continued

continued from previous page

be promptly convened to announce to the Filipinos our purpose to concede to them the independence for which they have so long fought and which of right is theirs.

The United States have always protested against the doctrine of international law which permits the subjugation of the weak by the strong. A self-governing state cannot accept sovereignty over an unwilling people. The United States cannot act upon the ancient heresy that might makes right. . . .

We deny that the obligation of all citizens to support their government in times of grave national peril applies to the present situation. If an administration may with impunity ignore the issues upon which it was chosen, deliberately create a condition of war anywhere on the face of the globe, debauch the civil service for spoils to promote the adventure, organize a truth-suppressing censorship, and demand of all citizens a suspension of judgment and their unanimous support while it chooses to continue the fighting, representative government itself is imperiled.

Platform of the American Anti-imperialist League, 1899

BUILDING CONTEXT

1. Compare Howells's analysis of women and morality to those of Stowe or Millet. Analyze whether each writer finds the belief in women's morality sincere or manipulative.

2. Compare Howells's attitude toward sexuality in literature with that of the court decision in *Ulysses*.

3. Argue whether or not Howells would condone government censorship of fiction. Compare your conclusion to another author's beliefs, or to your own opinion.

FURTHER STUDY

1. Explore the economic influences on popular and "high" culture. What are the implications of supply and demand on pornography, for example? On censorship?

2. Investigate the literary convention of the "American girl." Why did it develop when it did? Why was the American girl more noteworthy than the boy, woman, or man?

ADDITIONAL RESOURCES

Eschholz, Paul A. *Critics on William Dean Howells.* Coral Gables, Fla.: University of Miami Press, 1975.

Habegger, Alfred. *Gender, Fantasy, and Realism in American Literature.* New York: Columbia University Press, 1982.

Prioleau, Elizabeth Stevens. *The Circle of Eros: Sexuality in the Work of William Dean Howells.* Durham, N.C.: Duke University Press, 1983.

Rugoff, Milton. *Prudery and Passion.* New York: Putnam, 1971.

RESEARCH KEYWORDS

Realism	Novel	American literature
Atlantic Monthly	Sex in Literature	Sex Role in Literature
Censorship		

FREDERICK JACKSON TURNER
"The Significance of the Frontier in American History" (1893)

"America has been another name for opportunity, and the people of the United States have taken their tone from the incessant expansion which has not only been open but has even been forced upon them."

Frederick Jackson Turner (1861–1932) was a young professor at the University of Wisconsin when he shocked the scholarly world with his theory that the existence of the frontier shaped the character of the United States. The reigning theory of the day was that America reflected its English roots, which in turn grew from medieval Germanic seeds ("germs"). In contrast, Turner argued that America was unique among modern nations because of its frontier. America alone had room to expand into open land without clashing with other established states, as happened time and again in Europe whenever a country tried to extend its territory. In addition, as the frontier receded, each new settlement repeated the pattern of earlier frontier settlements: contemporary civilization was not simply planted in new soil; rather America relived, section by section, the entire process of birth and growth. Thus, frontier characteristics like ruggedness, independence, and creativity became typically American. Finally, lacking entrenched sectional loyalty, frontier settlers looked to the central government for support, thereby strengthening national identity.

This view, essentially optimistic, appealed to a nation eager to believe that its vigorous democracy had overtaken the decrepit empires of Europe, as evidenced by thriving industries and expansion into the Pacific. It was especially popular among the Midwestern states that still felt their pioneer origins, while Eastern intellectuals used it to explain the roughness and Populist politics of middle America.

Text: Frederick Jackson Turner, *The Significance of the Frontier in American History.* New York: Holt, Rinehart and Winston, 1962.

EXPLORING ISSUES IN THE TEXT

1. Summarize the features that Turner says make American development unique (pars. 1-2). How was the American frontier different from European frontiers (pars. 3-4)?

2. Explain how the frontier contributes to the creation of national identity (pars. 8-11).

3. Explain how the frontier promotes democracy (pars. 12–13) and shapes national character (par. 16).

THE SIGNIFICANCE OF THE FRONTIER IN AMERICAN HISTORY

1 In a recent bulletin of the Superintendent of the Census for 1890 appear these significant words: "Up to and including 1880 the country had a frontier of settlement, but at present the unsettled area has been so broken into by isolated bodies of settlement that there can hardly be said to be a frontier line. In the discussion of its extent, its westward movement, etc., it can not, therefore, any longer have a place in the census reports." This brief official statement marks the closing of a great historic movement. Up to our own day American history has been in a large degree the history of the colonization of the Great West. The existence of an area of free land, its continuous recession, and the advance of American settlement westward, explain American development.

2 Behind institutions, behind constitutional forms and modifications, lie the vital forces that call these organs into life and shape them to meet changing conditions. The peculiarity of American institutions is, the fact that they have been compelled to adapt themselves to the changes of an expanding people—to the changes involved in crossing a continent, in

winning a wilderness, and in developing at each area of this progress out of the primitive economic and political conditions of the frontier into the complexity of city life. Said Calhoun in 1817, "We are great, and rapidly—I was about to say fearfully—growing!" So saying, he touched the distinguishing feature of American life. All peoples show development; the germ theory of politics has been sufficiently emphasized. In the case of most nations, however, the development has occurred in a limited area; and if the nation has expanded, it has met other growing peoples whom it has conquered. But in the case of the United States we have a different phenomenon. Limiting our attention to the Atlantic coast, we have the familiar phenomenon of the evolution of institutions in a limited area, such as the rise of representative government; the differentiation of simple colonial governments into complex organs; the progress from primitive industrial society, without division of labor, up to manufacturing civilization. But we have in addition to this a recurrence of the process of evolution in each western area reached in the process of expansion. Thus American development has exhibited not merely advance along a single line, but a return to primitive conditions on a continually advancing frontier line, and a new development for that area. American social development has been continually beginning over again on the frontier. This perennial rebirth, this fluidity of American life, this expansion westward with its new opportunities, its continuous touch with the simplicity of primitive society, furnish the forces dominating American character. The true point of view in the history of this nation is not the Atlantic coast, it is the Great West. Even the slavery struggle, which is made so exclusive an object of attention by writers like Professor von Holst, occupies its important place in American history because of its relation to westward expansion.

3   In this advance, the frontier is the outer edge of the wave—the meeting point between savagery and civilization. Much has been written about the frontier from the point of view of border warfare and the chase, but as a field for the serious study of the economist and the historian it has been neglected.

4   The American frontier is sharply distinguished from the European frontier—a fortified boundary line running through dense populations. The most significant thing about the American frontier is, that it lies at the hither edge of free land. In the census reports it is treated as the margin of that settlement which has a density of two or more to the square mile. The term is an elastic one, and for our purposes does not need sharp definition. We shall consider the whole frontier belt, including the Indian country and the outer margin of the "settled area" of the census reports. This paper will make no attempt to treat the subject exhaustively; its aim is simply to call attention to the frontier as a fertile field for investigation, and to suggest some of the problems which arise in connection with it.

5   In the settlement of America we have to observe how European life entered the continent, and how America modified and developed that life and reacted on Europe. Our early history is the study of European germs developing in an American environment. Too exclusive attention has been paid by institutional students to the Germanic origins, too little to the American factors. The frontier is the line of most rapid and effective Americanization. The wilderness masters the colonist. It finds him a European in dress, industries, tools, modes of travel, and thought. It takes him from the railroad car and puts him in the birch canoe. It strips off the garments of civilization and arrays him in the hunting shirt and the moccasin. It puts him in the log cabin of the Cherokee and Iroquois and runs an Indian palisade around him. Before long he has gone to planting Indian corn and plowing with a sharp stick; he shouts the war cry and takes the scalp in orthodox Indian fashion. In short, at the frontier the environment is at first too strong for the man. He must accept the conditions which it furnishes, or perish, and so he fits himself into the Indian clearings and follows the Indian trails. Little by little he transforms the wilderness, but the outcome is not the old Europe, not simply the development of Germanic germs, any more than the first phenomenon was a case of reversion to the Germanic mark. The fact is, that here is a new product that is American. At first, the frontier was the Atlantic coast. It was the frontier of Europe in a very real sense. Moving westward, the frontier became more and more American. As successive terminal moraines result from successive glaciations, so each frontier leaves its traces behind it, and when it becomes a settled area the region still partakes of the frontier characteristics. Thus the advance of the frontier has meant a steady movement away from the influence of Europe, a steady growth of independence on American lines. And to study this advance, the men who grew up under these conditions, and the political, economic, and social results of it, is to study the really American part of our history. . . .

6   At the Atlantic frontier one can study the germs of processes repeated at each successive frontier. We have the complex European life sharply precipitated by the wilderness into the simplicity of primitive conditions. The first frontier had to meet its Indian question, its question of the disposition of the public domain, of the means of intercourse with older settlements, of the extension of political organization, of religious and educational activity. And the settlement of these and similar questions for one frontier served as a guide for the next. The American student needs not to go to the "prim little townships of Sleswick" for illustrations of the law of continuity and development. For example, he may study the origin of our land policies in the colonial land policy; he may see how the system grew by adapting the statutes to the customs of the successive frontiers. He may see how the mining experience in the lead regions of Wisconsin, Illinois, and Iowa was applied to the mining

laws of the Sierras, and how our Indian policy has been a series of experimentations on successive frontiers. Each tier of new States has found in the older ones material for its constitutions. Each frontier has made similar contributions to American character. . . .

7   Having now roughly outlined the various kinds of frontiers, and their modes of advance, chiefly from the point of view of the frontier itself, we may next inquire what were the influences on the East and on the Old World. A rapid enumeration of some of the more noteworthy effects is all that I have time for.

8   First, we note that the frontier promoted the formation of a composite nationality for the American people. The coast was preponderantly English, but the later tides of continental immigration flowed across to the free lands. This was the case from the early colonial days. The Scotch-Irish and the Palatine Germans, or "Pennsylvania Dutch," furnished the dominant element in the stock of the colonial frontier. With these peoples were also the freed indented servants, or redemptioners, who at the expiration of their time of service passed to the frontier. Governor Spotswood of Virginia writes in 1717, "The inhabitants of our frontiers are composed generally of such as have been transported hither as servants, and, being out of their time, settle themselves where land is to be taken up and that will produce the necessarys of life with little labour." Very generally these redemptioners were of non-English stock. In the crucible of the frontier the immigrants were Americanized, liberated, and fused into a mixed race, English in neither nationality nor characteristics. The process has gone on from the early days to our own. Burke and other writers in the middle of the eighteenth century believed that Pennsylvania was "threatened with the danger of being wholly foreign in language, manners, and perhaps even inclinations." The German and Scotch-Irish elements in the frontier of the South were only less great. In the middle of the present century the German element in Wisconsin was already so considerable that leading publicists looked to the creation of a German state out of the commonwealth by concentrating their colonization. Such examples teach us to beware of misinterpreting the fact that there is a common English speech in America into a belief that the stock is also English.

9   In another way the advance of the frontier decreased our dependence on England. The coast, particularly of the South, lacked diversified industries, and was dependent on England for the bulk of its supplies. In the South there was even a dependence on the Northern colonies for articles of food. Governor Glenn, of South Carolina, writes in the middle of the eighteenth century: "Our trade with New York and Philadelphia was of this sort, draining us of all the little money and bills we could gather from other places for their bread, flour, beer, hams, bacon, and other things of their produce, all which, except beer, our new townships begin to supply us with, which are settled with very industrious and thriving Germans.

This no doubt diminishes the number of shipping and the appearance of our trade, but it is far from being a detriment to us." Before long the frontier created a demand for merchants. As it retreated from the coast it became less and less possible for England to bring her supplies directly to the consumer's wharfs, and carry away staple crops, and staple crops began to give way to diversified agriculture for a time. The effect of this phase of the frontier action upon the northern section is perceived when we realize how the advance of the frontier aroused seaboard cities like Boston, New York, and Baltimore, to engage in rivalry for what Washington called "the extensive and valuable trade of a rising empire."

10 The legislation which most developed the powers of the national government, and played the largest part in its activity, was conditioned on the frontier. . . . The pioneer needed the goods of the coast, and so the grand series of internal improvement and railroad legislation began, with potent nationalizing effects. . . .

11 It was this nationalizing tendency of the West that transformed the democracy of Jefferson into the national republicanism of Monroe and the democracy of Andrew Jackson. The West of the War of 1812, the West of Clay, and Benton and Harrison, and Andrew Jackson, shut off by the Middle States and the mountains from the coast sections, had a solidarity of its own with national tendencies. On the tide of the Father of Waters, North and South met and mingled into a nation. Interstate migration went steadily on—a process of cross-fertilization of ideas and institutions. The fierce struggle of the sections over slavery on the western frontier does not diminish the truth of this statement; it proves the truth of it. Slavery was a sectional trait that would not down, but in the West it could not remain sectional. It was the greatest of frontiersmen who declared: "I believe this Government can not endure permanently half slave and half free. It will become all of one thing or all of the other." Nothing works for nationalism like intercourse within the nation. Mobility of population is death to localism, and the western frontier worked irresistibly in unsettling population. The effect reached back from the frontier and affected profoundly the Atlantic coast and even the Old World.

12 But the most important effect of the frontier has been in the promotion of democracy here and in Europe. As has been indicated, the frontier is productive of individualism. Complex society is precipitated by the wilderness into a kind of primitive organization based on the family. The tendency is anti-social. It produces antipathy to control, and particularly to any direct control. The tax-gatherer is viewed as a representative of oppression. Prof. Osgood, in an able article, has pointed out that the frontier conditions prevalent in the colonies are important factors in the explanation of the American Revolution, where individual liberty was sometimes confused with absence of all effective government. The same conditions aid in explaining the difficulty of instituting a strong

government in the period of the confederacy. The frontier individualism has from the beginning promoted democracy.

13   The frontier States that came into the Union in the first quarter of a century of its existence came in with democratic suffrage provisions, and had reactive effects of the highest importance upon the older States whose peoples were being attracted there. An extension of the franchise became essential. It was *western* New York that forced an extension of suffrage in the constitutional convention of that State in 1821; and it was *western* Virginia that compelled the tide-water region to put a more liberal suffrage provision in the constitution framed in 1830, and to give to the frontier region a more nearly proportionate representation with the tide-water aristocracy. The rise of democracy as an effective force in the nation came in with western preponderance under Jackson and William Henry Harrison, and it meant the triumph of the frontier—with all of its good and with all of its evil elements. . . .

14   The most effective efforts of the East to regulate the frontier came through its educational and religious activity, exerted by interstate migration and by organized societies. Speaking in 1835, Dr. Lyman Beecher declared: "It is equally plain that the religious and political destiny of our nation is to be decided in the West," and he pointed out that the population of the West "is assembled from all the States of the Union and from all the nations of Europe, and is rushing in like the waters of the flood, demanding for its moral preservation the immediate and universal action of those institutions which discipline the mind and arm the conscience and the heart. And so various are the opinions and habits, and so recent and imperfect is the acquaintance, and so sparse are the settlements of the West, that no homogeneous public sentiment can be formed to legislate immediately into being the requisite institutions. And yet they are all needed immediately in their utmost perfection and power. A nation is being 'born in a day.' . . . But what will become of the West if her prosperity rushes up to such a majesty of power, while those great institutions linger which are necessary to form the mind and the conscience and the heart of that vast world. It must not be permitted. . . . Let no man at the East quiet himself and dream of liberty, whatever may become of the West. . . . Her destiny is our destiny."

15   With the appeal to the conscience of New England, he adds appeals to her fears lest other religious sects anticipate her own. The New England preacher and school-teacher left their mark on the West. The dread of Western emancipation from New England's political and economic control was paralleled by her fears lest the West cut loose from her religion. Commenting in 1850 on reports that settlement was rapidly extending northward in Wisconsin, the editor of the *Home Missionary* writes: "We scarcely know whether to rejoice or mourn over this extension of our settlements. While we sympathize in whatever tends to increase the

physical resources and prosperity of our country, we can not forget that with all these dispersions into remote and still remoter corners of the land the supply of the means of grace is becoming relatively less and less." Acting in accordance with such ideas, home missions were established and Western colleges were erected. As seaboard cities like Philadelphia, New York, and Baltimore strove for the mastery of Western trade, so the various denominations strove for the possession of the West. Thus an intellectual stream from New England sources fertilized the West. Other sections sent their missionaries; but the real struggle was between sects. The contest for power and the expansive tendency furnished to the various sects by the existence of a moving frontier must have had important results on the character of religious organization in the United States. The multiplication of rival churches in the little frontier towns had deep and lasting social effects. The religious aspects of the frontier make a chapter in our history which needs study.

16   From the conditions of frontier life came intellectual traits of profound importance. The works of travelers along each frontier from colonial days onward describe certain common traits, and these traits have, while softening down, still persisted as survivals in the place of their origin, even when a higher social organization succeeded. The result is that to the frontier the American intellect owes its striking characteristics. That coarseness and strength combined with acuteness and inquisitiveness; that practical, inventive turn of mind, quick to find expedients; that masterful grasp of material things, lacking in the artistic but powerful to effect great ends; that restless, nervous energy; that dominant individualism, working for good and for evil, and withal that buoyancy and exuberance which comes with freedom—these are traits of the frontier, or traits called out elsewhere because of the existence of the frontier. Since the days when the fleet of Columbus sailed into the waters of the New World, America has been another name for opportunity, and the people of the United States have taken their tone from the incessant expansion which has not only been open but has even been forced upon them. He would be a rash prophet who should assert that the expansive character of American life has now entirely ceased. Movement has been its dominant fact, and, unless this training has no effect upon a people, the American energy will continually demand a wider field for its exercise. But never again will such gifts of free land offer themselves. For a moment, at the frontier, the bonds of custom are broken and unrestraint is triumphant. There is not *tabula rasa*. The stubborn American environment is there with its imperious summons to accept its conditions; the inherited ways of doing things are also there; and yet, in spite of environment, and in spite of custom, each frontier did indeed furnish a new field of opportunity, a gate of escape from the bondage of the past; and freshness, and confidence, and scorn of older society, impatience of its

restraints and its ideas, and indifference to its lessons, have accompanied the frontier. What the Mediterranean Sea was to the Greeks, breaking the bond of custom, offering new experiences, calling out new institutions and activities, that, and more, the ever retreating frontier has been to the United States directly, and to the nations of Europe more remotely. And now, four centuries from the discovery of America, at the end of a hundred years of life under the Constitution, the frontier has gone, and with its going has closed the first period of American history.

BUILDING CONTEXT

1. Compare Turner's view of the Indians to that of Stanley or another writer. For example, are Indians people or merely one of the obstacles to be overcome? What does Turner see as the place of the Indian in American development?
2. Analyze Turner's theory about creating group identity. How is a group defined? Compare this view to Justice Harlan's.
3. Examine the relevance of Turner's observations to Hoover's theory of rugged individualism. Consider, for example, whether the pioneer on the frontier is a rugged individual or requires governmental support.

FURTHER STUDY

1. Explore the popular image of the frontiersman or pioneer. What place did this image play in shaping America's history? What influence has it had on governmental policy concerning, for example, unemployment insurance and welfare?
2. Investigate the image of the frontier in popular movies. Compare this image—or these images—to Turner's description of the frontier.

ADDITIONAL RESOURCES

Billington, Ray Allen. *The American Frontier Thesis: Attack and Defense.* Washington: American Historical Association, 1971.

Taylor, George Rogers. *The Turner Thesis concerning the Role of the Frontier in American History.* 3rd ed. Lexington, MA: Heath, 1972.

RESEARCH KEYWORDS

Turner (Frederick Jackson)	Frontier	Frontier Thesis
Nationalism	Individualism	

HENRY M. STANLEY
My Early Travels and Adventures in America
(1895)

"*It* is useless to blame the white race for moving across the continent. . . . If we proceed in that manner, we shall presently find ourselves blaming Columbus for discovering America. . . ."

"Dr. Livingston, I presume." With these words, *New York Herald* reporter Henry Stanley, who had trekked through the uncharted wilds of "Darkest Africa" in search of the missing explorer, immortalized his greatest scoop—and fashioned his image as a steely-nerved adventurer.

Henry Stanley (1841–1904) was born John Rowlands in Wales, the illegitimate son of Elizabeth Parry, who left him in the care of relatives and the public almshouse. At 15, the boy ran away from the school-workhouse where he had learned the values of discipline and religious faith, and, in 1858, arrived as a cabin boy in New Orleans. There he was befriended by a wealthy merchant who eventually adopted him—and became his new namesake: Henry Morton Stanley.

When the Civil War broke out shortly afterwards, young Stanley was pressured by his friends to enlist in the Confederate Army. He was captured at Shiloh in 1862 and, while in prison in Chicago, agreed to join a newly formed Union regiment composed of foreign-born prisoners of war. He had contracted dysentery, however, and soon found himself honorably discharged from the army. After drifting from job to job, he enlisted in the Union Navy and wrote about some of the battles he saw, thus beginning his career in journalism, for which he is most remembered.

In 1867 Stanley covered the Indian territory for the St. Louis *Missouri Democrat,* traveling with the army and various Indian Peace Commissioners. He described life on the frontier and recorded the negotiations for a number of peace treaties. In 1895, when he was famous worldwide for his exploits in Africa, he collected these and other pieces to publish *My Early Travels and Adventures in America and Asia,* adding the retrospective introduction that is reprinted here.

Text: Henry M. Stanley, *My Early Travels and Adventures in America and Asia.* Vol. 1; London: S. Low, Marston, 1895.

EXPLORING ISSUES IN THE TEXT

1. Describe the changes to the frontier between 1867 and 1895 (pars. 3–4). What is Stanley's attitude toward these changes?

2. Explain why Stanley believes "it is useless to blame the white race" for the fate of the Indians (par. 5). What is his view of Native American history before the arrival of Europeans (par. 6)? According to Stanley, how were the natives affected by the Europeans (pars. 7–9)?

3. From what Stanley says in paragraph 7, what can you infer about white attitudes toward the Indians? What attitude does Stanley project in paragraphs 10 and 11?

MY EARLY TRAVELS
AND ADVENTURES IN AMERICA

1   The letters from the Indian country which are contained in the first volume were not written with a view to permanent publication, but for the exacting and imperious necessities of American newspapers, principally for the *Missouri Democrat* of St. Louis, and a New York paper. Previous to the period at which they begin, I had been only an Occasional Descriptist of battle scenes and important public events; but in my twenty-fifth year I was promoted to the proud position of a Special Correspondent, with the very large commission to inform the public regarding all matters of general interest affecting the Indians and the great Western plains.

2   The incidents to which the letters relate occurred in 1867, during two Indian Campaigns. When General Hancock's Expedition first set out from the Missouri River, it was generally expected that there would be a good deal of fighting; but the General's disposition, and management of the Indian chiefs, were such that he had only to conduct a series of tactical marches through the red men's domains. Later, General Sherman took charge of the operations. He was accompanied by several of the most renowned American Generals, such as old General Harney, Generals Augur, Terry, Sanborn and Hardie, who with a couple of Chief Indian Commissioners, and Senator Henderson, constituted a Peace Commission. On discovering that there was not much need of his military services, Sherman soon retired, and left the Indian affairs in the hands of the Peace Commissioners. To hold the councils with the principal Indian tribes, the Peace Commission made prolonged excursions through a wide tract of the plains, altogether travelling about 2000 miles. The incidents on these journeys afforded abundance of interesting matter to the press of the period, and were not without benefit to me in after years.

3   Scarcely twenty-eight years have elapsed since these letters were hastily written amid the bustle of military life, and yet what a change has

come over the face of the land! I find that many of the predictions then ventured upon have been more than realised. Kansas, which contained in 1867 only 350,000 inhabitants, now possesses a population of one and a half millions. The several isolated forts at which we halted have become thriving towns and cities, connected by railways. Dodge City, near old Fort Dodge, has 2000 people. Cheyenne City—then only a tented camp—numbers 12,000 inhabitants. Junction City and Abilene, its neighbour, have over 6000. Laramie City in 1890 contained 6400 inhabitants. The territory of Colorado, which in 1867 had only 35,000, is now a State with over half a million of people, while the population of Nebraska has increased from 122,000 to 1,100,000. In their respective capitals, Denver and Omaha, will be found the greatest marvels of growth and prosperity; for Denver has increased from 3500 to 106,000 people, while Omaha, from 11,000, has risen to 145,000. We may well look back "bewildered, and wondering how it is" that such prodigious and extraordinary results have taken place.

4   From the letters in the first volume it may be gathered what this portion of the United States—Nebraska, Eastern Colorado and Western Kansas—was like in 1867. It was chiefly an ocean of prairie untenanted by the white man, except at the Forts. It was one vast pasture plain, trodden by buffalo, and ranged over by thousands of audaciously hostile Indians. It is now intersected by railways—as many as nine lines cross Kansas—the buffalo have been exterminated, the Indians are rare visitants, and may be said to have disappeared; and over their hunting-grounds, about which they were so anxious and appealed so passionately, there are scattered 750,000 orderly and law-abiding white citizens.

5   Few can read the speeches of the Indian chiefs without feeling deep sympathy for them. They move us by their pathos and mournful dignity, for it must be admitted, now that we know what has happened, that the speech of Black Foot, for instance, is solemn and depressing reading. What has taken place was inevitable. It is useless to blame the white race for moving across the continent in a constantly increasing tide. If we proceed in that manner, we shall presently find ourselves blaming Columbus for discovering America, and the Pilgrim Fathers for landing on Plymouth Rock. The whites have done no more than follow the law of their nature and being. Moreover, they had as much right to the plains as the Indians, and it would not be a difficult task to prove that they had a better right.

6   The mounds in the Mississippi Valley, the temple ruins of Central America, and the silent cities in Arizona prove that there once existed in America semi-civilised millions. But the Pilgrim Fathers found no such people when they landed in America in 1620, they found only war-bred savages, who were devoted to internecine strife, descendants, probably, of those nomads who had dispossessed the true aborigines. When the white race appeared, it was the turn of the haughty savages to be dispossessed, and driven back to the West, where, in 1867, we find them cooped up between the Missouri River and the Rocky Mountains. The whites were, however, kinder to them

than their fathers had been to the industrious mound-builders. For two hundred and fifty years the whites persisted in offering terms of peace, but during all that time the slightest cause had been seized by the Indians for renewing the strife. Had not the American Government restrained them from their inter-tribal wars, protected them from unscrupulous traders, and from the just revenge of settlers, the tribes treated of in these letters had long ago been exterminated. Savage and implacable humanity of the Indian type need expect no other fate than that of extinction.

7   In commenting upon the causes of the red men's disappearance, writers have been in the habit of imputing the blame to the white colonists. From the pulpit and the press, as well as on the floors of the congressional halls, the diatribes have issued in eloquent streams. There is no doubt that the rifles and "firewater" of the colonists have slain a great many, but the principal causes of their disappearance have sprung from their own innate savagery. It was in their nature to destroy their own families, tribes and each other. The "firewater" of the whites undermined the constitutions of a comparative few, but with the firearms, of which they obtained possession by trade and war, and as peace offerings, the incorrigible Indian spirit of revenge led them, upon the most trivial affront, to remorseless slaughter of each other. It would be no exaggeration to state that twenty times more Indians fell by the hands of rifle-armed Indians than by the arms of the whites.

8   Added to the fatal habit of Indians to resent their petty spites with midnight massacre of entire families, communities—aye, even of tribes— were the thousand and one accidents of savage life, the ravages of infectious diseases, the cruel indifference to childhood and infirm age, the neglect of the sick, the lack of means and knowledge to arrest illness, their ignorance of medicine, and profound faith in the incantations of their "medicine-men," the insanitary condition of their camps, their coarse and precarious manner of existence, their sudden exposure to wintry blasts after being overheated in their wigwams, the brutal treatment and heavy labour to which they subjected their females, old and young, and the natural sterility of their women consequent upon privation and intermarriage between relations, or "breeding in." These, and hundreds of kindred causes, prove that the nature of Indian life and temper killed thousands where the whites killed scores.

9   When the hot-headed and fiery braves, whose chief glory lay in the number of scalps taken, exchanged their primitive weapons for the musket, their power of inflicting loss upon their race increased tenfold, but when they exchanged the flintlock or single-shot rifle for the fifteen-shot Winchester, any one who reasoned might perceive that their annihilation was not far off.

10   The lessons derived from the near extinction of the Indian are very applicable to Africa, and it was my principal reason for advocating the

prohibition of trade in breech-loading rifles with Africans. To produce the same effects on the African aborigines as have resulted in the almost total destruction of the North Americans, all we need do is to freely permit the carriage of modern rifles and their ammunition into Africa, and in a few years we shall find the same rapid process of depopulation going on there. Savages have the minds of children and the passions of brutes, and to place breech-loaders in their hands is as cruel an act as to put razors in the hands of infants.

11   These letters describe two great efforts made by the United States Government to save the unfortunate Indians from the consequences of their own rash and heedless acts. The speeches of Generals Hancock and Sherman and the Peace Commissioners faithfully reflect the sentiments of the most cultivated Americans towards them, and are genuine exhortations to the Indians to stand aside from the overwhelming wave of white humanity which is resistlessly rolling towards the Pacific, and to take refuge on the reservations, where they will be fed, clothed, protected, and educated in the arts of industry and Christian and civilised principles. The replies of the Indian chiefs no less faithfully reflect their savage, indomitable spirit, their proud contempt of danger, and betray in many instances a consciousness of the sad destiny awaiting them.

BUILDING CONTEXT

1. Compare Stanley's explanation for the destruction of the Native American cultures to those of Van Every and Cameron.

2. Contrast Stanley's views about educating and "civilizing" the Native Americans with those of Red Jacket.

3. Place Stanley's views within the context of America's mission or religious heritage. For example, do Stanley and Theodore Roosevelt share the same concept of America's destiny?

FURTHER STUDY

1. What was Stanley's tone and intent when he said "we shall presently find ourselves blaming Columbus for discovering America"? What had happened to this perception by the time of the Columbus Quincentenary in 1992? Account for this change of perspective by placing it in historical context.

2. Investigate the term "white man's burden." What was its original meaning? What mission did it reflect? What were its results? You might want to read Rudyard Kipling's poem, "The White Man's Burden."

ADDITIONAL RESOURCES

Brown, D. Alexander. *Bury My Heart at Wounded Knee.* New York: Holt, Rinehart and Winston, 1971.

Mardock, Robert W. *The Reformers and the American Indian.* Columbia: University of Missouri Press, 1971.

Moquin, Wayne, and Charles Van Doren, eds. *Great Documents in American Indian History.* New York: Praeger, 1973.

Nabakov, Peter, ed. *Native American Testimony.* New York: Viking, 1991.

RESEARCH KEYWORDS

Manifest Destiny   Anthropology
American Indians   Exploration

BOOKER T. WASHINGTON
"The Atlanta Address"
(1895)

"The wisest of my race understand that the agitation of questions of social equality is the extremest folly. . . . No race that has anything to contribute to the markets of the world is long in any degree ostracized."

Booker T. Washington (1856–1915) was born in a slave shack on a plantation in Virginia; his father was believed to be a neighboring white man. After the Emancipation, his mother took the family to join her husband in West Virginia, and Booker took his stepfather's first name as his own surname. Despite working in a salt furnace and a coal mine, Washington attended school at every opportunity. In 1872, he was considered promising enough to be admitted to the Hampton Normal and Agricultural Institute, which had been established four years earlier to provide freed slaves with practical vocational skills. Washington worked as a janitor at the school while training to be a brick mason and learning social manners. After receiving additional training at Weyland Seminary in Washington, he returned to Hampton as a teacher in an experimental program for Native Americans.

In 1881 he was asked to direct the newly founded—but as yet barely existing—Tuskegee Normal and Industrial Institute in Alabama. Starting with one teacher and about fifty students, over the next three decades Washington led students in literally constructing the school while attending classes. He also assembled a distinguished faculty, including, for example, the renowned botanist George Washington Carver as head of the Department of Agriculture. The success of Tuskegee made Washington a national hero and the leading spokesman of African Americans for a generation.

In 1895, at the Cotton States and International Exposition, Washington delivered what came to be called his "Atlanta Compromise," stating his belief that economic power had to precede social integration, which he felt would naturally follow once the freedmen proved their value. This position proved very popular among whites, since it promised to defuse demands for immediate equality, while holding the blacks accountable for their lack of progress. Needless to say, however, its reception among blacks was more ambivalent, and Washington's "Compromise" remains a source of bitterness among many—as exemplified by W. E. B. Du Bois in his famous critique (see Chapter 9).

Text: Booker T. Washington; *Up From Slavery;* N.Y.: Doubleday, 1901.

EXPLORING ISSUES IN THE TEXT

1. Interpret the story about the ship lost at sea (par. 5). Examine how Washington uses it to structure his argument (pars. 5–7).

2. What do you infer were the alternatives to blacks and whites "cast[ing] down your bucket where you are"?

3. Examine Washington's attitude toward immigrants (par. 7). Why should Southern whites feel more loyalty to blacks than to immigrants?

4. Analyze Washington's strategy in paragraphs 11 and 12. Why might this passage have offended African Americans? What was Washington's reaction to their objections?

THE ATLANTA ADDRESS

1 The Atlanta Exposition, at which I had been asked to make an address as a representative of the Negro race, as stated in the last chapter, was opened with a short address from Governor Bullock. After other interesting exercises, including an invocation from Bishop Nelson, of Georgia, a dedicatory ode by Albert Howell, Jr., and addresses by the President of the Exposition and Mrs. Joseph Thompson, the President of the Woman's Board, Governor Bullock introduced me with the words, "We have with us to-day a representative of Negro enterprise and Negro civilization."

2   When I arose to speak, there was considerable cheering, especially from the coloured people. As I remember it now, the thing that was uppermost in my mind was the desire to say something that would cement the friendship of the races and bring about hearty coöperation between them. So far as my outward surroundings were concerned, the only thing that I recall distinctly now is that when I got up, I saw thousands of eyes looking intently into my face. The following is the address which I delivered:—

MR. PRESIDENT AND GENTLEMEN OF THE BOARD OF DIRECTORS AND CITIZENS.

3   One-third of the population of the South is of the Negro race. No enterprise seeking the material, civil, or moral welfare of this section can disregard this element of our population and reach the highest success. I but convey to you, Mr. President and Directors, the sentiment of the masses of my race when I say that in no way have the value and manhood of the American Negro been more fittingly and generously recognized than by the managers of this magnificent Exposition at every stage of its progress. It is a recognition that will do more to cement the friendship of the two races than any occurrence since the dawn of our freedom.

4   Not only this, but the opportunity here afforded will awaken among us a new era of industrial progress. Ignorant and inexperienced, it is not strange that in the first years of our new life we began at the top instead of at the bottom; that a seat in Congress or the state legislature was more sought than real estate or industrial skill; that the political convention or stump speaking had more attractions than starting a dairy farm or truck garden.

5   A ship lost at sea for many days suddenly sighted a friendly vessel. From the mast of the unfortunate vessel was seen a signal, "Water, water; we die of thirst!" The answer from the friendly vessel at once came back, "Cast down your bucket where you are." A second time the signal, "Water, water; send us water!" ran up from the distressed vessel, and was answered, "Cast down your bucket where you are." And a third and fourth signal for water was answered, "Cast down your bucket where you are." The captain of the distressed vessel, at last heeding the injunction, cast down his bucket, and it came up full of fresh, sparkling water from the mouth of the Amazon River. To those of my race who depend on bettering their condition in a foreign land or who underestimate the importance of cultivating friendly relations with the Southern white man, who is their next-door neighbour, I would say: "Cast down your bucket where you are"—cast it down in making friends in every manly way of the people of all races by whom we are surrounded.

6   Cast it down in agriculture, mechanics, in commerce, in domestic service, and in the professions. And in this connection it is well to bear in mind that whatever other sins the South may be called to bear, when it

comes to business, pure and simple, it is in the South that the Negro is given a man's chance in the commercial world, and in nothing is this Exposition more eloquent than in emphasizing this chance. Our greatest danger is that in the great leap from slavery to freedom we may overlook the fact that the masses of us are to live by the productions of our hands, and fail to keep in mind that we shall prosper in proportion as we learn to dignify and glorify common labour and put brains and skill into the common occupations of life; shall prosper in proportion as we learn to draw the line between the superficial and the substantial, the ornamental gewgaws of life and the useful. No race can prosper till it learns that there is as much dignity in tilling a field as in writing a poem. It is at the bottom of life we must begin, and not at the top. Nor should we permit our grievances to overshadow our opportunities.

7   To those of the white race who look to the incoming of those of foreign birth and strange tongue and habits for the prosperity of the South, were I permitted I would repeat what I say to my own race, "Cast down your bucket where you are." Cast it down among the eight millions of Negroes whose habits you know, whose fidelity and love you have tested in days when to have proved treacherous meant the ruin of your firesides. Cast down your bucket among these people who have, without strikes and labour wars, tilled your fields, cleared your forests, builded your railroads and cities, and brought forth treasures from the bowels of the earth, and helped make possible this magnificent representation of the progress of the South. Casting down your bucket among my people, helping and encouraging them as you are doing on these grounds, and to education of head, hand, and heart, you will find that they will buy your surplus land, make blossom the waste places in your fields, and run your factories. While doing this, you can be sure in the future, as in the past, that you and your families will be surrounded by the most patient, faithful, law-abiding, and unresentful people that the world has seen. As we have proved our loyalty to you in the past, in nursing your children, watching by the sick-bed of your mothers and fathers, and often following them with tear-dimmed eyes to their graves, so in the future, in our humble way, we shall stand by you with a devotion that no foreigner can approach, ready to lay down our lives, if need be, in defence of yours, interlacing our industrial, commercial, civil, and religious life with yours in a way that shall make the interests of both races one. In all things that are purely social we can be as separate as fingers, yet one as the hand in all things essential to mutual progress.

8   There is no defence or security for any of us except in the highest intelligence and development of all. If anywhere there are efforts tending to curtail the fullest growth of the Negro, let these efforts be turned into stimulating, encouraging, and making him the most useful and intelligent citizen. Effort or means so invested will pay a thousand per cent interest. These efforts will be twice blessed—"blessing him that gives and him that takes."

9   There is no escape through law of man or God from the inevitable:—

> The laws of changeless justice bind
> Oppressor with oppressed;
> And close as sin and suffering joined
> We march to fate abreast.

10   Nearly sixteen millions of hands will aid you in pulling the load upward, or they will pull against you the load downward. We shall constitute one-third and more of the ignorance and crime of the South, or one-third its intelligence and progress; we shall contribute one-third to the business and industrial prosperity of the South, or we shall prove a veritable body of death, stagnating, depressing, retarding every effort to advance the body politic.

11   Gentlemen of the Exposition, as we present to you our humble effort at an exhibition of our progress, you must not expect overmuch. Starting thirty years ago with ownership here and there in a few quilts and pumpkins and chickens (gathered from miscellaneous sources), remember the path that has led from these to the inventions and production of agricultural implements, buggies, steam-engines, newspapers, books, statuary, carving, paintings, the management of drug-stores and banks, has not been trodden without contact with thorns and thistles. While we take pride in what we exhibit as a result of our independent efforts, we do not for a moment forget that our part in this exhibition would fall far short of your expectations but for the constant help that has come to our educational life, not only from the Southern states, but especially from Northern philanthropists, who have made their gifts a constant stream of blessing and encouragement.

12   The wisest among my race understand that the agitation of questions of social equality is the extremest folly, and that progress in the enjoyment of all the privileges that will come to us must be the result of severe and constant struggle rather than of artificial forcing. No race that has anything to contribute to the markets of the world is long in any degree ostracized. It is important and right that all privileges of the law be ours, but it is vastly more important that we be prepared for the exercises of these privileges. The opportunity to earn a dollar in a factory just now is worth infinitely more than the opportunity to spend a dollar in an opera-house.

13   In conclusion, may I repeat that nothing in thirty years has given us more hope and encouragement, and drawn us so near to you of the white race, as this opportunity offered by the Exposition; and here bending, as it were, over the altar that represents the results of the struggles of your race and mine, both starting practically empty-handed three decades ago, I pledge that in your effort to work out the great and intricate problem which God has laid at the doors of the South, you shall have at all times the patient, sympathetic help of my race; only let this

be constantly in mind, that, while from representations in these buildings of the product of field, of forest, of mine, of factory, letters, and art, much good will come, yet far above and beyond material benefits will be that higher good, that, let us pray God, will come, in a blotting out of sectional differences and racial animosities and suspicions, in a determination to administer absolute justice, in a willing obedience among all classes to the mandates of law. This, this, coupled with our material prosperity, will bring into our beloved South a new heaven and a new earth.

🙠

14 The first thing that I remember, after I had finished speaking, was that Governor Bullock rushed across the platform and took me by the hand, and that others did the same. I received so many and such hearty congratulations that I found it difficult to get out of the building. I did not appreciate to any degree, however, the impression which my address seemed to have made, until the next morning, when I went into the business part of the city. As soon as I was recognized, I was surprised to find myself pointed out and surrounded by a crowd of men who wished to shake hands with me. This was kept up on every street on to which I went, to an extent which embarrassed me so much that I went back to my boarding-place. The next morning I returned to Tuskegee. At the station in Atlanta, and at almost all of the stations at which the train stopped between that city and Tuskegee, I found a crowd of people anxious to shake hands with me.

15 The papers in all parts of the United States published the address in full, and for months afterward there were complimentary editorial references to it. Mr. Clark Howell, the editor of the Atlanta *Constitution,* telegraphed to a New York paper, among other words, the following, "I do not exaggerate when I say that Professor Booker T. Washington's address yesterday was one of the most notable speeches, both as to character and as to the warmth of its reception, ever delivered to a Southern audience. The address was a revelation. The whole speech is a platform upon which blacks and whites can stand with full justice to each other."

16 The Boston *Transcript* said editorially: "The speech of Booker T. Washington at the Atlanta Exposition, this week, seems to have dwarfed all the other proceedings and the Exposition itself. The sensation that it has caused in the press has never been equalled."

17 I very soon began receiving all kinds of propositions from lecture bureaus, and editors of magazines and papers, to take the lecture platform, and to write articles. One lecture bureau offered me fifty thousand dollars, or two hundred dollars a night and expenses, if I would place my services at its disposal for a given period. To all these communications I replied that my life-work was at Tuskegee; and that whenever I spoke it must be in the interests of the Tuskegee school and my race, and that I

would enter into no arrangements that seemed to place a mere commercial value upon my services.

18   Some days after its delivery I sent a copy of my address to the President of the United States, the Hon. Grover Cleveland. I received from him the following autograph reply:—

> GRAY GABLES, BUZZARD'S BAY, MASS.,
> October 6, 1895.

BOOKER T. WASHINGTON, ESQ.:

> MY DEAR SIR: I thank you for sending me a copy of your address delivered at the Atlanta Exposition.
> I thank you with much enthusiasm for making the address. I have read it with intense interest, and I think the Exposition would be fully justified if it did not do more than furnish the opportunity for its delivery. Your words cannot fail to delight and encourage all who wish well for your race; and if our coloured fellow-citizens do not from your utterances gather new hope and form new determinations to gain every valuable advantage offered them by their citizenship, it will be strange indeed.
> Yours very truly,
> GROVER CLEVELAND.

19   Later I met Mr. Cleveland, for the first time, when, as President, he visited the Atlanta Exposition. At the request of myself and others he consented to spend an hour in the Negro Building, for the purpose of inspecting the Negro exhibit and of giving the coloured people in attendance an opportunity to shake hands with him. As soon as I met Mr. Cleveland I became impressed with his simplicity, greatness, and rugged honesty. I have met him many times since then, both at public functions and at his private residence in Princeton, and the more I see of him the more I admire him. When he visited the Negro Building in Atlanta he seemed to give himself up wholly, for that hour, to the coloured people. He seemed to be as careful to shake hands with some old coloured "auntie" clad partially in rags, and to take as much pleasure in doing so, as if he were greeting some millionaire. Many of the coloured people took advantage of the occasion to get him to write his name in a book or on a slip of paper. He was as careful and patient in doing this as if he were putting his signature to some great state document.

21   Mr. Cleveland has not only shown his friendship for me in many personal ways, but has always consented to do anything I have asked of him for our school. This he has done, whether it was to make a personal donation or to use his influence in securing the donations of others. Judging from my personal acquaintance with Mr. Cleveland, I do not believe that he is conscious of possessing any colour prejudice. He is too great for that. In my contact with people I find that, as a rule, it is only the little, narrow people who live for themselves, who never read good books, who do not travel, who never open up their souls in a way to permit

them to come into contact with other souls—with the great outside world. No man whose vision is bounded by colour can come into contact with what is highest and best in the world. In meeting men, in many places, I have found that the happiest people are those who do the most for others; the most miserable are those who do the least. I have also found that few things, if any, are capable of making one so blind and narrow as race prejudice. I often say to our students, in the course of my talks to them on Sunday evenings in the chapel, that the longer I live and the more experience I have of the world, the more I am convinced that, after all, the one thing that is most worth living for—and dying for, if need be—is the opportunity of making some one else more happy and more useful.

22   The coloured people and the coloured newspapers at first seemed to be greatly pleased with the character of my Atlanta address, as well as with its reception. But after the first burst of enthusiasm began to die away, and the coloured people began reading the speech in cold type, some of them seemed to feel that they had been hypnotized. They seemed to feel that I had been too liberal in my remarks toward the Southern whites, and that I had not spoken out strongly enough for what they termed the "rights" of the race. For a while there was a reaction, so far as a certain element of my own race was concerned, but later these reactionary ones seemed to have been won over to my way of believing and acting.

BUILDING CONTEXT

1. Compare Washington's attitude toward African colonization or toward emigration to Canada to the attitude of Lincoln, Stowe, Douglass, or Du Bois.

2. Compare Washington's presentation of his personal odyssey to the autobiography of Franklin or Douglass. In what way(s) is Washington typically "American"?

3. Contrast Washington's improvement program for African Americans to that of Du Bois, or to Stanley's suggestion for helping Native Americans. To what extent have these ideas been implemented? What has been their impact?

FURTHER STUDY

1. Analyze the issues upon which Washington and Du Bois disagreed. Trace the history of these issues in the African-American community. To what extent are they still a source of controversy?

2. Investigate the history of Washington's reputation among African Americans. Has his esteem been subject to cyclical changes in popular opinion, or to generational differences?

3. Assess the effect of "American" education in improving the lot of African Americans and Native Americans. To what extent is the loss of traditional values or culture the cost of success in America? In your opinion, are these sacrifices worth their price?

ADDITIONAL RESOURCES

Harlan, Louis R. *Booker T. Washington*. Vol. I: *The Making of a Black Leader, 1856–1901*. Vol. II: *The Wizard of Tuskegee, 1901–1915*. New York: Oxford University Press, 1983.

Hawkins, Hugh, ed. *Booker T. Washington and His Critics: Black Leadership in Crisis*. 2nd. ed. Lexington, Mass.: Heath, 1974.

Schroeder, Alan. *Booker T. Washington*. New York: Chelsea House, 1992.

RESEARCH KEYWORDS

Tuskegee Institute	Black Colleges	Carver (George Washington)
Du Bois (W. E. B.)	NAACP	

Plessy v. *Ferguson*
(1896)

"If one race be inferior to the other socially, the Constitution of the United States cannot put them upon the same plane."

After the Civil War, the Constitution was amended to protect African-American citizens, and federal troops were stationed throughout the South to enforce the new civil rights laws. But the removal of the troops and a series of regressive Supreme Court decisions brought an end to black civil rights in the South. The *Slaughterhouse* cases of 1873 ruled that the Bill of Rights was not binding on the states. And the *Civil Rights* cases of 1883 overturned federal laws against segregation.

In 1890, Louisiana's law requiring separate railroad cars for whites and blacks was challenged by Homer Plessy, a member of a prominent creole family who was, in fact, only one-eighth black. Writing for the majority, Justice Henry B. Brown defended the principle of "separate but equal" accommodations. In a lonely dissent, Justice John Marshall Harlan argued that unless constitutional protection was "color-blind," it was meaningless.

Text: Leon Friedman and Fred L. Israel, eds.; *The Justices of the United States Supreme Court,. 1789–1969: Their Lives and Major Opinions;* New York: Chelsea House, 1969.

EXPLORING ISSUES IN THE TEXT

1. Explain the distinction between law and individual behavior (pars. 3, 6). According to the Court, how much control can—or should—the government have over the behavior of an individual?

2. Analyze the tone of paragraph 11. To what extent do you think it reflects law and to what extent contemporary prejudice?

3. Discuss the basis for Justice Harlan's disagreement with the Court's decision. How does his concept of government differ from the Court's? Comment in particular on his interpretation of "fellow-citizens" (par. 15).

PLESSY V. FERGUSON

1 The constitutionality of this act is attacked upon the ground that it conflicts both with the Thirteenth Amendment of the Constitution, abolishing slavery, and the Fourteenth Amendment, which prohibits certain restrictive legislation on the part of the States.

2 1. That it does not conflict with the Thirteenth Amendment, which abolished slavery and involuntary servitude, except as a punishment for crime, is too clear for argument. Slavery implies involuntary servitude—a state of bondage; the ownership of mankind as a chattel, or at least the control of the labor and services of one man for the benefit of another, and the absence of a legal right to the disposal of his own person, property and services. This amendment was said in the *Slaughter House cases,* 16 Wall. 36, to have been intended primarily to abolish slavery, as it had been previously known in this country, and that it equally forbade Mexican peonage or the Chinese coolie trade, when they amounted to slavery or involuntary servitude, and that the use of the word "servitude" was intended to prohibit the use of all forms of involuntary slavery, of whatever class or name. It was intimated, however, in that case that this amendment was regarded by the statesmen of that day as insufficient to protect the colored race from certain laws which had been enacted in the Southern States, imposing upon the colored race onerous disabilities and burdens, and curtailing their rights in the pursuit of life, liberty and property

to such an extent that their freedom was of little value; and that the Fourteenth Amendment was devised to meet this exigency.

3   So, too, in the *Civil Rights cases,* 109 U.S. 3, 24, it was said that the act of a mere individual, the owner of an inn, a public conveyance or place of amusement, refusing accommodations to colored people, cannot be justly regarded as imposing any badge of slavery or servitude upon the applicant, but only as involving an ordinary civil injury, properly cognizable by the laws of the State, and presumably subject to redress by those laws until the contrary appears. "It would be running the slavery argument into the ground," said Mr. Justice Bradley, "to make it apply to every act of discrimination which a person may see fit to make as to the guests he will entertain, or as to the people he will take into his coach or cab or car, or admit to his concert or theatre, or deal with in other matters of intercourse or business."

4   A statute which implies merely a legal distinction between the white and colored races—a distinction which is founded in the color of the two races, and which must always exist so long as white men are distinguished from the other race by color—has no tendency to destroy the legal equality of the two races, or reëstablish a state of involuntary servitude. . . .

5   2. By the Fourteenth Amendment, all persons born or naturalized in the United States, and subject to the jurisdiction thereof, are made citizens of the United States and of the State wherein they reside; and the States are forbidden from making or enforcing any law which shall abridge the privileges or immunities of citizens of the United States, or shall deprive any person of life, liberty or property without due process of law, or deny to any person within their jurisdiction the equal protection of the laws. . . .

6   The object of the amendment was undoubtedly to enforce the absolute equality of the two races before the law, but in the nature of things it could not have been intended to abolish distinctions based upon color, or to enforce social, as distinguished from political equality, or a commingling of the two races upon terms unsatisfactory to either. Laws permitting, and even requiring, their separation in places where they are liable to be brought into contact do not necessarily imply the inferiority of either race to the other, and have been generally, if not universally, recognized as within the competence of the state legislatures in the exercise of their police power. The most common instance of this is connected with the establishment of separate schools for white and colored children, which has been held to be a valid exercise of the legislative power even by courts of States where the political rights of the colored race have been longest and most earnestly enforced.

7   One of the earliest of these cases is that of *Roberts* v. *City of Boston,* 5 Cush. 198, in which the Supreme Judicial Court of Massachusetts held that the general school committee of Boston had power to make provision for the instruction of colored children in separate schools established exclusively for them, and to prohibit their attendance upon the

other schools. "The great principle," said Chief Justice Shaw, p. 206, "advanced by the learned and eloquent advocate for the plaintiff," (Mr. Charles Sumner), "is, that by the constitution and laws of Massachusetts, all persons without distinction of age or sex, birth or color, origin or condition, are equal before the law. . . . But, when this great principle comes to be applied to the actual and various conditions of persons in society, it will not warrant the assertion, that men and women are legally clothed with the same civil and political powers, and that children and adults are legally to have the same functions and be subject to the same treatment; but only that the rights of all, as they are settled and regulated by law, are equally entitled to the paternal consideration and protection of the law for their maintenance and security." It was held that the powers of the committee extended to the establishment of separate schools for children of different ages, sexes and colors, and that they might also establish special schools for poor and neglected children, who have become too old to attend the primary school, and yet have not acquired the rudiments of learning, to enable them to enter the ordinary schools. Similar laws have been enacted by Congress under its general power of legislation over the District of Columbia, Rev. Stat. D.C. §§ 281, 282, 283, 310, 319, as well as by the legislatures of many of the States, and have been generally, if not uniformly, sustained by the courts. . . .

8   Laws forbidding the intermarriage of the two races may be said in a technical sense to interfere with the freedom of contract, and yet have been universally recognized as within the police power of the State. *State* v. *Gibson,* 36 Indiana, 389.

9   The distinction between laws interfering with the political equality of the negro and those requiring the separation of the two races in schools, theatres and railway carriages has been frequently drawn by this court. Thus in *Strauder* v. *West Virginia,* 100 U.S. 303, it was held that a law of West Virginia limiting to white male persons, 21 years of age and citizens of the State, the right to sit upon juries, was a discrimination which implied a legal inferiority in civil society, which lessened the security of the right of the colored race, and was a step toward reducing them to a condition of servility. Indeed, the right of a colored man that, in the selection of jurors to pass upon his life, liberty and property, there shall be no exclusion of his race, and no discrimination against them because of color, has been asserted in a number of cases. . . .

10   So far, then, as a conflict with the Fourteenth Amendment is concerned, the case reduces itself to the question whether the statute of Louisiana is a reasonable regulation, and with respect to this there must necessarily be a large discretion on the part of the legislature. In determining the question of reasonablensss it is at liberty to act with reference to the established usages, customs and traditions of the people, and with a view to the promotion of their comfort, and the preservation of the public peace and good order. Gauged by this standard, we cannot say that a law which authorizes or even requires the separation of the two

races in public conveyances is unreasonable, or more obnoxious to the Fourteenth Amendment than the acts of Congress requiring separate schools for colored children in the District of Columbia, the constitutionality of which does not seem to have been questioned, or the corresponding acts of state legislatures.

11   We consider the underlying fallacy of the plaintiff's argument to consist in the assumption that the enforced separation of the two races stamps the colored race with a badge of inferiority. If this be so, it is not by reason of anything found in the act, but solely because the colored race chooses to put that construction upon it. The argument necessarily assumes that if, as has been more than once the case, and is not unlikely to be so again, the colored race should become the dominant power in the state legislature, and should enact a law in precisely similar terms, it would thereby relegate the white race to an inferior position. We imagine that the white race, at least, would not acquiesce in this assumption. The argument also assumes that social prejudices may be overcome by legislation, and that equal rights cannot be secured to the negro except by an enforced commingling of the two races. We cannot accept this proposition. If the two races are to meet upon terms of social equality, it must be the result of natural affinities, a mutual appreciation of each other's merits and a voluntary consent of individuals. As was said by the Court of Appeals of New York in *People* v. *Gallagher*, 93 N.Y. 438, 448, "this end can neither be accomplished nor promoted by laws which conflict with the general sentiment of the community upon whom they are designed to operate. When the government, therefore, has secured to each of its citizens equal rights before the law and equal opportunities for improvement and progress, it has accomplished the end for which it was organized and performed all of the functions respecting social advantages with which it is endowed." Legislation is powerless to eradicate racial instincts or to abolish distinctions based upon physical differences, and the attempt to do so can only result in accentuating the difficulties of the present situation. If the civil and political rights of both races be equal one cannot be inferior to the other civilly or politically. If one race be inferior to the other socially, the Constitution of the United States cannot put them upon the same plane. . . .

John Marshall Harlan, Dissenting

12   . . . In respect of civil rights, common to all citizens, the Constitution of the United States does not, I think, permit any public authority to know the race of those entitled to be protected in the enjoyment of such rights. Every true man has pride of race, and under appropriate circumstances when the rights of others, his equals before the law, are not to be affected, it is his privilege to express such pride and to take such action based upon it as to him seems proper. But I deny that any legislative

body or judicial tribunal may have regard to the race of citizens when the civil rights of those citizens are involved. Indeed, such legislation, as that here in question, is inconsistent not only with that equality of rights which pertains to citizenship, National and State, but with the personal liberty enjoyed by every one within the United States. . . .

13   The white race deems itself to be the dominant race in this country. And so it is, in prestige, in achievements, in education, in wealth and in power. So, I doubt not, it will continue to be for all time, if it remains true to its great heritage and holds fast to the principles of constitutional liberty. But in view of the Constitution, in the eye of the law, there is in this country no superior, dominant, ruling class of citizens. There is no caste here. Our Constitution is color-blind, and neither knows nor tolerates classes among citizens. In respect of civil rights, all citizens are equal before the law. The humblest is the peer of the most powerful. The law regards man as man, and takes no account of his surroundings or of his color when his civil rights as guaranteed by the supreme law of the land are involved. It is, therefore, to be regretted that this high tribunal, the final expositor of the fundamental law of the land, has reached the conclusion that it is competent for a State to regulate the enjoyment by citizens of their civil rights solely upon the basis of race. . . .

14   The arbitrary separation of citizens, on the basis of race, while they are on a public highway, is a badge of servitude wholly inconsistent with the civil freedom and the equality before the law established by the Constitution. It cannot be justified upon any legal grounds.

15   If evils will result from the commingling of the two races upon public highways established for the benefit of all, they will be infinitely less than those that will surely come from state legislation regulating the enjoyment of civil rights upon the basis of race. We boast of the freedom enjoyed by our people above all other peoples. But it is difficult to reconcile that boast with a state of the law which, practically, puts the brand of servitude and degradation upon a large class of our fellow-citizens, our equals before the law. The thin disguise of "equal" accommodations for passengers in railroad coaches will not mislead any one, nor atone for the wrong this day done.

BUILDING CONTEXT

1.   Draw parallels between the Court's opinion in *Plessy* and Washington's "Atlanta Address." What important attitudes do they share?

2.   Compare the Court's reasoning in *Plessy* to *Brown* v. *The Board of Education.* What do you think accounts for the reaching of such different conclusions by the Court?

3. Consider the importance of historical details in the Plessy decision. What does this say about history as a creation rather than the mere retelling of the past?

FURTHER STUDY

1. Discuss the implications of the statement that "legislation is powerless to eradicate racial instincts" (par. 11). What does this assume about the function of government? Is the law concerned with how people feel or how they act?

2. Explore the belief that the law must be color-blind (par. 13). How is this position reconciled with affirmative action, or voting districts that guarantee the election of members of certain groups?

ADDITIONAL RESOURCES

Cortner, Richard C. *The Supreme Court and Civil Liberties Policy.* Palo Alto, Calif.: Mayfield Publishing Co., 1975.

Konvitz, Milton R., ed. *Bill of Rights Reader: Leading Constitutional Cases.* 5th ed. Ithaca, N.Y.: Cornell University Press, 1973.

Latham, Frank Brown. *The Great Dissenter: John Marshall Harlan, 1833–1911.* New York: Cowles Book Co., 1970.

RESEARCH KEYWORDS

Separate but Equal	Civil Rights	Racial Equality
Civil Rights Cases	*Slaughterhouse* Cases	Creoles—Louisiana

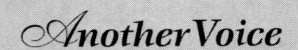

Another Voice

LIMITING THE BILL OF RIGHTS

. . . The first section of the fourteenth article, . . . opens with a definition of citizenship—not only citizenship of the United States, but citizenship of the States. No such definition was previously found in the Constitution, nor had any attempt been made to define it by act of Congress. . . .

The language is, "No State shall make or enforce any law which shall abridge the privileges or immunities of citizens of *the United States.*" It is a little remarkable, if this clause was intended as a protection to the citizen of a State against the legislative

continued

continued from previous page

power of his own State, that the word citizen of the State should be left out when it is so carefully used, and used in contradistinction to citizens of the United States, in the very sentence which precedes it. It is too clear for argument that the change in phraseology was adopted understandingly and with a purpose.

Of the privileges and immunities of the citizen of the United States, and of the privileges and immunities of the citizen of the State, and what they respectively are, we will presently consider; but we wish to state here that it is only the former which are placed by this clause under the protection of the federal Constitution, and that the latter, whatever they may be, are not intended to have any additional protection by this paragraph of the amendment.

If, then, there is a difference between the privileges and immunities belonging to a citizen of the United States as such, and those belonging to the citizen of the State as such, the latter must rest for their security and protection where they have heretofore rested; for they are not embraced by this paragraph of the amendment. . . .

Slaughterhouse Cases, 1873

Another Voice

LIMITING CIVIL RIGHTS

But is there any similarity between such servitudes and a denial by the owner of an inn, a public conveyance, or a theatre, of its accommodations and privileges to an individual, even though the denial be founded on the race or color of that individual? Where does any slavery or servitude, or badge of either, arise from such an act of denial? Whether it might not be a denial of a right which, if sanctioned by the state law, would be obnoxious to the prohibitions of the Fourteenth Amendment, is another question. But what has it to do with the question of slavery? . . .

Civil Rights Cases, 1883

> ### ALAN DAWLEY AND PAUL FALER
> *"Working-Class Culture and Politics in the Industrial Revolution: Sources of Loyalism and Rebellion"* (1988)

"Industrial morality was a general feature of the industrial class system as a whole, not the particular values of one class within the system."

By and large, American workers do not identify themselves as a proletariat locked in a class war with capitalists; they do not attack the concept of property, support socialist or workers' parties, or subscribe to a separate moral culture. Rather, they consider themselves to be middle-class citizens, sharing the religious loyalties and divisions of other groups and voting for candidates from the two major political parties.

One of the most intriguing questions asked by historians is why American workers lack—or even reject—class consciousness.

This situation requires explanation. The Industrial Revolution was, after all, a true revolution. The world we know today is no longer dominated by subsistence farming on family plots, with little need for hard currency because excess produce could be bartered for manufactured goods, which, in turn, were still, as the name implies, "made by hand." And, as Alan Dawley and Paul Faler note, revolutions usually change human behavior. In Europe, for instance, industrialized workers identify themselves as a class and elect governments committed to socialism and the welfare state. In America, on the other hand, industrialization has only reinforced individualism and other traditional values.

Alan Dawley (Trenton State College) and Paul Faler (the University of Massachusetts at Boston) have tried to trace the roots of this disparity by examining the shoe industry of Lynn, Massachusetts—from its beginnings as a cottage industry in 1635, to its shift from the hands of artisans to those of wage-earners. This study is part of their ongoing research into working-class history, a relatively new field that expands the scope of history beyond the mere study of national leaders and wars.

Text: Peter N. Stearns, ed.; *Expanding the Past: A Reader in Social History;* New York: New York University Press, 1988.

EXPLORING ISSUES IN THE TEXT

1. Summarize the characteristics of industrial morality (par. 2). How do they differ from the values of preindustrial society (pars. 3–5)?

2. Explain the two types of reaction to the new industrial culture (pars. 6–7). Explain why both reactions discouraged workers from challenging their employees (par. 8). What factors fostered challenge by workers (pars. 8–10)?

3. Summarize why radicalization did not spread (par. 13ff.). Try to analyze the uniquely American reasons.

WORKING-CLASS CULTURE AND POLITICS IN THE INDUSTRIAL REVOLUTION: SOURCES OF LOYALISM AND REBELLION

1 Lynn embarked on the path of industrialism in the 1820s and 1830s when a reorganization in the production of shoes underminded the old artisan/mercantile way of life and created a new social structure based on capitalist manufacturers and wage earners, the two core groups of the industrial class system. In the same two decades, the community saw the beginnings of industrial class conflict (strike organizations), the formation of working-class institutions (journeymen's societies and workingmen's parties), and the emergence of a new industrial culture—all before the advent of the factory system. The importance of this period is underlined by the fact that the main ideas, forms of organization, and social cleavages that developed before the factories would persist for a full generation under the factory system.

2 None of these early innovations was more far-reaching than a new industrial morality. This moral code was characterized by a panoply of individualist values: self-discipline, self-control, and self-reliance. "Trust thyself," Emerson intoned, "every heart vibrates to that iron string." The code promised self-fulfillment through the faithful devotion to regular habits of toil. It stressed the virtue of work for its own sake, not as an expression of some higher calling. It demanded industry (labor aimed at self-improvement), frugality (economic self-sacrifice), and temperance (sensual self-denial). In the new code of morality, the self was at once supreme and suppressed, deified and denied, liberated and enchained.

3 Industrial morality bore a certain resemblance to an earlier set of virtues. It is clear that industry, frugality, and temperance had preindustrial (though not precapitalist) origins, and that an ethic of competitive individualism had put in an appearance among eighteenth-century laboring classes (among mechanics, at any rate, if not slaves, servants, or common laborers). But it is equally clear that the moral universe in which these values appeared remained bounded by traditional forms, and that those forms were broken only by the rise of industrial capitalism in the nineteenth century. In preindustrial times, individualism had been incorporated into a pattern of deference to social superiors, but in

the new setting individualism was alloyed with a belief in equality of opportunity. At one time industry had meant hard work; now it was redefined as devotion to a methodical work routine. Frugality was once consistent with charity; now it became associated with a definition of poverty as crime and a new stringency in poor relief. Temperance once meant moderation in drinking habits and prudent sexuality; now it was redefined as total abstinence and prudish sexuality. Thus, the new values were the result of the reassertion of traditional attitudes in new surroundings and represent both the effort of preindustrial America to keep itself going along traditional lines and the failure of that effort. This paradox of change emerging from an effort to conserve the past pervades American history in the 1820s and 1830s. To take another example, the Jacksonian movement sought to restore the foundations of the old Republic, but instead fostered the new democratic styles in politics and the very expansion in industry that undermined it. The dialectical process of breakdown and repair thus resulted in the creation of something quite different than was intended.

4   We emphasize that industrial morality was a general feature of the industrial class system as a whole, not the particular values of one class within the system. It was neither bourgeois nor proletarian. It caused businessmen to organize the Society for the Promotion of Industry, Frugality, and Temperance, and prompted wage earners to join the Washingtonian Total Abstinence Society. It inspired businessmen to promote their new Institution for Savings with appeals to popular thriftiness, and it encouraged many working families to practice thrift at the expense of current living standards.

5   Because industrial morality defined what industrial workers and industrial capitalists had in common with one another, it also defined how their values differed from the libertine culture of preindustrial class systems. The contrast is most striking when we compare industrial morality with the culture of slavery: individualism versus paternalism; the work ethic versus an ethic of leisure; free labor versus bond labor. Just as the industrial classes drew upon a common cultural reservoir, so, too, the classes of slavery drew their values from common preindustrial sources. Despite vast inequalities between slaves and masters, they shared certain cultural outlooks that set them farther apart from the industrial classes than from each other. (This point will take on added importance later when we consider the political impact of the Civil War.)

6   Industrial morality was a source of cleavage within the working class between "traditional" and "modern" values. As each generation of preindustrial laborers came into contact with industrialism, some adopted the new code, while others rejected it and clung to preindustrial values. We term the latter "traditionalists" because they refused to give up their casual attitudes toward work, their pursuit of happiness in gaming and drinking, and the raucous revelry that accompanied fire and militia

musters. Traditionalists still deferred to the silk vest, the gold watch, and the ivory-handled cane, still expected a rum ration from their employers, and still claimed Saturday afternoon and Monday morning as their own time. In 1820 virtually all the shoemakers in Lynn were traditionalists, and continual infusions of people with preindustrial backgrounds from the hills of New Hampshire and the rills of County Cork insured that a variety of traditional customs would persist well into the industrial period.

7   A second group adopted the new morality, and we term them "modernists." In terms of moral character, modernist workers resembled their employers (most of whom were also modernists) more than they did their traditionalist coworkers. They joined their employers in shunning the very things traditionalists cherished—the warm sociability of the drinking club, the "wasteful" amusement of the circus and the Jim Crow show, the easygoing work rhythm.

8   If morality were the only determinant of behavior, then neither group of workers would have mounted an organized challenge to their employers—the traditionalists because they believed their employers were their betters and the modernists because they believed their employers were no different than themselves. But other factors threw wage earners into conflict with their employers and tapped industrial morality as both a motivation for struggle and as a means to wage that struggle. The economic changes of the industrial revolution intensified competition among wage earners, cheapened their skills, undercut their security, attacked their standard of living, increased their dependency, and lowered their social position. In each case these changes conflicted head-on with the values of industrial morality: self-reliance, self-discipline, and self-improvement. Given the situation in which scores of people were dependent upon a single individual for their livelihood, what other recourse was there for those who believed in equal rights and self-improvement but to take collective action? Social and economic changes impelled the individualism of the modernists in collective directions toward the mutualism of the benefit society, the fraternity of the lodge, the common front of collective bargaining, and the solidarity of the strike.

9   All the modernists were caught up in this process, but not all in the same way. Some hastened its work; they devoted all their spare time to the moral elevation of the laboring classes, sold subscriptions to labor newspapers, canvassed the town to promote support for a strike, and, after attending a temperance rally on Friday, spoke at a meeting of the journeymen's society on Saturday. Others, however, slowed the process; they subscribed to a community newspaper but not a labor journal, told the canvasser a strike was ill-advised, and spoke at the temperance rally, but probably did not attend the journeymen's meeting. In other words, the modernists subdivided into two different groups; the first we term "rebels," the second, "loyalists." The rebels laid the foundations of the labor movement, saw sobriety and literacy as matters of self-pride and as

means to proclaim their independence from the external commands of employer and liquor, and did not shrink from the prospect of a strike. On the other hand, loyalists held aloof from the labor movement (or joined only in a crisis), wore their sobriety and literacy as badges of middle-class respectability, and tried to evade the issue of class conflict altogether. It is this division between rebels and loyalists that commands our attention for the remainder of the essay.

10   Since rebels and loyalists shared the same underlying moral character, they did not part company with each other (or with their bosses) over this cultural issue. Rather, they divided over the question of political economy. Where the loyalists saw an overriding mutuality of interests between labor and capital, offset only by minor differences, the rebels saw an overriding antagonism, offset only by minor points of agreement. To the loyalist, capital and labor were mutually dependent, and each was entitled to a just reward—the entrepreneur a fair profit, the laborer a fair wage. To the rebel, however, capital and labor stood in direct opposition, since the interest of the former was to get as much work from the latter for the lowest possible wage. . . .

∽

11   By the 1870s workers in Lynn, as in other sections of the country, appeared ready to believe that the unequal distribution of wealth and power was caused by an interlocking economic, social, political, and cultural mechanism that brought about the oppression of all who labored with their hands.

12   But this potential was never fully realized. By the end of the century most workers probably linked their desire for collective self-help to a conception of labor as an interest group rather than a class. What, then, had contained the spread of radicalism? What historical alchemy had transformed rebellion into reconciliation? . . .

13   Our own answer focuses on the intersection of working-class culture and American politics and is divided into three parts: (a) the ritual of democracy, (b) the impact of the Civil War, and (c) the interclass character of the party system.

14   During the 1820s and 1830s American politics became a mass ritual for the expression of popular culture. For the first time anywhere in the world, ordinary folk (at least the white males among them) regularly expressed their values and beliefs in the ongoing political process through the hoopla of conventions, the pageantry of parades, the camp-meeting style of rallies, the frenetic electioneering of voting day, and the final victory celebrations. All the bunting, brass bands, banners, and flags that festooned election campaigns merely demonstrated that politics had become a popular form of mass entertainment.

15   Industrial morality had a key role to play in the new ritual of democracy. Working people who believed in their own self-worth, and no

longer deferred to the silk vest, the gold watch, or the ivory-handled cane, insisted that their own voices be heard and their own votes counted. Sooner or later most politicians learned to court them with phrases about the bone and sinew of society that flattered even their own high self-esteem. Democrats were the first to adopt the new style, but Whigs were not far behind, as they proved in the Log Cabin and Hard Cider campaign of 1840. The new style, with its banners, floats, and parades, thus incorporated into the election campaign itself many of the tamer features of old 'Lection day, a preindustrial festival of popular culture abolished by the Massachusetts General Court in 1831. In other words, the ritual of democracy reinforced the individualist code of ethics adopted by modernist workingmen, but also provided popular entertainment for the traditionalists.

16   Further, the ritual emphasized the common political culture workers and employers shared. In contrast to several European countries, political democracy did not arise in the United States from the class demands of dispossessed workers against the propertied interests that controlled the state. Instead, it arose from an interclass movement that included both propertyless workers and small entrepreneurs, and was dominated by property-owning artisans and farmers. Thus the first generation of industrial workers often cooperated with industrial employers in joint political ventures. Lynn shoemakers who saw the wealth and power of some manufacturers increasing daily at their expense could turn to politics and make common cause with other manufacturers against an enemy—real or imagined—of the democratic political culture. In this fashion, antimasonry swept Lynn with a call to alarm against a secret, conspiratorial aristocracy. Nativism arose out of the fear of an internal threat to American republicanism posed by an authoritarian foreign power that used ignorant Irish Catholics as its pawns for gaining control. The powerful Free Soil movement attacked the Southern slaveocracy on the grounds that it was the epitome of aristocratic power, a death threat leveled at the producing classes, and the antithesis of industrial morality. Finally, the conflict between workers and employers was frequently softened by their joint cooperation as producers against the parasitic money power. Just as inequality waxed in economics, it seemed to wane in politics.

17   Thus for the first generations of industrial workers, politics was a continual re-enactment of a ritual embodying the social relations of an earlier era of unity among the "producing classes." Industrial culture interacted with the political system in just the opposite way that it interacted with the economic system. The consequence was to retard the spread of rebellion and to advance the politics of loyalism.

18   The Civil War gave an enormous impetus to the politics of loyalism. At the outset of the War, Lynn was bitterly divided along class lines drawn during the strike of 1860. Strike passions boiled over into electoral

politics as strike leaders organized a Workingmen's party to vent their outrage against the use of out-of-town police and their frustration over losing on all their formal strike demands. As the economic struggle resolved into a political struggle, economic defeat was offset by an overwhelming political victory. The Workingmen's party captured nearly every position in the Lynn city government. But then, just at this decisive moment, Fort Sumter fell. Rebel workingmen got back in step with their employers, strikers and bosses submerged their differences in the Yankee cause, and together they marched off to fight confederate traitors. The effect of the War on class consciousness was written in the next election returns: the Republican party, dominated by local shoe manufacturers, won its first city election, and soon worker opposition withered away to nothing. Literally *nothing.* Not a single vote was cast against the incumbent Republican mayor in 1863.

19   The suffocating embrace of wartime unity persisted through the next decade as the issues created by the War continued to dominate the nation's political affairs, again despite massive economic dispute and division. Questions of reconstructing the Union overshadowed the social and economic issues of industrialization, so that when labor discontent re-emerged after the War, it did not define the main lines of political debate. Thus during the most critical years of industrialization, the United States was more keenly divided politically between industrialism and slavery than between industrial workers and industrial capitalists.

20   The War gave workers and manufacturers a common historical legacy. Both groups agreed that the history of their country after 1850 was, in effect, the history of class struggle. They regarded bleeding Kansas, the John Brown raid, the Civil War itself, and the military occupation of the South afterwards as incidents in a mortal battle for state power waged by antagonistic social and economic interests. Workers and manufacturers regarded their joint victory as a judgment on the superiority of the northern, industrial way of life. Both groups rejoiced in the defeat of the common enemy, the vindication of industrial morality, and the preservation of democratic values against their subversion by a would-be aristocracy. Both believed that the Federal government and the Union armies had served their basic interests well.

21   Class consciousness, like all forms of collective thought, is based on actual historical experience transformed into myth. The mythology that arose from the Civil War tended to persuade workers that their power and destiny were inexplicably linked to the military heroes, civilian leaders, and the existing frame of government that had won the war. It was not necessary for bourgeois ideologists to go about preaching a "false" consciousness to working people who had risked their lives to bring down the slave power; workers needed only to compare their death toll at the hands of the slaveocracy with their death toll at the hands of company guards, police, and militia. Although the violent suppression of the

Mollie Maguires and railroad workers in 1877 began to add up, the result was still dozens against thousands. Had the war ended differently, with the Union in disgrace, or had slavery not been rooted so deeply in American history that it required the greatest military effort of the nineteenth century to extirpate it, the experience and the myths would have been different. Perhaps the conflict between the industrial and preindustrial systems would have been less severe and the conflict between the industrial classes more severe, but as it turned out, things ran the other way. The War took grist from the rebels' mill and gave it to the loyalists.

22 Working-class political culture emerged from conflicting cross-pressures, some encouraging and others discouraging a class view. As the effect of the Civil War waned, perhaps the most crucial pressure against class consciousness and the major outlet for working-class discontent was electoral politics. Its effect derived from the interclass character of the political parties, and it was crucial because it bore directly on the rebel worker, without whom no widespread radical movement was possible. Whether a rebel became a Democrat, Republican, Labor Reformer, or Greenbacker, he invariably came into close contact with middle-class politicians (a point David Montgomery has emphasized in his perceptive analysis of postwar politics), and this itself demonstrated the openness of the political process. No one has captured the essential relation between social discontent and electoral politics better than Wendell Phillips, firebrand of social reform, Labor Reform candidate for governor of Massachusetts, and hero to rebel workers. "We rush into politics," Phillips explained, "because politics is the safety-valve."

23 The most powerful political organization in Lynn between 1878 and 1890 was a Workingmen's party that emerged under exactly the same circumstances as its predecessor in 1860: outrage and frustration in a strike launched a political movement for revenge against city officials that carried a Workingmen's candidate to overwhelming victory. The candidate, George P. Sanderson, was a man of clear rebel credentials. The son of a small-town, New Hampshire preacher, he had been a partner in a shoemakers' cooperative. His campaign was infused with rebel rhetoric about the conflict between labor and capital, a conflict personified by Sanderson himself, who had been a shoeworker most of his life, and his opponent, who was the owner of the largest shoe factory and the largest fortune in the city.

24 But soon after taking office, the rebellion petered out. Although Sanderson acted on his promise to fire the hated police chief, he brought forth nothing else in the way of a distinctive labor program. Having turned the rascals out of office and satisfied the popular taste for revenge, he had nothing further to do except reward the party faithful. Once in office, he became a loyalist by default.

25 The pattern set by Sanderson persisted throughout the Workingmen's reign. The party was effective in winning elections, manipulating city

contracts and patronage jobs, and in controlling the local police force. Each of these accomplishments was important to the city's labor movement, and it is not necessary to belittle the bread-and-butter benefits provided by the Workingmen's party to make the point that it did nothing to pursue the broader interests of the class or to take the rebel outlook into such areas as municipal ownership, health and safety regulations in the factories, or expanded assistance to the poor. The Workingmen's party avoided areas of potential friction between wage earners and middle-class supporters and, instead, sought out the areas of agreement between them. The Workingmen's party was not a party of the proletariat.

BUILDING CONTEXT

1. Examine the relationship between values and labor. Compare the observations of Dawley and Faler to those of Hymowitz and Weissman.

2. How do Dawley and Faler's observations about American class structure compare to those of Tocqueville or Crèvecoeur?

3. Relate Dawley and Faler's explanation of the American work ethic to the writings of Franklin.

4. Explore the influence of slavery upon group identification, as discussed by Dawley and Faler, Thoreau, Douglass, or Washington.

FURTHER STUDY

1. Research the history of the labor movement in the United States. To what extent was it home-grown and to what extent imported? Which group(s) was it designed to protect? How has membership in the labor movement changed over the years?

2. Investigate the role of women or African Americans in the labor movement. What has been their reception and status? Compare the labor movement in this respect to Abolitionism or the modern Civil Rights Movement.

ADDITIONAL RESOURCES

Dubofsky, Melvyn. *Industrialization and the American Worker, 1865–1920.* 2d ed. Arlington Heights, Ill.: H. Davidson, 1985.

Foner, Philip S. *History of the Labor Movement in the United States.* 2d ed. New York: International Publishers, 1975.

Yellowitz, Irwin. *Industrialization and the American Labor Movement.* Port Washington, N.Y.: Kennikat, 1977.

RESEARCH KEYWORDS

Labor and Laboring Classes	Working Class	Labor Unions
Trade Unions	Knights of Labor	Socialist Party
Woman's Rights Movement	AFL-CIO	Social Gospel

EXPLORING CRITICAL ISSUES THROUGH WRITING

1. How does economics influence popular and "high" culture? What are the implications of supply and demand on pornography, for example? On censorship?

2. Investigate the literary convention of the "American girl." Why did it develop when it did? Why was the American girl more noteworthy than the boy, woman, or man?

3. Examine the myth of the rugged individual. Consider, for example, whether the pioneer on the frontier is a rugged individual or requires governmental support.

4. Explore the popular image of the frontiersman or pioneer. What place did this image play in shaping America's history? What influence has it had on governmental policy concerning, for example, unemployment insurance and welfare.

5. Investigate the image of the frontier in popular movies. Trace how it has changed over the years and try to explain the reasons for the changes.

6. Stanley's ironic statement that "we shall presently find ourselves blaming Columbus for discovering America" was realized during the Columbus Quincentenary in 1992. Account for this change of perspective using historical context.

7. Define the term "white man's burden." What was its original meaning? What mission did it reflect? What were its results? You might want to read Rudyard Kipling's poem, "The White Man's Burden."

8. Analyze the issues upon which Booker T. Washington and W. E. B. Du Bois disagreed. Trace the history of these issues in the African-American community. To what extent are they still a source of controversy?

9. Investigate the history of Washington's reputation among African Americans. Has his standing been subject to rise and fall or to generational differences?

10. Assess the effect of "American" education in improving the lot of African Americans and Native Americans. To what extent is the loss of traditional values or culture the price for success in America? In your opinion, are these sacrifices worth their price? What accounts for the different experiences of different groups?

11. Discuss the implications of the statement in *Plessy* that "legislation is powerless to eradicate racial instincts." What does this assume about the function of government? Does this reflect the current view of the Supreme Court and the American government? What is your own view about the power of government to improve racial conflict?

12. Explore the conviction that the law must be color-blind. Examine the debate over reconciling this position with affirmative action, or voting districts that guarantee the election of members of certain groups.

13. Research the history of the labor movement in the United States. To what extent was it home-grown and to what extent imported? Which group(s) was it designed to protect? How has membership in the labor movement changed over the years?

14. Assess the role of women and African Americans in the labor movement. What has been their reception and status? Compare the labor movement in this respect to abolitionism or the modern Civil Rights Movement.

15. Pursue an idea from the reading selections that caught your interest, charmed or provoked you, or supported or challenged your own beliefs. Try to place this issue within a larger context, and explain its significance.

8

NINETEENTH-CENTURY LIVES: 1860–1900

"What had been would continue to be. . . . [A] system of society which had lasted since Adam would outlast one Adams more."

HENRY BROOKS ADAMS

"Fundamentally, I muse, all people are the same. My mother's race is as prejudiced as my father's."

EDITH MAUD EATON

The United States began the last half of the nineteenth century with a bloody civil war and concluded it as a world power, with holdings in both the Atlantic and Pacific oceans. The great challenge to equality in 1850 was slavery. By 1900, Americans were demanding equal rights for African Americans, Asians, southern and eastern Europeans, and women. In 1850, the United States was still a nation of farmers—where, as Henry Adams observed, every stroke of the axe made the immigrant a capitalist and his children gentlemen. By 1900, the frontier had closed and industrialization created teeming urban slums, and radicalized workers were turning to unions, socialism, and anarchism for relief. The vast social impact these fifty years had on people of every class and background is only hinted at in the autobiographical sketches that follow.

It is well to remember at this point that autobiography, like any writing, is more than the mere listing of dates and events. It has a thesis that determines what to include, in what order, with what emphasis. Benjamin Franklin gave these reasons for writing his own autobiography: to be a role model for future generations, to "correct" his errors in a so-called second edition of his life, and to indulge his vanity. Each of these motivates certain kinds of choices and imposes structure on the work. Other writers have different motivations, which must often be inferred by the reader.

At the height of his success, Mark Twain looked back at the years before the Civil War to recreate an idyllic small-town boyhood. In contrast, Henry Adams, who as a boy had every reason to assume he would be a president like his grandfather and great-grandfather, sees his childhood through the eyes of an old man alienated from a society that took a wrong turn and lost its way. In this same world, however, Abraham Cahan, an immigrant, finds friends, fame, and a political purpose that shapes his narrative.

Women, too, had varying experiences and reasons for writing. Elizabeth Custer makes it clear that civilization can come to the frontier only if soldiers like her husband protect helpless women and children from treacherous savages. And Edith Maud Eaton travels from place to place trying to find acceptance as an independent Chinese woman.

Each of these autobiographies, then, depicts a different aspect of America in the nineteenth century. By combining them, we get a fuller picture, but certainly not a complete one.

MARK TWAIN
Life on the Mississippi
(1874)

"*When I was a boy, there was but one permanent ambition among my comrades in our village. . . . That was, to be a steam-boatman.*"

America's most famous humorist was born Samuel Langhorne Clemens (1835-1910), but he took the name Mark Twain from the steamboatman's term for safe water. Although his works include sophisticated political satire, like *The Prince and the Pauper* and *A Connecticut Yankee in King Arthur's Court,* as well as books of travel sketches and autobiography, he is best remembered for his evocations of the mythic joy of boyhood. *The Adventures of Tom Sawyer* recasts Twain's boyhood hometown of Hannibal, Missouri, in idyllic hues, and even *The Adventures of Huckleberry Finn*—a mature condemnation of slavery and human cruelty—is treated today as a children's book because of the exuberance and charm of its young hero. Much of the setting in these two novels, as well as the nostalgia, comes from the recreation of persons and places of Twain's childhood. However, William Dean Howells, Twain's longtime friend and colleague in the anti-imperialist movement, often commented on the keenness of the satire beneath the pleasantries.

Twain received little formal education; he was apprenticed to a printer after his father died in 1847. Years later, responding to a query from *Harper's Bazaar,* Twain cited his father's death as "The Turning-point of My Life." In typical Twain fashion of "spinning a yarn," his reasoning went like this: His mother could not discipline him, so she sent him to live with the printer, from whom he wandered West, where he found a job as a printer, then a reporter, then a travel writer, then a novelist; thus, his father's death made him a writer.

Though this thumbnail sketch is tongue-in-cheek, it illustrates the art of autobiography. Writers do not simply record every event from every day of their lives. They choose details from the past that they consider significant from their current perspective. In the following excerpt from *Life on the Mississippi,* Twain describes the quintessential American childhood, free of adult problems and national crises. The tone of gentle humor is as important as the facts—some of which may not be quite accurate—because it shows us the mature man smiling at his youthful pretensions.

Text: Mark Twain; *Life on the Mississippi.* New York: Harper and Brothers, 1917.

EXPLORING ISSUES IN THE TEXT

1. Explain how paragraph 1 captures the enthusiasms of childhood. How does it establish the tone of this piece?

2. Summarize paragraph 2. Why do you think it is the longest paragraph in this excerpt?

3. What was the "eminence" achieved by the first boy who went away (par. 3)? Comment on some of the details that illustrate his "exalted" position. Explain the effect this boy's success had upon the narrator's religious training.

LIFE ON THE MISSISSIPPI

Chapter IV

THE BOYS' AMBITION

1   When I was a boy, there was but one permanent ambition among my comrades in our village on the west bank of the Mississippi River. That was, to be a steamboatman. We had transient ambitions of other sorts, but they were only transient. When a circus came and went, it left us all burning to become clowns; the first negro minstrel show that ever came to our section left us all suffering to try that kind of life; now and then we had a hope that, if we lived and were good, God would permit us to be pirates. These ambitions faded out, each in its turn; but the ambition to be a steamboatman always remained.

2   Once a day a cheap, gaudy packet arrived upward from St. Louis, and another downward from Keokuk. Before these events, the day was glorious with expectancy; after them, the day was a dead and empty thing. Not only the boys, but the whole village, felt this. After all these years I can picture that old time to myself now, just as it was then: the white town drowsing in the sunshine of a summer's morning; the streets empty, or pretty nearly so; one or two clerks sitting in front of the Water Street stores, with their splint-bottomed chairs tilted back against the walls, chins on breasts, hats slouched over their faces, asleep—with shingle-shavings enough around to show what broke them down; a sow and a litter of pigs loafing along the sidewalk, doing a good business in watermelon rinds and seeds; two or three lonely little freight piles scattered about the "levee"; a pile of "skids" on the slope of the stone-paved wharf, and the fragrant town

drunkard asleep in the shadow of them; two or three wood flats at the head of the wharf, but nobody to listen to the peaceful lapping of the wavelets against them; the great Mississippi, the majestic, the magnificent Mississippi, rolling its mile-wide tide along, shining in the sun; the dense forest away on the other side; the "point" above the town, and the "point" below, bounding the river-glimpse and turning it into a sort of sea, and withal a very still and brilliant and lonely one. Presently a film of dark smoke appears above one of those remote "points"; instantly a negro dray-man, famous for his quick eye and prodigious voice, lifts up the cry, "S-t-e-a-m-boat a-comin'!" and the scene changes! The town drunkard stirs, the clerks wake up, a furious clatter of drays follows, every house and store pours out a human contribution, and all in a twinkling the dead town is alive and moving. Drays, carts, men, boys, all go hurrying from many quarters to a common center, the wharf. Assembled there, the people fasten their eyes upon the coming boat as upon a wonder they are seeing for the first time. And the boat *is* rather a handsome sight, too. She is long and sharp and trim and pretty; she has two tall, fancy-topped chimneys, with a gilded device of some kind swung between them; a fanciful pilot-house, all glass and "gingerbread," perched on top of the "texas" deck behind them; the paddle-boxes are gorgeous with a picture or with gilded rays above the boat's name; the boiler-deck, the hurricane-deck, and the texas deck are fenced and ornamented with clean white railings; there is a flag gallantly flying from the jack-staff; the furnace doors are open and the fires glaring bravely; the upper decks are black with passengers; the captain stands by the big bell, calm, imposing, the envy of all; great volumes of the blackest smoke are rolling and tumbling out of the chimneys—a husbanded grandeur created with a bit of pitch-pine just before arriving at a town; the crew are grouped on the forecastle; the broad stage is run far out over the port bow, and an envied deck-hand stands picturesquely on the end of it with a coil of rope in his hand; the pent steam is screaming through the gauge-cocks; the captain lifts his hand, a bell rings, the wheels stop; then they turn back, churning the water to foam, and the steamer is at rest. Then such a scramble as there is to get aboard, and to get ashore, and to take in freight and to discharge freight, all at one and the same time; and such a yelling and cursing as the mates facilitate it all with! Ten minutes later the steamer is under way again, with no flag on the jack-staff and no black smoke issuing from the chimneys. After ten more minutes the town is dead again, and the town drunkard asleep by the skids once more.

3   My father was a justice of the peace, and I supposed he possessed the power of life and death over all men, and could hang anybody that offended him. This was distinction enough for me as a general thing; but the desire to be a steamboatman kept intruding, nevertheless. I first wanted to be a cabin-boy, so that I could come out with a white apron on and shake a table-cloth over the side, where all my old comrades could see me; later I thought I would rather be the deck-hand who stood on the end of the

stage-plank with the coil of rope in his hand, because he was particularly conspicuous. But these were only day-dreams—they were too heavenly to be contemplated as real possibilities. By and by one of our boys went away. He was not heard of for a long time. At last he turned up as apprentice engineer or "striker" on a steamboat. This thing shook the bottom out of all my Sunday-school teachings. That boy had been notoriously worldly, and I just the reverse; yet he was exalted to this eminence, and I left in obscurity and misery. There was nothing generous about this fellow in his greatness. He would always manage to have a rusty bolt to scrub while his boat tarried at our town, and he would sit on the inside guard and scrub it, where we all could see him and envy him and loathe him. And whenever his boat was laid up he would come home and swell around the town in his blackest and greasiest clothes, so that nobody could help remembering that he was a steamboatman; and he used all sorts of steamboat technicalities in his talk, as if he were so used to them that he forgot common people could not understand them. He would speak of the "labboard " side of a horse in an easy, natural way that would make one wish he was dead. And he was always talking about "St. Looy" like an old citizen; he would refer casually to occasions when he was "coming down Fourth Street," or when he was "passing by the Planter's House," or when there was a fire and he took a turn on the brakes of "the old Big Missouri"; and then he would go on and lie about how many towns the size of ours were burned down there that day. Two or three of the boys had long been persons of consideration among us because they had been to St. Louis once and had a vague general knowledge of its wonders, but the day of their glory was over now. They lapsed into a humble silence, and learned to disappear when the ruthless "cub"-engineer approached. This fellow had money, too, and hair-oil. Also an ignorant silver watch and a showy brass watch-chain. He wore a leather belt and used no suspenders. If ever a youth was cordially admired and hated by his comrades, this one was. No girl could withstand his charms. He "cut out" every boy in the village. When his boat blew up at last, it diffused a tranquil contentment among us such as we had not known for months. But when he came home the next week, alive, renowned, and appeared in church all battered up and bandaged, a shining hero, stared at and wondered over by everybody, it seemed to us that the partiality of Providence for an undeserving reptile had reached a point where it was open to criticism.

4   This creature's career could produce but one result, and it speedily followed. Boy after boy managed to get on the river. The minister's son became an engineer. The doctor's and the postmaster's sons became "mud clerks"; the wholesale liquor dealer's son became a barkeeper on a boat; four sons of the chief merchant, and two sons of the county judge, became pilots. Pilot was the grandest position of all. The pilot, even in those days of trivial wages, had a princely salary—from a hundred and

fifty to two hundred and fifty dollars a month, and no board to pay. Two months of his wages would pay a preacher's salary for a year. Now some of us were left disconsolate. We could not get on the river—at least our parents would not let us.

5   So, by and by, I ran away. I said I would never come home again till I was a pilot and could come in glory. But somehow I could not manage it. I went meekly aboard a few of the boats that lay packed together like sardines at the long St. Louis wharf, and humbly inquired for the pilots, but got only a cold shoulder and short words from mates and clerks. I had to make the best of this sort of treatment for the time being, but I had comforting day-dreams of a future when I should be a great and honored pilot, with plenty of money, and could kill some of these mates and clerks and pay for them.

Chapter V

I WANT TO BE A CUB-PILOT

6   Months afterward the hope within me struggled to a reluctant death, and I found myself without an ambition. But I was ashamed to go home. I was in Cincinnati, and I set to work to map out a new career. I had been reading about the recent exploration of the river Amazon by an expedition sent out by our government. It was said that the expedition, owing to difficulties, had not thoroughly explored a part of the country lying about the headwaters, some four thousand miles from the mouth of the river. It was only about fifteen hundred miles from Cincinnati to New Orleans, where I could doubtless get a ship. I had thirty dollars left; I would go and complete the exploration of the Amazon. This was all the thought I gave to the subject. I never was great in matters of detail. I packed my valise, and took passage on an ancient tub called the *Paul Jones,* for New Orleans. For the sum of sixteen dollars I had the scarred and tarnished splendors of "her" main saloon principally to myself, for she was not a creature to attract the eye of wiser travelers.

7   When we presently got under way and went poking down the broad Ohio, I became a new being, and the subject of my own admiration. I was a traveler! A word never had tasted so good in my mouth before. I had an exultant sense of being bound for mysterious lands and distant climes which I never have felt in so uplifting a degree since. I was in such a glorified condition that all ignoble feelings departed out of me, and I was able to look down and pity the untraveled with a compassion that had hardly a trace of contempt in it. Still, when we stopped at villages and wood-yards, I could not help lolling carelessly upon the railings of the boiler-deck to enjoy the envy of the country boys on the bank. If they did not seem to discover me, I presently sneezed to attract their attention, or moved to a position where they could not help seeing

me. And as soon as I knew they saw me I gaped and stretched, and gave other signs of being mightily bored with traveling.

8   I kept my hat off all the time, and stayed where the wind and the sun could strike me, because I wanted to get the bronzed and weather-beaten look of an old traveler. Before the second day was half gone I experienced a joy which filled me with the purest gratitude; for I saw that the skin had begun to blister and peel off my face and neck. I wished that the boys and girls at home could see me now.

9   We reached Louisville in time—at least the neighborhood of it. We stuck hard and fast on the rocks in the middle of the river, and lay there four days. I was now beginning to feel a strong sense of being a part of the boat's family, a sort of infant son to the captain and younger brother to the officers. There is no estimating the pride I took in this grandeur, or the affection that began to swell and grow in me for those people. I could not know how the lordly steamboatman scorns that sort of presumption in a mere landsman. I particularly longed to acquire the least trifle of notice from the big stormy mate, and I was on the alert for an opportunity to do him a service to that end. It came at last. The riotous pow-wow of setting a spar was going on down on the forecastle, and I went down there and stood around in the way—or mostly skipping out of it—till the mate suddenly roared a general order for somebody to bring him a capstan bar. I sprang to his side and said: "Tell me where it is—I'll fetch it!"

10   If a rag-picker had offered to do a diplomatic service for the Emperor of Russia, the monarch could not have been more astounded than the mate was. He even stopped swearing. He stood and stared down at me. It took him ten seconds to scrape his disjointed remains together again. Then he said impressively: "Well, if this don't beat h____l!" and turned to his work with the air of a man who had been confronted with a problem too abstruse for solution.

11   I crept away, and courted solitude for the rest of the day. I did not go to dinner; I stayed away from supper until everybody else had finished. I did not feel so much like a member of the boat's family now as before. However, my spirits returned, in installments, as we pursued our way down the river. I was sorry I hated the mate so, because it was not in (young) human nature not to admire him. He was huge and muscular, his face was bearded and whiskered all over; he had a red woman and a blue woman tattooed on his right arm—one on each side of a blue anchor with a red rope to it; and in the matter of profanity he was sublime. When he was getting out cargo at a landing, I was always where I could see and hear. He felt all the majesty of his great position, and made the world feel it, too. When he gave even the simplest order, he discharged it like a blast of lightning, and sent a long, reverberating peal of profanity thundering after it. I could not help contrasting the way in which the average landsman would give an order with the mate's way of doing it. If the landsman should wish the gangplank moved a foot farther forward, he would probably say:

"James, or William, one of you push that plank forward, please"; but put the mate in his place, and he would roar out: "Here, now, start that gang-plank for'ard! Lively, now! *What*'re you about! Snatch it! *snatch* it! There! there! Aft again! aft again! Don't you hear me? Dash it to dash! are you going to *sleep* over it!' '*Vast* heaving. 'Vast heaving, I tell you! Going to heave it clear astern? WHERE 're you going with that barrel! *for'ard* with it 'fore I make you swallow it, you dash-dash-dash-*dashed* split between a tired mudturtle and a crippled hearse-horse!"

12   I wished I could talk like that.

13   When the soreness of my adventure with the mate had somewhat worn off, I began timidly to make up to the humblest official connected with the boat—the night watchman. He snubbed my advances at first, but I presently ventured to offer him a new chalk pipe, and that softened him. So he allowed me to sit with him by the big bell on the hurricane-deck, and in time he melted into conversation. He could not well have helped it, I hung with such homage on his words and so plainly showed that I felt honored by his notice. He told me the names of dim capes and shadowy islands as we glided by them in the solemnity of the night, under the winking stars, and by and by got to talking about himself. He seemed over-sentimental for a man whose salary was six dollars a week— or rather he might have seemed so to an older person than I. But I drank in his words hungrily, and with a faith that might have moved mountains if it had been applied judiciously. What was it to me that he was soiled and seedy and fragrant with gin? What was it to me that his grammar was bad, his construction worse, and his profanity so void of art that it was an element of weakness rather than strength in his conversation? He was a wronged man, a man who had seen trouble, and that was enough for me. As he mellowed into his plaintive history his tears dripped upon the lantern in his lap, and I cried, too, from sympathy. He said he was the son of an English nobleman—either an earl or an alderman, he could not re-member which, but believed was both; his father, the nobleman, loved him, but his mother hated him from the cradle; and so while he was still a little boy he was sent to "one of them old, ancient colleges"—he couldn't remember which; and by and by his father died and his mother seized the property and "shook" him, as he phrased it. After his mother shook him, members of the nobility with whom he was acquainted used their influ-ence to get him the position of "loblolly-boy in a ship"; and from that point my watchman threw off all trammels of date and locality and branched out into a narrative that bristled all along with incredible ad-ventures; a narrative that was so reeking with bloodshed, and so crammed with hair-breadth escapes and the most engaging and uncon-scious personal villainies, that I sat speechless, enjoying, shuddering, wondering, worshiping.

14   It was a sore blight to find out afterward that he was a low, vulgar, ig-norant, sentimental, half-witted humbug, an untraveled native of the

wilds of Illinois, who had absorbed wildcat literature and appropriated its marvels, until in time he had woven odds and ends of the mess into this yarn, and then gone on telling it to fledglings like me, until he had come to believe it himself.

BUILDING CONTEXT

1. Analyze how the boys define success. What seems to be their most important goal? What significance does this have to group identity?
2. Relate Twain's vision of childhood to that of Jacobs. Explain the reasons for their similarities and their differences.
3. Compare Twain's and Adams's interpretations of their childhoods. What makes Twain's happy and Adams's—despite its humor—sad?

FURTHER STUDY

1. Investigate Twain's experience during the Civil War. What was his attitude then and later toward slavery?
2. Evaluate the controversy surrounding *Huckleberry Finn.* What is the source of the conflict? What is the message of the novel? How does the response to Huck Finn compare to the reactions to *The Merchant of Venice,* or to Kate Millet's attack on the novels of Norman Mailer?
3. Explore the dark side of Mark Twain, as evident in "The Man That Corrupted Hadleyburg" and *What Is Man?* Associate this with his themes in *Huckleberry Finn* and other works.

ADDITIONAL RESOURCES

Eble, Kenneth Eugene. *Old Clemens and W. D. H.: The Story of a Remarkable Friendship.* Baton Rouge: Louisiana State University, 1985.
Emerson, Everett H. *The Authentic Mark Twain: A Literary Biography of Samuel L. Clemens.* Philadelphia: University of Pennsylvania Press, 1984.
Fishkin, Shelley Fisher. *Was Huck Black?: Mark Twain and African-American Voices.* New York: Oxford University Press, 1993.
Howells, William Dean. *My Mark Twain.* New York, 1910.
Kesterson, David B., ed. *Critics on Mark Twain.* Coral Gables, Fl.: University of Miami Press, 1973.

RESEARCH KEYWORDS

American Fiction	African Americans in Literature
Humor	Howells (William Dean)

ELIZABETH BACON
CUSTER
Boots and Saddles
(1885)

"It would be expected that army women would know a great deal about fire-arms. . . . I am compelled to confess that the holster of a pistol gave me a shiver."

Though George Armstrong Custer graduated last in his class at West Point, he won national attention for his daring as a cavalry officer at the battles of Bull Run and Gettysburg and for his part in forcing the surrender of General Robert E. Lee.

Elizabeth Bacon Custer (1842–1933), of Monroe, Michigan, met her future husband in the winter of 1863, shortly before the 23-year-old captain from Ohio was promoted to brigadier-general of a Michigan volunteer cavalry unit. They became engaged the following autumn, while Custer was on three weeks leave recovering from a wound, and were married in February during another brief leave. This time, however, when Custer returned to the front, his bride insisted on going along, thus establishing the pattern that she maintained for the twelve years of their marriage: she traveled with the army to Texas and Kansas, and was at an outpost in the Dakota Territory on June 25, 1876, when Custer and his entire command of 267 men of the 7th Cavalry died at the Little Bighorn river.

Moving to New York, Elizabeth Custer discovered that her new acquaintances were interested in life on the frontier, but ignorant. She therefore wrote *Boots and Saddles: or, Life in Dakota with General Custer* and, when this was well received, *Tenting on the Plains:, or General Custer in Kansas and Texas.* While the books concentrate on "the domestic life of an army family . . . our occupations, amusements, and mode of house-keeping," they also polished the legend of Custer, portraying him as perfect in mind and bearing, and always referring to him as "the general" even though his rank in the post-war regular army was colonel. Most of all, however, the books present the frontier and army life from the point of view of the women who had to improvise a community in the wilderness, arrange social gatherings, calm each other's fears, and comfort the victims of tragedy. Notably, the army wives are depicted as helpless and giddy, and dependent on the brave and long-suffering men for protection—leaving the reader to wonder about the author's intended message.

Text: Elizabeth B. Custer, *Boots and Saddles: or, Life in Dakota with General Custer,*. 1885.

EXPLORING ISSUES IN THE TEXT

1. Analyze the significance of "our gasping and wild heart-beating" and "wily, creeping savages" (par. 5) and similar expressions throughout.

2. How would you characterize the women's response to their danger (pars. 6–9)? What is the significance of the passage about firearms? How are the women being portrayed?

3. Analyze the interaction of the women and the officer who had remained behind (pars. 9–10, 18).

A DAY OF ANXIETY AND TERROR

1 When the air became milder it was a delight, after our long housing, to be able to dawdle on the piazza. The valley below us was beginning to show a tinge of verdure. Several hundred mules belonging to the supply-wagon train dotted the turf and nibbled as best they could the sprouting grass. Half a dozen citizens lounged on the sod, sleepily guarding the herd, for these mules were hired by the Government from a contractor. One morning we were walking back and forth, looking, as we never tired of doing, down the long, level plain, when we were startled by shouts. We ran to the edge of the piazza, and saw the prisoners, who had been working outside the post, and the guard who had them in charge, coming in at a double-quick. A hatless and breathless herder dashed up to the officer on an unsaddled mule. With blanched face and protruding eyeballs he called out that the Indians were running off the herd.

2 The general came hastily out, just in time to see a cloud of dust rising through a gap in the bluffs, marking the direction taken by the stampeded mules. Instantly he shouted with his clear voice to the bugler to sound the call, "Boots and saddles," and keep it up until he told him to stop. The first notes of the trumpet had hardly sounded before the porches of the company quarters and the parade were alive with men. Every one, without stopping to question rushed from the barracks and officers' quarters to the stables. The men threw their saddles on their horses and galloped out to the parade-ground. Soldiers who were solely on garrison duty, and to whom no horse was assigned, stole whatever ones they could find, even those of the messengers tied to the hitching-posts. Others vaulted on to mules barebacked. Some were in jackets, others in their flannel shirt-sleeves. Many were hatless, and occasionally a head was tied up with a handkerchief. It was anything but a military-looking crowd, but every one was ready for action, and such spirited-looking creatures it is rarely one's lot to see. Finding the reason for the hasty summons when they all gathered together, they could hardly brook even a few moments' delay.

3   The general did not tarry to give any but brief directions. He detailed an officer to remain in charge of the garrison, and left him some hurried instructions. He stopped to caution me again not to go outside the post, and with a hasty good-bye flung himself into the saddle and was off. The command spurred their horses towards the opening in the bluff, not a quarter of a mile away, through which the last mules had passed. In twenty minutes from the first alarm the garrison was emptied, and we women stood watching the cloud of dust that the hoofs of the regimental horses had stirred as they hurled themselves through the cleft in the hills.

4   We had hardly collected our senses before we found that we were almost deserted. As a rule, there are enough soldiers on garrison duty, who do not go on scouts, to protect the post, but in the mad haste of the morning, and impelled by indignant fury at having the herd swept away from under their very noses as it were, all this home-guard had precipitately left without permission. Fortunately for them, and his own peace of mind regarding our safety, the general did not know of this until he returned. Besides, the officers never dreamed the pursuit would last for more than a mile or so, as they had been so quick in preparing to follow.

5   After our gasping and wild heart-beating had subsided a little, we realized that, in addition to our anxiety for those who had just left us, we were in peril ourselves. The women, with one instinct, gathered together. Though Indians rarely attack a post directly, the pickets that were stationed on the low hills at the rear of the garrison had been fired upon previously. We also feared that the buildings would be set on fire by the wily, creeping savages. It was even thought that the running off of the herd was but a ruse to get the garrison out, in order to attack the post. Of course we knew that only a portion of the Indians had produced the stampede, and we feared that the remainder were waiting to continue the depredations, and were aware of our depleted numbers.

6   Huddled together in an inner room, we first tried to devise schemes for secreting ourselves. The hastily-built quarters had then no cellars. How we regretted that a cave had not been prepared in the hill back of us for hiding the women in emergencies. Our means of escape by the river were uncertain, as the ferry-boat was in a shocking condition; besides, the citizens in charge would very naturally detain the boat upon some pretext on the safe side of the river. Finally, nervous and trembling over these conferences, we returned to the piazza, and tried to think that it was time for the return of the regiment. Our house being the last in the line, and commanding an extended view of the valley, we kept our lookout there. Each of us took turns in mounting the porch railing, and, held there in place by the others, fixed the field-glass on the little spot of earth through which the command had vanished. With a plaintive little laugh, one of our number called out the inquiry that has symbolized all beleaguered women from time immemorial, "Sister Anne, do you see any one coming?"

7   All of us scanned the horizon unflaggingly. We knew the Indian mode of taking observation. They pile a few stones on the brow of the hill after dark; before dawn they creep up stealthily from the farther side, and hiding behind the slight protection, watch all day long with unwearying patience. These little picket posts of theirs were scattered all along the bluffs. We scarcely allowed ourselves to take our eyes off them. Once in a while one of our group on watch called out that something was moving behind the rocks. Chairs were brought out and placed beside her, in order that a second pair of eyes might confirm the statement. This threw our little shivering group into new panics.

8   There was a window in the servants' room at the rear of the house, to and from which we ascended and descended all day long. I do not think the actual fear of death was thought of so much as the all-absorbing terror of capture. Our regiment had rescued some white women from captivity in Kansas, and we never forgot their stories. One of our number became so convinced that their fate awaited us, that she called a resolute woman one side to implore her to promise that, when the Indians came into the post, she would put a bullet through her heart, before she carried out her determination to shoot herself. We sincerely discussed whether, in extreme danger, we could be counted upon to load and fire a carbine.

9   It would be expected that army women would know a great deal about fire-arms; I knew but few who did. I never even went into the corner of my husband's library, where he kept his stand of unloaded arms, if I could help it. I am compelled to confess that the holster of a pistol gave me a shiver. One of our ladies, however, had a little of the Mollie Pitcher spirit. She had shot at a mark, and she promised to teach us to put in the cartridges and discharge the piece. We were filled with envy because she produced a tiny Remington pistol that heretofore she had carried in her pocket when travelling in the States. It was not much larger than a lead-pencil, and we could not help doubting its power to damage. She did not insist that it would kill, but even at such a time we had to laugh at the vehement manner in which she declared that she could disable the leg of an enemy. She seemed to think that sufficient pluck would be left to finish him afterwards. The officer who had remained in command was obliged to see that the few troopers left were armed, and afterwards he visited the pickets. Then he came to us and tried to quiet our fears, and from that time his life became a burden.

10   We questioned twenty times his idea as to *where* he thought the command had gone, *when* it would come back, and such other aimless queries as only the ingenuity of frightened women can devise. He was driven almost desperate. In assuring us that he hoped there was no immediate danger, he asked us to remember that the infantry post was near enough to give assistance if we needed it. Alas, that post seemed miles away, and we believed the gulleys that intervened between the two gar-

risons would be filled with Indians. After a prolonged season of this experience, the officer tried to escape and go to his quarters. We were really so anxious and alarmed that he had not the heart to resist our appeals to him to remain near.

11   And so that long day dragged away. About five o'clock in the afternoon a faint haze arose on the horizon. We could hardly restrain our uneasy feet. We wanted to run up over the bluff to discover what it meant. We regretted that we had given our word of honor that we would not leave the limits of the post. Soon after the mules appeared, travelling wearily back through the same opening in the bluffs through which so many hours before they had rushed headlong. We were bitterly disappointed to find only a few soldiers driving them, and they gave but little news. When the regiment overtook the stock these men had been detailed to return with the recaptured animals to the garrison; the command had pushed on in pursuit of the Indians.

12   The night set in, and still we were in suspense. We made a poor attempt to eat dinner; we knew that none of the regiment had taken rations with them, and several of the officers had not even breakfasted. There was nothing for us to do but to remain together for the night.

13   From this miserable frame of mind we were thrown into a new excitement, but fortunately not of fear: we heard the sound of the band ringing out on the still evening air. Every woman was instantly on the piazza. From an entirely different direction from that in which they had left, the regiment appeared, marching to the familiar notes of "Garryowen."

14   Such a welcome as met them! The relief from the anxiety of that unending day was inexpressible. When the regiment was nearing the post, the general had sent in an orderly to bring the band out to meet them. He cautioned him to secrecy, because he wished us to have a joyous release from the suspense he knew we had endured.

15   The regiment had ridden twenty miles out, as hard as the speed of the horses would allow. The general, and one other officer mounted like himself on a Kentucky thorough-bred, found themselves far in advance, and almost up to some of the Indians. They seeing themselves so closely pressed, resorted to the cunning of their race to escape. They threw themselves from their ponies, and plunged into the underbrush of a deep ravine where no horse could follow. The ponies were captured, but it was useless to try any further pursuit. All the horses were fagged, and the officers and men suffering from the want of food and water.

16   When the herders were questioned next day, it was found that the Indians had started the stampede by riding suddenly up from the river where they had been concealed. Uttering the wildest yells, they each swung a buffalo robe about the ears of the easily excited mules.

17   An astonishing collection of maimed and halt appeared the next morning; neither men nor officers had been in the saddle during the winter. This sudden ride of so many miles, without preparation, had so

bruised and stiffened their joints and flesh that they could scarcely move naturally. When they sat down it was with the groans of old men. When they rose they declared they would stand perpetually until they were again limber and their injuries healed.

18   As to the officer who had been left behind, he insisted that their fate was infinitely preferable to his. We heard that he said to the others in confidence, that should he ever be detailed to command a garrison where agitated women were left, he would protest and beg for active duty, no matter if his life itself were in jeopardy.

BUILDING CONTEXT

1. Compare Elizabeth Custer's view of herself to that of Harriet Jacobs or Elizabeth Cady Stanton. What "feminine" traits do the three authors value? What is their sense of hierarchy or equality?

2. Try to place Custer's memoir in the context of her time and place. Compare her purpose to that of Franklin or Booker T. Washington.

3. Compare Custer's racial attitudes to those described in the selections by Edith Maud Eaton or Abraham Cahan.

FURTHER STUDY

1. What political purpose—even if unintentional—might Custer have served by her memoirs? Consider the theories of Kolodny and Millett.

2. Investigate racial (including ethnic) attitudes at the end of the nineteenth century. Which earlier "outside" groups had by that time become insiders? Which groups were now the object of bias? Try to account for the changes.

3. Contrast Custer's depiction of women to the "American girl" or to contemporary feminists. Try to find parallel contrasts in today's television or movie portrayals.

ADDITIONAL RESOURCES

Ambrose, Stephen E. *Crazy Horse and Custer: The Parallel Lives of Two American Warriors.* Garden City, NY: Doubleday, 1975 .

Deloria, Vine. *Custer Died for Your Sins: An Indian Manifesto.* New York: Macmillan, 1969.

Fairbanks, Carol. *Prairie Women: Images in American and Canadian Fiction.* New Haven, CN: Yale University Press, 1986.

Riley, Glenda. *Women and Indians on the Frontier, 1825–1915.* Albuquerque: University of New Mexico Press, 1984.

RESEARCH KEYWORDS

Frontier Women	Women Pioneers
Frontier and Pioneer Life	West—Race Relations
Heroes—U.S.	Legends
U. S. Army—Military Life	Indians of North America
Oglala Indians	

> **HENRY BROOKS
> ADAMS**
> *The Education of
> Henry Adams* (1907)

"*What had been would continue to be. . . . [A] system of society which had lasted since Adam would outlast one Adams more.*"

Grandson of one president of the United States and great-grandson of another, with the best education and access to the powerful, Henry Adams (1838–1918) should have felt that his own success would be inevitable. Instead, all around him he perceived decay and disintegration—the result of the nation's failure to achieve the moral idealism and responsible individualism embodied by his ancestors. In *The Degradation of the Democratic Dogma,* he argues that a loss of spiritual and intellectual energy has made future social progress impossible. In *Mont-Saint-Michel and Chartres,* he longs for the unifying spirit of the Catholic Middle Ages. And in *The Education of Henry Adams,* subtitled "A Study of 20th-Century Multiplicity," he laments his—and by extension modern man's—alienation in a hostile world.

In part, at least, Adams' pessimism resulted from his feeling that the world had passed him by: His class deserved to lead and to be honored for its achievements, but a new breed, with the wrong values, had usurped power. In the excerpt that follows, Adams, standing at the threshold of a new century, looks back at a childhood spent alternating between the homes of his Adams and Brooks grandparents. Explaining events as he understands them sixty years later, rather than from his childhood perspective, Adams compares his grandfather the president to his grandfather the wealthy businessman; life in rural Quincy to life in urban Boston; idealistic individualism to political expediency; and eighteenth-century spirituality to twentieth-century materialism. In each case, the former has been defeated by the latter, the noble to the less-than-noble—leaving Henry Adams confused and adrift.

Text: Henry Adams, *The Education of Henry Adams;* Boston: Houghton Mifflin, 1918.

EXPLORING ISSUES IN THE TEXT

1. Why does Adams call himself an "eighteenth-century child" who could never "care for nineteenth-century style" (par. 1)? How does this establish the pervasive sense of alienation in this selection?

2. Interpret the significance of the incident in which Adams's grandfather takes him to school (pars. 3–4). What does Adams see as the purpose of education (par. 2)? How does this explain his attraction to the old and his uneasiness with the modern?

3. Explain the significance of Adams's recollection of the weekly church service, and the Irish gardener's comment (par. 5).

4. What lesson did Adams learn in Quincy about America's mission (par. 11)? Why does the chapter end on a note of uncertainty?

THE EDUCATION OF HENRY ADAMS

1 . . . The President's place at Quincy was the larger and older and far the more interesting of the two; but a boy felt at once its inferiority in fashion. It showed plainly enough its want of wealth. It smacked of colonial age, but not of Boston style or plush curtains. To the end of his life he never quite overcame the prejudice thus drawn in with his childish breath. He never could compel himself to care for nineteenth-century style. He was never able to adopt it, any more than his father or grandfather or great-grandfather had done. Not that he felt it as particularly hostile, for he reconciled himself to much that was worse; but because, for some remote reason, he was born an eighteenth-century child. The old house at Quincy was eighteenth century. What style it had was in its Queen Anne mahogany panels and its Louis Seize chairs and sofas. The panels belonged to an old colonial Vassall who built the house; the furniture had been brought back from Paris in 1789 or 1801 or 1817, along with porcelain and books and much else of old diplomatic remnants; and neither of the two eighteenth-century styles—neither English Queen Anne nor French Louis Seize—was comfortable for a boy, or for any one else. The dark mahogany had been painted white to suit daily life in winter gloom. Nothing seemed to favor, for a child's objects, the older forms. On the contrary, most boys, as well as grown-up people, preferred the

new, with good reason, and the child felt himself distinctly at a disadvantage for the taste. . . .

2   The attachment to Quincy was not altogether sentimental or wholly sympathetic. Quincy was not a bed of thornless roses. Even there the curse of Cain set its mark. There as elsewhere a cruel universe combined to crush a child. As though three or four vigorous brothers and sisters, with the best will, were not enough to crush any child, every one else conspired towards an education which he hated. From cradle to grave this problem of running order through chaos, direction through space, discipline through freedom, unity through multiplicity, has always been, and must always be, the task of education, as it is the moral of religion, philosophy, science, art, politics, and economy; but a boy's will is his life, and he dies when it is broken, as the colt dies in harness, taking a new nature in becoming tame. Rarely has the boy felt kindly towards his tamers. Between him and his master has always been war. Henry Adams never knew a boy of his generation to like a master, and the task of remaining on friendly terms with one's own family, in such a relation, was never easy.

3   All the more singular it seemed afterwards to him that his first serious contact with the President should have been a struggle of will, in which the old man almost necessarily defeated the boy, but instead of leaving, as usual in such defeats, a lifelong sting, left rather an impression of as fair treatment as could be expected from a natural enemy. The boy met seldom with such restraint. He could not have been much more than six years old at the time—seven at the utmost—and his mother had taken him to Quincy for a long stay with the President during the summer. What became of the rest of the family he quite forgot; but he distinctly remembered standing at the house door one summer morning in a passionate outburst of rebellion against going to school. Naturally his mother was the immediate victim of his rage; that is what mothers are for, and boys also; but in this case the boy had his mother at unfair disadvantage, for she was a guest, and had no means of enforcing obedience. Henry showed a certain tactical ability by refusing to start, and he met all efforts at compulsion by successful, though too vehement protest. He was in fair way to win, and was holding his own, with sufficient energy, at the bottom of the long staircase which led up to the door of the President's library, when the door opened, and the old man slowly came down. Putting on his hat, he took the boy's hand without a word, and walked with him, paralyzed by awe, up the road to the town. After the first moments of consternation at this interference in a domestic dispute, the boy reflected that an old gentleman close on eighty would never trouble himself to walk near a mile on a hot summer morning over a shadeless road to take a boy to school, and that it would be strange if a lad imbued with the passion of freedom could not find a corner to dodge around, somewhere before reaching the school door. Then and always, the boy insisted

that this reasoning justified his apparent submission; but the old man did not stop, and the boy saw all his strategical points turned, one after another, until he found himself seated inside the school, and obviously the centre of curious if not malevolent criticism. Not till then did the President release his hand and depart.

4   The point was that this act, contrary to the inalienable rights of boys, and nullifying the social compact, ought to have made him dislike his grandfather for life. He could not recall that it had this effect even for a moment. With a certain maturity of mind, the child must have recognized that the President, though a tool of tyranny, had done his disreputable work with a certain intelligence. He had shown no temper, no irritation, no personal feeling, and had made no display of force. Above all, he had held his tongue. During their long walk he had said nothing; he had uttered no syllable of revolting cant about the duty of obedience and the wickedness of resistance to law; he had shown no concern in the matter; hardly even a consciousness of the boy's existence. Probably his mind at that moment was actually troubling itself little about his grandson's iniquities, and much about the iniquities of President Polk, but the boy could scarcely at that age feel the whole satisfaction of thinking that President Polk was to be the vicarious victim of his own sins, and he gave his grandfather credit for intelligent silence. For this forbearance he felt instinctive respect. . . .

5   Till his twelfth year, the child passed his summers there, and his pleasures of childhood mostly centered in it. Of education he had as yet little to complain. Country schools were not very serious. Nothing stuck to the mind except home impressions, and the sharpest were those of kindred children; but as influences that warped a mind, none compared with the mere effect of the back of the President's bald head, as he sat in his pew on Sundays, in line with that of President Quincy, who, though some ten years younger, seemed to children about the same age. Before railways entered the New England town, every parish church showed half-a-dozen of these leading citizens, with gray hair, who sat on the main aisle in the best pews, and had sat there, or in some equivalent dignity, since the time of St. Augustine, if not since the glacial epoch. It was unusual for boys to sit behind a President grandfather, and to read over his head the tablet in memory of a President great-grandfather, who had "pledged his life, his fortune, and his sacred honor" to secure the independence of his country and so forth; but boys naturally supposed, without much reasoning, that other boys had the equivalent of President grandfathers, and that churches would always go on, with the bald-headed leading citizens on the main aisle, and Presidents or their equivalents on the walls. The Irish gardener once said to the child: "You'll be thinkin' you'll be President too!" The casualty of the remark made so strong an impression on his mind that he never forgot it. He could not remember ever to have thought on the subject; to him, that there

should be a doubt of his being President was a new idea. What had been would continue to be. He doubted neither about Presidents nor about Churches, and no one suggested at that time a doubt whether a system of society which had lasted since Adam would outlast one Adams more.

6   The Madam was a little more remote than the President, but more decorative. She stayed much in her own room with the Dutch tiles, looking out on her garden with the box walks, and seemed a fragile creature to a boy who sometimes brought her a note or a message, and took distinct pleasure in looking at her delicate face under what seemed to him very becoming caps. He liked her refined figure; her gentle voice and manner; her vague effect of not belonging there, but to Washington or to Europe, like her furniture, and writing-desk with little glass doors above and little eighteenth-century volumes in old binding, labelled "Peregrine Pickle" or "Tom Jones" or "Hannah More." . . .

7   Such a figure was even less fitted than that of her old husband, the President, to impress on a boy's mind, the standards of the coming century. She was Louis Seize, like the furniture. . . .

8   A boy who began his education in these surroundings, with physical strength inferior to that of his brothers, and with a certain delicacy of mind and bone, ought rightly to have felt at home in the eighteenth century and should, in proper self-respect, have rebelled against the standards of the nineteenth. The atmosphere of his first ten years must have been very like that of his grandfather at the same age, from 1767 till 1776, barring the battle of Bunker Hill, and even as late as 1846, the battle of Bunker Hill remained actual. The tone of Boston society was colonial. The true Bostonian always knelt in self-abasement before the majesty of English standards; far from concealing it as a weakness, he was proud of it as his strength. The eighteenth century ruled society long after 1850. Perhaps the boy began to shake it off rather earlier than most of his mates.

9   Indeed this prehistoric stage of education ended rather abruptly with his tenth year. One winter morning he was conscious of a certain confusion in the house in Mount Vernon Street, and gathered, from such words as he could catch, that the President, who happened to be then staying there, on his way to Washington, had fallen and hurt himself. Then he heard the word paralysis. After that day he came to associate the word with the figure of his grandfather, in a tall-backed, invalid armchair, on one side of the spare bedroom fireplace, and one of his old friends, Dr. Parkman or P. P. F. Degrand, on the other side, both dozing.

10   The end of this first, or ancestral and Revolutionary, chapter came on February 21, 1848—and the month of February brought life and death as a family habit—when the eighteenth century, as an actual and living companion, vanished. If the scene on the floor of the House, when the old President fell, struck the still simple-minded American public with a sensation unusually dramatic, its effect on a ten-year-old boy, whose boy-life

was fading away with the life of his grandfather, could not be slight. One had to pay for Revolutionary patriots; grandfathers and grandmothers; Presidents; diplomats; Queen Anne mahogany and Louis Seize chairs, as well as for Stuart portraits. Such things warp young life. Americans commonly believed that they ruined it, and perhaps the practical common-sense of the American mind judged right. Many a boy might be ruined by much less than the emotions of the funeral service in the Quincy church, with its surroundings of national respect and family pride. . . .

11   Thus already, at ten years old, the boy found himself standing face to face with a dilemma that might have puzzled an early Christian. What was he?—where was he going? Even then he felt that something was wrong, but he concluded that it must be Boston. Quincy had always been right, for Quincy represented a moral principle—the principle of resistance to Boston. His Adams ancestors must have been right, since they were always hostile to State Street. If State Street was wrong, Quincy must be right! Turn the dilemma as he pleased, he still came back on the eighteenth century and the law of Resistance; of Truth; of Duty, and of Freedom. He was a ten-year-old priest and politician. He could under no circumstances have guessed what the next fifty years had in store, and no one could teach him; but sometimes, in his old age, he wondered— and could never decide—whether the most clear and certain knowledge would have helped him. Supposing he had seen a New York stock-list of 1900, and had studied the statistics of railways, telegraphs, coal, and steel—would he have quitted his eighteenth-century, his ancestral prejudices, his abstract ideals, his semi-clerical training, and the rest, in order to perform an expiatory pilgrimage to State Street, and ask for the fatted calf of his grandfather Brooks and a clerkship in the Suffolk Bank?

12   Sixty years afterward he was still unable to make up his mind.

BUILDING CONTEXT

1. Contrast Adams's interpretation of his childhood with Twain's. What accounts for Adams's melancholy, as opposed to Twain's bright cheerfulness?

2. How do Adams and Twain use humor to contribute to the theme or thesis in each of their reminiscences?

3. Compare the educations of Adams and Abraham Cahan. What did they both have to learn? What similar discoveries did they make about their places in society?

4. In what way(s) is the situation of Elizabeth Custer similar to that of Adams? How well do they fit into their societies? How aware are they of alienation?

FURTHER STUDY

1. Deduce the reasons for Adams's sense of alienation. Research the responses of other writers to the changes taking place at the end of the nineteenth century. What were some of the social or political responses to these changes?

2. Explore the relevance of Adams's *Education* to modern society. Do people today experience similar feelings of alienation? If so, what are their reactions?

ADDITIONAL RESOURCES

Levenson, J. C. *The Mind and Art of Henry Adams.* Boston: Houghton-Mifflin, 1957.

Lyons, Melvin. *Symbol and Idea in Henry Adams.* Lincoln: University of Nebraska Press, 1970.

Stevenson, Elizabeth. *Henry Adams: A Biography.* New York: Macmillan, 1955.

Wasser, Henry. *The Scientific Thought of Henry Adams.* Thessaloniki: 1956.

RESEARCH KEYWORDS

Adams (John Quincy)
Immigration
Nativism

EDITH MAUD EATON
Leaves from the Mental Portfolio of an Eurasian
(1909)

"Fundamentally, I muse, all people are the same. My mother's race is as prejudiced as my father's."

The short stories of Edith Maud Eaton (1865–1914), written under the pseudonym Sui Sin Far, describe the mixture of fear and hope, attraction and revulsion that many Chinese—and other—immigrants feel toward their new country and its alien ways. At a time when the Chinese Exclusion Act was still in effect, Eaton was the first American of Chinese ancestry to attack in print the many misconceptions about and injuries to the Chinese. Significantly, her sister Winnifred wrote under the Japanese name Onoto Watanna because Japanese were then held in higher esteem in North America.

Eaton's autobiography depicts a strong-willed woman carving a place for herself despite society's preconceptions regarding the proper behavior for her sex and race. The following excerpt traces her developing consciousness of discrimination and her decision—despite her Eurasian ancestry and European education—to cast her lot with the Chinese.

Text: Edith Maud Eaton; *Leaves from the Mental Portfolio of an Eurasian; Heath Anthology of American Literature,* Vol. II; Lexington, Mass.: D.C. Heath, 1990.

EXPLORING ISSUES IN THE TEXT

1. Interpret Eaton's comment that at eighteen she was troubled that people were ignorant of her superiority (par. 7). Contrast this with her remarks about the appearance of Chinese men (par. 12). What traits does she consider handsome? What insight does this give the reader into her value system?

2. Why does Eaton say that her mother's race is as prejudiced as her father's (pars. 13–14)?

3. Why do "sporty" people seek out Eaton when they learn that she is not all white (par. 28)? What is the significance of the anecdote about the naval officer who stops by Eaton's hotel one day (pars. 29–31)?

4. Comment on the suggestion that Eaton should trade on her nationality if she wishes to succeed in literature (par. 36).

LEAVES FROM THE MENTAL PORTFOLIO OF AN EURASIAN

1 My brother is remarkably bright; my sister next to me has a wonderful head for figures, and when only eight years of age helps my father with his night work accounts. My parents compare her with me. She is of sturdier build than I, and, as my father says, "Always has her wits about her." He thinks her more like my mother, who is very bright and interested in every little detail of practical life. My father tells me that I will never make half the woman that my mother is or that my sister will be. I am not as strong as my sisters, which makes me feel somewhat ashamed, for I am the eldest little girl, and more is expected of me. I have no organic disease, but the strength of my feelings seems to take from me the strength of my body. I am prostrated at times with attacks of nervous

sickness. The doctor says that my heart is unusually large; but in the light of the present I know that the cross of the Eurasian bore too heavily upon my childish shoulders. I usually hide my weakness from the family until I cannot stand. I do not understand myself, and I have an idea that the others will despise me for not being as strong as they. Therefore, I like to wander away alone, either by the river or in the bush. The green fields and flowing water have a charm for me. At the age of seven, as it is today, a bird on the wing is my emblem of happiness.

2   I have come from a race on my mother's side which is said to be the most stolid and insensible to feeling of all races, yet I look back over the years and see myself so keenly alive to every shade of sorrow and suffering that it is almost a pain to live.

3   If there is any trouble in the house in the way of a difference between my father and mother, or if any child is punished, how I suffer! And when harmony is restored, heaven seems to be around me. I can be sad, but I can also be glad. My mother's screams of agony when a baby is born almost drive me wild, and long after her pangs have subsided I feel them in my own body. Sometimes it is a week before I can get to sleep after such an experience.

4   A debt owing by my father fills me with shame. I feel like a criminal when I pass the creditor's door. I am only ten years old. And all the while the question of nationality perplexes my little brain. Why are we what we are? I and my brothers and sisters. Why did God make us to be hooted and stared at? Papa is English, mamma is Chinese. Why couldn't we have been either one thing or the other? Why is my mother's race despised? I look into the faces of my father and mother. Is she not every bit as dear and good as he? Why? Why? She sings us the songs she learned at her English school. She tells us tales of China. Tho a child when she left her native land she remembers it well, and I am never tired of listening to the story of how she was stolen from her home. She tells us over and over again of her meeting with my father in Shanghai and the romance of their marriage. Why? Why?

5   I do not confide in my father and mother. They would not understand. How could they? He is English, she is Chinese. I am different to both of them—a stranger, tho their own child. "What are we?" I ask my brother. "It doesn't matter, sissy," he responds. But it does. I love poetry, particularly heroic pieces. I also love fairy tales. Stories of everyday life do not appeal to me. I dream dreams of being great and noble; my sisters and brothers also. I glory in the idea of dying at the stake and a great genie arising from the flames and declaring to those who have scorned us: "Behold, how great and glorious and noble are the Chinese people!"

6   My sisters are apprenticed to a dressmaker; my brother is entered in an office. I tramp around and sell my father's pictures, also some lace which I make myself. My nationality, if I had only known it at that time, helps to make sales. The ladies who are my customers call me "The Little

Chinese Lace Girl." But it is a dangerous life for a very young girl. I come near to "mysteriously disappearing" many a time. The greatest temptation was in the thought of getting far away from where I was known, to where no mocking cries of "Chinese!" "Chinese!" could reach.

7   Whenever I have the opportunity I steal away to the library and read every book I can find on China and the Chinese. I learn that China is the oldest civilized nation on the face of the earth and a few other things. At eighteen years of age what troubles me is not that I am what I am, but that others are ignorant of my superiority. I am small, but my feelings are big—and great is my vanity.

8   My sisters attend dancing classes, for which they pay their own fees. In spite of covert smiles and sneers, they are glad to meet and mingle with other young folk. They are not sensitive in the sense that I am. And yet they understand. One of them tells me that she overheard a young man say to another that he would rather marry a pig than a girl with Chinese blood in her veins.

9   In course of time I too learn shorthand and take a position in an office. Like my sister, I teach myself, but, unlike my sister, I have neither the perseverance nor the ability to perfect myself. Besides, to a temperament like mine, it is torture to spend the hours in transcribing other people's thoughts. Therefore, altho I can always earn a moderately good salary, I do not distinguish myself in the business world as does she.

10   When I have been working for some years I open an office of my own. The local papers patronize me and give me a number of assignments, including most of the local Chinese reporting. I meet many Chinese persons, and when they get into trouble am often called upon to fight their battles in the papers. This I enjoy. My heart leaps for joy when I read one day an article signed by a New York Chinese in which he declares "The Chinese in America owe an everlasting debt of gratitude to Sui Sin Far for the bold stand she has taken in their defense."

11   The Chinaman who wrote the article seeks me out and calls upon me. He is a clever and witty man, a graduate of one of the American colleges and as well a Chinese scholar. I learn that he has an American wife and several children. I am very much interested in these children, and when I meet them my heart throbs in sympathetic tune with the tales they relate of their experiences as Eurasians. "Why did papa and mamma born us?" asks one. Why?

12   I also meet other Chinese men who compare favorably with the white men of my acquaintance in mind and heart qualities. Some of them are quite handsome. They have not as finely cut noses and as well developed chins as the white men, but they have smoother skins and their expression is more serene; their hands are better shaped and their voices softer.

13   Some little Chinese women whom I interview are very anxious to know whether I would marry a Chinaman. I do not answer No. They

clap their hands delightedly, and assure me that the Chinese are much the finest and best of all men. They are, however, a little doubtful as to whether one could be persuaded to care for me, full-blooded Chinese people having a prejudice against the half white.

14 Fundamentally, I muse, all people are the same. My mother's race is as prejudiced as my father's. Only when the whole world becomes as one family will human beings be able to see clearly and hear distinctly. I believe that some day a great part of the world will be Eurasian. I cheer myself with the thought that I am but a pioneer. A pioneer should glory in suffering.

∽

15 "You were walking with a Chinaman yesterday," accuses an acquaintance.

"Yes, what of it?"

"You ought not to. It isn't right."

"Not right to walk with one of my mother's people? Oh, indeed!"

I cannot reconcile this notion of righteousness with my own.

∽

16 I am living in a little town away off on the north shore of a big lake. Next to me at the dinner table is the man for whom I work as a stenographer. There are also a couple of business men, a young girl and her mother.

17 Some one makes a remark about the cars full of Chinamen that past that morning. A transcontinental railway runs thru the town.

18 My employer shakes his rugged head. "Somehow or other," says he, "I cannot reconcile myself to the thought that the Chinese are humans like ourselves. They may have immortal souls, but their faces seem to be so utterly devoid of expression that I cannot help but doubt."

19 "Souls," echoes the town clerk. "Their bodies are enough for me. A Chinaman is, in my eyes, more repulsive than a nigger."

"They always give me such a creepy feeling," puts in the young girl with a laugh.

"I wouldn't have one in my house," declares my landlady.

"Now, the Japanese are different altogether. There is something bright and likeable about those men," continues Mr. K.

20 A miserable, cowardly feeling keeps me silent. I am in a Middle West town. If I declare what I am, every person in the place will hear about it the next day. The population is in the main made up of working folks with strong prejudices against my mother's countrymen. The prospect before me is not an enviable one—if I speak. I have no longer an ambition to die at the stake for the sake of demonstrating the greatness and nobleness of the Chinese people.

21 Mr. K. turns to me with a kindly smile.

"What makes Miss Far so quiet?" he asks.

"I don't suppose she finds the 'washee washee men' particularly interesting subjects of conversation," volunteers the young manager of the local bank.

22   With a great effort I raise my eyes from my plate. "Mr. K.," I say, addressing my employer, "the Chinese people may have no souls, no expression on their faces, be altogether beyond the pale of civilization, but whatever they are, I want you to understand that I am—I am a Chinese."

23   There is silence in the room for a few minutes. Then Mr. K. pushes back his plate and standing up beside me, says:

24   "I should not have spoken as I did. I know nothing whatever about the Chinese. It was pure prejudice. Forgive me!"

25   I admire Mr. K.'s moral courage in apologizing to me; he is a conscientious Christian man, but I do not remain much longer in the little town.

26   I am under a tropic sky, meeting frequently and conversing with persons who are almost as high up in the world as birth, education and money can set them. The environment is peculiar, for I am also surrounded by a race of people, the reputed descendants of Ham, the son of Noah, whose offspring, it was prophesied, should be the servants of the sons of Shem and Japheth. As I am a descendant, according to the Bible, of both Shem and Japheth, I have a perfect right to set my heel upon the Ham people; but tho I see others around me following out the Bible suggestion, it is not in my nature to be arrogant to any but those who seek to impress me with their superiority, which the poor black maid who has been assigned to me by the hotel certainly does not. My employer's wife takes me to task for this. "It is unnecessary," she says, "to thank a black person for a service."

27   The novelty of life in the West Indian island is not without its charm. The surroundings, people, manner of living, are so entirely different from what I have been accustomed to up North that I feel as if I were "born again." Mixing with people of fashion, and yet not of them, I am not of sufficient importance to create comment or curiosity. I am busy nearly all day and often well into the night. It is not monotonous work, but it is certainly strenuous. The planters and business men of the island take me as a matter of course and treat me with kindly courtesy. Occasionally an Englishman will warn me against the "brown boys" of the island, little dreaming that I too am of the "brown people" of the earth.

28   When it begins to be whispered about the place that I am not all white, some of the "sporty" people seek my acquaintance. I am small and look much younger than my years. When, however, they discover that I am a very serious and sober-minded spinster indeed, they retire quite gracefully, leaving me a few amusing reflections.

29   One evening a card is brought to my room. It bears the name of some naval officer. I go down to my visitor, thinking he is probably some one

who, having been told that I am a reporter for the local paper, has brought me an item of news. I find him lounging in an easy chair on the veranda of the hotel—a big, blond, handsome fellow, several years younger than I.

30   "You are Lieutenant _____?" I inquire.

He bows and laughs a little. The laugh doesn't suit him somehow—and it doesn't suit me, either.

"If you have anything to tell me, please tell it quickly, because I'm very busy."

"Oh, you don't really mean that," he answers, with another silly and offensive laugh. "There's always plenty of time for good times. That's what I am here for. I saw you at the races the other day and twice at King's House. My ship will be here for _____ weeks."

31   "Do you wish that noted?" I ask.

"Oh, no! Why—I came just because I had an idea that you might like to know me. I would like to know you. You look such a nice little body. Say, wouldn't you like to go out for a sail this lovely night? I will tell you all about the sweet little Chinese girls I met when we were at Hong Kong. They're not so shy!" . . .

∽

32 The proprietor of one of the San Francisco papers, to whom I have a letter of introduction, suggests that I obtain some subscriptions from the people of Chinatown, that district of the city having never been canvassed. This suggestion I carry out with enthusiasm, tho I find that the Chinese merchants and people generally are inclined to regard me with suspicion. They have been imposed upon so many times by unscrupulous white people. Another drawback—save for a few phrases, I am unacquainted with my mother tongue. How, then, can I expect these people to accept me as their own countrywoman? The Americanized Chinamen actually laugh in my face when I tell them that I am of their race. However, they are not all "doubting Thomases." Some little women discover that I have Chinese hair, color of eyes and complexion, also that I love rice and tea. This settles the matter for them—and for their husbands.

33   My Chinese instincts develop. I am no longer the little girl who shrunk against my brother at the first sight of a Chinaman. Many and many a time, when alone in a strange place, has the appearance of even an humble laundryman given me a sense of protection and made me feel quite at home. This fact of itself proves to me that prejudice can be eradicated by association.

34   I meet a half Chinese, half white girl. Her face is plastered with a thick white coat of paint and her eyelids and eyebrows are blackened so that the shape of her eyes and the whole expression of her face is changed. She was born in the East, and at the age of eighteen came West in answer to an advertisement. Living for many years among the working class, she had heard little but abuse of the Chinese. It is not difficult, in a land like California, for

a half Chinese, half white girl to pass as one of Spanish or Mexican origin. This the poor child does, tho she lives in nervous dread of being "discovered." She becomes engaged to a young man, but fears to tell him what she is, and only does so when compelled by a fearless American girl friend. This girl, who knows her origin, realizing that the truth sooner or later must be told, and better soon than late, advises the Eurasian to confide in the young man, assuring her that he loves her well enough not to allow her nationality to stand, a bar sinister, between them. But the Eurasian prefers to keep her secret, and only reveals it to the man who is to be her husband when driven to bay by the American girl, who declares that if the halfbreed will not tell the truth she will. When the young man hears that the girl he is engaged to has Chinese blood in her veins, he exclaims: "Oh, what will my folks say?" But that is all. Love is stronger than prejudice with him, and neither he nor she deems it necessary to inform his "folks."

35   The Americans, having for many years manifested a much higher regard for the Japanese than for the Chinese, several half Chinese young men and women, thinking to advance themselves, both in a social and business sense, pass as Japanese. They continue to be known as Eurasians; but a Japanese Eurasian does not appear in the same light as a Chinese Eurasian. The unfortunate Chinese Eurasians! Are not those who compel them to thus cringe more to be blamed than they? . . .

36   I secure transportation to many California points. I meet some literary people, chief among whom is the editor of the magazine who took my first Chinese stories. He and his wife give me a warm welcome to their ranch. They are broadminded people, whose interest in me is sincere and intelligent, not affected and vulgar. I also meet some funny people who advise me to "trade" upon my nationality. They tell me that if I wish to succeed in literature in America I should dress in Chinese costume, carry a fan in my hand, wear a pair of scarlet beaded slippers, live in New York, and come of high birth. Instead of making myself familiar with the Chinese-Americans around me, I should discourse on my spirit acquaintance with Chinese ancestors and quote in between the "Good mornings" and "How d'ye dos" of editors

> *"Confucius, Confucius, how great is Confucius, Before Confucius, there never was Confucius. After Confucius, there never came Confucius," etc., etc., etc.,*

or something like that, both illuminating and obscuring, don't you know. They forget, or perhaps they are not aware that the old Chinese sage taught "The way of sincerity is the way of heaven."

37   My experiences as an Eurasian never cease; but people are not now as prejudiced as they have been. In the West, too, my friends are more ad-

vanced in all lines of thought than those whom I know in Eastern Canada—more genuine, more sincere, with less of the form of religion, but more of its spirit.

38 So I roam backward and forward across the continent. When I am East, my heart is West. When I am West, my heart is East. Before long I hope to be in China. As my life began in my father's country it may end in my mother's.

39 After all I have no nationality and am not anxious to claim any. Individuality is more than nationality. "You are you and I am I," says Confucius. I give my right hand to the Occidentals and my left to the Orientals, hoping that between them they will not utterly destroy the insignificant "connecting link." And that's all.

Another Voice

THE MIDDLE CLASS WIFE
THORSTEIN VEBLEN

It is a fact of common observation that in this lower middle class there is no pretence of leisure on the part of the head of the household. Through force of circumstances it has fallen into disuse. But the middle-class wife still carries on the business of vicarious leisure, for the good name of the household and its master. . . .

The leisure rendered by the wife in such cases is, of course, not a simple manifestation of idleness or indolence. It almost invariably occurs disguised under some form of work or household duties or social amenities, which prove on analysis to serve little or no ulterior end beyond showing that she does not and need not occupy herself with anything that is gainful or that is of substantial use. . . .

The wife, who was at the outset the drudge and chattel of the man, both in fact and in theory—the producer of goods for him to consume—has become the ceremonial consumer of goods which he produces. But she still quite unmistakably remains his chattel in theory; for the habitual rendering of vicarious leisure and consumption is the abiding mark of the unfree servant.

The Theory of the Leisure Class, 1899

BUILDING CONTEXT

1. Why does Eaton come close to "mysteriously disappearing" (par. 6)? How is this danger or experience similar to that of free blacks under the Fugitive Slave Act? What comparable situations exist today?
2. Compare the evolution of ethnic identity experienced by Eaton and Cameron or Mohr. To what extent were they motivated by both positive and negative stimuli? Is ethnic identity self-created or imposed by others?
3. Relate Du Bois's belief that "beauty is black" to the attitudes expressed by Eaton, Cameron, and minority or ethnic groups today.

FURTHER STUDY

1. Explore the psychology of self-identification. For example, Eaton was as much Caucasian as she was Chinese, yet she chose to consider herself Chinese. Why?
2. Eaton discovers that it is better to "pass" as Mexican or Japanese than Chinese. Analyze the implications of "passing"—racial, ethnic, religious, or sexual.
3. Explore society's fluctuating attitudes toward ethnicity or particular groups. To what extent is there "fashion" in prejudice? How, for example, did Asians go from "yellow peril" to "model immigrants" (to use Mazumdar's observation)?

ADDITIONAL RESOURCES

Kingston, Maxine Hong. *The Woman Warrior: Memoir of a Girlhood among Ghosts.* New York: Knopf, 1976.

Ling, Amy. *Between Worlds: Women Writers of Chinese Ancestry.* New York: Pergamon Press, 1990.

Ruoff, A. LaVonne Brown, and Jerry W. Ward, Jr., eds. *Redefining American Literary History.* New York: Modern Language Association of America, 1990.

Yap, Stacey, G. H. *Gather Your Strength, Sisters: The Emerging Role of Chinese Women Community Workers.* New York: AMS Press, 1989.

RESEARCH KEYWORDS

American Literature—Chinese-American Authors
Chinese-American Women
Chinese-Americans in Literature
American Literature—Chinese Influence
Emigration and Immigration
Minorities—U.S.

ABRAHAM CAHAN
The Education of
Abraham Cahan (1926)

"*America had no censor, nor was it engaged in a bitter struggle for freedom. . . . There was not the same motivation for an earnest interest in literary matters.*"

Famous as a writer in both Yiddish and English, Abraham Cahan (1860–1951) moved comfortably in three societies: Jewish, American, and socialist. While studying at the Teachers' Seminary in Vilna, Lithuania (then part of Russia), he became interested in anarchism, and when some of his acquaintances were implicated in the assassination of Czar Alexander II, he fled the country one step ahead of the police. Arriving in America in 1882, he was stunned to see anarchist publications for sale at newsstands. America, he discovered, was not Russia.

But neither was it the Garden of Eden. Cahan found much suffering among the tens of thousands of Russian-Jewish immigrants who escaped from the czarist pogroms to New York's Lower East Side. He believed that socialism offered one solution; Americanization was another. In the Yiddish-language *Jewish Daily Forward,* which he helped found in 1897 and edited from 1902 until his death, he included columns on English grammar, citizenship, and good manners; as well as socialist tracts and fiction by Sholem Asch, Isaac Bashevis Singer (who later won the Nobel Prize), and other masters of Yiddish literature. At its peak, the *Forward* was perhaps the most influential foreign-language newspaper in America.

Cahan's emphasis on self-help and cultural accommodation—but not total assimilation—mirrors his own life. He learned English, joined literary clubs and debating societies, worked as a reporter for English-language newspapers, and lectured on the importance of unions and the corruption of capitalism. His first English novel, *Yekl: A Tale of the New York Ghetto* (1896), was praised by William Dean Howells as a milestone of realism, and *The Rise of David Levinsky* (1917) remains a classic study of the immigrant experience.

Cahan's five-volume autobiography focuses on his poltical education and the evolution of his philosophy. Intellectual life in Russia meant banned pamphlets, secret cells, and exile to Siberia. In America, ideas are free, even if conditions need improvement. And, as Cahan discovers in the following excerpt, anti-Semitism is not pervasive among intellectuals. If there is a fault with the young men he meets, it is a flippancy born of safety, a sense that ideas are not life-and-death issues.

Text: Abraham Cahan; *The Education of Abraham Cahan;* Trans. Leon Stein et al.; Philadelphia: Jewish Publication Society, 1969.

EXPLORING ISSUES IN THE TEXT

1. Who were the "nihilists" (par. 10)? Explain the significance of the date November 11, 1887, and Cahan's reason for leaving the club. Contrast the Russian intellectuals with the members of Cahan's debating society (pars. 9–10).

2. Why is it significant that the members of Cahan's literary society had not heard of Howells and James (pars. 15–16)? Why wouldn't this happen in Russia (pars. 17–18)? Why does Cahan believe that literature is more important to Russians than to Americans (pars. 18–19)?

3. Summarize Cahan's analysis of anti-Semitism in America (pars. 25–35).

THE EDUCATION OF ABRAHAM CAHAN

1   I was also a member of another club, one which had no political connections. Most of its members were young American schoolteachers. One of them was Carls, a gentile who taught in the classroom next to mine in the evening school on Chrystie Street. He was a handsome young man with a round face and rosy cheeks. We often chatted before class. Several times I visited him at his father's house on East 106th Street which was then a gentile neighborhood lined by rows of narrow wooden houses. Carls' parents were German immigrants; he had been born in New York.

2   Through Carls I joined a club which consisted of young Irish and native Americans who had graduated together from City College. They met in one of the clubrooms of Congress Hall on Third Avenue and Eighteenth Street. I liked the company of these young men and I joined their club and remained a member for more than two years. This was before I joined the Socialist Labor party.

3   The club had about thirty members. I was the only one who was not a City College graduate. All except three were gentiles. Only about five of us were not schoolteachers.

4   The club was really a literary debating society. At each of the Saturday evening meetings the subject for the following meeting would be announced. Then the speakers for and against the subject were named by the chairman. Our purpose was to develop our skills as speakers and debaters.

5   In addition, we would have readings of poems, essays and stories written by the members. This would be followed by group criticism. After the formal part of the meeting there was warm camaraderie, the telling of jokes, anecdotes and singing.

6   I participated as an equal. The only concession made in my behalf was that, unlike the others, I was allowed to choose the side of the resolution I wished to defend in the debate. At one of the meetings the topic for debate was: "*Resolved,* That the capitalist system of production and distribution is a just one." Before I could choose, the chairman assigned the negative to me.

7   My friend Carls protested. "Cahan will win it hands down," he told the others. "He's a specialist on that subject. Let one of us show what we can do with it."

8   He asked the chairman to assign the negative to him. He had no real interest in the matter, but out of friendship for me he wanted to show how he could handle the topic. I yielded to him. I armed him with some pamphlets and briefed him with explanations. He was a fine speaker and won the debate, surprising his opponent and the others with the effectiveness of his preparation.

9   In this way the club "officially" went on record as agreeing that the capitalist system was unjust. But this was only a formality that was required in order to conclude the debate. Actually, these young men were not at all concerned with social problems.

10   I thought of young men in Russia, their profound interest in these matters, their readiness to suffer exile in Siberia or death itself on the gallows. How different things were in Russia and how different were the young intellectuals of that country. Once, I tried to picture the difference for Carls and the others. The drama of the Russian struggle for freedom immediately interested them. They began to ask many questions, especially about the nihilists. They listened so avidly that we never got around to our formal meeting that night. That was shortly before November 11, 1887.

11   On the evening of November 12 I went to the meeting of our club. I had decided to explain the meaning of the Chicago executions to my fellow club members, to prove that these deaths constituted bloody class vengeance and thus to arouse sympathy for the hanged ones.

12   But before the meeting started I overheard two of the club members joking about the Chicago anarchists. One of them ran his finger across his throat and stuck out his tongue, making a choking sound.

13   I felt sick. Suddenly the club became unclean to me. I felt bitter over my plan to win sympathy for the hanged ones. I left the hall quietly. I stopped going to the club.

14   The first time Carls asked why I wasn't coming to meetings anymore, I offered some lame excuse. But later I blurted out the truth. Carls was deeply apologetic. He prevailed on me to return to the club, where the others also apologized for the conduct of the two members.

15 Two of the most important American authors at the time were William Dean Howells and Henry James. Both were realists. It was then the fashion to boast about them. Important visitors from Europe, when interviewed,

were asked by the reporters whether they were familiar with "our writers Howells and James."

16   But among the young men of our literary club not one had read the works of these two writers. They were familiar enough with the English classics. But Howells and James were of the avant-garde and were outside their ken. I had read the works of both men. When I tried to talk about them at the club no one recognized the names.

17   This kind of thing would have been impossible in Russia. It was unimaginable that a young man in that country just out of the university would not know the finest and most important belletrists of the day. This was the startling difference between the young, educated men of the two countries.

18   The profound interest of the Russian students in the contemporary literature of their country reflected their deep interest in social problems. Russian literature was a weapon in the Russian struggle for freedom. Because Russian censorship made criticism of Russian life impossible, one engaged instead in literary criticism and belles lettres. Criticism of tales, fables and essays became, in effect, crticism of social life in Russia. For this reason, interest in literature in Russia was more serious than in other nations.

19   America had no censor, nor was it engaged in a bitter struggle for freedom. Political and social problems were openly discussed in the press, in magazines and books and from the lecture platform. There was not the same motivation for an earnest interest in literary matters.

20   Though the club members showed little interest in the country's social problems, they were greatly interested in politics. Each of them was a warm defender of one of the two major parties, more often than not the party for which his father voted. Every year, as election time approached, their excitement rose. But they did not bring their party differences into the club.

21   Many of them intended to study law. Some had already started. This aroused dreams of a political career, of a job in Washington, perhaps even of a seat in Congress. By coincidence, our meeting place was called Congress Hall, and one of our slogans became "Congress Hall is our preparation for the Halls of Congress." Even those not studying law had a deep interest in politics. From his youth, politics is every American's passion.

22   But again politics had one meaning for these young Americans and quite another for the youthful Russian intellectuals. In Russia, politics meant a challenge to tyranny; it meant students risking their lives for freedom; it meant martyrdom.

23   But to the young American, politics was a game, a sport, a means for making money directly or indirectly, a way of acquiring power and influence. So it is in republics or in monarchies with parliaments.

24   The young members of the club, hitching their dreams of a career to politics, were thoroughly informed about political life in New York and

Washington. They knew the names of important politicians, their past and their present circumstances. They were loaded with names and facts and anecdotes and statistics, everything concerning congressmen, senators, assemblymen, aldermen, leaders—their fights, their intrigues, their prospects, their victories, their defeats.

25 In our club I never saw the slightest trace of anti-Semitism. Our relations were most comradely. We visited with each other. There was little anti-Semitism in America at that time.

26 　In Europe the greatest source of hatred of the Jew is competition in business or the professions. But Americans had no reason to fear competition by the Jews. First of all, the Yankee is himself a pretty smart businessman. Secondly, the number of Jews was so small that most Americans had never seen one.

27 　Finally, there was little hostility based on differences in religion. This is a land of many faiths with a heterogeneous population. No politician scurrying for votes is going to reveal hostile feelings.

28 　In his heart the Yankee proudly feels that he is in fact the only genuine American. Therefore, he holds himself aloof from the others, but no more aloof from the Jew than from the Irishman. Having fought the Catholics in the old country, he has no fondness for them here. Nevertheless, for a long time Jews were to be found in the wealthy American organizations—wealthy Jews, naturally.

29 　Snobbish anti-Semitism or aristocratic anti-Semitism was imported to America from Europe; it was as much a thing of fashion as the new hats and styles that are brought over from Paris. As wealth spread in America, high society here began to imitate royal society overseas. Since Jews were banned from European high society, they were gradually excluded here too.

30 　In 1877 the family of the Jewish millionaire Joseph Seligman was not admitted to a fancy summer hotel at Saratoga Springs, New York. Several years later, Laurel House in Lakewood, New Jersey, closed its doors to the Jewish millionaire Nathan Straus. But the fashion had not yet really spread.

31 　During my first years in the United States, millionaires were few in number. They were still "new arrivals" at their high status and had not yet developed snobbish tastes and pretensions. Among them were a few old Jewish millionaires. No new ones were admitted to the society of millionaires.

32 　When I arrived the immigration committee included one wealthy young Jewish lady who belonged to the cream of the monied aristocracy. She was Emma Lazarus. She often visited the immigrants' camp on Ward's Island in the East River, but this never undermined her status as an aristocrat.

33 She was of the Portuguese Jews, the oldest Jewish families in America. Today, even a Portuguese Jewish family would not be admitted to the "400." This is a list of 400 New York families considered to be the aristocracy of the wealthy. The "400" and aristocracy have become synonymous.

34 In the South, where the pride of status is even stronger than in the North, there was less anti-Semitism than in the North. Jewish families mixed freely with even the highest level of the non-Jewish aristocracy. Several Jews were elected governors.

35 The young men of the literary club of which I was a member in 1887 were not members of the "400." They were from ordinary families. But today even such young men would be infected with anti-Semitism, unless they were radicals—which they were not.

Another Voice

A NEW YORK TENEMENT
JACOB RIIS

It is said that nowhere in the world are so many people crowded together on a square mile as here. The average five-story tenement adds a story or two to its stature in Ludlow Street and an extra building on the rear lot, and yet the sign "To Let" is the rarest of all there. Here is one seven stories high. The sanitary policeman whose beat this is will tell you that this building here contains thirty-six families, but the term has a widely different meaning here and on the avenues. In this house, where a case of small-pox was reported, there were fifty-eight babies and thirty-eight children that were over five years of age. In Essex Street two small rooms in a six-story tenement were made to hold a "family" of father and mother, twelve children and six boarders. . . . These are samples of the packing of the population that has run up the record here to the rate of three hundred and thirty thousand per square mile. The densest crowding in Old London, I pointed out before, never got beyond a hundred and seventy-five thousand. . . .

How the Other Half Lives, 1902

BUILDING CONTEXT

1. Evaluate Cahan's economic explanation for bigotry (par. 26). Consider relevant observations by Booker T. Washington, Hymowitz and Weissman, or Millett. How would you associate the experience of Henry Adams?

2. Compare Cahan's analysis of religious commitment in America to that of Crèvecoeur or Tocqueville.

3. Compare Cahan's belief in the importance of literature to that of Howells. Analyze his theory of censorship in light of the case of *Ulysses* or other books.

FURTHER STUDY

1. Review the history of anti-Semitism in America. Distinguish snobbish, economic, political, and religious anti-Semitism. Investigate especially Cahan's belief that anti-Semitism did not affect radicals.

2. Research the theory of anarchism and its history in America. Who were its supporters in America? Why was the official response to this particular movement so vigorous?

3. Examine the controversy surrounding the Haymarket incident of 1886. Why were feelings on both sides so intense? Try to place the emotions in the context of their time. What recent event provoked a similar public reaction?

ADDITIONAL RESOURCES

Chametzky, Jules. *From the Ghetto: The Fiction of Abraham Cahan.* Amherst: University of Massachusetts Press, 1977.

Goren, Arthur A. *New York Jews and the Quest for Community.* New York: Columbia University Press, 1970.

Howe, Irving. *World of Our Fathers: The Journey of the East European Jews to America and the Life They Found and Made.* New York: Harcourt Brace Jovanovich, 1976.

Sanders Ronald. *The Downtown Jews: Portraits of an Immigrant Generation.* New York: Dover, 1987.

RESEARCH KEYWORDS

Forward (Forverts)	Immigrants	Jews—New York
Lower East Side	New York—Ethnic Relations	Anti-Semitism

Exploring Critical Issues Through Writing

1. Evaluate the controversy surrounding *Huckleberry Finn* or another work that some people find offensive, such as a novel by Norman Mailer or a movie by Spike Lee. What is the source of the conflict? How might it be resolved?

2. Explore the nativist or America First movements. Identify the social situations that give rise to these movements. What psychological needs do they satisfy?

3. Explore alienation. What are its psychological causes? List both its positive and negative aspects. How does it influence individual behavior and public policy?

4. Investigate racial and ethnic attitudes at the end of the nineteenth century in America. Which previously excluded groups had by that time become insiders? Which groups had become new objects of bias? Account for these changes.

5. Analyze the image of the "American girl," or other depictions of American womanhood. Trace their origins and current manifestations in literature, television, or film.

6. Review the history of anti-Semitism in America, distinguishing between the snobbish, economic, political, and religious forms for this prejudice. Consider both the right-wing and left-wing manifestations of American anti-Semitism.

7. Research the theory of anarchism and its history in America. Who were its supporters? Why was the official response so vigorous?

8. Explore the psychology of self-identification. Why do individuals often define themselves on the basis of one particular aspect out of many—including sex, race, religion, region, and occupation?

9. Explore society's fluctuating attitudes toward ethnicity or particular groups. To what extent is there "fashion" in prejudice? How, for example, did Asians go from "yellow peril" to "model immigrants"?

10. Explore an idea from the reading selections that caught your interest, charmed or provoked you, or supported or challenged your own beliefs. Place the issue within a larger context and explain its significance.

9

SEEDS OF MODERNITY: 1900–1940

"Mr. Washington represents in Negro thought the old attitude of adjustment and submission."

W. E. B. Du Bois

". . . nothing will help us keep . . . the peace more than a knowledge that our men can shoot straight."

Theodore Roosevelt

". . . Government . . . exists to serve individual men and women."

Franklin D. Roosevelt

The twentieth century dawned upon an America well on its way to becoming a superpower, with the foreign involvements and domestic shape that would inform the entire century.

The colonies of visionaries, refugees, and adventurers hugging the Atlantic coast in the seventeenth century had absorbed three thousand miles of "howling wilderness" inland, as well as the North American territories of Spain and France. During the nineteenth century, moreover, the quest for empire spread beyond the continental boundaries of Manifest Destiny, to include islands in the Pacific and the Caribbean. American sugar planters overthrew Queen Liliuokalani of Hawaii in 1893, with annexation of the islands following five years later. The Spanish-American War ended with the United States in control of Spain's colonies in Puerto Rico and the Philippines. If this period can be said to have a mythic embodiment, it would be in the person of Theodore Roosevelt, who captured the national imagination as the dashing leader of the Rough Riders charging up San Juan Hill—and whose guiding principle as president was "Speak softly and carry a big stick."

Access to markets in South America and Asia, coupled with industrialization, created huge fortunes for enterprising individuals and corporations. But millions of immigrants, drawn by the promise of work in the factories, lived in urban poverty. Whereas Crèvecoeur could claim that freedom and ambition soon made the poor immigrant a wealthy landowner, that promise, as Turner noted, disappeared with the closing of the frontier. Now, laborers had to create a better future for themselves as laborers, and with that realization came radical changes and even more radical theories. Thoreau could argue that "That government is best which governs not at all," but now workers wanted government to reduce the overwhelming power of corporations, and business wanted government to control the riotous masses. Previously, group identity had been defined in terms of religion, nationality, and race. Now "workers of the world" and "middle class" became theoretical constructs, and Upton Sinclair could write polemics against "wage slavery."

The influx of new ideas like socialism and communism threatened many Americans, who found comfort in isolationism and nativism. A longing for what were perceived as traditional values—*ours,* not *theirs*—affected literature as well. In the previous century, the very American Walt Whitman had shocked readers with the explicit sexuality of the *Leaves of Grass,* and the British critic George Saintsbury had to defend the work by noting that "the treatment, though outspoken, is eminently 'clean.'" But now, some believed the government had to protect Americans by prohibiting decadent European books like James Joyce's *Ulysses.*

The role of government changed in race relations as well. By 1900 blacks had lost most of the rights and power they had gained during Reconstruction. The Supreme Court had ruled in *Plessy* v. *Ferguson* that being required to ride in separate railway cars did not violate laws protecting the rights of blacks. And Booker T. Washington had seemed to agree with this government withdrawal, assuring whites that blacks wanted decent jobs, not forced social integration. However, other black leaders, including the brilliant firebrand W. E. B. Du Bois, rejected such compromises and demanded instead an end to discrimination in education, employment, trade unions, and public accommodations. In 1905 they launched the Niagara Movement, which, with the assistance of sympathetic whites, became the National Association for the Advancement of Colored People in 1909.

Finally, in the first half of the twentieth century, World War I destroyed the old order in Europe, leaving the United States a world power. As the philosopher William James argued that pacifism could be "the moral equivalent of war," President Woodrow Wilson fought for establishment of the League of Nations, an international forum that would keep the world safe for democracy. But this was not to be. A worldwide economic collapse aggravated the social unrest and national rivalries that would eventually lead to World War II just before mid-century. In the meantime, the Great Depression became a new battleground between the hands-off policies of Herbert Hoover and the activist government theories of Franklin D. Roosevelt.

Another Voice

CONSCRIPTION FOR NATIONAL SERVICE
WILLIAM JAMES

If now—and this is my idea—there were, instead of military conscription a conscription of the whole youthful population to form for a certain number of years a part of the army enlisted against *Nature,* the injustice would tend to be evened out, and numerous other goods to the commonwealth would follow. The military ideals of hardihood and discipline would be wrought into the growing fibre of the people; no one would remain blind as the luxurious classes now are blind, to man's relations to the globe he lives on, and to the permanently sour and hard foundations of his higher life. To coal and iron mines, to freight trains, to fishing fleets in December, to dishwashing, clothes-washing, and window-washing, to road-building and tunnel-making, to foundries

continued

continued from previous page

and stoke-holes, and to the frames of skyscrapers, would our gilded youths be drafted off, according to their choice, to get the childishness knocked out of them, and to come back into society with healthier sympathies and soberer ideas. They would have paid their blood-tax, done their own part in the immemorial human warfare against nature; they would tread the earth more proudly, the women would value them more highly, they would be better fathers and teachers of the following generation. . . .

The martial type of character can be bred without war. Strenuous honor and disinterestedness abound elsewhere. Priests and medical men are in a fashion educated to it, and we should all feel some degree of it imperative if we were conscious of our work as an obligatory service to the state.

The Moral Equivalent of War, 1910

UPTON SINCLAIR
The Jungle (1906)

"There are a million people, men, women and children, who share the curse of the wage-slave; who toil every hour they can stand and see for just enough to keep them alive."

Born in Baltimore in 1878, Upton Sinclair (1878–1968) moved to New York City, where he graduated from the tuition-free College of the City of New York and pursued advanced studies at Columbia University while working as a journalist. He was a prolific writer and a leading muckraker, exposing the dark side of society in the hope of forcing the government to make improvements. After many years as a member of the Socialist Party, in 1933 he founded the End Poverty in California movement. The following year he ran unsuccessfully for governor as a Democrat, a campaign that saw leading Hollywood film studios create false "documentaries" to discredit his programs and supporters.

The Jungle, published in 1906, grew out of Sinclair's investigation of the Chicago stockyards for the socialist weekly *Appeal to Reason.* It follows the exploitation and disintegration of a fictional immigrant family. Only the leading character is saved, through his conversion to socialism after hearing the climactic speech reprinted here. Like *Uncle Tom's Cabin* and only a few other books, *The Jungle* immediately became a political force, other than a mere work of fiction—leading, for example, to the passage of the Pure Food and Drug Act. However, because the book is most remembered for its portrayal of filth in meat-packing plants, and not for its socialist message, Sinclair lamented, "I aimed at the public's heart and by accident I hit it in the stomach."

Text: Upton Sinclair, *The Jungle;* New York: Bantam Books, 1981.

EXPLORING ISSUES IN THE TEXT

1. What does Sinclair mean by "wage-slave" (par. 4)? How does he develop and add power to this image?

2. Why does a description of the horrors of war precede the section on wage-slavery? What connection does Sinclair want the reader to make?

3. Does Sinclair define equality in terms of opportunity or results? What does he say accounts for the equality or inequality in America? According to Sinclair, what is the government's responsibility to its citizens?

THE JUNGLE

1 "You listen to these things," the man was saying, "and you say, 'Yes, they are true, but they have been that way always.' Or you say, 'Maybe it will come, but not in my time—it will not help me.' And so you return to your daily round of toil, you go back to be ground up for profits in the world-wide mill of economic might! To toil long hours for another's advantage; to live in mean and squalid homes, to work in dangerous and unhealthful places; to wrestle with the specters of hunger and privation, to take your chances of accident, disease, and death. And each day the struggle becomes fiercer, the pace more cruel; each day you have to toil a little harder, and feel the iron hand of circumstance close upon you a little tighter. Months pass, years maybe—and then you come again; and again I am here to plead with you, to know if want and misery have yet done their work with you, if injustice and oppression have yet opened your eyes! I shall still be waiting—there is nothing else that I can do. There is no wilderness where I can hide from these things, there is no haven where I can escape them; though I

travel to the ends of the earth, I find the same accursed system—I find that all the fair and noble impulses of humanity, the dreams of poets and the agonies of martyrs, are shackled and bound in the service of organized and predatory Greed! And therefore I cannot rest, I cannot be silent: therefore I cast aside comfort and happiness, health and good repute—and go out into the world and cry out the pain of my spirit! Therefore I am not to be silenced by poverty and sickness, not by hatred and obloquy, by threats and ridicule—not by prison and persecution, if they should come—not by any power that is upon the earth or above the earth, that was, or is, or ever can be created. If I fail tonight, I can only try tomorrow; knowing that the fault must be mine—that if once the vision of my soul were spoken upon earth, if once the anguish of its defeat were uttered in human speech, it would break the stoutest barriers of prejudice, it would shake the most sluggish soul to action! It would abash the most cynical, it would terrify the most selfish; and the voice of mockery would be silenced, and fraud and falsehood would slink back into their dens, and the truth would stand forth alone! For I speak with the voice of millions who are voiceless! Of them that are oppressed and have no comforter! Of the disinherited of life, for whom there is no respite and no deliverance, to whom the world is a prison, a dungeon of torture, a tomb! With the voice of the little child who toils tonight in a Southern cotton mill, staggering with exhaustion, numb with agony, and knowing no hope but the grave! Of the mother who sews by candlelight in her tenement garret, weary and weeping, smitten with the mortal hunger of her babes! Of the man who lies upon a bed of rags, wrestling in his last sickness and leaving his loved ones to perish! Of the young girl who, somewhere at this moment, is walking the streets of this horrible city, beaten and starving, and making her choice between the brothel and the lake! With the voice of those, whoever and wherever they may be, who are caught beneath the wheels of the Juggernaut of Greed! With the voice of humanity, calling for deliverance! Of the everlasting soul of Man, arising from the dust; breaking its way out of prison—rending the bands of oppression and ignorance—groping its way to the light!"

2   "I plead with you," he said, "whoever you may be, provided that you care about the truth; but most of all I plead with workingmen, with those to whom the evils I portray are not mere matters of sentiment, to be dallied and toyed with, and then perhaps put aside and forgotten—to whom they are the grim and relentless realities of the daily grind, the chains upon their limbs, the lash upon their backs, the iron in their souls.

3   To you, workingmen! To you, the toilers, who have made this land, and have no voice in its councils! To you, whose lot it is to sow that others may reap, to labor and obey, and ask no more than the wages of a beast of burden, the food and shelter to keep you alive from day to day. It is to you that I come with my message of salvation, it is to you that I appeal. I know how much it is to ask of you—I know, for I have been in your place, I have lived your life, and there is no man here before me tonight who

knows it better. I have known what it is to be a street-waif, a bootblack, living upon a crust of bread and sleeping in cellar stairways and under empty wagons. I have known what it is to dare and to aspire, to dream mighty dreams and to see them perish—to see all the fair flowers of my spirit trampled into the mire by the wild-beast powers of my life. I know what is the price that a workingman pays for knowledge—I have paid for it with food and sleep, with agony of body and mind, with health, almost with life itself; and so, when I come to you with a story of hope and freedom, with the vision of a new earth to be created, of a new labor to be dared, I am not surprised that I find you sordid and material, sluggish and incredulous. That I do not despair is because I know also the forces that are driving behind you—because I know the raging lash of poverty, the sting of contempt and mastership, 'the insolence of office and the spurns.' Because I feel sure that in the crowd that has come to me tonight, no matter how many may be dull and heedless, no matter how many may have come out of idle curiosity, or in order to ridicule—there will be some one man whom pain and suffering have made desperate, whom some chance vision of wrong and horror has startled and shocked into attention. And to him my words will come like a sudden flash of lightening to one who travels in darkness—revealing the way before him, the perils and the obstacles—solving all problems, making all difficulties clear! The scales will fall from his eyes, the shackles will be torn from his limbs—he will leap up with a cry of thankfulness, he will stride forth a free man at last! A man delivered from his self-created slavery! A man who will never more be trapped—whom no blandishments will cajole, whom no threats will frighten; who from tonight on will move forward, and not backward, who will study and understand, who will gird on his sword and take his place in the army of his comrades and brothers. Who will carry the good tidings to others, as I have carried them to him—the priceless gift of liberty and light that is neither mine nor his, but is the heritage of the soul of man! Workingmen, workingmen—comrades! open your eyes and look about you! You have lived so long in the toil and heat that your senses are dulled, your souls are numbed; but realize once in your lives this world in which you dwell—tear off the rags of its customs and conventions—behold it as it is, in all its hideous nakedness! Realize it, *realize it!* Realize that out upon the plains of Manchuria tonight two hostile armies are facing each other—that now, while we are seated here, a million human beings may be hurled at each other's throats, striving with the fury of maniacs to tear each other to pieces! And this in the twentieth century, nineteen hundred years since the Prince of Peace was born on earth! Nineteen hundred years that his words have been preached as divine, and here two armies of men are rending and tearing each other like wild beasts of the forest! Philosophers have reasoned, prophets have denounced, poets have wept and pleaded—and still this hideous Monster roams at large! We have schools and colleges, newspapers and books; we have searched the heavens and the earth, we have weighed and probed and reasoned—and all to equip men to destroy each other! We call it War, and pass it by—but do not put me off with platitudes and conventions—come with me, come with me—*realize it!* See the bodies of men pierced by bullets, blown into pieces by bursting shells! Hear the crunching of the bayonet, plunged into human flesh; hear the groans and shrieks of agony, see the faces of men crazed by pain, turned into fiends by fury and hate! Put your hand upon that piece of flesh—it is hot and quivering—just now it was part of a man! This blood is still streaming—it was driven by a human heart! Almighty God! and this goes on—it is systematic, organized, premeditated! And we know it, and read of it, and take it for granted; our papers tell of it, and the presses are not stopped—our churches know of it, and do not close their doors—the people behold it, and do not rise up in horror and revolution!

4   "Or perhaps Manchuria is too far away for you—come home with me then, come here to Chicago. Here in this city tonight ten thousand women are shut up in foul pens, and driven by hunger to sell their bodies to live. And we know it, we make it a jest! And these women are made in the image of your mothers, they may be your sisters, your daughters; the child whom you left at home tonight, whose laughing eyes will greet you in the morning—that fate may be waiting for her! Tonight in Chicago there are ten thousand men, homeless and wretched, willing to work and begging for a chance, yet starving, and fronting in terror the awful winter cold! Tonight in Chicago there are a hundred thousand children wearing out their strength and blasting their lives in the effort to earn their bread! There are a hundred thousand mothers who are living in misery and squalor, struggling to earn enough to feed their little ones! There are a hundred thousand old people, cast off and helpless, waiting for death to take them from their torments! There are a million people, men and women and children, who share the curse of the wage slave; who toil every hour they can stand and see, for just enough to keep them alive; who are condemned till the end of their days to monotony and weariness, to hunger and misery, to heat and cold, to dirt and disease, to ignorance and drunkenness and vice! And then turn over the page with me, and gaze upon the other side of the picture. There are a thousand—ten thousand, maybe—who are masters of these slaves, who own their toil. They do nothing to earn what they receive, they do not even have to ask for it—it comes to them of itself, their only care is to dispose of it. They live in palaces, they riot in luxury and extravagance—such as no words can describe, as makes the imagination reel and stagger, makes the soul grow sick and faint. They spend hundreds of dollars for a pair of shoes, a handkerchief, a garter; they spend millions for horses and automobiles and yachts, for palaces and banquets, for little shiny stones with which to deck their bodies. Their life is a contest among themselves for supremacy in ostentation and recklessness, in the destroying of useful and necessary

things, in the wasting of the labor and the lives of their fellow creatures, the toil and anguish of the nations, the sweat and tears and blood of the human race! It is all theirs—it comes to them; just as all the springs pour into streamlets, and the streamlets into rivers, and the rivers into the oceans—so, automatically and inevitably, all the wealth of society comes to them. The farmer tills the soil, the miner digs in the earth, the weaver tends the loom, the mason carves the stone; the clever man invents, the shrewd man directs, the wise man studies, the inspired man sings—and all the result, the products of the labor of brain and muscle, are gathered into one stupendous stream and poured into their laps! The whole of society is in their grip, the whole labor of the world lies at their mercy—and like fierce wolves they rend and destroy, like ravening vultures they devour and tear! The whole power of mankind belongs to them, forever and beyond recall—do what it can, strive as it will, humanity lives for them and dies for them! They own not merely the labor of society, they have bought the governments; and everywhere they use their raped and stolen power to intrench themselves in their privileges, to dig wider and deeper the channels through which the river of profits flows to them!—And you, workingmen, workingmen! You have been brought up to it, you plod on like beasts of burden, thinking only of the day and its pain—yet is there a man among you who can believe that such a system will continue forever—is there a man here in this audience tonight so hardened and debased that he dare rise up before me and say that he believes that it can continue forever; that the product of the labor of society, the means of existence of the human race, will always belong to idlers and parasites, to be spent for the gratification of vanity and lust—to be spent for any purpose whatever, to be at the disposal of any individual will whatever—that somehow, somewhere, the labor of humanity will not belong to humanity, to be used for the purposes of humanity, to be controlled by the will of humanity? And if this is ever to be, how is it to be—what power is there that will bring it about? Will it be the task of your masters, do you think— will they write the charter of your liberties? Will they forge you the sword of your deliverance, will they marshal you the army and lead it to the fray? Will their wealth be spent for the purpose—will they build colleges and churches to teach you, will they print papers to herald your progress, and organize political parties to guide and carry on the struggle? Can you not see that the task is your task—yours to dream, yours to resolve, yours to execute? That if ever it is carried out, it will be in the face of every obstacle that wealth and mastership can oppose—in the face of ridicule and slander, of hatred and persecution, of the bludgeon and the jail? That it will be by the power of your naked bosoms, opposed to the rage of oppression! By the grim and bitter teaching of blind and merciless affliction! By the painful gropings of the untutored mind, by the feeble stammerings of the uncultured voice! By the sad and lonely hunger of the spirit, by seeking and striving and yearning, by heartache and despairing, by agony and sweat of blood! It will be by money paid for with hunger, by knowledge stolen from sleep, by thoughts communicated under the shadow of the gallows! It will be a movement beginning in the far-off past, a thing obscure and unhonored, a thing easy to ridicule, easy to despise; a thing unlovely, wearing the aspect of vengeance and hate—but to you, the workingman, the wage slave, calling with a voice insistent, imperious—with a voice that you cannot escape, wherever upon the earth you may be! With the voice of all your wrongs, the voice of all your desires; with the voice of your duty and your hope—of everything in the world that is worth while to you! The voice of the poor, demanding that poverty shall cease! The voice of the oppressed, pronouncing the doom of oppression! The voice of power, wrought out of suffering—of resolution, crushed out of weakness—of joy and courage, born in the bottomless pit of anguish and despair! The voice of Labor, despised and outraged; a mighty giant, lying prostrate—mountainous, colossal, but blinded, bound, and ignorant of his strength. And now a dream of resistance haunts him, hope battling with fear; until suddenly he stirs, and a fetter snaps—and a thrill shoots through him, to the farthest ends of his huge body, and in a flash the dream becomes an act! He starts, he lifts himself; and the bands are shattered, the burdens roll off him; he rises—towering, gigantic; he springs to his feet, he shouts in his newborn exultation—"

BUILDING CONTEXT

1. According to Sinclair, who is responsible for a person's poverty or wealth? What part does, or should, government play? Compare his position to those of Booker T. Washington, Franklin D. Roosevelt, or a modern politician.

2. What determines a person's identity or group membership for Sinclair? Relate his approach to those of Rowlandson, Van Every, Crèvecoeur, or others.

3. Compare the arguments in this speech to those surrounding the statement in Weber that "they make tallow out of cattle and money out of men."

4. What does Sinclair claim is the attitude of the established church toward labor? Associate this with what other selections say about the church's role in slavery or civil rights.

FURTHER STUDY

1. Critics say that the main character in *The Jungle* is "converted" to socialism. Explore the appropriateness of this religious image. In what way is socialism a type of religion? How does this speech use the vocabulary and techniques of religion?

2. In the early 1990s, Communism collapsed in Eastern Europe. Was socialism also abandoned? What is the difference between communism and socialism? Between socialism and capitalism? Argue whether or not the United States is a purely capitalist society.

3. The excerpted speech, the climax of *The Jungle,* is a blatant political polemic. Debate whether politics, propaganda, and other persuasive purposes have a valid place within art. Consider the works of Sinclair, Stowe, Rowlandson, Franklin, Thoreau, or others.

ADDITIONAL RESOURCES

Blinderman, Abraham, ed. *Critics on Upton Sinclair: Readings in Literary Criticism.* Coral Gables, Fl.: University of Miami Press, 1974.
Bloodworth, William A. *Upton Sinclair.* Boston: Twayne, 1977.
Mitchell, Greg. *The Campaign of the Century: Upton Sinclair's Race for Governor of California and the Birth of Media Politics.* New York: Random House, 1992.

RESEARCH KEYWORDS

Socialism
Politics and Government—U.S.

W. E. B. DU BOIS
"*Of* Mr. *Booker T. Washington and Others*"
(1903)

"*Mr. Washington represents in Negro thought the old attitude of adjustment and submission.*"

William Edward Burghardt Du Bois (1868–1963) was an African-American leader who rejected the compromises of Booker T. Washington. After helping establish the Niagara Movement and the NAACP, he edited the NAACP journal, *The Crisis,* from 1910 to 1932.

Born in Massachusetts after the Civil War, Du Bois enjoyed many privileges but also vividly recalled the rejection he suffered from being "different."

He won scholarships to Fisk, the University of Berlin, and Harvard, where, in 1895, he became the first African American to earn a Ph.D. His dissertation, *The Suppression of the African Slave Trade to the U.S.A., 1638–1870,* was a ground-breaking investigation that is still studied today. His 1903 book, *The Souls of Black Folk,* in which the following selection appeared, established his reputation as a brilliant radical thinker. This essay argues that Washington was not a valid black leader, that he blamed the victim instead of the oppressor, and that his economic program was a poor substitute for equality—charges that are still hotly debated.

Throughout his life he urged blacks to organize their own businesses, run their own schools, preserve their identity, respect their heritage, and remember that "beauty is black." He died in 1963 at the age of 95, shortly after becoming a citizen of Ghana.

Text: W. E. B. Du Bois; *The Souls of Black Folk;* New York: Library of America, 1990.

EXPLORING ISSUES IN THE TEXT

1. Summarize Du Bois's explanation for the rise of Booker T. Washington to African-American leadership (pars. 1–2).

2. Summarize the opposition of blacks to Washington (pars. 4–6). How does he represent the "old attitude of adjustment and submission"?

3. According to Du Bois, what characterizes Washington's program (par. 7)? Which of its aspects does Du Bois particularly attack? Why does he think Washington proposed this program?

4. Du Bois accuses Washington of shifting "the burden of the Negro problem to the Negro's shoulders." What sacrifices did Washington ask of African Americans? What alternative does Du Bois propose?

OF MR. BOOKER T. WASHINGTON AND OTHERS

1 Easily the most striking thing in the history of the American Negro since 1876 is the ascendancy of Mr. Booker T. Washington. It began at the time when war memories and ideals were rapidly passing; a day of astonishing commercial development was dawning; a sense of doubt and hesitation overtook the freedmen's sons,—then it was that his leading began. Mr. Washington came, with a simple definite programme, at the psychological moment when the nation was a little ashamed of having bestowed so much sentiment on Negroes, and was concentrating its energies on Dollars. His programme of industrial education, conciliation of the South, and submission and silence as to civil and political rights, was not wholly original; the Free Negroes from 1830 up to wartime had

striven to build industrial schools, and the American Missionary Association had from the first taught various trades; and Price and others had sought a way of honorable alliance with the best of the Southerners. But Mr. Washington first indissolubly linked these things; he put enthusiasm, unlimited energy, and perfect faith into this programme, and changed it from a by-path into a veritable Way of Life. And the tale of the methods by which he did this is a fascinating study of human life.

2   It startled the nation to hear a Negro advocating such a programme after many decades of bitter complaint; it startled and won the applause of the South, it interested and won the admiration of the North; and after a confused murmur of protest, it silenced if it did not convert the Negroes themselves.

3   To gain the sympathy and cooperation of the various elements comprising the white South was Mr. Washington's first task; and this, at the time Tuskegee was founded, seemed, for a black man, well-nigh impossible. And yet ten years later it was done in the word spoken at Atlanta: "In all things purely social we can be as separate as five fingers, and yet one as the hand in all things essential to mutual progress." This "Atlanta Compromise" is by all odds the most notable thing in Mr. Washington's career. The South interpreted it in different ways: the radicals received it as a complete surrender of the demand for civil and political equality; the conservatives, as a generously conceived working basis for mutual understanding. So both approved it, and to-day its author is certainly the most distinguished Southerner since Jefferson Davis, and the one with the largest personal following.

4   Among his own people, however, Mr. Washington has encountered the strongest and most lasting opposition, amounting at times to bitterness, and even to-day continuing strong and insistent even though largely silenced in outward expression by the public opinion of the nation. Some of this opposition is, of course, mere envy; the disappointment of displaced demagogues and the spite of narrow minds. But aside from this, there is among educated and thoughtful colored men in all parts of the land a feeling of deep regret, sorrow, and apprehension at the wide currency and ascendancy which some of Mr. Washington's theories have gained. These same men admire his sincerity of purpose, and are willing to forgive much to honest endeavor which is doing something worth the doing. They cooperate with Mr. Washington as far as they conscientiously can; and, indeed, it is no ordinary tribute to this man's tact and power that, steering as he must between so many diverse interests and opinions, he so largely retains the respect of all.

5   . . . But Booker T. Washington arose as essentially the leader of not one race, but of two,—a compromiser between the South, the North, and the Negro. Naturally the Negroes resented, at first bitterly, the signs of compromise which surrendered their civil and political rights, even though this was to be exchanged for larger chances of economic development.

The rich and dominating North, however, was not only weary of the race problem, but was investing largely in Southern enterprises, and welcomed any method of peaceful cooperation. Thus, by national opinion, the Negroes began to recognize Mr. Washington's leadership; and the voice of criticism was hushed.

6   Mr. Washington represents in Negro thought the old attitude of adjustment and submission; but adjustment at such a peculiar time as to make his programme unique. This is an age of unusual economic development, and Mr. Washington's programme naturally takes an economic cast, becoming a gospel of Work and Money to such an extent as apparently almost completely to overshadow the higher aims of life. Moreover, this is an age when the more advanced races are coming in closer contact with the less developed races, and the race-feeling is therefore intensified; and Mr. Washington's programme practically accepts the alleged inferiority of the Negro races. Again, in our own land, the reaction from the sentiment of war time has given impetus to race-prejudice against Negroes, and Mr. Washington withdraws many of the high demands of Negroes as men and American citizens. In other periods of intensified prejudice all the Negro's tendency to self-assertion has been called forth; at this period a policy of submission is advocated. In the history of nearly all other races and peoples the doctrine preached at such crises has been that manly self-respect is worth more than lands and houses, and that a people who voluntarily surrender such respect, or cease striving for it, are not worth civilizing.

7   In answer to this, it has been claimed that the Negro can survive only through submission. Mr. Washington distinctly asks black people to give up, at least for the present, these things.

First, political power,

Second, insistence on civil rights,

Third, higher education of the Negro youth, —

and concentrate all their energies on industrial education, the accumulation of wealth, and the conciliation of the South. This policy has been courageously and insistently advocated for over fifteen years, and has been triumphant for perhaps ten years. As a result of this tender of the palm-branch, what has been the return? In theses years there have occurred:

1. The disfranchisement of the Negro.

2. The legal creation of a distinct status of civil inferiority for the Negro.

3. The steady withdrawal of aid from institutions for the higher training of the Negro.

8   These movements are not, to be sure, direct results of Mr. Washington's teachings; but his propaganda has, without a shadow of doubt, helped their speedier accomplishment. The question then comes: Is it

possible, and probable, that nine millions of men can make effective progress in economic lines if they are deprived of political rights, made a servile caste, and allowed only the most meagre chance for developing their exceptional men? If history and reason give any distinct answer to these questions, it is an emphatic *No.* And Mr. Washington thus faces the triple paradox of his career:

1. He is striving nobly to make Negro artisans business men and property-owners; but it is utterly impossible, under modern effective methods, for workingmen and property-owners to defend their rights and exist without the right of suffrage.

2. He insists on thrift and self-respect, but at the same time counsels a silent submission to civic inferiority such as is bound to sap the manhood of any race in the long run.

3. He advocates common-school and industrial training, and depreciates institutions of higher learning; but neither the Negro common-schools, nor Tuskegee itself, could remain open a day were it not for teachers trained in Negro colleges, or trained by their graduates. . . .

9   It would be unjust to Mr. Washington not to acknowledge that in several instances he has opposed movements in the South which were unjust to the Negro; he sent memorials to Louisiana and Alabama constitutional conventions, he has spoken against lynching, and in other ways has openly or silently set his influence against sinister schemes and unfortunate happenings. Notwithstanding this, it is equally true to assert that on the whole the distinct impression left by Mr. Washington's propaganda is, first, that the South is justified in its present attitude toward the Negro because of the Negro's degradation; secondly, that the prime cause of the Negro's failure to rise more quickly is his wrong education in the past; and, thirdly, that his future rise depends primarily on his own efforts. Each of these propositions is a dangerous half-truth. The supplementary truths must never be lost sight of: first, slavery and race-prejudice are potent if not sufficient causes of the Negro's position; second, industrial and common-school training were necessarily slow in planting because they had to await the black teachers trained by higher institutions,—it being extremely doubtful if any essentially different development was possible, and certainly a Tuskegee was unthinkable before 1880; and, third, while it is a great truth to say that the Negro must strive and strive mightily to help himself, it is more equally true that unless his striving be not simply seconded, but rather aroused and encouraged by the initiative of the richer and wiser environing group, he cannot hope for great success.

10   In his failure to realize and impress this last point, Mr. Washington is especially to be criticised. His doctrine has tended to make the whites, North and South, shift the burden of the Negro problem to the Negro's shoulders and stand aside as critical and rather pessimistic spectators;

when in fact the burden belongs to the nation, and the hands of none of us are clean if we bend not our energies to righting these great wrongs.

BUILDING CONTEXT

1. Contrast the positions of Du Bois and Washington concerning the part the government should play in fostering racial equality and harmony.

2. To what extent are the differing perspectives of Du Bois and Washington based upon changes in societal attitudes? Is their disagreement merely generational, or is it based on other causes?

3. Du Bois accuses Washington of, in essence, blaming the victim. How does this idea relate to the attitudes of Van Every and Cameron toward the Indians?

FURTHER STUDY

1. Debate whether the problems in race relations described by Du Bois have been resolved. Research the efforts made to implement the solutions proposed by both Du Bois and Washington. What have been the results?

2. Consider how the contrasting experiences of different generations influence their values. Why are some people willing to settle for any job, while others demand career satisfaction? Why do certain voters prefer political candidates with military backgrounds? Why are some people more concerned than others about the economic clout of Japan or the reunification of Germany?

ADDITIONAL RESOURCES

Aptheker, Herbert. *The Literary Legacy of W. E. B. Du Bois.* White Plains, N.Y.: Kraus International Publications, 1989.

Broderick, Francis L. *W. E. B. Du Bois: Negro Leader in a Time of Crisis.* Stanford: Stanford University Press, 1959.

Du Bois, Shirley Graham. *His Day Is Marching On: A Memoir of W. E. B. Du Bois.* Philadelphia: Lippincott, 1971.

Horne, Gerald. *Black and Red: W. E. B. Du Bois and the Afro-American Response to the Cold War, 1944–1963.* Albany: State University of New York, 1986.

RESEARCH KEYWORDS

African Americans Race Relations—U.S.
World Politics   Foreign Policy—U.S.

THEODORE
ROOSEVELT
"World Feats" (1910)

" . . . nothing will help us keep in a state of profound peace more than a knowledge that our men can shoot straight, and will, if they have to."

Best known as the leader of the Rough Riders during the Spanish-American War, and the twenty-sixth president of the United States, Theodore Roosevelt (1858–1919) is immortalized in the gigantic "shrine to democracy" on Mount Rushmore. Roosevelt joins George Washington, Thomas Jefferson, and Abraham Lincoln to represent the founding, expansion, preservation, and unification of the United States.

As a Republican member of the New York State Assembly, Roosevelt opposed the corruption of party machines. After a series of defeats, he served on the U.S. Civil Service Commission from 1889 to 1895, and then became the Police Commissioner of New York City—where he enhanced his reputation as a progressive reformer and advocate of clean government. He was appointed the Assistant Secretary of the Navy, but, when the Spanish-American war broke out in 1898, he gave up this post to organize the 1st U.S. Volunteer Cavalry—the "Rough Riders." His exploits at San Juan Hill, while probably insubordinate from a military point of view, made him a national hero. Elected governor of New York, he instituted a civil service system and so enraged the political bosses that they arranged to have him nominated for vice president, a position with no power to hurt them. In 1901, however, President McKinley was assassinated, and Roosevelt became president. His administration fought vigorously against corporate monopolies, favored an equitable balance of power between labor and management, and supported conservation.

A prolific writer and lecturer, Roosevelt published over 2,000 articles and many books on politics, travel, and natural history. He compared foreign affairs to the jungle, where the strong survived and the weak perished. He therefore expanded the navy and backed—or engineered—a revolution in Panama that brought to power a government that supported the building of a canal by the United States. His pride in these two accomplishments is evident in the selection that follows, written in 1910.

Text: Theodore Roosevelt; *The New Nationalism;* New York: The Outlook Company, 1910.

EXPLORING ISSUES IN THE TEXT

1. What are the two accomplishments Roosevelt praises? What, according to him, makes them world feats (pars. 1–3)?

2. What mission does Roosevelt imply for America in paragraph 4? How does this mission affect American identity?

3. Explain why the Panama Canal is "one of the great achievements of modern times" (pars. 5–7). According to Roosevelt, what feat must follow the building of the Panama Canal (par. 9)? Why?

4. Identify Roosevelt's attitude toward foreign countries and mutual assistance treaties (par. 10). What insight does this offer concerning his image of America?

WORLD FEATS

1   In traveling in Europe last spring, one thing which especially struck me was the fact that the two feats which made the deepest impression abroad were the cruise of the battle fleet around the world and the digging of the Panama Canal. Wherever I went, wherever I met the great statesmen of foreign nations, I found out that these two feats, among all the feats credited to the American people during the last two decades, had most deeply and favorably affected foreign judgment of our people.

2   Remember, friends, that foreign judgment of us depends not in the least upon what we say we can do, but upon what we can do. I hate to see an American boast in the presence of a foreigner; it exposes him and his country to laughter. It does no good to boast that we are the greatest nation on the face of the earth; but it does help us when we do a great deed that no other nation has done.

3   During the past fifteen years we have built up our Navy, and the building up of that Navy has been the most potent means of making the United States respected abroad. Some time after we began to build it up the great military missions abroad sneered and said, "Yes; the Yankees can build ships; but they don't know how to handle them; they cannot do anything with them when they have been built." No nation had ever ventured on the experience of sending a great battle fleet around the world. Other nations have tried it with small squadrons halfway around the world, and they had plenty of difficulties and plenty of failures even with such a small task; but Uncle Sam once for all put an end to this talk about his fleet when he had that fleet undertake a cruise that is to the credit of no other nation under the sun.

4   Now there is no use of a nation claiming to be a great nation unless it is prepared to play a great part. A nation such as ours cannot possibly

play a great part in international affairs, cannot expect to be treated as a weight in either the Atlantic or the Pacific, or to have its voice as to the Monroe Doctrine, or the management of the Panama Canal, heeded, unless it has a strong and thoroughly efficient Navy. Within the last decade the American Navy has been about trebled in strength and much more than trebled in efficiency, due to its extraordinary progress in marksmanship and maneuvering. And, friends, that Navy is not an affair of the seacoast only. There is not a man who lives in the grass country, in the cattle country, or among the Great Lakes, or alongside the Missouri who is not just as keenly interested in that Navy as if he dwelt on the New England coast, or the Gulf coast, or on Puget Sound. The Navy belongs to all of us. If it wins credit for the nation, it wins for all of us. . . . Now, so far from this growth of our Navy representing on our part either a menace of aggression to weaker nations or a menace of war to stronger nations, it has told most powerfully for peace. Everywhere in Europe the cruise of the battle fleet around the world was accepted not only as an extraordinary feat, reflecting the highest honor upon our Navy, but as one of the movements which tended markedly to promote peaceful stability in international relations. No nation regarded the cruise as fraught with any menace of hostility to itself; and yet every nation accepted it as proof that we were not only desirous ourselves to keep the peace, but able to prevent the peace being broken at our expense. No cruise in any way approaching it has ever been made by any fleet of any other power; and the best naval opinion abroad had been that no such feat was possible; that is, that no such cruise as that we actually made could be undertaken by a fleet of such size without innumerable breakdowns and accidents. The best naval people on the other side sneered when I said "The fleet will start"; and they said that the battleships and torpedo boats would be strewed around every part of the globe making repairs. As a matter of fact, the fleet was never, in the whole year and a quarter of its absence in its circumnavigation of the globe, excepting once when there was a typhoon, five minutes late in keeping the schedule time every day, and never did a single vessel fail to put in its appearance at the appointed time of visit. The success of the cruise, performed as it was without a single accident, immeasurably raised the prestige, not only of our fleet, but of our nation; and was a distinct help to the cause of international peace.

5   As regards the Panama Canal, I really think that outside nations have a juster idea than our own people of the magnitude and success of the work. I wish our people realized what is being done on the Isthmus. If a man of intelligence who had never left the country asked me whether I would advise him to make a short trip to Europe or a trip to the Panama Canal, I would without hesitation advise him to go to the Panama Canal. He would there see in operation the completing of one of the great achievements of modern times. Colonel Goethals, and the men working

under him, are rendering a service to this country which can only be paralleled in our past history by some of the services rendered in certain wars. No feat of the kind or of anything like the magnitude has ever been successfully carried out, and hardly ever been attempted. No other nation has to its credit a task of such magnitude, of such importance, as we will have three years hence when that canal is completed.

6   Six years ago last spring the American government took possession of the Isthmus. The first two years were devoted to the sanitation of the Isthmus, to assembling the plant and working force, and providing quarters, food, and water supplies. In all these points the success was extraordinary. From one of the plague spots of the globe, one of the most unhealthy regions in the entire world, the Isthmus has been turned into a singularly healthy place of abode, where the death rate is small, and where hundreds of children are now being raised under as favorable conditions as in most parts of the United States. The quarters, food, and water supply are excellent, and the plant the best ever gathered for such a purpose. Active excavation on a large scale did not begin until January, 1907. Three and a half years have gone by since then, and three-fifths of the total excavation has already been accomplished. I had no idea that such a rate of progress was possible. Our people are really not awake to the fact that such a rate has obtained. The amount taken out has passed anything which previous experience warranted us in believing to be possible. In 1908 and 1909 the monthly average of rock and earth removed was three million yards, notwithstanding the fact that nine months of each year constituted a season of very heavy rainfall. There remains to be excavated only about sixty million cubic yards. If we could keep up the past average of excavation, this should be done in twenty months; but it is impossible to maintain such a ratio as the depth increases, for the output necessarily diminishes as the field of operation narrows. Still, it is certain that such a rate can be maintained as will enable the workers to finish the excavation considerably in advance of the date fixed for the opening of the canal, January 1, 1915. When I announced on the authority of the experts that the canal would be opened on New Year's Day, 1915, even the friends of the canal said, "And of course, it is very nice to say so; but these things are never done as quickly as people hope; and it will be some years after." Well, instead of being some time after the date fixed, it will be some time before the date fixed. I believe that the canal will be opened from six months to a year before.

7   The work has two great features: the Culebra Cut, which I have been considering; and the great dam at Gatun. The latter is to imprison the waters of the Chagres and other streams into a lake with an area of one hundred and sixty-four square miles. This work is advancing steadily, and just as successfully as the work on the Culebra Cut. The water which is ultimately to fill the lock is now flowing through the concrete spillway in the center of the dam, the Chagres having been diverted from its bed and placed under complete control. The construction of the dam has advanced

sufficiently to convince the engineers in charge of the work of its absolute stability and imperviousness. The concrete work on the lock is advancing so rapidly that the first double-set at Gatun will be completed this coming November, and the engineer in charge has announced that all the concrete in all the locks will be in place two years hence. The date of final completion and formal opening of the canal to the commerce of the world will be determined by the time consumed in placing one great steel gate, emergency dams, and all appliances for operating the docks. But those in charge of the work announce without hesitation that everything will be finished well in advance of January 1, 1915.

8   This is a stupendous record of achievement. As a people, we are rather fond of criticizing ourselves, and sometimes with very great justice; but even the most pessimistic critic should sometimes think of what is to our credit. Among our assets of the past ten years will be placed the extraordinary ability, integrity, and success with which we have handled all the problems inherited as the result of the Spanish War; the way we have handled ourselves in the Philippines, in Cuba, in Porto Rico, in San Domingo, and in Panama. The cruise of the battle fleet around the world was a striking proof that we had made good with the Navy; and what we have done at Panama represents the accomplishment of one of the great feats of the ages. It is a feat which reflects the highest honor upon our country; and our gratitude is due to every man who has taken an honorable part in any capacity in bringing about its performance.

9   So far, I have been speaking of what we have done, and you have applauded it. It is very interesting to tell what we have done; but that is not the important thing. The important thing is to do the next job well. We have now a further duty to perform in connection with the canal, and that is fortifying it. We took that canal upon the ground that Uncle Sam was big enough to tackle the job, and now we have got to show that Uncle Sam is big enough to make a good job of it. We are in honor bound to fortify it ourselves, and only by so doing can we effectively guarantee its neutrality; and, moreover, effectively guarantee that it shall not be used against us. I want the good will of every nation; I want to deserve it; but in vital matters I do not want to trust to it. The good will is felt immensely if we have a first-class Navy and adequate fortifications; but nothing will help us keep in a state of profound peace more than a knowledge that our men can shoot straight, and will, if they have to. The chief material advantage—certainly one of the chief material advantages—which we shall gain by the canal's construction is the way in which it will, for defensive purposes, double the power of the United States Navy. We must either have a Navy so big that we shall be able to put half in the Atlantic and half in the Pacific, or must be able to put into either ocean a Navy of the present size. It is not a blunder, but a crime, to divide the present Navy between the two. We must either double it, or we must be able to transfer our fleet from the Pacific to the Atlantic when we need it. That can be done only through a canal.

10   To refuse to fortify the canal, and, above all, to consider for a moment such an act of utter weakness and folly as to invite other nations to step in and guarantee the neutrality of this purely American work (and thereby really to make it certain that, in the event of war, we should find the canal used against us, as our fleets would be forbidden to pass through it, or else our opponent's fleets permitted to) would be to incur, and quite rightfully, the contempt of the world. It would mean the complete abandonment of the Monroe Doctrine; it would be a wicked blow to our prestige in the Pacific; and, moreover, it would be in its essence treason to the destiny of this republic. We built that canal ourselves, and we do not have to have anybody else to come in and say how it shall be used. If it was not our intention to have our sayso in the management of the canal, we had no business to undertake it, or to go into the expenditure of the scores of millions involved. It is not an act showing a peaceful disposition to ask other nations to come in and do all that we ought to do. I want Uncle Sam to be peaceful; I want Uncle Sam to show scrupulous regard for the rights of others; but I want to see Uncle Sam owe his safety to two facts: in the first place, that he will do nothing but good to men; and, in the second place, that he will submit to wrong from no man. Therefore, I am glad we have an efficient fleet; therefore, I am glad that we have completed in such splendid and successful fashion the Panama Canal; and, therefore, I say that unless, as a people, we intend to occupy a contemptible attitude, we will fortify and police and defend that canal ourselves, and see that it is used impartially by all the nations of the earth, and at the same time see that no nation shall use it against our own interests.

BUILDING CONTEXT

1. Contrast Roosevelt's view of America's mission to that of Bradford or Jefferson.

2. How does Roosevelt's concept of American identity compare to the beliefs of Crèvecoeur or Acosta-Belén?

3. How does Roosevelt view the function of government? Compare this to the view of Thoreau, Hoover, or Franklin D. Roosevelt.

FURTHER STUDY

1. Among America's "assets," Roosevelt lists (par. 8) "the way we handled ourselves in the Philippines, in Cuba, in Porto Rico, in San Domingo, and in Panama." Explain the United States's involvement in these countries. What alternative interpretations can you offer regarding America's actions?

2. In paragraph 10, Roosevelt outlines his plans for the future of the Panama Canal. Investigate whether history has fulfilled his intentions. Compare differing opinions about the consequences of building the Canal.

3. Theodore Roosevelt belonged to the Republican Party, as did Abraham Lincoln, Herbert Hoover, and Ronald Reagan. Examine how the ideals and platforms of that party have evolved.

4. Theodore Roosevelt was recognized as a progressive, "clean government" reformer in domestic issues. Place his views on foreign and domestic affairs within the context of American values.

ADDITIONAL RESOURCES

Berman, Jay Stuart. *Police Administration and Progressive Reform: Theodore Roosevelt as Police Commissioner of New York.* New York: Greenwood Press, 1987.

Harbaugh, William Henry. *Power and Responsibility: The Life and Times of Theodore Roosevelt.* Rev. ed. New York: Oxford University Press, 1975.

McCullough, David G. *The Path between the Seas: The Creation of the Panama Canal, 1870–1914.* New York: Simon & Schuster, 1977.

RESEARCH KEYWORDS

U.S.—Politics and Government   Progressive Party
Police Administration   Panama Canal

*U*nited States v. One
Book Called Ulysses
(1933)

" . . . *in* Ulysses, *in spite of its unusual frankness, I do not detect anywhere the leer of the sensualist.*"

Published in Paris in 1922 by the Irish author James Joyce, *Ulysses* is recognized as one of the great novels of the twentieth century. Using stream of consciousness and other experimental techniques, it records an average day in the lives of several residents of Dublin, Ireland, in 1904. The three main characters—Leopold Bloom, his wife Molly, and Stephen Dedalus— recreate in a modern milieu the supposed relationship of the classical Greek hero Ulysses (Odysseus), his wife Penelope, and their son Tele- machus. In mining the most mundane activities for their dramatic possibil- ities, and exploring the complex longings of husband/father, wife/mother, and replacement/son, Joyce described sex—especially female sexuality— in language and detail that revolutionized literature. Many people were shocked, and the book was banned in the United States as pornographic. The case ended in 1934 with the decision that follows. But the issues at its core have hardly been resolved.

Text: Milton R. Konvitz; *Bill of Rights Reader: Leading Constitutional Cases,* 5th ed.; Ithaca, N.Y.: Cornell University Press, 1973.

EXPLORING ISSUES IN THE TEXT

1. Describe the criteria by which the decision defines pornography (pars. 4, 20). Analyze how a reader can perceive an author's intent, or how a critic can determine a reader's likely reaction.

2. Summarize the reasons given for calling *Ulysses* pornographic (pars. 12–13). Explain why the court rejects this interpretation.

3. Describe Judge Woolsey's attitudes toward the Irish and the working class.

UNITED STATES v. *ONE BOOK CALLED* ULYSSES

1   The motion for a decree dismissing the libel herein is granted, and, con- sequently, of course, the Government's motion for a decree of forfeiture and destruction is denied. . . .

2   II. I have read *Ulysses* once in its entirety and I have read those pas- sages of which the Government particularly complains several times. In fact, for many weeks, my spare time has been devoted to the considera- tion of the decision which my duty would require me to make in this matter.

3   *Ulysses* is not an easy book to read or to understand. But there has been much written about it, and in order properly to approach the con- sideration of it, it is advisable to read a number of other books which have now become its satellites. The study of *Ulysses* is, therefore, a heavy task.

4   III. The reputation of *Ulysses* in the literary world, however, warranted my taking such time as was necessary to enable me to satisfy myself as to the intent with which the book was written, for, of course, in any case

where a book is claimed to be obscene it must first be determined, whether the intent with which it was written was what is called, according to the usual phrase, pornographic,—that is, written for the purpose of exploiting obscenity.

5   If the conclusion is that the book is pornographic that is the end of the inquiry and forfeiture must follow.

6   But in *Ulysses,* in spite of its unusual frankness, I do not detect anywhere the leer of the sensualist. I hold, therefore, that it is not pornographic.

7   IV. In writing *Ulysses,* Joyce sought to make a serious experiment in a new, if not wholly novel, literary genre. He takes persons of the lower middle class living in Dublin in 1904, and seeks not only to describe what they did on a certain day in June of that year as they went about the City bent on their usual occupations, but also to tell what many of them thought about the while.

8   Joyce has attempted—it seems to me, with astonishing success—to show how the screen of consciousness with its ever-shifting kaleidoscopic impressions carries, as it were on a plastic palimpsest, not only what is the focus of each man's observation of the actual things about him, but also in a penumbral zone residua of past impressions, some recent and some drawn up by association from the domain of the subconscious. He shows how each of these impressions affect the life and behavior of the character which he is describing.

9   What he seeks to get is not unlike the result of a double or, if that is possible, a multiple exposure of cinema film which would give a clear foreground with a background visible but somewhat blurred and out of focus in varying degrees.

10   To convey by words an effect which obviously lends itself more appropriately to graphic technique, accounts, it seems to me, for much of the obscurity which meets a reader of *Ulysses.* And it also explains another aspect of the book, which I have to consider, namely, Joyce's sincerity and his honest effort to show exactly how the minds of his characters operate.

11   If Joyce did not attempt to be honest in developing the technique which he has adopted in *Ulysses* the result would be psychologically misleading and thus unfaithful to his chosen technique. Such an attitude would be artistically inexcusable.

12   It is because Joyce has been loyal to his technique and has not funked its necessary implications, but has honestly attempted to tell fully what his characters think about, that he has been the subject of many attacks and that his purpose has been so often misunderstood and misrepresented. For his attempt sincerely and honestly to realize his objective has required him incidentally to use certain words which are generally considered dirty words and has led at times to what many think is a too poignant preoccupation with sex in the thoughts of his characters.

13   The words which are criticized as dirty are old Saxon words known to almost all men and, I venture, to many women, and are such words as would be naturally and habitually used, I believe, by the types of folk whose life, physical and mental, Joyce is seeking to describe. In respect of the recurrent emergence of the theme of sex in the minds of his characters, it must always be remembered that his locale was Celtic and his season Spring.

14   Whether or not one enjoys such a technique as Joyce uses is a matter of taste on which disagreement or argument is futile, but to subject that technique to the standards of some other technique seems to me to be little short of absurd.

15   Accordingly, I hold that *Ulysses* is a sincere and honest book and I think that the criticisms of it are entirely disposed of by its rationale.

16   V. Furthermore, *Ulysses* is an amazing *tour de force* when one considers the success which has been in the main achieved with such a difficult objective as Joyce set for himself. As I have stated, *Ulysses* is not an easy book to read. It is brilliant and dull, intelligible and obscure by turns. In many places it seems to me to be disgusting, but although it contains, as I have mentioned above, many words usually considered dirty, I have not found anything that I consider to be dirt for dirt's sake. Each word of the book contributes like a bit of mosaic to the detail of the picture which Joyce is seeking to construct for his readers.

17   If one does not wish to associate with such folk as Joyce describes, that is one's own choice. In order to avoid indirect contact with them one may not wish to read *Ulysses;* that is quite understandable. But when such a real artist in words, as Joyce undoubtedly is, seeks to draw a true picture of the lower middle class in a European city, ought it to be impossible for the American public to legally see that picture?

18   To answer this question it is not sufficient merely to find, as I have found above, that Joyce did not write *Ulysses* with what is commonly called pornographic intent, I must endeavor to apply a more objective standard to his book in order to determine its effect in the result, irrespective of the intent with which it was written.

19   VI. The statute under which the libel is filed only denounces, in so far as we are here concerned, the importation into the United States from any foreign country of "any obscene book." Section 305 of the Tariff Act of 1930, Title 19 United States Code, Section 1305. It does not marshal against books the spectrum of condemnatory adjectives found, commonly, in laws dealing with matters of this kind. I am, therefore, only required to determine whether *Ulysses* is obscene within the legal definition of that word.

20   The meaning of the word "obscene" as legally defined by the Courts is: tending to stir the sex impulses or to lead to sexually impure and lustful thoughts.

21   Without letting either of my assessors know what my decision was, I gave to each of them the legal definition of obscene and asked whether in his opinion *Ulysses* was obscene within that definition.

22   I was interested to find that they both agreed with my opinion: that reading *Ulysses* in its entirety, as a book must be read on such a test as this, did not tend to excite sexual impulses or lustful thoughts but that its net effect on them was only that of a somewhat tragic and very powerful commentary on the inner lives of men and women.

23   It is only with the normal person that the law is concerned. Such a test as I have described, therefore, is the only proper test of obscenity in the case of a book like *Ulysses* which is a sincere and serious attempt to devise a new literary method for the observation and description of mankind.

24   I am quite aware that owing to some of its scenes *Ulysses* is a rather strong draught to ask some sensitive, though normal, persons to take. But my considered opinion, after long reflection, is that whilst in many places the effect of *Ulysses* on the reader undoubtedly is somewhat emetic, nowhere does it tend to be an aphrodisiac.

2   *Ulysses* may, therefore, be admitted to the United States.

BUILDING CONTEXT

1. Compare Judge Woolsey's theory of literature to that of Howells. Examine how the two men determine literary merit and acceptability.

2. Connect the banning of pornography to America's mission or to the relationship between the individual and the state. Examine the role of the government as protector, whether of morals or welfare. Consider the opinions of Sinclair, Hoover, Franklin D. Roosevelt, or Booker T. Washington.

3. Relate Judge Woolsey's analysis of consciousness (par. 8) to the theory of reading that we discussed in Chapters 1 and 2—namely that readers are expected to recognize how early events and documents form the context for later ones.

FURTHER STUDY

1. Explore the conflict between freedom of speech and laws against pornography. Evaluate whether some types of speech—immoral, sexual, political, or offensive—should be outlawed.

2. Argue whether art should test the boundaries of taste and sexual, religious, or political acceptability. Examine whether all art necessarily takes sides for or against social conventions. Consider the works of Joyce, Sinclair, Stowe, or others.

3. Investigate how the standards of taste and the laws of pornography have changed since the 1930s.

ADDITIONAL RESOURCES

De Grazia, Edward. *Censorship Landmarks.* New York: Bowker, 1969.

Klausler, Alfred. *Censorship, Obscenity and Sex.* St. Louis: Concordia Publishing House, 1967.

McClellan, Grant S., ed. *Censorship in the United States.* New York: H. W. Wilson Company, 1967.

Oboler, Eli M. *The Fear of the Word.* Metuchen, N.J.: Scarecrow Press, 1974.

RESEARCH KEYWORDS

Censorship	Obscenity (Law)
Freedom of the Press	Freedom of Speech

HERBERT HOOVER
"The American System of Rugged Individualism"
(1928)

" . . .only through ordered liberty, freedom and equal opportunity to the individual will his initiative and enterprise spur on the march of progress."

When World War I broke out in 1914, Herbert Hoover (1874–1964) was an engineer working in Europe. As an American, and therefore the citizen of a neutral country, he was able to organize volunteer relief efforts for the millions of refugees. After the United States entered the war in 1917, Hoover returned home and was appointed Food Administrator, a position from which he urged voluntary conservation and increased production; he also served as director general of Allied relief services. After the war, he replaced these official activities with a voluntary organization to aid children and displaced persons. These experiences led to a book, *American Individualism,* in which Hoover argued that individualism combined with equal opportunity was a moral ideal, with proven benefits; they also explain his emphasis on voluntary cooperation as Secretary of Commerce under Presidents Harding and Coolidge.

In 1928 Hoover was elected president on the Republican ticket. During the campaign, his opponent demanded greater governmental involvement in the economy. As in the following selection, Hoover defended what he saw as the American system of government, warned against Socialism and putting the government into business, and described how governmental bureaucracy threatened freedom, equality and individual opportunity. Nonetheless, the Stock Market crash of 1929 and the Great Depression that followed challenged his lifelong belief in the power of individual initiative.

Text: Richard Hofstadter and Beatrice K. Hofstadter, eds. *Great Issues in American History.* Rev. ed. Vol. III. New York: Vintage Books, 1969.

EXPLORING ISSUES IN THE TEXT

1. What distinctions does Hoover draw between the American and European systems of government (pars. 1–3)? How does he say the American system evolved?

2. Under what circumstances does Hoover accept governmental involvement in business and daily life (pars. 2–3)?

3. What does Hoover mean by "liberalism" (pars. 8–9)?

4. What result does Hoover predict if the government becomes a player rather than an umpire in the economic game (par. 9)?

5. Examine how Hoover uses personal experience to support his thesis (pars. 11–13).

RUGGED INDIVIDUALISM

1 After the war, when the Republican party assumed administration of the country, we were faced with the problem of determination of the very nature of our national life. During 150 years we have builded up a form of self-government and a social system which is particularly our own. It differs essentially from all others in the world. It is the American system. It is just as definite and positive a political and social system as has ever been developed on earth. It is founded upon a particular conception of self-government in which decentralized local responsibility is the very base. Further than this, it is founded upon the conception that only through ordered liberty, freedom and equal opportunity to the individual will his initiative and enterprise spur on the march of progress. And in our insistence upon equality of opportunity has our system advanced beyond all the world.

2   During the war we necessarily turned to the Government to solve every difficult economic problem. The Government having absorbed every energy of our people for war, there was no other solution. For the

preservation of the State the Federal Government became a centralized despotism which undertook unprecedented responsibilities, assumed autocratic powers, and took over the business of citizens. To a large degree we regimented our whole people temporarily into a socialistic state. However justified in time of war if continued in peace time it would destroy not only our American system but with it our progress and freedom as well.

3   When the war closed, the most vital of all issues both in our own country and throughout the world was whether Governments should continue their wartime ownership and operation of many instrumentalities of production and distribution. We were challenged with a peacetime choice between the American system of rugged individualism and a European philosophy of diametrically opposed doctrines—doctrines of paternalism and state socialism. The acceptance of these ideas would have meant the destruction of self-government through centralization of government. It would have meant the undermining of the individual initiative and enterprise through which our people have grown to unparalleled greatness.

4   . . . When the Republican Party came into full power it went at once resolutely back to our fundamental conception of the State and the rights and responsibilities of the individual. Thereby it restored confidence and hope in the American people, it freed and stimulated enterprise, it restored the Government to its position as an umpire instead of a player in the economic game. For these reasons the American people have gone forward in progress while the rest of the world has halted, and some countries have even gone backwards. If anyone will study the causes of retarded recuperation in Europe, he will find much of it due to the stifling of private initiative on one hand, and overloading of the Government with business on the other.

5   There has been revived in this campaign, however, a series of proposals which, if adopted, would be a long step toward the abandonment of our American system and a surrender to the destructive operation of governmental conduct of commercial business. Because the country is faced with difficulty and doubt over certain national problems—that is, prohibition, farm relief and electrical power—our opponents propose that we must thrust government a long way into the businesses which give rise to these problems. In effect, they abandon the tenets of their own party and turn to State socialism as a solution for the difficulties presented by all three. It is proposed that we shall change from prohibition to the State purchase and sale of liquor. If their agricultural relief program means anything, it means that the Government shall directly or indirectly buy and sell and fix prices of agricultural products. And we are to go into the hydro-electric-power business. In other words, we are confronted with a huge program of government in business.

6   There is, therefore, submitted to the American people a question of fundamental principle. That is: shall we depart from the principles of

our American political and economic system, upon which we have advanced beyond all the rest of the world, in order to adopt methods based on principles destructive of its very foundations? And I wish to emphasize the seriousness of these proposals. I wish to make my proposition clear; for this goes to the very roots of American life and progress.

7   I should like to state to you the effect that this projection of government in business would have upon our system of self-government and our economic system. The effect would reach to the daily life of every man and woman. It would impair the very basis of liberty and freedom not only for those left outside the fold of expanded bureaucracy but for those embraced within it. . . .

8   It is false liberalism that interprets itself into the Government operation of commercial business. Every step of bureaucratizing of the business of our country poisons the very roots of liberalism—that is, political equality, free speech, free assembly, free press, and equality of opportunity. It is the road not to more liberty, but to less liberty. Liberalism should be found not striving to spread bureaucracy but striving to set bounds to it. True liberalism seeks all legitimate freedom, first in the confident belief that without such freedom the pursuit of all other blessings and benefits is vain. That belief is the foundation of all American progress, political as well as economic.

9   Liberalism is a force truly of the spirit, a force proceeding from the deep realization that economic freedom cannot be sacrificed if political freedom is to be preserved. Even if Governmental conduct of business could give us more efficiency instead of less efficiency, the fundamental objection would remain unaltered and unabated. It would destroy political equality. It would increase rather than decrease abuse and corruption. It would stifle initiative and invention. It would undermine the development of leadership. It would cramp and cripple the mental and spiritual energies of our people. It would extinguish equality and opportunity. It would dry up the spirit of liberty and progress. For these reasons primarily it must be resisted. For a hundred and fifty years liberalism has found its true spirit in the American system, not in the European systems.

10   I do not wish to be misunderstood in this statement. . . . Nor do I wish to be misinterpreted as believing that the United States is free-for-all and devil-take-the-hindmost. The very essence of equality of opportunity and of American individualism is that there shall be no domination by any group or combination in this Republic, whether it be business or political. On the contrary, it demands economic justice as well as political and social justice. It is no system of laissez faire.

11   I feel deeply on this subject because during the war I had some practical experience with governmental operation and control. I have witnessed not only at home but abroad many failures of Government in business. I have seen its tyrannies, its injustices, its destructions of self-government, its undermining of the very instincts which carry our people forward to

progress. I have witnessed the lack of advance, the lowered standards of living, the depressed spirits of people working under such a system. My objection is based not upon theory or upon a failure to recognize wrong or abuse, but I know the adoption of such methods would strike at the very roots of American life and would destroy the very basis of American progress. . . .

12   And what have been the results of our American system? Our country has become the land of opportunity to those born without inheritance, not merely because of the wealth of its resources and industry, but because of this freedom of initiative and enterprise. Russia has natural resources equal to ours. Her people are equally industrious, but she has not had the blessings of 150 years of our form of government and of our social system.

13   By adherence to the principles of decentralized self-government, ordered liberty, equal opportunity, and freedom to the individual, our American experiment in human welfare has yielded a degree of well-being unparalleled in all the world. It has come nearer to the abolition of poverty, to the abolition of fear of want, than humanity has ever reached before. Progress of the past seven years is the proof of it. This alone furnishes the answer to our opponents who ask us to introduce destructive elements into the system by which this has been accomplished. . . .

BUILDING CONTEXT

1. Compare Hoover's ideas about government and the American character to those of Jefferson, Thoreau or Turner.

2. Compare Hoover's economic ideas to those of Crèvecoeur, Sinclair or Franklin Roosevelt.

3. In light of what was going on in Europe and of the types of immigrants coming to America at the time, why does Hoover emphasize that individualism is 1) a bona fide theory, and 2) an *American* theory? Examine other reading selections which discuss similar contrasts.

4. Compare Hoover's use of the term "liberal" to its current meaning.

FURTHER STUDY

1. Many of the programs that Hoover opposed have come into being. Choose one or two and explore what the results have been.

2. Hoover speaks of individualism combined with equal opportunity. What are the implications of this policy for minority civil rights and affirmative action programs? What was the situation of racial and ethnic minorities in 1928?

ADDITIONAL RESOURCES

Burner, David. *Herbert Hoover: A Public Life.* New York: Knopf, 1979.

Cohen, Robert. *When the Old Left Was Young: Student Radicals and America's First Mass Student Movement, 1929–1941.* New York: Oxford University Press, 1993.

Gregory, James N. *American Exodus: The Dust Bowl Migration and Okie Culture in California.* New York: Oxford University Press, 1989.

RESEARCH KEYWORDS

Depressions—1929   U. S.—Politics and Government
Migration   Agricultural Laborers
Student Movements

FRANKLIN D. ROOSEVELT
"Government and Economic Life" (1932)

"The issue of Government has always been whether individual men and women will have to serve some system of Government . . . or whether a system of Government . . . exists to serve . . . individual men and women."

Franklin D. Roosevelt (1882–1945) transformed the relationship between the American government and the individual. The Great Depression that began in 1929 proved deeper and longer than politicians had predicted. With millions of people unemployed, the presidential election of 1932 pitted Hoover's theory of laissez-faire against Roosevelt's belief in governmental intervention. At issue were many of the programs that we now take for granted: minimum wage, Social Security, unemployment benefits, welfare programs, funding for jobs and training, and massive public works projects. Roosevelt instituted recovery measures—the New Deal—after his reelection, and thus profoundly changed the face of American government. He explains his philosophy in the campaign speech that follows.

Text: Richard Hofstadter and Beatrice K. Hofstadter, eds.; *Great Issues in American History,* Rev. ed., Vol. III; New York: Vintage Books, 1969.

EXPLORING ISSUES IN THE TEXT

1. According to Roosevelt, what were the results of the Industrial Revolution (par. 3)? How did this affect expectations about government? How did government meet these expectations (par. 4)? Does Roosevelt approve or disapprove of the government's solution?

2. What change in conditions does Roosevelt claim requires a change in the government's approach to business (pars. 5–6)?

3. How were the early railroads and industries financed (par. 5)? What irony, or inconsistency, does Roosevelt say this demonstrates in the attitude of business toward government?

4. Explain the evolution in business concentration that troubles Roosevelt (pars. 7–8).

5. What is the mission that Roosevelt outlines for business and government (pars. 10–11)? How does he define the relationship between the individual and the state (pars. 16–17)?

GOVERNMENT AND ECONOMIC LIFE

1 I want to invite you, to consider with me in the large, some of the relationships of Government and economic life that go deeply into our daily lives, our happiness, our future and our security.

2 The issue of Government has always been whether individual men and women will have to serve some system of Government or economics, or whether a system of Government and economics exists to serve individual men and women. This question has persistently dominated the discussion of Government for many generations. On questions relating to these things men have differed, and for time immemorial it is probable that honest men will continue to differ.

3 It was in the middle of the nineteenth century that a new force was released and a new dream created. The force was what is called the industrial revolution, the advance of steam and machinery and the rise of the forerunners of the modern industrial plant. The dream was the dream of an economic machine, able to raise the standard of living for everyone; to bring luxury within the reach of the humblest; to annihilate distance by steam power and later by electricity, and to release everyone from the drudgery of the heaviest manual toil. It was expected that this would necessarily affect Government. Heretofore, Government had merely been called upon to produce conditions within which people could live happily, labor peacefully, and rest secure. Now it was called upon to aid in the consummation of this new dream. There was, however, a shadow over the dream. To be made real, it required use of the talents of men of tremendous will and tremendous ambition, since by no

other force could the problems of financing and engineering and new developments be brought to a consummation.

4   So manifest were the advantages of the machine age, however, that the United States fearlessly, cheerfully, and, I think, rightly, accepted the bitter with the sweet. It was thought that no price was too high to pay for the advantages which we could draw from a finished industrial system. The history of the last half century is accordingly in large measure a history of a group of financial Titans, whose methods were not scrutinized with too much care, and who were honored in proportion as they produced the results, irrespective of the means they used. The financiers who pushed the railroads to the Pacific were always ruthless, often wasteful, and frequently corrupt; but they did build railroads, and we have them today. It has been estimated that the American investor paid for the American railway system more than three times over in the process; but despite this fact the net advantage was to the United States. As long as we had free land; as long as population was growing by leaps and bounds; as long as our industrial plants were insufficient to supply our own needs, society chose to give the ambitious man free play and unlimited reward provided only that he produced the economic plant so much desired.

5   During this period of expansion, there was equal opportunity for all and the business of Government was not to interfere but to assist in the development of industry. This was done at the request of business men themselves. The tariff was originally imposed for the purpose of "fostering our infant industry," a phrase I think the older among you will remember as a political issue not so long ago. The railroads were subsidized, sometimes by grants of money, oftener by grants of land; some of the most valuable oil lands in the United States were granted to assist the financing of the railroad which pushed through the Southwest. A nascent merchant marine was assisted by grants of money, or by mail subsidies, so that our steam shipping might ply the seven seas. Some of my friends tell me that they do not want the government in business. With this I agree; but I wonder whether they realize the implications of the past. For while it has been American doctrine that the Government must not go into business in competition with private enterprises, still it has been traditional, particularly in Republican administrations, for business to ask the Government to put at private disposal all kinds of Government assistance. The same man who tells you that he does not want to see the Government interfere in business—and he means it, and has plenty of good reason for saying so—is the first to go to Washington and ask the Government for a prohibitory tariff on his product. When things get just bad enough, as they did two years ago, he will go with equal speed to the United States Government and ask for a loan; and the Reconstruction Finance Corporation is the outcome of it. Each group has sought protection from the Government for its own special interests,

without realizing that the function of Government must be to favor no small group at the expense of its duty to protect the rights of personal freedom and of private property of all its citizens.

6   In retrospect we can now see that the turn of the tide came with the turn of the century. We were reaching our last frontier; there was no more free land and our industrial combinations had become great uncontrolled and irresponsible units of power within the State. Clear-sighted men saw with fear the danger that opportunity would no longer be equal; that the growing corporation, like the feudal baron of old, might threaten the economic freedom of individuals to earn a living. In that hour, our anti-trust laws were born. The cry was raised against the great corporations. Theodore Roosevelt, the first great Republican Progressive, fought a Presidential campaign on the issue of "trust busting" and talked freely about malefactors of great wealth. If the Government had a policy it was rather to turn the clock back, to destroy the large combinations and to return to a time when every man owned his individual small business.

7   Just as freedom to farm has ceased, so also the opportunity in business has narrowed. It still is true that men can start small enterprises, trusting to native shrewdness and ability to keep abreast of competitors; but area after area has been preempted altogether by the great corporations, and even in the fields which still have no great concerns, the small man starts under a handicap. The unfeeling statistics of the past three decades show that the independent business man is running a losing race. Perhaps he is forced to the wall; perhaps he cannot command credit; perhaps he is "squeezed out," in Mr. Wilson's words, by highly organized corporate competitors, as your corner grocery man can tell you. Recently a careful study was made of the concentration of business in the United States. It showed that our economic life was dominated by some six hundred odd corporations who controlled two-thirds of American industry. Ten million small business men divided the other third. More striking still, it appeared that if the process of concentration goes on at this rate, at the end of another century we shall have all American industry controlled by a dozen corporations, and run by perhaps a hundred men. But plainly, we are steering a steady course toward economic oligarchy, if we are not there already.

8   Clearly, all this calls for a reappraisal of values. A mere builder of more industrial plants, a creator of more railroad systems, an organizer of more corporations, is as likely to be a danger as a help. The day of the great promoter or the financial Titan, to whom we granted anything if only he would build, or develop, is over. Our task now is not discovery or exploitation of natural resources, or necessarily producing more goods. It is the soberer, less dramatic business of administering resources and plants already in hand, of seeking to reestablish foreign markets for our surplus production, of meeting the problem of underconsumption, of adjusting production to consumption, of distributing wealth and products

more equitably, of adapting existing economic organizations to the service of the people. The day of enlightened administration has come.

9　　Just as in older times the central Government was first a haven of refuge, and then a threat, so now in a closer economic system the central and ambitious financial unit is no longer a servant of national desire, but a danger. I would draw the parallel one step further. We did not think because national Government had become a threat in the 18th century that therefore we should abandon the principle of national Government. Nor today should we abandon the principle of strong economic units called corporations, merely because their power is susceptible of easy abuse. In other times we dealt with the problem of unduly ambitious central Government by modifying it gradually into a constitutional democratic Government. So today we are modifying and controlling our economic units.

10　　As I see it, the task of Government in its relation to business is to assist the development of an economic declaration of rights, an economic constitutional order. This is the common task of statesman and business man. It is the requirement of a more permanently safe order of things.

11　　I feel that we are coming to a view through the drift of our legislation and our public thinking in the past quarter century that private economic power is, to enlarge an old phrase, a public trust as well. I hold that continued enjoyment of that power by any individual or group must depend upon the fulfillment of that trust. The men who have reached the summit of American business life know this best; happily, many of these urge the binding quality of this greater social contract.

12　　The terms of that contract are as old as the Republic, and as new as the new economic order.

13　　Every man has a right to life; and this means that he has also the right to make a comfortable living. He may by sloth or crime decline to exercise that right; but it may not be denied him. We have no actual famine or dearth; our industrial and agricultural mechanism can produce enough and to spare. Our Government formal and informal, political and economic, owes to everyone an avenue to possess himself of a portion of that plenty sufficient for his needs, through his own work.

14　　Every man has a right to his own property; which means a right to be assured, to the fullest extent attainable, in the safety of his savings. By no other means can men carry the burdens of those parts of life which, in the nature of things, afford no chance of labor; childhood, sickness, old age. In all thought of property, this right is paramount; all other property rights must yield to it. If, in accord with this principle, we must restrict the operations of the speculator, the manipulator, even the financier, I believe we must accept the restriction as needful, not to hamper individualism but to protect it.

15　　These two requirements must be satisfied, in the main, by individuals who claim and hold control of the great industrial and financial combinations which dominate so large a part of our industrial life. They have undertaken to be, not business men, but princes of property. I am not prepared to say that the system which produces them is wrong. I am very clear that they must fearlessly and competently assume the responsibility which goes with the power. So many enlightened business men know this that the statement would be little more than a platitude, were it not for an added implication.

16 This implication is, briefly, that the responsible heads of finance and industry instead of acting each for himself, must work together to achieve the common end. They must, where necessary, sacrifice this or that private advantage; and in reciprocal self-denial must seek a general advantage. It is here that formal Government—political Government, if you choose—comes in. Whenever in the pursuit of this objective the lone wolf, the unethical competitor, the reckless promoter, the Ishmael or Insull whose hand is against every man's, declines to join in achieving an end recognized as being for the public welfare, and threatens to drag the industry back to a state of anarchy, the Government may properly be asked to apply restraint. Likewise, should the group ever use its collective power contrary to the public welfare, the Government must be swift to enter and protect public interest.

17 The Government should assume the function of economic regulation only as a last resort, to be tried only when private initiative, inspired by high responsibility, with such assistance and balance as Government can give, has finally failed. As yet there has been no final failure, because there has been no attempt; and I decline to assume that this nation is unable to meet the situation.

18 The final term of the high contract was for liberty and the pursuit of happiness. We have learned a great deal of both in the past century. We know that individual liberty and individual happiness mean nothing unless both are ordered in the sense that one man's meat is not another man's poison. We know that the old "rights of personal competency," the right to read, to think, to speak, to choose and live a mode of life, must be respected at all hazards. We know that liberty to do anything which deprives others of those elemental rights is outside the protection of any compact; and that Government in this regard is the maintenance of a balance, within which every individual may have a place if he will take it; in which every individual will find safety if he wishes it; in which every individual may attain such power as his ability permits, consistent with his assuming the accompanying responsibility.

BUILDING CONTEXT

1. Analyze how Roosevelt redefines Jefferson's words in the Declaration of Independence (pars. 12–15).

2. Explore how Roosevelt's analysis of American industrial policy uses the ideas of Turner.

3. In running against Hoover, why does Roosevelt emphasize the American contribution to this theory of government? What aspects of the New Deal, or liberalism, had been attacked as "un-American"?

FURTHER STUDY

1. What does Roosevelt have in mind when he says that a change in circumstance must lead to a change in values? Analyze other historical, or recent, situations that have required similar responses.

2. Roosevelt asks whether people exist to serve government or government exists to serve people. How does his answer correspond to those offered by other American and international politicians?

ADDITIONAL RESOURCES

Dubofsky, Melvyn. *American Labor since the New Deal*. Chicago: Quadrangle Books, 1971.
Leuchtenburg, William E. *Franklin D. Roosevelt and the New Deal, 1932–1940*. New York: Harper & Row, 1963.
McElvaine, Robert S. *The Great Depression: America, 1929–1941*. New York: Times Books, 1983.

RESEARCH KEYWORDS

New Deal	Depressions—1929
Labor Movement	Trade Unions

EXPLORING CRITICAL ISSUES THROUGH WRITING

1. Religion has played a large part in American history, but America has also secularized religion: work, patriotism, health care, and the economy are all discussed in religious terms. Explore how current public discussion of one of these areas employs religious concepts. Or, compare how two or three writers—for example Franklin, Stowe, and Sinclair—use religious vocabulary for secular purposes.

2. In the early 1990s, Communist powers collapsed in Eastern Europe. Was socialism also abandoned? What is the difference between communism and socialism? Between socialism and capitalism? Explore whether socialism is compatible with democracy. What about communism? What kind of a system do we have in the United States?

3. Explore whether politics, propaganda, and other persuasive purposes have a valid place within art. Consider whether pornography and certain

types of speech should be prohibited. If so, on what grounds—moral, sexual, political, or other reasons?

4. Argue whether art should test the boundaries of taste and sexual, religious, or political acceptability. Explore whether art necessarily sides with—or defies—social conventions. Consider the works of Joyce, Sinclair, Stowe, Eaton, and others.

5. How do the contrasting experiences of different generations shape their values? Why are some people willing to settle for any job, while others demand career satisfaction? Why do certain voters prefer political candidates with military backgrounds? Why are some people more concerned than others about the economic clout of Japan or the reunification of Germany?

6. Trace the evolution of ethnic identity experienced by various writers. To what extent were they motivated by both positive and negative stimuli? To what extent is ethnic identity self-created or imposed by others? Consider, for example, Du Bois's belief that "beauty is black." Compare this attitude to those of minority or ethnic groups today.

7. The late nineteenth and early twentieth centuries saw the rise of a number of utopian movements, among them socialism, pacifism, and internationalism. What is utopianism? What threads run through all these movements?

8. Universal conscription for public service presupposes that individuals owe something to their government. How does this belief conform to American values? What, if anything, do you believe citizens owe to their country? What do some of the writers you have read say about this? How have people reacted to proposals for this type of system in America, or elsewhere?

9. In light of events in Europe and the types of immigrants coming to America at the time, why does Hoover emphasize that individualism is an *American* theory? Why does Franklin D. Roosevelt emphasize the American contribution to his theory of government? What aspects of the New Deal, or liberalism, have been attacked as "un-American"?

10. Explore an idea from the reading selections that caught your interest, charmed or provoked you, or supported or challenged your own beliefs. Place the issue within a larger context and explain its significance.

10

EARLY TWENTIETH CENTURY LIVES: 1900–1950

"The real or imaginary danger was used as an excuse not to promote Puerto Rican workers. . . ."

BERNARDO VEGA

"The Black female is . . . caught in the tripartite crossfire of masculine prejudice, white illogical hate and Black lack of power."

MAYA ANGELOU

We have already seen that by the beginning of the twentieth century the United States was a world power. It was also a country facing many of the social problems that still confront us today.

Women, who had put their own demands aside in order to crusade for abolition of slavery and equal rights for blacks, now renewed their own movement. The more moderate organizations, like the American Women's Suffrage Association, fought only for the right to vote. Others, however, demanded equality in work, pay, marriage, and sex. To them, the Nineteenth Amendment, ratified in 1920, addressed less than half of the problem. Working-class and radical women, such as Emma Goldman, coming from countries where class structure was more entrenched, were also likely to view solutions to these inequities in terms of revolutionary struggle. They believed that retaining the political structure could only guarantee, at best, equality of oppression. To them, achieving meaningful equality required the sweeping away of all hierarchies—not only those of individual and state, but also those of owner and worker, man and woman. Such foreign ideas frightened many segments of the population.

The fear of new or newly visible groups surfaced in other ways as well. The annexation of the Hawaiian Islands in 1898 gave America a substantial Polynesian and Japanese population. The Spanish-American War left America with Puerto Rico and the Philippines—and their diverse peoples. In addition, political upheavals and natural disasters resulted in millions of refugees. The acceptance of these immigrants into American society varied, with those from Western Europe being considered more desirable than those from Southern and Eastern Europe and Asia. Yet, "undesirables" came in greater numbers. More than 350,000 immigrants from Great Britain and Germany entered the country in 1882, as opposed to 32,000 from Italy and 17,000 from Russia. In 1907, however, 285,000 people emigrated from Italy and 258,000 from Russia, but only 116,000 from Britain and Germany. As early as 1882, the Chinese Exclusion Act had sought to stem the tide of Oriental immigration. In 1921, the government instituted the Per Centum Limit Plan, or "quota law," to set proportional limits upon immigrants from all countries.

Reaction among private citizens also was not always positive. In a series of sketches collected in *The American Scene,* the novelist Henry James bemoaned the destruction of the America he knew. Touring New York's Lower East Side, he could see only the crime and filth. The plight of the victims—poverty, sickness, and rejection—drew few notes of pity.

For all his lack of sympathy, however, James was civilized, resigning himself and his class to defeat. More violent responses were common. Nativist political parties and secret organizations lobbied for the exclusion of foreigners—defined as Catholics, Jews, Southern and Eastern Europeans, Asians, and Africans—or physically attacked them. Blacks were lynched with horrifying frequency. *Birth of a Nation,* one of the most popular American movies of the period, glorified the activities of the Ku Klux Klan.

The readings in this section reflect this dynamic period of change and conflict, belief in the future and longing for the past, with new groups gaining influence while others saw their own power slip away. The autobiography of Edna Ferber reveals an assimilated American Jew identifying herself with her co-religionists in a time of trouble; the essay by Emma Goldman exemplifies the call for radical change; the memoirs of Bernardo Vega show a Puerto Rican labor leader fighting racism and misguided good intentions; and the work of Maya Angelou illustrates the plight of African-American women struggling against discrimination aimed at both their race and their sex.

Another Voice

THE FUTURE OF ENGLISH
HENRY JAMES

Henry James feared that the English language would be changed because of the intellectuals among the immigrants. He believed that "the mere mob" could be ignored, but was frightened by the "possibilities of the waiting spring of intelligence":

It was the incurable man of letters . . . who gasped, I confess; for it was in the light of letters, that is in the light of our language as literature has hitherto known it, that one stared at this all-unconscious impudence of the agency of future ravage. . . . [T]he dragon most rousing, over the land . . . is just this immensity of the alien presence climbing higher and higher, climbing itself into the very light of publicity. . . . The accent of the very ultimate future, in the States, may be destined to become the most beautiful on the globe and the very music of humanity (here the "ethnic" synthesis shrouds itself thicker than ever); but whatever we shall know it for, certainly, we shall not know it for English—in any sense for which there is an existing literary measure.

The American Scene, 1907

Another Voice

HOW ALIENS THREATEN
AMERICA
HIRAM W. EVANS

The Imperial Wizard of the Ku Klux Klan used moderate language to explain the sometimes violent behavior of his followers:

In spite of it, however, these Nordic Americans for the last generation have found themselves increasingly uncomfortable, and finally deeply distressed. There appeared first confusion in thought and opinion, a groping and hesitancy about national affairs and private life alike, in sharp contrast to the clear, straightforward purposes of our earlier years. . . .

They saw, too, that the alien was tearing down the American standard of living, especially in the lower walks. It became clear that while the American can out-work the alien, the alien can so far under-live the American as to force him out of all competitive labor. So they came to realize that the Nordic can easily survive and rule and increase if he holds for himself the advantages won by strength and daring of his ancestors in times of stress and peril, but that if he surrenders those advantages to the peoples who could not share the stress, he will soon be driven below the level at which he can exist by their low standards, low living and fast breeding. And they saw that the low standard aliens of Eastern and Southern Europe were doing just that thing to us.

They learned, though more slowly, that alien ideas are just as dangerous to us as the aliens themselves, no matter how plausible such ideas may sound. With most of the plain people this conclusion is based simply on the fact that the alien ideas do not work well for them. Others went deeper and came to understand that the differences in racial background, in breeding, instinct, character and emotional point of view are more important than logic. So ideas which may be perfectly healthy for an alien may also be poisonous for Americans.

"The Klan's Fight for Americanism," 1926

EMMA GOLDMAN
"The Tragedy of Woman's Emancipation"
(1910s)

"The greatest shortcoming of the emancipation of the present day lies in its artificial stiffness and its narrow respectabilities, which produce an emptiness in woman's soul that will not let her drink from the fountain of life."

Born in Lithuania in 1869, Emma Goldman fled to the United States in 1885 to escape political repression and anti-Semitic persecution. Ten-hour days in a factory for $2.50 a week convinced her that America was as much in need of reform as Russia, and an unhappy marriage at age seventeen added a feminist plank to her revolutionary platform. She soon became the most radical and charismatic woman lecturer in America. *Mother Earth,* which she founded in 1906, became her vehicle for continuous criticism of the political, economic, religious, and sexual status quo. Her advocacy of birth control brought her to the attention of a wider public than most anarchists enjoyed, and her vocal opposition to the military draft during World War I led to her imprisonment and deportation to the Soviet Union in 1919.

Always skeptical of absolutes, she spoke against the utopian calls for centralized government; instead, she espoused anarchism because she believed that the State destroyed individual freedom in favor of conformity. Though she supported the theoretical economic equality of communism, she denounced Soviet suppression of civil rights. She also antagonized feminists by attacking both those who merely sought equal rights in what she considered a corrupt society, and those who denied women's desire for love and motherhood. As in the following essay, she argued that women *as women* should join the struggle for a better world.

Text: *Red Emma Speaks: Selected Writings and Speeches by Emma Goldman;* ed. Alix Kates Shulman; New York: Vintage Press, 1972.

EXPLORING ISSUES IN THE TEXT

1. How does Goldman distinguish between "forgiving" one another and "understanding" one another (par. 3)? Why is this fundamental to her position about the emancipation of women?

2. According to Goldman, what were the original aims of the movement for woman's emancipation (par. 4)? Why had emancipation turned women into artificial beings (par. 5)? What did women lose by the emancipation of her day? What was wrong with economic independence?

3. Why does Goldman consider professional women—lawyers, doctors, teachers—to be worse off than working-class women (pars. 10–12)? In what way have they lost "life's essence" (par. 13)?

4. Explain Goldman's objection to "ethics" (pars. 14–15). What is she advocating in this discussion?

5. According to Goldman, why do many emancipated women still cling to ideas that are detrimental to them (pars. 16–18)? Identify the "greatest" shortcoming of the emancipation" (par. 19).

THE TRAGEDY OF WOMAN'S EMANCIPATION

1   I begin with an admission: Regardless of all political and economic theories, treating of the fundamental differences between various groups within the human race, regardless of class and race distinctions, regardless of all artificial boundary lines between woman's rights and man's rights, I hold that there is a point where these differentiations may meet and grow into one perfect whole.

2   With this I do not mean to propose a peace treaty. The general social antagonism which has taken hold of our entire public life today, brought about through the force of opposing and contradictory interests, will crumble to pieces when the reorganization of our social life, based upon the principles of economic justice, shall have become a reality.

3   Peace or harmony between the sexes and individuals does not necessarily depend on a superficial equalization of human beings; nor does it call for the elimination of individual traits and peculiarities. The problem that confronts us today, and which the nearest future is to solve, is how to be one's self and yet in oneness with others, to feel deeply with all human beings and still retain one's own characteristic qualities. This seems to me to be the basis upon which the mass and the individual, the true democrat and the true individuality, man and woman, can meet without antagonism and opposition. The motto should not be: Forgive one another; rather, Understand one another. The oft-quoted sentence of Madame de Staël: "To understand everything means to forgive everything," has never particularly appealed to me; it has the odor of the confessional; to forgive one's fellow-being conveys the idea of pharisaical superiority. To understand one's fellow-being suffices. The admission partly represents the fundamental aspects of my views on the emancipation of woman and its effect upon the entire sex.

4   Emancipation should make it possible for woman to be human in the truest sense. Everything within her that craves assertion and activity should reach its fullest expression; all artificial barriers should be broken, and the road towards greater freedom cleared of every trace of centuries of submission and slavery.

5   This was the original aim of the movement for woman's emancipation. But the results so far achieved have isolated woman and have robbed her of the fountain springs of that happiness which is so essential to her. Merely external emancipation has made of the modern woman an artificial being, who reminds one of the products of French arboriculture with its arabesque trees and shrubs, pyramids, wheels, and wreaths; anything, except the forms which would be reached by the expression of her own inner qualities. Such artificially grown plants of the female sex are to be found in large numbers, especially in the so-called intellectual sphere of our life.

6   Liberty and equality for woman! What hopes and aspirations these words awakened when they were first uttered by some of the noblest and bravest souls of those days. The sun in all his light and glory was to rise upon a new world; in this world woman was to be free to direct her own destiny—an aim certainly worthy of the great enthusiasm, courage, perseverance, and ceaseless effort of the tremendous host of pioneer men and women, who staked everything against a world of prejudice and ignorance.

7   My hopes also move towards that goal, but I hold that the emancipation of woman, as interpreted and practically applied today, has failed to reach that great end. Now, woman is confronted with the necessity of emancipating herself from emancipation, if she really desires to be free. This may sound paradoxical, but is, nevertheless, only too true.

8   What has she achieved through her emancipation? Equal suffrage in a few States. Has that purified our political life, as many well-meaning advocates predicted? Certainly not. Incidentally, it is really time that persons with plain, sound judgment should cease to talk about corruption in politics in a boarding-school tone. Corruption of politics has nothing to do with the morals, or the laxity of morals, of various political personalities. Its cause is altogether a material one. Politics is the reflex of the business and industrial world, the mottos of which are: "To take is more blessed than to give"; "buy cheap and sell dear"; "one soiled hand washes the other." There is no hope even that woman, with her right to vote, will ever purify politics.

9   Emancipation has brought woman economic equality with man; that is, she can choose her own profession and trade; but as her past and present physical training has not equipped her with the necessary strength to compete with man, she is often compelled to exhaust all her energy, use up her vitality, and strain every nerve in order to reach the market value. Very few ever succeed, for it is a fact that women teachers,

doctors, lawyers, architects, and engineers are neither met with the same confidence as their male colleagues, nor receive equal remuneration. And those that do reach that enticing equality generally do so at the expense of their physical and psychical well-being. As to the great mass of working girls and women, how much independence is gained if the narrowness and lack of freedom of the home is exchanged for the narrowness and lack of freedom of the factory, sweat-shop, department store, or office? In addition is the burden which is laid on many women of looking after a "home, sweet home"—cold, dreary, disorderly, uninviting—after a day's hard work. Glorious independence! No wonder that hundreds of girls are so willing to accept the first offer of marriage, sick and tired of their "independence" behind the counter, at the sewing or typewriting machine. They are just as ready to marry as girls of the middle class, who long to throw off the yoke of parental supremacy. A so-called independence which leads only to earning the merest subsistence is not so enticing, not so ideal, that one could expect woman to sacrifice everything for it. Our highly praised independence is, after all, but a slow process of dulling and stifling woman's nature, her love instinct, and her mother instinct.

10   Nevertheless, the position of the working girl is far more natural and human than that of her seemingly more fortunate sister in the more cultured professional walks of life—teachers, physicians, lawyers, engineers, etc., who have to make a dignified, proper appearance, while the inner life is growing empty and dead.

11   The narrowness of the existing conception of woman's independence and emancipation; the dread of love for a man who is not her social equal; the fear that love will rob her of her freedom and independence; the horror that love or the joy of motherhood will only hinder her in the full exercise of her profession—all these together make of the emancipated modern woman a compulsory vestal, before whom life, with its great clarifying sorrows and its deep, entrancing joys, rolls on without touching or gripping her soul.

12   Emancipation, as understood by the majority of its adherents and exponents, is of too narrow a scope to permit the boundless love and ecstasy contained in the deep emotion of the true woman, sweetheart, mother, in freedom.

13   The tragedy of the self-supporting or economically free woman does not lie in too many, but in too few experiences. True, she surpasses her sister of past generations in knowledge of the world and human nature; it is just because of this that she feels deeply the lack of life's essence, which alone can enrich the human soul, and without which the majority of women have become mere professional automatons.

14   That such a state of affairs was bound to come was foreseen by those who realized that, in the domain of ethics, there still remained many decaying ruins of the time of the undisputed superiority of man; ruins that

are still considered useful. And, what is more important, a goodly number of the emancipated are unable to get along without them. Every movement that aims at the destruction of existing institutions and the replacement thereof with something more advanced, more perfect, has followers who in theory stand for the most radical ideas, but who, nevertheless, in their every-day practice, are like the average Philistine, feigning respectability and clamoring for the good opinion of their opponents. There are, for example, Socialists, and even Anarchists, who stand for the idea that property is robbery, yet who will grow indignant if anyone owe them the value of a half-dozen pins.

15   The same Philistine can be found in the movement for woman's emancipation. Yellow journalists and milk-and-water littérateurs have painted pictures of the emancipated woman that make the hair of the good citizen and his dull companion stand up on end. Every member of the woman's rights movement was pictured as a George Sand in her absolute disregard of morality. Nothing was sacred to her. She had no respect for the ideal relation between man and woman. In short, emancipation stood only for a reckless life of lust and sin, regardless of society, religion, and morality. The exponents of woman's rights were highly indignant at such misrepresentation, and, lacking humor, they exerted all their energy to prove that they were not at all as bad as they were painted, but the very reverse. Of course, as long as woman was the slave of man, she could not be good and pure, but now that she was free and independent she would prove how good she could be and that her influence would have a purifying effect on all institutions in society. True, the movement for woman's rights has broken many old fetters, but it has also forged new ones. The great movement of *true* emancipation has not met with a great race of women who could look liberty in the face. Their narrow, puritanical vision banished man, as a disturber and doubtful character, out of their emotional life. Man was not to be tolerated at any price, except perhaps as the father of a child, since a child could not very well come to life without a father. Fortunately, the most rigid Puritans never will be strong enough to kill the innate craving for motherhood. But woman's freedom is closely allied with man's freedom, and many of my so-called emancipated sisters seem to overlook the fact that a child born in freedom needs the love and devotion of each human being about him, man as well as woman. Unfortunately, it is this narrow conception of human relations that has brought about a great tragedy in the lives of the modern man and woman. . . .

16   A rich intellect and a fine soul are usually considered necessary attributes of a deep and beautiful personality. In the case of the modern woman, these attributes serve as a hindrance to the complete assertion of her being. For over a hundred years the old form of marriage, based on the Bible, "Till death doth part," has been denounced as an institution that stands for the sovereignty of the man over the woman, of her

complete submission to his whims and commands, and absolute dependence on his name and support. Time and again it has been conclusively proved that the old matrimonial relation restricted woman to the function of man's servant and the bearer of his children. And yet we find many emancipated women who prefer marriage, with all its deficiencies, to the narrowness of an unmarried life; narrow and unendurable because of the chains of moral and social prejudice that cramp and bind her nature.

17　The explanation of such inconsistency on the part of many advanced women is to be found in the fact that they never truly understood the meaning of emancipation. They thought that all that was needed was independence from external tyrannies; the internal tyrants, far more harmful to life and growth—ethical and social conventions—were left to take care of themselves; and they have taken care of themselves. They seem to get along as beautifully in the heads and hearts of the most active exponents of woman's emancipation, as in the heads and hearts of our grandmothers.

18　These internal tyrants, whether they be in the form of public opinion or what will mother say, or brother, father, aunt, or relative of any sort; what will Mrs. Grundy, Mr. Comstock, the employer, the Board of Education say? All these busybodies, moral detectives, jailers of the human spirit, what will they say? Until woman has learned to defy them all, to stand firmly on her own ground and to insist upon her own unrestricted freedom, to listen to the voice of her nature, whether it call for life's greatest treasure, love for a man, or her most glorious privilege, the right to give birth to a child, she cannot call herself emancipated. How many emancipated women are brave enough to acknowledge that the voice of love is calling, wildly beating against their breasts, demanding to be heard, to be satisfied. . . .

19　The greatest shortcoming of the emancipation of the present day lies in its artificial stiffness and its narrow respectibilities, which produce an emptiness in woman's soul that will not let her drink from the fountain of life. I once remarked that there seemed to be a deeper relationship between the old-fashioned mother and hostess, ever on the alert for the happiness of her little ones and the comfort of those she loves, and the truly new woman, than between the latter and her average emancipated sister. The disciples of emancipation pure and simple declared me a heathen, fit only for the stake. Their blind zeal did not let them see that my comparison between the old and the new was merely to prove that a goodly number of our grandmothers had more blood in their veins, far more humor and wit, and certainly a greater amount of naturalness, kind-heartedness, and simplicity, than the majority of our emancipated professional women who fill the colleges, halls of learning and various offices. This does not mean a wish to return to the past, nor does it condemn woman to her old sphere, the kitchen and the nursery.

20   Salvation lies in an energetic march onward towards a brighter and clearer future. We are in need of unhampered growth out of old traditions and habits. The movement for woman's emancipation has so far made but the first step in that direction. It is to be hoped that it will gather strength to make another. The right to vote, or equal civil rights, may be good demands, but true emancipation begins neither at the polls nor in courts. It begins in woman's soul. History tells us that every oppressed class gained true liberation from its masters through its own efforts. It is necessary that woman learn that lesson, that she realize that her freedom will reach as far as her power to achieve her freedom reaches. It is, therefore, far more important for her to begin with her inner regeneration, to cut loose from the weight of prejudices, traditions, and customs. The demand for equal rights in every vocation of life is just and fair; but, after all, the most vital right is the right to love and be loved. Indeed, if partial emancipation is to become a complete and true emancipation of woman, it will have to do away with the ridiculous notion that to be loved, to be sweetheart and mother, is synonymous with being a slave or subordinate. It will have to do away with the absurd notion of the dualism of the sexes, or that man and woman represent two antagonistic worlds.

21   Pettiness separates; breadth unites. Let us be broad and big. Let us not overlook vital things because of the bulk of trifles confronting us. A true conception of the relation of the sexes will not admit of conqueror and conquered; it knows of but one great thing: to give of one's self boundlessly, in order to find one's self richer, deeper, better. That alone can fill the emptiness, and transform the tragedy of woman's emancipation into joy, limitless joy.

BUILDING CONTEXT

1. Goldman notes (par. 8) that allowing women to vote did not purify politics. Why did people think it would? Try to locate such a claim by Stanton, Stowe or Millett.

2. Goldman was an early advocate of birth control. How does this stance correspond to the views she expresses in this essay? For what reasons was birth control important?

3. Compare Goldman's description of working women to that of Hymowitz and Weiss.

FURTHER STUDY

1. Goldman claims that in answering their critics, feminists overstated the virtues and purity of women (par. 15). Explain her reasoning. Why did

this undermine the position of women? What similar situations exist today?

2. Which of Goldman's ideas are accepted as mainstream today? Which are still considered to be radical?

ADDITIONAL RESOURCES

Bardwick, Judith. *Psychology of Women: A Study of Bio-Cultural Conflicts.* New York: Harper & Row, 1971.

Becker, Susan D. *The Origins of the Equal Rights Amendment.* Westport, Conn.: Greenwood Press, 1981.

Rossi, Alice S., ed. *The Feminist Papers: From Adams to Beauvoir.* Boston: Northeastern University Press, 1973.

RESEARCH KEYWORDS

Woman's Rights
Feminism
Women—History

EDNA FERBER
A Peculiar Treasure
(1939)

" . . . the gorgeous irony of it is this: Adolf Hitler has done more to strengthen, to unite, to solidify and to spiritualize the Jews of the world than any other man since Moses."

The author of more than thirty plays and works of fiction, Edna Ferber is best known for her depictions of frontier and small town life in middle

America. *So Big,* about a woman's quest for independence, won the Pulitzer Prize in 1924; her best-selling novels *Cimarron* and *Giant* became popular movies; *Show Boat* was made into a hit musical; and *Dinner at Eight* and *Stage Door* were successful plays that also became film classics.

Though her father was a Jewish immigrant from Hungary and her mother descended from a German-Jewish family that settled in Chicago, Ferber wrote little about Jewish topics. The heroines of her early works are Dawn O'Hara and Emma McChesney; after *Fanny Herself,* which follows the life of a Jewish girl in a small town, mythic Americans—pioneers, settlers, farmers, gamblers, working girls—peopled her work. However, when Hitler came to power in Germany and anti-Semitism was on the rise in America, Ferber published her autobiography, *A Peculiar Treasure,* which she described as "about being a Jew."

The following excerpt illustrates Ferber's skill as a social critic, as she moves back and forth in time using the present to illuminate the past—and the past to explain the present.

Text: Edna Ferber; *A Peculiar Treasure;* Literary Guild of America, 1939.

EXPLORING ISSUES IN THE TEXT

1. Explain how the details in the first three paragraphs support the conclusion that Appleton was "the American small town at its best."

2. Summarize Ferber's theory about the consequence of anti-Semitism (par. 5). Why does she include this in a paragraph that begins by describing Jewish life in a small town? What point is Ferber making about the nature of group identity?

3. Assess Ferber's theory about the creativity of the Jews (pars. 6–7). What does she suggest would actually reduce Jewish self-expression (par. 5)?

4. How does Ferber believe anti-Semitism originated (pars. 8–12)? In what way does she relate this theory to her own experience?

5. Consider Ferber's discussion about women in business (par. 17). How is this connected to her memories of childhood and the factories in the Fox River Valley (pars. 18–20)?

A PECULIAR TREASURE

1 Perhaps pioneer families of sixty years before, coming upon a cool green oasis after heart-breaking days through parched desert and wind-swept plains, must have felt much as the Ferber family did as it arrived in Appleton, Wisconsin, and looked about at the smiling valley in whose arms

the town so contentedly nestled. A lovely little town of sixteen thousand people; tree-shaded, prosperous, civilized. Its waterways hummed with huge paper mills fed by the forests of Michigan and Wisconsin. All about it lay small prosperous towns like itself—Kaukauna, Neenah, Menasha, Little Chute. Giant elms and oaks, arching overhead, made cool green naves of the summer streets. The townspeople owned their houses, tended their lawns and gardens. They were substantial, intelligent, progressive. They read, they traveled, they went to the theater, heard music, educated their children at the local college, a Methodist institution called Lawrence University, or sent them to Beloit College, or Notre Dame, or the University of Wisconsin at Madison.

2 My parents rented a comfortable white frame house on Drew Street, across from the quiet tree-shaded City Park, and immediately the hospitable town came calling.

3 There never was such a town for sociability. At the least provocation Japanese lanterns burst into bloom on a hundred lawns, and lemonade-punch bowls were encircled by organdie-clad girls, and boys in white duck pants (peg-top) and blue serge coats (with silk revers). The dour days—the seven lean years through which we had just passed—were dispelled like fog before the sun of Appleton's warm-generous friendliness. If Ottumwa had seemed like some foreign provincial town in its narrowness and bigotry, Appleton represented the American small town at its best. A sense of well-being pervaded it. It was curiously modern and free in the best sense of the words. Cliques, malice, gossip, snobbishness—all the insular meannesses—were strangely lacking in this thriving community. Trouble, illness and death were to come upon us there in the next few years, but sympathy and friendship leavened them and made them bearable.

4 The mayor of Appleton that year, and for many years thereafter, was old David Hammel, a Jew. A handsome patriarch with a high-bridged nose, a bearded leonine head, ruddy color, a superb physique. He and his handsome white-haired wife and their sons and daughters lived in a big Victorian frame house on North and Durkee streets. Later, when we moved to North Street, just across the way from the Hammel house, I saw much of their family life as I read and rocked and munched cookies and played on our own front porch. It was a lesson in loyalty and family devotion. . . .

5 In Appleton most of the Jewish families were interrelated and even intermarried. With the exception of ourselves and two or three other families they hailed from the little German town of Gemünden. There was a snarl of brothers, sisters, uncles, cousins, very puzzling to the outsider. The children and grandchildren had been born in Appleton. The men were, for the most part, in the business of buying and selling Wisconsin farm lands and horses—all sorts of horses from beautiful spirited carriage chestnuts or blacks to mammoth pudding-footed draught animals. They

were a full-blooded open-handed sort, these husbands and fathers. They smelled too pungently of the horse barns even when dressed in their Sabbath blacks. Their wives were placid, home-loving; their sons and daughters well educated and intelligent. The children did not stand spectacularly high in their studies, in the athletic field, or in any of the arts, probably because they never had experienced racial or religious oppression. It is usually the persecuted Jew who naturally tries to compensate for oppression. It always has been my contention that the Jew, left in peace for two hundred years throughout the world, would lose his aggressiveness, his tenacity and neurotic ambition; would be completely absorbed and would vanish, as a type, from the face of the earth. The Jew, like the Protestant or the Catholic, fights the battles of his own country, be it America, Germany, Italy, France, England; he works for his living, educates his children, travels, lives the normal life of his country as richly as his condition permits. Suddenly, from the headlines of every newspaper in the so-called civilized world, blaring out of the radio, screaming from a thousand platforms, he sees and hears quoted, to his amazement and heartsick despair, "Jew! Jew! Jew! Down! Down!" If these fools really want to destroy us they need only leave us alone. Incredibly adaptable, gregarious, imitative, we soon would be absorbed by the world about us. Yet invariably, just as we are slipping into the world mass, our identity to be forever lost, along comes a despot who singles us out as an object on which to vent his hate or to satisfy his own or his country's psychological perversion. So then, outnumbered but terribly persistent, we again muster what defense we can, draw close together for protection, the stronger helping the weak as we stumble along. Thus for centuries we have been saved from complete absorption or utter oblivion by such fanatics, megalomanics or perverts as Pharaoh, Hitler, Ivan of Russia, Philip of France or Edward I of England. If one must build bricks without straw or die, one contrives, somehow, to build bricks without straw. So, through the centuries, the weakest of us have perished; the strong, the courageous, the cunning, the tenacious have survived the repeated blasts of hatred and prejudice. Any biologist or horticulturalist will tell you that that is not the way to weaken or destroy a strain; that is the way to strengthen it. If, in past centuries, the Jew has grown pale of skin, undersized, rather badly articulated, overeager, oversensitive, it is because the ghetto to which he was condemned was the tenement of the Middle and Dark Ages—crowded, airless, mean, dark. Tenements then and now do not make for stature, beauty, health or self-confidence. The German Jew, following these past few years of torture, will need a century to recuperate, if ever he is given the opportunity at all.

6   So, then, again and again deprived of property, of liberty, of land, of human rights, we have turned to the one thing of which only death can rob us: creative self-expression. An old Chassidic book says:

> There are three ways in which a man expresses his deep sorrow: the
> man on the lowest level cries; the man on the second level is silent,
> but the man on the highest level knows how to turn his sorrow into
> song.

7   So then, because of a Hitler, the Jew of Europe (and of the world) has
perforce become more intensely racial. In the mercantile class and in
the professions he has clung to the last to his rights; he will emerge more
tenacious, more aggressive unless he is completely destroyed. But before
that happens let us hope that, seeking in self-expression some relief for
our pain, we may again, as in the past, produce for the delight of the
whole world another Mozart, another Mendelssohn, another Bernhardt,
golden-voiced; another Heifetz, another Rachmaninoff, another
Menuhin, another Zimbalist, another Gershwin, turning centuries of
sorrow into song. And by that legacy of beauty justify our living and our
dying; justify even those who, by torturing us, have produced our
poignantly beautiful death cry. For, paradoxical though it may seem, in
spite of the degradation of the body, the humiliation of the spirit, the
agony of mind, the torture of the soul which has been visited upon the
Jews of the so-called civilized world in the past five years, the gorgeous
irony of it is this: Adolf Hitler has done more to strengthen, to unite, to
solidify and to spiritualize the Jews of the world than any other man
since Moses.

8   I never have heard a satisfactory answer to the riddle of the world's attitude toward the Jew. I remember my shock of horror when, having
been taken to an early-morning Mass by the hired girl Sarah, in Ottumwa, I looked upon my first sight of agony and bloodshed—a church
statue of the crucifixion. I have wondered many times since just how
deep and widespread an effect in later life this same experience has had
upon hundreds of millions of children.

9   It is generally accepted among intelligent people that very early impressions, deeply implanted, influence us for the remainder of our lives.
Certainly the psychiatrist is interested in fishing up, not the events and
people and thoughts that occupied us at fifteen, twenty, twenty-five, but
when we were three years old, four, five, six.

10   Small children are ordinarily shielded from sights and sounds of horror. Even the rhymes and the pictures in Mother Goose are sometimes
seriously debated.

> There was a man in our town,
> And he was wondrous wise.
> He jumped into a bramble bush,
> And scratched out both his eyes.

11   Dear me! says the child-psychologist. No good can come of that. The
child will grow up suspecting hidden horrors in every bush it encounters,

and probably will develop eye trouble at fifteen. But at the age of four or five this child is deliberately confronted with its first vision of sanguine tragedy. In a picture or a statue he sees a man's nude figure drawn and distorted in agony. Nails through the hands and feet pin him to a cross of wood. On his head is a crown of thorns. From head, hands and feet the scarlet blood streams over the tortured body.

The child's face is a mask of fascinated revulsion. "What is that?"

"That is Our Lord Jesus Christ."

"What is the matter with him? Why is he like that?"

"He is nailed to the cross. He died for you and me."

"Who nailed him?"

"The Jews."

12   This has gone on for hundreds of years. The fact that Jesus was tried by Pontius Pilate, the Roman governor, and sentenced by law according to the court proceedings of that day, and that he was then crucified by Roman soldiers is universally ignored. He was one of thousands of that period who died on the cross. The life and death of this Jew, distorted through the centuries, has deeply affected the life and death of millions of Jews, and will until the historical truth is generally accepted.

13   These Appleton townspeople of Jewish faith—first-, second-, and third-generation Americans—owned big comfortable houses, richly furnished; they lived well, had carriages and horses. The horses were well matched high-stepping beauties, the carriages beige- or plum-cushioned victorias with silver-trimmed harness, the whole topped by a coachman on the box. The wives used these for afternoon shopping, for paying calls, for rather aimless drives east to the end of College Avenue, then west to where the Chute ended in the state road.

14   Appleton boasted its millionaires, but none of these was a Jew. The McNaughtons, the Van Nortwicks, the Pattens, the Peabodys—of Dutch, Scotch or New England descent—these were the really moneyed people of the town.

15   During the first year or two of our coming to Appleton my mother rather grandly established Friday afternoons At Home. Our hired girl of that day was of German descent: Tillie Schultz, a treasure of purest ray serene. Tillie was a naturally gifted cook. On Friday mornings the house was fragrant with the scent of baking dough; of sugar and spice, of fruits bubbling on the bosom of plum, apricot and apple kuchen. The cheese kuchen, made from a recipe in which cottage cheese was smartened by lemon juice and grated lemon peel, was a specialty of the house. At about four o'clock the tantalizing fragrance of coffee would be added to the rest. These Friday afternoons became something of a stampede.

16   My mother was rather a bombshell in this placid society. American-born, alert, original, she found she had little in common with these somewhat slow-thinking and sheltered wives. She gravitated toward two

families in the Jewish community: one named Lyons who had come up to Wisconsin from the South; the other named Spitz. Mrs. Spitz, tiny, quick-witted, top-heavy with a magnificent crown of braided red hair, was, like my mother, married to a Hungarian.

17 Two reasons caused the discontinuance of the Fridays At Home. First, the lively Julia became bored with them; second, there was no staying sociably at home, surrounded by coffee cake and feminine chatter, when the business needed her energies and intelligence more and more. Curiously enough, for so advanced a town, there were very few business women in the Appleton of that day. But then, the woman in business had not yet taken her astonishing place in the American commercial, financial and professional world. Even fourteen years later, when I wrote the first of the Emma McChesney stories, a series whose chief character was a traveling saleswoman with a line of Featherloom petticoats, they were greeted as something completely fresh and novel in fiction. . . .

18 The Fox River Valley from Oshkosh to Green Bay hummed with commerce, yet it was serene and lovely with its ravines and woods and jewel-like lakes. The ravines, characteristic of the region, were things of especially enchanting beauty. The town dipped and swooped into hollows that once had been Indian camping grounds. Little brooks tinkled through these green recesses. The monster falsely called Progress was presently to come along with his oily promises and counsel the filling of these natural parks, and soon they were used as dumping grounds, their lovely slopes were foul with ashes, tin cans and garbage. Solid now with buildings whose utility can never compensate for lost beauty, the vanished valleys should be haunted by the grim ghosts of Indian braves and squaws. Their revenge lies in the desecration that the white man has himself wrought.

19 The region abounded both in manufacturing and agriculture, but the huge paper and pulp mills were the valley's chief industry. The vast plants stretched for miles along the river; when you neared them your nostrils were pricked with the acid smells of the churning pulp tubs. Some of the mills made rag paper, others pulp paper. One saw a pair of ragged blue overalls made into a snowy sheet of writing paper or a great rugged tree emerge as wrapping or news paper. Many years later, in 1934, when I was writing the novel Come and Get It, I again made use, as always, of the old yellow-trunk method by fishing up out of my memory the paper-mill lore and knowledge acquired in the girlhood years spent in the Fox River Valley. I knew the mill hands, I knew the mill millionaires, first in my casual childhood, later as they came as customers to Ferber's store for one thing or another, still later when I became a reporter on the Appleton Crescent.

20 If the girls who worked in the rag-sorting rooms were a trifle pale and inclined to cough, no one paid any particular attention. Dust and lint poured out of the bins. Those were the good old days. On the other hand,

if a mill owner wanted to chop down a thousand acres of forest, with never a thought of reforesting, or if his mill acids polluted a river, or if he found it convenient to divert a waterway, a complaisant world made no objection. A few years later, in the governor's chair at Madison, a fiery little man named La Follette was to stir up considerable dust of his own which got into the eyes and throats of the wealthy Wisconsinites. Their bellows could be heard for miles—as far as Washington, in fact. . . .

21   At the card parties you saw Jacob Ferber seated behind the players at this table or that. They played whist, but not he. The red and black symbols and the pictures on the cards now were only little smeary spots to him. He hadn't even the doubtful diversion of kibitzing as he sat there, apart.

22   The kindly itinerant eye doctor of the Ottumwa days had been all too right. My father's eyes were growing steadily worse. My mother was in the store now almost all day. She had developed a rather surprisingly shrewd head for business—surprising because her direct heritage and background had taught her nothing of this. Perhaps one of the Berlin banking or business Neumanns were cropping up in this, their descendant. By now she realized that she must take the helm or the business would founder altogether.

23   There now appeared in the house as part of our daily lives a monster known as the Pain. The Pain was like a fifth person in the house—an evil prowling thing never absent, though often hidden; quick to pounce on its helpless victim as he sat, as he lay sleeping, as he ate at table. As the Pain delivered its preliminary crashing blow, a low moan would be wrung from my father. He would reel to the nearest chair. I early discovered that my hands could help, or could give the effect of helping. I had, even then, unusually long, strong fingers through which seemed to flow, for this suffering man, an electric and soothing quality. I would go to him as he lay groaning, his face scarlet, his eyes glazed with agony, his breath coming in gasps. Standing behind his chair I would take his head in my two hands, my fingers pressing hard on his temples and forehead, tighter and tighter until it seemed to me that the very pressure must crush the skull that was bursting with pain. Then I would begin to stroke the head with a firm deliberate motion from the center of the forehead to the temples and down to the neck. After five minutes of torture the tense body would slowly relax, the twisted face would become gray-white, a cold clammy sweat would break out on his forehead. The Pain had had its way, and had retreated, glutted for the moment, to its dark corner. This would occur perhaps a dozen or more times daily. . . .

24   Usually, on summer evenings, he and I took a walk, but I was impatient to be off with my friends. Children have no curiosity about their parents as human beings. They are merely household necessities, like chairs and beds and food. I wish I had talked to him about his childhood and his youth in Hungary, and his high hopes as he crossed the ocean, a lad, to find fortune and happiness in this golden new land. But I didn't.

BUILDING CONTEXT

1. According to Ferber, how is group identity formed? Compare this view with those of Crèvecoeur, Van Every, Cameron, or Acosta-Belén.

2. Compare Ferber's observations about women (or women in business) to those of Goldman and Angelou.

3. How do Ferber's ideas about religion in America relate to those of Crèvecoeur, O'Brien, or King?

FURTHER STUDY

1. Ferber commented that Hitler encouraged Jewish solidarity before World War II. Do you think that the destruction of European Jewry during the war reinforces or negates her observation? What was the reaction of Jews and the world to the discovery of the Holocaust?

2. What was your reaction to reading that at the turn of the twentieth century the mayor of Appleton, Wisconsin, was Jewish? What was the cause of his election—minority bloc voting, political power, or something else? Where are minorities most often elected today? What caused the change?

3. In paragraph 5, Ferber mentions Pharaoh, Hitler, Ivan of Russia, Philip of France, and Edward I of England. Look up these names in an encyclopedia or history book to see if the description supports her characterization of them as "fanatics, megalomaniacs or perverts." Explain the reason for any discrepancies.

ADDITIONAL RESOURCES

American Jewish History. Quarterly Journal of the American Jewish Historical Society. Waltham, Mass.

Feingold, Henry L., ed. *The Jewish People in America.* 5 vols. Baltimore: The Johns Hopkins University Press, 1992.

Ribalow, Harold U., ed. *Autobiographies of American Jews.* Philadelphia: Jewish Publication Society, 1973.

Rubin, Steven J. *Writing Our Lives: Autobiographies of American Jews, 1890–1990.* Philadelphia: Jewish Publication Society, 1991.

RESEARCH KEYWORDS

Jews—U.S.   Jewish Authors—U.S.
Immigration—Jews   U.S. Jews—Identity
Ethnic Relations—U.S.

BERNARDO VEGA
Memoirs (1940s [1977])

"*The real or imaginary danger was used as an excuse not to promote Puerto Rican workers. . . .*"

Bernardo Vega (1885–1965), a native of Puerto Rico, moved to New York City in 1916, during the beginning of a significant migration from the island to the mainland. His *Memoirs,* written during the 1940s but not published until 1977, is possibly the most detailed and perceptive account of Puerto Rican life in New York during the first half of the twentieth century. While Vega naturally focuses most of his attention on the growing Puerto Rican community, he also exposes the conditions of other immigrant groups— partly because immigrants lived in neighboring slums and vied for the same jobs, and partly because, as he says, being "white," he was often mistaken for a Russian, Jewish, or Japanese man.

A cigar-maker, Vega was also an intellectual and labor activist. His perceptive views about politics, unions, and Socialism also included surprising sympathies for competing ethnic communities. His involvement with a range of well-organized social and political institutions provides glimpses into the early history of the Puerto Rican community in New York and its place within larger immigration and labor issues.

The following chapter of the *Memoirs* captures much of this discussion, as well as the irony of the inadvertent setback of the Puerto Rican community by the good intentions of Eleanor Roosevelt, a well-known philanthropist and wife of the president.

Text: *Memoirs of Bernardo Vega,* ed. Cesar Andreu Iglesias, trans. Juan Flores; New York: Monthly Review Press, 1984.

EXPLORING ISSUES IN THE TEXT

1. Describe how Mrs. Roosevelt's intended philanthropy led to unfortunate consequences (pars. 1, 4–5). How did the media react to the Puerto Ricans' protests (pars. 2–3)?

2. Summarize the "trial" discussed in paragraphs 7–9. What was your reaction to the verdict? To the consequence of the verdict?

3. Examine the efforts made to unionize Puerto Rican workers (pars. 10–14). What was the reaction of the major labor unions to these efforts?

4. How does Vega analyze the Harlem riot of 1935 (pars. 15–16)? What is his opinion of the official response (par. 17)?

5. Discuss the issues surrounding the intelligence test given to Puerto Rican children (pars. 19–20).

MEMOIRS

Of how even the best of intentions can sometimes do more harm than good, and other events

1 The correlation between tuberculosis and Puerto Ricans established by Mrs. Roosevelt after her trip to Puerto Rico had immediate, and prejudicial, consequences. The New York City Department of Health tightened its restrictions on the little cigar factories where so many of our countrymen worked, whether as owners or as employees. Countless domestic workers lost their jobs, and so did those in hotels and restaurants. The real or imaginary danger was used as an excuse not to promote Puerto Rican workers and to condemn them to menial jobs as dishwashers and the like.

2 We were quick to respond to Mrs. Roosevelt's ill-advised words. At the time I was chairman of the Club Hostos and president of the Liga Puertorriqueña, and in those capacities I sent the First Lady a telegram informing her of the distressing result of her statements. She either didn't— or didn't want to—understand, and brushed aside our objections in rather angry terms.

3 The newspapers, both in New York and San Juan, reported our protest, labeling us "ingrates" for failing to appreciate "the humanitarian lady's show of generosity." Needless to say, it was people whose children would not be affected by the consequences of Mrs. Roosevelt's statements who repudiated our position! But I refused to be intimidated, and carried on my press campaign with comments like, "The portrait offered by Mrs. Roosevelt is not favorable, on the contrary, it is damaging to us . . ." "Anyone who has taken the trouble to study the impoverished conditions in which our people live knows full well what it is that caused it . . ." "We sons of Puerto Rico did not come here because we wanted to. We live in New York out of necessity. Our problems cannot be solved by doing what Mrs. Roosevelt has done and portraying Puerto Ricans as a racial group afflicted with contagious diseases so that a few charitable Americans can give us alms while the rest—the majority—do nothing but insult us . . ."

4 Shortly thereafter something happened that, unfortunately for us, only confirmed our worst fears about what Mrs. Roosevelt's remarks might lead to. There were several religious groups that recruited children from the Puerto Rican community to attend their summer camps.

Around six thousand Puerto Rican children were able to enjoy a week or two of summer vacation in the country in upstate New York. Churches of all denominations, especially in El Barrio, signed up the children, giving special consideration to the neediest families.

5   Now it happened that on May 22, 1934, a letter was received by the Reverend Joseph Haviland, who each year sent a large number of Puerto Rican children from his parish to the church's summer camp. The letter read as follows: "Dear Mr. Haviland: Your communication of May 16, addressed to the Gould Foundation, has been submitted to our office, as we are presently making arrangements for the children's accommodation in the summer camps. I understand that most of your children are Puerto Rican. Such being the case, I regret to inform you that the Gould Foundation will not be in a position to accept them this year, as we have been asked not to send any Puerto Rican children. Sincerely yours, Edith May Holmes, Director of Applications."

6   The letter was sent by nothing less than the Federation of Protestant Welfare Agencies.

7   As soon as the news broke, the Liga Puertorriqueña called a mass public demonstration. Practically every social, political, and religious group in El Barrio showed up for the planning meeting.

8   It was agreed to hold a rally in the form of a public hearing at which the accused would be the Gould Foundation and the religious agencies that practiced such harsh discrimination against Puerto Rican children. The Park Palace was jammed with people as the hearing began. It fell on me to preside over the tribunal. The first thing was to select a jury composed of twenty-three delegates from various labor and religious organizations. The distinguished lawyers Jacobo Bohana and H. Tower were named as judges. León Abramaguer, Esq., acted as defense attorney on behalf of the accused institutions, and the Reverend S. Martínez of the Hispanic clergy as "friend of the court." And arguing for the prosecution, as district attorneys acting for the Puerto Rican community, were H. Brideman, Julio Medina, and Jesús Colón. All of the accused were duly informed of the trial and invited to name their defenders should they desire to do so.

9   As you can imagine, the event turned out to be very dramatic, and held the interest of everyone present. Need it be said that the prosecution's argument convinced the jury—as well as the audience—that the attitude toward Puerto Rican children shown by the Gould Foundation and the religious agencies had been "abusive, discriminatory, and cruel." Those institutions were ordered by the court to "issue a public retraction of that vicious and inhuman attitude and to give to the Protestant congregations in El Barrio the opportunity to send their children to summer camps, as has been the case in the past . . ." And indeed, the convicted agencies responded favorably and corrected their behavior. . . .

10   As president of the Liga Puertorriqueña and chairman of the Club Hostos, I continued to press for the unionization of Puerto Rican workers. But despite interest on the part of the workers themselves, the leading

officials of the A. F. of L. unions proved indifferent, if not actually hostile. Among the women working in the needle trades, a spontaneous movement arose in which the Puerto Rican rank-and-file of Local 22 of the International Ladies' Garment Workers' Union appealed to the top leadership—in a letter signed by 187 members—to authorize the formation of a local for Spanish-speaking workers. The same thing had been done earlier with Italian workers so as to facilitate organizing among them. The executive council of the International effectively killed the proposal by refusing to put it on the agenda.

11   Another such spontaneous organizing drive arose among workers in several cardboard box factories, where there were also a lot of Puerto Ricans. A work stoppage began in one plant and soon spread to others owned by the same company. There were quite a few scuffles between strikers and scabs. Spanish-speaking workers, mostly Puerto Ricans, who made up over half the workforce, were loyal to the strike. Many were arrested and beaten by the police. Nevertheless, the strike was fairly successful.

12   In January 1935 we received news of a strike called by the dockworkers in San Juan. Simultaneous strikes hit the sugar industry across Puerto Rico. In several places there were violent clashes between workers and guards hired by the companies. The news sparked a strike solidarity movement in New York: we formed a united front of several labor union federations, some civic groups, the Harlem Section of the Communist Party, and the Junta Nacionalista de Puerto Rico en Nueva York. This movement proved to be significant for several reasons: not only did it lead to a rapprochement between the Puerto Rican nationalists and the labor movement, but it also helped overcome the hostilities that Feliú's death had provoked between the nationalists and the Communists in New York.

13   One of our major acts was setting up a picketline supporting the strike in front of the shipping companies that transport cargo between San Juan and New York. Protest letters were sent to the authorities in San Juan and in Washington, and messages of solidarity and support went to the striking workers. At several places in the city committees were formed to collect aid for the strikers.

14   This mass effort in support of the strikes in Puerto Rico had positive results. The coming together of the different organizations opened up the possibility of closer collaboration in the future, which in turn broadened the horizon of the Puerto Rican independence struggle. The impressive parade that took place on September 14 of the same year in the streets of Harlem and El Barrio was one sign of this. The massive turnout was a result of the wide range of organizations that took part: from the Harlem section of the Communist Party, the Junta Nacionalista, and the Asociación Pro Independencia de Puerto Rico, to the Unemployed Councils, the International Workers' Order, the Centro Obrero Español, and the Church of the Seventh Day Adventists.

15   On March 21, 1935, Harlem was hit by a major riot. It was sparked off by the arrest of León Rivera, a young boy accused of stealing from the Kress store on 125th Street off Lenox Avenue. Several women who witnessed the event thought Rivera was a black American, although he was of course Puerto Rican, and rushed out into the street to protest the abusive manner in which the private guards (whites, of course) made the arrest. Hundreds of people gathered around the women, anger flared, and rocks started sailing through the store's windows. Violence spread throughout the neighborhood and lasted for several hours. When order was finally restored, Harlem looked like a city in ruins and was in a state of siege.

16   The roughing-up of the young boy by the guards and the women's outburst was like pulling a cork, and all of the pain and suffering of the black people rose to the surface. There were thousands of businesses in the area, all of them run by whites. In none of them—from the largest to the smallest—was there a single Afro-American person working. Discrimination was rampant, and was all the more abusive and humiliating because Harlem had the greatest concentration of blacks in New York City. The refusal to hire Negroes, even in businesses largely patronized by them, and at a time when the most severe unemployment was among black people—who, on top of all that, also had to pay higher rents than whites—made racial discrimination all the more disgusting.

17   Fortunately, Fiorello La Guardia was mayor of New York at the time. As soon as he heard about the riot, he went up to Harlem himself, restrained the police—who thought they could solve the problem with billy clubs—and stated publicly that black people were victims of a grave injustice. He called a meeting right there on the spot, spoke in conciliatory tones, and pledged the resources of the city government to alleviate the most pressing problems afflicting the Negro population—immediate assistance, jobs, and so forth. His quick action prevented a repetition of the violence.

18   That riot of March 21 seemed to strike panic into the managers of companies operating in Harlem. From then on, nearly all the stores began to hire blacks for menial work. The recently established "relief agencies" recruited blacks to conduct some of their investigations, and employment became available at the Board of Education and in the Police Department. These were some of Fiorello La Guardia's achievements during his first term in City Hall.

19   If anything taught the Puerto Ricans—including white Puerto Ricans—what life is like in the United States, it was the awareness of discrimination. As we have come to see, racial prejudice takes on many different faces. One form it took, around that time, was exemplified by the New York City Chamber of Commerce. Claiming that it needed to determine the "intelligence quotient" of Puerto Rican children, it sponsored a series of experimental tests. After administering the exam to 240 students, the Chamber announced in the papers that Puerto Rican children were "deficient" and lacked "intellectual development."

20   That "experiment" provoked a protest from groups representing the Puerto Rican community. In a message to the Chamber of Commerce, we proposed that they name a committee of teachers, to include representatives of our community, that would draw up an examination to be administered to an equal number of Puerto Rican and North American children. We were certain that our children would not come out any worse as far as natural intelligence is concerned. But the Chamber of Commerce showed little or no interest, and turned to other matters. Our suggestion was never followed up.

21   By that time the Puerto Rican community had spread out considerably. In addition to El Barrio in Harlem, thickly populated neighborhoods had sprung up in the Bronx, Washington Heights, and on parts of Long Island. The owners and managers of apartment buildings actively resisted this Puerto Rican expansion. In many cases, especially up in Washington Heights, they refused to rent to families who had come from Puerto Rico, which is what gave rise to the Comité de Defensa de Derechos de los Hispanos. Its membership included such prominent figures as Drs. E. Verges Casals, Max Ríos, and Vando de León, and attorneys Enrique Sarabals and Carlos Rodríguez.

22   In 1935 I reached my fiftieth birthday. I had been in New York for nearly twenty years. Counting my years of struggle in Puerto Rico, it could be said that I had spent no fewer than thirty years striving to "improve the world." . . .

BUILDING CONTEXT

1. Vega says (par. 3), "We sons of Puerto Rico did not come here because we wanted to. We live in New York out of necessity." Do other groups immigrate out of desire, or necessity, or both? How would you distinguish between the two? For example, does immigrating in search of religious freedom, or a better life, constitute desire or necessity? Compare the experiences of Bradford, Crèvecoeur, Goldman, and others.

2. What distinction does Vega imply existed between "white" and "nonwhite" Puerto Ricans? What led to the breakdown of this distinction? Find other examples of an ethnic group being divided against itself. Which reading selections describe similar situations?

FURTHER STUDY

1. Why does Vega consider it was fortunate that Fiorello La Guardia was mayor of New York in 1935? What can you discover about La Guardia that might explain his behavior?

2. Vega describes a situation in which good intentions lent support to a negative stereotype. Provide similar examples and theorize as to when and why these incidents occur.

ADDITIONAL RESOURCES

Dinnerstein, Leonard, and David M. Reimers. *Ethnic Americans: A History of Immigration and Assimilation.* New York: Dodd, Mead, 1975.

Fitzpatrick, Joseph P. *Puerto Rican Americans.* Englewood Cliffs, N.J.: Prentice-Hall, 1971.

Mohr, Eugene. *The Nuyorican Experience: Puerto Rican Minority Literature in the United States.* Westport, Conn.: Greenwood Press, 1982.

Sanchez Korrol, Virginia. *From Colonia to Community: A History of Puerto Ricans in New York City, 1917–1948.* Westport, CT: Greenwood Press: 1983.

RESEARCH KEYWORDS

Puerto Ricans
Emigration and Immigration
Ethnic Relations

MAYA ANGELOU
I Know Why the Caged Bird Sings (1970)

"The Black female is . . . caught in the tripartite crossfire of masculine prejudice, white illogical hate and Black lack of power."

Honored for her acting on Broadway and in film, as well as for her musical productions and poetry, Maya Angelou is perhaps best known for her autobiographical writing, an early attempt at converting the slave narrative into a modern literary vehicle. She was nominated for a Pulitzer prize in poetry in 1972 for *Just Give Me a Cool Drink of Water 'fore I Diiie* and for a Tony Award for her performance in *Roots* in 1977.

The chapter excerpted here, which traces her attempt—supported by her mother but not by the local civil rights organizations—to become the first black conductor on the San Francisco streetcars, clearly illustrates her belief that "a good autobiographer seems to write about herself but is in fact writing about the temper of the times." It also captures her credo: "I am feminist. I am black. I am a human being. The three are inseparable."

Text: Maya Angelou, *I Know Why the Caged Bird Sings.* New York: Random House, 1970.

EXPLORING ISSUES IN THE TEXT

1. What does Angelou mean when she writes, "pride had kept me from selecting typing, shorthand or filing as subjects in school" (par. 3)? Explain the insight this offers regarding her character, and how it prepares us for the dynamics that follow.

2. Interpret the "emotional ladder" that Angelou climbs (pars. 6–7). How does her reaction relate to her mother's terse answer in paragraph 5?

3. Why does Angelou at first consider the receptionist as much a victim as herself (pars. 15–16)? What later changes her mind (pars. 17–18)?

4. Summarize Angelou's experience with the civil rights organizations and her new feelings about San Francisco (pars. 21–22).

5. Why was this episode the beginning of "mutual adult admiration" between Angelou and her mother (par. 23)? How did it change her relationship with her peers (pars. 31–33)?

A JOB ON THE STREETCARS

1   Later, my room had all the cheeriness of a dungeon and the appeal of a tomb. It was going to be impossible to stay there, but leaving held no attraction for me, either. Running away from home would be anticlimactic after Mexico, and a dull story after my month in the car lot. But the need for change bulldozed a road down the center of my mind.

2   I had it. The answer came to me with the suddenness of a collision. I would go to work. Mother wouldn't be difficult to convince; after all, in school I was a year ahead of my grade and Mother was a firm believer in self-sufficiency. In fact, she'd be pleased to think that I had that much gumption, that much of her in my character. (She liked to speak of herself as the original "do-it-yourself girl.")

3   Once I had settled on getting a job, all that remained was to decide which kind of job I was most fitted for. My intellectual pride had kept me from selecting typing, shorthand or filing as subjects in school, so office work was ruled out. War plants and shipyards demanded birth certificates, and mine would reveal me to be fifteen, and ineligible for work. So

the well-paying defense jobs were also out. Women had replaced men on the streetcars as conductors and motormen, and the thought of sailing up and down the hills of San Francisco in a dark-blue uniform, with a money changer at my belt caught my fancy.

4 Mother was as easy as I had anticipated. The world was moving so fast, so much money was being made, so many people were dying in Guam, and Germany, that hordes of strangers became good friends overnight. Life was cheap and death entirely free. How could she have the time to think about my academic career?

5 To her question of what I planned to do, I replied that I would get a job on the streetcars. She rejected the proposal with: "They don't accept colored people on the streetcars."

6 I would like to claim an immediate fury which was followed by the noble determination to break the restricting tradition. But the truth is, my first reaction was one of disappointment. I'd pictured myself, dressed in a neat blue serge suit, my money changer swinging jauntily at my waist, and a cheery smile for the passengers which would make their own work day brighter.

7 From disappointment, I gradually ascended the emotional ladder to haughty indignation, and finally to that state of stubbornness where the mind is locked like the jaws of an enraged bulldog.

8 I would go to work on the streetcars and wear a blue serge suit. Mother gave me her support with one of her usual terse asides, "That's what you want to do? Then nothing beats a trial but a failure. Give it everything you've got. I've told you many times, 'Can't do is like Don't Care.' Neither of them have a home."

9 Translated, that meant there was nothing a person can't do, and there should be nothing a human being didn't care about. It was the most positive encouragement I could have hoped for.

10 In the offices of the Market Street Railway Company the receptionist seemed as surprised to see me there as I was surprised to find the interior dingy and the décor drab. Somehow I had expected waxed surfaces and carpeted floors. If I had met no resistance, I might have decided against working for such a poor-mouth-looking concern. As it was, I explained that I had come to see about a job. She asked, was I sent by an agency, and when I replied that I was not, she told me they were only accepting applicants from agencies.

11 The classified pages of the morning papers had listed advertisements for motorettes and conductorettes and I reminded her of that. She gave me a face full of astonishment that my suspicious nature would not accept.

12 "I am applying for the job listed in this morning's *Chronicle* and I'd like to be presented to your personnel manager." While I spoke in supercilious accents, and looked at the room as if I had an oil well in my own

backyard, my armpits were being pricked by millions of hot pointed needles. She saw her escape and dived into it.

13 "He's out. He's out for the day. You might call tomorrow and if he's in, I'm sure you can see him." Then she swiveled her chair around on its rusty screws and with that I was supposed to be dismissed.

"May I ask his name?"

She half turned, acting surprised to find me still there.

"His name? Whose name?"

"Your personnel manager."

We were firmly joined in the hypocrisy to play out the scene.

"The personnel manager? Oh, he's Mr. Cooper, but I'm not sure you'll find him here tomorrow. He's . . . Oh, but you can try."

"Thank you."

"You're welcome."

14 And I was out of the musty room and into the even mustier lobby. In the street I saw the receptionist and myself going faithfully through paces that were stale with familiarity, although I had never encountered that kind of situation before and, probably, neither had she. We were like actors who, knowing the play by heart, were still able to cry afresh over the old tragedies and laugh spontaneously at the comic situations.

15 The miserable little encounter had nothing to do with me, the me of me, any more than it had to do with that silly clerk. The incident was a recurring dream, concocted years before by stupid whites and it eternally came back to haunt us all. The secretary and I were like Hamlet and Laertes in the final scene, where, because of harm done by one ancestor to another, we were bound to duel to the death. Also because the play must end somewhere.

16 I went further than forgiving the clerk, I accepted her as a fellow victim of the same puppeteer.

17 On the streetcar, I put my fare into the box and the conductorette looked at me with the usual hard eyes of white contempt. "Move into the car, please move on in the car." She patted her money changer.

18 Her Southern nasal accent sliced my meditation and I looked deep into my thoughts. All lies, all comfortable lies. The receptionist was not innocent and neither was I. The whole charade we had played out in that crummy waiting room had directly to do with me, Black, and her, white.

19 I wouldn't move into the streetcar but stood on the ledge over the conductor, glaring. My mind shouted so energetically that the announcement made my veins stand out, and my mouth tighten into a prune.

20 I WOULD HAVE THE JOB. I WOULD BE A CONDUCTORETTE AND SLING A FULL MONEY CHANGER FROM MY BELT. I WOULD.

21 The next three weeks were a honeycomb of determination with apertures for the days to go in and out. The Negro organizations to whom I appealed for support bounced me back and forth like a shuttlecock on a

badminton court. Why did I insist on that particular job? Openings were going begging that paid nearly twice the money. The minor officials with whom I was able to win an audience thought me mad. Possibly I was.

22   Downtown San Francisco became alien and cold, and the streets I had loved in a personal familiarity were unknown lanes that twisted with malicious intent. Old buildings, whose gray rococo façades housed my memories of the Forty-Niners, and Diamond Lil, Robert Service, Sutter and Jack London, were then imposing structures viciously joined to keep me out. My trips to the streetcar office were of the frequency of a person on salary. The struggle expanded. I was no longer in conflict only with the Market Street Railway but with the marble lobby of the building which housed its offices, and elevators and their operators.

23   During this period of strain Mother and I began our first steps on the long path toward mutual adult admiration. She never asked for reports and I didn't offer any details. But every morning she made breakfast, gave me carfare and lunch money, as if I were going to work. She comprehended the perversity of life, that in the struggle lies the joy. That I was no glory seeker was obvious to her, and that I had to exhaust every possibility before giving in was also clear.

24   On my way out of the house one morning she said, "Life is going to give you just what you put in it. Put your whole heart in everything you do, and pray, then you can wait." Another time she reminded me that "God helps those who help themselves." She had a store of aphorisms which she dished out as the occasion demanded. Strangely, as bored as I was with clichés, her inflection gave them something new, and set me thinking for a little while at least. Later when asked how I got my job, I was never able to say exactly. I only knew that one day, which was tiresomely like all the others before it, I sat in the Railway office, ostensibly waiting to be interviewed. The receptionist called me to her desk and shuffled a bundle of papers to me. They were job application forms. She said they had to be filled in triplicate. I had little time to wonder if I had won or not, for the standard questions reminded me of the necessity for dexterous lying. How old was I? List my previous jobs, starting from the last held and go backward to the first. How much money did I earn, and why did I leave the position? Give two references (not relatives).

25   Sitting at a side table my mind and I wove a cat's ladder of near truths and total lies. I kept my face blank (an old art) and wrote quickly the fable of Marguerite Johnson, aged nineteen, former companion and driver for Mrs. Annie Henderson (a White Lady) in Stamps, Arkansas.

26   I was given blood tests, aptitude tests, physical coordination tests, and Rorschachs, then on a blissful day I was hired as the first Negro on the San Francisco streetcars.

27   Mother gave me the money to have my blue serge suit tailored, and I learned to fill out work cards, operate the money changer and punch transfers. The time crowded together and at an End of Days I was swinging on

the back of the rackety trolley, smiling sweetly and persuading my charges to "step forward in the car, please."

28   For one whole semester the street cars and I shimmied up and scooted down the sheer hills of San Francisco. I lost some of my need for the Black ghetto's shielding-sponge quality, as I clanged and cleared my way down Market Street, with its honky-tonk homes for homeless sailors, past the quiet retreat of Golden Gate Park and along closed undwelled-in-looking dwellings of the Sunset District.

29   My work shifts were split so haphazardly that it was easy to believe that my superiors had chosen them maliciously. Upon mentioning my suspicions to Mother, she said, "Don't worry about it. You ask for what you want, and you pay for what you get. And I'm going to show you that it ain't no trouble when you pack double."

30   She stayed awake to drive me out to the car barn at four thirty in the mornings, or to pick me up when I was relieved just before dawn. Her awareness of life's perils convinced her that while I would be safe on the public conveyances, she "wasn't about to trust a taxi driver with her baby."

31   When the spring classes began, I resumed my commitment with formal education. I was so much wiser and older, so much more independent, with a bank account and clothes that I had bought for myself, that I was sure that I had learned and earned the magic formula which would make me a part of the gay life my contemporaries led.

32   Not a bit of it. Within weeks, I realized that my schoolmates and I were on paths moving diametrically away from each other. They were concerned and excited over the approaching football games, but I had in my immediate past raced a car down a dark and foreign Mexican mountain. They concentrated great interest on who was worthy of being student body president, and when the metal bands would be removed from their teeth, while I remembered sleeping for a month in a wrecked automobile and conducting a streetcar in the uneven hours of the morning.

33   Without willing it, I had gone from being ignorant of being ignorant to being aware of being aware. And the worst part of my awareness was that I didn't know what I was aware of. I knew I knew very little, but I was certain that the things I had yet to learn wouldn't be taught to me at George Washington High School.

34   I began to cut classes, to walk in Golden Gate Park or wander along the shiny counter of the Emporium Department Store. When Mother discovered that I was playing truant, she told me that if I didn't want to go to school one day, if there were no tests being held, and if my school work was up to standard, all I had to do was tell her and I could stay home. She said that she didn't want some white woman calling her up to tell her something about her child that she didn't know. And she didn't want to be put in the position of lying to a white woman because I wasn't woman enough to speak up. That put an end to my truancy, but nothing appeared to lighten the long gloomy day that going to school became.

35   To be left alone on the tightrope of youthful unknowing is to experience the excruciating beauty of full freedom and the threat of eternal indecision. Few, if any, survive their teens. Most surrender to the vague but murderous pressure of adult conformity. It becomes easier to die and avoid conflict than to maintain a constant battle with the superior forces of maturity.

36   Until recently each generation found it more expedient to plead guilty to the charge of being young and ignorant, easier to take the punishment meted out by the older generation (which had itself confessed to the same crime short years before). The command to grow up at once was more bearable than the faceless horror of wavering purpose, which was youth.

37   The bright hours when the young rebelled against the descending sun had to give way to twenty-four-hour periods called "days" that were named as well as numbered.

38   The Black female is assaulted in her tender years by all those common forces of nature at the same time that she is caught in the tripartite crossfire of masculine prejudice, white illogical hate and Black lack of power.

39   The fact that the adult American Negro female emerges a formidable character is often met with amazement, distaste and even belligerence. It is seldom accepted as an inevitable outcome of the struggle won by survivors and deserves respect if not enthusiastic acceptance.

BUILDING CONTEXT

1. Why is it significant to Angelou, as a woman and a black, that this experience occurred during World War II? In what ways did the war change things for women and blacks? For other groups?

2. Trace the formation of Angelou's sense of identity. With which group(s) does she originally identify? What makes her reject these and align herself with others? Compare her experience to those of Cameron and Ferber.

FURTHER STUDY

1. Compare the relationship of Angelou and the receptionist to other situations in which women, minorities, ethnic groups, or subordinates are pitted against each other by powerful, but invisible, forces.

2. Why does Angelou believe that it is inevitable that "the adult American Negro female emerges a formidable character"? Does the same reasoning apply to other "survivors"? Compare and contrast other groups with similar experiences.

ADDITIONAL RESOURCES

Cade, Toni, ed. *The Black Woman.* New York: Bantam Books, 1970.

Franklin, John Hope. *Racial Equality in America.* Chicago: University of Chicago Press, 1976.

Sterling, Dorothy. *We Are Your Sisters.* New York: W. W. Norton, 1984.

RESEARCH KEYWORDS

African Americans   Feminism

Women—U.S.   Race Relations

EXPLORING CRITICAL ISSUES THROUGH WRITING

1. Explore the formation of self-image and group identity. What makes a person choose allegiance to a group, or change allegiances? To what extent is identity imposed by others? You might want to compare two or three of the autobiographical selections.

2. Analyze the connection between equality and identity. Trace how equality in America has changed in response to the changing definitions of "us versus them." Associate this to the experiences of groups that achieve equality while retaining their identities.

3. Explore the place of immigration and attitudes toward immigrants in the history of the United States. Compare, for example, the views of Crève-coeur, Booker T. Washington, Sinclair, or Goldman.

4. Goldman claims that in answering their critics, feminists overstated the virtues and purity of women. Why did this undermine the position of women? What similar situations exist today? Relate Goldman's beliefs about women to those of Stowe, Angelou, Millet, or current feminists and politicians.

5. Some critics argue that Americans ascribe nobility to victims; that is, we assume that defeated natives must have been innocent, that people who suffer discrimination learn compassion, and that the election of women and minorities will clean up politics. Discuss and evaluate reading selections, books, or movies that seem to perpetuate this reasoning. You might want to start with Garrison's disagreement with Douglass about the status of slaves in abolitionism.

6. Examine the dynamics of situations in which women, minorities, ethnic groups, or subordinates are pitted against each other by powerful, but invisible, forces. Recall the incident involving Angelou and the receptionist, or include an experience of your own.

7. Why does Angelou believe that it is inevitable that "the adult American Negro female emerges a formidable character"? Does the same reasoning

apply to other "survivors"? Compare and contrast other groups with similar experiences.

8. Research the history of nativist or populist parties in the United States. What issues concern them? What influence have they had in this country? Consider, for example, the end of the nineteenth century or the period between the two world wars.

9. To what extent was the fear expressed by Henry James justified? How have immigrants and minorities changed English language and literature?

10. Investigate the American reaction to Nazism or fascism during the 1930s. In what ways are these movements similar to American nativist and populist movements?

11. Argue whether certain ideas are inherently foreign to particular cultures or races. Why is democracy, for example, successful in some countries but not in others? Why was communism never very popular in the United States?

12. Explore an idea that caught your interest, charmed or provoked you, or supported or challenged your own beliefs. Place this issue within a larger context and explain its significance.

11

$\mathcal{P}$URSUING EQUALITY:
1950–1980

"We conclude that in the field of public education the doctrine of 'separate but equal' has no place."

Brown v. Board of Education

"One of the chief effects of class within patriarchy is to set one woman against another."

Kate Millett

"The first requirement for . . . the Positive Woman is to understand the differences between men and women."

Phyllis Schlafly

After World War II, the United States enjoyed a burst of economic growth and prosperity. Opportunity abounded—for with all of Europe in ruins, only America could supply the money and materials to rebuild the devastated nations. At home, industries freed from war production could finally satisfy the pent-up demands of consumers. Homes, cars, and televisions were bought as fast as they could be produced. Demand created jobs that put money in the hands of workers who in turn created more demands and more jobs. The circle seemed endless, and Americans took for granted that they would be better off than their parents, and their children would enjoy even greater wealth.

African Americans also shared in the general prosperity, though to a lesser degree. During the war, President Roosevelt had banned racial discrimination in defense industries; after the war, President Truman ended segregation in the armed forces. Then in *Brown* v. *Board of Education,* the Supreme Court ruled that "separate but equal" schools were inherently unequal, thus setting the stage to overturn all the Jim Crow laws that had been sanctioned for sixty years by *Plessy* v. *Ferguson.*

The fly in the ointment of good times was communism. Russia, America's wartime ally against Germany and Japan, occupied the lands her armies liberated. Communist regimes were established in East Germany, Poland, Hungary, and elsewhere. The Red Chinese drove the Nationalists from the mainland. There was fear that the Communist Bloc had or would soon acquire the atomic bomb. The United States found herself fighting a war in Korea and hunting communists at home. A deep malaise gripped the country as people wondered which was worse, the possibility of subversion or the excesses of McCarthyism.

The election of John F. Kennedy in 1960 revived the hopes of many Americans. His youthfulness seemed to signal the passing of the torch to a new generation. His vision of a New Frontier invoked the myth of pioneers forging America's destiny, and his call for national service brought thousands of volunteers into the Peace Corps. He also supported the African Americans' struggle for full civil rights.

The leader of that struggle was Martin Luther King, Jr., a Southern pastor committed to nonviolent disobedience of unjust laws. Under his moral guidance, thousands of black and white "Freedom Riders" attempted to desegregate bus terminals, restaurants, and other public facilities. Many were beaten or arrested; several were killed. King himself was murdered in 1968, an act that ignited riots in many cities.

Encouraged by the Civil Rights Movement, women also found new strength. Feminists rediscovered Simone de Beauvoir's *The Second Sex,* first published in 1949, which surveyed the contributions of biology, anthropology, sociology, and literature to an understanding of sex differences. Betty Friedan taught in *The Feminine Mystique* (1963) that feelings that had been dismissed as neuroses in women actually stemmed from structural flaws in

society. The power of Kate Millett's *Sexual Politics* also received an overwhelming response. Victory followed victory. Congress approved the Equal
Rights Amendment during the 1971 and 1972 sessions; ratification by the
states seemed assured. And in 1973, the Supreme Court declared in *Roe* v.
Wade that state laws prohibiting abortion violate the constitutional right of
privacy.

But not all women supported every feminist issue. Some women, for example, supported equal pay for equal work but opposed abortion; others
wanted stricter alimony laws but did not want to see women in combat.
And some, like Phyllis Schlafly in *The Power of the Positive Woman,* believed
that sex differences serve a divine plan.

Brown **v. Board of
Education (1954)**

"We conclude that in the field of public education the doctrine
of 'separate but equal' has no place. Separate educational facilities
are inherently unequal."*

The primary racial issue in the early nineteenth century had been slavery;
by the first half of the twentieth century, it was segregation. Soon after
Plessy v. *Ferguson* had given judicial sanction to "separate but equal" facilities on trains and public accommodations, blacks and whites throughout
the South had separate restrooms, water fountains, and entrances to stores.
Social interaction between the races was blocked to every possible extent;
when it did occur, blacks were clearly subordinated to the whites.

While Booker T. Washington had disavowed any social "forcing," his prediction that economic freedom would lead to integration did not materialize.
His theory was not disproved; rather, African Americans were not given the
opportunity to compete as equals and thus develop an economic base. As the
President's Committee on Civil Rights noted in its 1947 report, the South's
segregated school system was the major cause of inequality. By whatever
criterion one used—expenditure per student, breadth of curriculum, length
of school year, ratio of students to teachers, or adequacy of facilities—the

Committee found that "separate but equal" schools did not exist, and urged that schools for blacks be improved.

As early as 1905, leaders of the Niagara Movement demanded an end to racial discrimination, and with the banning of white-only primaries in 1927, the Supreme Court started moving slowly in that direction. When, therefore, the parents of Linda Brown and other African-American children sued for the right of blacks to attend the better equipped white schools, the Court decided that the time had come to examine the very doctrine of "separate but equal." In the 1954 case of *Brown* v. *Board of Education,* Chief Justice Earl Warren applied historical analysis and the science of psychology in defending the legal decision that would change the entire public social structure of America.

Text: Leon Friedman and Fred L. Israel, eds.; *The Justices of the United States Supreme Court 1789–1969: Their Lives and Major Opinions,* Vol. IV; New York: Chelsea House, 1969.

EXPLORING ISSUES IN THE TEXT

1. Explain the complaint of the plaintiffs (pars. 2–3). Why did they feel their children's schools were inadequate?

2. Summarize the Court's finding about the context in which the Fourteenth Amendment was passed (par. 4).

3. Trace the changing nature of public schools (pars. 5, 8–9). How is this change central to the Court's reasoning? Connect this rationale to the idea of America's mission.

4. Analyze how the Court decided that "separate but equal" schools are "inherently unequal" (pars. 10–11). What is the Court's concept of equality?

BROWN v. *BOARD OF EDUCATION*

1   These cases come to us from the States of Kansas, South Carolina, Virginia, and Delaware. They are premised on different facts and different local conditions, but a common legal question justifies their consideration together in this consolidated opinion.

2   In each of the cases, minors of the Negro race, through their legal representatives, seek the aid of the courts in obtaining admission to the public schools of their community on a nonsegregated basis. In each instance, they have been denied admission to schools attended by white children under laws requiring or permitting segregation according to race. This segregation was alleged to deprive the plaintiffs of the equal protection of the laws under the Fourteenth Amendment. In each of the cases other than the Delaware case, a three-judge federal district court denied relief to the plaintiffs on the so-called "separate but equal" doctrine announced by this

Court in *Plessy* v. *Ferguson,* 163 U.S. 537. Under that doctrine, equality of treatment is accorded when the races are provided substantially equal facilities, even though these facilities be separate. In the Delaware case, the Supreme Court of Delaware adhered to that doctrine, but ordered that the plaintiffs be admitted to the white schools because of their superiority to the Negro schools.

3   The plaintiffs contend that segregated public schools are not "equal" and cannot be made "equal," and that hence they are deprived of the equal protection of the laws. Because of the obvious importance of the question presented, the Court took jurisdiction. Argument was heard in the 1952 Term, and reargument was heard this Term on certain questions propounded by the Court.

4   Reargument was largely devoted to the circumstances surrounding the adoption of the Fourteenth Amendment in 1868. It covered exhaustively consideration of the Amendment in Congress, ratification by the states, then existing practices in racial segregation, and the views of proponents and opponents of the Amendment. This discussion and our own investigation convince us that, although these sources cast some light, it is not enough to resolve the problem with which we are faced. At best, they are inconclusive. The most avid proponents of the post-War Amendments undoubtedly intended them to remove all distinctions among "all persons born or naturalized in the United States." Their opponents, just as certainly, were antagonistic to both the letter and the spirit of the Amendments and wished them to have the most limited effect. What others in Congress and the state legislatures had in mind cannot be determined with any degree of certainty.

5   An additional reason for the inconclusive nature of the Amendment's history, with respect to segregated schools, is the status of public education at that time. In the South, the movement toward free common schools, supported by general taxation, had not yet taken hold. Education of white children was largely in the hands of private groups. Education of Negroes was almost nonexistent, and practically all of the race were illiterate. In fact, any education of Negroes was forbidden by law in some states. Today, in contrast, many Negroes have achieved outstanding success in the arts and sciences as well as in the business and professional world. It is true that public school education at the time of the Amendment had advanced further in the North, but the effect of the Amendment on Northern States was generally ignored in the congressional debates. Even in the North, the conditions of public education did not approximate those existing today. The curriculum was usually rudimentary; ungraded schools were common in rural areas; the school term was but three months a year in many states; and compulsory school attendance was virtually unknown. As a consequence, it is not surprising that there should be so little in the history of the Fourteenth Amendment relating to its intended effect on public education.

6   In the first cases in this Court construing the Fourteenth Amendment, decided shortly after its adoption, the Court interpreted it as proscribing all state-imposed discriminations against the Negro race. The doctrine of "separate but equal" did not make its appearance in this Court until 1896 in the case of *Plessy* v. *Ferguson, supra,* involving not education but transportation. American courts have since labored with the doctrine for over half a century. In this Court, there have been six cases involving the "separate but equal" doctrine in the field of public education. . . . In none of these cases was it necessary to re-examine the doctrine to grant relief to the Negro plaintiff. And in *Sweatt* v. *Painter, supra,* the Court expressly reserved decision on the question whether *Plessy* v. *Ferguson* should be held inapplicable to public education.

7   In the instant cases, that question is directly presented. Here, unlike *Sweatt* v. *Painter,* there are findings below that the Negro and white schools involved have been equalized, or are being equalized, with respect to buildings, curricula, qualifications and salaries of teachers, and other "tangible" factors. Our decision, therefore, cannot turn on merely a comparison of these tangible factors in the Negro and white schools involved in each of the cases. We must look instead to the effect of segregation itself on public education.

8   In approaching this problem, we cannot turn the clock back to 1868 when the Amendment was adopted, or even to 1896 when *Plessy* v. *Ferguson* was written. We must consider public education in the light of its full development and its present place in American life throughout the Nation. Only in this way can it be determined if segregation in public schools deprives these plaintiffs of the equal protection of the laws.

9   Today, education is perhaps the most important function of state and local governments. Compulsory school attendance laws and the great expenditures for education both demonstrate our recognition of the importance of education to our democratic society. It is required in the performance of our most basic public responsibilities, even service in the armed forces. It is the very foundation of good citizenship. Today it is a principal instrument in awakening the child to cultural values, in preparing him for later professional training, and in helping him to adjust normally to his environment. In these days, it is doubtful that any child may reasonably be expected to succeed in life if he is denied the opportunity of an education. Such an opportunity, where the state has undertaken to provide it, is a right which must be made available to all on equal terms.

10   We come then to the question presented. Does segregation of children in public schools solely on the basis of race, even though the physical facilities and other "tangible" factors may be equal, deprive the children of the minority group of equal educational opportunities? We believe that it does.

11   In *Sweatt* v. *Painter, supra,* in finding that a segregated law school for Negroes could not provide them equal educational opportunities, this Court relied in large part on "those qualities which are incapable of objective

measurement but which make for greatness in a law school." In *McLaurin v. Oklahoma State Regents, supra,* the Court, in requiring that a Negro admitted to a white graduate school be treated like all other students, again resorted to intangible considerations: ". . . his ability to study, to engage in discussions and exchange views with other students, and, in general, to learn his profession." Such considerations apply with added force to children in grade and high schools. To separate them from others of similar age and qualifications solely because of their race generates a feeling of inferiority as to their status in the community that may affect their hearts and minds in a way unlikely ever to be undone. The effect of this separation on their educational opportunities was well stated by a finding in the Kansas case by a court which nevertheless felt compelled to rule against the Negro plaintiffs:

> Segregation of white and colored children in public schools has a detrimental effect upon the colored children. The impact is greater when it has the sanction of the law; for the policy of separating the races is usually interpreted as denoting the inferiority of the negro group. A sense of inferiority affects the motivation of a child to learn. Segregation with the sanction of law, therefore, has a tendency to [retard] the educational and mental development of negro children and to deprive them of some of the benefits they would receive in a racial[ly] integrated school system.

Whatever may have been the extent of psychological knowledge at the time of *Plessy* v. *Ferguson,* this finding is amply supported by modern authority. Any language in *Plessy* v. *Ferguson* contrary to this finding is rejected.

12   We conclude that in the field of public education the doctrine of "separate but equal" has no place. Separate educational facilities are inherently unequal. Therefore, we hold that the plaintiffs and others similarly situated for whom the actions have been brought are, by reason of the segregation complained of, deprived of the equal protection of the laws guaranteed by the Fourteenth Amendment. . . .

BUILDING CONTEXT

1. Contrast the *Brown* and *Plessy* interpretations of the constitutional guarantee of equality. Describe how each decision reflects its era and social context.

2. Compare the views of *Brown* and *Plessy* regarding the relationship between the government and the individual. On what basis does *Brown* overturn *Plessy?*

3. Compare *Brown* to another reading selection that expands the concept of equality. Analyze the reasoning used in both selections.

Another Voice

SOUTHERN CONGRESSMEN
OPPOSE *BROWN*

Negative reaction to Brown *was swift and often violent. White parents kept their children away from integrated schools, black students were spat upon and attacked, police even barred black students from entering schools. In 1957, President Eisenhower sent federal troops to Little Rock, Arkansas, to end this defiance of the court decision.*

In the midst of the crisis, in March 1956, ninety-six Southern congressmen issued the following statement:

. . . As admitted by the Supreme Court in the public school case (*Brown* v. *Board of Education*), the doctrine of separate but equal schools "apparently originated in *Roberts* v. *City of Boston* (1849), upholding school segregation against attack as being violative of a state constitutional guarantee of equality." This constitutional doctrine began in the North—not in the South—and it was followed not only in Massachusetts but in Connecticut, New York, Illinois, Indiana, Michigan, Minnesota, New Jersey, Ohio, Pennsylvania and other northern states until they, exercising their rights as states through the constitutional processes of local self-government, changed their school systems.

In the case of *Plessy* v. *Ferguson* in 1896 the Supreme Court expressly declared that under the Fourteenth Amendment no person was denied any of his rights if the states provided separate but equal public facilities. This decision has been followed in many other cases. It is notable that the Supreme Court, speaking through Chief Justice Taft, a former President of the United States, unanimously declared in 1927 in *Lum* v. *Rice* that the "separate but equal" principle is ". . . within the discretion of the state in regulating its public schools and does not conflict with the Fourteenth Amendment."

This interpretation, restated time and again, became a part of the life of the people of many of the states and confirmed their habits, customs, traditions and way of life. It is founded on elemental humanity and common sense, for parents should not be deprived by Government of the right to direct the lives and education of their own children.

continued

continued from previous page

Though there has been no constitutional amendment or act of Congress changing this established legal principle almost a century old, the Supreme Court of the United States, with no legal basis for such action, undertook to exercise their naked judicial power and substituted their personal political and social ideas for the established law of the land

This unwarranted exercise of power by the court, contrary to the Constitution, is creating chaos and confusion in the states principally affected. It is destroying the amicable relations between the white and Negro races that have been created through ninety years of patient effort by the good people of both races. It has planted hatred and suspicion where there has been heretofore friendship and understanding.

Without regard to the consent of the governed, outside agitators are threatening immediate and revolutionary changes in our public school systems. If done, this is certain to destroy the system of public education in some of the states.

With the gravest concern for the explosive and dangerous condition created by this decision and inflamed by outside meddlers:

We reaffirm our reliance on the Constitution as the fundamental law of the land.

We decry the Supreme Court's encroachments on rights reserved to the states and to the people, contrary to established law and to the Constitution.

We commend the motives of those states which have declared the intention to resist forced integration by any lawful means. . . .

Congressional Record, 84th Congress

FURTHER STUDY

1. Investigate the social and economic changes that took place in America during the first half of the twentieth century. Assess how these changes might have influenced the decision in *Brown.*

2. Explore the relevance of *Brown* to the contrasting views of Frederick Douglass, Booker T. Washington, and W. E. B. Du Bois. For example, can African Americans receive justice from an all-white court? Can—or must—social integration be forced?

3. Investigate the impact of *Brown* upon the history of segregation after 1954.

ADDITIONAL RESOURCES

Franklin, John Hope. *Racial Equality in America.* Chicago: University of Chicago Press, 1976.

Kluger, Richard. *Simple Justice: The History of Brown v. Board of Education and Black America's Struggle for Equality.* New York: Alfred A. Knopf, 1976.

Woodward, C. Vann. *The Strange Career of Jim Crow,* 3d ed. New York: Oxford University Press, 1974.

RESEARCH KEYWORDS

Separate but Equal	Segregation	Jim Crow
Fourteenth Amendment	Warren (Earl)	Supreme Court
Civil Rights		

JOHN F. KENNEDY
Nomination Acceptance Speech **(1960)**

"We stand today on the edge of a New Frontier . . . a frontier of unknown opportunities and perils—a frontier of unfulfilled hopes and threats."

The public considered the election of John F. Kennedy (1917–1963) as president in 1960 to be particularly significant, with many sharing a sense that the torch had been passed to a new generation. While historians today find much to praise in the presidency of Dwight D. Eisenhower, by the end of his second term many Americans considered him a kindly old grandfather who ignored the nation's business while passing his time on the golf course. In contrast, Kennedy, only forty-three years old, projected an aura of youth, vigor, and passion. The young television industry worked especially in his favor, as his good looks and ready wit impressed viewers of the nation's first televised presidential debates.

Despite his strengths, however, his candidacy suffered because of religious prejudice: Kennedy was Catholic, and no Catholic had ever been elected president. Even Al Smith, the popular governor of New York, fell victim to nationwide anti-Catholic bias in the presidential campaign of 1928. In his nomination acceptance speech at the Democratic Party Convention in Los Angeles, Kennedy directly addressed this issue, assuring voters that his religion did not interfere with his loyalty to the nation. Ironically, in the manner

of seventeenth-century Puritan oratory, the speech is rich in Biblical allusions and quotations.

Although he supported the failed Bay of Pigs invasion of Cuba to overthrow its communist government, Kennedy's brief tenure in office was
marked by great enthusiasm and hope. Thousands of young people volun-
teered to serve in the Peace Corps that he established, and his bill to protect
the civil rights of African Americans was in congressional committee when
he was assassinated in 1963.

Text: John F. Kennedy; "Nomination Acceptance Speech"; in Charles Hurd, ed., *A Treasury of
Great American Speeches*, Rev. ed.; New York: Hawthorn Books, 1970.

EXPLORING ISSUES IN THE TEXT

1. Summarize how Kennedy confronts the problem of religious prejudice
   (pars. 1–2). What does his promise imply about his religious commitment? Why does he refer to the situations in other countries?

2. List the changes Kennedy identifies as taking place in the world (pars.
   4–5) and at home (pars. 6–11).

3. Explain how Kennedy uses the myth of the American frontier for his
   own purposes (pars. 13–15). How accurate is his statement that the
   motto of the pioneers was not "every man for himself"?

4. Define the New Frontier (pars. 17–24). In what ways does it differ from
   the New Freedom and the New Deal? How does it harness the nation's
   sense of mission?

5. Consider the significance of the biblical allusions throughout the speech
   (for example, pars. 18, 27).

NOMINATION ACCEPTANCE SPEECH

1   I am fully aware of the fact that the Democratic party, by nominating
someone of my faith, has taken on what many regard as a new and hazardous risk—new, at least, since 1928. But I look at it this way: the Democratic party has once again placed its confidence in the American people,
and in their ability to render a free, fair judgment. And you have, at the
same time, placed your confidence in me, and in my ability to render a
free, fair judgment—to uphold the Constitution and my oath of office—and
to reject any kind of religious pressure or obligation that might directly or
indirectly interfere with my conduct of the presidency in the national interest. My record of fourteen years supporting public education—supporting complete separation of church and state—and resisting pressure from
any source on any issue should be clear by now to everyone.

2   I hope that no American, considering the really critical issues facing this country, will waste his franchise by voting either for me or against me solely on account of my religious affiliation. It is not relevant, I want to stress, what some other political or religious leader may have said on this subject. It is not relevant what abuses may have existed in other countries or in other times. It is not relevant what pressures, if any, might conceivably be brought to bear on me. I am telling you now what you are entitled to know: that my decisions on every public policy will be my own—as an American, a Democrat and a free man. . . .

3   Today our concern must be with that future. For the world is changing. The old era is ending. The old ways will not do.

4   Abroad the balance of power is shifting. There are new and more terrible weapons—new and uncertain nations—new pressures of population and deprivation. One third of the world, it has been said, may be free—but one third is the victim of cruel repression—and the other one third is rocked by the pangs of poverty, hunger and envy. More energy is released by the awakening of these new nations than by the fission of the atom itself.

5   Meanwhile, Communist influence has penetrated further into Asia, stood astride the Middle East and now festers some ninety miles off the coast of Florida. Friends have slipped into neutrality—and neutrals into hostility. . . .

6   Here at home, the changing face of the future is equally revolutionary. The New Deal and the Fair Deal were bold measures for their generations—but this is a new generation.

7   A technological revolution on the farm has led to an output explosion—but we have not yet learned to harness that explosion usefully, while protecting our farmers' right to full parity income.

8   An urban population revolution has overcrowded our schools, cluttered up our suburbs, and increased the squalor of our slums.

9   A peaceful revolution for human rights—demanding an end to racial discrimination in all parts of our community life—has strained at the leashes imposed by timid executive leadership.

10   A medical revolution has extended the life of our elder citizens without providing the dignity and security those later years deserve. And a revolution of automation finds machines replacing men in the mines and mills of America, without replacing their income or their training or their need to pay the family doctor, grocer and landlord.

11   There has also been a change—a slippage—in our intellectual and moral strength. Seven lean years of drouth and famine have withered the field of ideas. Blight has descended on our regulatory agencies—and a dry rot, beginning in Washington, is seeping into every corner of America—in the payola mentality, the expense account way of life, the confusion between what is legal and what is right. Too many Americans have lost their way, their will and their sense of historic purpose.

12   It is time, in short, for a new generation of leadership—new men to cope with new problems and new opportunities. . . .

13   For I stand tonight facing West on what was once the last frontier. From the lands that stretch three thousand miles behind me, the pioneers of old gave up their safety, their comfort and sometimes their lives to build a new world here in the West. They were not the captives of their own doubts, the prisoners of their own price tags. Their motto was not "every man for himself"—but "all for the common cause." They were determined to make that new world strong and free, to overcome its hazards and its hardships, to conquer the enemies that threatened from without and within.

14   Today some would say that those struggles are all over—that all the horizons have been explored—that all the battles have been won—that there is no longer an American frontier.

15   But I trust that no one in this vast assemblage will agree with those sentiments. For the problems are not all solved and the battles are not all won—and we stand today on the edge of a New Frontier—the frontier of the 1960's—a frontier of unknown opportunities and perils—a frontier of unfulfilled hopes and threats.

16   Woodrow Wilson's New Freedom promised our nation a new political and economic framework. Franklin Roosevelt's New Deal promised security and succor to those in need. But the New Frontier of which I speak is not a set of promises—it is a set of challenges. It sums up not what I intend to *offer* the American people, but what I intend to *ask* of them. It appeals to their pride, not their pocketbook—it holds out the promise of more sacrifice instead of more security.

17   But I tell you the New Frontier is here, whether we seek it or not. Beyond that frontier are uncharted areas of science and space, unsolved problems of peace and war, unconquered pockets of ignorance and prejudice, unanswered questions of poverty and surplus. It would be easier to shrink back from that frontier, to look to the safe mediocrity of the past, to be lulled by good intentions and high rhetoric—and those who prefer that course should not cast their votes for me, regardless of party.

18   But I believe the times demand invention, innovation, imagination, decision. I am asking each of you to be new pioneers on that New Frontier. My call is to the young in heart, regardless of age—to the stout in spirit, regardless of party—to all who respond to the Scriptural call: "Be strong and of good courage; be not afraid, neither be thou dismayed."

19   For courage—not complacency, is our need today—leadership—not salesmanship. And the only valid test of leadership is the ability to lead, and lead vigorously. A tired nation, said David Lloyd George, is a Tory nation—and the United States today cannot afford to be either tired or Tory.

20   There may be those who wish to hear more—more promises to this group or that—more harsh rhetoric about the men in the Kremlin—more assurances of a golden future, where taxes are always low and subsidies ever high. But my promises are in the platform you have adopted—our ends will not be won by rhetoric and we can have faith in the future only if we have faith in ourselves.

21   For the harsh facts of the matter are that we stand on this frontier at a turning-point in history. We must prove all over again whether this nation—or any nation so conceived—can long endure—whether our society—with its freedom of choice, its breadth of opportunity, its range of alternatives—can compete with the single-minded advance of the Communist system.

22   Can a nation organized and governed such as ours endure? That is the real question. Have we the nerve and the will? Can we carry through in an age where we will witness not only new breakthroughs in weapons of destruction—but also a race for mastery of the sky and the rain, the ocean and the tides, the far side of space and the inside of men's minds?

23   Are we up to the task—are we equal to the challenge? Are we willing to match the Russian sacrifice of the present for the future—or must we sacrifice our future in order to enjoy the present?

24   That is the question of the New Frontier. That is the choice our nation must make—a choice that lies not merely between two men or two parties, but between the public interest and private comfort—between national greatness and national decline—between the fresh air of progress and the stale, dank atmosphere of "normalcy"—between determined dedication and creeping mediocrity.

25   All mankind waits upon our decision. A whole world looks to see what we will do. We cannot fail their trust, we cannot fail to try.

26   It has been a long road from that first day in New Hampshire to this crowded convention city. Now begins another long journey, taking me into your cities and homes all over America. Give me your help, your hand, your voice, your vote. Recall with me the words of Isaiah: "They that wait upon the Lord shall renew their strength; they shall mount up with wings as eagles; they shall run, and not be weary."

27   As we face the coming challenge, we too, shall wait upon the Lord, and ask that He renew our strength. Then shall we be equal to the test. Then we shall not be weary. And then we shall prevail.

BUILDING CONTEXT

1. What does Kennedy's plight say about the predictions of Crèvecoeur and Tocqueville regarding religion in America? How does Conor Cruise O'Brien respond to Kennedy's situation?

2. Compare the function of religious imagery in the selections by Kennedy and Stowe. How integral is religion to each?

3. Relate Kennedy's image of the frontier to Turner's. Which is probably more accurate. Why?

FURTHER STUDY

1. Consider the place of religion in American politics since Kennedy's election. For example, how significant are religious arguments in the debate over abortion? How many politicians today feel compelled to disavow their religious commitments? Account for this change of perspective.

2. Explore the "Camelot" aspect of the Kennedy era. Why did he evoke such feelings in Americans? Connect this reaction to the image shared by many Americans of their country and its mission.

ADDITIONAL RESOURCES

Brown, Thomas. *JFK: History of an Image.* Bloomington: Indiana University Press, 1988.

Parmet, Herbert S. *JFK: The Presidency of John F. Kennedy.* New York: Dial Press, 1983.

White Theodore H. *The Making of the President, 1960.* New York: New American Library, 1967.

Wicker. Tom. *JFK and LBJ: The Influence of Personality upon Politics.* Baltimore: Penguin Books, 1969.

RESEARCH KEYWORDS

Kennedy Family	New Frontier	War on Poverty
Bay of Pigs Invasion	Cuban Missile Crisis	Historiography—U.S.
Presidents—U.S.	African Americans	

Another Voice

BIRMINGHAM CLERGYMEN APPEAL FOR LAW AND ORDER

In January 1963, eight clergymen issued "An Appeal for Law and Order and Common Sense," expressing their understanding of African-American grievances and urging a peaceful resolution through the courts. King's famous "Letter from Birmingham Jail" is a response to another public statement issued by these same clerics that April:

. . . Responsible citizens have undertaken to work on various problems which cause racial friction and unrest. In Birmingham, recent public events have given indication that we all have op-

continued

continued from previous page

portunity for a new constructive and realistic approach to racial problems.

However, we are now confronted by a series of demonstrations by some of our Negro citizens, directed and led in part by outsiders. We recognize the natural impatience of people who feel that their hopes are slow in being realized. But we are convinced that these demonstrations are unwise and untimely.

We agree rather with certain local Negro leadership which has called for honest and open negotiation of racial issues in our area. And we believe this kind of facing of issues can best be accomplished by citizens of our own metropolitan area, white and Negro, meeting with their knowledge and experience of the local situation. All of us need to face that responsibility and find proper channels for its accomplishment.

Just as we formerly pointed out that "hatred and violence have no sanction in our religious and political traditions," we also point out that such actions as incite to hatred and violence, however technically peaceful those actions may be, have not contributed to the resolution of our local problems. We do not believe that these days of new hope are days when extreme measures are justified in Birmingham. . . .

MARTIN LUTHER KING, JR.
"Letter from Birmingham Jail" (1963)

"*One has not only a legal but a moral responsibility to obey just laws. Conversely, one has a moral responsibility to disobey unjust laws.*"

Dr. Martin Luther King, Jr. (1929–1968) was the soul, and most visible martyr, of the Civil Rights struggle of the 1960s. As a young pastor in 1957, he led a black boycott against the segregated bus system of Montgomery, Alabama, later making such economic tactics a mainstay of the Southern Christian Leadership Conference, which he organized. By integrating Mahatma Gandhi's belief in nonviolence with Thoreau's civil disobedience, King captured a moral high ground—insisting that his followers would fill the nation's jails rather than acknowledge the legitimacy of unjust laws.

In April of 1963, during demonstrations in Birmingham, Alabama, King once again found himself in jail. When eight local clergymen released a statement calling the demonstrations "untimely" and labeling them incitements to "hatred and violence," King smuggled out a "letter" of reply. With concrete and piercing examples, he invokes the numerous humiliations suffered by African Americans—lynchings, poverty, exclusion, fear, emotional distress, and loss of identity. And, echoing the Biblical prophets and moral leaders of the past, he attacks the unethical behavior that hides behind unjust laws.

The following August, 200,000 black and white Americans demonstrated their support of civil rights in a march on Washington. In the shadow of the Lincoln Memorial, King electrified the nation with his "I Have a Dream" speech, a prophetic vision of "that day when all of God's children, black men and white men, Jews and Gentiles, Protestants and Catholics, will be able to join hands and sing in the words of the old Negro spiritual, 'Free at last! Free at last! Thank God Almighty, we are free at last!'"

Though opposed by "Black Power" militants, King was recognized as the preeminent African-American leader of his day. He won the Nobel Peace Prize in 1964—and was assassinated four years later.

Text: Thomas Klein et al., eds., Martin Luther King; "Letter from Birmingham Jail"; in *Great Ideas: Conversations between Past and Present;* Fort Worth, TX: Holt, Rinehart and Winston, 1991.

EXPLORING ISSUES IN THE TEXT

1. According to King, why is it unfair to ask blacks to be patient (pars. 13–14)?

2. Analyze the distinction between just and unjust laws (pars. 15–22). Explain the importance of King's willingness to accept punishment for breaking the law.

3. Discuss King's belief that his is the middle approach between two extremes in the African-American response to racism (pars. 27–28). Trace the logic by which King accepts the label of extremist (pars. 29–31).

4. Summarize King's disappointment with the churches' response (pars. 33–37). How does his identification with the church bolster his argument? Explain his use of irony to contrast the power of the early, outlawed church with the weak modern church (pars. 40–41).

5. Consider King's use of terms like "brother" and "sister" (for example, par. 23). Show the significance of this usage to his concept of equality and identity.

LETTER FROM BIRMINGHAM JAIL

My Dear Fellow Clergymen:

1 While confined here in the Birmingham city jail, I came across your recent statement calling my present activities "unwise and untimely." Seldom do I pause to answer criticism of my work and ideas. If I sought to answer all the criticisms that cross my desk, my secretaries would have little time for anything other than such correspondence in the course of the day, and I would have no time for constructive work. But since I feel that you are men of genuine good will and your criticisms are sincerely set forth, I want to try to answer your statement in what I hope will be patient and reasonable terms.

2 I think I should indicate why I am here in Birmingham, since you have been influenced by the view which argues against "outsiders coming in." I have the honor of serving as president of the Southern Christian Leadership Conference, an organization operating in every southern state, with headquarters in Atlanta, Georgia. We have some eighty-five affiliated organizations across the South, and one of them is the Alabama Christian Movement for Human Rights. Frequently we share staff, educational, and financial resources with our affiliates. Several months ago the affiliate here in Birmingham asked us to be on call to engage in a nonviolent direct-action program if such were deemed necessary. We readily consented, and when the hour came we lived up to our promise. So I, along with several members of my staff, am here because I was invited here. I am here because I have organizational ties here.

3 But more basically, I am in Birmingham because injustice is here. Just as the prophets of the eighth century B.C. left their villages and carried their "thus saith the Lord" far beyond the boundaries of their home towns, and just as the Apostle Paul left his village of Tarsus and carried the gospel of Jesus Christ to the far corners of the Greco-Roman world, so am I compelled to carry the gospel of freedom beyond my own home town. Like Paul, I must constantly respond to the Macedonian call for aid.

4 Moreover, I am cognizant of the interrelatedness of all communities and states. I cannot sit idly by in Atlanta and not be concerned about what happens in Birmingham. Injustice anywhere is a threat to justice everywhere. We are caught in an inescapable network of mutuality, tied in a single garment of destiny. Whatever affects one directly, affects all indirectly. Never again can we afford to live with the narrow, provincial

"outside agitator" idea. Anyone who lives inside the United States can never be considered an outsider anywhere within its bounds.

5   You deplore the demonstrations taking place in Birmingham. But your statement, I am sorry to say, fails to express a similar concern for the conditions that brought about the demonstrations. I am sure that none of you would want to rest content with the superficial kind of social analysis that deals merely with effects and does not grapple with underlying causes. It is unfortunate that demonstrations are taking place in Birmingham, but it is even more unfortunate that the city's white power structure left the Negro community with no alternative.

6   In any nonviolent campaign there are four basic steps: collection of the facts to determine whether injustices exist; negotiation; self-purification; and direct action. We have gone through all these steps in Birmingham. There can be no gainsaying the fact that racial injustice engulfs this community. Birmingham is probably the most thoroughly segregated city in the United States. Its ugly record of brutality is widely known. Negroes have experienced grossly unjust treatment in the courts. There have been more unsolved bombings of Negro homes and churches in Birmingham than in any other city in the nation. These are the hard, brutal facts of the case. On the basis of these conditions, Negro leaders sought to negotiate with the city fathers. But the latter consistently refused to engage in good-faith negotiation.

7   Then, last September, came the opportunity to talk with leaders of Birmingham's economic community. In the course of the negotiations, certain promises were made by the merchants—for example, to remove the stores' humiliating racial signs. On the basis of these promises, the Reverend Fred Shuttlesworth and the leaders of the Alabama Christian Movement for Human Rights agreed to a moratorium on all demonstrations. As the weeks and months went by, we realized that we were the victims of a broken promise. A few signs, briefly removed, returned; the others remained.

8   As in so many past experiences, our hopes had been blasted, and the shadow of deep disappointment settled upon us. We had no alternative except to prepare for direct action, whereby we would present our very bodies as a means of laying our case before the conscience of the local and the national community. Mindful of the difficulties involved, we decided to undertake a process of self-purification. We began a series of workshops on nonviolence, and we repeatedly asked ourselves: "Are you able to accept blows without retaliating?" "Are you able to endure the ordeal of jail?" We decided to schedule our direct-action program for the Easter season, realizing that except for Christmas, this is the main shopping period of the year. Knowing that a strong economic-withdrawal program would be the by-product of direct action, we felt that this would be the best time to bring pressure to bear on the merchants for the needed change.

9   Then it occurred to us that Birmingham's mayoral election was coming up in March, and we speedily decided to postpone action until after election day. When we discovered that the Commissioner of Public Safety, Eugene "Bull" Connor, had piled up enough votes to be in the run-off, we decided again to postpone action until the day after the run-off so that the demonstrations could not be used to cloud the issues. Like many others, we wanted to see Mr. Connor defeated, and to this end we endured postponement after postponement. Having aided in this community need, we felt that our direct-action program could be delayed no longer.

10   You may well ask, "Why direct action? Why sit-ins, marches, and so forth? Isn't negotiation a better path?" You are quite right in calling for negotiation. Indeed, this is the very purpose of direct action. Nonviolent direct action seeks to create such a crisis and foster such a tension that a community which has constantly refused to negotiate is forced to confront the issue. It seeks so to dramatize the issue that it can no longer be ignored. My citing the creation of tension as part of the work of the nonviolent-resister may sound rather shocking. But I must confess that I am not afraid of the word "tension." I have earnestly opposed violent tension, but there is a type of constructive, nonviolent tension which is necessary for growth. Just as Socrates felt that it was necessary to create a tension in the mind so that individuals would rise from the bondage of myths and half-truths to the unfettered realm of creative analysis and objective appraisal, so must we see the need for nonviolent gadflies to create the kind of tension in society that will help men rise from the dark depths of prejudice and racism to the majestic heights of understanding and brotherhood.

11   The purpose of our direct-action program is to create a situation so crisis-packed that it will inevitably open the door to negotiation. I therefore concur with you in your call for negotiation. Too long has our beloved Southland been bogged down in a tragic effort to live in monologue rather than dialogue.

12   One of the basic points in your statement is that the action that I and my associates have taken in Birmingham is untimely. Some have asked: "Why didn't you give the new city administration time to act?" The only answer that I can give to this query is that the new Birmingham administration must be prodded about as much as the outgoing one, before it will act. We are sadly mistaken if we feel that the election of Albert Boutwell as mayor will bring the millennium to Birmingham. While Mr. Boutwell is a much more gentle person than Mr. Connor, they are both segregationists, dedicated to maintenance of the status quo. I have hoped that Mr. Boutwell will be reasonable enough to see the futility of massive resistance to desegregation. But he will not see this without pressure from devotees of civil rights. My friends, I must say to you that we have not made a single gain in civil rights without determined legal

and nonviolent pressure. Lamentably, it is an historical fact that privileged groups seldom give up their privileges voluntarily. Individuals may see the moral light and voluntarily give up their unjust posture; but, as Reinhold Niebuhr has reminded us, groups tend to be more immoral than individuals.

13 We know through painful experience that freedom is never voluntarily given by the oppressor; it must be demanded by the oppressed. Frankly, I have yet to engage in a direct-action campaign that was "well timed" in the view of those who have not suffered unduly from the disease of segregation. For years now I have heard the word "Wait!" It rings in the ears of every Negro with piercing familiarity. This "Wait" has almost always meant "Never." We must come to see, with one of our distinguished jurists, that "justice too long delayed is justice denied."

14 We have waited for more than 340 years for our constitutional and God-given rights. The nations of Asia and Africa are moving with jetlike speed toward gaining political independence, but we still creep at horse-and-buggy pace toward gaining a cup of coffee at a lunch counter. Perhaps it is easy for those who have never felt the stinging darts of segregation to say, "Wait." But when you have seen vicious mobs lynch your mothers and fathers at will and drown your sisters and brothers at whim; when you have seen hate-filled policemen curse, kick, and even kill your black brothers and sisters; when you see the vast majority of your twenty million Negro brothers smothering in an airtight cage of poverty in the midst of an affluent society; when you suddenly find your tongue twisted and your speech stammering as you seek to explain to your six-year-old daughter why she can't go to the public amusement park that has just been advertised on television, and see tears welling up in her eyes when she is told that Funtown is closed to colored children, and see ominous clouds of inferiority beginning to form in her little mental sky, and see her beginning to distort her personality by developing an unconscious bitterness toward white people; when you have to concoct an answer for a five-year-old son who is asking, "Daddy, why do white people treat colored people so mean?"; when you take a cross-country drive and find it necessary to sleep night after night in the uncomfortable corners of your automobile because no motel will accept you; when you are humiliated day in and day out by nagging signs reading "white" and "colored"; when your first name becomes "nigger," your middle name becomes "boy" (however old you are) and your last name becomes "John," and your wife and mother are never given the respected title "Mrs."; when you are harried by day and haunted by night by the fact that you are a Negro, living constantly at tiptoe stance, never quite knowing what to expect next, and are plagued with inner fears and outer resentments; when you are forever fighting a degenerating sense of "nobodiness"—then you will understand why we find it difficult to wait. There comes a time when the cup of endurance runs over, and

men are no longer willing to be plunged into the abyss of despair. I hope, sirs, you can understand our legitimate and unavoidable impatience.

15   You express a great deal of anxiety over our willingness to break laws. This is certainly a legitimate concern. Since we so diligently urge people to obey the Supreme Court's decision of 1954 outlawing segregation in the public schools, at first glance it may seem rather paradoxical for us consciously to break laws. One may well ask: "How can you advocate breaking some laws and obeying others?" The answer lies in the fact that there are two types of laws: just and unjust. I would be the first to advocate obeying just laws. One has not only a legal but a moral responsibility to obey just laws. Conversely, one has a moral responsibility to disobey unjust laws. I would agree with St. Augustine that "an unjust law is no law at all."

16   Now, what is the difference between the two? How does one determine whether a law is just or unjust? A just law is a man-made code that squares with the moral law or the law of God. An unjust law is a code that is out of harmony with the moral law. To put it in the terms of St. Thomas Aquinas: An unjust law is a human law that is not rooted in eternal law and natural law. Any law that uplifts human personality is just. Any law that degrades human personality is unjust. All segregation statutes are unjust because segregation distorts the soul and damages the personality. It gives the segregator a false sense of superiority and the segregated a false sense of inferiority. Segregation, to use the terminology of the Jewish philosopher Martin Buber, substitutes an "I-it" relationship for an "I-thou" relationship and ends up relegating persons to the status of things. Hence segregation is not only politically, economically, and sociologically unsound, it is morally wrong and sinful. Paul Tillich has said that sin is separation. Is not segregation an existential expression of man's tragic separation, his awful estrangement, his terrible sinfulness? Thus it is that I can urge men to obey the 1954 decision of the Supreme Court, for it is morally right; and I can urge them to disobey segregation ordinances, for they are morally wrong.

17   Let us consider a more concrete example of just and unjust laws. An unjust law is a code that a numerical or power majority group compels a minority group to obey but does not make binding on itself. This is *difference* made legal. By the same token, a just law is a code that a majority compels a minority to follow and that it is willing to follow itself. This is *sameness* made legal.

18   Let me give another explanation. A law is unjust if it is inflicted on a minority that, as a result of being denied the right to vote, had no part in enacting or devising the law. Who can say that the legislature of Alabama which set up that state's segregation laws was democratically elected? Throughout Alabama all sorts of devious methods are used to prevent Negroes from becoming registered voters, and there are some counties in which, even though Negroes constitute a majority of the population,

not a single Negro is registered. Can any law enacted under such circumstances be considered democratically structured?

19   Sometimes a law is just on its face and unjust in its application. For instance, I have been arrested on a charge of parading without a permit. Now, there is nothing wrong in having an ordinance which requires a permit for a parade. But such an ordinance becomes unjust when it is used to maintain segregation and to deny citizens the First-Amendment privilege of peaceful assembly and protest.

20   I hope you are able to see the distinction I am trying to point out. In no sense do I advocate evading or defying the law, as would the rabid segregationist. That would lead to anarchy. One who breaks an unjust law must do so openly, lovingly, and with a willingness to accept the penalty. I submit that an individual who breaks a law that conscience tells him is unjust, and who willingly accepts the penalty of imprisonment in order to arouse the conscience of the community over its injustice, is in reality expressing the highest respect for law.

21   Of course, there is nothing new about this kind of civil disobedience. It was evidenced sublimely in the refusal of Shadrach, Meshach, and Abednego to obey the laws of Nebuchadnezzar, on the ground that a higher moral law was at stake. It was practiced superbly by the early Christians, who were willing to face hungry lions and the excruciating pain of chopping blocks rather than submit to certain unjust laws of the Roman Empire. To a degree, academic freedom is a reality today because Socrates practiced civil disobedience. In our own nation, the Boston Tea Party represented a massive act of civil disobedience.

22   We should never forget that everything Adolf Hitler did in Germany was "legal" and everything the Hungarian freedom fighters did in Hungary was "illegal." It was "illegal" to aid and comfort a Jew in Hitler's Germany. Even so, I am sure that, had I lived in Germany at the time, I would have aided and comforted my Jewish brothers. If today I lived in a Communist country where certain principles dear to the Christian faith are suppressed, I would openly advocate disobeying that country's antireligious laws.

23   I must make two honest confessions to you, my Christian and Jewish brothers. First, I must confess that over the past few years I have been gravely disappointed with the white moderate. I have almost reached the regrettable conclusion that the Negro's great stumbling block in his stride toward freedom is not the White Citizen's Counciler or the Ku Klux Klanner, but the white moderate, who is more devoted to "order" than to justice; who prefers a negative peace which is the absence of tension to a positive peace which is the presence of justice; who constantly says, "I agree with you in the goal you seek, but I cannot agree with your methods of direct action"; who paternalistically believes he can set the timetable for another man's freedom; who lives by a mythical concept of time and who constantly advises the Negro to wait for a "more convenient

season." Shallow understanding from people of good will is more frustrating than absolute misunderstanding from people of ill will. Lukewarm acceptance is much more bewildering than outright rejection.

24   I had hoped that the white moderate would understand that law and order exist for the purpose of establishing justice and that when they fail in this purpose they become the dangerously structured dams that block the flow of social progress. I had hoped that the white moderate would understand that the present tension in the South is a necessary phase of the transition from an obnoxious negative peace, in which the Negro passively accepted his unjust plight, to a substantive and positive peace, in which all men will respect the dignity and worth of human personality. Actually, we who engage in nonviolent direct action are not the creators of tension. We merely bring to the surface the hidden tension that is already alive. We bring it out in the open, where it can be seen and dealt with. Like a boil that can never be cured so long as it is covered up but must be opened with all its ugliness to the natural medicines of air and light, injustice must be exposed, with all the tension its exposure creates, to the light of human conscience and the air of national opinion, before it can be cured.

25   In your statement you assert that our actions, even though peaceful, must be condemned because they precipitate violence. But is this a logical assertion? Isn't this like condemning a robbed man because his possession of money precipitated the evil act of robbery? Isn't this like condemning Socrates because his unswerving commitment to truth and his philosophical inquiries precipitated the act by the misguided populace in which they made him drink hemlock? Isn't this like condemning Jesus because his unique God-consciousness and never-ceasing devotion to God's will precipitated the evil act of crucifixion? We must come to see that, as the federal courts have consistently affirmed, it is wrong to urge an individual to cease his efforts to gain his basic constitutional rights because the quest may precipitate violence. Society must protect the robbed and punish the robber.

26   I had also hoped that the white moderate would reject the myth concerning time in relation to the struggle for freedom. I have just received a letter from a white brother in Texas. He writes: "All Christians know that the colored people will receive equal rights eventually, but it is possible that you are in too great a religious hurry. It has taken Christianity almost two thousand years to accomplish what it has. The teachings of Christ take time to come to earth." Such an attitude stems from a tragic misconception of time, from the strangely irrational notion that there is something in the very flow of time that will inevitably cure all ills. Actually, time itself is neutral; it can be used either destructively or constructively. More and more I feel that the people of ill will have used time much more effectively than have the people of good will. We will have to repent in this generation not merely for the hateful words and

actions of the bad people, but for the appalling silence of the good people. Human progress never rolls in on wheels of inevitability; it comes through the tireless efforts of men willing to be co-workers with God, and without this hard work, time itself becomes an ally of the forces of social stagnation. We must use time creatively, in the knowledge that the time is always ripe to do right. Now is the time to make real the promise of democracy and transform our pending national elegy into a creative psalm of brotherhood. Now is the time to lift our national policy from the quicksand of racial injustice to the solid rock of human dignity.

27   You speak of our activity in Birmingham as extreme. At first I was rather disappointed that fellow clergymen would see my nonviolent efforts as those of an extremist. I began thinking about the fact that I stand in the middle of two opposing forces in the Negro community. One is a force of complacency, made up in part of Negroes who, as a result of long years of oppression, are so drained of self-respect and a sense of "somebodiness" that they have adjusted to segregation; and in part of a few middle-class Negroes who, because of a degree of academic and economic security and because in some ways they profit by segregation, have become insensitive to the problems of the masses. The other force is one of bitterness and hatred, and it comes perilously close to advocating violence. It is expressed in the various black nationalist groups that are springing up across the nation, the largest and best-known being Elijah Muhammad's Muslim movement. Nourished by the Negro's frustration over the continued existence of racial discrimination, this movement is made up of people who have lost faith in America, who have absolutely repudiated Christianity, and who have concluded that the white man is an incorrigible "devil."

28   I have tried to stand between these two forces, saying that we need emulate neither the "do-nothingism" of the complacent nor the hatred and despair of the black nationalist. For there is the more excellent way of love and nonviolent protest. I am grateful to God that, through the influence of the Negro church, the way of nonviolence became an integral part of our struggle.

29   If this philosophy had not emerged, by now many streets of the South would, I am convinced, be flowing with blood. And I am further convinced that if our white brothers dismiss as "rabblerousers" and "outside agitators" those of us who employ nonviolent direct action, and if they refuse to support our nonviolent efforts, millions of Negroes will, out of frustration and despair, seek solace and security in black-nationalist ideologies—a development that would inevitably lead to a frightening racial nightmare.

30   Oppressed people cannot remain oppressed forever. The yearning of freedom eventually manifests itself, and that is what has happened to the American Negro. Something within has reminded him of his birthright of freedom, and something without has reminded him that it

can be gained. Consciously or unconsciously, he has been caught up by the *Zeitgeist,* and with his black brothers of Africa and his brown and yellow brothers of Asia, South America, and the Caribbean, the United States Negro is moving with a sense of great urgency toward the promised land of racial justice. If one recognizes this vital urge that has engulfed the Negro community, one should readily understand why public demonstrations are taking place. The Negro has many pent-up resentments and latent frustrations, and he must release them. So let him march; let him make prayer pilgrimages to the city hall; let him go on freedom rides—and try to understand why he must do so. If his repressed emotions are not released in nonviolent ways, they will seek expression through violence; this is not a threat but a fact of history. So I have not said to my people, "Get rid of your discontent." Rather, I have tried to say that this normal and healthy discontent can be channeled into the creative outlet of nonviolent direct action. And now this approach is being termed extremist.

31   But though I was initially disappointed at being categorized as an extremist, as I continued to think about the matter I gradually gained a measure of satisfaction from the label. Was not Jesus an extremist for love: "Love your enemies, bless them that curse you, do good to them that hate you, and pray for them which despitefully use you, and persecute you." Was not Amos an extremist for justice: "Let justice roll down like waters and righteousness like an ever-flowing stream." Was not Paul an extremist for the Christian gospel: "I bear in my body the marks of the Lord Jesus." Was not Martin Luther an extremist: "Here I stand: I cannot do otherwise, so help me God." And John Bunyan: "I will stay in jail to the end of my days before I make a butchery of my conscience." And Abraham Lincoln: "This nation cannot survive half slave and half free." And Thomas Jefferson: "We hold these truths to be self-evident, that all men are created equal. . . ." So the question is not whether we will be extremists, but what kind of extremists we will be. Will we be extremists for hate or for love? Will we be extremists for the preservation of injustice or for the extension of justice? In that dramatic scene on Calvary's hill three men were crucified. We must never forget that all three were crucified for the same crime—the crime of extremism. Two were extremists for immorality, and thus fell below their environment. The other, Jesus Christ, was an extremist for love, truth, and goodness, and thereby rose above his environment. Perhaps the South, the nation, and the world are in dire need of creative extremists.

32   I had hoped that the white moderate would see this need. Perhaps I was too optimistic; perhaps I expected too much. I suppose I should have realized that few members of the oppressor race can understand the deep groans and passionate yearnings of the oppressed race, and still fewer have the vision to see that injustice must be rooted out by strong, persistent, and determined action. I am thankful, however, that some of

our white brothers in the South have grasped the meaning of this social revolution and committed themselves to it. They are still all too few in quantity, but they are big in quality. Some—such as Ralph McGill, Lillian Smith, Harry Golden, James McBride Dabbs, Ann Braden, and Sarah Patton Boyle—have written about our struggle in eloquent and prophetic terms. Others have marched with us down nameless streets of the South. They have languished in filthy, roach-infested jails, suffering the abuse and brutality of policemen who view them as "dirty nigger-lovers." Unlike so many of their moderate brothers and sisters, they have recognized the urgency of the moment and sensed the need for powerful "action" antidotes to combat the disease of segregation.

33   Let me take note of my other disappointment. I have been so greatly disappointed with the white church and its leadership. Of course, there are some notable exceptions. I am not unmindful of the fact that each of you has taken some significant stands on this issue. I commend you, Reverend Stallings, for your Christian stand on this past Sunday, in welcoming Negroes to your worship service on a nonsegregated basis. I commend the Catholic leaders of this state for integrating Spring Hill College several years ago.

34   But despite these notable exceptions, I must honestly reiterate that I have been disappointed with the church. I do not say this as one of those negative critics who can always find something wrong with the church. I say this as a minister of the gospel, who loves the church; who was nurtured in its bosom; who has been sustained by its spiritual blessings and who will remain true to it as long as the cord of life shall lengthen.

35   When I was suddenly catapulted into the leadership of the bus protest in Montgomery, Alabama, a few years ago, I felt we would be supported by the white church. I felt that the white ministers, priests, and rabbis of the South would be among our strongest allies. Instead, some have been outright opponents, refusing to understand the freedom movement and misrepresenting its leaders; all too many others have been more cautious than courageous and have remained silent behind the anesthetizing security of stained glass windows.

36   In spite of my shattered dreams, I came to Birmingham with the hope that the white religious leadership of this community would see the justice of our cause and, with deep moral concern, would serve as the channel through which our just grievances could reach the power structure. I had hoped that each of you would understand. But again I have been disappointed.

37   I have heard numerous southern religious leaders admonish their worshipers to comply with a desegregation decision because it is the law, but I have longed to hear white ministers declare: "Follow this decree because integration is morally right and because the Negro is your brother." In the midst of blatant injustices inflicted upon the Negro, I have watched white churchmen stand on the sideline and mouth pious irrelevancies

and sanctimonious trivialities. In the midst of a mighty struggle to rid our nation of racial and economic injustice, I have heard many ministers say: "Those are social issues, with which the gospel has no real concern." And I have watched many churches commit themselves to a completely otherworldly relation which makes a strange, un-Biblical distinction between body and soul, between the sacred and the secular.

38 I have traveled the length and breadth of Alabama, Mississippi, and all the other southern states. On sweltering summer days and crisp autumn mornings I have looked at the South's beautiful churches with their lofty spires pointing heavenward. I have beheld the impressive outlines of her massive religious-education buildings. Over and over I have found myself asking: "What kind of people worship here? Who is their God? Where were their voices when the lips of Governor Barnett dripped with words of interposition and nullification? Where were they when Governor Wallace gave a clarion call for defiance and hatred? Where were their voices of support when bruised and weary Negro men and women decided to rise from the dark dungeons of complacency to the bright hills of creative protest?"

39 Yes, these questions are still in my mind. In deep disappointment I have wept over the laxity of the church. But be assured that my tears have been tears of love. There can be no deep disappointment where there is not deep love. Yes, I love the church. How could I do otherwise? I am in the rather unique position of being the son, the grandson, and the great-grandson of preachers. Yes, I see the church as the body of Christ. But, oh! How we have blemished and scarred that body through social neglect and through fear of being nonconformists.

40 There was a time when the church was very powerful—in the time when the early Christians rejoiced at being deemed worthy to suffer for what they believed. In those days the church was not merely a thermometer that recorded the ideas and principles of popular opinion, it was a thermostat that transformed the mores of society. Whenever the early Christians entered a town, the people in power became disturbed and immediately sought to convict the Christians for being "disturbers of the peace" and "outside agitators." But the Christians pressed on, in the conviction that they were "a colony of heaven," called to obey God rather than man. Small in number they were big in commitment. They were too God-intoxicated to be "astronomically intimidated." By their effort and example they brought an end to such ancient evils as infanticide and gladiatorial contests.

41 Things are different now. So often the contemporary church is a weak, ineffectual voice with an uncertain sound. So often it is an archdefender of the status quo. Far from being disturbed by the presence of the church, the power structure of the average community is consoled by the church's silent—and often even vocal—sanction of things as they are.

42 But the judgment of God is upon the church as never before. If today's church does not recapture the sacrificial spirit of the early church, it will

lose its authenticity, forfeit the loyalty of millions, and be dismissed as an irrelevant social club with no meaning for the twentieth century. Every day I meet young people whose disappointment with the church has turned into outright disgust.

43   Perhaps I have once again been too optimistic. Is organized religion too inextricably bound to the status quo to save our nation and the world? Perhaps I must turn my faith to the inner spiritual church, the church within the church, as the true *ekklesia* and the hope of the world. But again I am thankful to God that some noble souls from the ranks of organized religion have broken loose from the paralyzing chains of conformity and joined us as active partners in the struggle for freedom. They have left their secure congregations and walked the streets of Albany, Georgia, with us. They have gone down the highways of the South on tortuous rides for freedom. Yes, they have gone to jail with us. Some have been dismissed from their churches, have lost the support of their bishops and fellow ministers. But they have acted in the faith that right defeated is stronger than evil triumphant. Their witness has been the spiritual salt that has preserved the true meaning of the gospel in these troubled times. They have carved a tunnel of hope through the dark mountain of disappointment.

44   I hope the church as a whole will meet the challenge of this decisive hour. But even if the church does not come to the aid of justice, I have no despair about the future. I have no fear about the outcome of our struggle in Birmingham, even if our motives are at present misunderstood. We will reach the goal of freedom in Birmingham and all over the nation, because the goal of America is freedom. Abused and scorned though we may be, our destiny is tied up with America's destiny. Before the pilgrims landed at Plymouth, we were here. Before the pen of Jefferson etched the majestic words of the Declaration of Independence across the pages of history, we were here. For more than two centuries our forebears labored in this country without wages; they made cotton king; they built the homes of their masters while suffering gross injustice and shameful humiliation—and yet out of a bottomless vitality they continued to thrive and develop. If the inexpressible cruelties of slavery could not stop us, the opposition we now face will surely fail. We will win our freedom because the sacred heritage of our nation and the eternal will of God are embodied in our echoing demands.

45   Before closing I feel impelled to mention one other point in your statement that has troubled me profoundly. You warmly commended the Birmingham police force for keeping "order" and "preventing violence." I doubt that you would have so warmly commended the police force if you had seen its dogs sinking their teeth into unarmed, nonviolent Negroes. I doubt that you would so quickly commend the policemen if you were to observe their ugly and inhumane treatment of Negroes here in the city jail; if you were to watch them push and curse old Negro women and

young Negro girls; if you were to see them slap and kick old Negro men and young boys; if you were to observe them, as they did on two occasions, refuse to give food because we wanted to sing our grace together. I cannot join you in your praise of the Birmingham police department.

46   It is true that the police have exercised a degree of discipline in handling the demonstrators. In this sense they have conducted themselves rather "nonviolently" in public. But for what purpose? To preserve the evil system of segregation. Over the past few years I have consistently preached that nonviolence demands that the means we use must be as pure as the ends we seek. I have tried to make clear that it is wrong to use immoral means to attain moral ends. But now I must affirm that it is just as wrong, or perhaps even more so, to use moral means to preserve immoral ends. Perhaps Mr. Connor and his policemen have been rather nonviolent in public, as was Chief Pritchett in Albany, Georgia, but they have used the moral means of nonviolence to maintain the immoral end of racial injustice. As T. S. Eliot has said, "The last temptation is the greatest treason: To do the right deed for the wrong reason."

47   I wish you had commended the Negro sit-inners and demonstrators of Birmingham for their sublime courage, their willingness to suffer, and their amazing discipline in the midst of great provocation. One day the South will recognize its real heroes. They will be the James Merediths, with the noble sense of purpose that enables them to face jeering and hostile mobs, and with the agonizing loneliness that characterizes the life of the pioneer. They will be old, oppressed, battered Negro women, symbolized in a seventy-two-year-old woman in Montgomery, Alabama, who rose up with a sense of dignity and with her people decided not to ride segregated buses, and who responded with ungrammatical profundity to one who inquired about her weariness: "My feets is tired, but my soul is at rest." They will be the young high school and college students, the young ministers of the gospel and a host of their elders, courageously and nonviolently sitting in at lunch counters and willingly going to jail for conscience sake. One day the South will know that when these disinherited children of God sat down at lunch counters, they were in reality standing up for what is best in the American dream and for the most sacred values in our Judeo-Christian heritage, thereby bringing our nation back to those great wells of democracy which were dug deep by the founding fathers in their formulation of the Constitution and the Declaration of Independence.

48   Never before have I written so long a letter. I'm afraid it is much too long to take your precious time. I can assure you that it would have been much shorter if I had been writing from a comfortable desk, but what else can one do when he is alone in a narrow jail cell, other than write long letters, think long thoughts, and pray long prayers?

49   If I have said anything in this letter that overstates the truth and indicates an unreasonable impatience, I beg you to forgive me. If I have said

anything that understates the truth and indicates my having a patience that allows me to settle for anything less than brotherhood, I beg God to forgive me.

50   I hope this letter finds you strong in the faith. I also hope that circumstances will soon make it possible for me to meet each of you, not as an integrationist or a civil-rights leader but as a fellow clergyman and a Christian brother. Let us all hope that the dark clouds of racial prejudice will soon pass away and the deep fog of misunderstanding will be lifted from our fear-drenched communities, and in some not too distant tomorrow the radiant stars of love and brotherhood will shine over our great nation with all their scintillating beauty.

Yours for the cause of Peace and Brotherhood,
Martin Luther King, Jr.

Another Voice

FIGHTING SELF-DEGRADATION
MALCOLM X

This was my first really big step toward self-degradation: when I endured all of that pain, literally burning my flesh to have it look like a white man's hair. I had joined that multitude of Negro men and women in America who are brainwashed into believing that the black people are "inferior"—and white people "superior"—that they will even violate and mutilate their God-created bodies to try to look "pretty" by white standards.

Look around today, in every small town and big city, from two-bit catfish and soda-pop joints into the "integrated" lobby of the Waldorf-Astoria, and you'll see conks on black men. And you'll see black women wearing these green and pink and purple and red and platinum-blonde wigs. They're all more ridiculous than a slapstick comedy. It makes you wonder if the Negro has completely lost his sense of identity, lost touch with himself.

You'll see the conk worn by many, many so-called "upper class" Negroes, and, as much as I hate to say it about them, on all too many Negro entertainers. One of the reasons that I've especially admired some of them, like Lionel Hampton and Sidney Poitier, among others, is that they have kept their natural hair and fought to the top. I admire any Negro man who has never

continued

continued from previous page

had himself conked, or who has had the sense to get rid of it, as I finally did.

I don't know which kind of self-defacing conk is the greater shame—the one you'll see on the heads of the black so-called "middle class" and "upper class," who ought to know better, or the one you'll see on the heads of the poorest, most downtrodden, ignorant black men. I mean the legal-minimum-wage ghetto-dwelling kind of Negro, as I was when I got my first one. It's generally among these poor fools that you'll see a black kerchief over the man's head, like Aunt Jemima; he's trying to make his conk last longer, between trips to the barbershop. Only for special occasions is this kerchief-protected conk exposed—to show off how "sharp" and "hip" its owner is. The ironic thing is that I have never heard any woman, white or black, express any admiration for a conk. Of course, any white woman with a black man isn't thinking about his hair. But I don't see how on earth a black woman with any race pride could walk down the street with any black man wearing a conk—the emblem of his shame that he is black.

To my own shame, when I say all of this I'm talking first of all about myself—because you can't show me any Negro who ever conked more faithfully than I did. I'm speaking from personal experience when I say of any black man who conks today, or any white-wigged black woman, that if they gave the brains in their heads just half as much attention as they do their hair, they would be a thousand times better off.

The Autobiography of Malcolm X, 1964

BUILDING CONTEXT

1. Determine King's stance in the disagreement between Booker T. Washington and W. E. B. Du Bois.
2. Evaluate Thoreau's influence upon King.
3. Analyze the function of Biblical allusions in the arguments of King and Douglass.
4. Compare the importance of "somebodiness" to King and another author, such as Eaton, Cameron, or Cahan.

FURTHER STUDY

1. Research the Civil Rights Movement of the 1960s. Explore its reception by both blacks and whites in the North, as well as the South.

2. Examine the philosophical and strategic differences between the Civil Rights and Black Power Movements. Evaluate their impact upon race relations today.

3. Investigate the psychology of identity creation, for example, construction of group identity, or loss of identity—"somebodiness" and "nobodiness."

ADDITIONAL RESOURCES

Branch, Taylor. *Parting the Waters: America in the King Years, 1954–1963.* New York: Simon & Schuster, 1988.

Garrow, David. *Bearing the Cross: Martin Luther King, Jr., and the Southern Christian Leadership Conference.* New York: Morrow, 1986.

Killian, Lewis M. *The Impossible Dream?—Black Power and the American Dream.* New York: Random House, 1968.

Malcolm X. *The Autobiography of Malcolm X.* New York: Grove Press, 1964.

RESEARCH KEYWORDS

Southern Christian Leadership Conference   Race Relations—U.S.
African-Americans—Civil Rights   Civil Disobedience
Nonviolence

KATE MILLETT
Sexual Politics (1970)

"One of the chief effects of class within patriarchy is to set one woman against another. . . . "

An accomplished sculptor and active feminist since 1966, Kate Millett (1934–   ) won national attention in 1970 with the publication of *Sexual*

Politics. This pioneering work, which began as a doctoral dissertation at Columbia University, argues that just as politics involves "power-structured relationships . . . whereby one group of persons is controlled by another," so too the social relationship between the sexes is one of dominance and subordination—a "birthright priority whereby males rule females"—that in many ways is more entrenched than racism. The book explores the psychology and sociology of patriarchy, illustrating how even such basic structures as the family serve ideological purposes, and includes scathing criticism of the works of D. H. Lawrence and Norman Mailer.

Other books by Millett include *Flying* (1974), a rumination on celebrity and bisexuality; *Sita* (1977), an autobiography; *The Basement: Meditations on Human Sacrifice* (1979); and *The Loony-bin Trip* (1990).

Text: Kate Millett; *Sexual Politics;* New York: Avon Books, 1970.

EXPLORING ISSUES IN THE TEXT

1. Who is Hannah Arendt (par. 8)? What makes her quotations in this context especially forceful?

2. According to Millett, how does socialization maintain patriarchy (par. 8)? How does it prevent many women from feeling oppressed (par. 21)?

3. Analyze how the family serves to maintain society and the state (pars. 9–14). Define the role of the family in socialization.

4. Summarize the relevance of race and class to sexual politics (pars. 15–22). What do you think of Millett's explanation for the importance of female purity (par. 17)?

5. How does Millett explain the fact that individual women or groups of women often dislike one another? What do you think of this explanation? What does it imply about the formation of identity?

SEXUAL POLITICS

1 In introducing the term "sexual politics," one must first answer the inevitable question "Can the relationship between the sexes be viewed in a political light at all?" The answer depends on how one defines politics. This essay does not define the political as that relatively narrow and exclusive world of meetings, chairmen, and parties. The term "politics" shall refer to power-structured relationships, arrangements whereby one group of persons is controlled by another. By way of parenthesis one might add that although an ideal politics might simply be conceived of as the arrangement of human life on agreeable and rational principles from

whence the entire notion of power *over* others should be banished, one must confess that this is not what constitutes the political as we know it, and it is to this that we must address ourselves.

2   The following sketch, which might be described as "notes toward a theory of patriarchy," will attempt to prove that sex is a status category with political implications. Something of a pioneering effort, it must perforce be both tentative and imperfect. Because the intention is to provide an overall description, statements must be generalized, exceptions neglected, and subheadings overlapping and, to some degree, arbitrary as well.

3   The word "politics" is enlisted here when speaking of the sexes primarily because such a word is eminently useful in outlining the real nature of their relative status, historically and at the present. It is opportune, perhaps today even mandatory, that we develop a more relevant psychology and philosophy of power relationships beyond the simple conceptual framework provided by our traditional formal politics. Indeed, it may be imperative that we give some attention to defining a theory of politics which treats of power relationships on grounds less conventional than those to which we are accustomed. I have therefore found it pertinent to define them on grounds of personal contact and interaction between members of well-defined and coherent groups: races, castes, classes, and sexes. For it is precisely because certain groups have no representation in a number of recognized political structures that their position tends to be so stable, their oppression so continuous.

4   In America, recent events have forced us to acknowledge at last that the relationship between the races is indeed a political one which involves the general control of one collectivity, defined by birth, over another collectivity, also defined by birth. Groups who rule by birthright are fast disappearing, yet there remains one ancient and universal scheme for the domination of one birth group by another—the scheme that prevails in the area of sex. The study of racism has convinced us that a truly political state of affairs operates between the races to perpetuate a series of oppressive circumstances. The subordinated group has inadequate redress through existing political institutions, and is deterred thereby from organizing into conventional political struggle and opposition.

5   Quite in the same manner, a disinterested examination of our system of sexual relationship must point out that the situation between the sexes now, and throughout history, is a case of that phenomenon Max Weber defined as *herrshaft,* a relationship of dominance and subordinance. What goes largely unexamined, often even unacknowledged (yet is institutionalized nonetheless) in our social order, is the birthright priority whereby males rule females. Through this system a most ingenious form of "interior colonization" has been achieved. It is one which tends moreover to be sturdier than any form of segregation, and more rigorous than class stratification, more uniform, certainly more enduring. However muted

its present appearance may be, sexual dominion obtains nevertheless as perhaps the most pervasive ideology of our culture and provides its most fundamental concept of power.

6   This is so because our society, like all other historical civilizations, is a patriarchy. The fact is evident at once if one recalls that the military, industry, technology, universities, science, political office, and finance—in short, every avenue of power within the society, including the coercive force of the police, is entirely in male hands. As the essence of politics is power, such realization cannot fail to carry impact. What lingers of supernatural authority, the Deity, "His" ministry, together with the ethics and values, the philosophy and art of our culture—its very civilization—as T. S. Eliot once observed, is of male manufacture.

7   If one takes patriarchal government to be the institution whereby that half of the populace which is female is controlled by that half which is male, the principles of patriarchy appear to be twofold: male shall dominate female, elder male shall dominate younger. However, just as with any human institution, there is frequently a distance between the real and the ideal; contradictions and exceptions do exist within the system. While patriarchy as an institution is a social constant so deeply entrenched as to run through all other political, social, or economic forms, whether of caste or class, feudality or bureaucracy, just as it pervades all major religions, it also exhibits great variety in history and locale. In democracies, for example, females have often held no office or do so (as now) in such minuscule numbers as to be below even token representation. Aristocracy, on the other hand, with its emphasis upon the magic and dynastic properties of blood, may at times permit women to hold power. The principle of rule by elder males is violated even more frequently. Bearing in mind the variation and degree in patriarchy—as say between Saudi Arabia and Sweden, Indonesia and Red China—we also recognize our own form in the U.S. and Europe to be much altered and attenuated by the reforms described in the next chapter.

Ideological

8   Hannah Arendt has observed that government is upheld by power supported either through consent or imposed through violence. Conditioning to an ideology amounts to the former. Sexual politics obtains consent through the socialization of both sexes to basic patriarchal politics with regard to temperament, role, and status. As to status, a pervasive assent to the prejudice of male superiority guarantees superior status in the male, inferior in the female. The first item, temperament, involves the formation of human personality along stereotyped lines of sex category ("masculine" and "feminine"), based on the needs and values of the dominant group and dictated by what its members cherish in themselves and find convenient in subordinates: aggression, intelligence, force, and efficacy

in the male; passivity, ignorance, docility, "virtue," and ineffectuality in the female. This is complemented by a second factor, sex role, which decrees a consonant and highly elaborate code of conduct, gesture and attitude for each sex. In terms of activity, sex role assigns domestic service and attendance upon infants to the female, the rest of human achievement, interest, and ambition to the male. The limited role allotted the female tends to arrest her at the level of biological experience. Therefore nearly all that can be described as distinctly human rather than animal activity (in their own way animals also give birth and care for their young) is largely reserved for the male. Of course, status again follows from such an assignment. Were one to analyze the three categories one might designate status as the political component, role as the sociological, and temperament as the psychological—yet their interdependence is unquestionable and they form a chain. Those awarded higher status tend to adopt roles of mastery, largely because they are first encouraged to develop temperaments of dominance. That this is true of caste and class as well is self-evident. . . .

9 Patriarchy's chief institution is the family. It is both a mirror of and a connection with the larger society; a patriarchal unit within a patriarchal whole. Mediating between the individual and the social structure, the family effects control and conformity where political and other authorities are insufficient. As the fundamental instrument and the foundation unit of patriarchal society the family and its roles are prototypical. Serving as an agent of the larger society, the family not only encourages its own members to adjust and conform, but acts as a unit in the government of the patriarchal state which rules its citizens through its family heads. Even in patriarchal societies where they are granted legal citizenship, women tend to be ruled through the family alone and have little or no formal relation to the state.

10 As cooperation between the family and the larger society is essential, else both would fall apart, the fate of three patriarchal institutions, the family, society, and the state are interrelated. In most forms of patriarchy this has generally led to the granting of religious support in statements such as the Catholic precept that "the father is head of the family," or Judaism's delegating of quasi-priestly authority to the male parent. Secular governments today also confirm this, as in census practices of designating the male as head of household, taxation, passports etc. Female heads of household tend to be regarded as undesirable; the phenomenon is a trait of poverty or misfortune. The Confucian prescription that the relationship between ruler and subject is parallel to that of father and children points to the essentially feudal character of the patriarchal family (and conversely, the familial character of feudalism) even in modern democracies. . . .

11 In contemporary patriarchies the male's *de jure* priority has recently been modified through the granting of divorce protection, citizenship,

and property to women. Their chattel status continues in their loss of name, their obligation to adopt the husband's domicile, and the general legal assumption that marriage involves an exchange of the female's domestic service and (sexual) consortium in return for financial support.

12   The chief contribution of the family in patriarchy is the socialization of the young (largely through the example and admonition of their parents) into patriarchal ideology's prescribed attitudes toward the categories of role, temperament, and status. Although slight differences of definition depend here upon the parents' grasp of cultural values, the general effect of uniformity is achieved, to be further reinforced through peers, schools, media, and other learning sources, formal and informal. While we may niggle over the balance of authority between the personalities of various households, one must remember that the entire culture supports masculine authority in all areas of life and—outside of the home—permits the female none at all.

13   To insure that its crucial functions of reproduction and socialization of the young take place only within its confines, the patriarchal family insists upon legitimacy. Bronislaw Malinowski describes this as "the principle of legitimacy" formulating it as an insistence that "no child should be brought into the world without a man—and one man at that—assuming the role of sociological father." By this apparently consistent and universal prohibition (whose penalties vary by class and in accord with the expected operations of the double standard) patriarchy decrees that the status of both child and mother is primarily or ultimately dependent upon the male. And since it is not only his social status, but even his economic power upon which his dependents generally rely, the position of the masculine figure within the family—as without—is materially, as well as ideologically, extremely strong.

14   Although there is no biological reason why the two central functions of the family (socialization and reproduction) need be inseparable from or even take place within it, revolutionary or utopian efforts to remove these functions from the family have been so frustrated, so beset by difficulties, that most experiments so far have involved a gradual return to tradition. This is strong evidence of how basic a form patriarchy is within all societies, and of how pervasive its effects upon family members. It is perhaps also an admonition that change undertaken without a thorough understanding of the sociopolitical institution to be changed is hardly productive. And yet radical social change cannot take place without having an effect upon patriarchy. And not simply because it is the political form which subordinates such a large percentage of the population (women and youth) but because it serves as a citadel of property and traditional interests. Marriages are financial alliances, and each household operates as an economic entity much like a corporation. As one student of the family states it, "the family is the keystone of the stratification system, the social mechanism by which it is maintained."

Class

15 It is in the area of class that the castelike status of the female within patriarchy is most liable to confusion, for sexual status often operates in a superficially confusing way within the variable of class. In a society where status is dependent upon the economic, social, and educational circumstances of class, it is possible for certain females to appear to stand higher than some males. Yet not when one looks more closely at the subject. This is perhaps easier to see by means of analogy: a black doctor or lawyer has higher social status than a poor white sharecropper. But race, itself a caste system which subsumes class, persuades the latter citizen that he belongs to a higher order of life, just as it oppresses the black professional in spirit, whatever his material success may be. In much the same manner, a truck driver or butcher has always his "manhood" to fall back upon. Should this final vanity be offended, he may contemplate more violent methods. The literature of the past thirty years provides a staggering number of incidents in which the caste of virility triumphs over the social status of wealthy or even educated women. In literary contexts one has to deal here with wish-fulfillment. Incidents from life (bullying, obscene, or hostile remarks) are probably another sort of psychological gesture of ascendancy. Both convey more hope than reality, for class divisions are generally quite impervious to the hostility of individuals. And yet while the existence of class division is not seriously threatened by such expressions of enmity, the existence of sexual hierarchy has been reaffirmed and mobilized to "punish" the female quite effectively.

16 The function of class or ethnic mores in patriarchy is largely a matter of how overtly displayed or how loudly enunciated the general ethic of masculine supremacy allows itself to become. Here one is confronted by what appears to be a paradox: while in the lower social strata, the male is more likely to claim authority on the strength of his sex rank alone, he is actually obliged more often to share power with the women of his class who are economically productive; whereas in the middle and upper classes, there is less tendency to assert a blunt patriarchal dominance, as men who enjoy such status have more power in any case.

17 It is generally accepted that Western patriarchy has been much softened by the concepts of courtly and romantic love. While this is certainly true, such influence has also been vastly overestimated. In comparison with the candor of "machismo" or Oriental behavior, one realizes how much a concession traditional chivalrous behavior represents—a sporting kind of reparation to allow the subordinate female certain means of saving face. While a palliative to the injustice of woman's social position, chivalry is also a technique for disguising it. One must acknowledge that the chivalrous stance is a game the master group

plays in elevating its subject to pedestal level. Historians of courtly love stress the fact that the raptures of the poets had no effect upon the legal or economic standing of women, and very little upon their social status. As the sociologist Hugo Beigel has observed, both the courtly and the romantic versions of love are "grants" which the male concedes out of his total powers. Both have had the effect of obscuring the patriarchal character of Western culture and, in their general tendency to attribute impossible virtues to women, have ended by confining them in a narrow and often remarkably conscribing sphere of behavior. It was a Victorian habit, for example, to insist the female assume the function of serving as the male's conscience and living the life of goodness he found tedious but felt someone ought to do anyway.

18   The concept of romantic love affords a means of emotional manipulation which the male is free to exploit, since love is the only circumstance in which the female is (ideologically) pardoned for sexual activity. And convictions of romantic love are convenient to both parties since this is often the only condition in which the female can overcome the far more powerful conditioning she has received toward sexual inhibition. Romantic love also obscures the realities of female status and the burden of economic dependency. As to "chivalry," such gallant gestures as still resides in the middle classes has degenerated to a tired ritualism, which scarcely serves to mask the status situation of the present

19   Within patriarchy one must often deal with contradictions which are simply a matter of class style. David Riesman has noted that as the working class has been assimilated into the middle class, so have its sexual mores and attitudes. The fairly blatant male chauvinism which was once a province of the lower class or immigrant male has been absorbed and taken on a certain glamour through a number of contemporary figures, who have made it, and a certain number of other working-class male attitudes, part of a new, and at the moment, fashionable life style. So influential is this working-class ideal of brute virility (or more accurately, a literary and therefore middle-class version of it) become in our time that it may replace more discreet and "gentlemanly" attitudes of the past.

20   One of the chief effects of class within patriarchy is to set one woman against another, in the past creating a lively antagonism between whore and matron, and in the present between career woman and housewife. One envies the other her "security" and prestige, while the envied yearns beyond the confines of respectability for what she takes to be the other's freedom, adventure, and contact with the great world. Through the multiple advantages of the double standard, the male participates in both worlds, empowered by his superior social and economic resources to play the estranged women against each other as rivals. One might also recognize subsidiary status categories among women: not only is virtue class, but beauty and age as well.

21 Perhaps, in the final analysis, it is possible to argue that women tend to transcend the usual class stratifications in patriarchy, for whatever the class of her birth and education, the female has fewer permanent class associations than does the male. Economic dependency renders her affiliations with any class a tangential, vicarious, and temporary matter. Aristotle observed that the only slave to whom a commoner might lay claim was his woman, and the service of an unpaid domestic still provides workingclass males with a "cushion" against the buffets of the class system, which incidentally provides them with some of the psychic luxuries of the leisure class. Thrown upon their own resources, few women rise above working class in personal prestige and economic power, and women as a group do not enjoy many of the interests and benefits any class may offer its male members. Women have therefore less of an investment in the class system. But it is important to understand that as with any group whose existence is parasitic to its rulers, women are a dependency class who live on surplus. And their marginal life frequently renders them conservative, for like all persons in their situation (slaves are a classic example here) they identify their own survival with the prosperity of those who feed them. The hope of seeking liberating radical solutions of their own seems too remote for the majority to dare contemplate and remains so until consciousness on the subject is raised.

22 As race is emerging as one of the final variables in sexual politics, it is pertinent, especially in a discussion of modern literature, to devote a few words to it as well. Traditionally, the white male has been accustomed to concede the female of his own race, in her capacity as "his woman," a higher status than that ascribed to the black male. Yet as white racist ideology is exposed and begins to erode, racism's older protective attitudes toward (white) women also begin to give way. And the priorities of maintaining male supremacy might outweigh even those of white supremacy; sexism may be more endemic in our own society than racism. For example, one notes in authors whom we would not term overtly racist, such as D. H. Lawrence—whose contempt for what he so often designates as inferior breeds is unabashed—instances where the lower-caste male is brought on to master or humiliate the white man's own insubordinate mate. Needless to say, the female of the nonwhite races does not figure in such tales save as an exemplum of "true" womanhood's servility, worthy of imitation by other less carefully instructed females. Contemporary white sociology often operates under a similar patriarchal bias when its rhetoric inclines toward the assertion that the "matriarchal" (e.g. matrifocal) aspect of black society and the "castration" of the black male are the most deplorable symptoms of black oppression in white racist society, with the implication that racial inequality is capable of solution by a restoration of masculine authority. Whatever the facts of the matter may be, it can also be suggested that analysis of this kind presupposes patriarchal values without questioning them, and tends to obscure

both the true character of and the responsibility for racist injustice toward black humanity of both sexes.

BUILDING CONTEXT

1. Compare Millett's view of women's morality to the opinions of Stowe and Howells.
2. How does Millett's analysis of sex, class, and race help to explain the negative reactions to Frederick Douglass's marriage to a white woman?
3. In what way does Millett's explanation of sexual socialization shed light on the behavior of the women described by Elizabeth Custer?

FURTHER STUDY

1. Explore how people—of any sex, race, or class—learn "their place" in society.
2. Investigate the belief that women contribute a greater sense of morality and cooperation to politics.
3. Analyze the relative importance of sex, race, and class to personal identity. Compare the ways people form their own identities to the manner in which they impose identity upon others.

ADDITIONAL RESOURCES

Cade, Toni, ed. *The Black Woman.* New York: Bantam Books, 1970.

Firestone, Shulamith. *The Dialectic of Sex.* New York: Bantam Books, 1971.

Friedan, Betty. *The Feminine Mystique.* New York: Dell, 1963.

Habegger, Alfred. *Gender, Fantasy, and Religion in American Literature.* New York: Columbia University Press, 1982.

Hole, Judith, and Ellen Levine. *Rebirth of Feminism.* New York: Quadrangle, 1971.

Morgan, Robin, ed. *Sisterhood Is Powerful.* New York: Random House, 1970.

RESEARCH KEYWORDS

Feminism	Sexual Politics	Patriarchy
Lesbianism	Women in Society	Equal Rights Amendment
Women—Legal Status	Sex Discrimination	Lawrence (D. H.)
Mailer (Norman)		

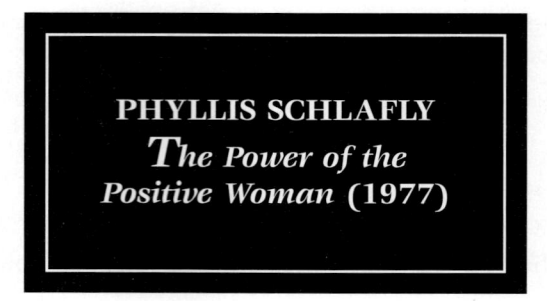

PHYLLIS SCHLAFLY
*The Power of the
Positive Woman* **(1977)**

"The first requirement for the acquisition of power by the Positive Woman is to understand the differences between men and women."

Phyllis Schlafly (1924–   ), is a fiery opponent of feminism who has been credited with almost single-handedly stopping ratification of the Equal Rights Amendment, which she derided as the "Men's Liberation Amendment" because it would remove men's financial obligation to their wives. Though in many ways she is the epitome of the liberated woman—she graduated from college Phi Beta Kappa, holds a master's degree from Harvard, and has published numerous books and articles—she considers herself first and foremost a wife and mother.

Schlafly is active in many conservative causes. An ardent anti-communist, she campaigned for Barry Goldwater in his race for the presidency in 1964, and she ran unsuccessfully for Congress in 1952, 1960 and 1970. But it was her opposition to feminism that propelled her to national prominence—and her reputation as "savior" to some, and the incarnation of betrayal to others. In *The Power of the Positive Woman,* Schlafly maintains that feminist notions of liberation actually reduce the influence of women; by denying that women have their own traits and strengths, she says, feminists insure that women lose to men because they are forced to compete in only the male arena. Moreover, she denies the feminist contention that "man is the enemy" and wryly argues that taken to its logical conclusion, feminism achieves fulfillment only in lesbianism.

Text: Phyllis Schlafly; *The Power of the Positive Woman;* New Rochelle, N.Y.: Arlington House, 1977.

EXPLORING ISSUES IN THE TEXT

1. Summarize Schlafly's fundamental premise about sexual equality (par. 1). According to her, how do feminists create a negative identity for themselves (pars. 2–3)?

2. Analyze Schlafly's conclusion that the highest form of feminism must be lesbianism (pars. 5–7). Why do you think she includes this argument? What gives it its force?

3. Analyze how Schlafly determines woman's true purpose (pars. 8–10, 25–27).

4. Interpret how, according to Schlafly, the premise of feminism forces women to compete on men's terms instead of their own (pars. 11–14).

5. Summarize the emotional and psychological differences that Schlafly claims exist between women and men (pars. 15–21). What is your reaction to her claim that public displays of emotion should be avoided by women as well as men (par. 22)?

THE POWER OF THE POSITIVE WOMAN

1 The first requirement for the acquisition of power by the Positive Woman is to understand the differences between men and women. Your outlook on life, your faith, your behavior, your potential for fulfillment, all are determined by the parameters of your original premise. The Positive Woman starts with the assumption that the world is her oyster. She rejoices in the creative capability within her body and the power potential of her mind and spirit. She understands that men and women are different, and that those very differences provide the key to her success as a person and fulfillment as a woman.

2 The women's liberationist, on the other hand, is imprisoned by her own negative view of herself and of her place in the world around her. This view of women was most succinctly expressed in an advertisement designed by the principal women's liberationist organization, the National Organization for Women (NOW), and run in many magazines and newspapers and as spot announcements on many television stations. The advertisement showed a darling curlyheaded girl with the caption: "This healthy, normal baby has a handicap. She was born female."

3 This is the self-articulated, dog-in-the-manger, chip-on-the-shoulder, fundamental dogma of the women's liberation movement. Someone—it is not clear who, perhaps God, perhaps the "Establishment," perhaps a conspiracy of male chauvinist pigs—dealt women a foul blow by making them female. It becomes necessary, therefore, for women to agitate and demonstrate and hurl demands on society in order to wrest from an oppressive male-dominated social structure the status that has been wrongfully denied to women through the centuries.

4 By its very nature, therefore, the women's liberation movement precipitates a series of conflict situations—in the legislatures, in the courts, in the schools, in industry—with man targeted as the enemy. Confrontation replaces cooperation as the watchword of all relationships. Women and men become adversaries instead of partners.

5 The second dogma of the women's liberationists is that, of all the injustices perpetrated upon women through the centuries, the most oppressive

is the cruel fact that women have babies and men do not. Within the confines of the women's liberationist ideology, therefore, the abolition of this overriding inequality of women becomes the primary goal. This goal must be achieved at any and all costs—to the woman herself, to the baby, to the family, and to society. Women must be made equal to men in their ability *not* to become pregnant and *not* to be expected to care for babies they may bring into the world.

6   This is why women's liberationists are compulsively involved in the drive to make abortion and child-care centers for all women, regardless of religion or income, both socially acceptable and government-financed. Former congresswoman Bella Abzug has defined the goal: "to enforce the constitutional right of females to terminate pregnancies that they do not wish to continue."

7   If man is targeted as the enemy, and the ultimate goal of women's liberation is independence from men and the avoidance of pregnancy and its consequences, then lesbianism is logically the highest form in the ritual of women's liberation. Many, such as Kate Millett, come to this conclusion, although many others do not.

8   The Positive Woman will never travel that dead-end road. It is self-evident to the Positive Woman that the female body with its baby-producing organs was not designed by a conspiracy of men but by the Divine Architect of the human race. Those who think it is unfair that women have babies, whereas men cannot, will have to take up their complaint with God because no other power is capable of changing that fundamental fact. On some college campuses, I have been assured that other methods of reproduction will be developed. But most of us must deal with the real world rather than with the imagination of dreamers.

9   Another feature of the woman's natural role is the obvious fact that women can breast-feed babies and men cannot. This functional role was not imposed by conspiratorial males seeking to burden women with confining chores but must be recognized as part of the plan of the Divine Architect for the survival of the human race through the centuries and in the countries that know no pasteurization of milk or sterilization of bottles.

10   The Positive Woman looks upon her femaleness and her fertility as part of her purpose, her potential, and her power. She rejoices that she has a capability for creativity that men can never have.

11   The third basic dogma of the women's liberation movement is that there is no difference between male and female except the sex organs, and that all those physical, cognitive, and emotional differences you *think* are there, are merely the result of centuries of restraints imposed by a male-dominated society and sex-stereotyped schooling. The role imposed on women is, by definition, inferior, according to the women's liberationists.

12   The Positive Woman knows that, while there are some physical competitions in which women are better (and can command more money) than men, including those that put a premium on grace and beauty, such

as figure skating, the superior physical strength of males over females in competitions of strength, speed, and short-term endurance is beyond rational dispute.

13 In the Olympic Games, women not only cannot win any medals in competition with men, the gulf between them is so great that they cannot even qualify for the contests with men. No amount of training from infancy can enable women to throw the discus as far as men, or to match men in push-ups or in lifting weights. In track and field events, individual male records surpass those of women by 10 to 20 percent.

14 Female swimmers today are beating Johnny Weissmuller's records, but today's male swimmers are better still. Chris Evert can never win a tennis match against Jimmy Connors. If we removed lady's tees from golf courses, women would be out of the game. Putting women in football or wrestling matches can only be an exercise in laughs. . . .

15 The differences between men and women are also emotional and psychological. Without woman's innate maternal instinct, the human race would have died out centuries ago. There is nothing so helpless in all earthly life as the newborn infant. It will die within hours if not cared for. Even in the most primitive, uneducated societies, women have always cared for their newborn babies. They didn't need any schooling to teach them how. They didn't need any welfare workers to tell them it is their social obligation. Even in societies to whom such concepts as "ought," "social responsibility," and "compassion for the helpless" were unknown, mothers cared for their new babies.

16 Why? Because caring for a baby served the natural maternal need of a woman. Although not nearly so total as the baby's need, the woman's need is nonetheless real.

17 The overriding psychological need of a woman is to love something alive. A baby fulfills this need in the lives of most women. If a baby is not available to fill that need, women search for a baby-substitute. This is the reason why women have traditionally gone into teaching and nursing careers. They are doing what comes naturally to the female psyche. The schoolchild or the patient of any age provides an outlet for a woman to express her natural maternal need.

18 This maternal need in women is the reason why mothers whose children have grown up and flown from the nest are sometimes cut loose from their psychological moorings. The maternal need in women can show itself in love for grandchildren, nieces, nephews, or even neighbors' children. The maternal need in some women has even manifested itself in an extraordinary affection lavished on a dog, a cat, or a parakeet.

19 This is not to say that every woman must have a baby in order to be fulfilled. But it is to say that fulfillment for most women involves expressing their natural maternal urge by loving and caring for someone.

20 The women's liberation movement complains that traditional stereotyped roles assume that women are "passive" and that men are "aggressive."

The anomaly is that a woman's most fundamental emotional need is not passive at all, but active. A woman naturally seeks to love affirmatively and to show that love in an active way by caring for the object of her affections.

21 The Positive Woman finds somebody on whom she can lavish her maternal love so that it doesn't well up inside her and cause psychological frustrations. Surely no woman is so isolated by geography or insulated by spirit that she cannot find someone worthy of her maternal love. All persons, men and women, gain by sharing something of themselves with their fellow humans, but women profit most of all because it is part of their very nature.

22 One of the strangest quirks of women's liberationists is their complaint that societal restraints prevent men from crying in public or showing their emotions, but permit women to do so, and that therefore we should "liberate" men to enable them, too, to cry in public. The public display of fear, sorrow, anger, and irritation reveals a lack of self-discipline that should be avoided by the Positive Woman just as much as by the Positive Man. Maternal love, however, is not a weakness but a manifestation of strength and service, and it should be nurtured by the Positive Woman. . . .

23 Finally, women are different from men in dealing with the fundamentals of life itself. Men are philosophers, women are practical, and 'twas ever thus. Men may philosophize about how life began and where we are heading; women are concerned about feeding the kids today. No woman would ever, as Karl Marx did, spend years reading political philosophy in the British Museum while her child starved to death. Women don't take naturally to a search for the intangible and the abstract. The Positive Woman knows who she is and where she is going, and she will reach her goal because the longest journey starts with a very practical first step.

24 Amaury de Riencourt, in his book *Sex and Power in History,* shows that a successful society depends on a delicate balancing of different male and female factors, and that the women's liberation movement, which promotes unisexual values and androgyny, contains within it "a social and cultural death wish and the end of the civilization that endorses it."

25 One of the few scholarly works dealing with woman's role, *Sex and Power in History,* synthesizes research from a variety of disciplines—sociology, biology, history, anthropology, religion, philosophy, and psychology. De Riencourt traces distinguishable types of women in different periods in history, from prehistoric to modern times. The "liberated" Roman matron, who is most similar to the present-day feminist, helped bring about the fall of Rome through her unnatural emulation of masculine qualities, which resulted in a large-scale breakdown of the family and ultimately of the empire.

26 De Riencourt examines the fundamental, inherent differences between men and women. He argues that man is the more aggressive, rational,

mentally creative, analytical-minded sex because of his early biological role as hunter and provider. Woman, on the other hand, represents stability, flexibility, reliance on intuition, and harmony with nature, stemming from her procreative function.

27 Where man is discursive, logical, abstract, or philosophical, woman tends to be emotional, personal, practical, or mystical. Each set of qualities is vital and complements the other. . . .

BUILDING CONTEXT

1. Contrast the positions of Schlafly and Millett on the question of whether our personalities are the product of nature or nurture.

2. What parallels can you draw between the conflicting approaches of women toward feminism and of African Americans toward civil rights?

3. Analyze Schlafly's use of religion in her argument. How do her religious allusions differ from those of King?

FURTHER STUDY

1. Trace the history of the Equal Rights Amendment. Explain why it elicited such conflicting responses from women.

2. Investigate the role of lesbians in the Woman's Rights Movement. Assess their effect upon the movement and its public reception. Trace the changes in the social reaction to lesbianism since the beginning of the movement.

3. Explore the special position of minority women in the Civil Rights and Woman's Movements. For example, account for their particular identity conflicts.

ADDITIONAL RESOURCES

Bird, Caroline. *What Do Women Want?* New York: Simon & Schuster, 1979.

Decter, Midge. *The New Chastity and Other Arguments against Women's Liberation.* New York: Coward, McCann & Geoghegan, 1972.

Greer, Germaine. *The Female Eunuch.* New York: McGraw-Hill, 1971.

Mathews, Donald G. *Sex, Gender and the Politics of ERA.* New York: Oxford University Press, 1990.

O'Neill, William L. *Everyone Was Brave: The Rise and Fall of Feminism in America.* New York: Quadrangle, 1969.

Slavin, Sarah, ed. *The Equal Rights Amendment.* New York: Haworth Press, 1982.

RESEARCH KEYWORDS

Feminism	Woman's Liberation
Woman's Movement	Equal Rights Amendment
Women—Legal Status	Sex Discrimination.

━━━━━━━━━━━━━━

EXPLORING CRITICAL ISSUES THROUGH WRITING

1. Investigate the social and economic changes that took place in America during the first half of the twentieth century. Assess how these changes might have influenced the decision in *Brown* and the progress of the Civil Rights Movement.

2. Debate whether African Americans can receive justice from an all-white court.

3. Argue whether social integration must be forced.

4. Assess the impact of *Brown* upon the history of segregation after 1954.

5. Consider the place of religion in American politics since Kennedy's election. For example, how significant are religious arguments in the debate over abortion? How many politicians today feel compelled to disavow their religious commitments?

6. Explore the "Camelot" aspect of the Kennedy era. Why did he evoke such feelings in Americans? Connect this reaction to the image shared by many Americans of their country and its mission.

7. Analyze the psychological importance of "being somebody." Interpret how this concept has affected schools and curricula, or other recent legislation. How is group identity constructed? How is it lost?

8. Examine the philosophical and strategic differences between the Civil Rights and Black Power Movements. Evaluate their impact upon race relations today.

9. Explain the psychology of identity creation, for example, the construction of group identity, or loss of identity.

10. Weigh the relative importance of sex, race, and class in the formation of personal identity. Compare the ways people form their own identities to the manner in which they impose identity upon others.

11. Describe how people—of any sex, race, or class—learn "their place" in society.

12. Argue whether or not women contribute a greater sense of morality and cooperation to politics.

13. Evaluate the role of lesbians in the Woman's Rights Movement. Assess their effect upon the movement and its public reception. Gauge the

changes in the social reaction to lesbianism since the beginning of the movement.

14. Explore the special position of minority women in the Civil Rights and Woman's Movements. For example, account for their particular identity conflicts.

15. Explore an idea from the reading selections that caught your interest, charmed or provoked you, or supported or challenged your own beliefs. Place the issue within a larger context and explain its significance.

12

FACING THE PRESENT: SINCE 1980

"I realized that I was the only Puerto Rican on the panel who writes in English."

NICHOLASA MOHR

"If the concept of the melting pot is outdated, what is to replace it?"

ROBERT REINHOLD

The decade of the 1980s was the Reagan-Bush era. In Washington, D.C., a social and political revolution, launched by President Ronald Reagan and continued by President George Bush, attempted to shrink the government intervention in private life and business: programs from the Great Society and civil rights legislation were cut back, and regulatory agencies were reduced or dismantled. In state legislatures, the Equal Rights Amendment failed to gain the votes needed for ratification. On Wall Street, "Yuppies"—young upwardly mobile professionals—led a buying frenzy that drove the stock market to record heights. In Europe, the Soviet empire collapsed, leading to jubilant claims that the West had won the Cold War.

At the same time, however, women and African Americans demanded greater power, and previously invisible minorities—Hispanics, Asian Americans, and gays and lesbians—joined them. These and other Americans became vocal proponents of multiculturalism: a perspective that welcomes racial and cultural differences as enriching all of society.

The earliest proponents of equal rights for blacks and women argued from religious and Enlightenment principles that all people are the same—created equal, equal in the eyes of God, and possessing of natural rights. The assumption was that everyone wanted to play the same game, but the field was not level. The obvious solution was to level the playing field—to remove any obstacles unfair to either side. During the 1980s, however, the game itself was challenged. Feminists and non-European minorities charged that American politics, scholarship, and culture all reflect the values of European men. Rather than trying to prove that they could play as well as white men, these groups demanded equal respect and societal support for other games—other values, cultures, and world views. No longer, for example, did a woman have to claim that she could be as tough and analytical as a man; now female sensitivity and empathy were defended as alternatives to male behavior.

The Women's and Black Studies movements of the 1970s challenged the academic arena that demanded the objective and impersonal study of facts, regardless of their political or emotional implications. Traditionally, specializing in an area of study—for example, Aztec ritual or medieval Italian art—indicated only an interest in the subject, not an identification with or defense of the people involved. The Women's and Black Studies movements, however, maintained that all scholarship is political: choosing to study medieval art implies, at the very least, a lack of interest in more pressing current problems and perpetuates the marginalization of ignored groups such as women and blacks. Study therefore grants legitimacy to its subject, and a student enrolled in a course about women or African Americans could expect to encounter the type of advocacy presented in Sucheta Mazumdar's woman-centered perspective of Asian-American history.

Literary canon formation—the process by which certain books achieve status in a community—has proven to be a vital battleground for the multicultural revolution. Reasons such as morality, insight, patriotism, literary merit, and political correctness have been offered to support the reading or teaching of particular books. The elevation of certain books to a higher status not only suggests that they contain these features in greater quantity than competing books, but also implies that these elements are universally valued. However, both of these assumptions are now under attack.

Arguing that the literary canon supported by critics and schools embodies the values of white, Protestant men from the upper middle class, feminist critics have championed lesser known women writers. Kate Millett's *Sexual Politics,* with its critique of D. H. Lawrence and Norman Mailer, insists that this canon validates misogyny and the subjugation of women. Nina Baym's *Woman's Fiction* resurrects the popular nineteenth-century writers whom Nathaniel Hawthorne, a cultural icon, had dismissed as a "damned mob of scribbling women."

Feminist critics also contend that value systems are not natural but cultural; many reject what Adrienne Rich calls "the false male universal" of abstraction and objectivity, demanding instead equal recognition of a female rhetoric grounded in experience and emotion. In the social sciences as well, feminists like Patricia Hill Collins have proposed a new theory of knowledge, or epistemology.

While some feminists, as well as African-American, Native-American, Hispanic, and other ethnic critics, have created counter-canons of forgotten and ignored writers, support has grown for the rejection of the entire idea of a literary canon in favor of an ethic of diversity, or multiculturalism.

A sense of urgency has been attached to revisionist criticism, because the canon itself represents power. Early on, feminism identified women as oppressed, naturally allied with groups suffering oppression on the basis of race, class, and sexual orientation. Thus, feminist and ethnic critics espouse theories that promise to change the balance of power. However, groups that are satisfied with the status quo vehemently oppose these efforts. And, of course, many Americans who want to do the right thing feel they are being pulled from two directions, as seen in the personal testimony of Nicholasa Mohr and the textbook controversy described by Robert Reinhold.

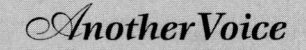

Another Voice

ENGLISH-ONLY AMENDMENT

In 1986, unhappiness with bilingual education, ballots, and official publications led 73 percent of voters to approve an amendment to

continued

continued from previous page

California's constitution making English the state's "official" language. Hispanic leaders condemned the amendment as racist, but it was supported by half of the Hispanic voting population.

SEC. 6. (a) *Purpose*

English is the common language of the people of the United States of America and the State of California. This section is intended to preserve, protect and strengthen the English language, and not to supersede any of the rights guaranteed to the people by this Constitution.

(b) *English as the Official Language of California.*

English is the official language of the State of California.

(c) *Enforcement.*

The Legislature shall enforce this section by appropriate legislation. The Legislature and officials of the State of California shall take all steps necessary to insure that the role of English as the common language of the State of California is preserved and enhanced. The Legislature shall make no law which diminishes or ignores the role of English as the common language of the State of California.

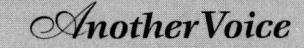

Another Voice

AMERICA'S DIVINE MISSION
RONALD REAGAN

In a speech at the dedication of the renovated Statue of Liberty in 1986, President Ronald Reagan, one of the most popular presidents of the twentieth century, gave voice to the still vital belief that the United States has a special, God-given, mission:

Well, the truth is, she's everybody's gal. We sometimes forget that even those who came here first to settle the new land were also strangers. I've spoken before of the tiny *Arabella*, a ship at

continued

continued from previous page

anchor just off the Massachusetts coast. A little group of Puritans huddled on the deck. And then John Winthrop, who would later become the first Governor of Massachusetts, reminded his fellow Puritans there on that tiny deck that they must keep faith with their God, that the eyes of all the world were upon them, and that they must not forsake the mission that God had sent them on, and they must be a light unto the nations of all the world—a shining city upon a hill.

Call it mysticism if you will, I have always believed there was some divine providence that placed this great land here between the two great oceans, to be found by a special kind of people from every corner of the world, who had a special love for freedom and a special courage that enabled them to leave their own land, leave their friends and their countrymen, and come to this new and strange land to build a new world of peace and freedom and hope.

Lincoln spoke about hope as he left the hometown he would never see again to take up the duties of the Presidency and bring America through a terrible civil war. At each stop on his long train ride to Washington, the news grew worse: The Nation was dividing; his own life was in peril. On he pushed, undaunted. In Philadelphia he spoke in Independence Hall, where 85 years earlier the Declaration of Independence had been signed. He noted that much more had been achieved there than just independence from Great Britain. It was, he said, "hope to the world, future for all time."

Well, that is the common thread that binds us to those Quakers on the tiny deck of the *Arabella,* to the beleaguered farmers and landowners signing the Declaration in Philadelphia in that hot Philadelphia hall, to Lincoln on a train ready to guide his people through the conflagration, to all the millions crowded in the steerage who passed this lady and wept at the sight of her, and those who've worked here in the scaffolding with their hands and with their love. . . .

100th anniversary of the Statue of Liberty, 1986

NICHOLASA MOHR

"Puerto Rican Writers in the U.S., Puerto Rican Writers in Puerto Rico: A Separation beyond Language" (1987)

"I realized that I was the only Puerto Rican on the panel who writes in English."

If the children of Greek immigrants to America are no longer Greek and are not expected to speak Greek, why are second and third generation descendants of Puerto Rican immigrants still called Puerto Ricans and expected to speak Spanish? Such questions of identity and group loyalty supply the motivation for the following essay.

Nicholasa Mohr was born in New York City and writes in English. Is she a bona fide member of the Puerto Rican community? Many of her acquaintances and professional colleagues think not. To them, her rejection of Spanish makes her an outsider; on visits to Puerto Rico, her Spanish is ridiculed as a corrupted dialect and she is dismissed as an intruder, a "Nuyorican." As indicated by the bilingual titles of her books *El Bronx Remembered* (1975) and *In Nueva York* (1977), she, in turn, feels that Puerto Rican identity includes more than the Spanish heritage; Puerto Rico, after all, has been part of the United States for over a century. How, she muses, does one honor both strands of this braided culture?

Mohr is also the author of *Rituals of Survival: A Woman's Portfolio* (1985) and *Going Home* (1986).

Text: Nicholasa Mohr; "Puerto Rican Writers in the U.S., Puerto Rican Writers in Puerto Rico: A Separation beyond Language"; *The Americas Review* 15, no. 2 (1987).

EXPLORING ISSUES IN THE TEXT

1. Account for the Puerto Ricans' unique position as United States citizens and members of the Latin American community (par. 4). Explain how this situation influences the Puerto Rican community in New York City (pars. 5–7).

2. Describe the experience of the postwar generation of Puerto Rican migrants (pars. 11–12). What were they taught about their ancestral home? What reality did they discover there? How did this discovery affect their sense of identity?

3. Analyze how the experience of being a Puerto Rican woman influenced Mohr as a writer (pars. 13–15). Explain why Mohr does not feel a sense of camaraderie with Puerto Rican authors who write in Spanish (pars. 16–17). Why does she identify with non-Puerto Rican writers like Alice Walker and Raymond Carver (par. 18)?

PUERTO RICAN WRITERS IN THE U.S., PUERTO RICAN WRITERS IN PUERTO RICO: A SEPARATION BEYOND LANGUAGE

1   As a writer of Puerto Rican parentage who was born, raised, educated, and is presently living in New York City, I often get asked, "Why don't you write in Spanish?" And this question is asked not only by those persons of non-Hispanic background but also by the Puerto Ricans residing on the Island of Puerto Rico.

2   In the fall of 1986, I was invited to be on a panel titled "Puerto Rican Women Fiction Writers," at Columbia University. As I began to work on my presentation, I realized that I was the only Puerto Rican on the panel who writes in English. I decided to examine the differences, which include and go beyond language, that exist between myself and those other Puerto Rican writers, writing in Spanish, who live in Puerto Rico or in other Spanish-speaking environments.

3   My birth makes me a native New Yorker. I write here in the United States about my personal experiences and those of a particular group of migrants that number in the millions. Yet, all of these actualities seem to have little or no bearing on those who insist on seeing me as an "intruder," or "outsider" who has taken on a foreign language: perhaps even taken it on much too forcefully, using it to document and validate our existence and survival inside the very nation that chose to colonize us.

4   Puerto Rico continues to use Spanish as its official language in spite of its status as a commonwealth of the U.S. Puerto Ricans born in Puerto Rico, unlike other immigrant or militant groups, hold the unique position of being United States citizens while still remaining part of the greater Latin American family. And even though their position in the hierarchy of Latin America is often assessed as one of low status because of their connected dependence to the United States (a sort of stepchild or impoverished relation of the Yankees) resulting in their government's dubious allegiance to Latin America, Puerto Rico is nonetheless considered a member of the Spanish-speaking world.

5   Thus, this status is singular in its kind, creating a dichotomous existence further exacerbated by the proximity of the Island and permitting Puerto Ricans as United States citizens to travel frequently and cheaply from the Island of Puerto Rico to and from the mainland United States. Con-

tact between the Islanders and the Puerto Ricans here is a common occurrence. It follows that Spanish continues to be spoken in areas of the U.S. that are heavily populated by Puerto Ricans and today by the new political refugees from Central and South America. One of the cities with the oldest Puerto Rican population that is today inhabited by the third and fourth generations of these early migrants, as well as other recently arrived Hispanic immigrants, is New York City.

6   Consequently, New York is fast becoming a bilingual city. Public service messages and advertisements are now written in Spanish and English. Hispanic food is available in luncheonettes as well as in fine restaurants. Many merchants speak Spanish or have bilingual employees to meet the needs of their customers.

7   In the U.S. and New York in particular, there are many other immigrants and political refugees and their children who are not Hispanic. However, it is unlikely that Greek-Americans, Irish-Americans, or Asian-Americans, for example, could conceivably have monthly or even weekend visits overseas with their relatives. This frequent traveling is not unusual within the Puerto Rican stateside and Island communities. Nor is it expected that these other ethnic Americans speak and write in the native language of their countries of origin. No matter how foreign these other groups may appear, their writers, when documenting injustices or illuminating accomplishments, all do so by writing in English. Some examples are Joseph Conrad, Vladimir Nabokov, and Jerzy Kozinski. Others born or raised here are Maxine Hong Kingston, Philip Roth, and Mario Puzo.

8   These writers are not chastised or rejected because they use English. Nor are they expected to use another language of expression. Indeed, they are applauded for the way in which they master the English language. Because I am a daughter of the Puerto Rican Diaspora, English is the language that gives life to my work, the characters I create, and that stimulates me as a writer. It has also been a vital component in the struggle for my very survival. However, it is much more than language that separates the Puerto Rican writers born and/or raised here from the writers in Puerto Rico. And I will endeavor, from my perspective, to describe what I perceive as some of the major reasons for this separation.

9   In the books I've published to date, I have dealt with a period in time that covers more than forty-five years of Puerto Rican history here in New York. When I started to write in 1972 I realized that, except for a book or two that concentrated on the Puerto Rican male's problems and misfortunes, there were no books in United States literature that dealt with our existence, our contributions, or what we Puerto Rican migrants were about. I, as a Puerto Rican child, never existed in North American letters. Our struggles as displaced migrants, working-class descendants of the *tabaqueros* (tobacco workers) who began coming here in 1916, were invisible in North American literature. As I proceeded to record

who we were, I addressed myself both to adults and to children—and, of course, to women.

10   In my first book, a novel entitled *Nilda,* I wrote about Puerto Ricans in New York City during the years of the second World War. Through the various adolescent stages of the youngest child, a girl, I trace one family's position as they deal with their alienation as despised migrants, as well as their psychological, emotional, and physical attempts to sustain the family in a traditional Puerto Rican manner. We also see the beginning of the assimilation of Puerto Ricans in the U.S.

11   The works that followed included books recounting the problems, failures, and successes of the greatest influx of Puerto Rican migrants that arrived on the shores of the mainland immediately after the second World War. My work continued to trace the postwar migrants, many of whom arrived as small children or were born here. As the process of assimilation began, they inevitably began to understand that there was no going back; "home" was here, where they were working to materialize their own domain alongside their peers and immediate families. The Puerto Rico that we were taught to believe in was largely based on the reminiscences of our parents and grandparents, many of whom had come from small towns and rural villages. They had nostalgically presented to their displaced offspring a "paradise" where sunshine, flowers, and ownership of one's business or plot of land brought everyone abundant food and eternal happiness. This mythical Island also boasted a population that knew no prejudice and within which neither the dark color of one's skin or one's humble birth were ever seen as a cause for rejection. All of this mythology had little or nothing to do with Puerto Rico, its inhabitants, and the reality of that culture.

12   Later, when some of us returned to the Island, it was clear to see that according to the position one's family held, and the color of one's skin, one could hold a better job and have a higher place in society. It was also evident that those children of the poor and dark migrants who had been forced out more than two generations before, and who returned either with intentions to relocate or merely to visit, were not always welcomed. They were quickly labeled and categorized as outsiders, as "gringos" and "Nuyoricans." Indeed, proof of the false legacy that so many of us had inherited from our elders was painfully clear.

13   The heart of my work has always dealt with my culture. Consequently, the players in my books have been the Puerto Ricans in this city, my people and my beloved Nueva York. Their failures and their triumphs are the core of what and who we are today.

14   In my work, I continue examining the values I have inherited, always aware of the fact that I have come from an Island people who have been colonized from the very onset of their being and who, to this day, continue their dependency. As a Puerto Rican woman, I must also reckon with the history of my patriarchal antecedents and work to heal the scars of machismo that have been etched into our fiber for centuries.

15   Within this framework, my obsession with people's ability to succeed and fail, to despise and cherish, to compromise and not yield, as well as all the other contradictions and incongruities inherent in the human species, fires me on to write. I often think I write very much as an investigative reporter, to find out in the end what happened, to get at an answer that might give me a hint of the "truth." Yet I persist in using fiction as my medium. Fiction, as it is defined in the dictionary is: "That which is feigned or imagined. An assumption of a possible thing as a fact irrespective of the question of its truth."

16   I am not an avid reader of the literature of Puerto Rico. However, throughout the years I have become mildly familiar with some of the work of these writers. Most of the time, I have found their work to be too obsessed with class and race, thus narrowing their subject matter into regional and provincial material. . . .

17   There are few writers from Puerto Rico with whom I feel I can share a sense of camaraderie. Most of what I read lacks the universality that bonds the common human family, regardless of language, class, or geography.

18   Here in the U.S., I find writers who continue to produce work that, although very specific, is also enlightening and inspiring. Their works introduce us to Americans who ultimately share similar goals. Let me cite a few examples. Alice Walker, in *The Color Purple,* speaks to the reader in an exquisite black English about the power of female survival against the harsh domination of black machismo. In his short stories, Raymond Carver, with his minimal but powerful prose, shares with his readers a wide spectrum of the lives of working-class white Americans. Tillie Olsen's books recount the personal struggles of European immigrants and their children, as well as the psychological and social obstacles women must overcome. Ishmael Reed's works explode with the rich vernacular of black English, creating a personal mythology that reflects the reality of the black male's struggles against emasculation in a white-dominated power structure. Finally, Denise Chávez, in *The Last of the Menu Girls* (Arte Público Press), opens the world of the Chicana from the 1950s to the present, incorporating the richness of Chicano Spanish and thereby further enhancing our literature with the language of the peoples of the U.S.

19   These are but a few examples of the writers (and there are many others I could include) who are not necessarily in the mainstream of the Anglo-American writers' empire but who, nonetheless, publish and speak about the realities and complexities of the varied ethnic groups who share our nation. All of these authors write in an American English that comes straight from their people. Their language represents and validates their experiences and those of the people who inhabit their books. None of them writes English like a "British subject," nor are they in any way trying to emulate the culture or values of England.

20   The rhythms of our American language are ever-changing, representing the many cultures that exist in the nation. Those whose works speak to and

about the peoples of color, and the other marginal communities that continue to struggle for equality in the U.S., are the writers I identify with.

21   Except for the attempts of a few writers, I do not see any significant literary movement on the Island of Puerto Rico that speaks for the common folk: the working-class population of the Island. I wonder if the obsession with race, class, Spain, and the use of baroque Spanish might not be a way for some intellectuals to attempt to safeguard their privilege and power against the strong North American influence that presently permeates Puerto Rico. If this should be the case, then it follows that in safeguarding such a status, a majority who are less fortunate must ultimately be excluded.

22   As I have stated, the separation between myself and the majority of Puerto Rican writers in Puerto Rico goes far beyond a question of language. The jet age and the accessibility of Puerto Rico brought an end to a time of innocence for the children of former migrants. There is no pretense that going back will solve problems or bring equality and happiness. This is home. This is where we were born, raised, and where most of us will stay. Notwithstanding is my affection and concern for the people and the land of my parents and grandparents that is my right and my legacy.

23   Who we are, and how our culture will continue to blossom and develop, is being recorded right here by our writers, painters, and composers and where our voices respond and resound, loud and clear.

BUILDING CONTEXT

1. Place Mohr's experience of having to defend the legitimacy of her culture within the context of the debate described by Robert Reinhold.

2. Compare Mohr's reaction to her double heritage to that of Edith Maud Eaton.

3. According to Mohr, what gives value to literature? Relate this attitude to those—either explicit or implied—in the essays by Collins and Mazumdar.

4. Evaluate the relative importance of feminism and race in the essays by Mohr, Collins, and Mazumdar.

FURTHER STUDY

1. Explore how immigrants create hybrid cultures, merging elements of their old and their new homes.

2. Research the history of the melting-pot ideal. Was there ever a time when all immigrants tried to assimilate into the original English culture? Was the English culture of America unchanged from that of England? In what way has official policy toward this issue changed in recent years?

3. Study the American fragmentation of identity. For example, examine how and why "Hispanic" identity in the United States has become particularized to Puerto Rican, Dominican, Chicano, Chicana, Latina, and others.

ADDITIONAL RESOURCES

Foner, Nancy, ed. *New Immigrants in New York.* New York: Columbia University Press, 1987.

Herrera-Sobek, Maria, and Maria Helena Viramontes, eds. *Chicana Creativity and Criticism: Charting New Frontiers in American Literature.* Houston: Arte Publico, 1988.

Horno-Delgado, Asuncion, et al. *Breaking Boundaries: Latina Writing and Critical Readings.* Amherst: University of Massachusetts Press, 1989.

National Association for Chicano Studies. *Chicana Voices: Intersections of Class, Race, and Gender.* Austin: The University of Texas Press, Center for Mexican American Studies, 1984.

RESEARCH KEYWORDS

Puerto Rican Women	Minorities	Immigration
Women—U.S.	Women—Fiction	

PATRICIA HILL
COLLINS
*"The Social Construction
of Black Feminist
Thought"* (1989)

"Since Black women have access to both the Afrocentric and the feminist standpoints, an alternative epistemology used to rearticulate a Black woman's standpoint reflects elements of both traditions."

Social behavior reflects the experience of a community. Language, culture, and manners all evolve over generations to serve the needs—even if only dimly understood or already forgotten—of a specific people. Because not everyone in a community is the same, however, societal norms usually serve one group better than others. Sociologists and anthropologists, while identifying dominant groups in various societies—most often men, priests, warriors, and property owners—have never considered it to be their responsibility to change the society they studied. In contrast, "radical" scholars argue that scholarship cannot be disinterested. As Patricia Hill Collins writes, black feminist thought "encourages all Black women to create new self-definitions that validate a Black woman's standpoint."

To achieve this validation, Collins argues that the concepts of knowledge and truth must be altered. The only theory of knowledge, or epistemology, currently accepted by scholars, publishers, scientists, and academic authorities is positivism—which values objectivity, strict methodological rules, and emotional distance from the subject. To Collins, this is a "Eurocentric masculine" cultural bias, contrary to both feminist and African values. When applied to the study of the black community, she asserts, "such criteria ask African-American women to objectify themselves, devalue their emotional life, displace their motivations for furthering knowledge about Black women, and confront, in an adversarial relationship, those who have more social, economic, and professional power than they." Instead, she offers an "Afrocentric feminist epistemology" that reflects the value that blacks place on dialogue, concrete experience, caring, and personal accountability. The following excerpt focuses on the last two issues. As you read, analyze whether she uses these Afrocentric principles or positivism to present her argument.

Collins (1948–   ) teaches African-American Studies and sociology at the University of Cincinnati. She has written *An Inclusive Curriculum: Race, Class, and Gender in Sociological Instruction* (1987), *Toward a New Vision: Race, Class and Gender as Categories of Analysis and Connection* (1989), and *Black Feminist Thought: Knowledge, Consciousness, and the Politics of Empowerment* (1991).

Text: Patricia Hill Collins; "The Social Construction of Black Feminist Thought"; *Signs: Journal of Women in Culture and Society* 14, no. 4 (1989).

EXPLORING ISSUES IN THE TEXT

1. Explain why Collins believes there is a distinctive black feminist epistemology (pars. 1–3). What experiences does she say have contributed to this view of the world?

2. Summarize the ethic of caring (pars. 7–11). What are its components? How does Collins use "concrete experience" to validate the existence of this ethic?

3. Analyze how Collins uses positivist and Afrocentric methods in presenting her argument. Which of her points do you find most convincing? Least satisfying? Why?

THE SOCIAL CONSTRUCTION OF BLACK FEMINIST THOUGHT

The Contours of an Afrocentric Feminist Epistemology

1   Africanist analyses of the Black experience generally agree on the fundamental elements of an Afrocentric standpoint. In spite of varying histories, Black societies reflect elements of a core African value system that existed prior to and independently of racial oppression. Moreover, as a result of colonialism, imperialism, slavery, apartheid, and other systems of racial domination, Blacks share a common experience of oppression. These similarities in material conditions have fostered shared Afrocentric values that permeate the family structure, religious institutions, culture, and community life of Blacks in varying parts of Africa, the Caribbean, South America, and North America. This Afrocentric consciousness permeates the shared history of people of African descent through the framework of a distinctive Afrocentric epistemology.

2   Feminist scholars advance a similar argument. They assert that women share a history of patriarchal oppression through the political economy of the material conditions of sexuality and reproduction. These shared material conditions are thought to transcend divisions among women created by race, social class, religion, sexual orientation, and ethnicity and to form the basis of a women's standpoint with its corresponding feminist consciousness and epistemology.

3   Since Black women have access to both the Afrocentric and the feminist standpoints, an alternative epistemology used to rearticulate a Black women's standpoint reflects elements of both traditions. The search for the distinguishing features of an alternative epistemology used by African-American women reveals that values and ideas that Africanist scholars identify as being characteristically "Black" often bear remarkable resemblance to similar ideas claimed by feminist scholars as being characteristically "female." This similarity suggests that the material conditions of oppression can vary dramatically and yet generate some uniformity in the epistemologies of subordinate groups. Thus, the significance of an Afrocentric feminist epistemology may lie in its enrichment of our understanding of how subordinate groups create knowledge that enables them to resist oppression.

4   The parallels between the two conceptual schemes raise a question: Is the worldview of women of African descent more intensely infused with the overlapping feminine/Afrocentric standpoints than is the case for either African-American men or white women? While an Afrocentric feminist epistemology reflects elements of epistemologies used by Blacks as a group and women as a group, it also paradoxically demonstrates features that may be unique to Black women. On certain dimensions, Black women may more closely resemble Black men, on others, white women,

and on still others, Black women may stand apart from both groups. Black feminist sociologist Deborah K. King describes this phenomenon as a "both/or" orientation, the act of being simultaneously a member of a group and yet standing apart from it. She suggests that multiple realities among Black women yield a "multiple consciousness in Black women's politics" and that this state of belonging yet not belonging forms an integral part of Black women's oppositional consciousness. Bonnie Thornton Dill's analysis of how Black women live with contradictions, a situation she labels the "dialectics of Black womanhood," parallels King's assertions that this "both/or" orientation is central to an Afrocentric feminist consciousness. Rather than emphasizing how a Black women's standpoint and its accompanying epistemology are different than those in Afrocentric and feminist analyses, I use Black women's experiences as a point of contact between the two.

5   Viewing an Afrocentric feminist epistemology in this way challenges analyses claiming that Black women have a more accurate view of oppression than do other groups. Such approaches suggest that oppression can be quantified and compared and that adding layers of oppression produces a potentially clearer standpoint. While it is tempting to claim that Black women are more oppressed than everyone else and therefore have the best standpoint from which to understand the mechanisms, processes, and effects of oppression, this simply may not be the case.

6   African-American women do not uniformly share an Afrocentric feminist epistemology since social class introduces variations among Black women in seeing, valuing, and using Afrocentric feminist perspectives. While a Black women's standpoint and its accompanying epistemology stem from Black women's consciousness of race and gender oppression, they are not simply the result of combining Afrocentric and female values—standpoints are rooted in real material conditions structured by social class. . . .

THE ETHIC OF CARING

7   "Ole white preachers used to talk wid dey tongues widdout sayin' nothin', but Jesus told us slaves to talk wid our hearts." These words of an ex-slave suggest that ideas cannot be divorced from the individuals who create and share them. This theme of "talking with the heart" taps another dimension of an alternative epistemology used by African-American women, the ethic of caring. Just as the ex-slave used the wisdom in his heart to reject the ideas of the preachers who talked "wid dey tongues widdout sayin' nothin'," the ethic of caring suggests that personal expressiveness, emotions, and empathy are central to the knowledge-validation process.

8   One of three interrelated components making up the ethic of caring is the emphasis placed on individual uniqueness. Rooted in a tradition of

African humanism, each individual is thought to be a unique expression of a common spirit, power, or energy expressed by all life. This belief in individual uniqueness is illustrated by the value placed on personal expressiveness in African-American communities. Johnetta Ray, an inner city resident, describes this Afrocentric emphasis on individual uniqueness: "No matter how hard we try, I don't think black people will ever develop much of a herd instinct. We are profound individualists with a passion for self-expression."

9   A second component of the ethic of caring concerns the appropriateness of emotions in dialogues. Emotion indicates that a speaker believes in the validity of an argument. Consider Ntozake Shange's description of one of the goals of her work: "Our [Western] society allows people to be absolutely neurotic and totally out of touch with their feelings and everyone else's feelings, and yet be very respectable. This, to me, is a travesty. . . . I'm trying to change the idea of seeing emotions and intellect as distinct faculties." Shange's words echo those of the ex-slave. Both see the denigration of emotion as problematic, and both suggest that expressiveness should be reclaimed and valued.

10 A third component of the ethic of caring involves developing the capacity for empathy. Harriet Jones, a sixteen-year-old Black woman, explains why she chose to open up to her interviewer: "Some things in my life are so hard for me to bear, and it makes me feel better to know that you feel sorry about those things and would change them if you could."

11 These three components of the ethic of caring—the value placed on individual expressiveness, the appropriateness of emotions, and the capacity for empathy—pervade African-American culture. One of the best examples of the interactive nature of the importance of dialogue and the ethic of caring in assessing knowledge claims occurs in the use of the call and response discourse mode in traditional Black church services. In such services, both the minister and the congregation routinely use voice rhythm and vocal inflection to convey meaning. The sound of what is being said is just as important as the words themselves in what is, in a sense, a dialogue between reason and emotions. As a result, it is nearly impossible to filter out the strictly linguistic-cognitive abstract meaning from the sociocultural psycho-emotive meaning. While the ideas presented by a speaker must have validity, that is, agree with the general body of knowledge shared by the Black congregation, the group also appraises the way knowledge claims are presented. . . .

12 The convergence of Afrocentric and feminist values in the ethic-of-care dimension of an alternative epistemology seems particularly acute. While white women may have access to a women's tradition valuing emotion and expressiveness, few white social institutions except the family validate this way of knowing. In contrast, Black women have long had the support of the Black church, an institution with deep roots in the African past and a philosophy that accepts and encourages expressiveness and an ethic of caring. While Black men share in this Afrocentric

tradition, they must resolve the contradictions that distinguish abstract, unemotional Western masculinity from an Afrocentric ethic of caring. The differences among race/gender groups thus hinge on differences in their access to institutional supports valuing one type of knowing over another. Although Black women may be denigrated within white-male-controlled academic institutions, other institutions, such as Black families and churches, which encourage the expression of Black female power, seem to do so by way of their support for an Afrocentric feminist epistemology.

THE ETHIC OF PERSONAL ACCOUNTABILITY

13 An ethic of personal accountability is the final dimension of an alternative epistemology. Not only must individuals develop their knowledge claims through dialogue and present those knowledge claims in a style proving their concern for their ideas, people are expected to be accountable for their knowledge claims. Zilpha Elaw's description of slavery reflects this notion that every idea has an owner and that the owner's identity matters: "Oh, the abominations of slavery! . . . every case of slavery, however lenient its inflictions and mitigated its atrocities, indicates an oppressor, the oppressed, and oppression." For Elaw, abstract definitions of slavery mesh with the concrete identities of its perpetrators and its victims. Blacks "consider it essential for individuals to have personal positions on issues and assume full responsibility for arguing their validity."

14 Assessments of an individual's knowledge claims simultaneously evaluate an individual's character, values, and ethics. African-Americans reject Eurocentric masculinist beliefs that probing into an individual's personal viewpoint is outside the boundaries of discussion. Rather, all views expressed and actions taken are thought to derive from a central set of core beliefs that cannot be other than personal. From this perspective, knowledge claims made by individuals respected for their moral and ethical values will carry more weight than those offered by less respected figures.

15 An example drawn from an undergraduate course composed entirely of Black women, which I taught, might help clarify the uniqueness of this portion of the knowledge-validation process. During one class discussion, I assigned the students the task of critiquing an analysis of Black feminism advanced by a prominent Black male scholar. Instead of dissecting the rationality of the author's thesis, my students demanded facts about the author's personal biography. They were especially interested in concrete details of his life such as his relationships with Black women, his marital status, and his social class background. By requesting data on dimensions of his personal life routinely excluded in positivist approaches to knowledge validation, they were invoking concrete experience as a criterion of meaning. They used this information to as-

sess whether he really cared about his topic and invoked this ethic of caring in advancing their knowledge claims about his work. Furthermore, they refused to evaluate the rationality of his written ideas without some indication of his personal credibility as an ethical human being. The entire exchange could only have occurred as a dialogue among members of a class that had established a solid enough community to invoke an alternative epistemology in assessing knowledge claims.

16   The ethic of personal accountability is clearly an Afrocentric value, but is it feminist as well? While limited by its attention to middle-class, white women, Carol Gilligan's work suggests that there is a female model for moral development where women are more inclined to link morality to responsibility, relationships, and the ability to maintain social ties. If this is the case, then African-American women again experience a convergence of values from Afrocentric and female institutions.

17   The use of an Afrocentric feminist epistemology in traditional Black church services illustrates the interactive nature of all four dimensions and also serves as a metaphor for the distinguishing features of an Afrocentric feminist way of knowing. The services represent more than dialogues between the rationality used in examining biblical texts/stories and the emotion inherent in the use of reason for this purpose. The rationale for such dialogues addresses the task of examining concrete experiences for the presence of an ethic of caring. Neither emotion nor ethics is subordinated to reason. Instead, emotion, ethics, and reason are used as interconnected, essential components in assessing knowledge claims. In an Afrocentric feminist epistemology, values lie at the heart of the knowledge-validation process such that inquiry always has an ethical aim.

Epistemology and Black Feminist Thought

18 Living life as an African-American woman is a necessary prerequisite for producing Black feminist thought because within Black women's communities thought is validated and produced with reference to a particular set of historical, material, and epistemological conditions. African-American women who adhere to the idea that claims about Black women must be substantiated by Black women's sense of their own experiences and who anchor their knowledge claims in an Afrocentric feminist epistemology have produced a rich tradition of Black feminist thought. . . .

19   As more Black women earn advanced degrees, the range of Black feminist scholarship is expanding. Increasing numbers of African-American women scholars are explicitly choosing to ground their work in Black women's experiences, and, by doing so, many implicitly adhere to an Afrocentric feminist epistemology. Rather than being restrained by their "both/and" status of marginality, these women make creative use of their outsider-within status and produce innovative Black feminist thought.

The difficulties these women face lie less in demonstrating the technical components of white male epistemologies than in resisting the hegemonic nature of these patterns of thought in order to see, value, and use existing alternative Afrocentric feminist ways of knowing.

20   In establishing the legitimacy of their knowledge claims, Black women scholars who want to develop Black feminist thought may encounter the often conflicting standards of three key groups. First, Black feminist thought must be validated by ordinary African-American women who grow to womanhood "in a world where the saner you are, the madder you are made to appear." To be credible in the eyes of this group, scholars must be personal advocates for their material, be accountable for the consequences of their work, have lived or experienced their material in some fashion, and be willing to engage in dialogues about their findings with ordinary, everyday people. Second, if it is to establish its legitimacy, Black feminist thought also must be accepted by the community of Black women scholars. These scholars place varying amounts of importance on rearticulating a Black women's standpoint using an Afrocentric feminist epistemology. Third, Black feminist thought within academia must be prepared to confront Eurocentric masculinist political and epistemological requirements.

21   The dilemma facing Black women scholars engaged in creating Black feminist thought is that a knowledge claim that meets the criteria of adequacy for one group and thus is judged to be an acceptable knowledge claim may not be translatable into the terms of a different group. Using the example of Black English, June Jordan illustrates the difficulty of moving among epistemologies: "You cannot 'translate' instances of Standard English preoccupied with abstraction or with nothing/nobody evidently alive into Black English. That would warp the language into uses antithetical to the guiding perspective of its community of users. Rather you must first change those Standard English sentences, themselves, into ideas consistent with the person-centered assumptions of Black English." While both worldviews share a common vocabulary, the ideas themselves defy direct translation.

22   Once Black feminist scholars face the notion that, on certain dimensions of a Black women's standpoint, it may be fruitless to try to translate ideas from an Afrocentric feminist epistemology into a Eurocentric masculinist epistemology, then the choices become clearer. Rather than trying to uncover universal knowledge claims that can withstand the translation from one epistemology to another, time might be better spent rearticulating a Black women's standpoint in order to give African-American women the tools to resist their own subordination. The goal here is not one of integrating Black female "folk culture" into the substantiated body of academic knowledge, for that substantiated knowledge is, in many ways, antithetical to the best interests of Black women. Rather, the process is one of rearticulating a preexisting Black women's standpoint

and recentering the language of existing academic discourse to accommodate these knowledge claims. For those Black women scholars engaged in this rearticulation process, the social construction of Black feminist thought requires the skill and sophistication to decide which knowledge claims can be validated using the epistemological assumptions of one but not both frameworks, which claims can be generated in one framework and only partially accommodated by the other, and which claims can be made in both frameworks without violating the basic political and epistemological assumptions of either. . . .

BUILDING CONTEXT

1. Compare how Collins and Maya Angelou analyze the relationship of black women to both white society and black men. Analyze whether any disagreements can be explained as stemming from generational differences.

2. Compare Collins's Afrocentric values with the values of Mohr, a Puerto Rican, and Mazumdar, an Asian American. What conclusion do you draw about the uniqueness of particular groups?

3. How do Collins's goals differ from those of the early Woman's and Civil Rights Movements, as illustrated, for example, by Stanton and King? What goals does she share with writers like Emma Goldman?

4. Place Collins's beliefs within the context of the debate over multiculturalism reported on by Reinhold.

FURTHER STUDY

1. Trace the conflict between the ideals of the melting-pot and multiculturalism. Examine their political fortunes, for example, when they were espoused as public policy by schools or the government.

2. Distinguish between multiculturalism and ethnic separatism. Explore, for example, Black Nationalism or the English-Only movement.

3. Explore the advantages and disadvantages of claiming that women, African Americans, or other groups each have a unique epistemology. How might this claim lead, for example, to greater job opportunities—or to exclusion from certain fields?

ADDITIONAL RESOURCES

Gilligan, Carol. *In a Different Voice.* Cambridge: Harvard University Press, 1982.

Giddings, Paula. *When and Where I Enter:The Impact of Black Women on Race and Sex in America.* New York: William Morrow, 1984.

Haan, Norma, et al., eds. *Social Science as Moral Inquiry*. New York: Columbia University Press, 1983.

Hooks, Bell. *Ain't I a Woman? Black Women and Feminism*. Boston: South End Press, 1981.

RESEARCH KEYWORDS

Epistemology	Social Classes	African-American Women
Feminism	Sex Roles	Intercultural Education
Ethnic Relations	Discrimination	

SUCHETA MAZUMDAR
"A Woman-Centered Perspective on Asian American History"
(1989)

"The political and social climate, in which blatantly racial violence against visible minorities has increased sharply, renders the challenges even more numerous and complex for Asian American women in the 1990s."

Patricia Hill Collins notes that in contrast to nominally objective traditional scholarship—which examines but does not necessarily defend its subject—black feminists consider advocacy a central aspect of scholarship. Similar identification with the subject characterizes most proponents of the Women's and Ethnic Studies movements. The purpose of this kind of scholarship is to grant legitimacy to the people studied and to relieve their oppression. Yet even as researchers identified themselves with the group they studied, membership within each group became more and more restrictive. Thus, instead of treating blacks as a group, scholars distinguished between African Americans, as Caribbeans, or black Cubans; similarly, Asian-American women were considered as a group distinct from Asians, Asian Americans, and women.

The following selection, from the introduction to *Making Waves: An Anthology of Writings by and about Asian American Women*, looks at the history of Asian immigrants to America through the eyes of women. What was it like to be the wife of a rich man in China who is reduced to being a laborer in San Francisco? What did it mean to be culturally inferior to a man who is the social inferior of everyone in the outside world? What is the implication of wanting to preserve an ethnic identity whose values have been a source of oppression for women? Throughout, the selection illustrates the new historiography, or theory of history: Mazumdar is not the cold observer, but the empathetic sister and advocate.

Text: Sucheta Mazumdar; "A Woman-Centered Perspective on Asian American History"; introduction to *Making Waves: An Anthology of Writings by and about Asian American Women;* Asian Women United of California; Boston: Beacon Press, 1989.

Another Voice

MAIL-ORDER BRIDES
VENNY VILLAPANDO

In the present matches bridges-to-be are generally Asian and husbands-to-be are Caucasians, mostly American, Australian, and Canadian. A majority of the women are poor and because of economic desperation become mail-order brides. Racial, as well as economic, factors define the marriage however. The new wife is relegated to a more inferior position than her picture bride counterpart. Plus the inequity of the partnership is further complicated by the mail-order bride's immigrant status. Consequently she is a foreigner not only to the culture, language, and society, but to her husband's race and nationality as well. . . .

"These men want women who will feel totally dependent on them," writes Dr. Gladys L. Symons of the University of Calgary. "They want women who are submissive and less intimidating." Aged between thirty and forty, these men grew up most likely before the rise of the feminist movement, adds Symons. She partially attributes the resurgence of the mail-order bride to a backlash against the 1980s high-pressure style of dating. . . .

The Japanese American Citizens League, a national civil rights group, . . . found that the men tend to be white, much older than the bride they choose, politically conservative, frustrated by the women's movement, and socially alienated. They experience feelings of personal inadequacy and find the traditional Asian value of deference to men reassuring.

continued

continued from previous page

In her interview in the *Alberta Report,* Symons points out that the men are also attracted to the idea of buying a wife, since all immigration, transportation, and other costs run to only about two thousand dollars. "We're a consumer society," says Symons. "People become translated into commodities easily." And commodities they are.

The Business of Selling Mail-Order Brides, 1989

EXPLORING ISSUES IN THE TEXT

1. Trace the evolution of American attitudes toward Asian immigrants from the label "yellow peril" to that of "model minority" (pars. 1–3). Why is the new label just as dangerous as the old one (par. 4)?

2. Explain how the Asian-American community is divided by class and other variables (par. 6). Why does Mazumdar believe that in the Asian community "ethnic identity supersedes gender and class" (par. 7)?

3. Evaluate the significance of gender in the Asian-American community (pars. 9–12). Why does Mazumdar warn against the generalization of "Asian women"?

4. Analyze Mazumdar's assertion that the experience of Asian-American professional women creates a new definition of success (par. 16). What is your opinion of this view?

A WOMAN-CENTERED PERSPECTIVE ON ASIAN AMERICAN HISTORY

From Yellow Peril to Model Minorities: The New Immigrants

1 The 1952 McCarran-Walter Act enabled Asians to acquire citizenship through naturalization, and changes in the 1965 immigration laws raised the quota of aliens permitted entry to twenty thousand from each Asian country. These liberalized policies meant that the immigrants entering after 1965 typically entered as families or could send for their families soon after arrival. However, the system has not been without biases.

2 Between the years 1943 and 1965, when the quota system was in effect, 50 percent of the quota was reserved for professionals. This selective process facilitated the immigration of those with post-secondary education, technical training, and specialized experience. It continued even after the 1965 liberalization of immigration laws, which permitted

entry based either on occupational skills needed by the United States or on the presence of relatives in this country. Professionals could immigrate under both types of preference categories; most other potential immigrants could apply only under the family reunification category. Without a relative willing to act as a sponsor, those who are unskilled may have to wait five to ten years for a visa. Complicated, time-consuming, and intimidating application procedures also favor the educated.

3   Though there are now more job opportunities available to these professionals and to second- and third-generation Asian Americans, one must be concerned that the sensationalized "yellow peril" cliché of poverty-stricken Asians not be replaced by yet another cliché, that of the "super successful model minority." This new success myth is dangerous because it does not tell the full story.

4   Despite various federal affirmative action policies and programs of the 1970s, 10.7 percent of all Asian Pacific families in 1979 had incomes below the poverty level. Statistics suggest that one-fifth of all employed Asian Pacific women work as waitresses, maids, and sewing machine operators. Many Asian Americans, including older immigrants and recent arrivals, live in Manilatowns and Koreatowns and Little Saigons, congested urban ghettoes like San Francisco Chinatown, where 77 percent of the housing does not even meet city codes and only 6 percent has adequate plumbing.

5   Many of these Asian ethnic ghettoes were on the decline in the 1950s and 1960s; their revival and proliferation in the 1970s and 1980s is not so much due to Chamber of Commerce promotion of tourist exotica as a genuine response to the needs of the new immigrants who live, work, or find support services there. Even highly trained professionals may find the language barrier overwhelming or their foreign credentials unacceptable here and be forced to turn to low-income housing and semiskilled jobs in ethnic markets, restaurants, and custodial services in order to survive.

6   Relationships between new arrivals and long-term residents or citizens and between professional and working classes can be complex and tense. The established working class sees new arrivals as competitors for the same scarce resources; the established professionals look askance at their limited English proficient or culturally ill-at-ease immigrant counterparts. Professionals dissociate themselves from the residents of ethnic ghettoes; working-class Asians view the professionals' tendency to be spokespersons for the community with suspicion. The new arrival from the middle class is often more politically conservative and may look to Asia for a frame of reference; the U.S.-born tends to view the world from an American perspective.

7   Race and ethnic origin are frequently the most cohesive forces in defining identity. Organizers in Chinatown have found, for example, that the paternalistic attitude of garment factory owners for their employees

is matched by a sense of obligation and loyalty among the workers. The isolation of workers and their lack of contact with the non-Chinese world make them all the more reluctant to trust outsiders or to challenge their Chinese employers. In times of crisis when an entire racial or national group has undergone severe trauma—such as during the World War II internment of Japanese Americans or the resettlement experience of Southeast Asians—ethnic identity supersedes gender and class. For women of color, concerns arising out of racial identity are an integral aspect of their overall identity.

8   For first-generation immigrants in particular, class issues can be quite confusing because class boundaries based on occupation can change dramatically with migration. For example, many of the early Japanese and Chinese immigrant women came from relatively wealthy land- and business-owning families. Once here, as wives of immigrant laborers, they often lived difficult and frequently impoverished lives. Similarly, among more recent immigrants, women from middle-class, white-collar backgrounds frequently only find work in semiskilled jobs as waitresses, cooks, shop clerks, or electronics assembly line workers. Their consciousness and aspirations nevertheless remain middle-class.

9   The impact of gender on Asian women in America varies enormously even within the same class and ethnic group. While the idea that female children are of less value than male children permeates all Asian cultures to greater or lesser degrees, the effect of this value system on an American-born woman is quite different than on an immigrant one. For immigrant women arrival in America can be liberating. Societal norms of the majority community frequently provide greater personal freedom than permitted in Asian societies. The young wife, though dependent on her husband in the unfamiliar environment, often finds she has greater control of her life when living apart from her mother-in-law. The stigma attached to divorce is also somewhat muted in the American setting, thus providing a measure of choice to women with adequate survival skills. In recalling her life in the 1920s, one Filipina echoed a theme found in many Asian American communities then and now: "When I finally ran away from him, it was only because we were far away from my parents and parents-in-law who would have insisted that I accept my fate and stay with him no matter what."

10   Individual freedom is especially palpable for women from the middle or upper classes, whose lives tend to be much more constricted in Asia. A Pakistani woman remarked recently: "I like the freedom for the woman in this country. . . . Women back home, they are kept so much inside the house and . . . things were very hard. . . . After living that kind of life . . . I came here and [found] so much freedom." A national survey of college-educated women from India living in the United States showed that 33.3 percent of the women working in technical fields and 50 percent in academic fields described themselves as feminists.

11   For second-, third-, and fourth-generation Asian American women, the chasm between traditional Asian familial values and mainstream values has often yielded conflict. Though some of this conflict is intergenerational and common to all societies, the disparate cultural values of East and West are a source of particular anguish. On the one hand, the preservation of ethnic identity within an environment often hostile to people of color has meant a closer allegiance to Asian cultural norms; on the other, these same cultural norms and values have been a source of oppression and discrimination, especially for women. Marrying outside the community has served as one way of expressing dissatisfaction with the traditional role. Interracial marriage among the earlier immigrants, such as Japanese Americans, is approaching a level of 50 percent; and among newer immigrants, one survey found that 12 percent of Korean women college students preferred non-Korean Asian Americans as spouses and another 13 percent preferred whites.

12   It would be inaccurate to talk about a homogeneous Asian American community when discussing class, education, national origin, economic status, or the potential for economic mobility. Similarly it would be erroneous to ascribe one common description to all Asian American women. The experiences of a Southeast Asian working-class woman and what she may perceive as the major causes of her oppression will differ greatly from those of a professional, middle-class Japanese American woman. Because it is difficult to capture the entire experience of Asian American women in this overview, what follows are but glimpses and facets of that experience.

From Serving Woman to Corporate Boardroom

13   Historically located in New York City, the garment industry expanded to California in the 1930s and is now also entrenched in Los Angeles and San Francisco. The industry draws workers from a continuous pool of Asian and Central American immigrants whose limited language and job skills keep them trapped in the low-paying industry. Though often perceived as just a first job, sewing is often their only job. Sui Sim Tom Yee started sewing in 1955, soon after she arrived in San Francisco. At first she earned 75¢ an hour and could only survive by working longer hours; in 1978, after twenty-three years in the industry, her wages were $2.50 an hour, minimum wage. In Hawaii the story is the same: Nora, a Filipina who has worked as a seamstress for twelve years, still has no job security and receives wages just 10¢ above minimum wage. Like her mainland counterparts, she cannot afford to take time off to acquire other job and language skills.

14   The electronics industry, another major employer of Asian immigrant women, also offers little chance for upward mobility. Whether in the United States or in Asia, the "women's place in the integrated circuit," is

typically on the lowest rung of the pay scale. Women comprise about 90 percent of the workers in semiconductor manufacturing and testing lines in California's Silicon Valley; about half of them are Filipinas, Vietnamese, Koreans, and South Asians. Workers in this largely nonunion industry often find minimum wage, forced overtime, work speedups, health hazards, stress, and plant closures a normal part of their work environment.

15 But there is another side to the profile of Asian American working women. For professional immigrant women and for second- and third-generation Asian American women who grew up in the expanding economy of post–World War II United States, reaping the benefits of a hard, long struggle by women and people of color, there have indeed been possibilities denied to earlier generations. Yet even this progress must be looked at closely. Though some Asian American women now work in positions of responsibility, visibility, and authority as lawyers, doctors, teachers, and businesswomen, most work "behind the scenes" as file clerks, office machine operators, typists, and cashiers. In 1970 Chinese women with four or more years of college were still concentrated in clerical work, as were about one-third of the native-born, college-educated Filipino women in 1980.

16 At this point it becomes necessary to question the concept of "success." Success is usually defined in terms of individual achievements—a recognition that one's undaunted spirit somehow beats the odds. But this paean to the individual disguises reality. The success of many women of color now in positions of power and visibility is not a fortuitous coincidence of opportunity and ability. Their individual achievements are founded on many years and many generations of struggle and pathmaking determination.

Immigrants and Survivors

17 The struggle of women of color for psychological and physical survival extracts a high price, and the cost goes up when the women are immigrants as well. Survival, as a woman and as a minority group member, is in itself a form of resistance. Survival for Asian women in America has taken many forms, from scrubbing floors to picking berries; from suppressing anger and swallowing loneliness to say it is all right to look the way they do. Yet there has been much more than mere survival; there has been a whole history of resistance. Private forms of resistance pass by unnoticed precisely because myths, such as the passive Asian woman, may cloud our vision. Portraits of resistance, of the struggle to preserve human dignity, abound when one begins to recognize them: mothers in Chinatown who lovingly tended little patches called "gardens" and grew flowers on windowsills as a statement of self instead of growing more "sensible" vegetables; mothers who miraculously found empty cardboard cartons to be used as screens for privacy at the intern-

ment camps. Private resistance may extend to refusing to speak English—a personal gesture that negates the world of the majority in which the immigrant woman is powerless and marginalized.

18   But there have also been individual and collective political forms of resistance, struggles largely unheralded except in the ethnic press. The history of labor union activism is nearly forgotten. Few remember the role of Asian immigrant women in the plantation strikes of turn-of-the-century Hawaii or know about recent struggles in the garment, hotel, and food-packaging industries. Few have heard of Esther Lau, a Chinese American whose 1970 charges of sexual harassment and physical assault by white policemen in Los Angeles brought to light scores of similar incidents perpetrated on other women of color; or Dr. Shymala Rajender, who won a class-action suit charging gender discrimination against the University of Minnesota in 1973; or of fifty-eight-year-old Helen Kim, a Korean American design engineer, who fought and won her seven-year sex discrimination suit against the Los Angeles Department of Transportation in 1980. Few know the names of the hundreds of Japanese American women who, in the 1982 hearings held to investigate the World War II internment of Japanese Americans, publicly spoke about their pain, humiliation, and degradation after forty years of agonizing silence. These Japanese American women broke their silence because they hoped "never again, would such wrong be done to a people, never again." Similarly engineer Kim stated, "It was never my intent to hurt anyone, not my department or the city. I just wanted the system to change. . . . Now, because of what I went through, maybe some other people will have an easier time of it."

19   Yet this sense of the larger political collective is no stranger to Asian American women, who have been involved in political issues both in the United States and their ancestral homelands. Prior to World War II, women from Asian countries under colonial rule were actively involved in independence struggles, forming support organizations, raising money. Korean women in Hawaii, for instance, raised $200,000 for the patriotic cause by working in the cane fields, doing needlework, and selling candies and Korean rice cakes. The handful of South Asian women in America at the turn of the century donated their gold bangles to finance the 1914–15 Gadhar (Revolution) against the British. And Chinese American women organized public marches and fundraisers and raised thousands of dollars for war relief in Japanese-occupied China.

20   The civil rights and anti-war movements motivated many younger Asian American women to become politically active over issues of discrimination because of race, sex, or place of origin. Others have become involved in the cause of the homeless and poor—many of whom are elderly immigrants—or in nuclear disarmament efforts. For some younger women the broader perspective of being Asian Americans, born of a dual heritage, has also meant involvement on international issues: Filipinas

and Korean women fighting to change political and social conditions in the Philippines and in Korea; women from many different communities working to stop the sex tourism trade in Asian countries.

31   For all these women, the chosen road is not easy. The political and social climate, in which blatantly racial violence against visible minorities has increased sharply, renders the challenges even more numerous and complex for Asian American women in the 1990s. But the women persevere. Many are taking assertive stances in defining solutions to local, national, and international issues affecting women of color. Working within their own communities or in new coalitions, they are ensuring that the voice of Asian women in America will be heard.

Another Voice

"WHAT ARE WOMEN'S ISSUES?"
DIANNE FEINSTEIN

But what are women's issues? Many people consider women's issues to be those areas intrinsically related to women, their bodies, and their families—like abortion and school issues. The E.R.A. has been an interesting departure. The campaign for ratification and its subsequent setbacks presented women with the opportunity to become a major political force in the country.

In my view, the time has come for us to draw a broader agenda. The time has come for women to reach out and grapple with the major issues of our day.

I submit to you that it is time women realize they are not a minority. We are a majority—in virtually every state, every city in this country, and in this world. We are a majority of voters, too. Let us not forget that.

War and peace, the economy, the national defense, housing, and jobs are all our issues, issues we should join today—right now. Let us stop building fences around ourselves and the questions facing our society: the issues belong to all of us. Issues like mortgage revenue bonds, programs for the homeless, urban reconstruction banks, tax reform and indexing, health care, and other such programs should be as familiar to us as that simple twenty-four-word amendment to the Constitution.

Women in Politics: Time for a Change, 1983

BUILDING CONTEXT

1. Compare the relative importance of race and gender in the theories of Mazumdar and Collins. For example, where do the authors place women in the hierarchy of their respective communities?
2. Compare and contrast Mazumdar's new definition of success to Collins's new definition of knowledge. What motivates their new suggestions?
3. Try to place Edith Maud Eaton in the Asian-American world described by Mazumdar. What problems do you encounter? What do you infer from them?

FURTHER STUDY

1. Compare the Asian-American experience to that of another immigrant group. Did both groups initially suffer discrimination? Did they eventually achieve the American dream? Did they try to assimilate, or did they attempt to retain their distinct cultural identities?
2. Examine the history of Asian women in America. Is it possible to define an "Asian" experience without distinguishing among the experiences of Indian, Japanese, Vietnamese, Korean, and Chinese women?
3. Analyze the immigrant experience in America. What common threads bind all immigrant groups? What accounts for the differences in successful acculturation or assimilation?
4. Consider the place of women in one or two ethnic communities. What is their position within their group? How does their relationship to the outside world compare to that of other members of their community?

ADDITIONAL RESOURCES

Amerasia. Journal published by the University of California, Los Angeles.

Daniels, Roger. *Coming to America: A History of Immigration and Ethnicity in American Life.* New York: HarperCollins, 1990.

Fisher, Dexter, ed. *The Third Woman: Minority Women Writers of the United States.* Boston: Houghton Mifflin, 1980.

Kim, Elaine H. *Asian American Literature: An Introduction to the Writings and Their Social Contexts.* Philadelphia: Temple University Press, 1982.

MELUS. Publication of the Society for the Study of Multiethnic Literature of the United States.

RESEARCH KEYWORDS

Asian-American Women	Immigration
Feminism, Sex Roles	Discrimination
U.S.—Social Conditions	Japanese
Indian	Korean
Filipino	

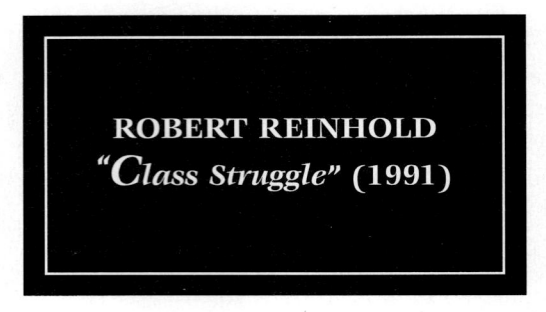

ROBERT REINHOLD
"Class Struggle" (1991)

"If the concept of the melting pot is outdated, what is to replace it?"

The California Board of Education told publishers that the state would only adopt elementary school textbooks that "accurately portray the cultural and racial diversity of our society" while clarifying the Western origin of American law and values. As Robert Reinhold—Los Angeles Bureau chief of the New York Times—reports, the resulting series has been attacked for both minimizing and emphasizing the European contribution to America, and for both slighting and exaggerating minority and non-Western influences. Some critics charge that the full extent of racism is not shown; others argue that American history should not be caricatured as endless exploitation and oppression. Ironically, Gary B. Nash, the principal historian for the project and an ardent supporter of multiculturalism, feels he is being attacked as a racist by the very people who should be his allies.

What does this experience tell us about the future of our country? Is it destined to become another Balkans—a patchwork of suspicious, hostile enclaves—or will we discover what Bill Honig, California's Superintendent of Public Instruction, calls "the political and moral values that are essential for us to live together"?

Text: Robert Reinhold; "Class Struggle"; *The New York Times Magazine,* September 29, 1991.

EXPLORING ISSUES IN THE TEXT

1. Summarize the Board of Education's framework (par. 2). Explain how its requirements were expected to improve the teaching of history. Do you think this expectation was reasonable?

2. What is the significance of the fact that non-Anglos will soon be a majority in California's schools (par. 6)? What does Reinhold imply are the goals of education (pars. 7–8)? What other, perhaps even contrary, goals are sought by some of the critics? What do you believe should be the goal of education?

3. Describe some of the objections to the new textbooks (pars. 18–26). Why did some people think that arguments in favor of slavery should have been omitted? How does this issue relate to the goals of education?

CLASS STRUGGLE

1 Four years ago, the State Board of Education adopted a history and social studies "framework," or curriculum, devised by a team that included Charlotte Crabtree, a professor of education at U.C.L.A., and Diane Ravitch, an Assistant Secretary of Education who was then an adjunct professor of history and education at Teachers College, Columbia University. It then invited publishers to submit a series of textbooks based on the new framework

2 By all accounts, it was an intimidating invitation. The framework called for stretching the study of world and American history to three years each, introduced social studies into the earliest grades, restored the study of religion as a key factor in world history, emphasized history as a dramatic chronicle to be taught as "a story well told," reintroduced literature in historical instruction and fully integrated geography with history. And it demanded that the public schools "accurately portray the cultural and racial diversity of our society" while emphasizing the "centrality of Western civilizations as the source of American political institutions, laws and ideology."

3 The new books are the most visible product yet of this campaign to inject new life and relevance into the teaching of history. The express purpose of the undertaking is to force a sharp reversal of the decades-old trend of watering down textbooks to avoid controversy and appeal to the widest possible market. . . .

4 While its critics have been numerous and vociferous, the project has enjoyed the forceful support of California's pugnacious Superintendent of Public Instruction, Bill Honig. In an interview in his office in Sacramento, Honig stoutly defended the framework against what he calls "the victimization crew," the "tribalists" and "separatists" in universities who "make a livelihood on discrediting broader cultural ideas."

5 And despite widespread complaints about its purported insensitivities to minorities, subtle and not-so-subtle stereotyping and outright biases, the California framework has begun to make wide ripples across American education. With 3.7 million pupils in grades kindergarten through eighth, California represents 11 percent of the $1.7 billion national market for school texts. Already the texts tailored to the California curriculum are beginning to be adopted elsewhere, in West Virginia, Indiana, Arkansas and Oregon, as well as Newark and Dubuque, Iowa.

6 The process by which these books were written, debated, adopted, amended and refined sheds light on the enormous complexity and political contentiousness of teaching history in this polyglot country. It is a debate that has gained urgency in New York and many other ethnically diverse states but nowhere more than in California. By the turn of the century, according to various projections, well under half the children of California will be "Anglos," or people of European origin, and more than a third will be Hispanic and one in eight Asian.

7   The question for educators and parents is this: Can these children, from the earliest school years, be exposed to the full diversity of cultures and traditions that make up the United States and still arrive at the conclusion that we are united by ideals, bonds and legal instruments that support the national motto, E pluribus unum, or "Out of many, one"?

8   Alternatively, are those common ideals, and the immigrant-absorption model on which they are based, fundamentally white European formulations that have excluded and failed the people of color whose ancestors came not in steamers from Europe but in shackles from Africa or, in the case of Indians, were here long before Columbus?. . . .

9   Critics and admirers alike agree that the new books are superior to the soporific history texts used by generations of American students. Never before have elementary-school texts made such an effort to include the broad sweep of history and the divergent cultures that flow into the American mainstream. The series consists of one book for each grade from first to eighth, and a separate fourth-grade book for six other states, including California. Each is filled with colorful charts, graphs, time lines, maps and photographs in a format suggestive of the newspaper USA Today. . . .

10   The series tries to correct the traditionally Eurocentric views of older texts. For example, the fifth-grade book (entitled "America Will Be," after a Langston Hughes poem) covers early American history and plunges students into the American ethnic rainbow with devices like a two-page color spread of different kinds of bread: pita for Greeks and Syrians, matzoh for Jews, corn bread for Indians, tortillas for Mexican and Central American Indians and so on.

11   The fifth-grade volume devotes roughly 50 pages to slavery in the South, with vivid, firsthand descriptions of its cruelty, and contains fairly frank treatment of the brutality visited on American Indians by European settlers. Among the primary sources quoted are Olaudah Equiano (an African slave), Abigail Adams, Marco Polo, Black Hawk and Jane Addams, the founder of Hull House. It quotes the writings of an escaped slave, the Rev. Josiah Henson, who described his mother, on her knees, begging the man who had just bought her to buy her baby too; she was kicked senseless.

12   The seventh-grade book, "Across the Centuries," devotes 51 pages to the history of Sub-Saharan Africa, tracing the Bantu migration, the rise of the Zimbabwe State and the Kongo Kingdom. It also covers Asian, pre-Columbian American and other civilizations, as well as Europe in the Renaissance, Reformation and the ages of colonialism and imperialism.

13   The fourth-grade book, "Oh, California," on the state's history, tries to describe the cruelties the Spanish mission system visited on the Indians of California. The books sometimes go to amusing lengths to achieve political correctness. The fourth-grade book has a full-page picture of a "vaquera"—a Mexican cowgirl—at a rodeo in 1820.

14   In the spring of 1990, nine publishers submitted entries to the state board's Curriculum Commission, which set up three panels of teachers to evaluate them. Only Houghton Mifflin offered books for all grades through eighth. In the end, the commission approved just the Houghton Mifflin series and a single eighth-grade entry from Holt, Rinehart & Winston Inc, "The Story of America: Beginnings to 1914." But it insisted upon certain changes, which started a process known in publishing jargon as "corrigenda," literally a list of errors to be corrected before publication.

15   For example, the original fifth-grade book credited John Wesley Powell with being the first person to lead a group the length of the Grand Canyon. That was changed to read that he was the first white person to do so, since Indians had traveled the route for centuries. And some changes were made to accommodate Muslim sensibilities. They deleted three pictures of Mohammed—in Islam, literal images of Mohammed are considered blasphemous—and a suggestion in the teacher's manual to have children impersonate Mohammed and his family, suggesting instead that they interview a Muslim scholar.

16   Other changes were made to avoid misinterpretations For instance, a sixth-grade lesson on the life of Jesus and the rise of Christianity was originally titled "An Age of Transition." To Jewish groups, this implied that Judaism was just a way station to Christianity. The lesson is now called "Religious Developments."

17   But the commission rebuffed numerous demands that it delete unhappy events or blemishes in history. "The purpose of history cannot be to expunge all such episodes from this record in the mistaken interest of filiopietism or children's self-esteem, but instead must be to help children to learn from them," the commission stated in its formal recommendations to the state board, which accepted the books last October.

18   The publishers were stunned by the bitterness of the protest that surrounded the process of public hearings and comment. That debate has now filtered down to nearly every one of the state's school districts, and even to every school in decentralized districts like Los Angeles Unified. Given little choice, most local boards have accepted the new books, with the notable exceptions of Oakland and Ravenswood City, a heavily minority school district in East Palo Alto. In those areas, they were rejected as insufficiently multicultural.

19   The debate this summer in San Francisco, where minorities make up 83 percent of the student population, typifies the controversy surrounding the books. While the school board ultimately voted 5 to 1 for adoption—joining the approximately 600 of California's 1,016 school districts that had approved the texts by Labor Day—it did so with no great enthusiasm. And it tacked on a lengthy supplementary reading list that included such titles as "Black Heroes of the Wild West," "Chinese Americans, Past and Present" and "Gays in America."

20   Even supplementary reading, however, is unlikely to placate all the critics, who understandably focus on religion and race issues as particularly problematic. Jewish groups complain about what they see as invidious comparisons between Judaism and Christianity. In one sentence about Jews, for example, the sixth-grade book refers to "their god," with a lower case "g." Three paragraphs later, discussing Christianity, the text refers to "a vision from God."

21   Muslims say they would like to see more pictures of people and fewer of camels when their religion is discussed. "When it comes to Islam, there are virtually no people," says Shabbir Mansuri, director of the Council of Islamic Education, based in Tustin. "The faces of real people disappear in the text. There is no relevance to the student. They will come away thinking this is a religion that does not deal with the rational thinking of the modern day, the religion of the terrorists."

22   Critics also have attacked the treatment of the Spanish missions in California, citing passages like this one in the fourth-grade texts about Father Junipero Serra: "Father Serra would also teach the Indians farming skills and trade crafts so that they would be able to support themselves." The Indians had no trouble getting by before Father Serra destroyed their culture, critics note sarcastically.

23   And many opponents say the books, for all their improvements over past materials, remain essentially, if unintentionally, racist. One of the most determined of these critics is Joyce E. King, director of teacher education at Santa Clara University, who was a dissenting member of the state Curriculum Development and Supplemental Materials Commission that approved the books.

24   She cites the sixth-grade book's treatment of the early development of human culture, starting two million years ago with Homo habilis on the plains of eastern Africa. The original version of the text urged children to imagine themselves there as "two naked dark-skinned people walk down to the lake not far from you. . . . You point to your open mouth to show them you are hungry. . . . One person walks off toward a field. . . . Soon the first person returns with a bloody bone. . . . They invited you to eat the red marrow oozing from the bone." (After complaints, the published version omitted the words "dark-skinned," "bloody" and "oozing.") Three pages later, the text moves forward to 12,011 B.C. and shows a Cro-Magnon man, a handsome clean-shaven fellow in buckskins. A few pages farther on, the text says, "In terms of physical features, the Cro-Magnons looked like people today."

25   King, who is black, finds that objectionable, saying it draws unfavorable comparisons between the savage Homo habilis of Africa and the clean-shaven Cro-Magnon of Europe. "The chapter begins with an imaginary excursion to Africa," she says. "Then three pages later we have a shaved white guy near a cave in France. That juxtaposition was prob-

lematic. They deleted 'dark- skinned,' but those kinds of problems cannot be fixed. We are putting these books in the hands of children who already have stereotypes."

26   She also criticizes sections on slavery, saying they depict slaves as animals devoid of human thoughts and emotions, and the black migration to the northern cities and the ghetto life they met there. "The discussion of the experiences of African Americans in the urban North perpetuates a negative stereotype of black life," she says. "Black ghettos appear to be just naturally crime-ridden and dirty."

27   The starkest paradox of the tempest aroused by the books is that the principal historian, Nash of U.CL.A., is a man with impeccable left-liberal credentials. His books, "Red, White, and Black: The Peoples of Early America" and "Forging Freedom: The Formation of Philadelphia's Black Community," have been widely admired by black and American Indian scholars. That Nash, who is white, should now be painted as a racist is a source of considerable frustration and pain to him. "If I'm the bad guy," he asks, "who are your allies?"

28   California casual in a sweatsuit one recent morning, Nash spreads the books over his dining-room table in the affluent Pacific Palisades section of Los Angeles. Nash counters the criticism about the Spanish missions by pointing out that the books also describe the whippings and other cruelties suffered by Indians at the hands of Father Serra. He concedes some of King's points but stoutly defends the overall treatment of African history and slavery.

29   "I had never heard of the Bantu migration and the rise of the Zimbabwe state when I got my Ph.D. at Princeton," he says. "We have 80 pages on African history for 12-year-olds. This is what bugs me. Joyce King and other critics will not take notice of this and continue to say this is a Eurocentric series."

30   Some critics have said the books should have omitted contemporary Southern arguments in favor of slavery. "I am not willing to make concessions on this," Nash says. "The Southern arguments are so patently false —the kids see this." He argues that the eighth-grade book offers as harsh a portrait of slavery as ever given in an elementary text, reprinting lengthy passages from the powerful autobiography of Frederick Douglass, an escaped slave. "I do not think anyone reading this would think this trivializes slavery," he says.

31   Ultimately, Nash argues, the issue comes down to the political one of whose vision of America one accepts. "You can turn American history unto a story of unremitting oppression of exploited minorities," he said. "That's just as distorted as the old view." Nash, at least, clings to the optimistic notion that all Americans can find common ground in the "ongoing struggle for greater equality and social justice—this society sooner or later must be what it says it intends to be."

32   This is where the books come under the toughest ideological attack from critics who argue that the immigrant model marginalizes people of color. Chief among them is a Jamaican woman, Sylvia Wynter, who holds a joint appointment in African and Afro-American Studies and Spanish and Portuguese at Stanford University. Her lengthy critique of the fifth-grade book, "America Will Be," argues that it tends to equate the prejudice once experienced by white immigrants from Europe with the racism suffered by black, brown and yellow peoples, thereby justifying their exploitation.

33   What is needed, she wrote in a commentary to the state Curriculum Commission, is an entirely new framework that "seeks to go beyond the model of a nation-state coterminous only with Euro-immigrant America, to one coterminous as a 'world' civilization, with all its peoples: and therefore, for the first time in recorded history, coterminous (as a land that's not been yet but yet must be) with humankind."

34   State Superintendent Honig bristles at such arguments. "They do not like the idea of common democratic principles," he says. "It gets in the way of their left point of view that this country is corrupt. This country has been able to celebrate pluralism but keep some sense of the collective that holds us together. Everything is not race, gender or class. The whole world cannot be seen just through those glasses.

35   "Democracy has certain core ideas—freedom of speech, law, procedural rights, the way we deal with each other," Honig continues. "If everything becomes hostile race and class warfare, we are going to lose this country. The issue is not multiculturalism. We agree with that. The question is, Are you also going to talk about the political and moral values that are essential for us to live together?". . . .

36   The issues that have been raised by muliticultural education have rubbed the rawest nerves, even in an America that is fundamentally pluralistic. A sharp debate broke out in New York State in late June over a paper prepared by a special panel for the State Commissioner of Education, Thomas Sobol, that urged a new curriculum that de-emphasizes the centrality of European thought and influence in the American experience. Noisy dissent came from some members of the panel, especially the historian Arthur Schlesinger Jr., who complained that "Europhobia" and a "cult of ethnicity" were turning America into a "quarrelsome splatter of enclaves"

37   The problem, in the view of Laurie Olsen, a former history teacher who is now with California Tomorrow, an educational group that develops and runs programs to deal with the increasingly multi-ethnic nature of California, is not the texts themselves. Rather, she says, it is "how polarized we are, how much fear there is about diversity, and how the schools have become the battleground." Lewis H. Butler, an Assistant

Secretary of Health, Education and Welfare in the Nixon Administration and now chairman of California Tomorrow, says the whole episode has been a "rather sad event" that pits white liberals against black and Indian scholars. "People who thought they were good guys found themselves bad guys, called racists or separatists," he says.

38   If the concept of the melting pot is outdated, what is to replace it? History, some say, is a kind of property whose owner controls the future. From that perspective, the future in California still belongs, however tenuously, to the proponents of traditional Western values. The current debate suggests, however, that an increasingly polyglot America has yet to come to grips with the full depth of its diversity.

BUILDING CONTEXT

1. What insights could the essays of Mohr and Eaton contribute to the debate over the California curriculum?

2. What parallels can you draw between the attacks on Gary Nash and the dispute between Frederick Douglass and William Garrison over the place of whites in the fight against slavery?

3. Relate the California curriculum debate to the concept of identity as understood, for example, by Eaton or Crèvecoeur.

FURTHER STUDY

1. Compare two or three theories of public education. For example, how should it benefit the individual? Is its main purpose to serve the individual or the state?

2. Do you think that an American history curriculum should reflect the relative contribution of each group to America, the proportion of each group in a particular student body, or something else? Defend your arguments.

ADDITIONAL RESOURCES

Banks, James A., and Cherry M. Banks, eds. *Multicultural Education: Issues and Perspectives.* Boston: Allyn & Bacon, 1988.

Spanier, Bonnie, et al. *Toward a Balanced Curriculum: A Sourcebook for Initiating Gender Integration Projects.* Cambridge, Mass.: Schenkman, 1984.

Takaki, Ronald. *A Different Mirror: A History of Multicultural America.* Boston: Little, Brown, 1993.

RESEARCH KEYWORDS

Multiculturalism	Intercultural Education
Ethnic Relations	Ethnicity
Race Relations—U.S.	

Exploring critical issues through writing

1. Analyze the immigrant experience in America. What common threads bind all immigrant groups? What accounts for differences in successful acculturation or assimilation? Explore how immigrants create hybrid cultures, merging elements of their old and their new homes.

2. Research the history of the melting pot ideal. Was there ever a time when all immigrants tried to assimilate into the original English culture? In what way has the American official policy toward assimilation changed in recent years?

3. Study the American fragmentation of identity. For example, examine how and why "Hispanic" identity in the United States has become particularized to Puerto Rican, Dominican, Chicano, Chicana, Latina and others.

4. Examine the conflict between the melting-pot ideal and multiculturalism. Evaluate the political response to both issues—for example, in the form of public policy enacted by schools or the government.

5. Distinguish between multiculturalism and ethnic separatism. Explore, for example, Black Nationalism or the English-Only movement.

6. Appraise the practice of attributing special virtues—for example, morality, empathy, or insight—to individuals because of the experience of their sex or ethnic group.

7. Calculate the advantages and disadvantages of claiming that women, African Americans, or other groups each have a unique epistemology. How might this claim lead, for example, to greater job opportunities—or to exclusion from certain fields?

8. Trace the history of Asian women in America. Is it possible to define an "Asian" experience without distinguishing among the experiences of Indian, Japanese, Vietnamese, Korean, or Chinese women?

9. Compare two or three theories of public education. For example, how should it benefit the individual? Is its main purpose to serve the individual or the state?

10. Do you think that an American history curriculum should reflect the relative contribution of each group to America, the proportion of each group in a particular student body, or something else? Defend your arguments.

11. Explore an idea from the reading selections that caught your interest, charmed or provoked you, or supported or challenged your own beliefs. Place this issue within a larger context and explain its significance.

CREDITS

Acosta-Belén, Edna. "From Settlers to Newcomers." From *The Hispanic Experience in the United States* by Edna Acosta-Belén. Copyright © 1988, Praeger Publishing, an imprint of Greenwood Publishing Group, Inc., Westport, CT. Reprinted with permission.

Adams, Alice Dana. "The Neglected Period of Antislavery." Copyright © 1908 by Radcliffe College Publishing. Reprinted by courtesy of Radcliffe College Archives.

Angelou, Maya. "A Job on the Streetcars." From *I Know Why the Caged Bird Sings* by Maya Angelou. Copyright © 1969 by Maya Angelou. Reprinted by permission of Random House, Inc.

Dawley, Alan, and Paul Faler. "Working Class Culture and Politics in the Industrial Revolution." From *Expanding the Past,* Peter N. Stearns, Editor. Copyright © 1988. Reprinted by permission of Peter N. Stearns.

de Tocqueville, Alexis. Pages 237–245, 287–301 from *Democracy in America* by Alexis de Tocqueville. Edited by J. P. Mayer and Max Lerner. Translated by George Lawrence. English translation copyright © 1965 by Harper & Row, Publishers, Inc. Copyright Renewed. Reprinted by permission of HarperCollins Publishers, Inc.

Feinstein, Dianne. "Women in Politics: Time for a Change." From *What Are Women's Issues?* Copyright © 1983. Reprinted by permission of Dianne Feinstein.

Goldman, Emma. "The Tragedy of Woman's Emancipation." From *Red Emma Speaks,* Alix Kates Shulman, Editor. Copyright © 1972. Reprinted by permission of Alix Kates Shulman.

Hill Collins, Patricia. "The Social Construction of Black Feminist Thought." From *Signs,* a University of Chicago Press Publication, copyright © 1989. Reprinted by permission of The University of Chicago and Patricia Hill Collins.

Hymowitz, Carol and Michaele Weissman. "A History of Women in America." From *A History of Women in America* by Carol Hymowitz and Michaele Weissman. Copyright © 1978 by the Anti-Defamation League of B'nai B'rith. Used by permission of Bantam Books, a division of Bantam Doubleday Dell Publishing Groups, Inc.

King, Jr., Martin Luther. "Letter From Birmingham Jail." Reprinted by arrangement with The Heirs to the Estate of Martin Luther King, Jr., c/o Joan Daves Agency as agent for the proprietor. Copyright © 1963 by the Estate of Martin Luther King, Jr. Copyright © renewed 1991 by Coretta Scott King.

Kolodny, Annette. "Among the Indians: The Uses of Captivity." Copyright © 1993 by The New York Times Company. Reprinted by permission.

Mazumdar. Sucheta. "A Woman Centered Perspective of Asian American History." From *Making Waves* by Asian Women United. Copyright © 1989 by Asian Women United. Reprinted by permission of Beacon Press.

Miller, Jr., James E. Excerpts from "A Narrative of the Captivity & Restoration of Mary Rowlandson" and "The General History of Virginia, New England, and The Summer Isles" in *Heritage of American Literature: Beginnings to the Civil War,* Volume I by James E. Miller, Jr., copyright © 1991 by Harcourt Brace & Company, reprinted by permission of the publisher.

Mohr, Nicholasa. "Puerto Rican Writers in the United States; Puerto Rican Writers in Puerto Rico" by Nicholasa Mohr is reprinted with permission from the publisher of *The Americas Review* Vol. 15, No. #2, 1987. Reprinted by permission.

Reinhold, Robert. "Class Struggle." From *The New York Times Magazine,* September 29, 1991. Copyright © 1991 by The New York Times Company. Reprinted by permission.

Strout, Cushing. "American Dilemma." From *Making American Tradition* by Cushing Strout. Copyright © 1990 by Cushing Strout. Reprinted by permission of Rutgers University Press.

Schlafly, Phyllis. Excerpt from *The Power of the Positive Woman* by Phyllis Schlafly. Copyright © 1977 by Phyllis Schlafly. Reprinted by permission of Crown Publishers, Inc.

Van Every, Dale. Chapter 2, pages 14–23 from *Disinherited: The Lost Birthright of the American Indian,* by Dale Van Every. Copyright © 1966 by Dale Van Every. Reprinted by permission of William Morrow & Company.

Villapando, Venny. "The Business of Selling Brides." From *Making Waves* by Asian Women United. Copyright © 1989 by Asian Women United. Reprinted by permission of Beacon Press.

Vega, Bernardo. "Memoirs." From *Monthly Review.* Copyright © 1984 by Monthly Review Press. Reprinted by permission of Monthly Review Foundation.

X, Malcolm. Excerpt from *The Autobiography of Malcolm X* by Malcolm X, with the assistance of Alex Haley. Copyright © 1964 by Alex Haley and Malcolm X and copyright © 1965 by Alex Haley and Betty Shabazz. Reprinted by permission of Random House, Inc.

$\mathcal{I}$NDEX OF AUTHORS, TITLES, AND THEMES